Effective Talent Management Strategies for Organizational Success

Mambo Mupepi
Grand Valley State University, USA

A volume in the Advances in Human Resources
Management and Organizational Development
(AHRMOD) Book Series

www.igi-global.com

Published in the United States of America by
    IGI Global
    Business Science Reference (an imprint of IGI Global)
    701 E. Chocolate Avenue
    Hershey PA, USA 17033
    Tel: 717-533-8845
    Fax: 717-533-8661
    E-mail: cust@igi-global.com
    Web site: http://www.igi-global.com

Library of Congress Cataloging-in-Publication Data

Names: Mupepi, Mambo, 1952- editor.
Title: Effective talent management strategies for organizational success /
  Mambo Mupepi, editor.
Description: Hershey : Business Science Reference, [2017] | Includes
  bibliographical references and index.
Identifiers: LCCN 2016049576| ISBN 9781522519614 (hardcover) | ISBN
  9781522519621 (ebook)
Subjects: LCSH: Manpower planning. | Intellectual capital. | Ability. |
  Personnel management. | Communication in management.
Classification: LCC HF5549.5.M3 E334 2017 | DDC 658.3/128--dc23 LC record available at https://lccn.loc.
gov/2016049576

This book is published in the IGI Global book series Advances in Human Resources Management and Organizational Development (AHRMOD) (ISSN: 2327-3372; eISSN: 2327-3380)

British Cataloguing in Publication Data
A Cataloguing in Publication record for this book is available from the British Library.

All work contributed to this book is new, previously-unpublished material. The views expressed in this book are those of the authors, but not necessarily of the publisher.

For electronic access to this publication, please contact: eresources@igi-global.com.

Advances in Human Resources Management and Organizational Development (AHRMOD) Book Series

Patricia Ordóñez de Pablos
Universidad de Oviedo, Spain

ISSN:2327-3372
EISSN:2327-3380

MISSION

A solid foundation is essential to the development and success of any organization and can be accomplished through the effective and careful management of an organization's human capital. Research in human resources management and organizational development is necessary in providing business leaders with the tools and methodologies which will assist in the development and maintenance of their organizational structure.

The **Advances in Human Resources Management and Organizational Development (AHRMOD) Book Series** aims to publish the latest research on all aspects of human resources as well as the latest methodologies, tools, and theories regarding organizational development and sustainability. The **AHRMOD Book Series** intends to provide business professionals, managers, researchers, and students with the necessary resources to effectively develop and implement organizational strategies.

COVERAGE

- Personnel Retention
- Employee Evaluation
- Personnel Policies
- Collaborative Method
- Job Enrichment
- Employee Benefits
- Coaching and Mentoring
- Succession Planning
- Work-Life Balance
- Change Management

IGI Global is currently accepting manuscripts for publication within this series. To submit a proposal for a volume in this series, please contact our Acquisition Editors at Acquisitions@igi-global.com or visit: http://www.igi-global.com/publish/.

Titles in this Series

For a list of additional titles in this series, please visit: www.igi-global.com

Handbook of Research on Human Resources Strategies for the New Millennial Workforce
Patricia Ordoñez de Pablos (University of Oviedo, Spain) and Robert D. Tennyson (University of Minnesota, USA)
Business Science Reference • copyright 2017 • 523pp • H/C (ISBN: 9781522509486) • US $310.00 (our price)

Management Education for Global Leadership
Neeta Baporikar (HP-GSB, Namibia University of Science and Technology, Namibia)
Business Science Reference • copyright 2017 • 321pp • H/C (ISBN: 9781522510130) • US $185.00 (our price)

Innovation and Shifting Perspectives in Management Education
Neeta Baporikar (HP-GSB, Namibia University of Science and Technology, Namibia)
Business Science Reference • copyright 2017 • 352pp • H/C (ISBN: 9781522510192) • US $190.00 (our price)

Strategic Labor Relations Management in Modern Organizations
Ana María Lucia Casademunt (Universidad Loyola Andalucía, Spain)
Business Science Reference • copyright 2016 • 313pp • H/C (ISBN: 9781522503569) • US $205.00 (our price)

Bridging the Scholar-Practitioner Gap in Human Resources Development
Claretha Hughes (University of Arkansas, USA) and Matthew W. Gosney (Hillcrest HealthCare Systems, USA)
Business Science Reference • copyright 2016 • 267pp • H/C (ISBN: 9781466699984) • US $185.00 (our price)

Quantitative Multidisciplinary Approaches in Human Capital and Asset Management
Meir Russ (University of Wisconsin-Green Bay, USA)
Business Science Reference • copyright 2016 • 317pp • H/C (ISBN: 9781466696525) • US $205.00 (our price)

Strategic Information Technology Governance and Organizational Politics in Modern Business
Tiko Iyamu (Cape Peninsula University of Technology, South Africa)
Business Science Reference • copyright 2015 • 326pp • H/C (ISBN: 9781466685246) • US $210.00 (our price)

Cross-Cultural Collaboration and Leadership in Modern Organizations
Nancy D. Erbe (California State University Dominguez Hills, California) and Anthony H. Normore (California State University Dominguez Hills, California)
Business Science Reference • copyright 2015 • 388pp • H/C (ISBN: 9781466683761) • US $225.00 (our price)

Handbook of Research on Internationalization of Entrepreneurial Innovation in the Global Economy
Luisa Cagica Carvalho (Universidade Aberta, Portugal & CEFAGE, Universidade de Évora, Portugal)
Business Science Reference • copyright 2015 • 547pp • H/C (ISBN: 9781466682160) • US $335.00 (our price)

www.igi-global.com

701 E. Chocolate Ave., Hershey, PA 17033
Order online at www.igi-global.com or call 717-533-8845 x100
To place a standing order for titles released in this series, contact: cust@igi-global.com
Mon-Fri 8:00 am - 5:00 pm (est) or fax 24 hours a day 717-533-8661

Table of Contents

Section 1
The Social Constructs of Effective Talent Management

Chapter 1
Mambo Mupepi, Grand Valley State University, USA
Francis Boachie-Mensah, University of Cape Coast, Ghana

Chapter 2
Mambo Mupepi, Seidman College, USA
Yalonda M. Ross-Davis, Seidman College, USA
Mark Davis, Self-employed Management Consultant, USA
Thomas S. Vachon, Grand Valley State University, USA

Chapter 3
Nana Yaw Oppong, University of Cape Coast, Ghana

Chapter 4
Mambo Mupepi, Seidman College of Business, USA

Chapter 5
Mambo Mupepi, Grand Valley State University, USA
Sylvia Mupepi, Grand Valley State University, USA

Section 3
Managing Talent in Global Environments

Detailed Table of Contents

Section 1
The Social Constructs of Effective Talent Management

Chapter 1

Mambo Mupepi, Grand Valley State University, USA
Francis Boachie-Mensah, University of Cape Coast, Ghana

The central precept of this chapter is to leverage the division of labor to create a talented workforce. The divided labor can be appreciated to acquire the knowledge and skills necessary to develop the talent useful to progress the job. Specialization arises in many situations such as when the experts share their experience, enabling the novice to constantly learn to improve systems thinking and personal mastery. It can also happen as a result of planned on-the-job training. Innovation can happen when individuals segment their knowledge about the job and increase their skillfulness to champion productivity. Technical know-how too can be described as highly structured skill-sets acquired from years of continuous learning and improvement leading to proficiency. Expertise can also refer to innovative and systems thinking, espousing the development of techniques and methods leading to increased productivity. A case study is deployed to understand how competencies were developed and implemented successfully in an enterprise. Appreciative Inquiry change management savoir-faire was deployed to pin-point at what gave life to the business. This information was used to promote the talent needed to boost output in the value creation system.

Chapter 2

Focusing strictly on negative organizational issues could constitute an obstacle to the improvement of key attributes, products, and or services offered. This chapter suggests that Appreciative Inquiry (AI) can be an effective and efficient strategic tool used to lead positive change and improve the talent of the organization by emphasizing what is successful rather than a deficit. AI is a well-developed methodology of examining, defining, implementing, and executing precise pans of improvement by applying positive psychology which will lead to the revitalization of productivity. Furthermore, available data suggests the employees within the organization can become resistant to change when there is an overemphasizing of the shortcoming areas of weakness. By using the AI assessment and evaluation technology, companies can pin-point and materialize desirable change.

Chapter 3

Although companies around the world have made talent management a top priority, most human resource professionals and senior executives believe their organizations have not fully resolved the talent management puzzle. The chapter investigates if there are any indicators that suggest that talent management is a puzzle. Applying mainly review of academic and popular literature, the assessment is done under five headings including talent and talent management definitions; the need for talent management; the root of talent management; talent management strategies and processes, and talent management-diversity integration. It is revealed that albeit being differentiator between organizations that succeed and those that do not, talent management is saddled with uncertainties, lack of clarity, and misunderstanding, which are hurdles that need to be cleared to pave way for more effective talent programs. To overcome these, organizations should avoid one common blueprint to all talent situations, but develop approaches that suit individual talent requirements.

Chapter 4

There are numerous approaches to developing organizational talent and all take different turns. In this chapter, meta-analysis and analytics techniques are contrasted to produce the explicit knowledge necessary to excel organization. Crafting the flair needed in winning corporations focuses on three specific areas in the value creation system: recruitment, training and development, and design and implementation of competitive conditions of service as critical in getting the people possessing the desirable competences and their retention to advance output. Data mined from the firms' activities can be organized in exploitable datasets which can be analyzed in tandem with research results to craft difficult to emulate practices leading to increased productivity.

This chapter advances a discourse on a co-constructed competency model referred to as the SCCM. The SCCM is an alternative competency management strategy designed to build talent needed to increase productivity. A competency model buttress talent management and how human resource management, can be designed and implemented. Arguments drawn indicate that competency models, in particular those concerned with organizational capabilities, are relatively ineffective when developed outside the organization. A contrast of the competency models developed elsewhere with those espoused within the organization by the knowledge communities (KC) and effectiveness demonstrated in the latter approach. By reviewing selections from the literature that established the competency development movement, a foundation on past knowledge is considered in the design and implementation of the capability required to champion organization. The SCCM approach is applicable to most organizations in creating explicit knowledge, skills, and behavior necessary to increase productivity.

This chapter makes a contribution to talent management literature by investigating the construction of a high-performance organization applying the structuration proposition. People remain as the source of value in all companies and increasingly the human factor is critical in making the difference. The structuration approach make it possible to include the collective experience of the people doing the work to leverage each employee's unique talents to boost productivity. The structuration ontology is applied to create structure and agency useful in making the competitive advantage real. The analysis of both structure and agency can lead to a reproduction of the competences that undergird high performance organization.

Chapter 7

The discourse in this presentation is about how talent can be viewed as appropriate techniques and explicit practices enhanced by experience useful in the value creation system. Talent can be deconstructed to progress the necessary efficacy in organization. A limited literature is drawn to understand the role of structures and technology in the value creation process. Value is created anytime an action is taken for which the benefits exceed the costs, or the moment an action can be prevented for which the costs exceed the benefits. A co-constructed competency model can be initiated to comprehend a systemic approach to enhancing performance and the design of strategy to retain talent and nurture the skillfulness and knowing necessary in boosting yields in diversified entities.

Section 2
Protecting the Intellectual Assets

The discussion progressed in this chapter is about the protection of organizational knowledge in competitive environments. Knowledge can leak in the value creation networks embedded in knowledge-intensive firms, and a collaborative approach can be utilized to minimize risk and increase sustainability. For knowledge to be preserved from unintentional outflow, its confidential nature and description must be understood at all levels. Loss of knowledge can occur at any point; whether it is through the process of consultation or when employees do their work. Forfeiture of information can be unintended or a planned effort. To prevent such unintended leakage, it is important to develop a shared mindset among employees to minimize the risk. The socio-technical system is a philosophical framework that enables companies to simultaneously consider both ethical and technical systems in order to best match the technology and the people involved. In this paper we show how the socio-technical system can be applied to prevent knowledge leakage.

This chapter discusses a framework to temper the impact of knowledge leakage and how losing the source of what gives life to the business can lead to its demise. Explicit practices should be sustained by limiting access and understood in averting loss. Explicit knowledge is expressed and categorized in work performance. In outsourced assignments, technical knowhow can be transferred accessed learnt and communicated throughout the entire organization. Viewed as technical know-how the firm can utilize it to make goods and services that are demanded by customers. Data generated from outsourcing should be analyzed to uncover data-driven pitfalls employing analytics to describe the nature of current talent, accurately forecasting staffing and material usage to leverage outsourcing of sustainable practices. Technical know-how permeates the firm in making the difference. It is pervasive in the value creation process and as such it is only prudent to prevent leakage to maintain productivity.

This article seeks to understand how a family enterprise was structured and positioned and grew into a successful global mining house. The focus is on how talent was managed drawing ontology from the mining industry founded in 1873 in South Africa by British and Dutch colonists. The founding families are those of Deidrick and Johannes De Beer, Alfred Beit, Cecil Rhodes, Nathaniel Rothschild and Ernest

Oppenheimer. The De Beer brothers sold out to Cecil Rhodes and his partners and the business was, amalgamated later with Anglo American Corporation. The business arrangement continued for four generations under the direction of the Oppenheimer family who were apprenticed by excellent craftsmen in the diamond trade, and educated in finance economics and law from Europe's best business schools, and a conducive segregated political environment which ended in a US Supreme Court judgment in 2012. However, the Oppenheimers nurtured the mining house to a successful international mining business that employs more than 20 000 people around the world today.

Chapter 11

Currently, new approaches for training can effectively adopt the "Flipped" model of instruction as an important means of organizing and developing workforce competencies. One of the goals in the university setting at Grand Valley State University is to improve skills and training opportunities which can most efficiently utilize training time. In order to improve cognitive practice and increase skillfulness in a value creation socio-technical system, the Zone of Proximal Development (ZPD) is deployed to progress the talent needed to advance productivity. Seeing much success is noticed in this newest pedagogy "flipped instruction" design, it has changed various disciplines in business education which can best be applied to the training component of the workforce today. The success of this model continues to create higher learner motivation resulting in desired outcomes. The technology of the ZPD juxtaposed with the flipped classroom technique can lead to the improvement of a highly talented workforce.

Chapter 12

Although human resources management is important in organization, its tenet of job evaluation is significant. Job evaluation is a management approach that enables employers to grade and reward jobs in comparison to what they are worth in the company in an equitable manner. The company will be able to craft a compensation plan aligned to performance. The Paterson derived job evaluation is a systemic way of determining the worth of a job in relation to other jobs in the organization using one single factor: decision making. This single factor is juxtaposed along the attributes of a selected multiple factors to progress the structuration of grades and compensation. Paterson defines six kinds of decisions or levels of work which are strategic intent, strategic execution, tactical management, advanced operational, operational and primary. These are found in any company and applied in the design and implementation of competitive conditions of employment to retain talent. There are more businesses floundering because of the failure to control costs. The single factor job evaluation system enables the firm to design and implement a sustainable performance strategy to retain talent in advancing the competitive advantage.

Chapter 13

This article progresses the argument that the core competences of the company must be created, diffused, and distributed and protected, to effectively exploit the market. Companies compete on what they know best and in management theory organizations draw a repertoire of multiple resources and skills to effectively differentiate the business in vying for market leadership. The core competence or capability of the firm can be described as talent and a special ability that allows the enterprise to produce the goods demanded by customers exceptionally well. The core competences can also be referred to as explicit practices constituting measurable or observable knowledge, skills, abilities, and behaviors critical in meeting the needs of clients. The capability should be crafted in a manner that makes imitation by similar entities impossible.

Section 3
Managing Talent in Global Environments

Chapter 14

The argument presented in this article is that highly productive workplaces can be inclusive, and purposefully built to produce the goods and services demanded by customers. A socio-technical system approach can be inclusive in terms of talent and technology and is subject to deconstruction. The characterization of diversity can be made in at least two ways: based on the attributes possessed by the employees; and racial composition of the workforce. A co-constructed competency model can be applied to understand the nature and description of prevailing cultural conditions to effectively engage people to be more productive. An inclusive circle of deeply involved people can design and support the necessary change and generate the synergy, techniques, and the heuristics, to increase productivity.

Chapter 15

Some leadership behaviors are more frequently applied by women than men in the management of teams. These attributes have been proven successful in enhancing corporate performance and will be a key factor in meeting tomorrow's business challenges. Talent is unevenly distributed in diversified work environments and promoting women and gender leadership variety is of strategic importance in companies. Results from a recent study show an unprecedented amount of CEO turnover in 2015 and a growing tendency to look for new leadership outside the company. Nearly a quarter of the world companies replaced their CEOs during the same year and it is the highest turnover for the past two decades. Those new top executives were increasingly hired from elsewhere even during planned leadership changes.

The data indicates that fewer women are the incoming list of top executives indicating that some of the old habits still linger in 21st century organizations. The organization development of effective capability deduces new viewpoints to advance the best talent for all time.

Chapter 16

In response to the call to elucidate the conditions necessary for successful multinational organization, this discussion is centered on effective communications between a subsidiary company located in China and an American parent organization (multinational company, MNC) based in the USA. Semi-structured interviews were conducted with 37 participants including the expatriate managers and the local employees. The findings show that the challenges facing the MNC mainly include confrontation in the contexts of conflict based on cultural differences and supervisor-subordinate interaction, and collectivity reflected in two themes including group dynamics and collective activities. The MNC incorporates local knowledge systems into its administration schema when conducting business worldwide. The study shows that perceptions of both management and employees vary. The challenge is to increase understanding of the job and what needs to be done in different environment as antecedent to increased outputs.

Chapter 17

This chapter explains the overview of talent management (TM); the characteristics of global talent management (GTM); TM and human capital; TM and career development; the emerging trends of TM in the modern workforce; and the significance of TM in the digital age. TM is a continuous process that involves sourcing, hiring, developing, retaining, and promoting talented employees while simultaneously meeting organization's requirements. TM involves individual and organizational development in response to a rapidly changing business environment. The best TM plans should be effectively aligned with organization's strategic goals and business needs. Business leaders who implement the best TM processes are more prepared than their competitors to compete in the global economy and quickly capitalize on new opportunities. Executives and HR managers need to support the TM-related development of their talented employees to make necessary progress in the modern workforce.

Chapter 18

Today, no country can claim that its business can be local or national due to the effects of globalization. The world of business has become international. In this new millennium, few economies can afford to ignore global business opportunities. The globalizing wind has broadened the mind sets of executives, extended the geographical reach of firms, and nudged international business into some new trajectories. One such new trajectory is the concern with national culture. This has a tremendous impact on the subject matter of talent management for any country, economy or nation. Africa is no exception. Though there is a considerable body of research suggesting a link between language, communication and how gender – and leadership – gets 'done' in organisations, there is very little research on global perspective for managing talent especially in the African context. This chapter intends to fill that gap and in particular deals with global perspective of talent management in the African context.

Chapter 19

Amplifying the Significance of Systems Theory: Charting the Course in High Velocity

Mambo Mupepi, Seidman College, USA

In system theory organizations are viewed as closed or open systems. An open system interacts with the environment for its sustainability. The closed system does not interact with its setting consequently its behavior depends largely on internal dynamics of its parts. The centricity of an open organizational structure is one created and empowered to learn and change very fast to successfully achieve desired goals. However open systems need to embrace change as follows: transform inputs of energy and information to produce the products demanded by the customers, transact with key stakeholders to access resources, regulate system behavior to achieve stable performance, and adapt to continuously changing high velocity competition to increase productivity.

Chapter 20

A Centricity on Survey Design Techniques: Advancing Talent Management in Emerging

Mambo Mupepi, Seidman College, USA

The primary objective of this paper is to demonstrate how questionnaire techniques can be applied to assess and evaluate data to develop the metrics necessary to progress efficiency and effectiveness in successful organization. An opinion poll is a tool associated with survey research and can be designed and employed to collect information pertaining to attitudes, practices, and skills prevailing in a given or random population. The information can be examined and construed to progress the efficacies necessary in triumphant enterprises. Surveys are used to measure behavior, knowledge, attitudes and opinions useful in the design and implementation of high performance organization. Opinion polls can be interpreted in crafting practices necessary in differentiating the business and making of goods and services demanded by customers.

Foreword

Defining Talent Management may seem to be vague and difficult as the definition is drawn from multidisciplinary perspectives. From the organizational development point of view, Talent Management is an approach towards enhanced productivity in which programs are designed to integrate various human resource and motivational efforts that exist across an organization into a comprehensive organizational strategy. In economics, talent is viewed as the intellectual capital of the firm employed to progress desirable goals. It is an asset that forms the main component of the competitive advantage.

The role of organizational developing and training in building effective intellectual assets is priceless. The ability to learn very fast makes it possible for companies to implement effective change within a short period of time. The field of organization development provides numerous interventions applicable in growing talent. This book attempts to incorporate methods and techniques useful in improving the talent needed to progress organizational goals. For example, on-the-job training provides the workforce the opportunity to acquire the skills necessary in their jobs. Another intervention is that of organizational learning. Managers attempt to maximize the ability of individuals and groups to think and behave creatively and thus maximize the potential for organizational learning to take place. Creating a shared mindset, systems thinking, role play, simulations, or project teams allow organization to share tacit experience useful in the design of explicit practices.

Talent management is viewed as an approach to motivating the organization. In this regards, Talent management programs differ across the organization but can be categorized in three distinct areas. The first concerns engaging members of the organization at each step of their employment to create explicit practices useful in differentiating the organization. They can include efforts to attract and select, retain, and development. The second programs include maintenance such as conditions of service, job evaluation, performance appraisals, on-the-job training and development, promotion and succession planning aimed at sustaining the competitive advantage. The third part includes a global perspective on how to remain competitive in international business environments.

In this book the authors have incorporated the knowledge, practices, and techniques that can be applied to enhance the company's ability to chart the rough terrains of the global markets and succeed in highly competitive environments.

Preface

OVERVIEW: WHAT THIS BOOK IS ALL ABOUT

Many companies have created positions focused on harnessing the intellectual capital necessary in advancing organizational goals. This book was influenced by my students who wanted a text that addressed how to develop and manage talent in entrepreneur environments. I have organized the book in three sections: the first examines methods and techniques of how to create and manage talent in any type of enterprise; the need to excel in small businesses has been propelled by fierce competition leading to many entrepreneurs to be innovative; and many are now opting for co-constructed competency models as means of gaining and sustaining the competitive advantage. This implies drawing on effective learning, system-wide thinking, and creating a shared mindset to sustain improvement.

BOOK'S VALUE AND HIGHLIGHTS

The field of Talent Management is developing a body of knowledge, research, good practices, tools, principles, and a diverse base of practitioners and researchers committed to bringing Talent Management to the fore as a viable methodology for creating and sustaining the competitive advantage in organizations. There is no quick and easy answer to building successful economies though able enterprises and free markets are the critical solutions.

Through eighteen chapters of this book, several critical insights emerge which help the reader find an answer for their own context. Different key themes and subjects are developed through three distinct parts of the book. Section 1, *The Social Constructs of effective Talent Management*, seven chapters in total, provide a general framework for uncovering critical insights into how to create diffuse and distribute explicit practices to nurture talent in varied cognitive environments where the know-how can be utilized to make goods and services demanded by customers.

Section 2, *Protecting the Intellectual Assets*, six chapters in total, illustrate how knowledge leakage can be contained in value creation systems. Intellectual capital can be appraised and appropriate human resource strategies can be applied to motivate and retain the talent needed in organization.

Finally, Section 3, *Managing Talent in Global Business Environments* five chapters in all, draw empirical evidence on global talent management from Southern Africa, Far East in Bangkok, China, and North America. I believe these experiences will support effective talent management in Global Business Environments.

Mambo Mupepi
Grand Valley State University, USA

Acknowledgement

To begin with I'm thankful to the resources made available to me that made the writing of this book possible. I'm thankful to the Chair, Management Department Jaideep Motwani for making the resources available for writing possible. The book would not have been published without the help of many people. I'm indebted to Aslam Modak, Kevin Barrons, Yalonda Ross-Davis, Monica Allen, Thomas McGinnis, Jim Sanford, and Robert Frey at the Seidman College, Grand Valley State University and Sylvia Mupepi Kirkhof College, Grand Valley State University, who made this book a reality.

I'm also thankful to the scholars Nana Yaw Oppong and Frances Boachie-Mensah, University of Cape Coast, Ghana; Yiheng Deng, Southwestern University, China; Kijpokin Kasemsap, Suan Sunandha Rajabhat University, Bangkok; and Neeta Baporikar, Namibia University of Science and Technology, Namibia, who contributed their knowledge, insights, and practices in writing this book.

I'm indebted to student assistants at Seidman College who answered my calls for keyboarding and Microsoft Suite expertise and these are Brianna Ward, Victoria Force and Kirsten Collins.

I had the rare opportunity of receiving expert support from Attorneys Jim Sanford and Robert Frey whose expertise on intellectual capital has added value to the book.

I would like to express my sincere thanks to Maria Rohde at IGI International Publisher of Progressive Information Science and Technology Research, whose word processing, editorial skills for both the book and bibliography, both with superb accuracy and speed. Her professionalism was unequalled.

To all those mentioned, and to those who were not but should be mentioned, thank you very much.

Mambo Mupepi
Grand Valley State University, USA

Section 1
The Social Constructs of Effective Talent Management

Chapter 1
Appreciating Specialization:
Nurturing Talent in the Division of Labor

Mambo Mupepi
Grand Valley State University, USA

Francis Boachie-Mensah
University of Cape Coast, Ghana

ABSTRACT

The central precept of this chapter is to leverage the division of labor to create a talented workforce. The divided labor can be appreciated to acquire the knowledge and skills necessary to develop the talent useful to progress the job. Specialization arises in many situations such as when the experts share their experience, enabling the novice to constantly learn to improve systems thinking and personal mastery. It can also happen as a result of planned on-the-job training. Innovation can happen when individuals segment their knowledge about the job and increase their skillfulness to champion productivity. Technical know-how too can be described as highly structured skill-sets acquired from years of continuous learning and improvement leading to proficiency. Expertise can also refer to innovative and systems thinking, espousing the development of techniques and methods leading to increased productivity. A case study is deployed to understand how competencies were developed and implemented successfully in an enterprise. Appreciative Inquiry change management savoir-faire was deployed to pin-point at what gave life to the business. This information was used to promote the talent needed to boost output in the value creation system.

INTRODUCTION

The discussion in this chapter is about appreciating knowledge, skills, and technology, in the division of labor to create specialists who can provide answers to the economic question of how to advance productivity. They can enable the divided labor to excel in their jobs and become talented in many aspects of the business. In a free market economy, the best producers are those that are able to supply goods and services valued by the consumers all the time. Adam Smith (1723-1790) envisioned a world of specialists native to the division of labor, who produce goods sold at greater profit margins. The

DOI: 10.4018/978-1-5225-1961-4.ch001

division of labor enables economies of scale that give the producer superiority in the production of the goods in demand. The competitive advantage can be created in many ways. For example, a company can make appropriate-in-technology investment, acquiring the tools, equipment and know-how to advance productivity. It can also invest in its people, allowing them to specialize in all aspects of doing the job. The company can have all the gadgets, tools and equipment, but people will make the difference. The discourse presented indicates that the edge can also be created by the business, using the knowledge and skills of the stakeholder specialists. Wealth can be realized by controlling costs and addressing taxation, all things being equal.

Background

The literature reviewed was limited. However, it provides an overview of Appreciative Inquiry (AI) and the Division of Labor to understand how the novice can be developed to become specialists. We realize that the organization during Adam Smith's time is different to the much-sophisticated corporations of 21st century. What remains consistently the same is how specialists can be developed to enable companies to increase productivity and more wealth. The AI Four- Dimension Model (4-D-Model) is a state-of-the-art assessment and evaluation technology, which can be applied to understand how desirable change can be co-constructed as strategy to increase productivity. The technique can also be employed to understand the talent needed to make increased output a reality. An entire company can pin-point desirable change in one large group meeting (see Figure 1). The literature describes some of the terms, methods and technology used in the AI methodology to engage people in organization. The AI techniques are juxtaposed in division of labor to understand what makes the novice become specialists.

What is Appreciative Inquiry?

AI is a change management methodology developed by David Cooperrider of Case Western Reserve University, Ohio. The technique focuses on what is working well in the organization such as the hypothetical divided labor in the Adam Smith Pin-production plant (see Figure 1) (Cooperrider, 1986).

Figure 1. The AI 4-D-Model (Mupepi, 2014)

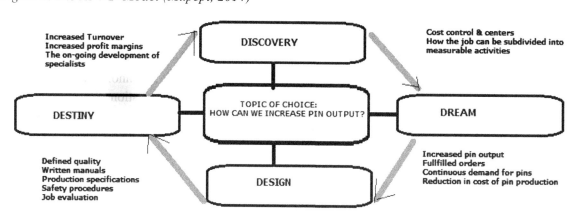

The AI Facilitator

AI can be facilitated by a few individuals trained on how to apply the techniques. The entire organization can all come together in one seating to deliberate. Depending on how fast they can learn, it can take about two days of deliberation to explain what AI is all about (Cooperrider & Whitney 2005). The AI facilitator can be an organization development consultant or one of the managers who is well-read in positive organizational scholarship (Cameron, Dutton, & Quinn 2003).

The 4-D Model can be modified to suit the goals of any organization. However, many scholars such as Yaeger & Sorensen (2001) propound that one of the strengths of AI is its versatility in implementation. The technique is easy to understand and apply. The design of the 4-D-Model enables the entire organization to effectively participate. The design can be modified to accommodate fifth and sixth phases which, in this discussion, are implementation and evaluation (see Figure 1). Complex projects that involve external input such as accreditation or compliance may require implementation and evaluation stages that require external input. AI is quite flexible to use in varied organizations. This flexibility makes it possible for companies to explore the value and challenges of collaboration when using AI to introduce and manage change. The organization will be able to use the adapted model to plan, execute, and control and close the work of a team to achieve specific goals and meet specific success criteria. In all cases, AI sanctions that change is to be implemented instantaneously.

Advantages of the AI Methodology

AI creates an environment that makes the company or group realize its potential and the capacity it needs to progress the business. It can be applied to examine work processes, systems and methods to allow the corporation to contextualize knowledge and encourage system-wide innovation in the making of specialists.

The AI ontology can be a strategy to advance organization-wide productivity. The chapter draws upon secondary data from a case study to show that effective technology can be created, diffused and distributed to all cognitive areas where it can be practical in producing goods and services that have more value for the business.

AI is useful in team building and working with people who do not get along together as well as those who work well but would like to increase their levels of productivity.

Unleashing the Power to Excel

There is an absent body of knowledge about value orientations in organizational performance management literature. In this debate, a proposition is made about value creation methods and practices using the social construct of Appreciative Inquiry (AI). The ontology on organizational performance is drawn from Cooperrider (1986), Cameron, Dutton, & Quinn (2003), Barrett (1995), and Mupepi & Mupepi (2016), among many others. A company is able to create the explicit knowledge necessary to advance goals and allow the business to sprout. AI is a stimulating and groundbreaking technique for pin-pointing the heart of what is working within the company in pursuit of desirable goals. As illustrated in Figure 1, the AI 4-D Model can be deployed to enhance the division of labor (Mupepi, 2014). The methodology can enable the understanding of the knowledge, skills, technology, and the behavior required to advance technology transfer, skills development and effective learning in making the specialists. The collective efforts of the specialist can lead to the creation of more wealth for the business and its owners. AI enables positive outcomes such as attributes of organizations and their members to happen. Cameron et al (2003) suggest that wealth creation and the resultant specialist in the division of labor is key indicator of success. Cameron et al propound that positive scholarship such as AI does not rely on a single theory, but focuses on dynamics that are typically described by words such as talent, prosperous, booming, or brilliance. AI provides an expanded perspective in the development of a thriving practice arising out of ideas of goodness and positive human potential.

The Discovery of Truths

The AI methodology uses data generated by the organization and focusing upon past successes, rather than what is missing; AI crafts an environment for change that is systemic, energizing and realistic. The 4-D-Model (see Figure 1) can be deployed to bring a better understanding of concepts and practices such as the Adam Smith Division of labor (Campbell & Skinner, 1976). The 4-D-Model can be used to determine the truth conditions for all statements made in each phase by asking affirmative questions about the pin making operations. The entire production system can be made to discover the practices, giving life to the new jobs in the hypothetical pin production factory. The contention of Adam Smith, in Campbell & Skinner, is to allow a systemic approach to knowledge and skills acquisition and appropriate on-the-job training to warrant increased output. On the topic of division of labor, in Campbell & Skinner (1976), Smith conceives a specialized workforce capable of earning more wages than the ordinary unskilled labor. He sees the corporations that employ specialized labor possessing the capacity to address the needs of society such as increased employment opportunities, a hype of economic activities leading to increased domestic productivity and international trade. We use the same approach to appreciate the division of labor in the company to discover more accurately what gives life to the business.

In Callinicos (2007), Adam Smith suggests that organizations are critical in economic life within the community they operate in many respects. For example, corporations impact education and training by determining the levels of education and skills required to do a job in those companies. Callinicos examines the ways in which the division of labor grew out of a time in history when societies in the West were moving away from the invocation of capitalism as the only means to validate organizations and the mastery of the world. Corporations of the day were created to exploit defined markets and had to create unique knowledge and practices to effectively exploit those markets. Ingham (2008) alludes to the fact that companies of the day had to be aggressive to engage in politics and protect their assets using all means to enter into trade relations. This was a great deviation from the norm. The companies in existence at the time could have been the likes of London Merchants Company and the East India Company, among many others, created to exploit new markets as the British Empire expanded. The organizations grew and, more often, had to make rules that enabled adaption to be comfortable. Ingham argues that the corporations had to emulate what they had done well in the past to bring about change in the future. Successful positive lessons were drawn from trading, and profit and loss accounts. The practice is still characteristic of organizational life today. The Discovery phase allows people to look into the positive past to identify the potentialities of business in defined markets.

Advancing Effectiveness and Efficiency

The affirmative topic of choice in the center of the 4-D-Model (see Figure1) is a state-of-the-art technique in pin-pointing at the risk the business faces by selecting certain courses of action. The organization is able to know what gives life to the business and to chart a full-proof modus operandi to increase productivity and, at the same time, minimizing loss. In Mupepi (2009), the affirmative topic of choice technique is Deployed to bring out the best in stakeholders. Groups and individuals make sense of their role in the business by understanding the relevance of their jobs and co-construction of the mission as a way to advance effectiveness and efficiency. The co-construction can also enable the transference of technology from the experts to the novices through the justification of systems and methods as affirmative topics. Of course, appropriate on-the-job training, and sharing of relevant information, can be initiated to complete technology transfer. Watkins (2011) asserts that co-construction of organizational reality is the key to increasing productivity. The 4-D-Model makes it possible for the entire organization to build a collective future, drawing upon those practices the company has successfully done in the past. Watkins argues that the corporation will be able to define specific competences and the modus operandi necessary to get the job done expeditiously.

Realizing the Dreams

Whitney et al (2010) describe the Dream phase as an organization in which people in the business care for their jobs and in being the best they can possibly be professionally as well as individually. AI creates an environment in which personal and organizational power can be separated. That creation enables the individual to unleash previously unknown capacity for organizational performance. Whitney et al argue that the 4-D-Model makes it possible for people to seek out and practice opportunities to be their best and to bring out the best in others.

Envisioning the Sales Pitch

The 4-D-Model as a tool is useful in strategy development. A pin-production sales team, for example, can discuss potential sales estimates using the data generated in the Discovery phase. For example, the pin-production sales-team affirmatively pin-points at all possible users of pins and defines pins by usage and creates a possible Adam Smith Corporate Services marketing and production database, illustrated in Figure 2. The Dream phase in sales planning can lead to a qualitative approach to a realistic sales forecast. People in the organization are encouraged to be innovative and envision fulfilled orders, continuous demand and new productive methods of doing the job. In describing AI as a successful methodology for transforming organizations, Bushe & Marshak (2009) allude to a scheme in which the resistance to the anticipated change is minimized as all relevant parties pitch in to a desired output. This reference is real because the people who actually do the job have a significant part to play in determining ways to increase productivity. Bushe & Marshak suggest that the Design phase entails determining the competences required for effectiveness to occur. It places a focus on business pragmatics of the corporation, which should entail humanistic as well as the technological values of the business.

Figure 2. The Adam Smith Pin-production Plant (Mupepi, 2014)

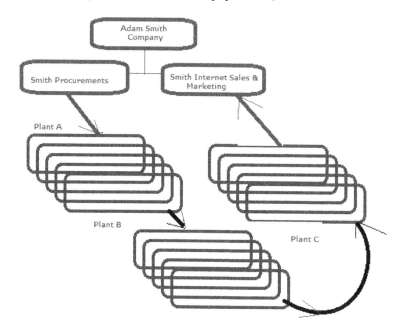

Designing Innovative Practices

In Mupepi & Mupepi (2013), the Design phase is viewed as the forum which espouses ingenuity. The pin-production system can have all the affordable technology, but people will make the difference. Tools such as metal presses, injection molding equipment or electroplating technology could have been developed by people in the same industries as an attempt to make sense of the job. The Design phase can allow the people to come up with innovative practices to get the job done at lower costs.

Appreciating the Entire Organization

AI allows the people in the organization to recognize the symbolic and relationally construct of the business and to pinpoint at what gives life to the company. Arguments developed for the AI methodology indicate that there is little about collective action that is preprogramed or unilaterally determined. There is a variety of different types of organizations. Each has its own beliefs and practices.

As Long as Customers Like it

In Erving Goffman's book, entitled *The Presentation of Self in Everyday Life*, published in 1959, he provides a detailed description and analysis of process and meaning in mundane interaction. Goffman writes from a symbolic interactionism perspective, which emphasizes roles each stakeholder is expected to play as part of the interactive organizational process. Arguments advanced resonate with Shakespeare's play "*As you like it*" in which the entire world is described as a stage in which every man and woman has a part to play (Garber, 2008). It makes organizational sense then to co-construct reality and, of course, to use the most efficient tools and technology in doing so. Creating goods and services that have more value requires a critical understanding of processes, systems and activities employed in the business. The need to know the needs of the customers cannot be overestimated. Basically, customers give life to the business, and it is imperative to design customer database to facilitate the constant flow of orders. Mupepi, Yim et al (2012) propose that AI enables all members of the organization to define their role and effectively contribute to defined organizational goals. In Cooperrider (1986), AI is designed to motivate teams and the entire organization to draw from what was done exceptionally in the past. This gives the opportunity to pose and benchmark future efforts. By reviewing the past, the firm can draw lessons to allow learning and continuous improvement. Cooperrider envisions a world full of possibilities in organization. Investigating the historical past offers the opportunity to ask questions as opinions are told at the same time, reiterating what is important to the business. Cooperrider argues that this is especially true in the context of creating the know-how needed to build and develop a successful business.

Advantages of Appreciative Inquiry

The advantages of employing the 4-D-Model of AI are many. One of them is the assertion that it allows everybody to have a say in the design and implementation of the required change. This approach minimizes the resistance to transformation. In Barrett (1995), people tend to do better when they are consulted is made. The 4-D-Model can enhance pin-production output, allowing the pin specialist to pin-point why his or her job exists and what sustains it in the scheme of pin production. Barrett (1995) holds the view that the pin specialist will be able to determine the performance criteria necessary to maintain output that has more value for the business.

Adam Smith Pin-making Corporation

The hypothetical Adam Smith Corporation is based upon the "Wealth of Nations," first published in 1774. The division of labor results in organization design referred to by Max Weber (1864–1920) in his book entitled "The Protestant Ethic and the Spirit of Capitalism," first published in 1904 and later in another book entitled "Economy and Society" published in 1914, as social structures (Mupepi, 2010). In McCreadie (2009), Adam Smith is asserted as the first classic economist to argue that the wealth of a nation was represented by a flow of goods and services in which many jobs and commercial activities allowed consumption and investment to happen concurrently. It was not an accumulated fund of precious metals or money deposited in bank accounts as viewed by mercantilists at that time in the 18th Century.

McCreadie argues that it was understandable to make such assumptions because wealth in those bygones was measured in gold bullion and other chattels held in bank accounts. Adam Smith revealed a link between exports and imports as part of economic process that made it possible for nations to create wealth. In this process, Smith identifies consumption as an integral part in which the division of labor played a critical role. In emphasizing labor as the source of the wealth of a nation Adam Smith differed from the mercantilists who stressed that land and money in the bank were the only sources of wealth. In this section of the discourse, AI is argued to have the capacity to allow the organization to rationalize processes in efforts that can allow more wealth to be created.

Conception of Enabling Organizational Design

The company can conceive the organizational structure or the much familiar hierarchical organizational structure as a division of labor controlled by defined rules and progressed by formal procedures. The plant has three sections A, B, and C. Each section is responsible for the design and implementation of the tools needed to progress the task. Each section is also responsible for understanding what the job entails. It is the responsibility of each divided labor to learn and improve the explicit practices needed to become a specialist. It is in the interest of both the employer and the employee to gain from the division of labor. The employee can become a specialist who earns a better wage from the dexterity of doing the job. The employers benefits from the increased out (See Figures 1 and 2). The organization structure is also made up of positions or jobs that have defined authority. In the organization, authority can be conferred on an individual by the organization in exchange for defined services. This conferred authority empowers the position holder to influence those who are responsible to him or her; and this influence is exercised via downward communications. In much earlier research, it is possible to advance efficiency and effectiveness in the division of labor, allowing the incumbent to understand the knowledge and skills required to increase productivity in his/her part of the structure or job.

Expanding the Knowledge and Skill Base

In Mupepi (2009), Adam Smith asserts that productivity in the pin-making factory can be increased by dividing labor into different areas of specialization. Productivity can be increased by allowing the budding specialists to enhance their job skills and to acquire the necessary knowledge, as illustrated in hypothetical Figure 2. AI can provide the answer to the economic question of scarcity by identifying the knowledge and skills required in each specialty area. It will allow a concerted effort of both the worker and employer to develop and participate in skills development efforts, which can impact the rate of the company's growth.

MAIN FOCUS OF THE CHAPTER

The main focus of this chapter is to apply the Four-Dimension Model of Appreciative Inquiry to assess and evaluate the change needed to enable specialization to occur in the division of labor. The assumption made includes a modified Six-Dimension Model (6-D-Model) to incorporate implementation and evaluation phases (see Figure 3). The first phase is the Discovery stage where everyone makes a contribution to describe the nature and description of a specialist. They all co-construct what a craftsman does, his dexterousness, and knowledge, and the type of tooling he improvises. Gergen (1999) propounds that the social construction format allows the minimization of the resistance to change.

The second phase is the Ideal stage. It is a modification of the dream to allow the organization to pin-point at the ideal product, process, or tool. If specialization has to happen, what kind of tools will the learner need to know how to use? This phase enables people in the business to think outside normal boundaries and be innovative (Bushe 2013). What the management believes to be true determines what the organization does, and thought and action emerge from relationships. Through the language and discourse of day to day interactions, people co-construct the organizations they inhabit. The purpose of inquiry is to stimulate new ideas, stories and images that generate new possibilities for action (Gergen, 1999).

Figure 3.

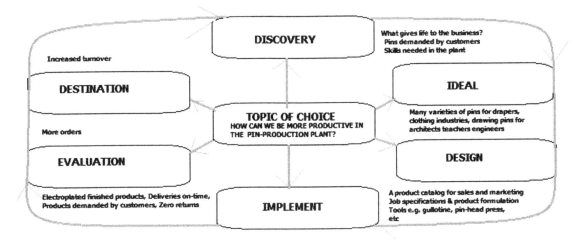

The third phase is the Design stage, interpreting the contributions made to produce a blueprint. The seeds of change and the things people think and talk about, what they discover and learn, are implicit in the very first questions asked. They will design things they have been talking about, and those discussions influence perceptions a great deal.

The Implementation phase puts the blue-print plans into action. The entire organization will anticipate positive results. Bushe (2013) suggests that the anticipatory principle posits that what we do today is guided by our image of the future. Human systems are forever projecting ahead of themselves a horizon of expectation that brings the future powerfully into the present as a mobilizing agent. Appreciative inquiry uses artful creation of positive imagery on a collective basis to refashion anticipatory reality.

The evaluation stage makes it possible for the organization to meet externally derived compliance such as rules and regulations in the industry. The evaluation phase can assist the business, or project to assess any aim, realizable concept/proposal, or any alternative, and to help in decision-making. AI normally does not wait for Implementation and Evaluation because once the desired change has been agreed upon transformation happens instantaneously. The positive principle proposes that momentum and sustainable change requires positive affect and social bonding. Sentiments, like hope, excitement, inspiration, camaraderie and joy, increase creativity, openness to new ideas and people, and cognitive flexibility. They also promote the strong connections and relationships between people, particularly between groups in conflict, required for collective inquiry and change.

The Destination Phase

The conclusion of the inquiry is arrival at the desired point. The aim is to build successful organization around what works, rather than attempting to fix what does not work

Case Study

A case study is employed to demonstrate how AI can be employed to expand the division of labor in developing specialists, and solving problems faced by a community or organization.

Controversies

AI focuses on the things the organization has done well in the past. It does ignore the mistakes made in the past. Many scholars argue that there are invaluable lessons to be learnt from past mistakes. History as a subject in management must be understood in order to design and implement a better future.

SOLUTIONS AND RECOMMENDATIONS

The following case study illustrates how useful AI is and highlights how the methodology can be applied to introduce and manage talent in organization.

The Zavaco Case Study

The paper draws empirical evidence from a company operating in the Zambezi Valley in Zimbabwe referred to as Zavaco Ltd (the Company). The research was conducted at the request of the management of Zavaco, an organization that can be described as an agro-business. The Company is situated in the Zambezi Valley, Zimbabwe. The management desired to build the capacity needed to advance its goals of poverty alleviation and food security in the region. The Management was also concerned about how that capacity could be built. The decision to use Appreciative Inquiry was made by the researchers for three reasons. The first reason is associated with the fact that AI is easy to explain and implement. The second reason is that collectivism in this part of the world is how society and its organization operate and is akin to some of the observations of Hofstede et al (2010). The third reason is that AI fitted into the scheme of what was needed to be done. Narratives form a significant part of the AI intervention. The rural community was lowly educated in the sense that they could not understand business plans and concepts without the translation of those ideas from the English to Shona Languages. The 4-D-Model was followed through in the Shona Language successfully. The assessment and evaluation techniques made it possible to identify the key performance areas in all the business activities. It allowed the focus group to participate in identifying what sustained the business. Thus, the community was ready to participate from day one.

Context-Everything Geographical Historical

Zavaco has its head office at Guruve, a small town developed during the colonial era, as the last railroad stop where cotton, tobacco, corn and other crops could be collected and transported from the Zambezi Valley to the urban and export markets. The agriculture produce would then be distributed to urban centers throughout the nation. The Guruve District is situated within the Zambezi Valley, with the Zambezi escarpment to the south, the Zambezi River to the north, and Mozambique to the east. Guruve is a low-lying area between 300 and 700 meters above sea level. The area, particularly around the Kanyemba border post, was used as a strategic entry point during Zimbabwe's protracted political and military struggle for independence by liberation forces based in Mozambique and Zambia. Hence, the villagers and farmers in the area were economically destabilized. The area is now a bastion of trade among traders from Angola, Botswana, Malawi, Mozambique, Namibia, South Africa, Zambia and Zimbabwe. The

Association is akin to the cooperative societies that have been promoted by post-independent governments in the Sub-Sahara African (SSA) region.

Background to Zavaco

Zavaco was formed in the late 1980s and at the time of its formation it employed five people. Zavaco was founded by five women who lost most of their families and asserts during the War of Liberation (1966-1980). Each of the founding members nominated an individual who joined the corporation as an employee. The Zavaco Company identified a niche in the Zambezi valley by providing food security and agro services to small plot holders and villagers. The Company's operations were expanding and the researchers were approached to build the competences the employees needed to articulate their new role in expanded activities. It can be argued that the company's growth was slow probably because of the socio-economic environment in which it was operating. However, the company's physical assets had increased from one truck to a fleet of 7 trucks and 5-ton trailers capable of moving huge amounts of grain and cotton from the small holder plots and village fields each month during the harvesting season. In addition, the company owned 5 tractors to fulfill all the tillage needs of the small plot holders and the villages. Many things, however, have changed since the company's inception in the late 1980s. Much of what Zavaco does is to meet the tillage, crop haulage, and farming equipment hardware needs of the local communities in the Zambezi Valley in Zimbabwe.

Technology Transfer

The post-independence administration embarked on a grand re-construction program after the War of Liberation (1966-1980) (or in the Shona Language Chimurenga, 1966-1980). Re-construction entailed rebuilding the infrastructure which had been destroyed in the fighting. It also meant building many social amenities such as schools, health clinics or sources, safe water supplies, which communal and rural areas had been deprived off by the minority Apartheid regimes (1890-1980).

Technology transfer made it possible for the Blair Toilets to be constructed in all communal areas. The Blair Toilet (aka Blair Latrine) is a pit toilet designed in 1971 by Peter Blair, a biologist at the Blair research Institute of the Ministry of Health, Zimbabwe. It was a result of large-scale projects to improve rural sanitation during the 1980s after Independence in Zimbabwe. There was mass deployment of the toilet design in the rural areas of the country. The villagers were shown how to erect the structures and were then given the rubrics to follow in the construction of the toilet. The Ministry of Health public health assistants helped the villagers to articulate the construction and maintenance of the toilet (Morgan, 2012).

Technology transfer initiatives were made by other public health organizations such as World Health Organization in the construction of water pumps and water boreholes.

The Creation of a Focus Group

The first step was to visit the company's operations in the Zambezi Valley and to conduct ethnography studies of how it did business, what each employee did and to put all that together in understanding production, administrative and marketing processes. The next step was to select a group of stakeholders from the non-management and management employees. The two groups were used to create the management community of practice (COP) and the non-management community of practice (COP2) and, subsequently, merged to form the Zavaco COP. All three COPs used Appreciative Inquiry in their deliberations.

Efficiency and Effectiveness

Successful companies are both efficient and effective. The Zavaco Company wanted to determine the competences it needed to create a business that efficiently met the needs of its customers. Most of these organizations focus on micro-enterprises and small businesses involved in the production of arts and crafts products. They attempt to address the poverty and diseases, and to impact economic activity in the Zambezi Valley. The current economic growth rate in Zimbabwe is given by the IMF as a negative figure of -0.5 (IMF, 2011). Where all things are equal, it also implies that the marginal propensity to consume is less than 0.5 or equal to it.

In Zimbabwe, organizations such as the Zavaco are referred to as "not-for-profit organizations" or "non-governmental organization (NGO)". Membership has been extended to villagers who are interested in self-reliance in poultry, animal husbandry, market gardening, honey production, small-scale cotton and corn production, among many other projects. All these members rally behind the Zavaco for technical and financial assistance. The Company employs more than 90 full-time employees in various capacities ranging from agronomy to grinding mill operations. It is the competencies of these employees that this study sought to address.

Capacity Building

First and foremost, the study seeks to determine the capacity required for an expanding and growing agro-based business. It is expanding, because it has increased the number of business units within a short period of its inception. Its growth can be attributed to the number of sustainable jobs that have been created from 5 to 90; another 2000 in each planting and harvesting season. The model of employment creation was adapted from the small business administration in the USA (Graves, 2012). Secondly, the study must determine the knowledge, skills, practices and behavior necessary to advance a small business operating in the remote parts of Africa where the infrastructure is very rudimentary. Explicit knowledge must be created for this company to fulfill its role as the advisor to the villagers, small-scale farmers, and the business community on micro-enterprise and small businesses (SME). In addition, the SMEs will also depend on good rainfall to be successful, something that is out of the control of either Zavaco or the state. Apart from creating direct and indirect employment, the SMEs provide opportunities for members of the community to participate meaningfully in the lives of their community, and improve the overall standard of life in the Zambezi Valley.

The Donor Community

The donor is made up of local and international organizations that support Zavaco and government departments in their efforts to secure food. Many things could have changed, since this study was revisited in 2009. The current political situation has forced some of these services to be withdrawn, causing shortages in recurrent expenditure and economic stagnation. The Company has pressed forward despite the prevailing economic hardships. The competencies required were charted using Appreciative Inquiry as the mode for pin-pointing at what mattered in the business. The results indicate that the knowledge and skills needed to do each job must be analyzed individually in order to pinpoint the levels of competency. Thus, it is important to assess pre-existing knowledge, skills and practices. Knowledge and skills gaps can be addressed by designing and implementation of appropriate competence programs. It is a truism that goods that have more value can only be produced by people who know what they are doing.

Data from the retrospective analyses and recorded narratives in field notebooks (FN1) and (FN2) as well as that obtained from the questionnaire were used to chart what was needed in a way of job competences. Narratives are applied to complement the statistical analysis, because people articulate their experiences through storytelling (Czarniawska, 2010), and those stories are particularly important in traditional African societies. Narratives have also been used in capacity building in Africa, particularly in the work of Mantel & Ludema (2000). Narratives have their own limitations, however, because not all experiences find their way to relevant level of discourse. Limitations can be recognized when using narratives to provide insight into the nature of competencies.

Creation of the Two Communities of Practice (COP1) and (COP2)

The sample size is 40 and within the sample a further eight management and eight non- management staff were randomly selected to be the COP 1 and COP 2 respectively. The samples were drawn and assessments designed to answer these research questions:

1. How does management rate itself in terms of competencies drawn by non-management?
2. How does management rate itself in terms of the competencies it draws for itself?
3. How does non-management rate itself in terms of competencies drawn by management?
4. How does non-management rate itself in terms of the competencies it draws for itself?

(These competencies are referred to later in this text as Management and Non-Management Perceived Competencies.)

Test of Significance and Interpretation of Results

This test investigated whether the competencies drawn by the COPs would represent statistically those of the population. The data was drawn from a random sample of 40 taken from a possible population of 90. The Communities of Practice sample size of eight in each group was randomly selected from the sample size of 40. Data was collected to test the hypothesis that competencies constructed by the communities of practice are more applicable than those developed elsewhere or by management alone.

The Pearson Chi-test

The Chi square test of statistical significance result of 0.146 rejects the hypothesis that Management alone can draw effective competencies. We accept the null hypothesis that only communities of practice can develop the knowledge appropriate for what the organization does. To prove this hypothesis requires in-depth analysis of all data. In Table 1, 50% of the responses were below the expert threshold, necessitating analyses of each category to determine individual competencies needs. The minimum expected

Table 1. N=40: The Pearson Chi-test

	Value	df	Asymp.sig. (2 sided)
Pearson Chi-Square	5.383[a]	3	0.146
Likelihood Ratio	6.416	3	0.093
Linear-by-Linear association	0.016	1	0.900
N of valid cases	40		

a. 4 cells (50,0%) have expected count less than 5. The minimum expected count is 1.20

count is 1.20 with a standard deviation of 3. The data can also mean that the Zavaco Company simply was not as competent as it should be.

Calibrating the Measurement Instrument

This research uses a competency range in the Likert Scale and is described below:

1=Little or No Skill
2= Basic Skill
3=Adequate Skill
4=Proficient Skill
5=Expert Skill
N/O=Not Observed.

Analysis of Individual Categories

Possibly, management in its self-rating was not drawing a distinction among strategic planning, crop production, and food and nutrition. The last two competences could be viewed by management as equal. Management might view the outcome of crop and food production as related. Is there any difference between how they rated themselves and how they were rated by non-management on the above competencies? Field observations indicate that there were no more than minimal reading and writing required in most of the jobs. Management did not go out daily to read and write about what was happening in the various programs. Production reports were produced at bi-weekly and monthly intervals. Field experience indicates that the tillage operations required the calculations of the area of the field that must be ploughed. The tractor driver and his assistant would measure the tillage area and report their findings to

Table 2. N=8 (COP1) Management self-rating on perceived competences

Competences	Total Respondents Average	1	2	3	4	5	N/A
Strategic planning		1	4	0	2	1	
Crop production		1	7	0	0	0	
Food & nutrition	8	1	0	0	2	5	

the tillage supervisor with the names and location of the customer for approval. The supervisor would either re-check the area to allow for fuel and time budgets. The actual work could only commence when the customer had made the 50% deposit required before the work can commence (FN1). There is very little writing at all, and these findings concur with Gergen (2009) and Mupepi (2005), whose contention is that language is much more important in such work environments. Gergen suggests that the technical language developed in the field of the profession is much more important in advancing effective communications. Mupepi posits that a language can impact the understanding of work practices as people coerce more with the spoken rather than the written word. Therefore, effective verbal communications are crucial in the transference of technology and the distribution of knowledge to all cognitive area where both will be processed to create goods and services that have more value.

Generally, the COP2 rated management lower on all competencies than management rated itself. But, unlike management, they made a huge distinction among the three competences. They accorded food and nutrition the highest rating. It appears that crop production was a potentially independent competence. It could imply that the entire Zavaco needed assistance to understand the agronomy of corn and cotton production. COPs have expertise in a defined expertise area. Tenkasi (2000) argues that knowledge requires contextual adaptation. COPs should disseminate their knowledge of best practices and experience to the rest of the organizational members.

Management rated itself high in Sanitation and HIV/AIDS and lowest on safe water supplies. The data draw a clear distinction between sanitation, HIV/AIDS virus and safe water supplies. Management might have rated itself lowest on safe water supplies because villagers have their own borehole or natural well water supplies. They do not need any assistance from the public health discourses on water supplies. The Ministry of Health had done a tremendous job in the construction of the so-called Blair toilets and in widespread health education programs that addressed the HIV/AIDS Pandemic. The entire Sub-Saharan Africa region has been devastated by the HIV/AIDS Pandemic. The Company needs to do a better job in promoting preventive health. The fight against the HIV/AIDS Pandemic should be viral

Table 3. N=8(COP2) Non-management self-rating on management perceived competences

Competencies	Total Respondents Average	1	2	3	4	5	N/A
Strategic planning	8	2	3	2	0	1	
Crop production	8	2	4	0	1	1	
Food & nutrition	8	1	0	0	2	5	

Table 4. N=8 (COP1) Management rating itself in its own perceived competencies

Competencies:	Total Respondents Average	Rating scale					N/A
		1	2	3	4	5	
Sanitation	8				4	4	
HIV/AIDS	8			2	3	3	
Safe water	8	2	3	1	1	1	

throughout the Zambezi Valley. Perceptions and behavior about families, and reproduction have to be changed through health education.

The cultural practices found in the region exacerbate the spreading of the HIV/AIDS virus. Health education should be a priority for the Company. Field observation indicates that the obstetrics and gynecology clinics held in collaboration with the Ministry of Health and Child Welfare have been impacted by lack of resources such as qualified community health cadres and transport. The international donor community has temporarily withdrawn technical support to Zimbabwe. But some of those preventive health programs can be achieved more with local rather than international donor support.

The low scores for safe water could cause concern. As explained under the perception of management on the same competency, villagers have their own fresh and safe water supplies. Water is drawn from boreholes and wells. Borehole construction was one of the items on rural and communal areas development immediately after independence in 1980. As noted in the introduction, the Zambezi Valley was part of the War of Liberation (1966-1980) theatre (Mupepi, 2015). The infrastructure was destroyed and the liberation government, led by Prime Minister Robert Mugabe, initiated a successful reconstruction program that included the construction of water boreholes, schools, roads, rural health centers and farm clinics. The government also initiated the delivery of health care through Primary Health Care (PHC). In this PHC discourse, preventive health is presented in many formats, including health education, in the construction of sanitation or water boreholes. Thus, the competency on HIV/AIDS is at expert level.

FUTURE RESEARCH DIRECTIONS

The Zavaco is doing all it can to provide the food security needs of the community in the Zambezi Valley. However, an interdisciplinary approach is required to benefit the stakeholders. The results from the questionnaire are limited only to the sampled population. The entire 90-100 stakeholders must be involved in determining what gives life to their organization.

The following are some of the recommendations in which Appreciative Inquiry can be useful in creating successful organization:

- The co-construction of the organizational mission.
- The design of effective organizational structure.
- The creation of explicit knowledge necessary for organizational structures to be effective.
- Large group interventions that could benefit from instantaneous change.
- Public health technology transfer e.g. in reproductive health, safe water and sanitation.
- The discussion of opportunities to expand business in the Zambezi Valley.
- The development of rubrics for micro-enterprise projects.

Table 5. N=8 (COP2) Non-Management rating on Management perceived competencies

Competencies:	Total Respondents	Rating scale					N/A
		1	2	3	4	5	
Sanitation	8	0	4	0	0	4	
HIVAIDS	8	0	0	0	3	5	
Safe water	8	1	1	2	2	2	

CONCLUSION

High performing organizations are characterized by increased productivity. AI can be successfully applied to create highly productive workplaces. The division of labor theory can be applied in tandem with other social construction intervention such as AI to advance specialization. The value creation system can be understood and enhanced using the assessment and evaluation technology of AI such as the modified 6-D-Model to focus on the efficacies needed in the business and in determining how to make those projections successful. For example, the value-chain analyses of the pin-production factory show how specialization has allowed the development of units, production departments or specialized divisions as efficient practices to enhance pin production. At the same time, effectiveness can also be achieved, recognizing the environment in which the business operates. The firm does not exist in isolation; there are stakeholders and competitors that form part of the value creation process. In addition, there are external factors that must be considered. All environments are not the same, as can be seen in the Zavaco Company. AI is an effective strategy that can progress the business to its desired destination, creating more wealth for the nation or shareholders all the same.

REFERENCES

Barrett, F. (1995). Creating appreciative learning cultures. *Organizational Dynamics*, *24*(2), 36–4. doi:10.1016/0090-2616(95)90070-5

Bushe, G. R. (2013). Generative process, generative outcome: The transformational potential of Appreciative Inquiry. In D. L. Cooperrider, D. P. Zandee, L. N. Godwin, M. Avital, & B. Boland (Eds.), Advances in Appreciative Inquiry. In *Organizational Generativity: The Appreciative Inquiry Summit and a Scholarship of Transformation* (Vol. 4, pp. 89–113). Bingley, UK: Emerald Group Publishing Limited. doi:10.1108/S1475-9152(2013)0000004003

Bushe, G. R. & Marshak, R. J. (2009). Re-visioning organization development: Diagnostic premises and patterns of practice. *Journal of Applied Behavioral Science On-line*. doi:10.1177/0021886309335070

Callinicos, A. (2007). *Social theory: A historical introduction*. Cambridge: Polity.

Cameron, K. S., Dutton, J. E., & Quinn, R. E. (2003). *Positive Organizational Scholarship: Foundations of a New Discipline*. San Francisco, CA: Berrett-Koehler.

Campbell, R. H., & Skinner, A. S. (Eds.). (1976). The wealth of nations. The Glasgow Edition of the Works and Correspondence of Adam Smith, 2b, 47

Cooperrider, D. L. (1986). *Appreciative inquiry: Toward a methodology for understanding and enhancing organizational innovation* [Unpublished doctoral dissertation]. Case Western Reserve University, Cleveland, Ohio.

Cooperrider, D. L. Jr, Sorensen, P. F., Whitney, D., & Yaeger, T. F. (2006). *Appreciative inquiry: Rethinking human organization: Toward a positive theory of change*. Champaign, Ill: Stipes LLC.

Cooperrider, D.L., & Whitney, D.K. (2005). *Appreciative Inquiry*. San Francisco, CA: Berrett-Koehler.

Czarniawska, B. (2010). *Organizing in the face of risk and threat.* Cheltenham: Edward Elgar Ltd.

Garber, M. B. (2008). *Profiling Shakespeare.* New York: Routledge.

Gergen, K. J. (2009). *Relational being: Beyond self and community.* New York: Oxford University Press.

Goffman, E. (1959). *The presentation of Self in everyday life.* London: Anchor Books.

Hofstede, G., Hofstede, G. J., & Minkov, M. (2010). *Cultures and organizations: Software of the mind* (3rd ed.). New York: McGraw-Hill.

IMF. (2011). IMF World Economics database. Retrieved from www.imf.org/external/na/ca.aspx?i.d.-28

Ingham, G. (2008). *Capitalism: reissued with a new postscript on the financial crisis.* Cambridge: Polity.

Mantel, M. J., & Ludema, J. D. (2000). From local conversations to global change: Experiencing the worldwide ripple effect of Appreciative Inquiry. *Organization Development Journal, 18*(2), 42–53.

McCreadie, K. (2009). *Adam Smith's The Wealth of Nations: A Modern-Day Interpretation of an Economic Classic.* Oxford: Oxford University Press.

Morgan, P. (2012). How to build a Blair Latrine. Retrieved from http://www.wikihow.com/Build-a-Blair-Latrine

Mupepi, M., & Mupepi, S. (2013). Creating high impact organization in the SADC: Adapting OD Methods and Practices. In J. Vogel et al. (Eds.), *Handbook for Strategic HR: Best Practices in Organization Development from the OD Network.* New York: AMACON.

Mupepi, M. G. (2005). *Transforming village entrepreneurs into sustainable organization. A case of Zimbabwe.* Ann Arbor, MI: ProQuest Inc.

Mupepi, M. G. (2009). The nature of a schematic description of a socially constructed organizational competency model (CCM). *International Journal of Collaborative Enterprise, 1*(2), 224–240. doi:10.1504/IJCENT.2009.029291

Mupepi, M. G. (2010). Appreciating social structures: a strategy for advancing the efficiency and effectiveness loci in organization. International Journal of Education Economics and Development, 1(4).

Mupepi, M. G. (2014). Can Human and Technical Resources be In Sync to Advance Resourceful Inclusive Enterprise? In F. Soliman (Ed.), *Learning Models for Innovation in Organizations: Examining Roles of Knowledge Transfer and Human Resources Management* (pp. 173–191). Hershey, PA, USA: IGI Global. doi:10.4018/978-1-4666-4884-5.ch009

Mupepi, M. G., & Motwani, J. (2015). Deconstructing the Value Creation Process: Positioning Diversity to Increase Output. *International Journal of Sociotechnology and Knowledge Development, 7*(4), 15–30. doi:10.4018/IJSKD.2015100102

Mupepi, M. G., & Mupepi, S. C. (2016). Applying Theory to Inform Competency Development: Bootstrapping Epistemic Communities in Growing Specialists. *International Journal of Productivity Management and Assessment Technologies, 4*(1), 28–38. doi:10.4018/IJPMAT.2016010103

Mupepi, M. G., & Mupepi, S. C. (2016). Applying Theory to Inform Competency Development: Bootstrapping Epistemic Communities in Growing Specialists. *International Journal of Productivity Management and Assessment Technologies*, 4(1), 28–38. doi:10.4018/IJPMAT.2016010103

Mupepi, M. G., Yim, J. Y., Mupepi, S. C. & Mupepi, K. B. (2012). Can a knowledge community situated in an African village create and advance human rights practices beyond love thy neighbor principle? *International Journal of Knowledge and Learning, 7*(3/4), 233 – 252.

Tenkasi, R. V. (2000). Some contextual antecedents of cognitive over-simplification processes in Research and Development environments: An exploration of the influence of social context on reasoning and knowledge creation practices in research and development teams. Retrieved from www2.warwick.ac.uk/fac/soc/wbs/conf/olkc/archive/oklc3/papers/id

Watkins, J. M., Mohr, B. J., & Kelly, R. (2011). *Appreciative inquiry: Change at the speed of imagination*. San Francisco: Pfeiffer. doi:10.1002/9781118256060

Whitney, D., Trosten-Bloom, A., & Rader, K. (2010). *Appreciative leadership: Focus on what works to drive winning performance and build a thriving organization*. New York: McGraw Hill.

Yaeger, T. F., & Sorensen, P. F. Jr. (2001). What Matters Most in Appreciative Inquiry. In D. Cooperider, P. Sorensen Jr, T. Yaeger, & D. Whitney (Eds.), *Appreciative Inquiry: An Emerging Direction For Organization Development* (pp. 129–142). Champaign, Illinois: Stipes Publishing L.L.C.

KEY TERMS AND DEFINITIONS

Appreciative Inquiry (AI): AI is a change management technique. AI seeks to identify sources of change that build on past successes and core organizational values through a process of recognizing positive attributes and sources of pride within the organization rather than problems or challenges.

Innovation: Is the introduction of something with new methods, techniques or tools to enhance productivity.

Personal Mastery: Means personal capacity as well as the principles one uses to produce goods and services valued by customers.

Proficiency: Is the skillfulness in the command of fundamental deriving practice and familiarity.

Resistance to Change: The process whereby individuals fail to recognize the value of a change and, thus, cling to old routines, habits or ways of thinking, rather than embrace changes.

Skill-Sets: Are a combination of skills, knowledge, and techniques one has developed to employ in doing a given job.

Specialization: In business administration, specialization is a technique of production where a business or area focuses on the production of a limited scope of products or services in order to gain greater degrees of productive efficiency within the entire system of businesses or areas.

Chapter 2
How to Effectively Apply Appreciative Inquiry in Developing Talent in Organizations

Mambo Mupepi
Seidman College, USA

Mark Davis
Self-employed Management Consultant, USA

Yalonda M. Ross-Davis
Seidman College, USA

Thomas S. Vachon
Grand Valley State University, USA

ABSTRACT

Focusing strictly on negative organizational issues could constitute an obstacle to the improvement of key attributes, products, and or services offered. This chapter suggests that Appreciative Inquiry (AI) can be an effective and efficient strategic tool used to lead positive change and improve the talent of the organization by emphasizing what is successful rather than a deficit. AI is a well-developed methodology of examining, defining, implementing, and executing precise pans of improvement by applying positive psychology which will lead to the revitalization of productivity. Furthermore, available data suggests the employees within the organization can become resistant to change when there is an overemphasizing of the shortcoming areas of weakness. By using the AI assessment and evaluation technology, companies can pin-point and materialize desirable change.

INTRODUCTION

Business entities in the 21st century are continuously faced with complex challenges that affect nearly every aspect within their organizations. In order to thrive in this modern environment, businesses are required to build the capacity necessary to progress the operations. Cooperrider (2012) provided an updated review of what Appreciated Inquiry (AI) can do when he asserted that the methodology is an innovative technique useful at building capacity in organizations. This paper considers an alternative change management technique hinged on the pragmatic ontology of AI with the goal of developing talent

DOI: 10.4018/978-1-5225-1961-4.ch002

in organizations. All companies are designed around specific goals, where entities strive to hire talented individuals to play exact roles in the production of goods and services valued most by customers. In addition, they understand social constructs (such as AI) as techniques that can be applied to pin-point the exact change needed to operate successful organizations. AI seeks to identify sources of change that will build on past successes and core organizational values. This identification happens through a process of recognizing positive attributes and sources of pride within the organization, rather than problems or challenges (Elsbach, Kayes & Kayes, 2016).

Background

AI has been used successfully world-wide to introduce and manage change. Leading consulting organizations such as Tim Rowe Price, and Booze Allan, among many others, have employed AI to grow the wealth for their clients. Leading business schools incorporating change management curricula have also adopted positive psychology in their curricula to build their students' capacity in the real world. Moreover, AI can help enhance understanding in many ways and enable organizations to build better futures.

What is Appreciative Inquiry?

What's working well? What isn't working? Although these two questions are often difficult to answer, they ultimately underline the difference between traditional Change Management Theory and Appreciative Inquiry (AI). Traditionally, in American Business conventional wisdom has led us to believe that improvement is the product of a series of identifying a problem, applying a diagnosis and developing a solution. The fundamental error of this theory is that problems are inevitable and that exposing them may lead to an overemphasis and amplification of them, hence having a negative impact on the mental processing on the talent within the organization. AI on the other hand seeks to identify sources of change that will build on past successes and core organizational values. This identification happens through a process of recognizing positive attributes and sources of pride within the organization, rather than the problems or challenges (Elsbach, Kayes & Kayes, 2016).

AI's inventors, Cooperrider & Srivastva (1987), suggested that AI is a universal (for all types of entities) model for analysis, decision-making, and the creation of strategic change. The technique at Case Western Reserve University by Cooperrider and Srivastva who felt that the overuse of "problem solving" as a model often held back essential analysis and understanding focusing on problems and limiting the discussion of new organizational models.

The Role of Talent Management in Organizations

At its core, talent management can simply be described as a matter of anticipating human capital and setting out a plan to meet it (Cappelli, 2008). Highly talented individuals can be characterized through a variety of characteristics, such as competencies, skills, abilities, experience, knowledge, intelligence, character, and/or the ability to learn and grow within the organization (Ulrich, 2008). The acquisition of talent helps organizations achieve a competitive advantage which plays a critical role in the overall success of an organization. However, due to their advantageous nature highly talented individuals are valuable, rare, and difficult to imitate (Barney, 1995). As a result, shortcomings in talent management practices remain an ongoing source of conflict which has limited the discussion of new and effective organizational models within many modern organizations.

Most limitations to talent management practices to date may rely on concerted efforts focused on subjective identification and mentorship of talents within a small portion of employees, which overlooks the overarching potential embracing the majority of the employees' talents. In addition, these approaches overlook human effects of this issue, in which human beings who react emotionally, cognitively, and behaviorally when treated differently from other people (Paauwe, 2004). Thus, we believe it's time for a fundamentally new approach to talent management and development that leverages Appreciative Inquiry (AI), a model where emphasis should be on identifying and nurturing specific talents in all employees, not the "chosen few". This approach suggests that every employee can be a top performer and should be treated as equals within the organization.

Fundamentals of the Four Stages of Appreciative Inquiry

The AI process encompasses four stages which have been labeled discovery, dream, design, and destiny most commonly known as the 4-D Cycle.

Discovery

The Discovery stage is a very broad and thorough search to explore the "best of what is". Through the utilization of data collection and narrative exploration, this phase serves to identify positive attributes, past successes and sources of pride within the organization. This process begins with a collaborative act of carefully crafting appreciative interview questions and creating an appreciative interview guide. These interview questions are written in an affirmative manner to highlight and enrich dialog among the participants and to instill a positive sense of identity of the organization.

Dream

The Dream stage of AI begins the process of "what might be": an energizing time to think about the possibilities beyond the realm of present day thinking. The dreaming process involves forming small groups (8-12 people) and encouraging these groups to review the summary sheets from the interviews. The intent of this phase is to cultivate common ground within the group based on the success stories and questions based on dreams, hopes, and visions of the future of the organization from the original interviews.

Design

The design phase begins to build the bridge from the best of "what is" (present) within the organization towards a more imaginative state of "what might be" (future). Thus, this stage essentially addresses the question "how can we make it happen?" The challenge of this phase is to ensure that everyone can find where they fit, a place where they feel valued and are enabled to contribute in a positive way of their choice. This phase is about giving form to the values, ideas and vision framed as provocative propositions and strategies. The focus is on how, but this stage will also clarify how we will know when we have achieved our goal.

Destiny

The final phase of appreciative inquiry is destiny. This phase concludes all that has been done in the discovery, dream, and design phases and through a lot of learning, adjusting and improvising, sets the stage for a new culture to form. Due to the sharing of the new image of the future in this phase, it is essential that everyone comes together to discuss what they can and will do to contribute to the realization of the organizational dream as articulated in the provocative propositions. These commitments then serve as the basis for ongoing activities. They key to sustaining the momentum here is to build an "appreciative eye" into all of the organization's systems, procedures, and ways of working.

Old Ways

Change management is common practice when solving workplace problems. All management theories hold a proper place to be utilized. Change management theory, as with all management theories, has many limitations. Common thought leads us to believe an answered problem most likely results in an absolute end to the issue. Change management exists in this realm of thought. Management determines an action to take and communicates the message to the employees. Although, employees are crucial to change management initiatives, they are often overlooked (Colletti & Chonko, 1997). This appears to be contradictory. However, management seeks to change employee behavior without the input of their employees. A primary focus on changing an individual's behavior fails to detect possible underlying issues. The change management theory tends to target symptoms of a potentially deeper problem to the workplace. Many managers seem to believe altering the company's systems and structure will lead to new employee behaviors (Colletti & Chonko 1997). For example, a manager institutes a new software to clock in hoping employees will no longer arrive late. The manager may be able to monitor arrival times more efficiently but has not determined the problem to be employee motivation rather than the time sheet system. The new systems fail and employees begin taking the blame. The most devastating effect on company culture is when fingers are pointed causing employees to take personal responsibility (Klie, 2008).

Workplace Culture Overview

Workplace culture evolves from the standard of which managers embody and enforce the values set forth by the company (Schein, 2004). Employees then agree on a framework of qualities to operate within. Therefore, a standard of operations is established whether dealing with customers, vendors, handling conflict, work ethic and any action in the workplace. It is known as culture. Companies flourish or decay by their culture. It becomes so heavily embedded in the company and each action molds the culture (Klie, 2008). While malleable, each action can have a very different effect on a company culture. Discipline is a major factor. Employees quickly learn acceptable behaviors which become commonplace. If one employee is never disciplined for showing up late, others will accept late arrival as acceptable. Then the culture develops into one of late arrivals. A manager can easily stop this with disciplinary action. Altering the workplace environment is difficult as employees will feel they are being personally attacked. This is where the old style of management has been successful on the surface. However, there may be an underlying issue to the tardiness which is AI and will be further discussed later in the chapter.

Strategic and Core Culture

A deeper level of culture is known as the strategic culture. Competitive advantages develop from a successful strategic culture. Therefore, managerial practices need to be in line with company strategic goals. For instance, a company focusing heavily on customer service will empower its employees to make independent decisions to help a customer in a time of need. Employees then learn to adapt to the situation enabling them to properly satisfy a customer rather than be dependent on a manager. Since strategy varies from company to company there is no universal beneficial strategic culture except trust (Klie, 2008). Trust along with knowledge, power, sharing, adaptability, and identity determine core culture and are commonly found in almost all companies (Klie, 2008). Without core culture, it is impossible to utilize a strategic culture.

Negative Culture

People with past experience in a poor workplace environment do not need a textbook to understand the damage it can do to a company. Poor corporate cultures create an uninspiring environment. Companies overly focused on micro-management along with environments built on heavy bureaucracies or a lack of constructive thought processes due to blame. (Cottrill, K. 2012). Since culture is determined by shared values, employees no longer maintain high values in the workplace. The result is reduced productivity and a lack of motivation, to name a few. Often overlooked, retention of employees becomes increasingly difficult. Few companies realize the missed opportunity to leverage company culture as a retention and even recruiting tool (Cottrill, K. 2012). The management is not focused on the larger issue of turnover because they are blinded by the costs associated with their poor company culture.

Qualitative Costs Associated with Poor Culture

Poor culture leads to increased costs to a company. Employees are no longer inspired to perform for the company. Due to the eroding culture, employee turnover increases. The firing process is very costly due to the paperwork and possible exit interview. The company then needs to rehire and train a new employee. Human Resources costs will be spent to recruit and interview potential candidates (Sinatra, 2015). Training a new employee will be one of the largest expenses. Companies may have to pay for a formal program or use time of current employees for on the job training. Employees preoccupied with training may fail to satisfy customers. Another possible customer disruption is a new employee interacting with a customer. Mistakes by the new employee or neglect from overburdened employees erode crucial trust build between the customer and the company. Sales numbers are likely to drop as a result. Until the training allows the new employee to fully fill the position, overtime will be paid to the employees working extra to pick up for the lost employee. Increasing the work burden heightens the potential for worker's compensation and unemployment claims. The most potentially dangerous effect is the cyclical decrease of employee morale (Sinatra, 2015).

Other Costs

Quantifiable costs are only a small portion of the damage. Employees possess knowledge, experience, and various skills. Employees may hold irreplaceable relationships with key vendors and customers (Sinatra,

M. 2015). Each skill and relationship lost may be impossible to account for the monetary impact on the company. Workers can become confused as to the reason coworkers left. Employees begin to develop their own idea which leads to further unnerving of employees. As a response, workers hold their ideas in order to not perform poorly and become the next to leave the company.

Talent becomes increasingly hard to manage when it disappears. Those with talent are overburdened with tasks because of their experience Employee satisfaction rapidly drops as stress levels from increased work load. Turnover becomes an endless cycle, multiplying with each departure of an employee, calling for immediate action by management (Sinatra, 2015).

How Appreciative Inquiry Creates a Prosperous Culture

Appreciative inquiry proposes an alternative solution to workplace issues. Myopically pointing fingers erodes the company culture. AI, on the other hand, builds up company culture. While AI does have its limitations when facing an urgent crisis a multitude of case studies illustrate the benefit gained by utilizing the AI approach (Drew & Wallis 2014). AI discovers the positive aspects of the company, envision a future state, design a plan, and then put it into action. To start, by utilizing a positive focus, morale is uplifted. The design stage delves deeper the underlying issues rather than each individual case. Design opens a new form of critical thinking which relies on more employee engagement. Excitement is drawn from an elevated way of thinking. The positive approach accompanied by inclusion of all ideas disarms those resistant to change (Drew, & Wallis, 2014). Employees reduce their dependence upon immediate solutions because they understand the overall plan in place. Managers no longer rely upon managing with a command and control style but rather focus on appreciation (Cwiklik, 2006).

Breaking the stagnant mold of problem solving breathes new light not only on the issue but into employees. New employee morale rapidly builds a positive culture which then creates a social reliability. Benefits of AI culminate into a culture focused on its strengths. Those who do not fall in line with the core values are phased out (Collins, 2001, p. 51). The system becomes a self-sufficient talent management system. Employees are drawn to, what Cooperrider & Sekerka (2003) call, the alluring future vision for the company. Those resistant to change will not agree with the values of the company. The newly released positive energy will cause those committed to stay and others to find employment elsewhere.

The Good and the Bad

Appreciative Inquiry process can be applied in a practical way within the business sector; with the central focus of the process being: searching for the best in people, within their organizations, and the applicable world around them.

How might the organization apply this principal? The first step is to understand and anticipate the strengths and limitations of AI, and how it might fit best within the organization. This process is designed to introduce an action based research that is both a problem solving method and process with activities and events strategically planned to avoid focusing strictly on the negative and what is not working. Several limitations were provided by Rogers & Fraser (2003) within practice and evaluation; underestimating the skills needed to implement this approach effectively, not being prepared to deal with potential problems, lack of time commitment to truly learn the environment of observation and lack of collaboration to identify a few.

How might the organization avoid those pit falls? Suggestions would be to make sure that the evaluators are familiar with the organization either as a third part consultant or an unbiased employee. For areas in which the evaluator is unclear of structure and processes, having a cross disciplinary team would be beneficial. Providing the evaluators with guidance on how they might involve several levels and layers of stakeholders is another important aspect. However those limitations provide areas of ambiguity and uncertainty in trusting that there is a balance in expected outcomes and the contributions to this process.

MAIN FOCUS OF THE CHAPTER

The focus of this discussion is how to design and implement successful talent management strategy in organization. AI is a positive psychology change management technique developed at Case Western Reserve University Ohio by David Cooperrider. Many scholars have contributed to the discourse of the methodology. For example, Mupepi, Tenkasi Sorensen & Mupepi (2013) have adapted the state-of-the-art assessment and evaluation technology of the 4-D Cycle as a tool that can be used by the participation of all stakeholders in one seating to pinpoint at the prevailing cultural conditions in the organization making it possible to instantaneously implement desirable change.

Controversy

One particular controversy surrounds AI. Its centricity is on focusing on the positive aspects in a history of an organization. It does not take into consideration how an organization could have failed to achieve a specific goal such as profitability. When that occurs, the organization does not learn from its past. The likelihood of the same mistake or errors occurring are greater.

SOLUTIONS AND RECOMMENDATIONS

Application Within the Company

In the first phase Discovery; the company should explore what their talent is best at. Asking questions such as "Tell me about a time when you performed at a high level of motivation?" or "What excites you the most about your job?" These types of questions are provocative and place the talent in a place where they are focusing on what traits, characteristics and moments made them the happiest—and as stated earlier productivity will increase when talent is happy.

In the second phase of AI—Dream, you will create small groups of people to process the interviews that were conducted during the Discovery phase. Within these small groups—cross disciplinary teams would be best—ideate about how might we create an environment or, consistently provide opportunities for our talent to truly occupy the space of satisfaction therefore improving the bottom line of the business. Once the small groups have begun to construct a common ground by looking for patterns, traits and characteristics of what makes their most successful—successful, they then can move into the Design.

In the Design phase, the bridge is built from ideation to prototyping—as in 'how might we' create this consistently in the future. By taking this next step, the organization is committing to finding the appropriate place for each of their current employees and making sure that they are maximizing their potential to the fullest; in addition to providing insight on where there is lack and why.

In the final phase of AI, Destiny, the organization has had an opportunity to gather information from individuals both top performers and those who are not; plus processed the information within small groups and ideate about the future. This phase allows for implementation of the information gathered and processed to be used as a catalyst for a new organizational culture. This is where management needs to have the awareness of their limitations, assumptions and become familiar with the notion that not every top performer needs to be promoted.

The Way Forward

In Mupepi (2017), the AI 4-D Cycle can be modified to suit each individual organizational needs. For example, two phases: implementation and valuation have been included in Figure 1 to enable the organization to implement and evaluate the desirable change after a given period of time (see Figure 1). The implementation phase is the process of putting a decision or plan into effect while the evaluation is the assessment of the outcome. It is a judgment about the amount, number, or value of the desirable change. It can be quantified or qualified with statements such as: increased turnover or met the sales target for the month or year. AI is very versatile and can be easy to understand and implement. The discovery phase provides participates to pin-point at the talent needed in effective organization. Drawing analog from the Adam Smith Pin-production factory, the talent required to advance pins production are many and can be confined within the division of labor include, pin-smiths, guillotine cutters, or electroplaters (See Figure 1). The idle situation is for the pin-production establishment to have experienced artisans. The move towards talent acquisition can include writing down the job descriptions and specifications of the artisans. These two documents can be used to provide on-job training to existing personnel within the divided labor or to advertise to hire such talent in the local media. The next phase would include the design and implementation of conditions of service necessary to recruit and retain the specialists (see

Figure 1. The 4-Cycle Model can be modified (Mupepi, 2017)

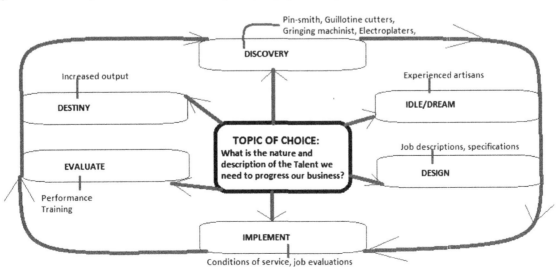

Figure1). Mupepi propounds that by constantly revisiting the Topic of Choice the organization is able to develop future scenarios in light of prevailing cultural conditions (see figure3).

When successfully used, AI will create a flourishing strategic culture resulting in a cultural draw. The company will be appealing to outsiders therefore attracting potential new recruits. Potential recruits will be unable to resist the flourishing culture. Employees will be committed to their workplace and enjoy the environment to a great extent ultimately lowering turnover. Employees will have a chance to stand out due to increased work ethic. Also, new ideas will be heard during the design process increasing the possibility of organizational breakthroughs (Drew & Wallis, 2014). Two new opportunities to evaluate and ultimately promote employees emerge. Since AI focusses on benefits, managers are encouraged to highlight the strengths of each employee and act upon them. Managers are encouraged in AI to shuffle employees around the company to find a better fit. A socially inclined employee may be given a chance in a customer facing role. Movement has the potential to increase employee satisfaction and performance. Highlighting strengths will eliminate company weaknesses. One of the most crucial elements to the change is the removal of resistance to change (Drew & Wallis 2014). Without AI removing the obstacle of stagnation, employees will resist actions in regards to talent management. When change becomes stagnant, a quick does of AI will rejuvenate the ideas of a company. Maintaining AI is crucial for sustained success (Cwiklik, 2006).

CONCLUSION

Appreciating talent in organization is one of the most challenging aspect of strategic planning and implementation. The model can be deployed to understand the talent that gives life to the business, and how it can be sustained to create the competitive advantage. The 4-D Cycle can be used continuously to enable management to appreciate the dynamics of intellectual capital prevailing in the business, how it can be protected and grown. In addition, the 4-D Cycle can be modified to suit the situation and needs of the organization. AI is one approach managers can apply to learn and continuously improve.

REFERENCES

Bareny, J. B. (1995). Looking inside for competitive advantage. *The Academy of Management Executive, 9*(4), 9–61.

Cappelli, P. (2014). *Strategic talent management: Contemporary issues in an international context.* Cambridge, UK: Cambridge University Press.

Colletti, J. A., & Chonko, L. B. (1997). Change management initiatives: Moving sales organizations from obsolescence to high performance. *Journal of Personal Selling & Sales Management, 17*(2), 1–30. Retrieved from http://search.proquest.com.ezproxy.gvsu.edu/docview/216748543?accountid=39473

Collins, J. C. (2001). *Good to Great: Why Some Companies Make the Leap--and Others Don't.* New York, NY: Harper-Business.

Cooperrider, D. L., & Sekerka, L. E. (2003). Toward a theory of positive organizational change. In K. S. Cameron, J. E. Dutton, & R. E. Quinn (Eds.), *Positive organizational scholarship: Foundations o f a new discipline. San Francisco: Berrett-Kohler.*

Cooperrider, D. L., & Srivastva, S. (1987). Appreciative Inquiry In Organizational Life. *Research in Organizational Change and Development, 1*, 129–169.

Cwiklik, J. S. (2006). *The story behind the numbers: How and why the appreciative inquiry summit process transforms organizational cultures.* Retrieved from http://search.proquest.com.ezproxy.gvsu.edu/docview/304910759?accountid=39473

Drew, S. W., & Wallis, J. L. (2014). The use of appreciative inquiry in the practices of large-scale organizational change. *Journal of General Management, 39*(4), 3–26.

Elsbach, K., Kaues, A., & Kayes, D. C. (2016). *Contemporary Organizational Behavior: From Ideas to Action.* Boston: Pearson.

Klie, Shannon (2008). Culture Guides Behaviors at Work. *Canadian HR Reporter.*

Mupepi, M. (2017). Using Communities of Practice to Identify Competencies. In K. Rasmussen, P. Northrup, & R. Colson (Eds.), *Handbook of Research on Competency-Based Education in University Settings* (pp. 157–167). doi:10.4018/978-1-5225-0932-5.ch008

Mupepi, Mambo Ram V. Tenkasi Peter F. Sorensen & Sylvia Mupepi (2013). *Creating High Impact Organizations in the SADC: Adapting OD Methods and Practices.* In J. Vogelsang & M. Townsend et al. (Eds.), *Handbook for Strategic HR best practices in Organization Development from OD Network.* New York: AMACON.

Paauwe, J. (2004). *HRM and performance: Achieving long-term viability.* New York, NY: Oxford University Press. doi:10.1093/acprof:oso/9780199273904.001.0001

Reid, J., & Crisp, D. (2007). The Talent Challenge: Creating a culture to recruit, engage and retain the best. *Ivey Business Journal Online.* Retrieved from http://search.proquest.com.ezproxy.gvsu.edu/docview/216185457?accountid=39473

Rogers, P.J., & Fraser, D. (2003). *Appreciating Appreciative Inquiry.* Wiley Periodicals, Inc.

Schein, E. H. (2004). *Organizational culture and leadership.* San Francisco: John Wiley & Sons, Inc.

Sinatra, M. (2015). Employee turnover: Costs and causes. *Air Conditioning, Heating & Refrigeration News, 255*(17), 30. Retrieved from http://search.proquest.com.ezproxy.gvsu.edu/docview/1718314845?accountid=39473

Ulrich, D. (2008). Call for talent: What is the best solutions? *Leadership Excellence, 25*(5), 17.

KEY TERMS AND DEFINITIONS

Appreciative Inquiry (AI): AI is about the co-evolutionary search for the best in people, their organizations, and the relevant world around them. It is a change management approach which involves systematic discovery of what gives life to a living system when it is most alive, most effective, and most constructively capable in economic, ecological, and human terms.

Positive Psychology: Positive psychology is the scientific study of human flourishing, and an applied approach to optimal functioning.

Talent Management: Talent management is the science of using strategic human resource planning to improve business value and to make it possible for companies and organizations to reach their goals.

Four-Dimension Assessment and Evaluation Technology (4-D Cycle Model): The 4-D Cycle Model is a state-of-the-art assessment and evaluation adaptable technology useful at pin-pointing the prevailing cultural conditions in organizations.

Chapter 3
Mastering Talent Management:
The Uncertainties, Lack of Clarity and Misunderstandings

Nana Yaw Oppong
University of Cape Coast, Ghana

ABSTRACT

Although companies around the world have made talent management a top priority, most human resource professionals and senior executives believe their organizations have not fully resolved the talent management puzzle. The chapter investigates if there are any indicators that suggest that talent management is a puzzle. Applying mainly review of academic and popular literature, the assessment is done under five headings including talent and talent management definitions; the need for talent management; the root of talent management; talent management strategies and processes, and talent management-diversity integration. It is revealed that albeit being differentiator between organizations that succeed and those that do not, talent management is saddled with uncertainties, lack of clarity, and misunderstanding, which are hurdles that need to be cleared to pave way for more effective talent programs. To overcome these, organizations should avoid one common blueprint to all talent situations, but develop approaches that suit individual talent requirements.

INTRODUCTION

The importance of talent management cannot be underestimated. It is obvious that structured TM program is expensive, especially when those developed are the ones likely to leave to bargain for high conditions of service with their newly acquired skills. This is informed by the looming talent shortage which will impact every organization without regard to industry, and that this stems from the fact that the skills set possessed by available workers may not match the advanced, more complex skills required by businesses in this information and knowledge economy. It is therefore advised that organizations should take specific initiatives to better position themselves to mitigate the operational challenges posed by the talent shortage. At the very least companies can start creating a culture as an employer of choice by accommodating individual differences and continually identifying and offering development opportunities

DOI: 10.4018/978-1-5225-1961-4.ch003

to employees. It is believed that talented individuals will be more likely attracted to organizations that invest in their employees (Busine & Watt, 2005).

Deloitte (2005) recounts the impending baby boomer retirements; widening skills gap between what organizations require and what is possessed by individuals; and ineffective approaches to talent management are combining forces enough to threaten the world business economy. Citing the result of a survey involving 123 HR executives to support this, the study revealed that incoming workers with inadequate skills (70%); baby boomer retirements (61%); and inability to retain key talent (51%) combine to pose the greatest threats to business performance. This result brings to the fore the need to provide relevant skills to younger employees and retain them for organizational success. This is the essence of TM which is believed to be the differentiator between organizations that succeed and those that do not. Talent management is however plagued with misunderstandings, uncertainties and lack of clarity, suggesting that the area is not grounded in practice, therefore highlighting why it is seen by many experts as a puzzle (Stahl et al., 2012) to realize the full benefits of the concept. It is the aim of this chapter to explore some of the issues that render TM a puzzle. This explanation is done under the following five sub-headings including talent and talent management definitions; the need for talent management; the root of talent management; talent management strategies and processes, and talent management-diversity integration.

TALENT AND TALENT MANAGEMENT DEFINITIONS

Many authors/researchers, a few being Cappelli (2008); Harris, Craig & Light (2011); Caravan, Barbery & Rock (2012);Swailes, Downs & Orr (2014) have written about talent management, with a few who have tried to define 'talent'. Notwithstanding, the definition of talent has been unclear. Literature suggests fundamental lack of clarity about what is meant by talent. This needs to be clarified because if organizations cannot compete successfully without talented people, then it becomes an unavoidable task to clarify who these talented people are. It is cited by Barlow (2006) that some organizations do forced ranking of people (not talent) into 'A', 'B' and 'C' as categories of talent but only the few rated 'A' grade are prioritized. Earlier, Michaels, Handfield-Jones & Axelrod (2001) had categorized talent as valuable, rare and hard-to-imitate. They however find it difficult to prescribe who talented employees are. More recently, Swailes et al. (2014) view talent from positive psychology perspective.

Generally, managers find it easier to indicate who their talented employees are than to explain what they mean by talent. When managers are asked to explain why employees appear on their talent list the commonest answer could be that they are good performers or promising. Due to the difficulty in pinpointing what talent is, many managers and authors attempt to describe who talented individuals are rather than what is talent. There are those who depart from the people categorization to identification of attributes of employees. For instance, Zingheim and Schuster (1999) compare talent to skills and competencies; Paprock (2006) compares it to skills, knowledge and capabilities; Fleming and Asplund (2008) compare talent to skills; while Ambrose (2003) compares it to capabilities. These descriptions offer some levels of understanding when considered individually but could be confusing when they are compared, trying to develop a common definition or understanding of talent. For instance, Fleming and Asplund (2008) distinguish between what is innate (talent) in individuals from what can be changed or acquired (knowledge, skills); while Gagné (2007) distinguishes between natural abilities (gifts, potentials) from systematically developed skills (talent). These distinctions suggest that while Fleming and Asplund see innate/natural abilities as talent as distinguished from what could be acquired or developed (skills), Gagné sees natural abilities as rather gifts/potentials as distinguished from developed skills (talent). Paprock's (2006) findings add to the confusion when skills, knowledge and talent are identified as different individual characteristics of people, the underutilization of which causes human resource development (HRD) problems.

This is enough literature to suggest differences in, and confusion about talent definition. These render the indicators of talent unclear and confusing. These become a challenge to effective implementation of talent management programmes. One could ask why organizations could identify talented individuals from within their team without a clear specification of exactly what made people 'talented'.

Despite the confusions and lack of clarity about indicators of talent or who talented employees are, few definitions of talent are identified. Considering a few of the definitions reveals how experts define talent to capture what indicates talent which, this author believes, are different things and should be distinguished. The former is the general meaning or understanding of talent as a concept while the latter has to do with what makes someone a talent i.e. talent as a concept as distinguished from talent as a resource. CIPD (2006) defines talent as a complex amalgam of employees' skills, knowledge, cognitive ability and potential. On their part, Fleming and Asplund (2008) define talent as those tendencies that exist deep within us, these are the aspects of personality or behavior most resistant to change, which could be considered together with acquired skills, experience and attitudes to polish talent. This implies that knowledge, skills and experience (acquired) are just used to polish talent (innate, natural abilities) to perform but knowledge, skills and experience will not mean much without talent. Deloitte (2005) defines talent from 'critical' point of view. Deloitte defines critical talent as the individuals and groups who drive a disproportionate share of their company's business performance and generate greater-than-average value for customers and shareholders. 'Critical talent' goes beyond performance as critical talent does not necessarily refer to high performers but represents those individuals who possess highly developed skills and deep knowledge of not only the work itself but how to make things happen within the organization. Once this is achieved, attraction and retention largely take care of themselves.

These three definitions, like many others, reveal the lack of clarity and uncertainty about the definition of talent. Thus, CIPD's (2006) definition is in a way refuted by Flaming & Asplund (2008) as incomplete because skills, knowledge and potentials are required to polish talent which is rather natural abilities. On the other hand, though Deloitte (2005) supports skills and knowledge they cannot be used to define talent – they are just the means to achievement of high organizational performance, which talents do. The definitions and descriptions of talent identified appear to be confusing and lack commonality. Thus, while Delloite (2005) considers talent from the perspective of what the person can do, CIPD (2006) and Fleming & Asplund (2008) consider it from perspective of what the person has which is subject to further distinction; what one has to be a talent as against what one has as a means of becoming a talent.

As with 'talent', the term talent management has also been admitted by many authors as difficult to define. Despite the popularity in recent years, a precise definition of talent management remains somewhat elusive and this raises significant concern about both the lack of common definition and the lack of evidence underpinning its practice. The lack of common definition is however not a surprise as this justifies the common problems associated with talent management. It is agreed that identifying, nurturing and growing the talent form critical part of talent management. How then can talent be effectively managed if it is difficult to define what should be identified, nurtured and grown? This definition challenge is confirmed by CIPD (2006) who admits that in the institute's 2006 learning and development survey, only 20% of respondents had a formal definition of talent management although 51% of respondents admitted undertaking talent management activities. Even with the 20%, the result revealed generally a lack of consistency in defining talent management. There are generally three primary perceptions of talent management. The first perception is that talent management is comprised of a collection and of typical human resource department practices such as recruitment, succession management and career development. This perception renders talent management as superfluous or a little more than a rebranding of human resource management (HRM) because these are what HRM seeks to do. The second perception is that talent management focuses on predicting or modelling the role of human resources throughout the organization based on such factors as workforce skills, supply and demand, and growth and attrition. This is an improvement on the first perception but portrays talent management to be more or less synonymous with human resource or workforce planning.

The third perception focuses on resourcing, developing and rewarding employee talent. This perception is problematic given the contradictory positions that are presented i.e. the focus on a select few versus all employees. These perceptions are indications that talent management is not well grounded in research, and not distinct from traditional HR practices or disciplines. It adds to the lack of clarity of talent management definition that many of the policies and practices underlying talent management are synonymous with the various components of HRM (e.g. recruitment, selection, compensation, performance management, development, succession planning). This makes it difficult to distinguish talent management from HRM (Hughes & Rog, 2008).

Let us consider these definitions:

1. Talent management as managing human capital, an intangible resource comprised of people's knowledge, skills and experience (Leisy & Pyron, 2009).
2. Talent management as a multi-faceted concept that has been championed by HR practitioners, fueled by the war for talent and built on the foundations of strategic HRM (Morton, 2005).
3. The accelerated development of a deliberately select proportion of employees, distinguished by their above average performance and promotability, and who have the potential to make substantial further contribution to the business and the alignment of the employees with key (strategically important) roles (Swailes et al., 2014).

While definition (1) is not different from the traditional HRM (Morton, 2005), the second definition was intended to depart from the rebranding of HRM. Even with this definition, emphasis is on whose responsibility it is to manage talent, the drivers of talent management and the role of talent management in organizations without actually revealing what talent management is. The third definition, which extends the first two, emphasizes those to develop (the select few); indication of being talented (above average performance); their contributions as talent; and exclusive role perspective (key roles in the organization). All these paint the picture that the definitions lack commonality, therefore fueling the definition battle.

THE NEED FOR TALENT MANAGEMENT

Considering the lack of certainty about talent and talent management, is there any need for the program in organizations? Despite the identified uncertainty, lack of clarity and misunderstanding, many studies support talent management programmes in organizations. In the fast-changing information technology and knowledge economy, talent is the differentiator between companies that succeed and those that do not. This is not being realized by organizations because many do not attach the required importance to talent management as they do to other resources. To quote Charan (2010: 14), "If businesses manage their finances as loosely as they manage their talent development, most would go bankrupt". This implies that businesses do not attach the needed seriousness to their talent management as they do to their finances and/or other aspects of business that they believe give them competitive advantage. It must be noted however that all company products and resources are time-perishable but the only thing that stays is the development of skills and capabilities in employees. Managing skills, especially of the right people in right roles at the right time should be nothing new to HR professionals, but done differently, talent management can create long-term organizational success and this is very important–creating talent mindset in organizations (Ashton & Morton, 2005). Talent management therefore goes further than the traditional HRM by "doing something differently" for competitive advantage. With this view of Ashton and Morton (2005), let us consider a fourth definition:

Identifying potentials and harnessing their (raw) talent towards the achievement of organizational goals. The harnessing process involves training and developing potentials; retaining and utilizing them; deploying them within the organization; and rewarding their contribution. (Oppong and Gold, 2013).

This definition is of two main parts – identification of potentials; and harnessing their talent. The harnessing processes include training and development; retention and utilization; deployment; and rewarding contribution.

The selected few; identification of the selected (not necessarily from within); the concept of raw talent (skills possessed, especially from outside) are raw and need to be harnessed to the required standard to drive organizational success. Identifying the talented; offering them company-specific skills that are less useful to competitors for further contribution to the organization; and retaining these talents to reap returns on investment are some of the additions that call for the need for talent management programmes. These, the authors believe, are the additions to the traditional HRM to move the process to talent management. With regards to the second part of the definition, which is the talent process, this takes the form of the traditional HRM but should be approached from strategic perspective.

There is no doubt that the need for talent management is appreciated by organizations. Even organizations without structured talent programmes could have hidden talent mechanisms in operation to identify, develop and utilize and retain employees. Regardless of knowing that they should have talent programmes in place, many business executives are not aware of the talent drivers though they regard talent as an HR risk, if not implemented. For instance, Ernst & Young's 2000 Global HR Risk Survey involving 150 global executives of Fortune 1000 companies revealed non-implementation of talent management as the top HR risk (Leisy & Pyron, 2009). What therefore are the forces that bring talent management to the forefront of today's HR risk concern focus? Some commonly cited factors include ageing workforce and globalization. Ageing workforce requires organizations to simultaneously manage older workers while attracting Generation Y talent as the baby boom generation is entering retirement. Impact of ageing workforce (and their increasing retirements) on talent needs to be well managed to find the right young replacements. Other than that, there is the risk of a massive loss of collective skills and experience. If not, the ageing population and inadequate supply of young talents will create a supply gap (between required and available talents) in many organizations. Another factor is globalization which is making 'talented' individuals no longer limited to marketing their skills within one country or region, but they can sell themselves to organizations across the world. In view of these factors contributing to a significant shift, experts should worry over the likelihood of intense global competition for talents – the need to worry over how talent is recruited, retained, developed, managed and retained.

On the contrary, other experts (including Uren, 2007; Hills, 2009) intimate that it is not talent shortage that prompts talent management in organizations and requires greater attention. They believe that the prime importance in this regard is a business process that is not dependent on any external factors.

The logic behind talent management is straightforward. Businesses are run by people. Processes, technology and capital are important, but it is people who make the decisions. It's people who create value by using these corporate assets to create products and services that people want. This must mean that the better the people an organization has, the better it will perform. This is the rationale behind talent management – attract, develop and utilize the best brains to get superior business results (Uren, 2007, p. 32).

Given this perspective, performance and business success are seen to depend more on effective utilization of human capital rather than on physical capital. It can be explained that despite their importance, technological and other material resources are generated by the industrious and creative efforts of people, whose ingenuity ensures that these resources are effectively deployed. Therefore, regardless of effects of external factors, organizations should still strive for effective management of their employees. As a matter of fact, effective talent management process helps people within an organization cross-skill so that there is well-equipped pool of suitably experienced talent for internal utilization and deployment. In short, the main idea of talent management is the focus on ensuring the organization is future-proofed in terms of the right skills, to ensure that the organization is able to grow and perform in the future that is increasingly unpredictable, but not to wait for future (and external) challenges before attempting to mitigate them through talent programmes. This suggests that the need for talent management is informed by internal factors but not external factors.

There is another school of thought that also departs from the external factors but equally departs from the business process perspective. It is explained that the current economic climate makes it less feasible to talk about war for talent (among organizations). For example, there is unemployment in the Far East (including China); and in East Asia (including India). Especially in Africa, there is production of large industrial 'reserve armies' due to foreign direct investments (FDIs) and redundancy exercises with resultant unemployment. Therefore, the world is gradually being filled by employable people that make the 'war for talent' a less critical issue. However, more people on the work market does not guarantee employers the needed talent. So, although the war for talent may no more be an appropriate talent jargon, there is still demand for talent in practice (Farndale, Scullion and Sparrow, 2010) which puts burden on organizations to develop in-company. Other supporters of the internal factor perspective, including Robinson (2001) and Stahl et al. (2012) criticize the external factors. They believe that even with the changing demographics tighter employment market could be compensated for, through productivity increases which are achieved through internal talent considerations. Also, the ageing population and effect on talent supply seems to be just projections and not something impacting on talent management today. For instance, it is revealed that by 2025 those aged 15 – 65 are projected to fall by 7% in Germany; by 9% in Italy; and by 14% in Japan (Stahl et al., 2012). Dr. Jacquelyn Robinson, community workforce development specialist (see Robinson, 2001) sums it up that organizations need to provide the specialized, job-specific training necessary for employees to cope with the company or industry, and also to take up challenging positions.

As has been noted, there is consensus on the need for talent management but authors differ greatly on the key drivers – either external factors or internal factors. Even those who are in the same camp differ on the actual factors. For instance, those who strongly favor external drivers are also 'at war' on whether it is the global employment trend or changing demographics. Further, those in support of changing demographics differ on whether age (the key demographic factor) impacts on talent shortage now or in future. The arguments communicate yet another area of uncertainty and lack of commonality in talent management.

THE ROOT OF TALENT MANAGEMENT

What is talent management rooted in – something that holds the concept, without which it will not exist? It is identified that the need to develop and manage talent is because organizations face skills deficiencies. This means without skills deficiency there will not be any justification for talent management. What are these deficiencies? 'Skills' is a combination of abilities and capabilities developed as a result of training and experience. Werner & DeSimone (2006) describe deficiencies that initiate talent management as skills gap, a situation where those entering the workforce are unable to meet current job requirements. Thus, they fall short of skills required to perform in their roles. Werner & DeSimone (2006) give an example that between 25% and 40% of hourly paid employees in the USA exhibit skills gap. This is more of individual skills gap. There could also be organizational skills gap, an example of which was described by Michael Mussallem, CEO and Chairman of Edward Lifesciences, a heart valve company based in the USA as quoted below.

We are evolving into a company that is going to drive more innovation and apply more technology to unmet patient needs. And that is going to require us to do more clinical studies than in the past to be able to demonstrate the value of our products. So as we increase the importance of clinical studies, we see that we don't have a strong enough clinical research function. We need more and better talent in that area, so we have made that a strategic priority (Bingham & Galagan, 2007, p. 33).

Skills gap therefore is the difference between skills required and (lower) skills available. The skills required usually go with what the organization or individual wants to achieve. The difference between the skills needed on the job and those possessed by applicants is of great concern to human resource managers and business owners looking to hire competent employees. While employers would prefer to hire people who are trained and ready to go to work, finding such people does not solve the skills gap problem entirely. Bloom et al. (2004), emphasize the root of talent management as skills challenge, which they note to include skills gap, skills shortage, and latent skills shortage. They explain skills gap as referring to skills deficiencies of employees, internal to a firm, hence working within the workplace. Skills shortage is defined as a shortage of suitably skilled people available in the labour market. While skills gap refers to skills people need to be able to perform, skills shortage refers to the people who require these skills. The most significant problem associated with skills is caused by latent skills shortage, which is skills challenge that goes unrecognized because the organization concerned has adapted to cope without these necessary skills (and potentially trapped itself in low skills equilibrium). This is similar to the outcome of Chan & Cooper's (2006) study that much research uncovering the skills gap however concentrates mainly on generic skills without much consideration for latent skills shortage.

Talent however should be quality talent (Q-Talent) within any organization as this has always been the key competitive differentiator and puts companies on competitive edge (Chan & Cooper, 2006).

There is consensus on 'skills deficiency' as what drives talent management. Varied skills are however identified, some of which are subsets of others. While Werner & DeSemone (2006) emphasize skills gap as the basis for talent management needs in organizations, Bloom et al. (2004) consider skills gap as subset of skills challenge and less important skills consideration for talent management programmes. Out of the three skill types mentioned by Bloom et al. (2004) including Werner and DeSemone's (2006) skills gap, latent skills shortage is considered the most significant. Surprisingly, Werner and DeSemone admit that these latent skills go unrecognized without identifying what these skills are. Similarly, Chan and Cooper (2006) emphasize the importance of latent skills shortage without identifying what they are. Chan and Cooper paint more uncertain picture when they discover skill gap as the parent skills which might include generic skills and latent skills shortage. In summary, while some authors agree on latent skills, it has been difficult to reveal what they are and therefore difficult to develop them during the talent process. Conversely, latent skills are considered less important and a subset of skills gap, which rather drives talent management. Therefore, although skills deficiency is collectively identified as talent management driver, the type of skills to be developed is uncertain.

TALENT MANAGEMENT STRATEGIES AND PROCESSES

Who or what should be the focus of talent management process? Should development be focused solely on an elite subgroup of future leaders, or on those capable of progressing through a number of levels on the organizational ladder? The question relates to the exclusive model of talent management (Delbridge, Gratton & Johnson, 2006) which is characterized by a concentration on one or a few segments (or talent pool) of the workforce who are either at the top or identified as having the potential to get to the top by exhibiting high levels of performance. There is however an 'inclusive' approach as opposed to the exclusive approach. The inclusive approach which is a competitive necessity (Warren, 2006) recognizes that there are various key positions to fill in any organization as well as a future pipeline of the appropriate skills required to fill these positions, whatever the level.

Who or What Should Be the Focus?

In the mist of the struggle over where the focus should be, there have been a range of conceptualizations. Most of these conceptualizations of talent fall into one of the following four perspectives (Iles et al., 2010).

- **Exclusive-People Perspective:** This is about key people with high potentials and/or performance. This perspective does not take into account positions or titles but a few talented individuals who are viewed as people with outstanding competence and ability and are therefore able to enhance the company's competitive advantage. This talent management perspective has it that not everyone in the company can be considered as talent because of differences in such characteristics as performance, competence and potential that distinguish talented from other employees. A striking feature here is the segmentation of the workforce into talents in whom the company invests scarce resources.

38

- **Exclusive-Position Perspective:** This perspective focuses on the identification of 'key' positions in the organization, usually referred to as 'A positions', and only the 'right' staff occupying these positions are deemed talents. These positions do not necessarily follow hierarchical titles or positions difficult to fill but positions that are of strategic importance and portray a wide variation in work quality.
- **Inclusive-People Perspective:** Contrary to the first two that focus on a few (people or positions), this perspective is formed on the premise that everyone in the organization has talent as they all have roles to play to contribute to organizational success. The belief is that every employee has the abilities, and is therefore required to be given the chance to demonstrate and use such abilities in the workplace.
- **Social Capital Perspective:** The first three perspectives concentrate on individual talent and ignoring the (complex) organizational structures within which individuals work. Those who hold the social capital perspective argue that the three perspectives downplay the social and organizational structures such as teams, roles, network, culture and leadership. The perspective therefore draws attention of talent management experts to social capital.

These four perspectives show how organizations struggle to choose an approach, or how experts find difficulty recommending what should be the focus of talent management programmes. This indecisions and varied views should be a worry because if organizations and experts can identify the need for talent management but fail to decide on the direction where resources should be channeled to achieve the purpose of the talent process, then it is not worth initiating because resources could be wasted and the purpose defeated.

To Communicate or Not to Communicate?

Despite the varied perspectives, it is believed that the exclusive person option is the most appropriate as selecting a few potentials and developing them to drive the organization is the essence of talent management (Uren, 2007). Other than that it just becomes synonymous with HRM. However, the task of evaluating employees for their skills development is riddled with dilemmas and emotive decisions that can never be fully reflected in a rational business process. This dilemma arises from the need to differentiate employees in terms of their performance and other characteristics in order to make investment decisions; versus the need to treat employees equally to promote solidarity. Round (2009), identifies two dilemmas in talent management which compliment views expressed by Uren (2007) and Iles et al. (2010).

The first dilemma (in the form of a question) is how to achieve a balance between the motivational impact of letting people know that they have been identified as having the potential and considered for the talent program versus the demotivational impact when they are not selected? This is perhaps the most hotly debated of all the questions that arise when designing and implementing talent management programmes. It is believed that the answer to this question depends on what the organization believes in (Uren, 2007). If managers know that employees believe in their potentials and can make decision about their career and their development within the organization, then they could be informed. However, if the organization thinks that by being transparent with individuals about their perceived potentials will inflate the expectations of one segment of the workforce, and/or crash the hopes of another, then there is cost to bear in opening up. Organizations need to choose one end of the spectrum – to be or not to be transparent because there is no such thing as being little bit transparent.

The second dilemma is more applicable during recessions or redundancies when organizations have to make a decision between the promises of people being the greatest assets versus wide-scale redundancies because people have become a luxury the company cannot afford. It becomes very difficult to communicate when affected employees have not done anything to warrant this. This dilemma could be resolved by an effective talent management system with robust data to enable the organization put in place effective workable processes for the identification of potentials. The two dilemmas reveal that even when management knows what to communicate to the selected and non-selected, they become uncertain how to handle the communication.

Should or Should Not Develop Subordinates?

Whose responsibility is it to manage talent? It is believed that the prime responsibility is on the HR department to build the framework and provide the tools, systems and resources but every manager, no matter the level, plays a role in strengthening the company's overall talent. Clarifying the 'responsibility list', Kamoche (2006) states that, "the idea of tapping into and managing the knowledge that resides in people should be a key responsibility for HR managers as well as line managers and corporate executives" (p.27). This means the commitment of senior management is especially important as management is a competitive differentiator and makes a commitment to devote time and resources to developing talent.

Leadership involvement in talent management is even more critical in relationship to retention of talent, which should be a strategy to justify investments in the talent process. Cappelli (2008), warns that retention should be well managed and should be one of the pivots of the talent management process because, as he puts it, a deep bench of talent has become expensive inventory these days – inventory that can walk through the door, and senior managers should not allow this to happen.

However, leaders or senior management identified as having the greatest responsibilities to see that talent management succeeds may rather thwart talent efforts in their organizations. Firstly, the skills that helped leaders to become successful at one level may impair their ability to excel to the next level (Ulrich & Smallwood, 2011). For instance, a great contributor in technical role such as a designer may entertain the fear that he/she cannot be a good CEO who will need the skills and experience of performing people management role; shaping the future of the organization, among others. This fear makes leaders/senior managers not moving up to ensure free flow of the talent pipeline. Secondly and more significantly, some leaders worry about succession (which is the essence of talent development) that talented subordinates could outshine them and take their place. So why leaders should be committed to a program that is likely to cause them their positions? This was the conclusion drawn by Oppong (2015) that expatriate managers were unwilling to develop their local managers to take over their positions. Although senior managers have the prime responsibility to develop talents they are less willing or unsure to do so due to the risk of losing their positions.

TALENT MANAGEMENT-DIVERSITY INTEGRATION

Good people management needs to embrace diversity because making the most of everyone's contribution in organization is not just a common sense but also vital to organizational success (CIPD, 2010a). This corroborates the popular view that diversity in talent management is about managing status shift, thus including people who might have been previously overlooked and progressing from historically 'out-group' to 'in-group' in the talent process (Gibbs, 2011). The business case for diversity is an important acknowledgement that it is no longer legitimate or profitable to exclude or marginalize women, physically challenged, racial and ethnic minorities and other identity groups from the workplace. This means businesses are required to ensure inclusion and non-discrimination of various identity groups (Kalonaityte, 2010) in the talent process.

However, as noted earlier in this chapter, war for talent means organizations have to compete to find and keep the few talents within them, implying that talent resides within certain individuals and only they are worth concentrating on (Blass & Maxwell, 2012). Exploring a balance between the inclusion and exclusion polarization, Ng and Burke (2005) believe that it may be that not everyone should be considered 'talent' but everyone should have the same opportunity to be considered for inclusion. By assuming that talent is nurtured but not as a result of nature, everyone should be from equal base point. Then ambition, experience, skills etc. determine whether someone is included in the talent pool at any given time.

Touching on the difficulty in achieving talent management-diversity integration, CIPD (2010b) revealed that there are numerous ways that organizations understand or approach talent management and diversity individually as concepts, and how they are integrated. For instance, in their study they revealed that three different organizations – Credit Suisse, British Telecom and the London Organizing Committee of the 2012 Olympic Games – had different approaches to diversity and inclusion (CIPD, 2010b).

Apart from difficulty of managing diversity and inclusion in the talent management process, there are many barriers to effectively integrate talent management and diversity. The current talent situation suggests that though businesses are increasingly realizing the need and benefits of diversity in talent management, there is misunderstanding as to why every employee should be included when the essence of talent management is to develop a few talented within an organization. Therefore, business owners and senior managers are either unsure how to implement this, or are simply unwilling to implement it.

SOLUTIONS AND RECOMMENDATIONS

The varied views identified and discussed reveal how talent management is yet to grow and mature and explain why some researchers, HR professionals and senior managers see talent management as a puzzle. The various views show that it is difficult, and not beneficial to all organizations, to have one common definition of talent management. The discussions further reveal that the difficulty of, and diminished benefits from talent management emanate from the various uncertainties, lack of clarity and misunderstandings surrounding the various aspects of the subject, which are hurdles that need to be cleared for effective talent management programmes. Albeit all these difficulties, experts still believe that talent management is the main differentiator between organizations that succeed and those that do not. These suggest that senior management of organizations that implement talent programmes should be more proactive in their approaches to the talent process, while those without structured talent programmes endeavor to develop same. These should be aligned with business strategy or operational parameters of strategy execution and to ensure that talent definitions, processes, and approaches change as strategic priorities change. Talent researchers also have the burden of undertaking rigorous empirical studies as a way of getting the reasons for, and solutions to these hurdles.

The author believes that most of the confusions, uncertainties and lack of clarities result from the fact that experts and organizations attempt to settle on common definitions, approaches, procedures and explanations – a universal best-fit approach. This could always create difficulties until it is realized that no one blueprint can be applied to all organizational contexts because organizations have varied talent requirements and expectations. As resourcing needs, as well as how best to meet these needs vary, talent management will continue to be plagued with the 'battle for commonality', if attempts continue to be made to apply universal approach to every organization. In this regard, it is advised that organizations should rather understand the context within which their talent management processed fit into their talent needs.

As the hurdles develop because of managers and experts' attempts of hunting for universal best-fit approach, it is recommended that management should identify their organization's talent needs and decide on the skills to develop, approaches to adopt and returns on talent investments that suit the organization's context. Despite being globally accepted, talent management would not work if attempts continue to be made to develop one blueprint for all organizations and industries. Organizations should therefore avoid definitions, approaches and processes that are too restrictive because the fact that one approach works for one organization does not mean it works for another. Talent practitioners should note that practices are not "best practices" unless they deliver results for an organization. Deciding which practice will suit your company is all about understanding the context within which your talent management process fits.

CONCLUSION

The chapter has identified and discussed varied views on many aspects of talent management. The author attempted to discuss these views and explained the uncertainties; lack of clarity; and misunderstandings that surround talent management as both concept and function. The discussions have been made under five main headings. These include: (1)Talent and talent management definitions, which have been found to lack commonality as authors and practitioners express varied views on meanings of talent and talent management; (2) the need for talent management which has been plagued by war over external versus internal factors as key drivers; (3) the root of talent management which although skills deficiency is identified, the type of skills to be developed remains uncertain; (4) talent management strategies and processes, which have revealed varied views and indecisions over the talent focus and how to communicate talent programmes; and (5) talent management-diversity integration which defeats the idea behind talent management – focus on select few. The author provides some reasons for these uncertainties, misunderstandings and lack of clarity and reveals that these happen mainly because authors and business executives attempt to settle on common definitions, approaches and processes of talent management, which should not be the case. Therefore, talent management should be approached based on talent needs of individual organizations (or industries) if the expected benefits are to be realized.

REFERENCES

Ambrose, D. (2003). Barriers to aspiration development and self-fulfilment: Interdisciplinary insights for talent discovery. *Gifted Child Quarterly, 47*(4), 282–29. doi:10.1177/001698620304700405

Barlow, L. (2006). Talent development: The new imperative? *Development and Learning in Organizations, 20*(3), 6–9.

Bingham, T. & Galagan, P. (2007). Finding the right talents for critical jobs. *T&D, 30*, 30-36.

Blass, E., & Maxwell, G. (2012). Inclusive talent management and diversity. In H. Francis, L. Holbeche, & M. Roddington (Eds.), *People and Organizational Development: A New Agenda for Organizational Effectiveness* (pp. 243–259). London: CIPD.

Bloom, N., Conway, N., Mole, K., Moslein, K., Neely, A., & Frost, C. (2004, March). Solving the skills gap. *Advanced Institute of Management Research*. Summary Report from the AIM/CIHE Management Research Forum.

Busine, M., & Watt, B. (2005). Succession management: Trends and current picture. *Asia Pacific Journal of Human Resources, 43*(2), 225–237. doi:10.1177/1038411105055060

Cappelli, P. (2008). Talent management for the twenty-first century. *Harvard Business Review, 86*(3), 76–81. PMID:18411966

Chan, P., & Cooper, R. (2006). Talent management in construction project organizations: Do you know where your experts are? *Construction Industry Quarterly, 194*, 12–18.

Charan, R. (2010). Banking on talent. *People Management*, October, 24-25.

CIPD. (2006). *Talent management: Understanding the dimensions. Change Agenda*. London: Chartered Institute of Personnel and Development.

CIPD (2010a). The PM guide to reward and benefits: Engagement. *People Management,* December, 33-50.

CIPD. (2010b). *Opening up for business success: Integrating talent management and diversity*. London: Chartered Institute of Personnel and Development.

Delbridge, R., Gratton, L., & Johnson, J. (2006). *The exceptional manager*. Oxford: Oxford University Press.

Deloitte (2005, February 15). Retiring workforce, widening skills gap, exodus of 'critical talent' threaten companies: Deloitte survey. *Canadian Corporate Newswire*.

Farndale, E., Scullion, H., & Sparrow, P. (2010). The role of the corporate HR function in global talent management. *Journal of World Business, 45*(2), 161–168. doi:10.1016/j.jwb.2009.09.012

Fleming, J.H. & Asplund, J. (2008, January 10). Understanding the nature of talent; managers must distinguish what's innate in their employees (talent) from what can be changed or acquired (knowledge and skills). *Gullup Management Journal*.

Gagné, F. (2007). Ten Commandments for academic talent development. *Gifted Child Quarterly, 51*(2), 93–118. doi:10.1177/0016986206296660

Garavan, T. N., Carbery, R., & Rock, A. (2012). Mapping talent development: Definition, scope and architecture. *European Journal of Training and Development, 36*(1), 5–24. doi:10.1108/03090591211192601

Gibb, S. (2011). *Human Resource Development: Foundations, Process, Contexts* (3rd ed.). London: Palgrave McMillan.

Harris, J. G., Craig, E., & Light, D. (2011). Talent and analytics: New approaches, higher ROI. *The Journal of Business Strategy, 32*(6), 4–13. doi:10.1108/02756661111180087

Hills, A. (2009). Succession planning – or smart talent management? *Industrial and Commercial Training, 41*(1), 3–8. doi:10.1108/00197850910927697

Hughes, J. C., & Rog, E. (2008). Talent management: A strategy for improving employee recruitment, retention and engagement within hospitality organizations. *International Journal of Contemporary Hospitality Management, 20*(7), 743–757. doi:10.1108/09596110810899086

Iles, P., Preece, D., & Chuai, X. (2010). Talent management as a management fashion in HRD: Towards a research agenda. *Human Resource Development International, 13*(2), 125–145. doi:10.1080/13678861003703666

Kalonaityte, V. (2010). The case of vanishing borders: Theorizing diversity management in internal border control. *Organization, 17*(1), 31–52. doi:10.1177/1350508409350238

Kamoche, K. (2006). Managing people in turbulent economic times: A knowledge-creation & appropriation perspective. *Asia Pacific Journal of Human Resources, 44*(1), 25–45. doi:10.1177/1038411106061506

Leisy, B., & Pyron, D. (2009). Talent management takes on new urgency. *Compensation and Benefits Review, 41*(4), 58–63. doi:10.1177/0886368709334323

Michaels, E., Handfield-Jones, H., & Axelrod, B. (2001). *The War for Talent*. Boston: Harvard Business School Press.

Morton, L. (2005). Talent management value imperatives: Strategies for successful execution (Research Report).

Ng, E. S. W., & Burke, R. J. (2005). Person-organization fit and the war for talent: Does diversity management make a difference? *International Journal of Human Resource Management, 16*(7), 1195–1210. doi:10.1080/09585190500144038

Oppong, N. Y. (2015). Localization of management in multinational enterprises in developing countries: A case study of policy and practice. *International Journal of Training and Development, 19*(3), 223–231. doi:10.1111/ijtd.12058

Oppong, N. Y., & Gold, J. (2013). Talent management in the Ghanaian gold mining industry: A critical exploration. *Universal Journal of Management and Social Sciences, 3*(10), 1–19.

Paprock, K. E. (2006). National human resource development in transitioning societies in the developing world: Introductory review. *Advances in Developing Human Resources, 8*(1), 12–27. doi:10.1177/1523422305283055

Robinson, J. (2001). Skills gap is big concern of employers today. *Alabama Cooperative Extension System*. Retrieved from www.aces.edu/dep/extcom

Stahl, G., Bjorkman, I., Farndale, E., Morris, S. S., Paauwe, J., Stiles, P., & Wright, P. et al. (2012). Six principles of effective global talent management. *Sloan Management Review, 53*(2), 25–42.

Swailes, S., Downs, Y., & Orr, K. (2014). Conceptualising inclusive talent management potentials, possibilities and practicalities. *Human Resource Development International, 17*(5), 529–544. doi:10.1080 /13678868.2014.954188

Ulrich, D., & Smallwood, N. (2011). *What is talent?* The RGL Group.

Uren, L. (2007, March). Uren, L. (2007). From talent compliance to talent commitment: Moving beyond the hype of talent management to realizing the benefits. *Strategic HR Review, 6*(3), 32–35. doi:10.1108/14754390780000970

Warren, C. (2006). Curtain call. *People Management, 12*(6), 24–29.

Werner, J. M., & DeSimone, R. L. (2006). *Human Resource Development* (4th ed.). Ohio: Thomson South-Western.

Zingheim, P., & Schuster, J. R. (1999). Dealing with scarce talent: Lessons from the leading edge (part 2 of 2). *Compensation and Benefits Review, 31*(2), 40–44.

ADDITIONAL READING

Buhler, P. M. (2008). Managing in the new millennium: Are you prepared for the talent shortage? *Super Vision, 69*(7), 19–21.

CIPD. (2007). *Employer branding: A non-sense approach. Research Guide*. London: Chartered Institute of Personnel and Development.

Cunningham, I. (2007). Talent management: Making it real. *Development and Learning in Organizations, 21*(2), 4–6.

D'Amico, E. (2008). Talent management. *Chemical Week, 170*(11), 22–23.

Fulmer, R. M., Gibbs, P. A., & Goldsmith, M. (2000). Developing leaders; how winning companies keep on winning. *Sloan Management Review*, Fall, 49–59.

Huselid, M. A., Beatty, R. W., & Becker, B. E. (2005). A players or A positions? The strategic logic of workforce management. *Harvard Business Review, 83*(2), 110–117. PMID:16334586

Lane, K., & Pollner, F. (2008). How to address China's talent shortage. *The McKinsey Quarterly, 3*, 2008.

Lewis, R. F., & Hackman, R. J. (2006). Talent management: A critical review. *Human Resource Management Review*, *16*(2), 139–154. doi:10.1016/j.hrmr.2006.03.001

McCauley, C., & Wakefield, M. (2006). Talent management in the 21ˢᵗ century: Help your company find, develop, and keep its strongest workers. *Journal for Quality and Participation*, *29*(4), 4–7.

Nyambegera, S. M. (2002). Ethnicity and human resource management practice in sub-Saharan Africa: The relevance of the managing diversity discourse. *International Journal of Human Resource Management*, *13*(7), 1077–1090. doi:10.1080/09585190210131302

Parry, K. W., & Proctor-Thomson, S. B. (2003). Leader career development: Who should take responsibility? *Asia Pacific Journal of Human Resources*, *41*(3), 316–337. doi:10.1177/1038411103041003005

Robertson, A., & Abbey, G. (2003). *Managing Talented People*. Edinburgh: Pearson Education Limited.

Round, S. (2009). Walking the talent tightrope. *Talent Management Review,* July/August, 14.

Stringer, H., & Rueff, R. (2006). *Talent force, a new manifesto for human side of business*. New Jersey: Prentice Hall.

Taylor, D.H. (2008, June 25). Keynote address. *Proceedings of the Informatology Conference.*

KEY TERMS AND DEFINITIONS

Root of Talent Management: Something that hold the talent management concept, without which there will be no justification for talent management programs and practices.

Skills Deficiency: It is lack of a combination of one's abilities and capabilities that are required for performance and contribution to organisational success.

Talent Communication: It involves how and why talent management decisions by management are conveyed to employees involved in the talent process.

Talent Management Puzzle: A term used to describe the challenges that make talent management less appreciated and less useful. These include issues that bring about misunderstanding and lack of clarity and uncertainty about talent definitions, approaches and processes.

Talent Management: A people management concept and function that is believed to create long-term organisational success, if well managed.

Talent Management-Diversity Integration: How managers could include all workplace identifiable groups such as women, physically challenged, ethnic minorities and even the less skilled in the talent process because it is believed that everyone is capable of being developed.

Talent: What an employee is made of that renders him/her capable to perform and contribute to organizational growth and competitiveness.

Chapter 4
Performance Analysis:
Crafting the Flair to Make the Difference

Mambo Mupepi
Seidman College of Business, USA

ABSTRACT

There are numerous approaches to developing organizational talent and all take different turns. In this chapter, meta-analysis and analytics techniques are contrasted to produce the explicit knowledge necessary to excel organization. Crafting the flair needed in winning corporations focuses on three specific areas in the value creation system: recruitment, training and development, and design and implementation of competitive conditions of service as critical in getting the people possessing the desirable competences and their retention to advance output. Data mined from the firms' activities can be organized in exploitable datasets which can be analyzed in tandem with research results to craft difficult to emulate practices leading to increased productivity.

INTRODUCTION

The plan of this discourse is in five parts. The first part offers an introduction and the definition of some of the key terms used in the discussion. As antecedence to progress the debate the questions asked are (1). What are the benefits of using analytics and results from organizational research? (2). what should organizations do to facilitate the use of this knowhow towards specific firm's objectives?

The second part provides the background information by reviewing a carefully selected literature that undergirds the application of information analytics and organizational research in building efficient and effective enterprise. Efficiency is a measure of how well resources are employed to achieve a goal. Effectiveness is a measure of the appropriateness of a goal the firm is pursuing and the degree to which the organization achieve that goal. Information deduced from mined data and research studies is applied to advance the efficacies necessary to increase productivity.

The third part produces a summary of the debate followed by the fourth part in which some of the problems in the design and implementation of credulous databases. The fifth part recommends a model of how to design and implement gullible databases. In the last part, a conclusion is drawn.

DOI: 10.4018/978-1-5225-1961-4.ch004

Background

The analytic framework is drawn from American academic philosophy contrasted with French or German philosophical traditions such as existentialism. The model has been influenced by Wilhelm von Humboldt and George Moore, among many others In Levy (1979), Moore is best known today for his defense of ethical non-naturalism, his emphasis on common sense in philosophical method and the paradox that bears his name. In Athanasopoulos, Damjananovic, Burnand & Bylund (2015), Wilhelm von Humboldt popularized the view that language is the fabric of thought. Thoughts are produced as a kind of intentional dialog using the same grammar as the thinker's native language. It emphasizes the importance of logical and linguistic analysis to solve problems. Athanasopoulos et al allude to the assumption that making shrewd business decisions is not driven by how much data one has – but by how quickly one can discover insights from all that data. In Toubia, Hauser, & Simester (2004) a suggestion was made about the usefulness of mining data from a firms' websites. Data could be collected from invoices, delivery notes, job applicants, and many others. This data can be organized into databases arranged to show customers and their locations, the products they buy from the company and the frequencies and prices of those purchases and may other information (see Figure 1). The databases can then be examined to produce information analytics useful to decision makers (see Figure 2). Mupepi & Mupepi (2016) posit that the information analytics can be juxtaposed with results from organizational research to increase the ability of management to make effective decisions. Qualitative research can generate data that can provide in depth insight into a question or topic. However, in order to draw conclusions from qualitative data, it is essential to quantify the data (see Figure 2). Qualitative data can be drawn from questionnaires emanating from customers or suppliers. Mupepi & Mupepi (2016) suggest that qualitative data provides the narrative layering and textual meaning in meta-analysis. It is however important to quantify the data obtained from qualitative research. Quantitative analysis of qualitative data involves turning the data from words or images into numbers. This can be done by coding ethnographic or other data and looking for emerging patterns. When combined with information analytics the picture drawn can become very clear. Management will be able to apply the results in the decision-making process to implement highly productive teams and appreciate with clarity the value creation system.

The data from human resources portals can be organized in relation to job applicants responding to specific job adverts and random job seekers (see Figure 1). The data can also be appreciated from two perspectives: internal and external applicants. Developing a multifaceted approach to talent management makes the alignment of the organization to competences real. Toubia, Hauser, & Simester (2004) suggested that a data mining process of inspecting cleaning transforming and modeling data with the goal of highlighting useful information suggesting conclusions and supporting decision making. In Dacinlyte & Stankevich (2015) it is suggested that recruiting talented people was not sufficient to accomplish desirable goals. A talent strategy need to be actionable, nimbly responsive to changing internal and external needs of the organization. A talent scheme must be specific to the ever changing needs of the business, appreciating the variety of skills, specialties and nuanced capabilities that make for successful execution within the context of the company.

Organizational Research

John Creswell & Vicki Plano Clark in their book entitled: *Designing and conducting research methods (2013)* suggested the following as a definition of mixed research methodology *a* research design with philosophical assumptions as well as methods of inquiry (2013:5). As a methodology, it involves philosophical assumptions that guide the direction of the collection and analysis and the mixture of qualitative and quantitative approaches in many phases of the research process. Thus, the data mined can be analyzed persuasively in tandem with data obtained from qualitative and quantitative studies based on the research questions. Creswell & Plano Clark proposed that the forms of data from analytics, quantitative and qualitative studies can be combined sequentially by having one build on the other or embedding one with the other.

Analytics is the discovery interpretation and communication of meaningful patterns in data (see Figure 1). Phillips (2013) suggests that analytics go beyond *web* or *site* analytics to encompass a wide spectrum of advanced techniques for using big data to reduce costs and increase profit. In building effective digital analytics in organizations, Phillips thoroughly explains digital analytics to business practitioners, and presents best practices for succeeding with it throughout the business. Phillips argues that everything from making the business case through defining and executing strategy, can be integrated successfully by analyzing processes, technology, and people skills and tasks in all aspects of operations. Manyika et al (2011) propound that analytics can focus on key issues facing the organization and lead towards the development of practical applications to solve organizational problems. Analytics can be employed to construct cutting-edge practices.

In Akella Marwaha & Sikes (2014), companies across industries are placing major bets on big data, expecting it could dramatically improve business processes and overall performance. As they move ahead, one issue that looms large is finding senior-leadership capacity to manage the huge program of organizational change that data analytics demands. Top-team members, fully engaged with their existing responsibilities, often find themselves straining to plan and implement big data strategies. Akella et all suggests that *informatics* a multidisciplinary and integrative approach that involves the computer cognitive and social sciences can be applied to understand the nature and description of organizational change resulting from big data informatics. Explicit knowledge to increase productivity and production and delivery of products and services demanded by customers, can be produced by analyzing and creating exploitable databases.

Growing Useful Customer Databases

Dias & Ioutiu et al (2016) suggested that useful customer databases could be constructed taking cognizance of costs, product design, and value generated for the company. Emerging analytics show key differentiators for customers such as prices and costs. They argued that companies often lacked guiding principles to shape those efforts. By analyzing and ranking correlations between customer satisfaction and operational factors (such as the reasons a customer chooses one company over others, cycle times, features offered, and the use of digital channels) in our survey, four pillars of great customer-experience performance stood out. Firstly, a focus on the few factors that moved the needle for customers. Dias & Ioutiu et al asked customers to assess different characteristics of the end-to-end experience, including the first interaction with the institution, the ease of identifying the right products, and the knowledge and professionalism of staff. They found that only a small number of characteristics such as three to five out of 15 had a material impact and accounted for the bulk of overall satisfaction.

Secondly, Ease and Simplicity: The Payoff Trade-Off

Today's pressured customer values convenience. Cutting down the time it takes to complete an individual journey, such as applying for an account, by making it easier and simpler has a deep effect on customer satisfaction. Dias & Ioutiu et al argued that as more processes are digitized, journey times will be cut back. But low cycle times alone do not equate to superior customer satisfaction. Rather, research results indicated that customers respond most positively to the ease of a transaction or process.

Thirdly, Different Customer Experience

Dias & Ioutiu et al analyzed different types of customer journeys: those that are completely online, those that start online and finish in a branch, those that start in a branch and finish online, and those that take place fully in a branch. The results showed that digital-first journeys led to higher customer-satisfaction scores and generated 10 to 20 percentage points more satisfaction than traditional journeys. For all the advantages of digital-first journeys, those journeys that are the most digitized across all the interactions lead to the greatest customer satisfaction. Nevertheless, many financial services do not provide fully digital services even when they exist, such as digital identification and verification. This finding indicates that financial-services providers can still significantly improve customer satisfaction by digitizing complete journeys.

Brands and Perceptions Matter

Dias & Ioutiu research considered the fourth pillar as brands and perception which were important consideration in customer satisfaction. Companies whose advertising inspired their customers with the power and appeal of their brand or generated word of mouth delivered 30 to 40 percentage points more satisfaction than their peers. But how advertising or word of mouth affects perceptions is crucial. Two banks in the US, for example, performed nearly identically across a set of customer journeys. However, customers viewed one bank as delivering a much better overall experience than its rival, because the higher-ranked institution's advertising promoted its user-friendliness.

That perception had an important effect on identifying promotions that were effective for attracting new customers but, on average, had a nearly neutral impact on satisfaction. The average, however, is misleading. Promotions are slightly negative for traditional banks but positive for purely online players. In the same vein, physical proximity to a financial-services provider tends to have, on average, little discernible influence on customer satisfaction. Again, though, the value to customers of physical proximity can vary widely from institution to institution and from country to country, pointing to a need for financial institutions to understand their customers at a more granular level.

Contrasting Data from Many Sources

In Aggarwal & Manuel (2016), data mining is an analytic process designed to explore data (usually large amounts of data - typically business or market related - also known as big data) in search of consistent patterns and/or systematic relationships between variables, and then to validate the findings by applying the detected patterns to new subsets of data (see Figure1). The ultimate goal of data mining is prediction - and predictive data mining is the most common type of data mining and one that has the most direct

Figure 1. Identifying clusters in databases: making sense of Bid data

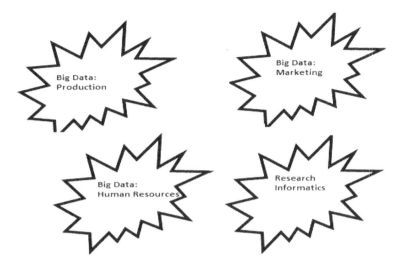

Figure 2. Cluster analysis to create exploitable database (Mupepi & Mupepi 2016)

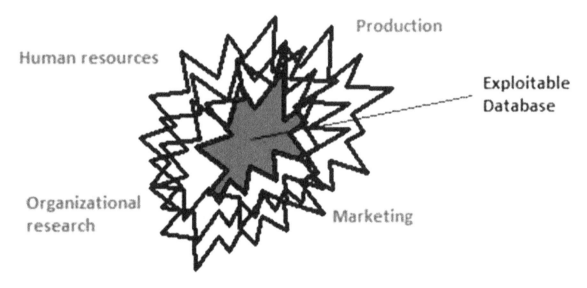

business applications. The process of data mining consists of three stages: (1) the initial exploration, (2) model building or pattern identification with validation/verification, and (3) deployment i.e., the application of the model to new data in order to generate predictions (see Figure 1).

Aggarwal & Manuel suggest that successful companies have gone beyond the excitement of big data and adopted an approach that centers on clear business cases. Business strategy and proven use cases –individual instances of practical applications –guide investments and deployment at these companies. For example, they target increased cross sales by using analytics that offer next-product-to-buy recommendations or improved pricing.

Clusters Analysis

In Management Association 1 (2016), the term cluster analysis was first used by Tryon, (1939) and it encompasses a number of different procedures and methods for grouping objects of similar kind into respective categories. A general question facing researchers in many areas of inquiry is how to organize observed data into meaningful structures, that is, to develop taxonomies. In other words, cluster analysis is an exploratory data analysis tool which aims at sorting different objects into groups in a way that the degree of association between two objects is maximal if they belong to the same group and minimal otherwise. Given the above, cluster analysis can be used to discover structures in data without providing an explanation/interpretation. In other words, cluster analysis simply discovers structures in data without explaining why they exist (see Figure 2).

In Achtert, Bohm, et al (2006), cluster analysis is widely used in market research when working with multivariate data from surveys and test panels. Clustering is a statistical application to group task or set of objects in such a way that the objects of same group are more similar to each other than to those in other groups. This approach is applied in creating exploitable databases from bid data (see Figures 1 & 2). Market researchers use cluster analysis to partition the general population of consumers into market segments and to better understand the relationships between different groups of consumers/potential customers, and for use in market segmentation, product positioning, new product development and selecting test markets. Businesses such as restaurant owners use clusters to organizing seating arrangements. A group of diners sharing the same table in a restaurant may be regarded as a cluster of people. In food stores items of similar nature, such as different types of meat or vegetables are displayed in the same or nearby locations. There is a countless number of examples in which clustering plays an important role. For instance, biologists have to organize the different species of animals before a meaningful description of the differences between animals is possible. According to the system approach employed in biology, man belongs to the primates, the mammals, the amniotes, the vertebrates, and the animals.

Efficiency and Effectiveness

Efficiency and effectiveness are two words that mean different things and yet they are used interchangeably in figurative speech to imply usefulness in organization. In the comparison of various statistical procedures, efficiency is a measure of the optimality of an estimator, of an experimental design or of a hypothesis testing procedure. Essentially, a more efficient estimator, experiment, or test needs fewer observations than a less efficient one to achieve a given performance. Effectiveness is a measure of the appropriateness of goals the firm is pursuing and the degree to which the organization achieves those goals. This debate focuses on the quality of being successful in producing intended result.

Clusters

Clustering techniques have been applied to a wide variety of research problems. Sibson (1973) and much later Achtest, Bohm, et al (2006) provide an excellent summary of the many published studies reporting the results of cluster analyses. For example, in the field of medicine, clustering diseases, cures for diseases, or symptoms of diseases can lead to very useful taxonomies. In the field of psychiatry, the correct diagnosis of clusters of symptoms such as paranoia, schizophrenia, etc. is essential for successful therapy. In archeology, researchers have attempted to establish taxonomies of stone tools, funeral objects, etc. by applying cluster analytic techniques. In general, whenever we need to classify a "mountain" of information into manageable meaningful piles, cluster analysis is of great utility (see Figure 1).

Big Data

In Jindal & Borah (2016), big data is a term used to mean data sets that are gigantic and complex. Handling big data requires sophisticated programming and powerful computers. Big data poses many defies in organization which include analysis, capture, data curation, search, sharing, storage, transfer, visualization, querying, updating, and information confidentiality. Jindal & Borah suggested that big data often referred to the use of predictive analytics, user behavior analytics, or certain other sophisticated data analytics methodologies useful at extracting data value from data, and seldom to a particular data set (see Figure 2).

In McMahon (2013), big data describes data sets so large and complex that it becomes difficult to process using traditional data processing methods like everyday databases. The sheer volume of data being tracked today is immense. One of the biggest challenges large organizations will face over the next decade will be finding ways to better analyze, monetize, and capitalize on Big Data. Businesses need a partner that can address the entire spectrum: data assessment, data retention, and data use requirements of this new environment. McMahon (2013) propounded that the big data revolution is letting companies identify trends, inefficiencies, IT security issues and opportunities, but it requires work, the right technology, and talented IT people to find the valuable needles in the haystacks of raw data.

Analysis of Big Data

Solnik (2008), the analysis of data sets can find new correlations to spot business trends, increase efficiency and effectiveness in organization, or benchmarking competitors' performance. Management regularly meet difficulties with large data-sets in areas including Internet search, finance, urban informatics, and business informatics. Solnik asserts that data sets grow rapidly in part because they are increasingly gathered by easily available information-sensing mobile devices, remote sensing, software logs, cameras, microphones, radio-frequency identification readers and wireless sensor networks, among many others.

MAIN FOCUS OF THE CHAPTER

The focus of this chapter is on how logic and performance technology can be applied to create clusters leading to useable databases that can be analyzed and the results applied to advance efficiency and effectiveness in organization. Language and logic are useful in making sense of big data and in the design and implementation of clusters in developing strategy.

Problems

The construct of linguistics suggests that a common language understood by all is needed in making organizational sense. At times organizations operate across national boundaries and many things change such as the law, customs, beliefs, and the spoken word. Translations are very possible but meaning can also be lost in transitioning words from one language to another.

SOLUTIONS AND RECOMMENDATIONS

Organizations can master four critical roles in using analytics and research results:

- As venture capitalist, showcasing the art of the possible" to internal customers by highlighting the most promising ideas to apply big data and advanced analytics.
- As product manager, assembling easy-to-use big data and advanced analytics "products" designed to match patterns of use by internal customers.
- As recruiter, motivating and retaining the best talent.
- As business leader, building the discipline to enable transformational change and impact at scale.

FUTURE RESEARCH DIRECTIONS

Big data is becoming a huge operation in many companies and the use of analytics is also increasing as many companies seek the information they need to keep abreast of competition. Is *logic* influenced by cultural differences or perception?

CONCLUSION

There is no one single method of conducting organizational research. Analytics techniques is one approach that can be applied to understand big data. The mixed research techniques can be understood in quantifying data from qualitative studies to make sense in organizational schemata. The performance and analytics techniques can be applied successfully to craft the flair required to make the difference in organization.

REFERENCES

Achtert, E., Böhm, C., Kriegel, H. P., Kröger, P., Müller-Gorman, I., & Zimek, A. (2006). Finding Hierarchies of Subspace Clusters. In *Knowledge Discovery in Databases. LNCS, 4213*, 446–453. doi:10.1007/11871637_42

Aggarwal, S., & Manuel, N. (2016). Big data analytics should be driven by business needs, not by technology. Retrieved from http://www.mckinsey.com/business-functions/mckinsey-analytics/our-insights/big-data-analytics-should-be-driven-by-business-needs-not-technology

Akella, J., Marwaha, S., & Sikes, J. (2014). How CIOs can lead their company's information business. Retrieved from http://www.mckinsey.com/business-functions/business-technology/our-insights/how-cios-can-lead-their-companys-information-business

Athanasopoulos, P., Damjanovic, L., Burnand, J., & Bylund, E. (2015). Learning to think in a second language: Effects of proficiency and length of exposure in English learners of German. *Modern Language Journal, 99*(S1Suppl. 1), 138–153. doi:10.1111/j.1540-4781.2015.12183.x

Creswell, J., & Plano Clark, V.L. (2013). *Designing and Conducting Mixed Methods Research*. London, UK: *Sage*.

Daciulyte, Ruta & Katazina Stankevich (2015). A systemic approach to talent management: managers' perceptions versus employees. *International Journal of Business and Emerging Markets, 7*(3), 223–236.

Dias, J., Ionutiu, O., Lhuer, X., & van Ouwerkerk, J. (2016). The four pillars of distinctive customer journeys. *McKinsey*. Retrieved from http://www.mckinsey.com/business-functions/digital-mckinsey/our-insights/the-four-pillars-of-distinctive-customer-journeys

Jindal, R., & Borah, M. D. (2016). A novel approach for mining frequent patterns from incremental data. *International Journal of Data Mining Modelling and Management, 8*(3), 244–264. doi:10.1504/IJDMMM.2016.079071

Levy, P. (1979). *Moore: G.E. Moore and the Cambridge Apostles*. London, UK: Weidenfeld and Nicolson.

Information Resources Management Association. (2016). Big Data: Concepts, Methodologies, Tools, and Applications. Hershey, PA, USA: IGI Global. doi:10.4018/978-1-4666-9840-6

Manyika, J., Chui, M., Bughin, J., Brown, B., Dobbs, R., Roxburgh, C., & Byers, A. H. (May, 2011). Big Data: The next frontier for innovation, competition, and productivity. Retrieved from http://www.mckinsey.com/business-functions/business-technology/our-insights/big-data-the-next-frontier-for-innovation

Mupepi, M., & Mupepi, S. (2016). Applying theory to inform competency development: Bootstrapping Epistemic Communities in Growing Specialists. *International Journal of Productivity Management and Assessment Technologies, 4*(1), 28–38. doi:10.4018/IJPMAT.2016010103

Phillips, J. (2013). *Building a Digital Analytics Organization: Create Value by Integrating Analytical Processes, Technology, and People into Business Operations*. London, UK: Pearson FT Press.

Sibson, R. (1973). An optimally efficient algorithm for the single-link cluster method. *The Computer Journal. British Computer Society, 16*(1), 30–34.

Siegel, E. (2013). *Predictive Analytics: The Power to Predict Who Will Click, Buy, Lie, or Die* (1st ed.). Hoboken, NJ: Wiley.

Solnik, B. (2008). *Global Investments* (6th ed.). Upper Saddle, NJ: Prentice Hall.

Toubia, O., Hauser, J. R., & Simester, D. I. (2004). Polyhedral methods for adaptive choice-based conjoint analysis. *JMR, Journal of Marketing Research, 41*(1), 116–131. doi:10.1509/jmkr.41.1.116.25082

KEY TERMS AND DEFINITIONS

Analytics: It is the detection and announcement of meaningful patterns in data.

Clusters: A group of people or things that are close together.

Existentialism: A philosophical theory that emphasizes the existence of the individual person as a free and responsible agent determining their own development through acts of the will.

Flair: A natural talent or aptitude.

Informatics: Information science.

Logic: A system of reasoning.

Big Data: This is a term used to describe data sets that are gigantic or complex.

Data Mining: Data mining is an interdisciplinary subfield of computer science.

Knowledge Management (KM): KM is the process of creating, sharing, using and managing the knowledge and information of an organization.

Chapter 5
The Structure of Talent:
A Co-constructed Competency Perspective

Mambo Mupepi
Grand Valley State University, USA

Sylvia Mupepi
Grand Valley State University, USA

ABSTRACT

This chapter advances a discourse on a co-constructed competency model referred to as the SCCM. The SCCM is an alternative competency management strategy designed to build talent needed to increase productivity. A competency model buttress talent management and how human resource management, can be designed and implemented. Arguments drawn indicate that competency models, in particular those concerned with organizational capabilities, are relatively ineffective when developed outside the organization. A contrast of the competency models developed elsewhere with those espoused within the organization by the knowledge communities (KC) and effectiveness demonstrated in the latter approach. By reviewing selections from the literature that established the competency development movement, a foundation on past knowledge is considered in the design and implementation of the capability required to champion organization. The SCCM approach is applicable to most organizations in creating explicit knowledge, skills, and behavior necessary to increase productivity.

INTRODUCTION

Global competition has forced many corporations to focus on the bottom-line and to recruit people who are effective from the beginning. This global competition has also created the demand for a better-organized workplace, competent workforce and the need for increased productivity. This chapter suggests an alternative method of differentiating what people do at work using the platform of social construction and its tenets of a knowledge community. Social construction founded on the premise that experience and collective knowing through the forum can progress organizational goals. The chapter proceeds to drawing the hypothesis: only the knowledge community (KC) can develop, distribute and diffuse the practices useful in organization.

DOI: 10.4018/978-1-5225-1961-4.ch005

Background

A Statement About the Literature Review

An assumption made about the predominant models of competencies is that they are not appropriate because the majority have no focus on any particular organization. The assumption is that the mainstream are inappropriate because they view knowledge and skills as universal. There is an uneven distribution of cognitive ability in organizations. One of the reason for this phenomenon is that in a normal distribution, that represents organizational knowledge and skills, people will fit into the four quarters according to their abilities and disposition to do the job. Cultural difference is another example why people at work may differ. For instance, high school graduates from different countries may have a different level of understanding of many subjects such as the games of soccer, basketball or lawn tennis compared to what local high school graduates may know about the same subjects. This may occur for many reasons, but the most the time culture in each country can be unique. For example, the curricula in two countries differ tremendously. Because of such diversity, organization takes different meaning in each situation. Corporations do their best to create or acquire the knowledge they perceive will put them in good stead, thus successful organizations must understand the environment in which they operate to be successful.

The SCCM is an alternative knowledge management model useful in aiding a firm to understand its business in relationship to what the people employed can do. The SCCM approach is applicable in the assessment and evaluation of prevailing cultural conditions in organization. Figure 1 depicts the proposed "co-constructed competency model" or the SCCM. The four circles are equal and represent the competency attributes of knowledge, attitudes, skills and technology. These are part of an organization's intellectual property. The behavior of each attribute affects the behavior of the whole structure. The attributes are all equal and competencies/expertise occurs where the four circles meet. If any of the attributes is misaligned from the center, the structure loses its essential properties, which are competencies.

Positive Reinforcement

Although technology is important in production systems, people who operate the tools, equipment or machines make the difference. People in the organization must have the mindset to work effectively. Positive reinforcement give people outcomes they desire when they do the job right all the time. Desirable outcomes include pay, praise or promotion. By linking rein-forcers to the performance of functional behaviors, managers motivate people to perform the desired job tasks correctly all the time.

Negative Reinforcement

Negative attitudes can cause the deflection of the competencies/expertise. The results can be undesirable outcomes such as re-working the job and creating extra costs. Customers normally do not like their time to be wasted; they will take their custom elsewhere. A SCCM is a tool managers can use to measure performance and to understand the gap between actual and desirable output. The Likert scales can be adapted to appreciate the distribution of culture in organization. In Table 1, an assessment of prevailing cultural conditions at Adam Smith Pin Production plant:

Figure 1. A socially constructed competency model (SCCM) Mupepi (2010)

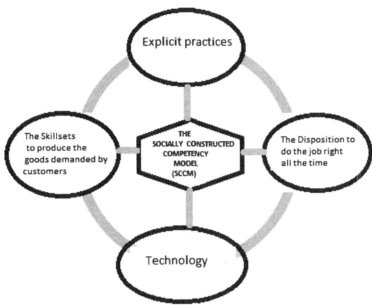

Table1. The Pin-makers role specific profile assessment tool

	Strongly Agree	Agree	Disagree	Strongly Disagree
Pin-makers do a great job				
Pin-makers are very innovative				
Pin-makers are always punctual				
Pin-makers are very skilled				
Pin-makers make great pins				
Pin-makers meet customers' needs				
Pin-makers are always helpful				

Competences can be grouped into specific combinations that are used to create job descriptions, guide behavioral interviews, generate training and development plans, and aid in selection for assignments and promotion. Viewing competences as talent necessary in designing jobs and product formulations, they form the intellectual capital in organization. The pin-makers can form a knowledge community focused on creating the explicit practices needed to produce the products demanded by the clothing manufactures and others. The core competences of the pin-factory reflect the set of critical abilities required throughout the firm to shape the organizational capabilities and culture to achieve the strategic intent.

The KC in the pin-production plant represent the ideal leadership texture for a particular context. It describes those pin smiths who perform well and deliver results in that particular context. The KC will be able to meet regularly to discuss the techniques to make the job easy and meet the demands of the customers accurately and punctually. The KC can create diffuse and distribute the practices needed to champion pin-production. The KC will need to spread the knowledge about the importance of customers as the main source of what gives life to the business and as such, they have a seat on the production management forum.

Drawing from Experience

Independent research on skills development and attitudes formation and change, and concur with the study done by Benjamin Bloom in 1956. Bloom's Taxonomy created to promote higher forms of thinking in education, such as analyzing and evaluating concepts, processes, procedures, and principles, rather than just remembering facts. What was good for learning in education is also excellent in organizational development and training. It is most often used when designing educational, training, and learning processes.

For example, Kaplan's (1972 & 1975) studies indicate that attitudes can collectively be formed changed and manipulated to suit the goals of the corporation or individual. Festinger & Smith (1959) postulate that people influence other people causing dissonance to result when those who have been influenced must choose between attitudes and behaviors that are contradictory. It can be part of the KC's role to ensure that people in corporation are receiving the right information and learn the correct things. The KC can actually develop the learning materials to ensure success. Individual attitudes can make or break success. In much later research, Mupepi & Mupepi (2016) found that the inability to read and write business plans did not deter a knowledge community, which had a limited knowledge of business, practices from acquiring entrepreneurial management skills. They suggest that change can happen when the learners are willing and able to learn. Logos, signs, pictures and narratives of success can be employed in enhancing knowledge –technology transfer in groups or corporations, which have varied cognitive abilities.

Technology is an important enabling attribute to the capability equation. Technology is made up of tools such as software, complex equipment and machinery, and other electronic or mechanical gadgets that enable people to increase productivity. Technology can allow organizations to manage competition with ease. The human aspect of technology application makes a difference in organization. Technology is human knowledge used to answer both material and spiritual needs. Knowledge, skills, and other resources combined to solve various existential and practical problems. The use of appropriate technology in expanding the CCK is suggested because companies and individuals do use what is affordable and suitable to what they do to improve economic viability. Technology is useful in extending a means of accomplishing defined goals. The KC can make their position clear by defining desired goals using the technology to enable that to happen. It is also important in determining the tooling and equipment necessary to accomplish desirable goals (see Figure 1).

Technology Can be Up-Dated

The Egyptians could have invented what could have been cutting-edge technology during their time. The *shaduf* a makeshift lever is a means to lift water from the canal and the tool could pull towards the vegetable patch or field of corn where the bucket of water emptied. The shaduf had a large pole balanced on a crossbeam, a rope and bucket on one end and a heavy counter weight at the other. Pulling the rope up and down lowered the bucket into the canal. The farmer then raised the bucket of water by pulling down on the weight (Potts, 2012). The concept of the shaduf could have inspired the development of submersible water pumps. Today the shaduf technology is applicable as appropriate technology in many parts of the developing world.

Beven & Raudebaugh (2004) posit that technology enables a people to design a better reality. They argue that failure to recognize the role of technology in learning and in the production of goods and services can result in slow-paced change and performance inefficiencies. Technology does not only assist in written communications and production. Brown et al. (2000) argue that a company should use technology to design and control its own destiny and sustenance. Many corporations have designed systems and methods of production that will sustain them until sometime when capital is available for up-grades. Derrida (2003) asserts that competencies represent the claimed truth and capabilities of the company. Derrida argues that such claims cannot be in writing alone. Logos, art, and meetings, can represent visible perspectives. For example, the Coca-Cola squiggle sign or logo is a famous marker for a corporation that produces thirst-quenching products. The role of symbols have been a source of information from time immemorial to signify what corporations and individuals stood for. The plaque written: *Senātus Populusque Rōmānus* (SPQR) was engraved in large letters could be viewed as the symbol of democracy by people from near and afar. Paterson (2004) argues that the role of symbols or logos in attaining total psychic growth in Carl Jung's psychological theories, explains the importance of logo-centric organizations. The understanding signs and symbols such as logos and abbreviated signs represent the culture of the business and its mission. Derrida propounded that the logo aided communication, and continual dialogue to learn and improve all the time.

There is an increased use of information technology (IT) in developing systems that enable people in the corporation to be more effective at what they do. For example, portals containing the firm's knowledge, success stories and other information can be made available to both external and internal stakeholders. Landberg (2004) argues that successful portals must combine personalization with self-service and supply the distinct information needs of all members of the organization. Portals should extend the organization's boundaries in a number of ways. For instance, the passing enquirer seeking product or service information creates an account which will stay with her/him through initial inquiries, purchasing and continuing supplies or product service maintenance, and data collection for developing the competitive advantage. Ulrich (1998) argues that human resources practitioners are now faced with designing portals that interface with the firm's strategies and enable change to take place quickly. Universal competency models can be developed by a few individuals within the corporation or purchased off the shelf or from the World Wide Web in many different formats that range from web-based training solutions to downloadable technology.

In terms of the social learning processes, the KC, through the agency relationship, assumes the role of the coordinator of knowledge the corporation requires in order to meet its objectives. Hasse (2004) contends that creativity and innovation cannot be confined to the individual alone if the ZPD is both an internal and an external relation between an actual and a potential developmental zone. Hasse suggests that corporations can smooth the progress of creativity and problem solving if the potential development zones for individuals can be identified. All the learning and training will then be focused at responding to the actual potential zones.

What should the community know? How best can this priori be disseminated? What is the ideal behavior given the training and learning? These questions are best answered by Senge et al. (1994) who see the creation of mental models in the KC as a prerequisite for successful learning; a forum for sharing knowledge and developing performance strategy. They argue that the commonalities among participants in any corporation should be a sense of shared vision. All the required learning then will be disseminated through the shared vision as mandates, goals, etc (1994:427).

Various research studies have shown that in the field of management the learning domain that is most in use is the cognitive. Many scholars have contested the constituents of competencies. The majority concur that the manager's job demands intellectual thinking and reasoning. For example, Bloom (1956) argued that a person's intellectual abilities were displayed in the First Domain, cognitive learning. The premise of cognitive learning is that managers can increase employee motivation and performance by how they link the outcomes that employees receive to the performance of desired behaviors and the attainment of goals. In most management practices, corporations deploy teams, groups or communities of practice to bring the entire corporation's talent together to produce goods valued by customers. Learning takes place when people learn to perform certain tasks to receive certain outcomes. Eggins et al (2007) suggest that the dimensions of group formation have significant effect on the ultimate success of any planning exercise. Groups learn by sharing experiences and working as teams. In teams, each member learns about his/her part and appreciates the role expectation he/she plays in that team. Teams differ from groups because teams have values, beliefs, and defined tasks. Eggens et al allude to the fact that the COP can be an effective focus group useful in creating the explicit knowledge required to increase team effectiveness. Because group members must conform to the performance criteria set by the group, it implies that there is continuous learning and improvement to increase performance.

Observing Performance

Casas (2004) contends that cognitive learning behaviors are characterized by observable and unobservable skills such as comprehending information, organizing ideas, and evaluating information and actions. Casas draws further arguments that indicate that the demand of intellectual reasoning in leadership jobs or managerial positions is driven by the need to keep abreast of competition and developments in areas of interest. In contrast, Kamei (2003) argues that long-term experience of farm menial work is associated with measurable psychomotor and cognitive deficits. Other studies such as Swan (2004) disputes both assumptions, arguing that in all cases, whether the job demands are highly literate or not, practice makes perfect. By engaging the students in activities such as practical problem solving and case studies among many, Swan contends that the students develop better competencies. Cognitive studies conducted by Perry (1970) have indicated that there are four distinct structures in cognition. Moore (1994) and Nilson (2001) provide a summary.

1. **Basic Dualism/Received Knowledge:** The assumption is that all problems can be solved; therefore, the learner must learn to find the right solution.
2. **Full Dualism:** Some authorities in literature and philosophy disagree with each other. Others in science and math agree. Therefore, there are right solutions but authorities differ. The learner's objective is to find the right solution and ignore the rest.
3. **Multiplicity-Subjective Knowledge:** The premise is that there are many solutions to problems. Some of these solutions conflict with one another.
4. Commitments in relativism imply that there are problems with known answers and some that do not have defined answers.

However, Perry's scheme speaks to epistemic issues underlying critical thinking and such assumptions can be applied to learners in organizations.

Latour (1987) suggests that organizations must observe technology in action and appreciate what it can do to further organizational goals. Latour alludes to the fact that action research can advance innovation in organization. In much later research, Mupepi (2005) found that organizations could develop technology that is both suitable and affordable. People did not require specialized literacy to do this, thus most of the tools found on the assembly lines evolved from those artisans who were doing the same repetitive work for a long period. Toolmakers translated the technology into objects like hammers, wrenches, or spanners. Such groups share the same syntax and a worldview dominated by automotive engineering technology perception.

Knowledge and Skills

Consistent with Polanyi (1944); Berger & Luckmann (1966); Latour (1987); Senge (1990); Brown & Duguid (1991); Lave & Wenger (1991); Boland & Tenkasi (1995); Nonaka & Takeuchi (1995); Mupepi (2005; 2009;2010); Mupepi & Mupepi (2016), among many others, organizational capabilities are a by-product of organizational learning. Baker (2008) suggests that collaboration and networking enable the collective experience of people in organization to be harnessed to mount significant situational ability. Successful global organizations such as IBM have recognized the importance of collaboration and networks in advancing productivity. Baker alludes to the fact that a community of practice can be strategically positioned to collect data, which can be decoded to reveal many things that can effectively influence behavior in organization. Communities of practice can use the data to create many organizational possibilities and select what can be effective in managing change. This emphasis on the need to change fast is typical of western organizations. They must do so to keep pace with an ever-changing business environment. Hiring able people and further training them to articulate what the organization does places competency growing at the forefront of organizational efforts (see figure1).

A Knowledge Community (KC)

The knowledge community has been recognized for its strength to enable people in organization to constantly learn and improve. Foucault (1969) suggested that a knowledge community's strength was its position to frame different perspectives in organization. Foucault argued that the analysis he outlined was only one possible procedure and that he was not seeking to displace other ways of analyzing discourse or render them as invalid.

In Earl (2001), a KC is a management construct stemming from the convergence of tacit knowledge as a field of study and social exchange theory. The collective experience of people is referred to as tacit knowledge which can be put into context to create innovation in organization. The knowledge community was formerly referred to as a discourse community because the forum had the capacity to develop innovative practices in organization. In this chapter the KC and COP imply the same thing, an organization within a company empowered to create, diffuse, and distribute explicit practices that render a business the competitive advantage. As with any field of study, there are various points of view on the motivations, organizing principles and subsequent structure of knowledge communities.

The community of practice (COP) was made popular by Lave & Wenger (1991) and is used the world over in co-construction of organizational reality. The COP concept has been improved upon by many scholars including Mupepi Mupepi Tenkasi & Sorensen (2013). Etienne Wenger in Ashkanasy (2002) describes a COP as "Groups of people who share a concern, a set of problems, or a passion about a topic and who deepen their knowledge and expertise by interacting on an ongoing basis" (p.1). The COP will have legitimate authority from the agency and functional relationships as defined by the management (Giddens, 1984).

Continuous Learning and Improvement

Lewin (1951) suggested that those organizations that failed to learn fast did not have much of a chance to succeed in their endeavors. The ability to learn and change pretty fast remains at the helm of successful organization. Learning is not an isolated practice, hence the role of social relations in the construction of knowledge and the continuity of learning in mergers and acquisitions (Barkema & Vermeulen, 1997). On one hand, knowledge grows organically from a synergy arising when different people bring to bear diverse skills and abilities to solve common pressing problems. Information technology has made it possible for teams, groups and individuals to meet more often and generate synergy focused on issues relating to the corporation. On the other hand, Yulong & Runyon (2004) contend that synergy or learning is not guaranteed when there are weak commitment-performance relationships within the new system. They argue that the effect of the Internet on learning and instruction is still marginal. Institutions still prefer conducting meetings and classes around the table and face-to-face rather than interactions on cyberspace. It is not known to what extent existing competency-based models (CBMs) take commitment and performance relationships into account but various scholars in postmodern literature have identified cognitive, motivational and organizational strategy as points where the dialogue of underlying arguments may start. For example, Thompson (2004) argues that research in biological and anthropological studies postulates that a certain amount of knowledge is inherent in the human genome. Thompson's argument alludes to the conclusion that the rest of the knowledge is acquired in the socialization process. Thompson's arguments concur with Rubiner (1997) asserting that the way humans develop and learn is dependent upon the interplay between genetic and environmental factors. Hofstede (2001) poses cognitive arguments that are related to culture. The argument developed is that cognition varies from individualism to collectivism as can be illustrated in traditional American culture versus what can be found in the nomadic groups that move from place to place in the Sahara Desert. DiMaggio (1997) concurs that there are variations in cognition as one moves from one culture to another and further argues that human behavior is strongly influenced by culture. For deep change to occur Quinn (2000) argues that a new set of values and a shared vision must be jointly developed by the people who will be affected by the change. Modified beliefs will be central to the success of the corporation. Our proposition is to incorporate the cultural variables into the competency development schema and build a cutting-edge supposition derived from learning, shared norms, beliefs and values.

The situation and environment in which the corporation operates is very important in determining the required organizational capabilities that can warrant success. Capaldo et al (2006) propose a methodological approach to competency management based on situational perspective. Situational analysis places emphasis on ensuring higher attention to organizational sense making and the nature of situated competencies. Capaldo et al argue that successful situation analysis demand collaboration and participative approaches. The participative and collaborative approaches are both characteristics of a knowledge community such as the COP.

Mupepi et al (2008b) assert that specialist knowledge produced and provided by a community of practice to the corporation is a source of collaborated information that encourages innovation in the corporation. The companies that collaborate and network across normal boundaries tend to be positioned to take advantage of globalization than those that follow traditional boundary lines. With the advent of modern information technology for communications such as the GIS or Internet, Mupepi et al suggest that membership to a community of practice cannot be restricted to those located within a specific geographic location but can be located anywhere in the world.

People in an organization can effectively learn as individuals or collectively in teams or groups. The studies that inform the CCK indicate that the best strategies evolve around people who share the same interests and meet regularly to further their passion. Organizational learning can be made ideal by a group of people within the same organization referred to as a community of practice (COP). Berger & Luckmann (1966) suggest that competencies in organization can be created by persons and groups interacting together in a beneficial manner. Their efforts are concerted, and through repeating the same things and understanding those things, they form a similar mindset. Berger & Luckmann argue that those mental representations become a mindset of each other's actions, and that these concepts eventually become habits.

In a much earlier research, Polanyi (1944) considers that greater transformation can be achieved through collaboration. Polanyi's arguments concur with Adam Smith's pin making factory in which the division of labor enables specialization to happen, in turn increases productivity, all things being equal. Polanyi suggests that organization of production and distribution can benefit from social networks. Communities of practice have been proven to be effective social networks. Henry Ford's automation philosophy is based on specialized social networks or productive systems. For example, in an assembly line the artisans range from electricians to specialized steel fabricators, welders, or spray painters. All the trades are socially linked to one product: the car, truck or bus. Boland & Tenkasi (1995) advances the notion that a community of practice can create many perspectives allowing the organization to select the best courses of action. Communities of practice can generate enormous synergy and focus efforts on collective goals, objectives, issues, problems, and results, if they are directed to do so. It is the synergy of an organization's convergent effect — people coming together to chart the way to address the challenges facing their organization. Knowledge creation and imagination become important and may constitute the factors that enhance the ability to outperform competition.

Senge (1990) considers that a systems thinking embraces the whole process, concluding that teamwork and social networks encourage learning and allow change to happen. In recent studies Easterby-Smith & Prieto (2008) assert that there is a strong relationship between the ability to collaborate across normal boundaries and the ability to create effective capabilities. They suggest that the firms that collaborate and learn have a higher degree of performance compared to those that are concerned with existing organizational structures. A vibrant COP can be made up of an effective intellectual team but is not limited to intellectualism alone. Combined organizational experience and knowledge can contribute effectively towards increasing capacity. Gasson (2005) proposes that tacit knowledge is equated with experience of acting in the world. Thus, on-the-job training, apprenticeship, or pupilage contributes enormously to the advancement of skills. Therefore, seating with the expert "Nelly" is an effective method of on-job training which comes with the acquisition of even the bad practices embedded in "Nelly's" behavior. Gasson suggests that what is important is the dissemination of "Nelly's" tacit knowledge and all the other undesirable habits can be weeded out in standardizing the practice. Mupepi et al (2008a) concur with Senge (1990) that collaboration nurtures a systems thinking process, leading to the creation of an organizational mindset. People in the organization can be made to think alike by being exposed to the same literature, practices, organizational mission or policy. The result can be positive action that impacts productivity. Lave & Wenger (1991) describe a perspective of human cognition that asserts competency development as an effort that results when people who share the same passion interact to advance their passion. Such assertion is a context and situation-bound theory of cognition.

Collaboration Within and Outside Normal Boundary Lines

The KC is a collaborative effort in which people within the organization can meet to discuss issues and problems they have a passion about. Collaboration is a recursive process whereby a community of practice or the entire organization can work together towards a common goal. In this process the organization can share selected knowledge, learn, and change. Wong (2004) and Mupepi et al (2008a), among many others, suggest that modern information technology can bring radical changes to what organizations can do. Wong (2004) asserts that IT can be used to harness the collective experience of people in organization, nurturing an environment conducive to collaboration and innovation. Competencies developed from the collective experience of a community of practice can be unique and hard for similar organizations to imitate. Wong argues that technology can be put into context by the people who use it. People carry their experience and what they know about certain trade technology and its many applications from one job to the other. The longer a person stays in one job location the more knowledge he acquires about that particular job, all things being equal. Fong & Tosi (2007) allude to the fact that micro-economics principles of utility maximization and human behavior can be increased through the agency of the KC. The KC can increase the opportunities in and decrease risk faced by the organization.

Mupepi et al (2008a) contest that situational experience can lead to the determination of the precise organizational needs. They agree with Tenkasi & Morhman (1999) in asserting that formidable strategy is dependent upon what the organization knows about its industry and how it might control the flux of things and establish stable beliefs. Many organizations are increasingly using information technology to control knowledge and establish databases necessary to advance organizational goals. In order to compete successfully the organization must be able to produce products and services efficiently. Tenkasi & Morhman contend that knowledge is unevenly distributed in organization. Information technology can help to address that abnormality. It can allow knowledge to be created, distributed, diffused and shared according to needs across cognitive environments where it is used to create more value for the organization. Knowledge may not constitute a competitive advantage in itself; what is important is how it is used to win in competition. The CCK is a technology that can facilitate the organization to succeed in competition. By allowing the precise assessment and evaluation of prevailing abilities and capacity the organization can be forewarned and get ready for competition.

Structuration Proposition

Structuration theory was developed by Giddens (1984) and he defines structures as rules and resources organized as properties of social systems. The theory employs a recursive notion of actions constrained and enabled by structures which are produced and reproduced by that action. Consequently, in this theory technology is not rendered as an artifact, but instead examines how people, as they interact with a technology in their ongoing practices, enact structures which shape their emergent and situated use of that technology. The main proponents include Mupepi (2010), Workman Ford & Allen (2008), DeSantis & Poole (1990), and Orlikowski (1992).

Giddens (1984) contends that the structure of the organization can be what the owners perceive to be the best corporation that can enable goals to be accomplished. Giddens propounds that organizational talent is a social construct. He examines phenomenology, hermeneutics, and social practices at the inseparable intersection of structures and agents. Workman Ford & Allen (2008) have adopted and expanded this balanced position. Though the theory has received much criticism, it remains a pillar of contemporary Sociological theory, and a tool entrepreneurs and governments have embraced in the design and implementation of strategy to grow useful businesses and economies.

Wenger (2004) suggests that if firms are to grow and expand then their strategic value has to be acknowledged and appreciated: (1) the value of community-enabled strategic planning must be appreciated as part of developing the competitive advantage. Among other things, this means that the COP must recognize the inputs from stakeholders such as customers, suppliers and others. These inputs have direct bearing on quality, sales, productivity, cost control, and delivery deadlines among others. (2) The COP is a source of innovation, co-creativity, and synergy efforts that increase organizational value. (3) The strategies developed by the COP can be aligned with the strategic intent of the organization, thereby developing tactics that will be difficult to imitate.

Mupepi (2015) conducted research among small scale farmers and found that stewardship was a way of assisting people to be assertive and be more alert about their time, talents and resources within the community. The argument is that stewardship should encourage the evolution of a culture of joint participation that would result in more diversity and higher productivity.

Many scholars and practitioners in the field of Organization Development view shared mental models as appealing ways to characterize the processes by which teams develop effective standards and practices. Shepard (2004) argues that teams must maintain a focus on the task or model and interactions among members. Teams must organize and share all information concerning the model or task and be aware of the limitations in the developed database. Attitudes form an important aspect of competency. Goleman et al. (2004:2) have shown the effects of attitudes in emotional intelligence. The ideal teams drawn from the community must share the same attitudes and expectations. Cannon-Bowers et al. (1995) in their study found that beliefs and attitudes are strongly associated with team processes and team performance. Goleman et al. concur that in work processes and team dynamics, emotions are crucial in job performance.

Coates et al. (2002) contend that the process of competency development lacks an empirical base; the argument is focused on core competences and contends that the existing research concentrates on illustrating that core competencies were developed rather than showing how they were developed. There are other scholars who argue that there is more than just one view of the world (Searle, 1997), who recognize that other perspectives may have validity. The COP will base the deconstruction of the process and standards of competency development on a proven social construction paradigm that includes action research and grounded theory.

This position is possible in democratic environments and may not work where (1) people are not free to express themselves; (2) there is no participatory management; (3) human rights are not recognized; and (4) censorship is exercised to control the population's moral values, creeds, and politics, thereby limiting access to knowledge and information. The COP will come across resistance to change, caused by organizational politics. If social construction is to succeed, organizations must empower the COP. The envisaged COP is akin to those depicted by Cooperrider et al. (2003) in which an interdisciplinary community is created to focus on changes in human, social, and environmental systems whose effects go beyond geographical and economic boundaries and require trans-boundary thinking and action. It is in such communities that competency strategies difficult to imitate will develop through grounded theory.

Prahalad & Hamel (2001:4) foresee the development of competencies centered on full communication, deep involvement, and commitment in working across boundaries. The development of the CCM will require the establishment of such partnerships with the community where low performers are helped by others to perform up to the required standards. Kreiner & Lee (2000) in their study of merger processes in hi-tech companies and communities saw that there were concealed knowledge and practices that were crucial to the development of the competitive advantage.

MAIN FOCUS OF THE CHAPTER

The objective of this discourse is three in number. The first part provides a schematic description of the skills, attitudes, technology, and typologies of knowledge necessary in building innovation or know-how referred to as a co-construct know-how (CCK). The second part determines methodologies appropriate to finding the balance between the particular knowledge attributes that form a minimum prerequisite for an organization's self-defined success. The third part reviews a selected literature suited to the advancement of competency and mounting the CCK. The arguments drawn do not maintain that the literature reviewed reflects all perspectives concerning competencies development. The arguments do not discuss whether universal competencies exist; rather, they show that only those championed through grounded theory and defined as appropriate by a KC ultimately matter to the organization. In progressing the CCK the focus is on emulating social construction principles, including elements such as collaboration, situated knowledge, and learning communities. The exploration of social constructivism can reveal how knowledge is articulated, created and put into organizational context, and expanded in response to specific tasks and challenges, i.e. in moments of historical confrontation such as war times. The discourse demonstrates that as knowledge is situational insight (Brown & Duguid (2000); Lave & Wenger (1991); Capaldo et al (2006); Mupepi et al (2008a) know-how is contextually bound.

Problems

Developing organizational strategy such as know-how or innovation requires more than just knowledge communities. Group dynamics is a system of behaviors and psychological processes occurring within a social group such as a KC. Group dynamics are at the core of understanding racism, sexism, and other forms of social prejudice and discrimination that can impact the gregariousness of the KC resulting in the resistance to change. There are three main things that can affect a team's cohesion. They are: environmental factors, personal factors and leadership factors. Environmental factors can include stress or physical health that impact individuals. Unhealthy individuals cannot effectively contribute to the success of the KC. Personal factors include interpersonal communications. An interpersonal relationship is a strong, deep, or close association or acquaintance between two or more people that may range in duration from brief to enduring. This association may be based on inference or regular business interactions, or some other type of social commitment such as the forum of the knowledge community. Interpersonal relationships are formed in the context of social, cultural and other influences. The context can vary from relations with associates or work colleagues. They may be regulated by law, custom, or mutual agreement, and are the basis of social groups and society as a whole. The third is related to leadership. Empowering the KC is critical in advancing the organizational mission. At times, leaders cannot let go the reins of power.

SOLUTIONS AND RECOMMENDATIONS

Innovative industries often succeed because they are proactive in find a better way to work. It has been argued that continuous learning and improvement were critical in organization and not an option. Highly productive organizations are those that synchronize task activities with the use of appropriate technology. What is appropriate technology depending on what the organization can manufacture, create, or afford to purchase. But it is critical to different the organization using techniques or explicit practices.

FUTURE RESEARCH DIRECTIONS

The Vygotskian ZPD principles place special emphasis on social activity and cultural practices as sources of thinking, synergy, psychological functioning of the firm, and the centrality of learning. Technology that can advance corporations can be easily acquired from external sources or through acquisition and mergers. Although we emulate much from child development and social learning from Vygotsky (1978); Bandura (1977); among many others, most of the theses were not developed with business corporations in mind. But the frameworks influence effective knowledge, technology and skill transfer. There are caveats too; the learner can also pick good or bad habits from the experts.

CONCLUSION

There are limits as to what the CCK can do. Assessments and evaluations are dependent upon what is being assessed. The paper is limited to a theoretical discussion of a competency-based-model and how it can be applied to enable the design and implementation of know-how or talent useful in organization. Future research can focus on growing effective technologies and innovation and the competencies necessary in sustaining high-tech or knowledge-intensive organization.

REFERENCES

Ashkanasy, N.A. (2002). Cultivating communities of practice. *Personnel Psychology, 55*(3), 739-743.

Bandura, A. (1977). *Social Learning Theory*. New York: General Learning Press.

Bandura, A., & Walters, R. (1959). *Social Learning and Personality Development*. New York: Holt, Rinehart & Winston.

Barkema, H.G., & Vermeulen, F. (1997). What differences in the cultural backgrounds? *Journal of International Business Studies, 28*(4), 84-104.

Berger, P. L., & Luckmann, T. (1966). *The Social Construction of Reality*. New York: Anchor Books.

Bevens, R.Q., & Raudenbaugh, R.A. (2004). A Model for Unified Science and Technology. *Journal of Technology Studies*.

Bloom, B. S. (Ed.). (1956). *Taxonomy of educational objectives: The classification of educational goals: Handbook I, cognitive domain*. New York: Longmans, Green.

Brown, L., Flavin, C., & French, H. (2000). *The State of the World 2000*. New York: Earthscan.

Cannon-Bowes, J., Tannenbaum, S. I., Salas, E., & Volpe, C. E. (1995). Defining team competencies. In R. Guzzo & E. Salas (Eds.), *Team effectiveness and decision making in organizations* (pp. 333–380). San Francisco, CA.

Capaldo, G., Iandoli, L., & Zollo, G. (2006). A situationalist perspective to competency management. *Human Resource Management*, *45*(3), 429–448. doi:10.1002/hrm.20121

Carruci, R.A., & Pasmore, W. (2002). *Relationships that enable enterprise change*. San Francisco, CA: Jossey-Bass/Pfeiffer.

Coates, E. (2004). Knowledge management: A primer. *Communications of the Association for Information Systems*, *14*, 406–489.

Cooperrider, D., Whitney, D., & Stavros, J. M. (2003). *Appreciative Inquiry Handbook*. Bedford Heights, OH: Lakeshore Publishers.

Derrida, J. (2003). The world of the Enlightenment to come (Exception, Calculation, Sovereignty). *Research in Phenomelogy*, *33*(1), 9–52. doi:10.1163/15691640360699591

DiMaggio, P. (1997). Culture and cognition. *Annual Review of Sociology*, *23*(1), 207–267. doi:10.1146/annurev.soc.23.1.263

Easterby-Smith, M., & Prieto, I. M. (2007). Dynamic capabilities and knowledge management: An integrative role for learning? *British Journal of Management*, *19*(3), 235–249. doi:10.1111/j.1467-8551.2007.00543.x

Eggens, R. A., O'Brien, A. T., Reynolds, K. J., Haslam, S. A., & Crocker, A. (2007). Refocusing the Focus Group: Airing as a basis for effective workplace planning. *British Journal of Management*, *19*(3), 235–249.

Farnhill, K. (2002). Guilds and the Parish Community in Late Medieval East Anglia, 1470-1550[book review]. *The Catholic Historical Review*, *88*(4), 769–771. doi:10.1353/cat.2003.0054

Festinger, L., & Carlsmith, J. M. (1959). Cognitive Consequences of Forced Compliance. *Journal of Abnormal and Social Psychology*, *58*(2), 203–210. doi:10.1037/h0041593 PMID:13640824

Foucault, M. (1969). *The Archaeology of knowledge*. London, UK: Routledge.

French, W.L., Bell, C.H., Jr., & Zawacki, R.A. (2000). *Organization development and transformation: Managing effective change*. Boston, MA: Irwin McGraw-Hill.

Gasson, Susan (2005). The dynamics of sensemaking, knowledge and expertise in collaborative, boundary spanning design. *Journal of computer-mediated Communications*, *10*(4).

Gergen, K. (1999). *An invitation to social construction*. London: Sage Publications Ltd.

Gergen, K. J. (2001). An invitation to Social Construction. *Social Forces*, *79*(3), 1190–1191.

Giddens, A. (1984). *Positivism and sociology*. London: Heinemann.

Goleman, D. (1998). *Working with emotional intelligence*. New York: Bantam Books.

Goleman, D., Boyatzis, R., & McKee, A. (2004). *Primal leadership: Learning to lead with emotional intelligence*. Boston, MA: Harvard Business School Press.

Hasse, C. (2004). Institutional Creativity: The Relational Zone of Proximal Development. *Culture and Psychology, 7*(2), 199–221. doi:10.1177/1354067X0172005

Heider, Fritz (1959). On Lewin's Methods and Theory. *Journal of Social Issues Supplementary Series.*

Hofstede, G. (1991). *Culture and Organization: Software of the mind: intercultural cooperation and its importance for survival*. New York: McGraw-Hill.

Hofstede, G. (2001). *Culture's consequences: comparing, values, behaviors, institutions and organizations across nations*. Thousand Oaks, CA: Sage.

Kaplan, H. B. (1975). *Self-attitudes and deviant behavior*. Pacific Palisades, CA: Goodyear.

Kaplan, K. J. (1972). From attitude formation to attitude change: Acceptance and impact as cognitive mediators. *Sociometry, 35*(3), 448–467. doi:10.2307/2786505

Kreiner, K., & Lee, K. (2000). Competence and community. *International Journal of Technology Management, 20*(5-8), 657. doi:10.1504/IJTM.2000.002886

Landberg, S. (2004). Enabling profitable growth. *Best's Review, 104*(11), 99.

Lewin, K. (1947). Frontiers in Group Dynamics: Concept, Method and Reality in Social Science; Social Equilibria and Social Change. *Human Relations, 1*(1), 36. doi:10.1177/001872674700100103

Lewin, K. (1948). Resolving social conflicts; selected papers on group dynamics (G.W. Lewin ed.). New York: Harper & Row.

Moore, W. S. (1994). Student and faculty epistemology in the college classroom: The Perry schema of intellectual and ethical development. In K. Pritchard & R. McLaren Sawyer (Eds.), *Handbook of college teaching: Theory and applications* (pp. 45–67). CT: Greenwood Press.

Mupepi, M. G. (2005). *Transforming village entrepreneurs into sustainable development using social constructs. A Case of Zimbabwe*. Ann Arbor, Michigan: ProQuest Publications Inc.

Mupepi, M.G., Mupepi, S.C., Tenkasi, R.V., & Jewell, G.D. (2012). Unlocking entrepreneurial capabilities: Appreciating knowledge and technology transfer in advancing micro-enterprises in Zimbabwe. In D. Laouisset (Ed.), Knowledge-Technology Transfer. New York: Hauppauge.

Mupepi, M.G., Mupepi, S.C., Tenkasi, R.V., & Jewell, G.D. (2008a). Precision in managing organizational change: identifying and analyzing needs using social constructs. *International Journal Management Practice, 3*(2), 150- 163.

Mupepi, M. G., Tenkasi, R. V., Sorensen, P. F. Jr, & Mupepi, S. C. (2007). Creating high impact organization in the SADC: Adapting Organization Development Methods and Practices. *OD Practitioner, 32*(2), 34–39.

Mupepi, S.C. Mupepi, M.G., Tenkasi, R.V., & Sorensen, P.F., Jr. (2006). Changing the mindset: transforming organizations into high energized and performance organization. *Proceedings of the 49th Midwest Academy of Management*, Louisville, KT, USA.

Nielsen, A. C. (2000). Nielson Net Ratings: Nielson Media Research. Retrieved from http://www.nielsen-netratings.com

Perry, W. G. Jr. (1970). *Forms of Intellectual and Ethical Development in the College Years: A Scheme.* New York: Holt, Rinehart, and Winston.

Perry, W. G. Jr. (1981). Cognitive and Ethical Growth: The Making of Meaning. In *The Modern American College* (pp. 76–116). San Francisco: Jossey-Bass.

Peterson, R. A., & Anand, N. (2004). The production of culture perspectives. *Annual Review of Sociology, 30*(1), 311–334. doi:10.1146/annurev.soc.30.012703.110557

Potts, D. T. (2012). *A Companion to the Archaeology of the Ancient Near East.* London, UK: John Wiley & Sons. doi:10.1002/9781444360790

Prahalad, C.K., & Hamel, G. (2001). The Core competence of the corporation. *Harvard Business Review*.

Quinn, R. (2000). *Change the world: How ordinary people can achieve extraordinary results.* San Francisco: Jossey Bass Publishers.

Rubiner, B. (1997). Brain study has wide implications. *Gannett News Service.*

Schaeffer, F. A. (1994). *Pollution and the Death of Man: The Christian View of Ecology.* Wheaton, IL: Crossway.

Searle, J. (1997). The Mystery of Consciousness. New York, New York Review Press Secretary of Labor Report (1918). Sixth Annual Report of the Secretary of Labor Report. Washington, D.C.: Department of Labor, Office of The Secretary. Retrieved from http://digital.library.arizona.edu/bisbee/docs2/dlrep.php

Senge, M.P., Kleiner, A., Roberts, C., Ross, R.B., & Smith, B.J. (1994). *The Fifth discipline fieldbook: Strategies and tools for building learning.*

Shepard, S. (2004). Teamwork and technology shift drilling performance paradigm. *World Oil 225*(4), 35-45.

Swan, B. (2004, May-June). Solving Problems through Action Research: Engaging the Teacher and Student through Exploratory Learning. *The Agricultural Education Magazine, 76*(6), 26–27.

Thompson, L. J. (2004). Moral leadership in a postmodern world. *Journal of Leadership & Organizational Studies, 11*(1), 27–37. doi:10.1177/107179190401100105

Ulrich, D. (1998). Intellectual Capital = Competence X Commitment. *Sloan Management Review, 39*(2).

Ulrich, D., & Brockbank, W. (2002). *Organization, people and HR: The General Manager agenda. Prepared for the Portable Executive Program.* Ann Arbor: University of Michigan Business School, Business School Press.

Van der Veer, R., & Valsiner, J. (1994). Introduction. In R. Van der Veer & J. Valsiner (Eds.), *The Vygotsky reader*. Oxford, England: Blackwell. doi:10.1016/S0070-2161(08)60974-0

Voyat, G. (1982). *Piaget systematized*. Hillsdale, N.J.: Earlbaum Associates.

Vygotsky, L. S. (1978). *Mind in Society. Cambridge*. MA: Harvard University Press.

Wenger, E. (2004). The community structure of large scale learning systems: Learning as a journey. Retrieved from http://www.efios.com/pdf/aerakeynote.pdf#search

Wenger, E. & Lave, Jean (2008). Communities of practice. Retrieved from http://www.infed.org/biblio/communities_of_practice.htm

Westmeyer, P. (1997). *A History of American Higher Education* (2nd ed.). Springfield, Illinois: C.C. Thomas.

Yulong, M. A., & Runyon, L. R. (2004). Academic synergy in the age of technology-A New paradigm. *Journal of Education for Business*, *79*(6), 367–371. doi:10.3200/JOEB.79.6.367-371

KEY TERMS AND DEFINITIONS

Group Dynamics: Group dynamics is a system of behaviors and psychological processes occurring within a social group or between teams or groups.

Know-How: Know-how is a term for practical knowledge on how to accomplish defined tasks. As a technology or techniques to do something others cannot easily do without copying those who own the technique.

Resistance to Change: The resistance to change is defined as the action taken by individuals and groups when they perceive that a change that is occurring as a threat to them.

Social Construction: Social constructionism or the social construction of reality (also social concept) is a theory of knowledge in sociology and communication theory that examines the development of jointly constructed understandings of the world that form the basis for shared assumptions about reality.

Structuration: The structuration theory is about how social systems based on structure and agents can be used to enact organizations useful at solving problems in society.

74

Chapter 6
Structuration Applications and Practice:
Restructuring High Impact Organization

Mambo Mupepi
Seidman College, USA

Sylvia Mupepi
Kirkhof College, USA

Aslam Modak
Seidman College, USA

ABSTRACT

This chapter makes a contribution to talent management literature by investigating the construction of a high-performance organization applying the structuration proposition. People remain as the source of value in all companies and increasingly the human factor is critical in making the difference. The structuration approach make it possible to include the collective experience of the people doing the work to leverage each employee's unique talents to boost productivity. The structuration ontology is applied to create structure and agency useful in making the competitive advantage real. The analysis of both structure and agency can lead to a reproduction of the competences that undergird high performance organization.

INTRODUCTION

The epistemology to effectively construct high performance organization is drawn from Giddens (1984; 2012), Berger & Luckmann (1966), Mupepi (2016, 2017), Contu & Willmott (2005), Mole & Mole (2010), Hansen (2006), Kuratko & Hodgetts (2004), Mupepi & Mupepi (2014, 2015, & 2016), Porter (1985), Prahalad & Hamel (1990), Sacab (2015).

The structuration theory was developed by Anthony Giddens in 1984 to explore the connection between individuals and social systems. This holistic view of modern societies has earned Giddens a reputation

DOI: 10.4018/978-1-5225-1961-4.ch006

for restructuring fledgling organizations around the world. Giddens & Sutton (2012) alluded to the demolition of apartheid in South Africa where racism and discrimination had been institutionalized. Since the ending of the apartheid regime the country implemented one of the most liberal constitutions in the world. In this consultation Giddens & Sutton applied the structuration approach to understand race and ethnicity, discrimination and prejudice, and ethnic conflicts in South Africa. Race is a widely-used term, often used in everyday language to describe biological differences. Racism is often blind of talent or it jibs what talent is. However, there is no scientific basis for the concept to be used within social science. Race is sociologically important because of racialization: the process by which race is used to classify individuals or groups of people within societies.

Ethnicity refers to the cultural practices and outlooks of a community, which identifies them as a distinctive social group. Ethnicity is a social phenomenon, which has no basis in human biology. However, ethnicity can also be problematic if it implies a contrast with some non-ethnic norm, or if ethnic groups are taken to be fixed and predetermined.

In South Africa organizations had to restructure to create enterprises that are functional in a new constitution. Organizations such the Vehicle Inspection Department (VID), Central Mechanical and Electrical Department (CMED), Public Works Department (PWD), had to be restructure and evaluated to allow the employment of a diverse workforce on equitable conditions of service. The Structuration approach deals with the evolution and development of groups and organizations. Giddens viewed groups and organizations as systems with observable patterns of relationships and communicative interaction among people creating the structures. Systems are produced by actions of people creating structures sets of rules and resources. The new organizations were designed and structured to provide services to the state in the form of contractors for specific jobs such as janitorial and building maintenance, the local car dealership took over the role of the CMED in procurement state vehicles and vehicle maintenance. Local building organizations such as construction engineers took over the PWD. These new organizations operate on a set of rules that acknowledge competition, equality, and talent in employment. The systems and structures now exist in a dual relationship with other civil service structures and have continued to reproduce each other in an on-going cycle, referred to as the structuration process (Giddens, 1984, p. 3).

All Star Performers

In Klein (2016) the South African all-star and all talent team was able to collect more medals than their segregated predecessors could in the Rio Olympics. The dismantling of apartheid rules unlocked the opportunities for South Africans to compete as a national team which brought home at least 10 medals. The focus on managing the all-White stars was not a key to sustained success. Talented individuals certainly help their organizations succeed, but organizations that rely primarily on the skills and abilities of top-performing individuals will not realize the full potential of their entire workforces. In an inclusive Olympic team, South Africa collected gold medals which could have been impossible for an exclusive team to achieve in Rio 2016 Olympics.

Deregulation is Part of Structuration

Deregulating the economy implies many things including getting rid of rules and regulations that thwart competition. Vibrant economies can be born out of structuralism that enables key players in the economy to grow businesses capable of creating sustainability. In Arnold (2014), deregulation is the process of removing or reducing state regulations, typically in the economic sphere. It is the undoing or repeal of governmental regulation of the economy. It became common in advanced industrial economies to deregulate industries resulting realistic growth patterns leading to employment levels below 5%. It can be argued that deregulation is akin to structuration which results in the creation of a new structure that can enable society to solve some of its perceived problems.

BACKGROUND

The Structuration Theory

The argument presented in this chapter is that the structuration theory can be applied to develop and implement high performance organization. High-performance organization is a concept within organization development referring to teams, organizations, or virtual groups that are highly focused on their goals and that achieve superior business results. High-performance teams outperform all other similar teams and they outperform expectations given their composition.

Sewell (1992) argued that successful economies were those that took into consideration of the duality of structures. In a book entitled the *Constitution of Society* first published in 1984, Anthony Giddens introduced his argument about the usefulness of structure and agency in advancing the wishes of a community in shaping human behavior. Giddens (1984) argued that structure was the recurrent patterned arrangements which influenced or limited the choices and opportunities that were available in any community. Agency was the enabling capacity by individuals to act independently and to make their own free choices. Giddens propounded that structure versus agency debate could be understood as an issue of socialization against autonomy in determining whether an individual acts as a free agent or in a manner dictated by social structure. The *Constitution of Society* examines empirical evidence wisdom literature and social practices at inseparable intersection of structure and agents. Its supporters have adopted and expanded this balanced position. The structuration theory has remained a pillar of contemporary sociological theory.

In Sewell (1992) a proponent of the structuration argument, Giddens contrasted Durkheim with Weber's approach — interpretative sociology and focused on understanding agency and motives of individuals. Sewell suggested that Giddens's ideas were much closer to those of Marx Weber than they are to Emile Durkheim although in his analysis he rejects both of those approaches, stating that while society is not a collective reality, nor should the individual be treated as the central unit of analysis. The chapter learns from Giddens (1984) and Giddens & Sutton (2012) about building effective economies in the UK, and USA, among many others, to progress a high performing global organization that recognizes competition to satisfy the needs of consumers (see Figure 1).

Agency and Structure

In Giddens (1984), *agency* is viewed as human action critical to both reproduction and transformation of society. *Structures* are the rules and resources embedded in agency memory traces and the modus operandi. The procedures and rules used to sustain the relationship between agency and structure. Giddens argued that the structuration theory enables a community to create an organization aimed at solving certain problems. He propounded that such organizations were bound to succeed because the

Figure 1. The Structuration proposition (Giddens, 1984)

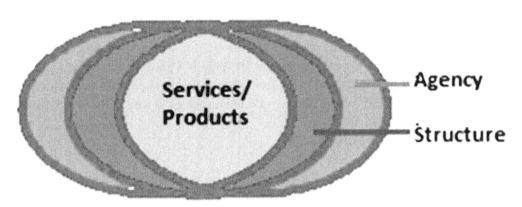

creators would provide the sustenance resources and authority necessary. Giddens separated memory traces into three parts. The first is dominion or power and authoritative resources which enable agents to control persons and material objects. The second memory trace is signification. This is the ability to make sense or meaning. In Marx Weber's bureaucratic structure a job incumbent must possess the right qualifications in order to make meaningful work (Desanctis & Poole 1994). The third memory trace is legitimation. Giddens interchanges rules to refer to either signification or legitimation. Rules in organization are referred to as norms. An agent draws upon these intellectual assets via memory to inform him or herself about the external context, conditions, and potential results of an action. Desanctis & Poole (1994) argue that the structuration theory can be applied successfully in growing organizations designed to solve economic problems such deregulation and structural unemployment.

Michael Porter published a book *Competitive Advantage* (1985) that changed the way entrepreneurs thought and behaved. Porter argued that the competitive advantage is a function of either providing comparable buyer value more efficiently than competitors (low cost), or performing activities at a comparable cost, but in unique ways that create more buyer value than competitors and, hence, command a premium price (differentiation). The entrepreneur wins either by producing and pricing goods lowly or by being different. Customers could perceive this entrepreneur as better or more relevant. There are no other ways. Porter's model can be applied to answer the research question: Does competency development play a critical role in establishing a successful fee-paying passenger car services?

The multidimensional approach to entrepreneurship propounded by Kuratko & Hodgetts (2004) advocated a multidimensional perspective to entrepreneurship. It provides four views to answer a research question such as: What are the required resources to necessary in establishing a successful business? Within this multidimensional approach, Kuratko & Hodgetts view entrepreneurship as a complex, framework that emphasizes the individual, the environment, the organization, and the venture process. Kuratko & Hodgetts approach suggested that entrepreneurship is a dynamic process of vision, change, and creation. It requires an application of energy and passion towards the creation and implementation of new ideas and creative solutions.

Kuratko & Hodgetts (2004) suggested that there are essential ingredients in entrepreneurship. These included the willingness to take calculated risks in terms of time, equity, or career; the ability to formulate an effective venture team; the creative skill to marshal needed resources; and the fundamental skill of building a solid business plan; and finally, the vision to recognize opportunity where others see chaos, contradiction, and confusion (see Figure 2). Kuratko & Hodgetts propounded that entrepreneurial and managerial domains were not mutually exclusive but overlap to a certain extent. The former is more opportunity-driven, and the latter is more resource- and driven. Thus the creation of an enterprise can take a multidimensional view drawn from all those participating in taking the risk. All the risk-takers would convene to structure their venture and provide the resources to sustain the new business.

Practices Can Become Habits

In Berger & Luckmann (1966), an approach to the defining and implementation of workplace relationships acquiescent to productivity is the application of a knowledge community KC or community of practice (COP). Rather than conceptualizing reality as existing outside our perceptions, social construction theory conceptualizes reality as socially constructed. Berger & Luckmann (1966) laid the foundation of social constructionism in their seminal work entitled: *The Social Construction of Reality: A Treatise in the Sociology of Knowledge.* Their proposition rests on three central assumptions. The first is that human behavior is grounded in knowledge; that is, our behavior is informed by our knowledge and understanding of the world around us. The second assertion is that knowledge, results from social processes. In later research Mupepi (2009) concurs with this notion and argues that only members of a KC can authenticate organizational practices. They can structure the organization as a tool to make ends meet. Thus, rather than being objective and real the KC view knowledge as a product of structuration resulting in a socially constructed existence of the organization. The third premise is that, social constructionism discards the idea that there is an objective reality and instead sustains that reality is socially constructed. As Berger and Luckmann (1966) stated, "The sociology of knowledge is concerned with the analysis of the social construction of reality" (p. 19). In contrast to post-positivism, human beings do not behave in and react to reality; they construct it via social practices. A structure influenced human behavior, and humans were capable of changing the social structures they inhabited and in particular the ones they created.

Figure 2. The multidimensional entrepreneurship (Kuratko & Hodgetts, 2004)

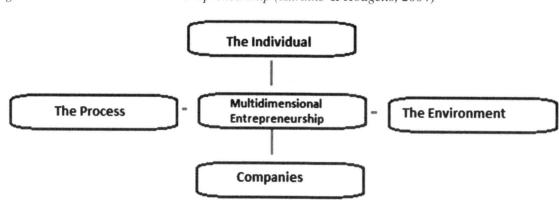

Bourdieu (1990) suggested that the *habitus* is a system of embedded dispositions, tendencies that organize the ways in which individuals perceived the social or business environment. The disposition was often shared by the entire organization, a knowledge community, or an entire profession. Bourdieu argued that the habitus was then acquired through imitation of reflected group culture, and personal history. Organizations were created through this process to solve a community's perceived problem. The habitus represents the way group culture and personal history shape the body and the mind, and as a result, shape social action in the present. As Bourdieu argues that the market is socially constructed by the state, which can decide, for example, whether to promote private housing or collective provision. And the individuals involved in the transaction are immersed in symbolic constructions which constitute, in a strong sense, the value of houses, neighborhoods and towns.

The Building Blocks

In Parsons (1996), structuration is viewed as a construction project with procedures for laying out the foundations and walls to support a roof. He suggested that the natural identification of interest led to the creation of organizations or structures. He viewed that effectiveness in organization occurred as a result of the concept of politics and influence which had/has roots in the community. Parsons propounded that solidarity was a bond among people who trusted each other and integrity remained as the value principle. In Mupepi (2017), the jig analogy is employed to produce product that are similar in dimension that also meet customer expectations. In the same debate competences are also viewed as a social construct. It implies that the forums of knowledge community (KC) or high performance teams can be empowered to progress the efficacies needed to champion organization. Mupepi (2017) argued that teams and teamwork represent very powerful mechanisms for getting results and achieving significant transformation in the business. Mupepi propounded that high performance teams could be self-managing to achieve dramatic results within a short space of time.

FOCUS OF THE CHAPTER

The focus of this chapter is on the structuration of the capability necessary in successful organization. The structuration theory can be applied to minimize risk and solve perceived problems. The structuration approach is employed to design and implement enterprises sensitive to the needs of the community and apparent markets. The structures created can be corporations or partnerships that are developed to make ends meet. The structures succeed as a result of the agency and structure relationship which is sustained by the creators who provide the resources necessary to make the outfit successful.

Controversies

Many organizations are created by a people who do not necessarily make the day-to-day decisions in the business but would like to know before certain decisions are made. This may be an advantage as a precautionary measure in risk management. But it may take a long time to get to those decisions and while time is of the essence opportunities do not wait for decision makers. A knowledge community (KC) can be represented by a board of directors whose main concern is a better return on investment. All other matters such as social responsibility and ethics programs may not matter that much.

RECOMMENDATIONS

The social construction of reality is a strategy that has been tested in creating successful enterprises. The structuration theory also derived from social construction can be applied to design and implement highly talented enterprise. High-performance teams outperform all other similar teams and they outperform expectations given their composition. The structuration theory is a framework for building high performance enterprises. The structuration proposition can be applied to nurture and grow the talent needed to take a business to the next level.

CONCLUSION

There are many caveats in managing talent and much so in developing a tailor-made workforce capable of producing the products and services demanded by customers. A company might spend resources in developing its intellectual capacity only to lose those intellectuals to the competition. The structuration must be understood in the design and implementation of structures and agency that give the company the competitive advantage. However, the competition do not wait while a similar company socially constructs its existence.

REFERENCES

Arnold, R. A. (2016). *Economics* (11th ed.). Mason, Ohio: South Western Inc.

Berger, P. L., & Luckmann, T. (1966). *The Social Construction of Reality: A Treatise in the Sociology of Knowledge*. Garden City, NY: Anchor Books.

Bourdieu, P. (1990). Structures, habitus, practices. In P. Bourdieu (Ed.), *The logic of practice* (pp. 52–79). Stanford, CA: Stanford University Press.

Contu, A., & Willmott, H. (2005). You spin me round: The realist turn in organization and management studies. *Journal of Management Studies*, *42*(8), 1645–1662. doi:10.1111/j.1467-6486.2005.00560.x

Desanctis, G., & Poole, M. S. (1994). Capturing the complexity in advanced technology use: Adaptive structuration theory. *Organization Science*, *5*(2), 121–147. doi:10.1287/orsc.5.2.121

Giddens, A. (1984). *The Constituency of Society*. Cambridge, UK: Cambridge University Press.

Giddens, A. (1989). A reply to my critics. In D. Held & J. B. Thompson (Eds.), *Social theory of modern societies: Anthony Giddens and his critics* (pp. 249–301). Cambridge: Cambridge University Press. doi:10.1017/CBO9780511557699.013

Giddens, A. (2009). *The Politics of Climate Change*. Cambridge, UK: Polity.

Giddens, A. (2014). *The role and nature of the European Union in Turbulent and Mighty Continent: What Future for Europe?* Cambridge, UK: Polity.

Klein, A. (1016). South Africa's 10 Biggest Moments of the Rio 2016 Olympic Games. Retrieved from www.okayafrica.com/sports/rio-2016/south-africa-rio-2016- olympic-games/

Kuratko, D. F., & Hodgetts, R. M. (2004). *Entrepreneurship: Theory, Process, Practice*. Mason, OH: South-Western Publishers.

Mole, K. F., & Mole, M. C. (2010). Entrepreneurship as the structuration of individual and opportunity: A response using a critical realist perspective. *Journal of Business Venturing, 25*(2), 230–237. doi:10.1016/j.jbusvent.2008.06.002

Mupepi, M. (2009). The nature of a schematic description of a socially constructed organizational competency model (CCM). *International Journal of Collaborative Enterprise, 1*(2), 224–240. doi:10.1504/IJCENT.2009.029291

Mupepi, Mambo (2010). Appreciating social structures: a strategy for advancing the efficiency and effectiveness loci in organization. *International Journal of Education Economics and Development, 1*(4), 306 – 319.

Mupepi, M. (2014). *Can the Division of Labor Be Re-Engineered to Advance Organizational Dynamism?* Wiley Open. Doi: doi:10.1177/2158244014536404

Mupepi, Mambo (2016). The passage of the coal train: the inevitable mosaic in technical systems in global and local organization. African J. of Economic and Sustainable Development, 5(2), 149-171.

Mupepi, M. (Forthcoming). *Using Communities of Practice to Identify Competencies.*

Mupepi, M. G., & Motwani, J. (2015). Deconstructing the Value Creation Process: Positioning Diversity to Increase Output. *International Journal of Sociotechnology and Knowledge Development, 7*(4), 15–30. doi:10.4018/IJSKD.2015100102

Mupepi, M. G., & Motwani, J. (2015). Deconstructing the Value Creation Process: Positioning Diversity to Increase Output. *International Journal of Sociotechnology and Knowledge Development, 7*(4), 15–30. doi:10.4018/IJSKD.2015100102

Mupepi, M. G., & Mupepi, S. C. (2015). Charting Highly Productive Organization: Wrapping it all in Social Constructs. *International Journal of Productivity Management and Assessment Technologies, 3*(1), 13–30. doi:10.4018/IJPMAT.2015010102

Mupepi, M. G., & Mupepi, S. C. (2016). Applying Theory to Inform Competency Development: Bootstrapping Epistemic Communities in Growing Specialists. *International Journal of Productivity Management and Assessment Technologies, 4*(1), 28–38. doi:10.4018/IJPMAT.2016010103

Parsons, T. (1996, Winter). The Theory of Human Behavior in its Individual and Social Aspects. *The American Sociologist, 27*(4), 13–23. doi:10.1007/BF02692048

Porter, M. E. (1985). *Competitive Advantage*. New York: Free Press.

Prahalad, C. K., & Hamel, G. (1990). The core competence of the corporation. Harvard Business Review, 68(3), 79–91.

Reed, M. (2005). The realist turn in organization and management studies. *Journal of Management Studies*, *42*(8), 1600–1644. doi:10.1111/j.1467-6486.2005.00559.x

Sewell, W. Jr. (1992). A Theory of Structure: Duality, Agency, and Transformation. *American Journal of Sociology*, *98*(1), 1–29. Retrieved from http://www.jstor.org/stable/2781191 doi:10.1086/229967

KEY TERMS AND DEFINITIONS

Agency: The agency relationship is a consensual relationship created when one person (agent) acts on behalf of and subject to the control of another (the principal)

Epistemology: This is the division of philosophy concerned with the theory of knowledge. It scrutinizes the nature of knowledge and how one can acquire it.

High performance: High performance organizations or teams are those that are highly focused on their goals and that achieve superior business results.

Ontology: Ontology is the philosophical study of the nature of being, becoming, existence, or reality, as well as the basic categories of being and their relations.

Positivism: Positivism is a philosophical dissertation that states that positive knowledge is based on natural occurrences and their properties and relations.

Structuralism: In organizational studies, structuralism is the methodology that elements of human culture must be understood in terms of their relationship to a larger, overarching system or structure.

Chapter 7
Deconstructing Talent:
Understanding know-how in organization

Mambo Mupepi
Seidman College, USA

Jaideep Motwani
Seidman College, USA

ABSTRACT

The discourse in this presentation is about how talent can be viewed as appropriate techniques and explicit practices enhanced by experience useful in the value creation system. Talent can be deconstructed to progress the necessary efficacy in organization. A limited literature is drawn to understand the role of structures and technology in the value creation process. Value is created anytime an action is taken for which the benefits exceed the costs, or the moment an action can be prevented for which the costs exceed the benefits. A co-constructed competency model can be initiated to comprehend a systemic approach to enhancing performance and the design of strategy to retain talent and nurture the skillfulness and knowing necessary in boosting yields in diversified entities.

INTRODUCTION

In four objectives, this paper will attempt to answer the question: Is it possible to increase yields in a diversified team? The first objective has two sub-objectives: An introduction to the discussion which will be followed by a definition of deconstruction and the value creation system as they are central to the appreciation of the arguments and conceptual framework developed in the discussion. The second objective reviews prudently selected literature about productivity in socio-technical systems characterized by talent or aptitudes distributed unevenly in diversity value creation systems. The literature review provides a platform to deconstruct the collective performance of groups and how such organization can co-construct different perspectives necessary to make ends meet. The third objective examines the application of the Social Construct Competency Model (SCCM), to appreciate how it can be applied to assess and measure knowing and skillfulness in winning corporations. In the final objective, the way forward is proposed and a conclusion is drawn mentioning the limitations of the arguments presented.

DOI: 10.4018/978-1-5225-1961-4.ch007

BACKGROUND

Understanding Some of the Key Dimensions

During the early 1980s, *Cultural differences* have been the subject of sizable research efforts in an attempt to understand how managers could sympathize with multiple ethnic groups with contrasting cultures compared to their own. It is important to recognize that people from different cultures perceive experiences differently. It implies that the way they were raised schooled and trained could be different from our own experience. Hofstede (1980) suggests that culture is the collective programming of the human mind that distinguishes the members of one human group from those of another. This assertion demonstrates that culture is the accumulation of values by a group of like-minded individuals. As times passes, these like-minded individuals will transfer their behaviors, beliefs, ideas etc., on to the new members of their culture; this is essentially how culture is built and sustained within a business entity. Culture more than leadership is the key to successful organizational performance. In concurrence Cameron (1999), propounds that leadership is a cultural variable that enables organizational effectiveness to be real. It is important to understand the prevailing cultural conditions in organization.

What is Multiculturalism in the Workplace?

Bell (2012) suggests that diversity can be viewed as real or perceived differences among people in race, ethnicity, sex, age, physical and mental ability, sexual orientation, religion, work and family status, weight and appearance, and other identity-based attributes that affect their interactions and relationships. It is a tall order description. But this variance if utilized correctly, can fortify the company's presence in the industry of operations, recruit and retain talented individuals in addition to positioning the company to surpass their desired goals.

Multiculturalism is about different ethnicities; it could be used to describe the ethnic makeup of an organization. This term can be deployed to describe Europeans who come from different parts of the European continent. It could be used too to describe Africans who could be affiliated to parts of the African continent. The same word can also be applied to describe Asian Americans who can speak different languages and possess differing views on religion, politics or customs, among many other cultural variables originating from specific places in Asia. For example, Indians or Chinese may have unique religious practices and all can be found in the modern American workplace.

Deconstruction is a method of critical analysis of philosophical and literary texts developed by Jacques Derrida in a book entitled *Of Grammatology* first published in 1967. Derrida's revolutionary theories contained in the book include deconstruction, phenomenology, psychoanalysis and structuralism which have become useful in developing sociotechnical systems perspectives such as shared distributed cognition, organizational capacity and competences, and knowledge community (KC), among numerous others (Derrida, 1998). In Mupepi, Mupepi & Motwani (2015), the co-construction of organizational capacity is suggested to yield realistic results when perspectives can be made and taken into the design context by a knowledge community (KC). Mupepi et al suggest that creating the dimensions required to progress output to desirable standards can be a collaborative effort. The shaping of technology, explicit practice, and the disposition to do the job accurately can be deconstructed using the forum of a KC. The KC can be composed of a diversified individuals elected to the forum for possessing specific talent needed in advancing the business. The KC can foster thinking in an unusual and un-stereotyped way to generate several possible solutions to solve organizational problems.

Deconstruction in the Construction Industry

Deconstruction has been adapted in the construction and design industries because applying the technique can yield viable projects. Muroe Hatamiya & Westwind (2006) employed as agents of federal state and municipal governments strive to reduce the volume of solid waste that is buried or incinerated, salvaging reusable and recyclable building materials through deconstruction. Munroe et al argue that until recently most contractors and developers have relied primarily on business profitability considerations when making the 'demolition vs. deconstruction' decisions which have favored demolition because demolition is often faster, less labor intensive, and usually more convenient. They posit that the balance was shifting – and an increasing number of deconstruction projects have shown that deconstructing buildings can be economically and technically viable. The lessons of these projects as well as public policies aimed at providing the appropriate incentives (as well as disincentives) can help in the maturation of a market-based deconstruction industry as part of the larger construction industry cluster.

Deconstruction of Diversity

The deconstruction technique emphasizes inquiry into the variable projection of what makes sense in organization. In Derrida (1998) organizational strategy is perceived as a construct of meaning making made possible through a language understood by all in the business. The focus of diversity in organization is to select and hire the best talent needed to make ends meet in the business. Beregszciszi & Hack-Polay (2015) suggest that large corporations can deconstruct operations to determine the best way toward a viable business plan. An additional reason for deconstructing organization has been to understand the drivers behind the creation of the competitive advantage. A company can have all the know-how money can buy but its people make the difference. The talent useful in organization is a construct when viewed from the organization's core competences. The KC is argued by Lave & Wenger (1991) and Mupepi et al (2015) to be the only qualified forum to authenticate the practices needed to make the difference. Beregszciszi & Hack-Polay (2015) propound that the reasons to acquire the technology needed to progress the business can be constructed with many goals such as minimizing risk and enhancing productivity in mind.

Deconstructing the Value Creation Process

Deconstructing human resources can lead to the acquisition or employment of the talent needed to grow the enterprise. The primary aim of businesses is to create goods and services that are demanded by customers (see Figure 1). In the Adam Smith Pin-production factory orders can come from different customers who could demand different products such as high street drapers' pins or safety pins demanded by high street companies such as Mother Care or Walgreens the Chemist, among many others. The value creation process begins with the materials manager in Plant A, who sources for different aluminum wire rims of varying dimensions suitable for making needles, pins, or hardware screws and nails. There are opportunities for the pin-smith to be innovative in plant A. For example, they can find out other drapers who need pins, school systems that use blackboard drawing pins and so forth. Plant A cuts the aluminum coil into the specifications obtained from customer e.g. 1000 one-inch drapery pins. Plant B receives the one inch stubs and proceeds to make pin-heads on each one. Innovation can also happen here when the pin-smith specialist thinks how to make his job easier. Plant C receives the one inch stubs and sharpens each one of them. The sharpened pins are passed on to Plant D for polishing. When done, the pins are

Figure 1. Adam Smith Pin-production factory…A value creation process (Mupepi, 2014)

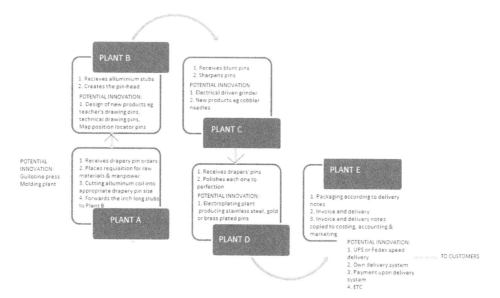

passed on to Plant E for packaging and onward delivery to customers. The argument presented by Adam Smith is that at each plant the pin-smith is able to increase output by thinking of how to make his job easier. New tools along with increased dexterity yield more output (see Figure1).

The knowledge, skills, and technology required in effective organization can be deconstructed to develop different scenarios and perspectives of how the job could be done successfully. Questions such as: What are the procedures in making pins demanded by customers? Or what are the product formulations in making drawing pins? The answers should reveal the materials tools and skills required to make the pins demanded by customers. The approach enables the design of useful on-job training and an appreciation of the product specifications which are the quality demanded by customers. According Adam Smith specialization results from the eagerness of the novice to learn and constantly practice and improve. The outcome benefits the employer when productivity increases and the worker earns more as a result of increased output.

In Mupepi (2014) the skills, technology, and knowledge required to progress effectiveness and efficiency in the plants can be understood by deploying the socially constructed competency model (SCCM). This knowledge can be applied to assess and evaluate the desirable performance The SCCM can be reconfigured to advance knowledge or skills acquisition which lead to the capacity an entity needs to meet the demands of customers (see Figure 2). Talent or organizational competency can be deconstructed by a knowledge community in constructing what gives the business the competitive advantage. It is a KC that can structure competencies raising the bar on inclusiveness to grow the talent a business needs to increase productivity. There are many strategies that companies could deploy to create the edge and a SCCM is an alternative technique that recognizes that a diversified team can make the difference in organization. For example, in understanding the knowledge, skills and technology needed to make the difference in the value creation process there is a need to recognize the fact that talent is unevenly distributed in races or ethnicity. Selecting the best talent can result in an organization that embraces multiculturalism.

Figure 2. Talent can be a co-construct (Mupepi, Mupepi, & Motwani 2015)

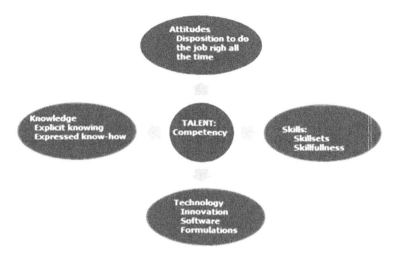

Mupepi (2010) argues that the SCCM is sustained for its effectiveness as a change management technique because competency models, in particular those concerned with organizational capabilities, are relatively ineffective when built outside the company without involving those who do the work. A contrast of the competency models established elsewhere is made with those espoused within the organization by the knowledge communities (KC) and effectiveness is demonstrated in the latter approach. In reviewing selections from the literature that established the competency development movement, a foundation on past knowledge is built. By taking this information into consideration and interpreting it, one may design and implement capabilities that advance the business. The resultant competencies can be applied in any entity (see Figure 2).

The Likert Scales

The Likert Scales have been identified as the most important and widely used recent approaches to assessment and evaluation technology (see Figure 3). Rensis Likert is one of the founding fathers of the field of organization development. He invented the assessment scales bearing his name as a technology that could be applied to assess and evaluate performance. Likert (1932) invented the assessment and evaluation tool which is a psychometric scale commonly involved in research that employs questionnaires. The format of a typical five-level Likert item, for example, could be: 1. Strongly disagree; 2. Disagree; 3. Neither agree nor disagree; 4. Agree; and 5. Strongly agree. Likert scaling is a bipolar scaling method, measuring either positive or negative response to a statement (Carifio & Perla, 2007).

Digital Analytics

Digital analytics relates to processing, storing and transmitting data in the form of numerical digits; a technique that evolved out of information technology management. It is now a tool useful in managing business information in a fast changing global market. Burby (2009) lists the capabilities of analysis as being goal oriented, actionable, insightful, impactful, inclusive, change base, ongoing and difficult.

Figure 3. The SCCM (Mupepi, 2010)

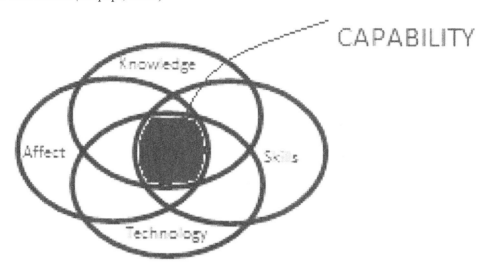

In digital analytics, quantitative and qualitative data mined from for instance human resources, can be analyzed as part of the recruitment process which can lead to the selection of the best talent. Data collected from the online sales portal can also be examined to understand the nature of demand generated by the customers. Such information has a bearing on the nature and description of the talent needed in successful organization. All the information can be used to advance sales and marketing efforts in addition to driving a continual learning and improvement of the online experience possessed by stakeholders.

Diversity and Sustainability

The concepts of sustainability and diversity have taken the center stage in describing a future workforce, one that is designed to succeed in the fast changing global economy. The diversified workforce can be viewed as an open system drawn from general systems theory in which Bertalanffy (1968) posits; that the main features of open systems where reproduction and identity can be the basis for differentials. Bertalanffy drew from Biology to describe resemblance in form or appearance between organisms of different ancestry or between different stages in the life cycle of the same organism. Systems theory can be applied to progress diversified workplaces by giving them a useful framework for looking at complex human groupings, including multi-racially structured workplaces. Deconstruction techniques can enable a group of people who share the same interests and meet together regularly in defined physical locations or in cyberspace at any time to develop alternative solutions to a problem. There is nearly an endless variety of ways in which members are unlike each other, ranging from dissimilarities in the both visible and invisible variances. But in organization all people can be employed for one unique reason... the competences useful in the business they possess.

Creating a Shared Mindset

Mupepi & Mupepi (2015) propound that organizations can create new perspectives about the job, how best to do it or what type of technology is required to make production easy by using the collective minds of the stakeholders. A mindset can be applied to mold a resilient company. It can be programmed for success. Mupepi & Mupepi (2015) suggest that the organization's mindset is a tool that can be disciplined. The success of the business can depend to a greater extent on the people doing the job. It can be argued that the same analyses perception and thinking in the division of labor can be mimicked to re-frame the value creation process to increase productivity.

System-Theoretical Re-Orientation

Scholars such as Green et al (2010) and Coelho, Goertzel, Pennachin & Heward (2010), among others have taken the systems thinking to the next level. Green et al suggest that human beings differentiate themselves from the ape animal communities as an example because they stand erect and can be described as Homo sapiens or thinking men. Coelho et al characterize the Homo sapiens as the model of a man, an active personality system, and tying up the psychophysiological organism as a whole into the focus of scientific endeavor. Aronson (1998) posits that systems thinking (ST) can lead to the creation of a shared mindset. Its designer a Professor Forrester at MIT in 1956 recognized the need for a better way of testing new ideas about social systems in the same way engineering products can be tested. Aronson (1998) argues that ST allows people in organization to make their understanding of the structures in their organization and improve them to yield increased outputs. They can also deploy engineering principles to make understanding of mechanical systems or the technology inherent in their particular value creation process.

Adam Smith the economist introduced the principles of the division of labor in his book "The Wealth of Nations" first published in 1776. Smith gave the world a niftier way to structure organizations that can improve productivity. The division of labor is a deliberate technique that can be applied to enhance systems thinking as a prerequisite to growing specialization. A specialized organization can be characterized by a joint enterprise that gives rise to a shared repertoire of knowledge, skillsets, and practices.

The Dynamics of a Diversified Workforce

Many individual elements affect the dynamics of diversified work groups; the reason why the group was formed, the personalities of the individual group members, the information the members have, how the group is skilled at doing the job assigned to it and how conflict is handled and resolved. In Mupepi &Taruvinga (2014), cultural differences and perceived risk-taking must be considered before charting organizational competences in household enterprises in the Southern African Development Communities and the USA. The consequences were that triumphant households were those that took cognizance of multiculturalism in assessing and measuring performance. Mupepi & Taruvinga (2014) argue that Multiple Linear Regression analysis demonstrated that capacity must be customized to suit organizational vision and that the vital predictor of perceived success in the USA was performance orientation while uncertainty avoidance topped the list in the SADC. Results indicate that diversity was understood in all successful enterprises.

Group Sensibility

Wilfred Bion is one of the pioneers in the field of organization development. His research at the Tavistock Institute in post-war Britain contributed to defining group dynamics. Kurt Lewin, Eric Trist, Fred

Emery, and Kenneth Bamworth, and others, worked with Bion to advance psychoanalysis as a concept that could be applied to understand groups at work. In much later research the study of groups have been expanded to product production as opposed to the military organization in which Wilfred Bion and his colleagues did much of their research. For example Driskell & Salas (2016) examine how the power of teams may be exploited by utilizing a distributed talent to pay more attention to issue-relevant information such as quality or safety in operational and production environments. Teams are ubiquitous in work situations in part because they offer the capacity to reduce workload and enhance performance in complex tasks. The perspective of group dynamics has remained central in organizational development. Bion's observations about the role of group processes in group dynamics are set out in Experiences in Groups (1961), where he refers to recurrent emotional states of groups as basic assumptions. Bion argues that in a formal group, two groups are actually present: the work group, and the basic assumption group. The work group is that aspect of group functioning which has to do with the primary task of the group—what the group has been formed to accomplish; will keep the group anchored to a sophisticated and rational level of behavior. Thus groups can be designed to enhance efficiency and effectiveness.

In pairing, Bion (1961) suggests that the development of the group is frozen by a hope of being rescued by two members who will pair-off and somehow create an alternative leader. This in-fighting can result in the formation of the second within the first group. In the fight or flight Bion propounds that the group might act as if its main task is to fight or flee from some common enemy who may be found either within or outside the group. In later research, Davis (2014) propounds that members of a group may seek the approval of the leader, others seek alliances within or outside their group and some could have developed strong feelings of love hate or comradeship, while others get cross or even cry. The argument Davis posits support the formation of a secondary group that has unique work ethics as part of their values within the original structure. Group dynamics can be applied usefully to advance talent and productivity in varied environments.

Schutt & Linegar (2016) build from the early experience of group dynamics to divide the organization into three broad areas. These areas are: groups working with organization development practitioners to improve performance; a self-managing project team working; and the organization in a distributed value creation process characterized with sophisticated hi-tech and information technology infrastructure. Schutt & Linegar suggest that these areas individually or in combination, can impact significantly on the success or otherwise of virtual world projects, and understanding them better offers the potential for greater success. However, these kinds of operational concerns do not guarantee high performance unless the groups move to becoming teams with defined norms and task expectations

Either Changing Pretty Fast or Perishing

The upshot to Productive Workplaces (1987), a book written by Marvin R. Weisbord which was voted by the OD Network as one of the influential Organization Development books of the last 40 years, was a re-edition in 2004. The edition includes nearly all of the earlier work plus 100 new pages. In the book Weisbord reports on what happened to organizations 15 to 30 years after major efforts to institutionalize changes for the better. He asserts that from the ten cases that he had examined 4 no longer existed, 4 were taken over by other stronger companies then, and only two had the same ownership in 2004 and only one in 2005. Marvin suggests that many of the companies perished because they were not structured to succeed. The inter-relations that made up the whole could have been misaligned and the blame lies equally well with the owners as well as those who drew a livelihood from those companies. In Mupepi & Mupepi (2015), organizational change is argued to be the only certainty in an organization, for this reason, failure to embrace this change can be disastrous. In earlier research Mupepi, Yim et al (2011) an assertion is made that groups can be customized to advance the goals of the company. The top management can be structured to allow three to five individuals to report directly to the CEO on matters pertaining to the key performance areas of the business. Mupepi & Yim et al argue that the collective experience of the organization can be applied to create cutting-edge practices. Weisbord (2004) indicates that the demise of a business entity is a result of the failure to share pertinent information necessary for the entity to embrace change.

Inspiration for Highly Productive Teams

In Lewin (1951), Bion (1961), Goleman (1996), Helm et al (2011), and Mupepi (2009), among many others, the study of supportive climate and emotional intelligence help to build exceptionally productive teams. The subjects in Bion (1961) research as well as those of Helm et al (2011) were psychiatric cases and the procedures applied can be replicated in normal groups too. As a field of study, group dynamics has roots in both psychology and sociology. Wilhelm Wundt (1832–1920), is credited as the founder of experimental psychology and had a particular interest in the psychology of communities, which he believed possessed phenomena (human language, customs, and religion) that could not be described through a study of the individual. On the sociological side, Émile Durkheim (1858–1917), who was influenced by Wundt, also recognized collective phenomena, such as public knowledge (Backstrom, et al 2006). Other key theorists include Gustave Le Bon (1841–1931) who believed that crowds possessed a racial unconscious with primitive, aggressive, and antisocial instincts, and William McDougall who believed in a group mind which had a distinct existence born from the interaction of individuals (Hogg, 2000).

Conducive Organizational Climate

In a study by Helm, Stams & Laan (2011), the construct validity and reliability of the Prison Group Climate Instrument (PGCI) in a sample of 77 adolescents placed in a youth prison and 49 adult prisoners living in a psychiatric prison with a therapeutic living group structure, is examined. Confirmatory factor analysis of a four-factor model—with "repression," "support," "growth," and "group atmosphere" as first-order factors—and "overall group climate" as a second order factor shows an adequate fit to the data, indicating construct validity of the PGCI. Cronbach's alpha reliability coefficients are good for all factors. The PGCI is a frugal instrument, enabling future research on group climate in youth prisons and secure forensic psychiatric institutions.

The PGCI instrument can be used as an assessment tool for judicial interventions that use group climate to improve outcomes in delinquent youth and adult delinquents receiving treatment for psychiatric problems. The Helm et al (2011) research indicates that a group atmosphere conducive to the business can be successfully designed and implemented to include the variables trust, cohesiveness and supportiveness. Cohesiveness refers to the attachment members feel toward each other, the group, and the task. Trust refers to the general belief that members can rely on each other. In a supportive climate, members encourage each other, care about each other, and treat each other with respect.

MAIN FOCUS OF THE CHAPTER

The focus of this chapter is to develop different perspectives to benchmark performance and enable continuous learning and improvement to happen in successful organization. Understanding the key dimensions in organization is critical in the design and implementation of effective enterprise. Deconstruction is a critical outlook technique developed by Derrida (1967) to understand the relationship between text and meaning. For example, a knowledge community can draw different perspectives in relation to the mandated realities of their organization. In Mupepi & Motwani (2015) deconstruction is employed to appreciate how aptitudes, explicit knowing, appropriate techniques, and efficacies to progress the enterprise. Value is created anytime an action is taken for which the benefits exceed the costs, or anytime an action can be prevented for which the costs exceed the benefits. A co-constructed competency model can be applied to understand the structures that enhance performance and the design of attractive conditions of service to retention talent and nurture the skillfulness and knowing necessary in boosting yields in diversified entities.

Controversies

Drawing from political science scholars such Breckman (2010) propounded that Law and Politics could not be separated. The legal text cannot be construed to imply other meanings apart from what the lawmakers have implied in writing. Arguing that law and politics cannot be separated Breckman suggested that it was difficult to deconstruct tensions and procedures by which they are expressed and deployed. Habermas (1972) argued that rationalism regarded reason as the main test of knowledge or any view developed from deconstruction. Habermas posited that deconstruction was limited in scope particularly in drawing perspectives from legal or political science text.

SOLUTIONS AND RECOMMENDATIONS

Scholars such as Cooperrider & Dutton (1999) suggested that in designing organizational talent positive scholarship technology such as a knowledge community can be employed to determine desirable change. By incorporating the views drawn from all stakeholders, it can be possible to chart practices that will be difficult for the competition to mimic for a long time. Practices that are unique to the organization can be deconstructed using the forum of a community of practice which is the only group authenticated to create, diffuse and distribute the explicit practices needed to differentiate the business.

The Way Forward

As today's world becomes increasingly global in its marketplace outlook, multiculturalism in the workplace could also increase. Cox & Blake (1991) suggest that organization workforces will be increasingly heterogeneous on dimensions such as race, ethnicity, gender and nationality. The benefits of becoming more diversity in those arenas are better decision making, higher creativity, and innovation, greater success in the marketing to foreign and ethnic minority communities, and a better distribution of economic opportunities. Productivity is measured by output; output is determined by the capability organization's objectives, including shareholder value, to improved business performance and solidifies a cohesive corporate culture. Productivity is not about working harder, yet it is about working smarter in all aspects; therefore using the information collected from the digital analysis will provide insight for change.

Successful Diversity Organization

Emotional Intelligence central concept has been identified by Mason & Leslie (2012) as the ability to focus on the perception and expression of emotion accurately and adaptively in both self and others. In addition to understanding the emotional knowledge and use of feeling to further thought and organization emotional intelligence has been noted over years of observation and research to be a key element in successful and positive outcomes for leadership, workplace environments, and team cohesion. This game changing factor in business can be developed and implemented in successful diverse organizations. Goleman (2013) suggests that emotional intelligence can also be assessed to understand behavior including how customers are treated or how products are made. Emotional Intelligence can be developed and implemented organization-wide to increase productivity. Goleman posits that his research overlaps between psychology and neuroscience and offers startling new insight into our two minds—the rational and the emotional—and how they together shape productivity in organization. Goleman (2013) delineates the five crucial skills of emotional intelligence, and shows how they determine our success in relationships, and work. Goleman recommends the following:

- Emotional and Social Competence Inventory (ESCI) – to assess the emotional and social competencies that distinguish outstanding leaders.
- ESCI Technical Manual – Describes the most recent findings using the ESCI as well as technical details such as reliability and validity.
- Emotional intelligence tests evaluated – To decide which EI assessment is most appropriate for a given use

The Socially Constructed Competency Model an Alternative Strategy

The four egg-shaped circles are equal and represent the threshold of capacity of the business. The SCCM is hinged on the platform of a knowledge community (KC), a group within the structure that meets regularly to solve organizational problems and create explicit practices to advance the business. The KC can be responsible for cross-teams or cross-divisional learning deploying systems thinking as a vehicle to share ideas, and design tools that can be employed to make the job easy. It can also be responsible for co-constructing a shared vision and in defining the drivers for successful value creation processes. Competences tend to increase and improve with continuous learning and skills upgrading (see Figure 3). Furthermore, an organization can have all the technology money can buy but its people will make the difference.

Assessment Tool

The SCCM can be converted into an assessment tool which can be applied to determine the distribution of explicit knowledge, skillfulness, and disposition prevailing in the organization. The Pin-production plant is drawn as an example where the Likert Scales can be adapted by calibrating the SCCM assessment tool to understand prevailing cultural conditions such as knowledge, attitudes, skills and technology (Likert, 1932). With the knowledge gained by the application of this model, the organization can reevaluate its organizational culture to reengineer performance (see Figure 4). Adapting the Likert Scale to understand pin-production and to effectively different on-job training and continuous learning and improvement (Mupepi, 2010).

Constructing a Group Climate

Group climate refers to the psychological atmosphere or environment within the group and is another key element in forging a team from a collection of diverse individuals. It is a co-construct and critical in a successful diverse organization. Group climate is the enveloping tone that is created by the way individual members communicate within groups. A positive climate exists when individuals perceive that they are valued, supported, and treated will by the group. A negative climate exists when group members do not feel valued, supported, and respected, when trust is minimal and when members perceive that they are not treated well (see Figure 4).

A Systemic Approach to Advancing Productivity

Talent and knowhow are scarce resources often unevenly distributed in organizations. These resources have to be managed efficiently and effectively to leverage the skillfulness, knowhow and tacit experience in sustaining the competitive advantage. Groups and teams operate interdependently within one another in furtherance of organizational goals (see Figure 5).

Figure 4. A sample of a survey instrument to measure climate (Mupepi, 2010)

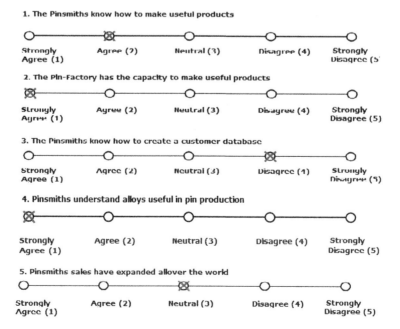

Figure 5. A systematic modeling of highly productive multicultural teams (Mupepi & Motwani, 2015)

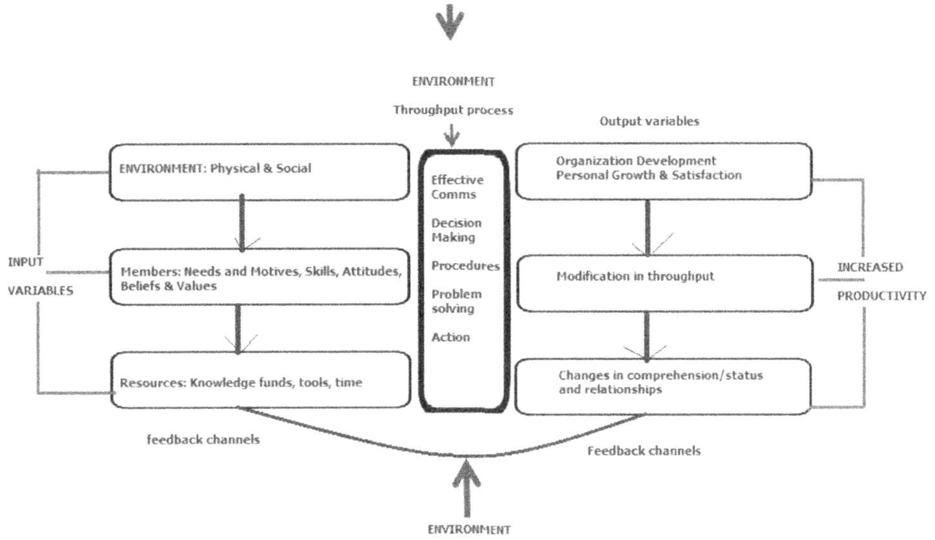

Implementation of Appropriate Databases

Human resources portals can be useful in mining all kinds of data and in hosting lesson plans to grow useful businesses. Statistical analysis of survey data suggests that certain attributes are driving good behaviors, and the demographic data suggests that this relationship holds irrespective of the geographic location of the site. Human resources portals can also be applied to mine data which can be analyzed in creating appropriate databases such as job and product specifications. Quality attributes such as product and job specifications can serve as surrogates for quality culture. Management communication should emphasize on appreciating the talent in a diverse workforce. The organization can have all the technology there is but its people will make the difference. Well-structured roles pave the way for clear performance criteria and feedback and continual learning and improvement and increased productivity (see Figure 5).

Building Expectation

The collectiveness of diverse work groups can be built. In most successful companies, individuals are hired to do specific jobs. There are specific rules of doing things useful to the organization the following can be some of the considerations:

- Equal opportunities can be incorporated in performance standards such promotion, and hiring of new personnel.
- Talented individuals can belong to any race or ethnicity…the employer should consider the contribution each employee can make to what gives life to the business
- Teams can be co-constructed successfully
- Teams that are highly cohesive are also effective at what they do
- Laid down procedures should be put into place to guide teams

The Essential Factors in High Performance Teams

Supportive members, who uphold the group's values and beliefs in the highest esteem, support the rest of the organization in advancing the mission. In a supportive climate, members have the freedom to disagree with their groups opinions. Hence, members feel safe from psychological assaults, they are free to direct most of their energies toward helping the group accomplish its task.

Building Trust and Cohesiveness

Where trust exists, members are more likely to create an open climate where members who trust one another are more likely to create an open space climate where people share freely. Trust impact the work of any group:

- Task related and interpersonal.
- A trustworthy member regarding the job can be relied upon in getting the job done professionally.
- He or she will be able to produce top notch work for the team/group consistently and respectfully.
- A member who does not contribute to the group forces the other members to pick up the slack; therefore, both the trust level and the cohesiveness of the group suffers.
- Team members can share the same sentiments about specialization and their profession for example that of the pin-smith. Thus, efforts to increase productivity can become a group goal, all things being equal.

FUTURE RESEARCH DIRECTIONS

There are many ways to create explicit practices. But differentiation in economics mean making products differently from the competition. In on-job training differentiation implies framing job instruction to allow the worker to understand his contribution he is required to make. Research could focus on on-job training and how instruction can be differentiated to allow effective techniques acquisition.

CONCLUSION

Deconstruction is a process that enables organizations to draw different perspectives about their enterprise. They will be able to appreciate the explicit knowledge, skills, technology, and the disposition to effectively do the job. Deconstruction will make realistic job at drawing the performance attributes necessary to differentiate the business accurately.

The company can have all the technology money can buy but its people will make the difference. An organization with an established level of productivity can increase their output by focusing on being highly cohesive, which will allow the group to customize their own tool and design work systems that will make the tasks easy to accomplish. In highly cohesive teams doing the job can be viewed as a pleasure, because each member has a heightened sense of awareness of their own strengths, but also those who work alongside them. Even though in work groups the caveats can be many; for example, if there is no trust among members, a talented group can be unproductive. Whereas, in a group that is not cohesive, members do not feel much sense of belonging. They may not be allegiant and can leave at short notice. This will leave the company with a consistent revolving door of new employees who may not possess the knowledge, skills, technology or attitude that will continue the momentum of the company moving forward, which can be expensive. By adopting an in-house evaluation and assessment tool/ technique, the organization can: identify their strengths, realign their inactivity and develop the competencies that will accelerate their productivity. In turn, it will position the company for an increase in productivity and a competitive stance in the global marketplace.

REFERENCES

Aronson, D. (1998). An Overview of Systems Thinking. *Thinking.net.* Retrieved from http://www.thinking.net/Systems_Thinking/OverviewSTarticle.pdf

Backstrom, L., Huttenlocher, D., Kleinberg, J., & Lan, X. (2006). Group formation in large social networks.*Proceedings of the 12th Annual International Conference on Knowledge Discovery and Data Mining.* doi:10.1145/1150402.1150412

Banton, M. (2007). Weber on Ethnic Communities: A critique. *Nations and Nationalism, 13*(1), 19–35. doi:10.1111/j.1469-8129.2007.00271.x

Bell, M. P. (2012). *Diversity on Organizations* (2nd ed.). Mason, OH: South Western.

Beregszaszi, J., & Hack-Polay, D. (2015). Off the overload: The growing HR outsourcing industry in emerging European economies - the case of Hungary. *European Journal of International Management, 9*(4), 409–424. doi:10.1504/EJIM.2015.070227

Bion, W. R. (1961). *Experiences in Groups.* London, UK: Tavistock Institute. doi:10.4324/9780203359075

Bizumic, B., & Duckitt, J. (2008). My group is not worthy of me: Narcissism and ethnocentrism. *Political Psychology, 29*(3), 437–453. doi:10.1111/j.1467-9221.2008.00638.x

Breckman, W. (2010, July). Times of Theory: On Writing the History of French Theory. *Journal of the History of Ideas, 71*(3), 339–361. doi:10.1353/jhi.0.0082

Burby, J. (2009, June 2). What is Digital Analysis? (Click Z). Retrieved from http://clickz.com/print_article/clickz/column/1717832/what-is-digital-analysis#

Cameron, K. (1999). A framework for organizational quality culture. *Quality Management Journal, 6*(4), 7–25.

Carifio, J., & Perla, R. J. (2007). Ten Common Misunderstandings, Misconceptions, Persistent Myths and Urban Legends about Likert Scales and Likert Response Formats and their Antidotes. *Journal of Social Sciences, 3*(3), 106–116. doi:10.3844/jssp.2007.106.116

Coelho, L., Goertzel, B., Pennachin, C., & Heward, C. (2010). Classifier Ensemble Based Analysis of a Genome-Wide SNP Dataset Concerning Late-Onset Alzheimer Disease. *International Journal of Software Science and Computational Intelligence, 2*(4), 60–71. doi:10.4018/jssci.2010100105

Cooperrider, D.L., & Dutton, J. (1999). *Organizational Dimensions of Global Change: No limits to Cooperation.* London, UK; Sage Publications

Cox, T., & Blake, S. (1991). Managing Cultural Diversity: Implications for Organizational Competitiveness. *The Journal of Academy of Management, 5*(3), 45–56.

Davis, T. E. (2014). Newly Created Heterogeneous Groups: The Time to Adjust to Significant Race and/or Gender Differences. In V. Wang (Ed.), *Advanced Research in Adult Learning and Professional Development: Tools, Trends, and Methodologies* (pp. 224–235). Hershey, PA: Information Science Reference; doi:10.4018/978-1-4666-4615-5.ch009

Derrida, J. (1967). *Of Grammatology.* Paris, France: Les Éditions de Minuit.

Derrida, J. (1998). *Of Grammatology (Corrected ed.).* Baltimore: John Hopkins University Press.

Driskell, T., & Salas, E. (2015). Investigative interviewing: Harnessing the power of the team. *Group Dynamics, 19*(4), 273–289. doi:10.1037/gdn0000036

Foschi, R., & Lombardo, G. P. (2006). Lewinian contribution to the study of personality as the alternative to the mainstream of personality psychology in the 20th century. In *J., Trempala, A. Pepitone, B. Raven (Eds.), Lewinian Psychology* (Vol. 1, pp. 86–98). Bydgoszcz: Kazimierz Wielki University Press.

Goleman, D. (1996). *Emotional Intelligence: Why It Can Matter More Than IQ.* Bantam Books.

Goleman, D. (1998). *Working with emotional intelligence.* New York: Bantam Books.

Goleman, D. (2013). *Focus: The Hidden Driver of Excellence.* New York: Harper.

Green, R. E., Krause, J., Briggs, A. W., Maricic, T., Stenzel, U., Kircher, M., & Paabo, S. et al. (2010). A Draft Sequence of the Neanderthal Genome. *The Science Journal, 328*(5979), 710–722. doi:10.1126/science.1188021 PMID:20448178

Habernas, J. (1972). *Knowledge and human interests.* Boston, MA: Beacon Press ISBN.

Hofstede, G. (1980). *Culture's consequences: International differences in work-related values.* Beverly Hills, CA, USA: Sage.

Hogg, M. A., & Williams, K. D. (2000). From me to us: Social identity and the collective self. *Group Dynamics, 4*(1), 81–97. doi:10.1037/1089-2699.4.1.81

James, P. (2015). Despite the Terrors of Typologies: The Importance of Understanding Categories of Difference and Identity. *International Journal of Postcolonial Studies., 17*(2), 174–195. doi:10.1080/1 369801X.2014.993332

Kasemsap, K. (2015). The Role of Total Quality Management Practices on Quality Performance. In A. Moumtzoglou, A. Kastania, & S. Archondakis (Eds.), *Laboratory Management Information Systems: Current Requirements and Future Perspectives* (pp. 1–31). Hershey, PA, USA: IGI Global. doi:10.4018/978-1-4666-6320-6.ch001

Katz, D., & Kahn, R. (1978). *The Social Psychology of Organizations* (2nd ed.). New York: Wiley.

Lave, J., & Wenger, E. (1991). *Situated Learning: Legitimate Peripheral Participation*. Cambridge, UK: Cambridge University Press. doi:10.1017/CBO9780511815355

Lewin, K. (1943). Defining the Field at a Given Time. *Psychological Review*, *50*(3), 292–310. doi:10.1037/h0062738

Lewin, K. (1951). *Field theory in social science; selected theoretical papers* (D. Cartwright, Ed.). New York: Harper & Row.

Likert, R. (1932). A Technique for the Measurement of Attitudes. *Archives de Psychologie*, *140*, 1–55.

Mason, D. C., & Leslie, J. B. (2012). The Role of Multicultural Competence and Emotional Intelligence in Managing Diversity. *The American Psychological Association*, *15*, 219–236.

Meltzer, D. (1978). *The Kleinian development Part I: Freud's Clinical Development; Part II: Richard Week-by-Week; Part III: The Clinical Significance of the Work of Bion*. London, UK: Harris Meltzer Trust Publishers Ltd.

Merriam-Webster. (2015). Definition of Subculture. Accessed 05/18/15 http://dictionary.reference.com/browse/subculture

Mupepi, M. (2009). The nature of a schematic description of a socially constructed organizational competency model (CCM). *International Journal of Collaborative Enterprise*, *1*(2), 224–240. doi:10.1504/IJCENT.2009.029291

Mupepi, M. (2010). The nature of a schematic description of a socially constructed organizational competency model (CCM). *International Journal of Collaborative Enterprise*, *1*(2), 224–240. doi:10.1504/IJCENT.2009.029291

Mupepi, Mambo (2014). Appreciating Rapid Technology Integration in Creating Value in Enterprises. *Journal of Electronic Commerce in Organizations*, *12*(1), 53-75.

Mupepi, M. (2015). *British Imperialism in Zimbabwe: Narrating the organization development of the First Chimurenga 1883-1904*. San Diego: Cognella.

Mupepi, M., & Mupepi, S. (2015). (in press). Is it possible to increase productivity in diversified workplaces? *Organization Development Journal*.

Mupepi, M., Mupepi, S., & Motiwan, J. (2015, March 10-14). Social constructs: Methods Tools and Applications: Re-engineering organizations successfully. *Proceedings of the Southwest Academy of Management 57th Annual Meeting*, Houston, Texas, USA.

Mupepi, M., Tenkasi, R., Sorensen, P., & Mupepi, S. (2007). Creating high impact organization in the SADC: Adapting OD Methods and Practices. *The OD Practitioner*, *32*(2), 34–39.

Mupepi, M., Yim, J., Mupepi, S., & Mupepi, K. (2011). Can a knowledge community situated in an African village create and advance human rights practices beyond love thy neighbor principles? *International Journal of Knowledge and Learning*, *7*(3/4), 233–252. doi:10.1504/IJKL.2011.044557

Mupepi, M. G., & Motwani, J. (2015). Deconstructing the Value Creation Process: Positioning Diversity to Increase Output. *International Journal of Sociotechnology and Knowledge Development, 7*(4), 15–30. doi:10.4018/IJSKD.2015100102

Mupepi, M. G., & Taruwinga, P. (2014). Cultural Differentials Modify Change: Comparativeness of the SADC and the US. *International Journal of Sustainable Economies Management, 3*(2), 50–79. doi:10.4018/ijsem.2014040105

Mupepi, S., & Mupepi, M. (2007, October 4-6). Creating a shared mindset: Advancing organizational effectiveness and efficiency. *Proceedings of the Midwest Academy of Management 50th Annual Conference*, Kansas City, Missouri, USA.

Muroe, T., Hatamiya, L., & Westwind, M. (2006). Deconstruction of structures: An overview of economic issues. *International Journal of Environmental Technology and Management, 6*(3-4). doi:10.1504/IJETM.2006.009002

Nolan, S. (2012). Analytics. *Strategic HR Review, 12*(1), 3. doi:10.1108/shr.2013.37212aaa.001

Schutt, S., & Linegar, D. (2016). Eight Years of Utilizing Virtual Worlds for Education: A View from the Trenches. In K. Terry & A. Cheney (Eds.), Utilizing Virtual and Personal Learning Environments for Optimal Learning (pp. 1–21). Hershey, PA, USA: IGI Global. doi:10.4018/978-1-4666-8847-6.ch001

van der Helm, P., Stams, G.J., & van der Laan, P. (2011). Measuring Group Climate in Prison. *The Prison Journal, 91*(2), 158-176. DOI: 10.1177/0032885511403595

von Bertalanffy, L. (1968). *General System Theory: Foundations, Development, Applications*. New York: George Braziller.

Von Bertalanffy, L. (1968). *General Systems Theory: Foundations, Developments, Applications*. New York: Braziller.

Weisbord, M. R. (1987). *Productive Workplaces: Organizing and Managing for Dignity, Meaning and Community*. San Francisco: Jossey-Bass.

Weisbord, M. R. (2004). *Productive Workplaces revisited: Dignity and Community in 21st Century*. New York: Wiley.

KEY TERMS AND DEFINITIONS

Aptitude: The ability to perform a job or play a game with natural skillfulness.

Competences: The desirable proficiency required to effectively do a job or play a game.

Deconstruction: The critical outlook concerned with the relationship between text and meaning useful approach in developing organizational strategy.

Socially Constructed Competency Model (SCCM): A framework useful in pinpointing the explicit knowledge, skills, technology, and the disposition required in effective organization.

Value Creation System: The business analysis perspective that describes social and technical resources used to produce the products and services demanded by customers.

Section 2
Protecting the Intellectual Assets

Chapter 8
Patents and Logocentric Differences:
Protecting the Competitive Advantage

Mambo Mupepi
Seidman College, USA

Robert Frey
Seidman College, USA

Jaideep Motwani
Seidman College, USA

ABSTRACT

The discussion progressed in this chapter is about the protection of organizational knowledge in competitive environments. Knowledge can leak in the value creation networks embedded in knowledge-intensive firms, and a collaborative approach can be utilized to minimize risk and increase sustainability. For knowledge to be preserved from unintentional outflow, its confidential nature and description must be understood at all levels. Loss of knowledge can occur at any point; whether it is through the process of consultation or when employees do their work. Forfeiture of information can be unintended or a planned effort. To prevent such unintended leakage, it is important to develop a shared mindset among employees to minimize the risk. The socio-technical system is a philosophical framework that enables companies to simultaneously consider both ethical and technical systems in order to best match the technology and the people involved. In this paper we show how the socio-technical system can be applied to prevent knowledge leakage.

INTRODUCTION

Knowledge-intensive companies are those that deploy intellectual capital to provide expert advice to corporations of all types. Since knowledge is the "capital" of most modern organizations, maintenance, protection, and optimization of this capital, has become a business necessity. Knowledge leakage is an

DOI: 10.4018/978-1-5225-1961-4.ch008

important issue that modern organizations have to deal with. This paper is arranged in four sections in an attempt to answer two questions (1) how can knowledge leakage be prevented?; (2) How should managers construct their discourse on knowledge leakage? The first part provides an introduction and explanation of some of the key terms used in this discussion. The notion that knowledge is a fundamental driver of the value creation process compels the organization to put a stop to knowledge leakage. The second part reviews a carefully selected literature to understand how knowledge is created, diffused, and distributed in pervasive socio-technical systems to avert risk of losing proprietary knowledge. The third part provides a socio-technical system (STS) framework to contain risk. We conclude in the last part by showing how STS can be applied to prevent knowledge leakage.

BACKGROUND

Explanation of Some of the Key Terms

In defining the term "epistemology," we draw from Armstrong (1989), and Lehrer (2000), among many others. Epistemology is the study of all types of knowledge such as tacit knowledge which is derived from experience. Armstrong (1989) posits that the theory on knowing can be divided into segments to make sense in learning and organization. It is these segments that are of interest in building effective talent in organization. Armstrong (1989) propounds that the knowledge expedient in a business can also be separated by subject to understand its expediency. It is then important to recognize what stakeholders imply when they say someone knows or fails to know. If this type of knowing leaks to the competition what does that also mean? Arguments projected by Prahalad & Hamel (1990) designate that companies compete on what they know best. Their best foot forward is dependent on the intellectual assets of the business. If those chattels are compromised the business could lose its livelihood. In the knowledge-intensive firms an epistemic community can be created composed of the experts in the organization. Its purpose will be to generate a pragmatic nuts-and-bolts competence that will help the organization to design innovative practices to make differentiation real.

In the second definition of knowledge, Armstrong suggests that tacit knowledge derived from the collective experience of the people doing the job, can be put into context in the value creation process (see Figure 1). In this debate an epistemic community or community of practice (COP) are defined as groups of individuals who collaborate on many fronts to advance productivity. It can be the role of the COP to contextualize tacit knowledge and turn it into explicit knowledge. The COP can be situated in areas where goods demanded by customers are made. When an order is received, it follows a process in which each man has a defined role to play. The COP can analyze the job description and the job specifiocation to understand many things including tooling and equipment requirements in the business model (see Figure 1). They can also understand the skillfulness and technology required in making certain products. By taking the socio-technical systems approach, a COP can shift the things that are often taken for granted to combine the interest of the people doing the job and the business. The socio-technical systems (STSD) approaches have strong roots in collaboration in the value creation processes in organization (Eijnatten, 1993).

Figure 1. A business model of the value creation system (Mupepi, 2016)

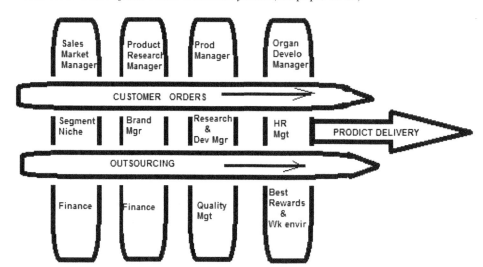

Socio-Technical System Design

The STSD approach in organization has its roots in Action Research developed by Lewin (1951) and Trist & Bamforth (1951), among others. In Organization Development (OD) the STSD is an approach to complex organizational work design that recognizes the interaction between people and technology in workplaces. It enables stakeholders to identify key success criteria, the steps and procedures in the value creation system and important variables in the processes. The STSD can be described as the structure that exists in organization where complex infrastructures, systems and human behavior interface. In this sense, the organization itself, and most of its substructures, are complex sociotechnical systems. The lens of the STSD offers some perspectives of how knowledge leakage occurs in complex socio-technical systems.

Creating a Shared Mindset by a COP

A shared mindset is a set of established attitudes held by key individuals in an organization. It can be co-constructed leading to a shared vision. Ulrich & Ulrich (2010) challenge that the highpoint of a shared mindest can be the co-construction of the organization's culture. That particular culture can constitute the explicit knowledge required in effective business operations. Lehrer (2000) maintains that for useful knowledge creation and implementation, there must be a belief or shared mindset as part of the organizational culture. Creating a shared mindset is an organized way for members to think about how the organization will work to minimize risk and increase output. It is also a successful way to sustain the organization.

Carvalho (2006) suggests that the STSD has two main principles. The first is that they are designed to have cause-and-effect relationships as a means to increase productivity. For example, the external auditor interfaces with different line managers as a means to understanding costs and revenue (see Figure 2). The interactions are designed to improve organizational performance in many ways. For example,

Figure 2. Knowledge leakage spots at the interface of technology and people doing the job

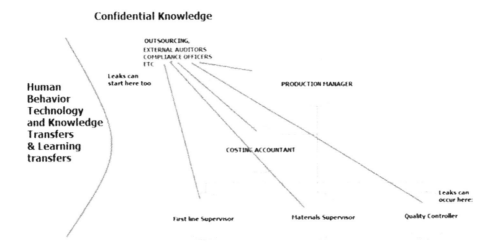

auditors frequently make suggestions on how to control costs. If this advice is taken, it could lead to increased profit margins. The second principle is to optimize output from each aspect of the socio or technical system to increase organizational yields. In Carvajal (1983), it is assumed that knowledge within socio-technical system is a social construct. Stakeholders can share job specifications, job descriptions or product formulations. They can share the same technical drawings, designs, or technology to grow the enterprise (Mupepi, Mupepi, & Motwani, 2015). These documents are part of social constructs and are useful in the design and implementation of effective training programs and as such, they are part of proprietary information which must be protected. These items are often removed from the business illegally under the pretext of "training" (see Figure 2).

In Eijnatten (1993), the soci-technical systems design is taken a step further to include how to design for analytical modeling that can incorporate an integral organizational redesign and implementation. This is called the STSD in short. Eijnatten suggested that the participative STSD takes into consideration methodology, structure, and technology used, in a parallel format to create goods and services needed by customers. Eijnatten alludes to a stricter control of know-how leakage in the parallel systems in the design that was tested and approved in the Netherlands to sustain the Integral Organizational Renewal Program.

However, the role of a COP in the STSD is to safeguard the interest of the business. An inventory of who has access to confidential information can be maintained to minimize the numbers of those who can access intellectual assets. The COP's role is both: to create, diffuse, and distribute knowledge, as well as to safeguard the deterioration of intellectual assets of the company. In Ruttan (2002), the knowledge diffusion process is viewed as a concentration of technology which can flow through a semipermeable membrane to another technology-less environment until there is equilibrium. The knowledge diffusion is similar to the biology osmosis process. In controlling the transfereability of the concentrate using the same analogy, the business has to become inpenetrable. Ruttan posited that langauge in discussions and meetings was attributed to knowledge leaking *consciously* or unconciously as members of a community of practice made sense of their environment, or deliberate to solve problems.

Knowledge Leakage

Frishammar Ericsson & Patel (2015) propound that knowledge leakage refers to loss of technological knowledge intended to stay within a firm's boundaries and may cause a "weakened state" in which a focal firm loses its competitive advantage and industry position. The change can happen very fast and the victim firm may fail to recover. Knowledge leakage is multidimensional and exists in three varieties. The first variety is a process whereby an external party assimilates knowledge from a local firm. This example typifies outsourcing firms distributed in varied advancing economies. For example, Walmart and other retail giant stores outsource the manufacture of some of the products they carry in their worldwide stores. Knowledge can leak to the manufacturers as a result of technology transfer and skills training. At the end of the contract, the technology recipient must find similar work and this can be the point of leakage when the technology developed by the first company can be used to secure another contract with a different company (see Figure 1). The second example describes a process whereby the local firm uses knowledge from another external party. The third example describes a process whereby the local firm applies knowledge already shared with an external party in such a way that it becomes sensitive.

As a more specific example, corporations in high-tech industries are increasingly investing in 3D and virtual reality packages to support customers in understanding and using their products. Annansingh (2015) suggested that the packages take the format of 3D virtual reality environments (VREs) where customers can navigate, browse and learn in an authentic close reality context. These products are supported by combinations of photographic techniques and virtual reality programming platforms and are increasingly popular and effective as training tools. Annansingh argues that this type of knowledge or technology is very expensive to outlay and when it is leaked to the competition, the founding firm could go bankrupt.

Sustainability

Prahalad & Hamel (1990) suggested that corporations can compete using what they know best, explicit practices or core competences. Firms will do their best to understand what they must know to produce the products demanded by their customers. They will capture, develop and share explicit practices in the value creation process to satisfy the needs of their clients and sustain their client's business. In later research Mupepi & Motwani (2015), argued that explicit practices could be de-constructed to progress the necessary efficacy in the structure of the value system. Value is created anytime an action is taken for which the benefits exceed the costs, or anytime an action can be prevented for which the costs exceed the benefits. Mupepi & Motwani argued that a collaborated competency model could be applied to understand the structures that enhance performance and the design of attractive conditions of service to retention talent and nurture the skillfulness and knowing necessary in boosting yields in diversified entities.

In Akpolat, Soliman, & Schweitzer (2014), it is suggested that sustainable growth can only happen in organization on condition that learning and innovation are vital process and capability. However, with increasingly unpredictable and dynamically changing business environments, it is imperative to better access and manage perceptions of uncertain environments in the context of the value creation system. Akpolat, Soliman, & Schweitzer suggested that the intricacies and implications of the need to protect proprietary information as part of continuous learning and development to minimize risk.

Tacit Knowing Reigns Supreme

Tacit knowledge (TK) is that type of epistemology that can be accumulated as a result of many years of relevant experience. The COP organization represents the collective experience of people who come together for many reasons such as employment. They can possess unique experience about their professions. In work situations, what they know can make an important difference in the organization. Tacit knowledge can be described as something that is hard to impart in writing. In organizations, tacit knowledge subsists in the minds of the people. It is illustrated in the skillfulness and dexterity of those who possess it. Tacit experience can be acquired after a long time of doing the same work in different environments. Most people build the knowledge of their practices or professions from a very early stage. Similar to the saying: charity begins at home, we particularly see that for the likes of famous entrepreneurs such as Steve Jobs or Richard Branson, their careers started in the basements or garages of their parents' homes.

Trespassers will be Prosecuted

Bandura (1986) and Vygotsky (1978) agree about one thing: socialization. When an individual is recruited to work in a company, the individual brings his or her own culture to the new work place. Such individuals will be inducted into the organization to learn how a job is done, where and when one goes to take a break or whom they should consult in case of difficulties. The induction training is basically a socialization process where the recruit will acquire a new culture necessary in effective performance. Bandura and Vygotsky concur that learning is how people acquire knowledge through observing others. Bandura (1986) argues that the concept of self-efficacy is central to cognitive development and the role of observational learning in building capacity in organizations. Vygotsky suggested a zone of proximal development as what the learner can do long after the expert has left. Both self-efficacy and the zone of proximal development can be points of knowledge leakage (see Figure 2). For example, the World Cup 2014 teams went into camps where they could develop and perfect tactics and strategy about the game of soccer. The winners were exceptional soccer players, but the winners differentiated their play by sharing tactics resulting in outplaying the competition. Reporters or observers are not permitted to attend the rehearsals lest the team's tactics are leaked to the opposition. A key characteristic of sports strategies is surprise or ambushing the opponent, and the same is true of organizations. If the element of surprise is not there, then there is no competition.

Bandura (1986) advances the concepts of COP mutuality which determine the connections among human behavior, environmental factors, and personal factors such as cognitive, affective, and biological events, and of reciprocal determinism, governing the causal relations between such factors. Bandura's emphasis on the capacity of agents to self-organize and self-regulate would eventually give rise to his later work on self-efficacy. In this situation, knowledge can leak in three places: the consultant agent and principal and customers (see Figure 3).

Bandura proposed that self-efficacy implies a lens to maintain confidentiality. Thus an agent must possess the capacity to produce the goods and services required by the principal's customers in consideration for a fee or agreed upon remuneration. Bandura's studies of self-efficacy form the rules governing the principal and agent relationship. Different paths in the development of self-efficacy, the dynamics of self-efficacy, and lack thereof can be the habits that add to, or detract from, self-efficacy and can be the points at which knowledge can leak (see Figure 3).

Figure 3. The fiduciary relationship among the customer, agent, and principal

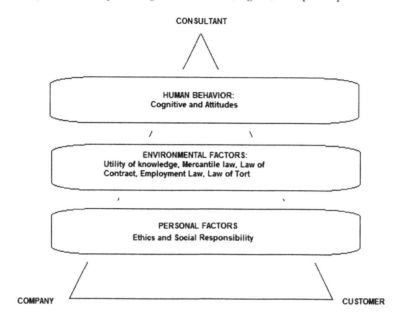

Sitting Next to Nellie

In much later research, Williams (2015) and Mupepi & Mupepi (2015) provide perspectives on how knowledge can leak within training environments. Williams (2015) suggested that on-job training facilitated by an existing member of staff known colloquially as 'sitting next to Nellie' is probably the most widely used development method. It enables the principal to impart what they know about how to do the job to the agent (see Figure 3). A trust and bonded relationship is supposed to exist between an apprentice and the trainer or between the principal and agent. The apprentice receives expert guidance to effectively perform his duties in consideration for a wage, and acquires the competences needed in a specific field.

In an example of an agent and a principal, trust is one of the consideration to make such an agreement valid. If an agent receives information such as job specifications, product formulations or work processes and technology to produce goods and services demanded by the principal's customers, it is expected that the information will not be shared with third parties. Knowledge can leak if the trust relationships break down. When this occurs, the assumption held by individuals and organizations called mental models collapses. In a second edition of his book: *The Fifth Discipline: The art and practice of the learning organization,* Senge (2006) re-asserts that the existence of trust between the expert and apprentice enables knowledge transfer to happen. The acquisition of the desirable competencies can be compromised when there are no amicable relations among principals and agents, and/ or no written confidentiality agreement between the expert and learner. A price can be placed on the value of knowledge or expertise. Like all products or services that have utility, they can be useful outside the triangle (principal, agent and customer), for a price (see Figure 1). Unethical behavior leading to theft of intellectual property could be classified in mercantile law as industrial espionage which can be heard in a law court as a criminal offense as well as civil torts of negligence and damage to intellectual property by removal or copying.

Work System Sabotage

Knowledge can leak if the relationship between the apprentice and employer is terminated prematurely. The apprentice might leave to go someplace where the grass could be greener. He can leave to go elsewhere, but does take with him, the tacit knowledge he acquired in that particular organization. He cannot be denied to earn a living. In Williams (2015), on-job training can work superbly; the old timers may have unrivalled knowledge and expertise and the desire and ability to pass it on. On the other hand, the old timer may be less than competent, uninterested in developing someone else or (justifiably) annoyed that training someone else will slow him down to the extent that he will fall behind with his own work or lose productivity-related bonus. This training activity explores benefits and potential problems, and involves checking written contracts for apprentices and the consequences of terminating those agreements before the time is up. Apprentices and other trainees are often exposed to the company's explicit practices. When they leave unceremoniously they take with them what they learned in the business and that can be a source of knowledge leakage.

Employee Induction Training

Induction training is very different from on-the-job training. Induction training is focused on the job the newly hired person is going to do. S/he is shown around what s/he must know to effectively do the job. S/he is shown around the place so that he can settle in properly and s/he is introduced to the person s/he reports to on a day-to-day basis, and the people s/he will be working with. Mupepi, Mupepi & Motwani (2015) propose that since knowledge is a social construct its control could start at the points it is produced (see Figure 3). Knowledge can come from consultant to employee or from customer to employee. It also implies that training programs start when knowledge is being transferred from those who possess it to those who need to know how to do the job. The value creation process and its STSD could be understood in terms of the role of each player. An induction program should integrate processes systems and structures into a comprehensive multi-dimensional framework for knowledge management strategies. Mupepi, Mupepi, & Motwani (2015) propound that process-oriented knowledge management initiatives can be focused on the provision to employees with task-related knowledge. This framework can address the integration of the resource-based view of a business – which is the main attention of knowledge management – with the market-oriented view – which is implicitly brought about by process orientation and learning. It can be argued that knowledge can leak if the human development system is not structured to recognize and retain talent. The incentives to retain talented individuals must be in place to stop useful know-how from leaving.

Faulty Towers

Giddens (1984) proposes that a business can be structured to provide a means to fulfill the goals of the owners of that particular enterprise. In civil engineering, faulty structures can be weak and can fail to hold the roof together and can collapse. Giddens argues that a business can be designed to do specific things and because of that the actions of the incumbents are inextricably linked. It implies that those job holders cannot ignore the way the company has been created and reproduced. The way knowledge is diffused and distributed in such an organization is to enable the incumbents to contextualize that knowledge to create goods demanded by the customers. Therefore, an organization's faulty human development systems can possibly abort its mission and the entire enterprise can potentially collapse. It is also in these structures that knowledge can leak, or get sabotaged through acts of cyberspace espionage which we discuss further below.

Cyberspace Espionage

In Etzioni (1998), cyber espionage is described as a practice of obtaining secrets without the permission of the holder of the information which can be personal, sensitive, proprietary or a classified nature. This information can be hacked from competitors, rivals, and enemies for personal economic, political or military advantage using methods on the internet, networks or individual computers through the use of hacking techniques and malicious software, including Trojan horses and spyware. Cyberspace espionage calls for even more sophisticated computer-based methods to secure the business's information system. Passwords and sign-in authentic identities still remain as vital methods to minimize the risk of unauthorized entries. Cyberspace espionage often takes place between western corporations and those from the socialist countries such as China. In Karaganis (2011), copyright infringements are referred to as disputes. Most of the cases that reach the law courts involve knowledge leakage in many different formats such as software piracy, reprinting books without permission, duplicating video games, films and music, among many other stolen intellectual property. Edwards & Waelde (2005) posit that global media piracy has become the scourge of developing economies. Media piracy has been attributed to price and the unavailability of the rule of law in certain countries. High prices for media goods, low incomes, and cheap digital technologies are the main ingredients of global media piracy. Edwards & Waelde assert that piracy is omnipresent in most parts of the world because some of the countries are at various levels of economic development and others have very low per capita income and cannot realistically afford some of the products such as various Microsoft software which are essential for commerce and industry.

Jiang et al (2013) propound that knowledge leakage can cause the company's competitiveness to falter because all companies rely on what they know how to do best in business. If their know-how leaks they stand to lose everything. In Prahalad & Hamel (1990), three things are attributed to constituting the core competencies (see Figure 1): the provision of potential access to a wide variety of markets; making a significant contribution to the perceived customer benefits of the end product; and the design and implementation of practices that are hard for the competitors to imitate. The discourse in this paper focuses on the third attribute, the design of practices that are hard to mimic.

Prahalad & Hamel suggest that explicit practices can be co-constructed. It does not always imply all co-constructs are full-proof of knowledge leakage. In Tan Wong & Chung (2015), knowledge leakages also happen in the supply chain where it is assumed that the individuals who are for example assigned to work with materials supply or product manufacture are trustworthy. Having laid down procedures of doing things is very useful in management. A shared mindset and a co-constructed mission could be one way to ensure behavior conformity. The COP could be composed of individuals who have the best interest of the business at heart. When trustworthy individuals constitute a COP, they can be relied upon to prevent unauthorized entries to the organization's network. The COP can be relied upon to scheme a practice that takes cognizant of the socio-technical system to design a hacker-proof information system.

Information obtained clandestinely can be used to damage the company's reputation as well as its finances. The competitive advantage can take enormous amount of resources to build and its structure is part of the business's assets. For example, Tan Wong & Chung (2015) argue that information used to create economies of scale should be safeguarded. If it is leaked to the competition, it can be used to replicate similar performance. Such action can cause a surge in demand for the competitor and could thus affect a business.

What Goes on in the Value Creation Process?

A value creation process is a concept that comprises the application of explicit practices to produce goods and services that are more valued by the customers (see Figure 2). The COP is a collaboration forum. It role is to create the explicit practices useful in organization. The COP can organize its work in teams often identified by task for example, the ITD (information technology department) is often composed of members with a number of different highly advanced discipline bases in information technology. They usually work in pairs or individually and trust each other in the work they do. Gardner, Gino & Staats (2011) propound that each knowledge worker carries values, systems, information and skills that may be only partially overlapping making inter-personal communications and collaboration difficult. The COP integrates the work of people doing the job. They provide them with the information they need to know to do their jobs effectively. Gardner et al argue that in knowledge-based environments, teams must develop a systems thinking approach to integrating knowledge resources throughout the production process in order to perform effectively. In competitive environments, many companies resort to the COP strategy to build and maintain high performance and foster innovation in the value creation processes (see Figure 2).

Numerous Causes of Leakages

Bian et al (2014) propound that leakages that occur outside the company's area of influence can happen when production is outsourced. When contracting with another company to do a particular function, that entity as part of the deal will receive job specifications, product formulations and labor specifications. At the end of the contractual agreement the contractor may request for the return of original documentation but they cannot erase the memories of their former partners who might want to use the same information in seeking new contracts. Burns & Janamanchi (2007) suggest that outsourcing requires a different approach to the management of information systems. In outsourcing projects, the task of estimations, and tracking completed tasks and work-in-progress can be managed effectively applying the Project Review Techniques (PERT). Burns & Janamanchi argue that PERT can be deployed as an accepted technique for tracking projects resource usage and budget management and for tighter integration and validity. PERT-based probabilistic approach to estimation and tracking is a knowledge management technique developed for use by the American Navy in WWII and it takes into consideration the critical path analysis in managing resource usage and budgetary constraints. The newer information technologies make PERT obsolete. However some of the project management techniques were developed and improved from the concepts of PERT and are useful in tracking users and making them accountable for alterations or downloads of proprietary information.

The absence of non-disclosure and confidential agreements can also be a reason for knowledge leakage. In this case there is no protection of confidential information. In most companies job specifications or production formulations are some of the best kept secrets. State employees often sign official secrets act contracts if their jobs entail working in certain environments where the chances of seeing information that is marked confidential or official secret are common.

Ununderstood Utilities

Knowledge leakages are often difficult to trace where its utility is not clearly understood. There are other leakages caused by departing stakeholders such as employees who take with them the experience they acquired during their tenure with the company. Those who decide to leave could have used their experience to leverage the chances of a lucrative employment contract. In some cases, headhunters are often on the lookout for talented individuals whom they can successfully lure to new pastures by offering them highly competitive remuneration. Firms that lose talented workers attempt to make counter-offers, but at times it can be too late. It is costly to let go an individual who has been trained and developed into a specialist by the company. He or she might leave behind the hard copies of product formulations or job specifications, but they take with them copies of proprietary information, and the experience they acquired during their tenure. They can reformat the explicit practices to improve upon the products they are now responsible for in their new jobs (Yang, 2011). Such seepage is hard to control because companies cannot stop ex-employees from earning a living. The best option is to constantly review conditions of service to maintain the competitive advantage. Hutt Bosworth & Hoyt (1995) suggest the following precautions: current employee needs should be addressed to avoid the temptation by them to leave the company; and outside contractors may represent security threats because their work is semiautonomous and performed with much skill and little supervision in the value creation processes where industrial espionage can be a reality.

Critical Business Skills

The skillfulness of employees is critical asset in advancing organizational goals. Mohamed et al (2007) propound that the concept of knowledge leakage, in its positive and negative forms need to be understood.

Possessing the right knowledge is not sufficient for organizations to maintain the edge. The individuals doing the work must be trustworthy to safeguard the interest of the business. Mohamed et al present results from in-depth interviews, with employees of manufacturing and services organizations and found that trust is a critical factor in stopping knowledge leakage. The results indicate that job specifications and product formulations change hands as employees and contractors interact in the interest of the company to solve productivity problems (see Figure 4).

Leakages in Management Consultation

It can be argued that a fiduciary relationship existed between the consultant and his client organization. The firm of Arthur Andersen had a fiduciary relationship with the Enron Corporation. In this relationship, the Enron Corporation relied on expert advice from Arthur Andersen to progress its mission (Benston, 2003). The Enron fraud revolutionized the way business ethics were viewed in the western world. There was loss of confidence and trust in the two parties as the massive fraud came to light. In Bratton (2002), the embezzlement ultimately led to the bankruptcy of the Enron Corporation, an American energy company based in Houston, Texas, and the de facto dissolution of Arthur Andersen, which was one of the five largest audit and accountancy partnerships in the world. Bratton asserts that in addition to being the largest bankruptcy reorganization in American history at that time, Enron was cited as the biggest audit failure.

Figure 4. A STSD incorporates human and technical systems together (Mupepi & Mupepi, 2016)

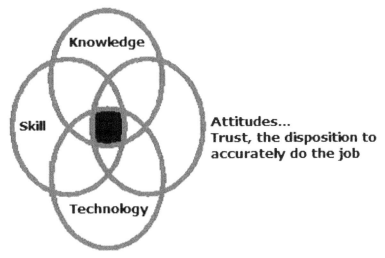

Knowledge Permeating in Value Creation Process

Explicit practices can be co-constructed by members of a KC who possess the knowledge, skillfulness, and disposition to accurately to the job.

Core competencies are made up of the knowledge and technology a company use to make ends meet. The KC can enable innovative thinking among the members who can then put this experience into the context of their jobs to make products and services demanded by customers. This assumption implies that explicit knowledge should be pervasive in all the value creation processes. This supposition also asserts that contextualized knowledge such as job specifications, product formulations, and customized tools useful in advancing productivity should be protected from leakage or loss. In the famous Adam Smith pin production factory (Mupepi, 2014), the value creation process includes explicit practices; the skills, knowledge and the disposition to effectively work are applied to make the drapers or apparel manufacturers' pins. In Figure 5, a referent of the Adam Smith Pin production factory is shown to elucidate how explicit knowledge can be created and applied to advance the skillfulness of the specialist. There is exchange of know-how, tools, job specifications, and formulations among Plants A, B, and C as they process the drapers' orders for pins. Seepage can occur between the plants as the workforces exchange information on how to effectively fulfill the order. Knowledge can leak when an employee takes job specifications to share the information freely or in exchange for other favors that can be equated with money, with the competition (see Figure 5).

Trust is a critical factor in establishing amicable relationship between the employer and employees (see Figure 1). Systems thinking is a social construct that can lead to a shared mindset, a description of how things are done. Such thinking is useful in reinforcing desirable behavior and creating an awareness of the need to know and make decisions that can lead to the accomplishment of the organization's mission. Mupepi, Tenkasi, & Sorensen (2007) posit that organizations that do not maintain confidential information are bound to fail. The amoeba is an organism that thrives in water and recreates itself by breaking into halves. Each part is a replication of the original organism complete with the same DNA. Mupepi et al argue that organizations that fail to recreate themselves all the time will not be very suc-

Figure 5. Understanding the utility of knowledge in organization (Mupepi, Mupepi, & Motiwan, 2015)

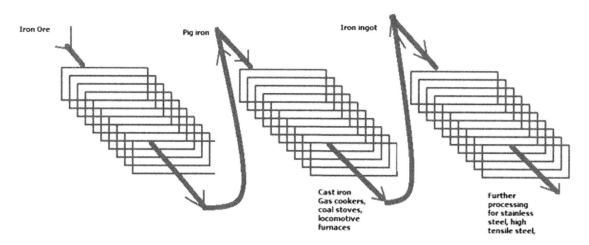

cessful. The environment of business is characterized by intensive competition. In this setting knowledge is used to make the difference.

Know-How Leakages

Knowledge leakage from the firm's practices can be very harmful because they pertain to specifications of doing something or producing goods and services valued by customers. Corporations have to safeguard the practices or know-how useful in their operations. Yang (2011) posits that corporations compete on what they know best and that includes technology, and skillfulness of its employees. The value creation process is ubiquitous in the organizational structure. Explicit practices are omnipresent in cost-centers; point of sale, and business units and systems thinking is priceless in such situations. The challenges of individual groups and teams working within the value creation process are to protect the knowledge that gives life to the organization. For example, Mupepi (2014) suggests that technology can be re-configured to systematically chart practicality in the business. Accidental leakage can happen in the practices but an astute COP can quickly repair leakages by closing the loopholes. Production plans can be contaminated with viruses by way of software, or those plans could be made available to the competition as an act of sabotage. The competitive advantage has to be protected one way or the other. In Pangartakar (2011), high performing companies such as Coca Cola and Starbucks have created a new organizational strategy that includes a completely outside-in approach to the market. They have replaced practices of the past with a new set of capabilities which enable them to be ahead of the curve in discovering new opportunities. Pangartakar argues that the new approach has enabled Coca Cola and Starbucks to apply new technologies in developing goods demanded by the market. These companies have not only patented successfully their past technologies, but they continue to learn and improve all the time and have protected the new proprietary technology.

Technology Transfer

In Chan & Daim (2012), international technology transfer is a direct approach to improve national technology level and strengthen national competence. Introducing advanced technologies from foreign countries can boost the speed of technology development in the host country. Leakage occurs when information that is supposed to be limited in its sharing is extended to third parties at the expense of foreign or local company. Knowledge leakage in technology transfer refers to loss of technological knowledge intended to stay within a firm's boundaries. A firm can easily go out of business if proprietary information is lost to the competition.

Multidisciplinary Approach

Knowledge Management refers to a multi-disciplined approach to achieving organizational objectives by making the best use of technical know-how and skills. This proposition assumes that knowledge can *leak* to undesirable environments where it can be re-configured to challenge a company's competitive advantage. It implies a multidisciplinary approach too to find solution to control leakage arising from numerous sources. Stein, Smith, & Lancionic, (2013) argue that customer relationship services generate critical data and the most important and comprehensive information available to management in many organizations. Stein et al contest that knowledge leakage is greater in business-to-business marketing, where the firm's extended working relationship with its customers is frequently crucial for the maintenance of a healthy business. Goodwill is also enhanced in two-way relationships where reciprocity is a modus operandi. Stein et al (2013) suggest that in agreements between suppliers of raw materials and manufacturers, the supplier often wants to plan ahead resulting in obtaining critical information from the production plans of the client. Those plans could show the product formulations content, and processes, which are of interest to the supplier.

MAIN FOCUS OF THE CHAPTER

The focus of the chapter is protecting the organizational knowledge to enhance the competitive advantage. Sustainable organizations are those that compete on what they know the best, explicit knowledge. If this intellectual capital is compromised a firm can easily go out of business. The socio-technical systems approach is deployed to make sense in organization and minimize risk.

Problems

Contracts for services are numerous and include partnerships, consulting, non-disclosure or independent contractor agreements and these should always be in writing. Non-disclosure clauses and proprietary information should be in a class of their own. Vetting users to access company proprietary information should be done to all those who must access this information in the course of their duties. The chances that knowledge can leak in these contracts are greater especially when the agreements have failed to be renewed. For example, a management consultant must seek another contract if his contract is not renewed. In this situation, the consultant will attempt to impress his prospective client about the work he has done in the past and in this way, knowledge can leak.

SOLUTIONS AND RECOMMENDATIONS

Knowledge leakage can be limited in many ways and the following can be effective:

- Creating awareness so that users promptly report any unusual occurrences and network restrictions. Although the primary purpose of any network is to facilitate communications among members of the COP, this very openness renders an unsecured network vulnerable to knowledge leakage and attack.
- Logos, copyrights, and patents constitute part of the organization's intellectual capital and people in the organization should be made aware of this
- Identifying those who have access to proprietary information, why they need it and to get them to sign non-disclosure agreements
- Understanding how knowledge is created and put into context in the value creation process
- Confidential information must be encrypted and a few individuals such as members of the COP be given exclusive access
- Access to the organization's information system must be through approved sign-in and passwords which must be renewed periodically.
- The Company's email system should be restricted to company business Communications and many other precautions will be dependent upon the technology employed by the organization.

CONCLUSION

Knowledge is one of the firms' best asset because people make the difference in organization. Managing this intellectual asset involves the process of capturing, developing, sharing, and using the explicit knowing possessed by a firm. Most businesses operating globally have partners across different regions they can rely on, a partner they can trust, for vital services, reliable products and customized solutions. This cannot happen outside the context of knowledge management. Like in many other business arrangements there are caveats the knowledge sharing parties must understand. Future research may focus on how knowledge leakage can best be controlled.

REFERENCES

Ahmad, A., Bosua, R., & Scheepers, R. (2015). Protecting organizational competitive advantage: A knowledge leakage perspective. *Computers & Security*, *42*, 27–39. doi:10.1016/j.cose.2014.01.001

Akpolat, C. K., Soliman, F., & Schweitzer, J. (2014). Learning and Innovation in Uncertain Times: The Role of Organizational Systems and Managerial Perceptions of Uncertainty. In F. Soliman (Ed.), *Learning Models for Innovation in Organizations: Examining Roles of Knowledge Transfer and Human Resources Management* (pp. 209–221). Hershey, PA, USA: IGI Global. doi:10.4018/978-1-4666-4884-5.ch011

Annansingh, F. (2015). Exploring the Risks of Knowledge Leakage: An Information Systems Case Study Approach. Retrieved from https://www.researchgate.net/publication/221924223_Exploring_the_Risks_of_Knowledge_Leakage_An_Information_Systems_Case_Study_Approach

Armstrong, D. M. (1989). *Universals: An Opinionated Introduction*. Melbourne, Australia: Westview Press.

Banathy, B. H. (1996). *Designing Social Systems in a Changing World*. New York: Plenum. doi:10.1007/978-1-4757-9981-1

Bandura, A. (1997). *Self-Efficacy: The Exercise of Control*. NY: W. H. Freeman and Company.

Benston, G. J. (2003). The Quality of Corporate Financial Statements and Their Auditors Before and After Enron. *Policy Analysis*, (497), 12.

Bian, J., Guo, X., Lai, K. K., & Hua, Z. (2014). The strategic peril of information sharing in Vertical-Nash Supply Chain: A note. *International. Journal of Production Management and Economics*, *158*, 37–43. doi:10.1016/j.ijpe.2014.07.016

Bratton, W. W. (2002, May). Does Corporate Law Protect the Interest of Shareholders and Other Stakeholders?: Enron and the Dark Side of Shareholder Value. *New Orleans. Tulane Law Review*, (1275), 61.

Burns, J. R., & Balaji, J. (2007). Improved methods for task estimation and project tracking. *International Journal of Information Systems and Change Management*, *2*(2), 167–189. doi:10.1504/IJISCM.2007.015118

Carvajal, R. (1983). Systemic net-fields: The systems paradigm crises. Part I. *Human Relations*, *36*(3), 227–246. doi:10.1177/001872678303600302

Chan, L., & Daim, T. (2012). High Technology Industrialization and Internationalization: Exploring International Technology Transfer. In A. Cakir & P. Ordóñez de Pablos (Eds.), *Social Development and High Technology Industries: Strategies and Applications* (pp. 70–98). Hershey, PA, USA: IGI Global. doi:10.4018/978-1-61350-192-4.ch006

De Carvalho, P.V.R. (2006). Ergonomic field studies in a nuclear power plant control room. *Progress in Nuclear Energy, 48*(1), 51-69.

Edwards, L., & Charlotte, W. (2005). *On-line Intermediaries and liability for copyright infringement*. Edinburgh, UK: University of Edinburgh.

Eijnatten, F. M. (1993). *The paradigm that changed the work place: Social Science for social action: Toward organizational renewal* (Vol. 4). Stockholm, Sweden: Swedish Center for Working Life.

Etzioni, A. (1998). *The Essential Communitarian Reader*. New York: Rowman & Littlefield.

Frishammar, J., Kristian E., & Pankaj C. (2015). The dark side of knowledge transfer: Exploring knowledge leakage in joint R&D projects. *Technovation, 41 & 42.*

Gardner, H. R., Gino, F., & Staats, B. R. (2011). *Dynamically Integrating Knowledge in Teams: Transforming Resources into Performance* (Working paper). Harvard Business School.

Giddens, A. (1984). *The constitution of society: Outline of the theory of structuration.* Cambridge, UK: Polity Press.

Golas, J. (2010). Effective teacher preparation programs: Bridging the gap between educational technology availability and its utilization. *International Forum of Teaching & Studies, 6*(1), 16-18.

Hua, T. K., Wong, W. P., & Chung, L. (2015). Information and knowledge leakage in supply chain. *Information Systems Frontiers.* doi:10.1007/s10796-015-9553-6

Hutt, A. E., Bosworth, S., & Hoyt, D. B. (1995). *Computer Security Handbook* (3rd ed.). Hoboken, NJ: Wiley.

Jiang, X., Li, M., Gao, S. X., Baob, Y. C., & Jiang, F. F. (2013). Managing knowledge leakage in strategic alliances: The effects of trust and formal contracts. *Industrial Marketing Management, 42*(6), 983–991. doi:10.1016/j.indmarman.2013.03.013

Jolly, R. (2015). *Systems Thinking for Business: Capitalize on Structures Hidden in Plain Sight. Portland.* Oregon: Systems Solutions Press.

Karaganis, J. (2011). *Media piracy in emerging economies.* New York: Social Science Research Council.

Lehrer, K. (2000). *Theory of knowledge.* Boulder, CO: Westview Press.

Lewin, K. (1947). Frontiers in Group Dynamics: Concept, Method and Reality in Social Science; Social Equilibria and Social Change. *Human Relations, 1*(1), 36. doi:10.1177/001872674700100103

Liam, M., & Scerri, M. et al.. (2013). Reframing social sustainability reporting: Towards an engaged approach. *Environment, Development and Sustainability, 15*(1), 225–243. doi:10.1007/s10668-012-9384-2

Mupepi, M. (2014). *Can the Division of Labor Be Re-Engineered to Advance Organizational Dynamism?* Sage Open. Doi:10.1177/2158244014536404

Mupepi, M., Motiwan, J., & Mupepi, S. (2015, April 13-15). Inside social constructs: Re-engineering organizations successfully. *Proceedings of the MBAA International Conference*, Palmer House, Chicago, USA.

Mupepi, M., & Mupepi, S. (2015). Charting Highly Productive Organization: Wrapping it all in Social Constructs. International Journal of Productivity Management and Assessment Technologies, 3(1).

Mupepi, M., & Mupepi, S. (2016). Applying Theory to Inform Competency Development: Bootstrapping Epistemic Communities in Growing Specialists. *International Journal of Productivity and Assessment Technologies, 4*(1), 27–37.

Mupepi, M., Tenkasi, R., Sorensen, P., & Mupepi, S. (2007). Creating high impact organization in the SADC: Adapting OD Methods and Practices. *The OD Practitioner, 32*(2), 34–39.

Mupepi, M. G., & Motwani, J. (2015). Deconstructing the Value Creation Process: Positioning Diversity to Increase Output. *International Journal of Sociotechnology and Knowledge Development, 7*(4), 15–30. doi:10.4018/IJSKD.2015100102

Pangarkar, N. (2011). *High performance companies: successful strategies from the world's top achievers*. San Francisco: Jossey-Bass.

Prahalad, C. K., & Hamel, G. (1990). The core competence of the corporation. Harvard Business Review, 68(3), 79–91.

Ruttan, V. W. (2003). *Social Science Knowledge and Economic Development An Institutional Design Perspective*. Ann Arbor: University of Michigan Press. doi:10.3998/mpub.22975

Scerri, M., Scerri, J., ... (2013). Reframing Social Sustainability Reporting: Towards an Engaged Approach. Retrieved from http://www.academia.edu/4362669/_Reframing_Social_Sustainability_Reporting_Towards_an_Engaged_Approach_

Senge, P. (2006). *The Fifth Discipline: The art and practice of the learning organization* (2nd ed.). New York: Random House Business.

Souad, M., Mynors, D., Grantham, A., Chan, P., Coles, R., & Walsh, K. (2007). Unearthing key drivers of knowledge leakage. *International Journal of Knowledge Management Studies*, 1(3/4), 456–470. doi:10.1504/IJKMS.2007.012535

Stein, A. D., Smith, M. F., & Lancionic, R. A. (2013). The development and diffusion of customer relationship management (CRM) intelligence in business-to-business environments. *Industrial Marketing Management*, 42(6), 855–861. doi:10.1016/j.indmarman.2013.06.004

Trist, E., & Bamforth, K. (1951). Some social and psychological consequences of the longwall method of coal getting. *Human Relations*, 4, 3–38. doi:10.1177/001872675100400101

Ulrich, D., & Ulrich, W. (2010). *Management by shared mindset* (1st ed.). New York: McGraw-Hill Education.

Ulrich, R., & Meier, R. (2001). Towards a framework for knowledge management strategies: process orientation as a strategic starting. Retrieved from http://citeseerx.ist.psu.edu/viewdoc/similar?doi=10.1.1.200.1086&type=ab

van Eijnatten, F. M., Hoevenaars, A. M., & Rutte, C. G. (1992). Holistic and participative (re)design: STSDD modeling in the Netherlands. In D. Hosking & N. Anderson (Eds.), *Organizing changes and innovations: European psychological perspectives* (pp. 183–207). London, UK: Routledge.

Vygotsky, L.S. (1978). *Mind in Society*. Cambridge, MA: Harvard University Press.

Williams, B. (2015). Sitting next to Nellie. *Fenman*. Retrieved from http://www.fenman.co.uk/traineractive/cat/login_dl.php?act_id=PED04

Yang, D. (2011). How does knowledge sharing and governances mechanism effect innovation capabilities?--from the coevolution perspectives. *International Business Research*, 4(1), 154–157.

KEY TERMS AND DEFINITIONS

Forfeiture: The penalty of losing something as a result of failure to comply or perform.

Knowledge Outflow: The loss of proprietary information to third parties.

Socio-Technical System (STS): Sociotechnical system is a management approach to complex organizational work design that recognizes the interaction between people and technology in workplaces.

Unintended Leakage: The loss of explicit practices to the competition which can cause detriment in the competitive advantage.

Chapter 9
Shielding the Corporation's Raison d'être:
Talent Management in Ubiquitous Value Creation Systems

Mambo Mupepi
Seidman College, USA

Aslam Modak
Seidman College, USA

Sylvia Mupepi
Kirkhof College, USA

ABSTRACT

This chapter discusses a framework to temper the impact of knowledge leakage and how losing the source of what gives life to the business can lead to its demise. Explicit practices should be sustained by limiting access and understood in averting loss. Explicit knowledge is expressed and categorized in work performance. In outsourced assignments, technical knowhow can be transferred accessed learnt and communicated throughout the entire organization. Viewed as technical know-how the firm can utilize it to make goods and services that are demanded by customers. Data generated from outsourcing should be analyzed to uncover data-driven pitfalls employing analytics to describe the nature of current talent, accurately forecasting staffing and material usage to leverage outsourcing of sustainable practices. Technical know-how permeates the firm in making the difference. It is pervasive in the value creation process and as such it is only prudent to prevent leakage to maintain productivity.

DOI: 10.4018/978-1-5225-1961-4.ch009

INTRODUCTION

This chapter is spread out in four parts. The first part provides an introduction and background information. The second reviews a selected literature to appreciate the management of knowledge in its various forms including proprietary information and talent and how it can be applied to make ends meet. Arguments developed indicate how knowledge leakage detrimental to the business can occur in the value creation process. In the third part we synthesize the information to advance a conceptual model that characterizes how knowledge leakage can be contained to minimize risk to increase the value of intellectual assets. The supposition adds new techniques of managing information in firms operating in boundary-less and varied environments. A conclusion is drawn in the fourth part mentioning the limitations of the arguments presented. The objective of the chapter is to demonstrate the need to contain knowledge leakage as a precondition to advancing the efficacies required in successful organization.

BACKGROUND

In Golden (2016), the term archetype is deployed to represent fundamental human motifs of experiences. Archetypes represent fundamental human motifs of our experience as we evolved; consequentially, they evoke deep emotions and impact the way the job is done, and how customers are served, among many other outcomes associated with productivity. The archetype means original or old and typos, which imply pattern, model or type. The combined meaning is an original pattern, of which all other similar persons, objects, or concepts are derived, copied, modeled, or emulated (Golden, 2016). The psychologist, Carl Gustav Jung, used the concept of archetype in his theory of the human psyche. He believed that universal, mythic characters—archetypes—reside within the collective unconscious of people the world over (Senge et al., 1994). Understanding the archetype in business organization is critical to its success. For example, invoices bills of laden or contracts for employment possess archetypical information managers need to recognize instantaneously and be weary of any deviations from the norm.

In Senge et al. (1994), tools and methods referred to as archetypes and stock-and-flow modeling are useful in limiting knowledge leakage in large-scale human systems. An archetype is a protocol model of a desirable construct. For example, a protocol for receiving dignitaries at one's function includes a greeting method such as: We welcome your Excellency to our fund raising event and this can be followed by escorting the visitors to their seats and so forth. An archetype can also include an acceptable way to behave. For example, all contracts should show the place where the agreement took place, be signed and dated by the parties in the agreement.

Proprietary Information

Explicit knowledge is expressed and recorded as words, numbers, or codes in organizations. It is written in job specifications, product formulations and when applied can lead to the products and services demanded by customers. It can be described too as proprietary information. It is sensitive information that is owned by an enterprise and it gives the business certain advantages. Explicit knowledge is part of proprietary information and all successful enterprise compete using what they know best. In Lave & Wenger (1991), explicit knowledge is co-constructed from the collective experience of the people who make up the organization. It is derived from situated learning, and can be acquired to augment practices in the format of technology useful in increasing performance. If this explicit practice is misappropriated a company can lose its market share. Proprietary information comes in many formats such as information contained on a computer hard drive about practices and procedures for making goods and services demanded by customers. It can also be defined as explicit practices that constitute the core business of a company. For example a foundry plant processing iron ore into steel ingots possesses job specifications, code of conduct, and many other specifications which can be contained in operation manuals on-line or hard copies. The placement of this proprietary information in the wrong hands jeopardizes the chances of the business from competing on what it knows because the competition might use the lost information to improve its own performance which debilitates the owner of the misplaced proprietary information from effective competition. Explicit knowledge can be presented visually in logos or orally in adverts on television or radio. Mimicry of proprietary information is prohibited by law.

How are Explicit Practices Modeled and Protected?

Explicit practices define professions or the core business of a company. A practice can be described as an organization requiring mastery of a complex set of knowledge and skills through formal education and/or practical experience. Explicit practices can be understood as proprietary information which can be stored in software or work specifications. The practices can be protected legally by patents. Formalized and patented practices constitute proprietary information. In an article that has become a Harvard Business Journal classic entitled *The Core Competency of the Corporation* written by Prahalad & Hamel (1990), a suggestion is made that explicit knowledge can be created by continuous learning and improvement.

Possessing explicit practices can enable a business to access to a wide variety of markets, make a significant contribution to the perceived customer benefits of the end product and make it difficult for similar businesses to imitate. Prahalad & Hamel argue that a core competency results from a specific set of skills or production techniques that deliver additional value to the customer. In Mupepi (2017), core competences can be illustrated in the Adam Smith pin-production plant where pin-smiths specialists, electro-plating experts, or precision grinders are useful at increasing productivity in pin production using skills, knowledge, tools, and the disposition to effectively do the job (see Figure 1).

Proprietary Know-How or Technical Know-How

The Collins Dictionary (2016) defines technical know-how as the ingenuity or skillfulness necessary in producing useful products or services. This technical know-how has synonyms such as dexterity or talent. In other organization narratives talent is referred to as competences (see Figure 1). In Ahmed, Bosua & Scheepers (2014), proprietary know-how is described as confidential concepts, formulae, software code, or technical information, among other explicit practices, that provide competitive advantage to a business. Proprietary know-how is usually protected under law against unauthorized disclosure, misuse, or stealing for an indefinite period, provided all reasonable care is taken to prevent its becoming public knowledge. It is also known as proprietary technology. Ahmad et al argue that proprietary know-how is an intangible organizational competitive resource that should be developed and protected in the same manner as other competitive firm resources.

Figure 1. The Core Competences in effective organization (Mupepi, 2017)

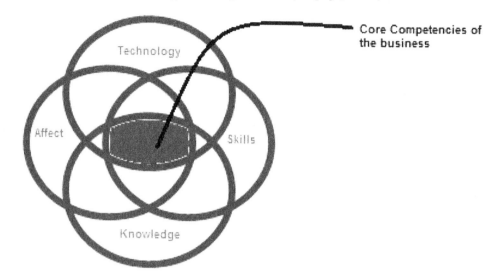

Operating from the Same Pages

Karl Ludwig von Bertalanffy was an American biologist is known as one of the founders of general systems theory (GST). Bertalanffy (1934) developed a mathematical model of the amoeba organism. The results indicated that the amoeba grew over time replicating itself as a form of reproduction. The organism's growth illustrated how the amoeba replicated itself very fast in water to ensure survival of the species. The amoeba breaks into two identical parts which continue to break into two parts and within no time a pond or lake can be infested with the amoeba organism who genetics and mutation are all the same. The amoeba theory of reproduction is still valid to this day. Systems thinking involves the use of various techniques to study systems of many kinds. In nature, examples of the objects of systems thinking include ecosystems - in which various elements (such as air, water, movement, plants, and animals) interact.

In Jolly (2015), systems thinking is argued to be a critical contributor to a company's competitive advantage. Emergent system effects are often driving decisive inflection points. Without proper training, Jolly suggested that the mechanisms at work may be hidden in plain sight. Using the methods described in the book, the reader can identify unanticipated leverage points and solutions. In these situations, standard business practice may not work or may even produce unexpected and damaging side effects.

Systems thinking includes a body of methods tools and principles focused at the inter-relatedness of forces, and seeing them as part of a common process. It can lead an organization to divergent thinking in an unusual and un-stereotyped way useful in developing strategy or generating several solutions to a problem. The field of systems thinking includes cybernetics, chaos theory, and gestalt therapy, among many others. Kurt Lewin, Eric Trist, and Ludwig von Bertalanffy, among others, contributed to the practical techniques for process mapping, or environmental scanning to understand flows of work and environmental threats. Organizations can also learn about systems thinking and how the techniques can be adapted to minimize risk and knowledge leakage.

Knowledge Leakage

Confidential proprietary information can be found in many places within the structure of the organization. In Figure 2, knowledge can leak through two-way communications, when employees and third parties are doing their work. Confidential information or proprietary information is typically found in product formulations or job specifications in the production marketing or finance department. As illustrated in Figure 1, what the customer wants is described fully in stage A and it is translated on to diagrams, models, and plans in B1 and B2. Knowledge in the form of specifications and product formulations can further leak in C, C1, and C2 when the confidential or sensitive information clause is breached. Knowledge leakage can occur in any of the stages in production. We use those stages to describe three knowledge leakage ways. The first occurs when confidential or sensitive information is disclosed to the competition or other third parties as a result of leakage. The third party may use this information to progress their own strategies against those of the company. The result can be disastrous for the company. In Blasco & Jorge (2013), this leakage is suggested to result from data used during the creation of databases, and analyzing the information. They suggest leakage in this situation can be controlled by limiting those who have access to the data and those who use the analytics to create the databases. This type of leakage can cause market share loss to the competition. Senge, Kleiner, Roberts, et al. (1994), propound that systems thinking can be a useful tool to solve problems such as knowledge seepage. System thinking is viewed as a powerful language that enables people in the organization to change the way they think and talk about complex issues. Senge et al argue that the system language can become a second nature when the members of a department or unit find themselves *thinking* in it.

The second definition is drawn from accounting management. In Sharif (2012), knowledge leakage controls can include risk assessments, weekly or monthly audits to prevent fraud or theft by conversion. Accounting personnel look for activities and figures to make meaningful reports. Negative cash flow does not necessarily mean loss, and may be due only to a mismatch of expenditure and income. However, a serious organizational harm can occur because of ineffective credit management, leakage of funds through fraud, or actual loss.

A third explanation can arise when proprietary information constituting job and product specifications is leaked to the competition or third parties. This information can be used to replicate performance to produce similar products and services and the end result can be a loss of market share. Sharif suggests

Figure 2. Knowledge can leak in production environments

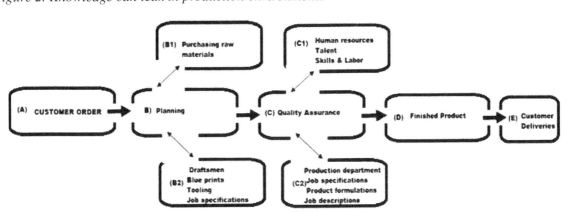

that technical controls can be firewalls, intrusion detection systems, and other devices that can regulate access to resources while informal controls include training and education that influence the creation diffusion and distribution of an organization-wide security culture. The internet shopper is attracted to on-line shopping because the space is perceived to be safe and secure against all types of hackers. Thus, the companies trading on-line seek to protect the privacy of their customers in the interests of their own business.

Outsourcing

The activities of purchasing goods and services from external sources, as opposed to internal sourcing either by internal production or by purchasing from subsidiaries of the business, is referred to as outsourcing (see Figure 3). In Chang (2007), outsourcing tends to be used in connection with a purchasing decision to change from an internal source to an external source.

Using Haddon & Sly of South Africa (see Figure 3), and some other international trading (French) Walmart (USA) and Kiko Espana (Spain), as examples, we see that outsourcing part of manufacturing and distribution operations could be cost-effective to an organization. By purchasing certain activities as contracts for the provision of specific services such as producing goods according to provided specifications and delivery of finished goods or raw materials according to specifications on delivery notes, the companies can realize remarkable savings in operational costs. The advantages of outsourcing can include cost reduction, access to specialist expertise and greater concentration on an organization's *core competence* by avoiding peripheral operations. Chang (2007) suggests that the potential disadvantage of outsourcing can include reduced control over operations involved and so less flexibility in responding to unexpected developments.

Outsourcing could have had its beginnings in Europe during the rise of trade unionism. The unions raised wages which are part of prime costs and the action leads to a reduction in the marginal productivity and managers could not determine the short-run optimal level of employment of capital and labor in the production process. They were left with no other choice but to outsource to places such as India, Bangladesh, or Swaziland in South Africa, where there were/are viable operations due to workforce

Figure 3. Outsourcing

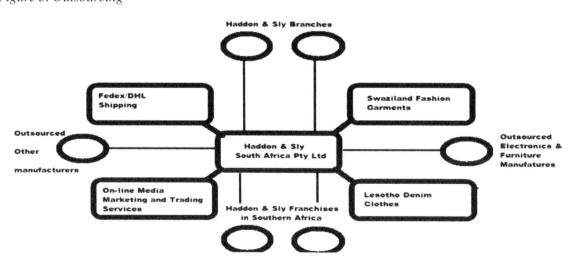

flexibility, low rent and wages and potential greater returns on investment (see Figure 3). Essentially economies of scale exist when increasing all inputs in production causes output to rise by more than the percentage change in inputs. These advantages existed in India and Swaziland, among many other fast developing economies. The European and North American unions sustained a work-to-rule philosophy that brought governments to a halt in Britain and other states (Webb & Webb, 2005).

Raison D'être

The reason why a company exists can be referred to as the *raison d'être* in the French Language. In most organizations it is reflected, if not mentioned directly, in mission statements. The *raison d'être* as part of the organizational vision is used to communicate the purpose and goals of the organization in many written and visual formats such as mission statements or logos. Organizations are evolving entities and as such they must change and adapt to changing cultural conditions. When this happens the *raison d'être* and the mission statements will also need to be modified to reflect changing cultural conditions.

The Importance of the Zebra's Hoofs and Stripes

Sometimes a company may need to take additional steps to protect a *brand* or its raison d'être. For example, we see Adidas successfully protecting the exclusivity of its logo by suing Payless Shoes to prevent it from selling shoes with stripes that may seem similar to those of the Adidas shoes (Daly, 2010). Tomorrow, we may find a horse suing a zebra for having similar hoofs.

Patents Protect Intellectual Assets

Companies can protect intellectual property that may differentiate them from their competitors by patenting any significant innovations. Patenting prevents competitors from using similar technology. Amazon was granted a patent for 1-click technology (or one-click buying) that allows customers to make an online purchase in a single click, using a previously stored billing address and payment info. Barnes & Noble offered a checkout option called "Express Lane," which also enabled shoppers to make an online purchase with one click. Amazon sued Barnes & Noble successfully and forced them to stop using technology that seemed similar to one that Amazon had patented just a few weeks earlier (Bostwick, 2009).

Patents Can be Gold Mines: Google Purchase of Motorola

Google purchased Motorola for $12.5 billion and sold it to Lenovo at loss of $2.8 billion. Rarely does a company offload a $12.5 billion purchase for less than $3 billion and call the deal "a success," but that's exactly what Google's head of mergers and acquisitions Don Harrison called the Motorola deal. In an interview with Forbes, Harrison did the math on the deal and said that in the end, Google came out on top. Jain (2014) took a closer look and examined the deal to understand Google's claim of success. What Google received from Motorola was a treasure trove of Motorola's patents that it retained after selling the company to Lenovo. Jain lists 5 points why Google was thinking in terms of acquiring the elephant in order to get to the ivory. The first was that Google's mobile strategy was to get their Android operating system onto as many phones as possible, as almost all of the company's revenue came from advertising, including on mobile devices. This was very different from Apple, BlackBerry, and Microsoft, which are all now integrated hardware-software businesses. The second point was related to patents. Google wanted Motorola for the patents, not for the manufacturing. Apple's patent attack on Android licensees was slowing down and worrying Google's customers. Motorola had a massive patent library that can be used defensively. The third reason was that once Google bought Motorola, some of its major licensees started hedging their bets by developing or buying their own non-Google operating systems: Samsung with Tizen and LG with WebOS, for instance. They were worried Google would compete directly with them. Lastly, by reselling Motorola, Google could be seen by other phone companies as a reliable provider of operating systems, and make money doing so.

Apple Versus Samsung: Squabbling Bedfellows

Apple and Samsung have a deep business relationship as Samsung provides 75% of the chips used in Apple's iPhones (Reisinger, 2015). Yet they bicker continuously in court over their competitive consumer electronic devices. In Mintz (2015), the Samsung Electronics Co Ltd and Apple corporations have agreed to scale down their international legal war and withdraw patent lawsuits outside the United States. This agreement does not involve any licensing arrangements, and the companies are continuing to pursue the existing cases in U.S. courts. However, in what may be a symbolic legal win, a federal appeals court blocked the sale of an older line of Samsung smartphones found by a San Jose jury last year to have copied key technology in Apple's iPhones. The U.S. Federal Circuit Court of Appeals, in a divided 2-1 ruling, backed a permanent injunction sought by Apple that would force Samsung to remove the copied features from the devices or take them off the shelves. Samsung has indicated that it could do such a "design around," but had urged the Washington, D.C.-based appeals court to reject the bid for an injunction in the ongoing patent war between the two tech giants. Mintz argues that the global smartphone leaders Apple and Samsung had been at each other's throats in courts around the world for several years accusing each other of infringing patents in their popular handsets and other mobile devices. Mintz asserts that in May 2015, a U.S. jury left the total damages Samsung must pay U.S.-based Apple unchanged at $119.6 million, after additional deliberations in a trial where the South Korean smartphone maker was found to have infringed three Apple patents.

In Ungurean (2016), Apple agreed to purchase 100 million OLED displays from Samsung for its 2017 iPhone 7s plus. Samsung and Apple have shown that they cannot live with each other and they cannot survive without each other.

Knowledge Protection Areas

In Ahmed, Bosua & Scheepers (2014), specific areas within the structure can be categorized in terms of risk. They can also be designated potential leakage areas that require stringent access control. The same areas are where explicit practices can be utilized to create value for the business. Ahmed at al identifies knowledge protection strategic level management, operational-level knowledge protection processes, supporting technology infrastructure, and legal structures for knowledge protection (see Figure 4). Top management is responsible for the overall strategic plans of the organization. They recognize valuable rare inimitable and non-substitutable knowledge assets. Unethical behavior leading to theft of intellectual property could be classified in mercantile law as industrial espionage which can be heard in a law court as a criminal offense as well as civil torts of negligence and damage to intellectual property by removal

Figure 4. Knowledge creation & protection in ubiquitous value creation processes

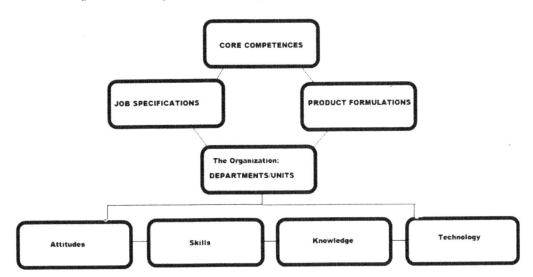

or copying. For example GM (General Motors Company) and VW (Volkswagen Company) were involved in litigating an industrial espionage case concerning theft of intellectual property (Bradsher, 1996).

Alijafari & Sarnikar (2009) posit that top management are responsible for developing, implementing and resourcing policies procedures and guidelines on knowledge protection. This includes defining the roles each member of the organization has to play regarding knowledge protection and the mechanism to shield processes and activities in which they are involved. In Majchrzak & Zjrvenpaa (2010), knowledge leakage protection at operational level involves the compartmentalization of sensitive knowledge. This can be done, for example, by limiting access to sensitive information and specifying off-limit knowledge, deliberately keeping knowledge tacit to mitigate leakage, making knowledge explicit to prevent loss such as when employees leave (see Figure 4). Large organizations such as Staples do it this way (Modak, 2016).

Blasco & Jorge (2013) provide a supporting technology framework for identification, configuration, and deployment of tools and technologies to authenticate control and track access to sensitive information. In Alijafari & Sarnikar (2009) collaboration technologies are making it easier for organizations and knowledge workers to collaborate across organizational boundaries. However, it is necessary for organizations to monitor, regulate and build appropriate security mechanisms in collaboration systems to prevent loss of strategic knowledge and competitive advantage. Alijafari & Sarnikar present a risk assessment framework that can help organizations identify valuable knowledge assets that can be exposed through collaboration technologies, and help prioritize security strategies that can be used to secure the collaboration systems to prevent the loss of valuable knowledge assets. Collaboration efforts exist in outsourcing business operations to third party organizations usually situated where operational costs can be low.

At the departmental level in Figure 4, knowledge protection is characterized by legal structures for knowledge protection. Each department has rules and regulations about how things are done. The human resources department is responsible for the organization's code of conduct. For example, employees can be made to sign confidential agreements intended to protect the interest of the company. In government, civil servants are made to sign official secrets act to stop the incumbents from leaking or sharing government information with outsiders or third parties. In Olander & Hurmelinna-Laukunnen (2010), activities that involve the flow and transfer of knowledge and accompanying potential for knowledge to leak between different parties and at different levels in an organization, are identified to be: at entry level, induction training and on-job training, and in actually doing the job. The job incumbent gets to understand work processes, product formulations, tools and equipment, and techniques deployed to produce goods and services valued by customers.

Zhang, He, & San (2014) propound that outsourcing has forced many corporations to review their operations against external firms to identify knowledge seepage fluxes along the value creation chain. Within these integrated relationships between external and internal parties where explicit knowledge has become an important production resource. Zhang et al (2014) suggest that existence and success of an increasing number of firms strongly depends on their capabilities to utilize knowledge and information for profit generation. In April 2016, one of the world's leading outsourcing companies, Tata Consulting Services (TCS), was fined $100 million for misappropriating trade secrets (Mendonca, 2016). These are the kind of issues a company should be wary of.

MAIN FOCUS OF THE CHAPTER

The focus of this chapter is to highlight the importance of protecting proprietary information in business organization. Proprietary information is also known as trade secrets, information a company wishes to keep confidential. Proprietary information can include secret formulas, processes, and methods used in production. Proprietary information constitutes explicit practices and when those practices fall in the wrong hands, it is common to hear the phrase "knowledge leak". When knowledge leaks it means a company's closely guarded secret can be lost and when that happens, the competitive advantage is lost too.

Controversies

When civil engineers were refurbishing the Van Andel Institute in Grand Rapids Michigan, they asked the users for their opinions so that they could use the ideas in the new design. There were a number of researchers who had won grants exceeding millions of dollars from the National Health or Center for Disease Control. In each office space there was a deep freezer with space enough to accommodate two to three beef carcasses locked up with huge bronze padlocks. These freezers contained work-in-progress and completed experiments waiting for write-ups. Each of the researcher was interested in protecting *explicit knowledge* from leakage. The researchers competed on building a reputation and it was then imperative to lock-up what gave the researchers life and recognition.

Experienced employees can be made responsible for the training of new recruits in the organization. Tacit knowledge which arises from many years of experience is very difficult to share. However, when the novice learn from the old-timers they can end up acquiring even some of the bad habits as well.

SOLUTIONS AND RECOMMENDATIONS

Strategic alliances can be some of the ways companies use to gain knowledge. These alliances can also be used to protect the loss of knowledge to third parties in at least two ways. The first is to mark documents containing proprietary information "Confidential" kept under "lock and key" and to create a room where this information could be viewed by authorized personnel only. There will be a register where those who access this information could complete and sign. The second is to do with proprietary information available on-line. Computer access can be controlled using passwords and sign-ins in a cascading manner. There can be first-, second-, or third-level sign-in allowing the user to use access different proprietary information such as product formulations or job specifications. Information security management is constantly evolving around newer IT. It can be treated as on-going vigilance exercise in shrewd organizations.

FUTURE RESEARCH DIRECTIONS

Enterprise architecture varies from one business to another. Meaningful research can be to do with innovation in each organization. Research on the usefulness of a knowledge community approach in protecting proprietary information could be useful.

CONCLUSION

Companies compete on what they know best and those are the reasons why they exist. If what they know is stolen or lost to third parties, then all their capability to compete with be gone. The strategic management literature emphasizes the importance of protecting organizational knowledge and information, especially in terms of maintaining competitive advantage. If the knowledge used by a company is leaked the chances are that the company could be out of business pretty soon. There is a need for more comprehensive frameworks to address knowledge leakage from a strategic perspective.

REFERENCES

Ahmad, A., Bosua, R., & Scheepers, R. (2014). Protecting organizational competitive advantage: A knowledge leakage perspective. *Computers & Security*, *42*, 27–39. doi:10.1016/j.cose.2014.01.001

Alijafari, R., & Sarnikar, S. (2009). A framework for assessing knowledge sharing risks in inter- organizational networks. *Proceedings of the Americas Conference on Information Systems*. Retrieved from http://aisel.aisnet.org/amcis2009/572/

Blasco, A., & Jorge, X. (2013). Bypassing information leakage protection with trusted applications. *Computers & Security*, *31*(4), 557–568. doi:10.1016/j.cose.2012.01.008

Bradsher, K. (1996, March 9). G.M. Files a Lawsuit against VW and Some Executives. *New York Times*.

Brown, R. S. (2013). Beyond the Evolutionary Paradigm in consciousness Studies. *Journal of Transpersonal Psychology*, *45*(2), 159–171.

Chang, H. (2007). *Cultural Communities in a Global Labor Market: Immigration Restrictions as Residential Segregation*. Pittsburgh: University of Pennsylvania Law School.

Collins Dictionary (2016). Technical know-how. Retrieved from http://www.collinsdictionary.com/dictionary/english

Daly, E. M. (2010). Payless drops appeal of $305 million Adidas Trademark win. Retrieved from http://www.law360.com/articles/145508/payless-drops-appeal-of-305m-Adidas-trademark-win

Ferrer, D. (2016). A quiet role model for kids. *Acttwomagazine.com*. Retrieved from http://acttwomagazine.com/david-ferrer-quiet-role-model-kids/

Ferrer, J. N. (2011). Participatory spirituality and transpersonal theory: A ten year retrospective. *Journal of Transpersonal Psychology*, *43*(1), 1–34.

Golden, C. (2016). Introduction to Soul Craft. Retrieved from http://www.soulcraft.co/

Hurmelinna-Laukunnen, P., & Puumalainen, K. (2007). Formation of appropriate regime: Strategic and practical considerations. *Innovation Management Policy Practices*, *9*(1), 2–13. doi:10.5172/impp.2007.9.1.2

Jain, A. (2014). Why did Google buy Motorola for $12.5 billion and sell it off for $2.91 billion? Retrieved from https://www.quora.com/Why-did-Google-buy-Motorola-for-12-5-billion-and-sell-it-off-for-2-91-billion

Majchrzak, M., & Jarvenpaa, S. L. (2010). Safe context for inter-organizational collaboration among homeland security professionals. *The Journal of Strategic Information Systems*, *27*(2), 55–86.

Mendonca, J. (2016). US Court slapping nearly $1billion penalty TCS could impact entire Indian IT sector. Retrieved from http://economictimes.indiatimes.com/tech/ites/us-court-slapping-nearly-1-billion-penalty-on-tcs-could-impact-entire-indian-it-sector/article show/51870656.cms

Mintz, H. (2015). Apple Vs Samsung: Samsung slapped with injunction. Retrieved from http://www.siliconvalley.com/apple-vs-samsung/ci_28829405/apple-v-samsung-samsung-slapped-injunction

Modak, F. (2016). *Policy: Protection of Confidential & Proprietary Information*. Denver, CO: Staples Inc.

Mupepi, M. (Forthcoming). Using Communities of Practice to Identify Competencies.

Mupepi, M.G. (2014, May). Can the Division of Labor Be Re-Engineered to Advance Organizational Dynamism? *SAGE Open*. doi:10.1177/2158244014536404

Oxman, J. (2007). *Preventing value leakage in outsourcing through an alternative model for invoicing reporting and data ownership*. New York: Technology Partners International.

Prahalad, C. K., & Hamel, G. (1990). The core competence of the corporation. Harvard Business Review, 68(3), 79–91.

Reisinger, D. (2015). Apple, Samsung to remain bedfellows for next iPhone. Retrieved from http://www.cnet.com/news/apple-samsung-still-bedfellows-as-they-eye-next-iphone-report-says/

Senge, P., Kleiner, A., Roberts, C., Ross, R. B., & Smith, B. (1994). *The Fifth Discipline Field book: Strategies and Tools for Building a Learning Organization*. New York: Doubleday.

Sharif, K. (2012). A Value Centric Study of Intention to use Internet as a Shopping Channel in an Introductory Online Market. *International Journal of Online Marketing*, 2(3), 1–20. doi:10.4018/ijom.2012070101

Ungureanu, H. (2016). Samsung Reportedly Making 100 Million OLED Displays for Apple's iPhone 7s Plus. *Techtimes.com*. Retrieved from http://www.techtimes.com/articles/150568/20160416/samsung-reportedly-making-100-million-oled-displays-for-apples-iphone-7s-plus.htm

Webb, S., & Webb, B. (2005). D. Martin (Ed.), The Webbs on Industrial Democracy. London, UK: Palgrave Macmillan.

KEY TERMS AND DEFINITIONS

Explicit Knowledge: Explicit knowledge constitutes the knowledge which can be readily understood, codified, accessed, and verbalized. It can be shared with others and stored in certain media such as computer hard drives. In a company this knowledge can be stored in job specifications or product formulations.

Know-How: Know-how is the practical skill or technology possessed by a company.

Knowledge Leakage: Knowledge leakage is the loss of the methods, and techniques that gives a company the competitive advantage. When such proprietary information leaks to the competition a company can lose its market share or even go out of business.

Outsourcing: In business organization outsourcing is an opportunity to contract out certain activities to a third party who are able to do the work at competitive prices. Outsourcing sometimes involves transferring employees and assets from one firm to another in the form of technology transfer.

Proprietary Information: A trade secret or piece of information used in a business that the company has taken strong measures to keep confidential, represents something of economic value, required effort or cost to develop, and has some degree of uniqueness or novelty.

Raison D'être: This the reason that justifies why an organization exists. The statement is usually embodied in the mission statement.

Ubiquitous: This term implies something that is present everywhere. For example, job specifications are present in the value creation process.

Chapter 10
Diamonds Are Not for Forever:
Talent Development at De Beers

Mambo Mupepi
Seidman College, USA

ABSTRACT

This article seeks to understand how a family enterprise was structured and positioned and grew into a successful global mining house. The focus is on how talent was managed drawing ontology from the mining industry founded in 1873 in South Africa by British and Dutch colonists. The founding families are those of Deidrick and Johannes De Beer, Alfred Beit, Cecil Rhodes, Nathaniel Rothschild and Ernest Oppenheimer. The De Beer brothers sold out to Cecil Rhodes and his partners and the business was, amalgamated later with Anglo American Corporation. The business arrangement continued for four generations under the direction of the Oppenheimer family who were apprenticed by excellent craftsmen in the diamond trade, and educated in finance economics and law from Europe's best business schools, and a conducive segregated political environment which ended in a US Supreme Court judgment in 2012. However, the Oppenheimers nurtured the mining house to a successful international mining business that employs more than 20 000 people around the world today.

INTRODUCTION

The objective of this article is to provide an overview of how talent in family owned enterprise was boosted to succeed in the early stages of company formation. Results from a review of selected literature indicate that talent management is critical in driving and sustaining the competitive advantage. The Oppenheimer family has grown for four generations of what was a local excavating enterprise to an international mining house with a network of retail outlets in major cities as well as a defined clientele (see Figure 1).

The names De Beers, Cecil Rhodes, Alfred Beit, Charles Rudd, Nathaniel Mayer Rothschild, are synonymous with the mining industry and colonization of Africa. In Southern Africa, the De Beers Company and Anglo American Corporation are entrenched in the economies of Botswana, South Africa, Namibia, Zambia, and Zimbabwe. Their interest is in several other countries including Australia, Brazil, Israel, and North and South America (Cowell, 2000). Up to the ruling of the Supreme Court (2012),

DOI: 10.4018/978-1-5225-1961-4.ch010

Figure 1. The US Supreme Court antitrust ruling in May 2012 compelled Anglo American Corporation to take charge

the De Beers Corporation controlled at least 90% of the world's diamond market. The questions asked to progress the discussion are: What were the political and economic factors leading to the creation of an environment conducive to business development? What is the nature and description of talent in a family owned enterprise? In addition, how can is it be enhanced?

The literature reviews a carefully selected literature on southern African history and biographies of four Oppenheimer generations to understand how they developed and implemented the strategy to advance the De Beers Company. The analyses also examine how the two De Beer brothers sold their company to Cecil Rhodes and his partners and illustrate how the Oppenheimer family took over when Rhodes and Beit had passed on in 1902 and 1906 respectively (Rubinstein, 2001). The discussion includes how the concept of segregation was hatched in the Boer Republics and British Cape Colony in the early state formation of South Africa. The dialogue continues until the decision of the Supreme Court (2012) to dissolve the company's monopolistic arrangements that enriched the oligarchy and its De Beers leadership for many years long after Cecil Rhodes Alfred Beit, Ernest and Harry Oppenheimer had passed on.

A Remarkable Beginning

The history of the De Beers Company begins with the two brothers Deidrick and Johannes De Beers who founded the company when diamonds had been discovered on their farm in Northern Cape in 1873. It caused commotion when many people moved in to purchase possible diamond claims. The discovery made it possible to develop a capitalist society in southern Africa. The European colonists and settlers built commercial enterprises based on mining and agriculture. The De Beer brothers sold their stake to Cecil John Rhodes and Barney Barnato an Italian financier leading to the formation of De Beers Consolidated Mines in 1888. In Chilvers (1939), Barney Barnato financed Cecil Rhodes and became a partner in the De Beers Company. Rhodes later bought Barnato out and became the sole owner of a very promising diamond mining operation in South Africa during that period in time.

BACKGROUND

In 1890, Rhodes elected the prime minister of the British Cape Colony and his grandiose mission was to expand the British Empire and get rich in the process. He and his partners formed the British South Africa Company (BSAC), an organization that created to be the instrument to negotiate treaties and even fight where necessary (Mupepi, 2015). As part of its many projects, the BSAC raised a commando group made up of people of English, Dutch, French and other European origin to occupy the lands north of the Limpopo and Zambezi rivers. The BSAC was created by a royal charter and it lasted until 1923 (Becker, 1979). The charter empowered the BSAC to organize a British colony later named Rhodesia, after Rhodes. The De Beers Company had preferential shares in the BSAC or the Chartered Company a name frequently called. As at end of 1890, the Cecil Rhodes and Alfred Beit portfolio included the Consolidated Goldfields, De Beers Diamond Company, and BSAC. Technology and tooling companies that grew as the British Empire expanded were numerous. They include the diamond oligarchy in Israel, London, New York or Zurich. The oligarchy was a group of diamond mining specialists and their job entailed securing diamonds for the De Beers Company at pre-agreed prices. The assignments included the design and cutting of diamonds according to customer specifications. Other organizations that thrived were the heavy equipment companies such as Caterpillar Corporation or De Wit Tooling Company, among many others (Mupepi, 2016).

In Mupepi (2015), the Jameson Raid (1895-1896) became a drama, when Rhodes's plan to topple the Dutch failed dismally. The Transvaal Boer Republic had been alerted by its Ndebele allies about the plot. The failed plot was an attempt to control the mining industry with its center in the Rand, Johannesburg. Rhodes and his partner Beit wanted to control the Kimberly Reef and Johannesburg Rand the largest diamond and gold producing settlements of all time. The BSAC had already established control of the Great Dyke gold, and emeralds in 1890. However, Diamonds and platinum discovered in post-independence Zimbabwe and were not part of the AAC or De Beers operations. The land re-distribution program nationalized the interest of Anglo American Corporation in Zimbabwe beginning in 1980. The issue Rhodes foresaw was that, his companies were located in areas influenced by the Dutch municipalities. Thus the Jameson Raid (29 December 1895 – 2 January 1896) was intended to stage a coup and topple the legitimate government of President Paul Kruger of the Transvaal (Parsons, 1993:3). The intention of the raid was to trigger an uprising by the British expatriate workers known then as *uitlanders* in Dutch Language or *outlander* or foreigner in English Language, who worked in the Transvaal. The raid failed to materialize because the outlanders did not respond positively and those, who responded to Rhodes's call arrested. The repercussions led Rhodes to resign from his premier position and had to bail out the entire captured raiders which included his brother for an amount exceeding £900 000 (Parsons, 1993:4). The raid was ineffective and no uprising took place, but it was an inciting factor in the Second Boer War and the Second Matabele War north of the Limpopo River, in Rhodesia. Cecil Rhodes passed on in 1902 and Alfred Beit took over as the Chairman of De Beers until his death in 1906. At this time, Ernest Oppenheimer was a partner in the Dunkelsbuhler & Company when consolidated with the De Beers Corporation.

Ernest Oppenheimer (1880 – 1957)

In Roberts (2003) Ernest Oppenheimer was a diamond and gold mining entrepreneur, and financier who controlled the De Beers Company and founded the Anglo-American Corporation of South Africa. Oppenheimer was born in Friedberg, Germany, the son of Edward Oppenheimer who was a cigar merchant. Oppenheimer began his working life at 17, when he entered Dunkelsbuhler & Company, a diamond brokerage in London. His efforts impressed his employer and in 1902, at the age of 22, he was send to South Africa to represent the company as a buyer in Kimberley, where he eventually rose to the position of mayor (Roberts, 2003).

Birds of the Same Feather

In South Africa, Oppenheimer joined the Jewish community most of whom had escaped Nazism in Europe. Among them were Alfred Beit, Nathan Rothschild and Barney Barnato, among others. Rhodes had built his mining and political career with the most help from the Jewish community and Afrikaners. He won the premiership of South Africa on an Afrikaner party ticket. His English compatriots played their part in public relations in Britain. For example, the Duke of Abercom, James Hamilton was the first chair of the British South Africa Company (BSAC) created specifically as a project to exploit the mineral wealth of what became British Central Africa. A royal charter effected the company 1889-1923. After its dissolution, the mining business remained in a company referred to as the Chartered Company, a predecessor to Anglo American Corporation (AAC) later created by Ernest Oppenheimer.

In 1927, Ernest Oppenheimer as the CEO and Chairman of De Beers Company and his first concern was to sustain the vision of the founding fathers. He proceeded to build the company's global monopoly over the world's diamond industry until his retirement. Oppenheimer pledged to continue to sustain the visionary leadership of Cecil Rhodes and Alfred Beit. This effort made the De Beers Company a premier diamond trading company. In Mlambo (2014), Oppenheimer drew lessons from past chairs such as Alfred Beit or Charles Rudd. De Beers was set to be the leading voice in diamond mining and trading. In this respect, Oppenheimer was involved in a number of controversies, including price fixing, antitrust behavior and an allegation of not releasing industrial diamonds for the US war effort during World War II (Roberts, 2003:1). However, he continued the legacy of growth.

Flexibility

In Britannica (2016), Ernest Oppenheimer was knight by King George V. Oppenheimer served as mayor of Kimberley from 1912 to 1915 and was a member of the Union of South Africa Parliament from 1924 to 1938. A philanthropist and an outstanding figure in South African life, he furthered Commonwealth studies at Oxford University. He was knighted in 1921under the recommendations made by Prime Minister David Lloyd George by King George V. Sir Ernest Oppenheimer knighted for his contribution to industry in South Africa, Israel, Europe and North America. A tactic useful in growing effective enterprise is responding to environmental pressure. Mupepi (2010) propounded that sociocultural factors emanating from the social structure of a country or society could either constrain or facilitate the way a business operates and behaves. By joining, the civic society in Kimberley Johannesburg and Cape Town Oppenheimer was able to influence the South African government legislation and regulation of labor in the mining industry. When apartheid was official in 1945, Oppenheimer was a member of parliament in Cape Town representing Kimberly and as a mayor of the same city 1924-1938. Some of the legislation enacted during his career were the Native Trust Act and Land Acts 1936 or Native Representation Act 1936 (Gregory, 2013). However, Oppenheimer cannot be accountable for the decisions passed by the South African legislature at that time in moment. He probably examined his own history to support parliamentary deliberations that sustained a future for his family.

Oppenheimer passed on in Johannesburg in 1957 at a young age of 77. His son Harry Oppenheimer succeeded him in the business. Oppenheimer's brother, Sir Bernard Oppenheimer, was also heavily involved in the diamond industry. In 1964, the Oppenheimer Diamond was named in his honor by its owner, Harry Winston, who donated the stone (not a gem, as it remains uncut and unpolished) to the Smithsonian Institution as a memorial (Gregory, 2013).

An obituary published on 15 November 1957 by the Royal African Society who was Vice-President of the Royal African Society reads:

Sir Ernest was a quiet prophet whose fellow-countrymen had the good sense to listen to and honor. His unpretentious manner in private and public life alike sprang from a kindliness and warmth which power- and riches only served to strengthen, bringing as they did a wider field for their exercise His was not the flamboyant temperament of an earlier generation of mining magnates in South Africa; but subtle in mind, and blessed with a delicate sense of the age, he dismissed any show of ostentation and was affronted by vulgarity and excess. Although he moved by bent within his own mind, Sir Ernest had the gift of judging men, and he surrounded himself with the most remarkable among them. This power was exercised quietly and surely, but it never led to the creation of a "court "into which the less-gifted. Such a possibility would have appalled that general humanity of spirit with which he kept faith throughout his life. (Royal African Society, 1957, p. 1).

The obituary stated some of the good deeds of Oppenheimer to society. He sustained all the trusts left by Rhodes and Beit to the last words. In 1917, with J Pierpont Morgan, he formed the Anglo-American Corporation of South Africa and at the time of his death, his interests covered 95 per cent of the world's supply of diamonds. He was Mayor of Kimberley (1912-15), raised the Kimberley Regiment and, a friend of Jan Smuts, and was a Member of Parliament for Kimberley (1924-38). He endowed university chairs and funded many social amenities schemes including housing in Johannesburg (Roger & Bakewell, 2011)

Harry Oppenheimer Reminisces of his Father, Ernest

Harry Oppenheimer could comment much about the life and business of his father Ernst Oppenheimer. He noted that the De Beers Company and Anglo American Corporation were two companies that were so profound to the Oppenheimer family.

Humble Beginnings

Ernest co-founded Anglo American Corporation on 25 September 1917, and remained Chairman of the two entities until his death forty years later. For all that time, he was in full control of policy and had detailed grip of its affairs. The whole organization is still marked with his ideas and his personality.

However, change like in most companies was imminent in an environment that was changing politically. Like a number of the other Johannesburg mining finance houses, Anglo American had its roots in the diamond trade. Ernest arrived in London for apprenticeship at a young age of sixteen. His elder brother Louis of ten years his senior had organized the artisan training in the firm of A. Dunkelsbuhler & Company one of the firms that made up the syndicate of De Beers Diamond Company. Oppenheimer's new boss had a similar first name to his, Ernest Dunkles, who had been born Ernest Dunkelsbuhler in London, Middlesex in 1880 to German parents Anton and Minna Dunkelsbuhler (St. Georges Church, 2016). Anton was a famous diamond dealer who owned Anton Dunkelsbuhler & Company. Ernest became a barrister and assumed the surname Dunkles in 1895; perhaps he felt it would be easier for his clients and neighbors than Dunkelsbuhler. The chapter informed that Ernest Oppenheimer had a sister who was married to the Dunkles and as was the custom of Jews, they kept the business within the family (St. Georges Church, 2016).

Harry reported that his father's first wage was a meagre 17s. 6d. per week and he used to enjoy enlarging on his humble start in business in London.

In Wrigley (2002), powerful interest groups and corporation began to emerge inform 1890s onward until 1938 at the beginning of the Second World War. Important entrepreneurs identified Britain's imperial possessions as an economic asset that jointly made ends meet for enterprises such as the Pioneer Column 1890 an outfit of colonizers funded by Cecil Rhodes and his company, the British South Africa Company. Wrigley asserted that the concept of an imperial economy centered on Britain, but encompassing all the major colonies of settlement and of conquest, reached its peak at the Imperial Economic Conference at Ottawa in August 1932, and played a crucial part in policy making for the rest of that decade.

Wrigley argued that the Conservative Party or the Tories benefited from British success in the Boer War or Anglo-Dutch War 1899-1902 and returned to power. The city of Kimberly sieged and the Transvaal and Orange River became part of the Union of South Africa with constitutional changes in 1910 (Gregory, 2013). Cecil Rhodes companies were thriving in Kimberly and Johannesburg long after he had passed on in 1902. The De Beers Consolidated Company and the Consolidated Goldfields Company were also excelling at the end of the Anglo-Dutch War. Lord Salisbury remained as prime minister in 1902 and became the last premier to sit in the House of Lords. Lord Salisbury had facilitated the Royal Charter in 1889 for the British South Africa Company (BSAC) owned by Cecil Rhodes and Alfred Beit. The BASC was the tool used by the BSAC to found the country then known as Rhodesia (now Zimbabwe).

Apprenticeship

Ernst Oppenheimer joined the staff of A. Dunkelsbuhler Inc. initially as an apprentice. After completing, he was a diamond buyer stationed in Kimberly South Africa. An apprenticeship remains as one of the methods useful in acquiring artisan expertise in different trades. He must have done well to be a buyer for his company at that time located in London. The jewelry and fashion industries were then in European cities of London, Zurich, Paris, Dusseldorf or Frankfurt. The industries of diamonds, gold, silver, and fashion went hand in hand. The rich could afford new clothes as well as jewelry, accessories and haberdasheries to match their tastes. The Jewelers of the day competed for this lucrative market.

In Whitworth (1985) apprenticeship as a means of acquiring specific skills in a given trade has its foundation in the Dark Ages in Europe (6th-14th centuries). When Ernest joined A Dunkelsbuhler & Company. An apprenticeship was a system of training a new generation of practitioners of a trade or profession with on-the-job training and often some accompanying study in classroom, work, and reading. This technique of knowledge-technology transfer is still in existence to this day. Whitworth asserted that apprenticeship enabled practitioners to gain a license to practice in a regulated profession. Aldrich (2005) gives an example of the legal profession. One could become a barrister or attorney after serving articles of clerkship for at least four or five years. The qualified barrister could also continue to study under a judge to become a prosecutor or judge. This period of training was also referred to as pupillage and available to those who aspired to be accountants or bankers too. In family owned enterprises, talent as an intellectual asset preserved in many ways. For example, the family medical practices affiliated to a teaching hospital where family members aspiring to be medical practitioners can pursue their ambitions.

The Division of Labor

For Ernest, management training must have focused on the principles of the division of labor propounded by Adam Smith (1723-1790). The specialization needed by De Beers Diamond Company follows Adam Smith assertion that a divided labor when allowed to specialize increased productivity. The argument leads to an illustration of how innovation happens within a divided labor as each man and woman think more about how to improve themselves in order to make better wages. One of the building blocks of competitive advantage is innovation. In a book first published in 1774 entitled: *The Wealth of Nations*, Smith laid the foundations of classical free market economic theory. *The Wealth of Nations* was a precursor to the modern academic discipline of economics. In this and other works, he expounded upon how rational self-interest and competition can lead to economic prosperity. Smith was controversial in his own day and Tory writers in the moralizing tradition of William Hogarth and Jonathan Swift (Davis, Figgins, Hedengren, Klein, 2011) often satirized his general approach and writing style. In 2005, *The Wealth of Nations* named among the 100 Best Scottish Books of all time (Otteson, 2002). Rhodes who had taken study leave to fulfill his ambition left the Consolidated Goldfields in the care of Charles Rudd and Alfred Beit and attended Oxford University Oriel College early 1870s. It is from here that he acquired knowledge about political science and economics. He left to found the De Beers Company and became a prime minister of South Africa. Ernest Oppenheimer was nominated to become the Vice-president of the Royal African Society at Oxford University where he was the principal of the Rhodes Fellowship until his death in 1957.

Efficacies in Organization

Ernest Oppenheimer built the competitive advantage of De Beers Diamond Company and Anglo American Corporation as efficient and effective organizations. American Engineer Frederick W. Taylor (1856-1915) could have influenced the management development of Oppenheimer and the structuration of the De Beers and AAC companies. Efficiency in these organizations meant control prime costs constituted by wages and raw materials. The environmental factors such as the economy played a critical role in how organizations could operate efficiently to deliver the goods and services demanded by customers. The legislation existing in South Africa sustaining the mining industry were many. They include Mines and Works Act (1913) and Natives (Urban Areas) (1923), among many others, characterized how the industry designed to excel at an expense of the indigenous people. The industry was effective at delivery of products demanded by customers.

In Hughes (1989), Taylor was one of the intellectual leaders of the efficiency movement and his ideas, broadly conceived, were highly influential in the Progressive Era (1890s-1920s). Taylor summed up his efficiency techniques in his 1911 book: *The Principles of Scientific Management*. His pioneering work in applying engineering principles to the work done on the factory floor was instrumental in the creation and development of the branch of engineering now known as industrial engineering. The process of mining gold and diamonds followed a structure and technology, which are the foundation in mining engineering today. The processes come complete with tools, equipment, and expertise useful in exploiting mineral wealth. This knowledge was important to Ernest Oppenheimer and all those who came to the helm of the Company later.

Succession Planning

The interaction of the family, ownership, and business subsystems, particularly at general transition points can be problematic. A number of ways to secure continuity in family enterprises are available in succession planning. Where the business system overlaps as family members come together as owners both inside and outside of the business, there are potential interface issues, potential conflicts, and always dilemmas to overcome.

Mupepi & Motwani (2016) suggest three perspectives of change as follows: (1) The present or current state: identification of key elements of the business and family that will be wedged by the change (2) The second is the transitioning period moving from one state to the next. The change process occurs in the family, business, and ownership. (3) The third phase is about the future stated in terms of time… one, two or three years. For the Oppenheimers there has always been an heir ready to take over at any given time. Their family controlled organization recruited professional people to manage the day-to-day affairs of the De Beers Company. The Oppenheimers focused on policy and keeping the stakeholders, particularly the customers and suppliers informed of the Company's plans. In Cummings & Worley (2015), family members are the best option to take over the business. De Beers Company secured family rights by owning more than 40% of the ordinary shares. Cummings & Worley argue that family members are a convenient workforce and may be the only option in the start-up phase of the founding generation but businesses that successfully integrate family members over the long-run do not base selection practices only on genetics. Policies on entering the family business, options for career paths, and multiple points of exposure to the family firm are a few of the best practices.

Clear Roles

Goffman (1959) propounded that every man and woman has a role to play in life more or so in a family owned business. There are distinct roles accorded, to those who possess the right attributes. For example,

Figure 2. De Beers Company: Succession plan for the Oppenheimers

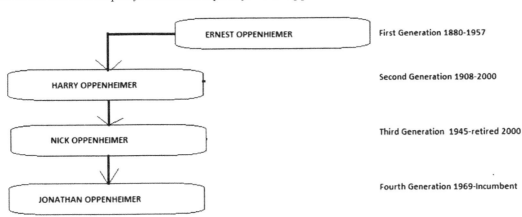

the recruitment and training of every member who chooses to be part of the family business should be a priority. With mentoring, those who chose to work for the family enterprise could assume greater responsibilities by and by. Cummings & Worley reported that nearly 37% of family owned businesses had a succession plan. They also found that 88% of family business respondents their families were going to continue controlling the business in the next five or more years.

Developing the Specialist

The Zone of Proximal Development (ZPD) inside the workshop or plant setting or cyberspace continuous learning environments has barrowed practices and techniques from Vygotsky (1978), Bandura (1977), Senge (1990), and Mupepi & Mupepi (2015), among many others. In Mupepi (2014), an apprenticeship enables practitioners to gain a license to practice in a regulated profession. Thus, a potential successor could start by undergoing training as an apprentice. When the time is ripe, the trainee accorded a lesser role at start, gradually takes more and more responsibilities by and by. Most of their training is done while working for an employer who helps the apprentices learn their trade or profession, in exchange for their continued labor for an agreed period after they have achieved measurable competencies. Ernest Oppenheimer served an apprenticeship for more than three years in England. He could have attended a technical secondary school, which were popular in Germany at the time. People who successfully complete an apprenticeship reach the journeyman level of competence. Normally persons earmarked for a managerial are provided guidance on a one-on-one basis to tailor-make the curriculum according to the needs of the learner as well as the organization.

In Britain, there were private grammar schools such as Charterhouse Grammar School for boys and King Edward VI Handsworth School for girls. In Bandura (1977) students in such learning environment are socialized to behave according to the school curricula. Socialization is argued to be a continuous process starting at home. The family enterprise can do the same for members of the family. They can be socialized or raised with certain expectations. Where seniority by birth is important it implies that the eldest child groomed to take over. Apprenticeships typically last three to six years and grooming someone to occupy a defined position can start with education. All the Oppenheimer children starting with Harry, Nicky, and Jonathan received private school education and attended Oxford University. The new specialist had to understand the role of trade unions, the state, and employers in collective bargaining agreements. Most of all he or she had to appreciate his role as part of management. Harry had to show Nicky the ropes in the mining industry. Harry also learnt his lessons from Ernest his father.

In Yasnitsky & Van Der Veer (2015), Vygotsky (1978) is deconstructed to make the zone of proximal development understood widely in competency development. Even though Vygotsky (1978) and Bandura (1986) were researched among a student population and not business organizations, their assumptions about human development are still viable today. Yasnitsky & Van Der Veer suggested that Vygotsky's study of children illustrated human development by what a child can do independently and by what that child could do when assisted by an adult or more competent peer. Ernest Oppenheimer served an apprenticeship where he learnt the state-of the-art diamond cutting and design. In Senge (1990), the time one serves an apprenticeship provides opportunities to improve personal mastery, and create a shared mindset with the experts. When one's time is up, he or she will be able to go it alone without relying much from the experts. In Bandura (1977), social learning assumes that people learn through observing others. It can be argued that the apprentice learns by observing the master doing the job. He is then given the opportunity to put into practice what he learned by observation. An example of social learning theory would be the students imitating the teacher. Self-efficacy is the belief in one's capabilities to organize and execute the courses of action required to manage prospective situations. In later research Bandura (1986), argued that the social cognitive theory focused on how behavior and growth were affected by the cognitive operations that occur during social activities. Thus, dexterity can be perfected by constant practice and improvement resulting in changed desirable performance.

Mupepi & Mupepi (2016), suggested that a knowledge community could be formed to keep the new graduates and their masters connected to further their interests. The centricity of a continuous learning and improvement discourse is enhanced through a knowledge community. Mupepi & Mupepi argue that understanding job specifications and the competencies required to do certain jobs were elaborated in knowledge community forums. The division of labor enabled the managers and those doing the work to understand the skills dexterity in the task to be successful.

Understanding Cultural Differences

The apprenticeship Oppenheimer served was critical in understanding what needed done in the diamond trade to make the most profits. He was a Jew in an industry dominated by many like him. The idea of leaving his homeland in Germany foe England was to escape persecution of the Jews by the Nazis. England became his adopted country and South Africa became his second citizenship. He acquired an expert knowledge of diamonds that impressed most merchants and miners including Rhodes. He was multilingual speaking English Dutch and German fluently. Oppenheimer built upon the foundation Rhodes made about the future of the diamond trade in the world. This multilingualism made it possible for Ernest to build amicable business relationships in Europe North America and around the British Empire.

Customer-Centric Organization

Oppenheimer became an expert of diamonds and maintained his relationships with his native Germany and Britain the country he was a citizen. In these relationships, Oppenheimer was able to consolidate his supplier base and technology transfer. For example, companies that were part of the De Beers success stories were American, Dutch, English, Dutch, French or Germany. Corporations such as Avery, Bosch, Caterpillar, De Witt, and Pneumatic Drilling Company, among many others. Oppenheimer was able to pinpoint at those organizations classified as customers and suppliers. It was easy to transfer technology within the suppliers to make the needs of customers a reality.

Creating a World Currency

As discussed earlier, the diamond main customers during the formations of the De Beers Company were companies and individuals who invested in precious metals and stones. The Company created a unique network of alliances which included suppliers of precious stones, suppliers of know-how, and special retail outlets for finished products (see Figure 3). This clientele is unevenly distributed all over the world and concentrated in Europe and Americas, and South Africa. The De Beers Company kept creating databases, which analyzed to construct two groups: current and potential customers and current suppliers. Rhodes had set the motion for this monopoly beginning in 1888. Political conflicts such

Figure 3. De Beers Company: A customer-centric organization

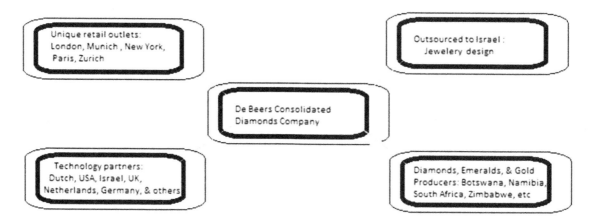

as WW1 disrupted mining activities in the British Empire (Turner, 1970). The mining industries in German Southwest Africa and commercial enterprises in Germany East Africa; and South Africa; and Rhodesia were later consolidated using finance from Nathaniel Rothschild and Chase Manhattan Bank to create the Anglo American Corporation in 1927. The British government in the reconstruction of Europe also consulted this company after WW1 and it became the holding company for the De Beers Company (Roth, 2007).

Ernest's management style could have caused controversy regarding the diamond monopoly. When he founded the Anglo-American Corporation, he received financial support from Rothschild Merchant Bank and other shareholders who equally had a stake in the De Beers Company and Consolidated Gold Fields Corporation. During the WW1, Ernest refused to supply the US military with industrial diamonds because he did not want to offend his German compatriots. Ernest could have used a stockpile of diamonds to leverage his way to the top. He served his community in many ways such on the board of Barclay's Bank as a director.

Lobbying the State

Ernest was a supporter of the South African Party under the leadership of General Jan Smut between 1924 and 1938. Ernest represented Kimberley in Parliament during this period. He kept aloof of parliamentary debates on racial issues, focusing his attention instead on financial and economic issues until his retirement from politics. Following independence from England, an uneasy power sharing between the English and Dutch groups held sway until the 1940's, when the Afrikaner National Party was able to gain a strong majority. Ernest sustained the National Party, which created apartheid as a means to cement their control over the economic and social system. Initially, aim of the apartheid was to maintain white domination while extending racial separation. The National Party received financial support from Ernest's companies. Apartheid made sense on the bottom line where companies did not provide benefits such as pensions, healthcare or other benefits. It was an opportunity to increase profit margins and reaping huge profits (Stanford University, 2016).

Minimizing Uncertainty

In post-war Southern Africa, uncertainties in business governments that oppressed the majority minimized organizations artificially. Certain laws enacted to advance separate economic development policies that defined the White minority as the main beneficiary of the economy. In South Africa, apartheid became a reality in 1948 (Mandela, 1995). In Southern Rhodesia, Northern Rhodesia, and Nyasaland, brought together under the British Central Africa Federation in 1952. Germany Southwest Africa and East Africa became British colonies. Southwest Africa entrusted to the government in South Africa for administration purposes became part of the lands, which De Beers Company exploited for mineral wealth. Ernest Oppenheimer worked with the South African government and shareholders of those Germany mines, confiscated at the end of WW1 in Southwest Africa. He brought those diamond producers under his control at De Beers Company. In South Africa and the British Central Africa Federation, there were many laws that protected the interests of the White race in mining and other industries. There were laws that made it legal for governments to grab African land willy-nilly. Africans were removed, from their own land, to pave way for the mining industry and European settlement. When the Chartered Company or BSAC opened Wankie Colliery (now Hwange Colliery) in 1899, intended to support the mining industry with energy resources. Rhodes's vision was to make both Northern and Southern Rhodesia self-sufficient economies. When Ernest cofounded Anglo American Corporation in 1917, he took over some of the assets of the Chartered Company including Hwange Colliery. The discovery of coal eased some of the concerns of the mining industry at places such as Mazowe, Penhalonga or Globe and Phoenix gold mines.

Civic Contribution

Ernst Oppenheimer served his community in three specific roles: first as mayor of Kimberley 1912-1915; second as member of parliament representing Kimberly 1924-1938; and third, as a lobbyist for the De Beers Company and Anglo American Corporation. His organizations funded special interest groups such as those created by the South African governments to destabilize Mozambique, Angola, and Zimbabwe whose liberations sustained, by communist governments of China or USSR (Simpson, 2002). It was felt that communist neighbors could influence the dismantling of the White minority rule in Southern Africa (Mupepi, 2016:5)

The Wenela Coal Train

Most of the industries established in South Africa after colonization sought to minimize operational costs so that they could get rich very quickly. Labor inputs are part of prime costs and rewarded according to what the job is worth in comparison to similar jobs in the organization. In the mining industries in South Africa, Botswana, Namibia, Zimbabwe and Zambia there were many individuals who could do menial jobs but required training and close supervision to undertake mining tasks on their own. The Mine Workers Act 1911 made it possible to discriminate based on race. The colonization of Africa 1884-1885 had left Africans as conquered people. Slavery had just ended in British colonies in 1833 and in some parts of the world but the subjugation of African labor continued. There was a paradigm shift in the way Africans had lived prior to colonization. The economies moved from a barter exchange to cash-driven economy. Those who had lived off the land found themselves in need of cash. South Africa and Rhodesia were the only economies that were developing fast because of industrialization efforts of companies such as those Ernest Oppenheimer represented. The mining industry in South Africa created an agent referred to as Wenela. This agent recruited labor on behalf of employers in South Africa, Rhodesia, Botswana, and Namibia. In Mupepi (2014), African labor drawn from southern African states such as Tanganyika or Angola and were not always willing to leave their homes to work on the mines. In Dube (2016), the South African government agreed to pay a pension to the survivors of the Wenela employees. The Wenela Company was the recruitment agent of the mining industry in the Rand, Kimberly and Great Dykes and Southwest Africa. The wages accorded to the African miner were very low and they made the mining companies realize a somewhat bigger profit margin. The Wenela Company was responsible for sourcing African labor and providing transportation and a travelling stipend for the recruits. The provision of social amenities such as healthcare or housing is mostly a post-independence legally forced restitution for surviving employees and dependents of those who passed on during and after retirement (Dube, 2016).

Strategy and Organizational Model (Kurt Lewin 1890-1947)

From the creation of Anglo American Corporation (AAC) in 1927, Ernest Oppenheimer built upon what his predecessors had put in place. One of the challenges Oppenheimer faced was converting the AAC to customer-centric organization. The De Beers Company had been created with a centricity on its suppliers to meet the needs of a then defined clientele (Roberts, 2007). Many businesses spent time to define customers. It was not the same for AAC. It was a company built around the needs of a specific stakeholder base. Kurt Zadek Lewin a German-American psychologist known as one of the modern pioneers of organization development (Altrichter, & Gstettner, 1993). Kurt Lewin, exiled from the land of his birth, made a new life for himself in the USA. Ernest Oppenheimer and his brothers did the same escaping from Nazi Germany to start a new life in England. In this new life, Lewin defined himself and his contributions within three lenses of analysis; applied research, action research, and group communication were his major offerings to the field of communication. AAC was a forward-looking organization and could have adapted Kurt Lewin's thinking. In South Africa, the field of industrial psychology was also growing very fast in the late 1950s.

In Erne (2016), the barriers that exist to changing to customer-centric organization include competition, the supplier chain, and government legislation. Emi suggested that scholars such as Lewin (1951) and many others, proposed reasons for the resistance to change (Blanchard, 2010; Keller, Meany, & Pung, 2010; and Kotter, 2012, among many others): a lack of a clearly defined project structure for the change initiative, failure to commit top management to desirable change, and undefined visions and goals regarding the intended outcomes and effects. Based on these insights, a number of models have been proposed in view of how to manage planned organizational changes (Lewin, 1951).

Strategic planning should be in sync with people structure rewards and the value creation process Lewin's change management model can be interpreted differently but for the predominant models, Lewin's (1951) three steps of change in social systems: to begin with, the need for change has to be established, e.g. by revealing and broaching the different social forces with their divergent intentions ("unfreezing") (See figure 5). Secondly, after the social system has been prepared for change, new practices can be tested and evaluated ("change"). In the third part the elaborated beneficial and feasible outcomes can then be anchored in the behavior and structures of a social system ("refreezing") (see Figure 5)

Figure 4. A Customer-centric strategy (Mupepi, 2009)

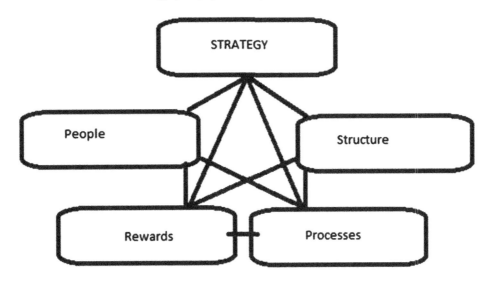

Figure 5. Kurt Lewin change management strategy (1951)

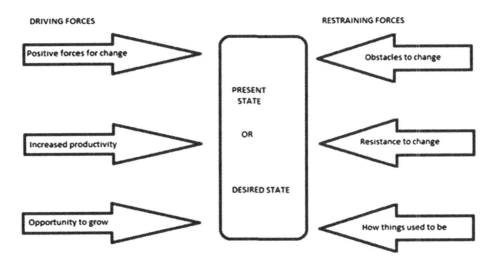

In Swanson 2014) the Field Force Theory, was developed by Lewin and introduces typical problems associated with how an organism must adapt to its environment in order to survive. An analogy of the amoeba an organism that thrives in water recreates itself by breaking into two parts repeatedly. The amoeba reproduces itself very fast and each piece has the same DNA as the original. Lewin features a systematic presentation of the physical and mathematical models established over the last 50 years. Written to foster an understanding of how theoretical analyses in practical situations and how organizations that fail to adapt to their environments fail. By joining political organizations, Ernest Oppenheimer had to build a company that would excel in the environment in South Africa. The South African governments from its inception in the Union was not pro-democracy. It sought to provide for the welfare of the White minority at the expense of the Blacks (Mandela, 1995). The creation of apartheid laws begun in

1890 during the premier of Cecil Rhodes. He too had to respond to the needs of the electorate in which only the Whites could vote.

In Tollefsen (2015), companies viewed as groups can systematically introduce change in society. They can create jobs to grow the economy. Groups can co-construct organizational reality different from that of society as a whole. Tollefsen argued that groups should be accountable for their moral responsibilities such as the perpetration of racialism in organizations. The Federal Trades Act 1914 amended in 1938 and 1975; and Civil Rights Act 1964 passed by Congress to enforce the constitutional right for fair trade practices and the rights to and fair treatment in organizations in the United States. This chapter informed that these legislations among many others affected the activities of Anglo American Corporation and De Beers Company because Americans held fifty percent of the shareholding of Anglo since 1927. In American mercantile law, the onus to prove a monopoly should be proved by the aggrieved party. The cartel finally took their case to the Supreme Court and the De Beers monopoly, was restrained in 2012.

Core Business

In the Economists (2004), the De Beers defined its core business as finding and selling diamonds. It had no interest in polishing stones. The Company identified the strategy consisting of people, structure, processes, and rewards as necessary in its diamond business. The Company sold sorted rough diamonds to invited clients only. In that way, it remained as the chief beneficiary in fixing prices and controlling supply. Sales take place ten times a year. The favored clients were rich individuals around the world. These customers worked with jewelry designers to tailor-make products according to their needs.

The Economist (2004) suggested that with its near monopoly as a trader of rough stones, De Beers has been able to maintain and increase the prices of diamonds by regulating their supply. It has never done much to create jobs or generate skills (beyond standard mining employment) in diamond-producing countries, but it delivered big and stable revenues for their governments. Botswana, Namibia, Tanzania and South Africa are four of Africa's richest and most stable countries, in part because of De Beers.

The Economist (2004:1) propounded that one family got extremely rich too. The Oppenheimers created the "single-channel marketing" system of shoveling all available stones to the clearinghouse. They came to dominate De Beers after Ernest Oppenheimer took control of most of Namibia's diamond mines nearly a century ago. He formed a mining conglomerate called Anglo American, before grabbing the Chairmanship of De Beers. The family is worth around $4.5 billion today; Nicky Oppenheimer, Ernest's grandson, is Africa's richest man. The family still owns a more than 40% direct stake in De Beers, and its members—Nicky Oppenheimer and his son, Jonathan—ran the firm up until Supreme Court (2012) ruling forced them to sell majority of the De Beers shares to its existing shareholders including Anglo American Corporation (Economist, 2004:2)

Harry Oppenheimer (1908-2000)

Harry inherited a viable business, an entity that was pretty much of a monopoly. He had joined his father's company in 1931 soon after graduating from Oxford University where he was an economics and philosophy major. He had a different upbringing to that of his father, Ernest who literally came from a blue-collar background. Earnest could have been involved in supporting a political system that sustained apartheid. Harry was just the opposite. He supported human rights such as Helen Suzman and Colin Eglin, who had become powerful symbols of liberal opposition to apartheid within South Africa and abroad.

The liberal values that Suzman and Eglin espoused are included in the constitution of democratic South Africa. However, true to characters Suzman and Eglin have not hesitated to criticize the governments of the post–1994 period (Mupepi, 2014:4).

Inheritance

The companies Harry Oppenheimer inherited organizations shaped to be what they were in 1931 when he joined the workforce. De Beers once controlled (though did not mine directly) some 80% of the world supply of rough stones. As recently as 1998, it accounted for nearly two-thirds of supply. Today production from its own mines gives it a mere 45% share. Only a contract to sell Russian stones lifts its overall market share to around 55% (Forbes, 2016).

Drastic Political Change

The National Party created the system of racial segregation in South Africa known as apartheid. It was implemented and enforced by a large number of parliament legislation and delegated by-laws. This legislation served to institutionalize racial discrimination and the dominance of White people over people of other races. In Mandela (1995, p. 4), the bulk of apartheid laws passed after the election of National Party government in 1948; it preceded by discriminatory legislation, enacted under earlier British and Afrikaner administrations. For example, the African Hut Tax 1894 is a legislation created by the Cecil Rhodes administration to tax the number of huts owned by the African family at $1 each (Mupepi, 2015, p. 3). Another example is that of Black Land Act 1913, which aimed at regulating the acquisition of African land to pave way for industrialization and urban settlements. There was no compensation to loss of land. Harry Oppenheimer saw some of these injustices and decided to support liberal values argued by Helen Suzman and Colin Eglin in South African legislature. As a businessperson, he had enormous wealth acquired as Chairman of the Anglo-American Corporation (1957–82) and De Beers Consolidated Mines, Ltd. (1957–84). Harry controlled one of the world's largest suppliers of diamonds, gold, platinum, coal, and other strategic mineral resources. The complex family conglomerate, which he had inherited from his father, also included banking, real estate, and other industrial concerns. Although Oppenheimer was, criticized for the working conditions of nonwhite employees, he remained an outspoken opponent of the racial segregation policy known as apartheid and a supporter of labor unions, education, and improved housing for blacks (Britannica, 2016).

Black Indigenization in Industries

In 1994, South African became a sovereign state after the African National Council (ANC) led by Nelson Mandela won the first democratic general elections. There was hope by the majority for equal opportunities and the doing away with racism in employment including the church. The pre-independence administrations had barricaded all facets of life into separatist policy. The ANC government sought to dismantle apartheid in all aspects of life in South Africa. Change was imperative for De Beers Company and Anglo American Corporation. The complaints charged that De Beers had created a global cartel in the markets of rough and polished diamonds – with a market share that reached nearly as high as 90% - through aggressive management of supply and prices, and collusive agreements with competitors, suppliers, and distributors. This was a quintessential antitrust violation of the Sherman Act 1890 a landmark federal statute in the history of United States antitrust law. This law prohibits certain business activities that federal government regulators deem to be anti-competitive, and requires the federal government to investigate and pursue trusts. The federal investigations ended when the Supreme Court ruled the De Beers operations to be a monopoly in 2012. Harry Oppenheimer did not live to hear this decision but it led his son Nicky Oppenheimer to withdraw from as the heir of the third Oppenheimer dynasty.

Nicky Oppenheimer

There is very little literature on Nicholas Oppenheimer probably this because his time at the top as chair of both De Beers and Anglo American Corporation has been limited. The chapter draws discourse from Minchon (2013), Balihouse (2016), Diamond Experts (2012), and Roberts (2007), among few others.

Nick is the son of Bridget and Harry Oppenheimer, and grandson of Ernest Oppenheimer, founder of Anglo American and the first generation of the family to Chair (from 1929) the De Beers Diamond Mining Company, established by Cecil John Rhodes in 1888 (Roberts, 2007). Nicky Oppenheimer was educated at Harrow School and Christ Church, Oxford, where he read Philosophy, Politics and Economics at graduate level. He followed example of his father, who was also the first in his family to graduate from Oxford University.

Nicky Oppenheimer joined the Anglo-American Corporation in 1968 and appointed a director in 1974. He became Deputy Chairman in 1983. He subsequently resigned as Deputy Chairman in 2001 but remained a non-executive director of the Anglo-American board until 2011 (Minchon, 2013).

Oppenheimer appointed as the Deputy Chairman of the then Central Selling Organization (now Diamond Trading Company) in 1984 and Deputy Chairman of De Beers Consolidated Mines in 1985, assumed the top position of De Beers and Anglo American Corporation. He later became the Chairman of the Diamond Trading Company in the same year. He was Chairman of the De Beers Group from 1998 to 2012, at which point he retired when the family stake was, sold, to Anglo American Corporation (Minchon, 2013).

The Antwerp Facets (2012) suggested that only after two months the Oppenheimer family sold its 40-percent stake in De Beers Company for $5.1 billion to Anglo American Corporation. The focus has moved to what led the family to exit diamonds after more than a century of involvement. The Antwerp Facets (2012) propounded that on quitting the Anglo-American Corporation board, De Beers Chairman Nicky Oppenheimer stated that it was time to quit amidst inevitable political change in South Africa. Nicky added that it was an extraordinarily emotional and difficult thing for the Oppenheimers who had been in the diamond business since his grandfather Ernest arrived in South Africa in 1902.

According to reports, the decision of the family to sell its stake based on three main factors: succession planning, the drop in the value of its mining interests and the possible need to inject capital, and the possibility of taking the money and investing in much more profitable enterprises throughout Africa.

For Nicky Oppenheimer the dream had been for his son Jonathan to become the fourth generation of the esteemed family to chair the De Beers Company. Educated at Oxford University, just like his father and grandfather, Jonathan had been involved with De Beers for 20 years, gaining experience in a range of areas of the company's operations. Currently he is networking with African Development Bank to inject investment in many parts of Africa not just South Africa.

Designing Performance to Create Wealth

In Berger and Berger (2011), suggested that strategy must be decoded into specific implications for future roles and people in the organization. They argued that high-potential individuals must show success at the three modes of leadership: operational, advisory, and collaborative roles. In Balibouse (2016), the room in the Four Seasons Hotel des Bergues was filled with multi-millionaire collectors and diamond dealers, listening intently as the bidders, each speaking by phone to a Christie's representative, took turns adding a few hundred thousand dollars in a tense struggle dragging on for more than half an hour. When the auctioneer's hammer came down, spontaneous applause broke out as the winner, who retained anonymity, bought the 14.62-carat Oppenheimer Blue for a world record $57.5 million for any jewel sold at auction. The Oppenheimers had set a trend for a new currency centered on precious stones and metals. They in their time demonstrated the three role expectations of operations, advisory, and collaboration. The oligarchy was founded on collaboration and trust and the capability of the Oppenheimers to meet the expectations of its partners (Balihouse, 2016).

Ending the Diamond Dynasty

Ending the diamond monopoly was also the end of the Oppenheimer as a diamond dynasty. In 2005, De Beers Consolidated Mines announced that it would turn over more than 15 percent of the company to Ponahalo Investment Holdings, a black-owned investment group, in compliance with South Africa's Black Economic Empowerment (BEE) mining charter. In 2007 De Beers began operations in Canada at Snap Lake Mine in the Northwest Territories—the company's first mine outside Africa. The company opened the Victor Mine in Ontario in 2008. Since the late 20th century the De Beers Company, has been criticized and indicted for various alleged criminal acts. During the 1990s, the company came under scrutiny for dealing in conflict—i.e., diamonds mined in areas controlled by forces opposed to the legitimate government of a country and illegally sold to fund military action against that government. In 1999, De Beers stopped purchasing diamonds from producers outside the CSO to ensure that it no longer traded in conflict diamonds (Britannica, 2016).

In 2004, De Beers entered an agreement with the U.S. Department of Justice in which it pleaded guilty to price fixing and agreed to pay a $10 million fine. Four years later the company paid $295 million to settle several class-action lawsuits charging it with misleading advertising, human rights violations, conspiracy to fix and raise diamond prices, and unlawfully monopolizing the supply of diamonds (Roberts, 2007).

In 2011 Joseph R. Saveri of the national plaintiff's law firm Lieff Cabraser Heimann & Bernstein LLP, announced that the U.S. Court of Appeals for the Third Circuit, issued an opinion upholding the settlement in the class action litigation against the South African company De Beers, the world's largest diamond supplier, for allegedly conspiring to monopolize the sale of rough diamonds (De Beers Settlement, 2013).

The appellate court affirmed an order by U.S. District Judge Stanley R. Chesler of the District of New Jersey that approved a settlement under which De Beers agreed to pay $295 million to U.S. jewelry makers, retailers, and consumers who purchased diamonds and diamond jewelry beginning in 1994. The settlement also prevents De Beers from continuing its illegal business practices and requires De Beers to submit to the jurisdiction of the Court to enforce the settlement (De Beers Settlement, 2013).

MAIN FOCUS OF THE CHAPTER

This article focused on how one family set about to create a successful enterprise that lasted for more than a century. Although the historical foundation of De Beers Consolidated Diamonds Company and Anglo American Corporation organizations trace to Cecil Rhodes and Alfred Beit and many others, the molding of a De Beers and Anglo American Corporation as successful enterprise has been the commitment of the Oppenheimer families. The success of their organization can be argued to have been sustained by a conducive environment. The Company provided support to the National Party in making apartheid official in 1948. The oppressive laws enabled organizations to lower operational costs in many ways such as paying minimal wages, use of forced labor, or not contributing to the health and welfare of the workforce. The De Beers Company was structured and sustained as a cartel. It had many suppliers of diamonds situated globally whom were paid pre-agreed prices. It became a monopoly which was sued successfully in a class lawsuit beginning in 2005 and settled in the Supreme Court in the US in 2012. Although the Oppenheimers are no longer at the helm of the Company, they still have interests in the diamond gold and platinum mining industry in Africa and around the world.

Issues, Controversies, Problems

During World War II Britain and its allies needed industrial diamonds to progress the war effort. The De Beers Company possessed these diamonds as they controlled at that time nearly 90% of the market. Although the company was registered in the USA, it did not have a physical presences in states and as such it could not be prosecuted under unfair trade practices. But the attempted to negotiate a way around the Sherman Antitrust Act by proposing that De Beers register a US branch of the Diamond Syndicate Incorporated. In a way his company could provide the US with the industrial diamonds, it desperately sought for the war effort in return for immunity from prosecution after the war. However, his proposal was rejected by the US Justice Department, when it was discovered that De Beers did not intend to stockpile any industrial diamonds in the US (Epstein, 1982). In 1945, the Justice Department finally filed an antitrust case against De Beers, but the case was dismissed, as the company had no presence on US soil.

The Oppenheimer family has since redirected much of its philanthropic efforts towards preserving the heritage and cultural importance of the Southern African region, as well as to broader community up-liftment in the areas of education, health, nature conservation and the arts. Nicky Oppenheimer and his son Jonathan Oppenheimer established the Brenthurst Foundation in 2005 as a way to contribute to the debate around strategies and policies for strengthening Africa's economic performance and enabling inclusive and sustainable development. The family has also long been involved in environmental and conservation issues (Forbes, 2016). The Oppenheimer family collaborated with De Beers to establish the Diamond Route in 2006 to maximize the potential of their properties for conservation, research and environmental awareness purposes. The Diamond Route in which the Oppenheimers have withdrawn their land, linked eight sites across northern South Africa, stretching from Namaqualand on the west coast, to Kimberley, north to Tswalu in the Kalahari, and to the Brenthurst Gardens in Johannesburg, eastwards to Ezemvelo Nature Reserve and northwards to the Venetia Limpopo Nature Reserve in Limpopo Province (Forbes, 2016).

SOLUTIONS AND RECOMMENDATIONS

The reconfiguration of national and racial identity in fluid colonial environments is illustrated in novels poems or prose. Chinua Achebe in his book entitled: *Things Fall Apart* first published in 1958. The time in which Achebe conceived and wrote his book, was also a time of anxiety and crisis. The ANC had been banned and was operating underground. Things fall apart can be viewed as an idiom implying the realities of cultural relativism. In Boaz (1963), cultural relativism is defined as a principle that an individual person's beliefs and activities should be understood by others in terms of that individual's own culture. So which cultures should be understood? All of them should be articulated in the construction of highly productive organizations. The core of integration begins where people reside, worship, work, and attend school or college, and where they relax. The way forward in building sustainable family enterprise is to draw strategy from environmental analyses and recognize that change can come from the economy and political, societal, and technological factors. Succession plans need to be designed and implemented taking cognizance of imminent environmental factors. The enterprise must be viewed boldly to determine the capacity it needs to effectively compete. The country must understand its comparative advantages and to provide organizational support to national industries. Job creation is best done by the private sector and the state's role is to develop the infrastructure. The mining industry has unique advantages such as technology, explicit practices in exploiting diamonds, gold, or platinum. Family enterprises should focus at competences necessary to progress the business. Succession plans should be designed and implemented as part of the company's overall strategy. Neither Rhodes nor Beit left apparent heir to the corporations they helped to found. The legacies made in their Wills are upheld by the courts, despite the demise of the Oppenheimers.

A Diamond Monopoly

In the reports pre4sented by Associated Press (2004), the De Beers Company started selling diamonds in the United States only through intermediaries shortly after World War II, when it was first charged with price fixing. The company was charged along with General Electric Co. in 1994. A judge later dismissed the charges against GE, stating that the government had failed to prove its case. Lawsuits against the De Beers Company started shortly after WW2 but the law courts ruled that the Company was not physically situated on US soil to warrant prosecution. From 2001 onwards several lawsuits were filed against De Beers in US State and Federal courts. These alleged that De Beers unlawfully monopolized the supply of diamonds and conspired to fix, raise and control diamond prices. Additionally, there were allegations of misleading advertising. While De Beers denied all allegations that it violated the law, in November 2005, it announced that an agreement had been reached to settle civil class action suits filed against the company in the United States and, in March 2006, three other civil class action suits were added to the November agreement. In April 2008, De Beers confirmed that Judge Chesler of the US Federal District Court in New Jersey had entered an order approving the Settlement, resulting in a settlement arrangement totaling US$295 million. De Beers does not admit liability. As part of the settlement, persons who purchased gem diamonds from 1 January 1994 to 31 March 2006, may be eligible for compensation. However, claimants were generally not pleased with the amounts they received from the settlement.

Company Problems Spanned Nations

In the EEC vs De Beers Company, the applicant contested that the Commission's decision of 26 January 2007 in competition Case COMP/39.221/B-2 - BVGD/De Beers, by which the Commission rejected the applicant's complaint regarding violations of Articles 81 and 82 EC in connection with the Supplier of Choice system applied by the De Beers Group for the distribution of rough diamonds, with the reasoning that there is not sufficient Community interest to act further on the applicant's complaint. The applicant alleged that De Beers - a producer of rough diamonds who, according to the applicant, was mainly involved upstream with the sale of rough diamonds – was trying through its Supplier of Choice system to extend its control of the market to cover the entire diamond pipeline from mine to consumer, i.e. also the downstream markets. In February 2006, De Beers entered into legally binding commitments with the European Commission to cease purchasing rough diamonds from Russian mining company Alrosa as of the end of 2008. In January 2007, the European Commission announced that it had closed the file due to lack of Community Interest. The commission decision is under appeal before the Court of First Instance in Luxembourg (European Court of Justice, 2007).

CONCLUSION

Family enterprises remain as the most viable businesses in generating employment and reviving the economy. The state effectively participates in capitalism by enacting conducive regulations. The majority of established enterprises have roots in families of the founding fathers in the US. For example, Ford, General Motors, De Beers Diamond Company, Oppenheimer Funds, Du Pont, or Anglo American Corporation.

REFERENCES

Achebe, C. (1958). *Things Fall Apart*. New York: William Heinemann.

AFNS. (2008). Bush family relation in diamond ring dispute. Retrieved from http://londonantwerpdiamonds.com/diamond-news-archive.php

Aldrich, R. (2005). Apprenticeship in England: Lessons from History of Education. In A. Heikkinen & R. Sultana (Eds.), *Vocational Education and Apprenticeships in Europe* (pp. 195–205). London, UK: Routledge.

Alford, C. J. (1906). Mining law of British Empire. Retrieved from https://archive.org/details/mininglaw-britis01alfogoog

Altrichter, H., & Gstettner, P. (1993). Action research: A closed chapter in the history of German social science. *Educational Action Research*, *1*(3), 329–360. doi:10.1080/0965079930010302

Bandura, A. (1977). *Social learning theory*. Englewood Cliffs, NJ: Prentice Hall.

Bandura, A. (1986). *Social Foundations of Thought and Action: A Social Cognitive Theory*. Englewood Cliffs, NJ: Prentice-Hall.

Berger, L. A., & Berger, D. R. (2011). *The Talent Management Handbook* (2nd ed.). New York: McGraw-Hill.

Berger, M. (2000, August 21). Harry Oppenheimer, 91, South African Industrialist, Dies. *New York Times.*

Berger, R., & Gavish, Y. (2015). A gem in a hostile world: an evolutionary analysis of the diamonds industry: the case of the Israeli diamond industry. *International Journal of Strategic Change Management, 6*(3/4), 268–291. doi:10.1504/IJSCM.2015.075906

Blake, R. (1977). *A History of Rhodesia.* London, UK: Eyre Methuen.

Boas, F. (1963). *[1911]. The Mind of Primitive Man.* New York: Collier Books.

Britannica (2016). Sir Ernest Oppenheimer: South African Industrialist. Retrieved from www.britannica.com/biography/Ernest-Oppenheimer

Cabraser, L. Heimann & Bernstein (December 21, 2011). Court Upholds $295 million settlement in De Beers Antitrust suit. Retrieved from http://www.diamonds.net/News/NewsItem.aspx?ArticleID=38343http://www.diamonds.net/News/NewsItem.aspx?Article ID=38343

Church, S. G. (2016). Beneath Thy feet: Secrets from the grave. *Beneaththyfeet.* Retrieved from http://beneaththyfeet.blogspot.com/2012/06/dunkelsbuhler-angels-and-diamonds.html

Cowell, A. (2000). Controversy Over Diamonds Made Into Virtue by De Beers. *New York Times.* Retrieved from http://www.nytimes.com/2000/08/22/business/controversy-over-diamonds-made-into-virtue-by-de-beers.html?pagewanted=all

Davenport, T. R. H. (1991). *South Africa: A modern history* (4th ed.). London, UK: Macmillan. doi:10.1007/978-1-349-21422-8

Davis, W. P., Figgins, B., Hedengren, D., & Klein, D. B. (2011). Economics Professors' Favorite Economic Thinkers, Journals, and Blogs (along with Party and Policy Views). *Econ Journal Watch, 8*(2), 133.

De Beers Company Settlement. (2013). De Beers Company Settlement. Retrieved from https://www.diamongsclassaction.com

de Rothschild, D. (1979). Rothschilds at Waddesdon Manor. New York: Viking Penguin.

Diamond, L. L. (2016). The early days of the De Beers Company. Retrieved from http://www.gemgate.com/originalgemgate/Diamond/Advanced/Section1/early_De_Beers

Drastal, M. (2010). The End of Apartheid: A racial revolution in South Africa. Retrieved from https://issuu.com/masondrastal/docs/the_end_of_apartheid_-_a_racial_rev

Dube, S. (2016). Ex-Wenela employees demand pension dues. *Chronicle.* Retrieved from http://www.chronicle.co.zw/ex-wenela-workers-demand-dues/

Dubow, S. (2014). *Apartheid 1948-1994.* New York: Oxford University Press.

Epstein, E. J. (1982). *The rise and fall of diamonds: The Shattering of a Brilliant Illusion.* New York: Simon & Schuster.

Erne, R. (2016). Change Management Revised. In A. Goksoy (Ed.), *Organizational Change Management Strategies in Modern Business* (pp. 1–23). Hershey, PA, USA: IGI Global. doi:10.4018/978-1-4666-9533-7.ch001

Fastiff, E. B. (2016). A determined Advocate for Fair Competition. Retrieved from http://www.lieffca-braser.com/attorneys/eric-b-fastiff/

Forbes (2016). Africa's top 50 wealthy people. Retrieved from http://www.forbes.com/profile/nicky-oppenheimer/

Giliomee, H., & Mbenga, B. (2007). *A New History of South Africa*. Cape Town: Tafelberg Pty Ltd.

Goldschein, E. (2011). The Incredible Story Of How De Beers Created And Lost The Most Powerful Monopoly Ever. Retrieved from http://www.businessinsider.com/history-of-de-beers-2011-12

Gregory, E. T. (2013).Ernest Oppenheimer and the economic development of Southern Africa. White-fish, MT: Literary Licensing, LLC.

Hughes, T. P. (1989). *American genesis: A century of invention and technological enthusiasm, 1870-1970*. New York: Viking.

Keays, A. (2011). *The Crown Jewels* (Special Edition). London, UK: Thames & Hudson.

Lewin, K. (1943, May). [1997]. Defining the Field at a Given Time.[Republished in Resolving Social Conflicts & Field Theory in Social Science. Washington, D.C.: American Psychological Association.]. *Psychological Review, 50*(3), 292–310. doi:10.1037/h0062738

Mandela, N. (1995). *Long Walk to Freedom: The Autobiography of Nelson Mandela Kindle Edition*. Cape Town: Little, Brown and Company.

Meredith, M. (2008). *Diamonds, Gold and War: The British, the Boers, and the making of South Africa*. New York: Public Affairs.

Minchon, C. (2013). Diamonds may not be forever…but now, they look pretty good. Retrieved from http://jewishbusinessnews.com/2013/06/11/diamonds-may-not-be- for-ever-but-at-the-moment-they-look-pretty-good/

Mlambo, A. S. (2014). A History of Zimbabwe. Cambridge, UK; Cambridge University Press.

Mupepi, Mambo (2014). Can the Division of Labor Be Re-Engineered to Advance Organizational Dynamism? *SAGE Open*. DOI:10.1177/2158244014536404

Mupepi, M. (2015). *British Imperialism in Zimbabwe: The Organization Development of the First Chimurenga (1883-1904)*. San Diego, CA: Cognella.

Mupepi, Mambo (2016). The passage of the coal train: the inevitable mosaic in technical systems in global and local organization. *African Journal of Economic and Sustainable Development, 5*(2), 149 – 171.

Mupepi, M., & Mupepi, S. (2014).Certain change: multi-democratic movements punctuate the tyrannical paradigm in Africa. *African Journal of Economic and Sustainable Development, 3*(1), 1–30.

Mupepi, M. G., & Mupepi, S. C. (2016). Applying Theory to Inform Competency Development: Bootstrapping Epistemic Communities in Growing Specialists.[IJPMAT]. *International Journal of Productivity Management and Assessment Technologies, 4*(1), 28–38. doi:10.4018/IJPMAT.2016010103

Oppenheimer, H. (2008). Sir Ernst Oppenheimer 1880-1957. Retrieved from http://www.brenthurst.org.za/sirernest.cfm

Otteson, J. R. (2002). *Adam Smith's Marketplace of Life*. Cambridge, UK: Cambridge University Press. doi:10.1017/CBO9780511610196

Parsons, N. (1993). *A New History of Southern Africa*. London, UK: Palgrave Macmillan.

Pouroulis, A. (2008). Chairman of Petra Diamonds Company Annual Report. Retrieved from http://londonantwerpdiamonds.com/diamond-news-archive.php

Reports, E. (2012). After De Beers, What's next for the Oppenheimers? Accessed 07/26/16http://rough-polished.com/en/expertise/58666.html?print=Y

Roberts, J. P. (2007). *Glitter & Greed: The secret world of the Diamond Cartel (Kindle ed.)*. Disinformation Books.

Rodger, L. & J. Bakewell, J. (2011). Sir Ernest Oppenheimer. *Chambers Biographical Dictionary*. London, United Kingdom: Chambers Harrap.

Roth, C. (2007). *The Magnificent Rothschild*. New York: Kissinger.

Senge, P. M. (1990). *The art and practice of the learning organization*. New York: Random House.

Sharfman, M.P., & Dean, J.W. (1991). Conceptualizing and measuring the organizational environment: a multidimensional approach. *Journal of Management, 17*(4), 681-701.

Simpson, C. (2002). Obituary: Jonas Savimbi, UNITA's local boy. *BBC News*. Retrieved from http://news.bbc.co.uk/2/hi/africa/264094.stm

Stanford University. (2016). The History of Apartheid in South Africa. Retrieved from http://www-cs-students.stanford.edu/~cale/cs201/apartheid.hist.html

Swanson, D. J., & Creed, A. S. (2014, January). Sharpening the focus of force field analysis. *Journal of Change Management, 14*(1), 28–47. doi:10.1080/14697017.2013.788052

Turner, L. C. F. (1970). *Origins of the First World War*. New York: W. W. Norton & Co.

Vygotsky, L. S. (1978). *Mind and society: The development of higher mental processes*. Cambridge, MA: Harvard University Press.

Whitworth, A. (1985). *A Centenary History, A History of the City and Guilds College, 1885 to 1985*. London, UK: University of London Press.

Wrigley, C. (2002). *A companion to Twentieth-Century Britain*. London, UK: Blackwell Ltd. doi:10.1111/b.9780631217909.2002.x

Yasnitsky, A., & Van Der Veer, R. (2015). *Revisionist Revolution in Vygotsky Studies: The State of the Art*. London, UK: Routledge.

KEY TERMS AND DEFINATION

Alfred Beit: Alfred Beit (1853-1906) was a very successful British South African businessman who founded the British South Africa Company together with Cecil Rhodes. Beit was the main partner of Cecil Rhodes in the colonization of Southern Africa.

Cartel: A cartel is an association of manufacturers or suppliers with the purpose of maintaining prices at a high level and restricting competition.

Cecil Rhodes: Cecil John Rhodes (1853-1902) was a very enterprising British South African technocrat and politician in Southern Africa. He served as Prime Minister of the Cape Colony from 1890 to 1896 and was a passionate believer in British imperialism. Rhodes and his British South Africa Company founded the southern African territory of Rhodesia (now Zimbabwe and Zambia), which the company named after him in 1895. South Africa's Rhodes University was named after him. Rhodes set up the provisions of the Rhodes scholarship funded by his estate, and put much effort towards his vision of a Cape to Cairo Railway through British territory.

Monopoly: A monopoly has the exclusive rights to the supply of certain goods in the market.

Nathaniel Mayer von Rothschild: Nathan Mayer von Rothschild (1777–1836) founded the Rothschild banking family of England in 1798. Rothschild first settled in Manchester running away from the persecution of Jews in Germany. His home was Frankfurt before he moved to London. His parents wanting the safety and success of their children sent Nathan to England. Wanting his sons to succeed on their own and to expand the family business in different European cities by establishing financial institution to invest in business and provide banking services. Nathan Mayer von Rothschild, the third son, first established a textile jobbing business in Manchester and from there went on to establish N M Rothschild & Sons Bank in London.

Oligopoly: A small group of people or businesses that control the supply of a specific product in the market.

Organizational design: A process by which managers make specific organizing choices that result in a particular kind of organizational structure.

The De Beer Brothers: In Epstein (1982), the first diamond was discovered near the Orange River in South Africa in 1870. These were the first diamond mines were the first in Northern Cape. Rather than finding by chance an occasional diamond in a river, diamonds could now be scooped out of these mines by huge steam shovels. Suddenly, the market was deluged a growing flood of diamonds. The British financiers who had organized the South African mines quickly came to realize that their investment was endangered: diamonds had little intrinsic value, and their price depended almost entirely on their scarcity. They feared that when new mines developed in South Africa, diamonds would become at best only a semi-precious gem. On Lovelady Diamond (2016) website, the 83.50-carat diamond crystal now known as the Star of South Africa instigated the international diamond rush to South Africa in 1868. A Dutch digger named Cornelia was allowed to prospect a farm for a 25% fee to the owners, the De Beer brothers. News traveled fast and in a very short time, the de Beer farm was inundated with diggers racing to stake their claims on and beyond the farms boundaries. In October 1871, the de Beer brothers sold their farm for 6,300 pounds, not realizing the vast wealth that lay beneath the farmland. In 1880, after years of aggressive claim buying, Cecil Rhodes founded what was then called the De Beers Mining Company. Barney Barnato, like Rhodes, came to South Africa with insight and vision and was eventually able to start a large diamond mining operation called Barnato Diamond Mining Company. He quickly gained control of the Kimberly Central Mining Company, at that time the largest mining company operating.

Rhodes and Barnato had to fight it out for ultimate control over the mining and in the end; Rhodes came out on top with his larger financial backing and perhaps sharper wit. The Lovelady Diamond (2016) suggested that in 1888 the De Beers Consolidated Mines Ltd. was born. Even though Barnato did not win the game, he still ended up as a major player. Barnato was a key figure in the development of the South African diamond trade and was involved in some of the gold mine developments including the Rand gold fields. Unfortunately, at the age of 44, under the stress of running the large financial empire and suffering from mental illness, he jumped overboard from a ship on a journey to England.

Chapter 11
Building Capability:
Flipping the Zone of Proximal Development For Talent Management

Kevin Paul Barrons
Seidman College, USA

Thomas C. McGinnis
Seidman College, USA

ABSTRACT

Currently, new approaches for training can effectively adopt the "Flipped" model of instruction as an important means of organizing and developing workforce competencies. One of the goals in the university setting at Grand Valley State University is to improve skills and training opportunities which can most efficiently utilize training time. In order to improve cognitive practice and increase skillfulness in a value creation socio-technical system, the Zone of Proximal Development (ZPD) is deployed to progress the talent needed to advance productivity. Seeing much success is noticed in this newest pedagogy "flipped instruction" design, it has changed various disciplines in business education which can best be applied to the training component of the workforce today. The success of this model continues to create higher learner motivation resulting in desired outcomes. The technology of the ZPD juxtaposed with the flipped classroom technique can lead to the improvement of a highly talented workforce.

INTRODUCTION

Many organizations continue to investigate ways in which talent management can be accelerated in their companies. While many approaches are presently applied, one alternative suggested is to implement the flipped classroom instructional strategy to improve a company's talent pool. While minimal pedagogical approaches are currently used to manage talent, the flipped instructional model provides a satisfactory alternative to training and skills development in the workforce. As we consider the options to increase our choices for talent management, we can apply the flipped classroom strategy and define

DOI: 10.4018/978-1-5225-1961-4.ch011

the complexity of the "zone of proximal development" (ZPD) and experiential learning theory (Figure 1). To guide the discourse, we must:

1. Conceptually frame how talent management is presently approached
2. Present the ZPD theoretical approach create value to the learner/talent and the organization
3. The shared experience to enable learning
4. Draw a conclusion, mentioning the limitations of the arguments provided in the debate, and a final suggestion can be supported for future research in "flipped" instructional pedagogy as it relates to talent management

BACKGROUND

Defining Key Dimensions

- **Flipped Instruction:** A model that allows for the traditional format of a classroom to be transformed into more of a hybrid design for learning. The focus of the model is to provide reading and the preview of content which needs to be completed before the class meeting. Individuals are then allowed time in class to work on projects individually and in teams as part of the learning process which promotes more of a problem-solving atmosphere (see Figure 1).

Figure1. The Zone of Proximal Development (Barrons, 2015)

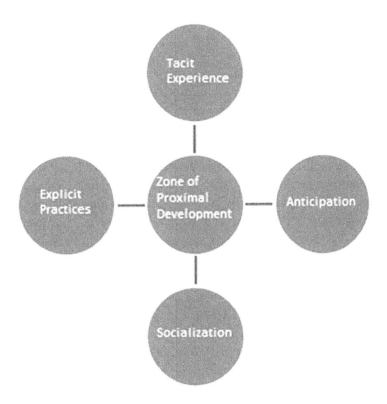

- **A "Flipped Classroom" Educational Model:** Exchanges the traditional format of a classroom lecture and homework problem set. We piloted two flipped classroom sessions in our emergency medicine (EM) residency didactic schedule. We aimed to learn about resident and faculty impressions of the sessions, in order to develop them as a regular component of our residency curriculum (Young, Bailey, Guptill et al., 2014). In Barrons (2015), the flipped classroom is viewed as a zone of proximal development where the novice can increase their skillfulness in job performance. The flipped classroom provides an opportunity to nurture talent (see Figure 1). The relationships of the key elements illustrated are tacit knowledge, anticipation, socialization and explicit practices.

- **Tacit Knowledge:** Is fundamentally difficult to transfer from one person to another by means of writing or speaking. Tacit knowledge can be defined as skills, ideas, and experiences that people have in their minds and are, therefore, difficult to access because it is often not codified and may not necessarily be easily expressed (Chugh, 2015).

- **Anticipation:** Is associated with predictions, desires or intentions which can strongly influence behavior, adaptation, and learning. Since Pavlov, there has been an appreciation of the link between anticipation and learning. Briefly, in typical Pavlovian conditioning, an unconditioned stimulus (US) has some natural or a prior unconditioned response (UR). Classic examples of US-UR pairs include food-related salivation and vasoconstriction due to exposure to cold. Any stimulus that is regularly contingent, either preceding or concurrent, with the US is a potential conditioned stimulus (CS), for example, the ringing of a bell. The result of Pavlovian conditioning is a conditioned response (CR), which either mimics or compensates for the UR. In either case, the CR is anticipatory with respect to the US. Anticipation is most clear when the CR and UR are of the same kind, for example, salivation, but compensatory responses, such as those that play a role in drug tolerance, have an anticipatory coping function discussed at length by the functional school of Pavlovian conditioning (Domjan, 2005).

- **Socialization:** In the learning process is known to improve the environment to increase knowledge. For decades, educational institutions have promoted and practiced the socialization components supported by John Dewey. By interacting with others, individuals receive feedback on their activities; they learn socially appropriate behaviors, and they understand what is involved in cooperating and working together (Dewey, 1940, 1966).

- **Explicit Practices:** In this context applies to the knowledge relevance of sharing information regarding intrinsic motivation. In public sector work, the idea of public sector motivation (PSM) assists individuals in their skill levels. With the introduction of PSM, the present study connects knowledge sharing with public administration. Public service as a calling leads civil servants to share knowledge to create more advanced organizational knowledge and accordingly improve public service performance. Compared to situational factors (e.g. the use of information technology and rewards), PSM plays an even more pivotal role in promoting knowledge sharing, according to the results of our empirical research. Thus, altruistic motivation should be addressed and emphasized if knowledge sharing in the public sector is to be encouraged (Chen & Hsieh, 2015).

Maintaining the Competitive Advantage

The current strategies in the job market require a level talent management that is lacking attention in the job market today. Currently, there is no consistent framework for employers to adhere to to manage a successful talent pool. Presently, standards vary from one company to another on how talent can be managed according to the most current literature review. In light of the extreme competitiveness in the global business environment, maintaining a competitive advantage is critical to a company's success. However, many businesses are failing to properly utilize their arguably most important asset- human capital (Axelrod, Handfield-Jones, & Michaels, 2001). The inability to develop employees, assist poor performers and identify leaders is dampening the performance of businesses worldwide. It is time for companies to realize that talent management is not a job that should be contained to the human resources department, but rather a role which should be taken on by senior leaders company-wide (Donahue, 2001).

There are many actions organizations can take to utilize their workforce more effectively. Overall, corporations should market the brand that they seek to promote, to attract people that mesh with their culture. Once employees are retained, training programs should also stress and embed the corporate culture. In this way, talent management will be better aligned with a company's strategy (Bjorkman, et al., 2012). Within the organization, senior leaders should be extensively trained in talent management and take an active role in developing their teams (Axelrod, Handfield-Jones, & Michaels, 2001). This includes identifying high and low performers and developing them accordingly. Special attention should be paid to ensure that each employee is facing proper challenges and is given the appropriate resources and freedom to execute their tasks (Donahue, 2001). If all senior leaders worked diligently to manage the skills of their teams, talent would permeate throughout the workforce, and the organization would reap tremendous success (Axelrod, Handfield-Jones, & Michaels, 2001).

Talent management can be categorized into two approaches:

1.   Differentiated
2.   Inclusive

Under the differentiated approach, energy is focused most heavily on the high performers while weeding out those who do not meet expectations. The inclusive approach, on the other hand, focuses on leveraging value from all different employee levels under the belief that each person has something unique to contribute. In reality, most companies utilize a hybrid system of talent management that looks to combine both mindsets (Bjorkman et al., 2012). Whether using the differentiated or inclusive approach, global companies must ensure that their method allows for both global and local talent standards to be implemented. It is helpful for these businesses to maintain a consistent approach to the overall strategy while simultaneously leaving smaller matters up to local discretion to appease local customs and preferences (Bjorkman et al., 2012).

In addition to focusing on the development of individual employees, businesses need to focus on investing in social capital through increasing group loyalty and developing trust. The implementation of this social capital will allow for increased employee motivation, productivity, and longevity. Some employees, of course, will maintain a "free agent" mentality and be willing to leave the company anytime they believe they will reap higher rewards elsewhere. It is important for managers to identify the both the free agents and the loyalists, as important decisions, such as layoffs, may be well-suited to take this information into consideration (Donahue, 2001).

An Overview of Talent Management Strategies and Flipped Approaches to Learning

The "Flipped Classroom" approach is applied during the instructional delivery of the Management 351-Management Information Systems course at GVSU located Pew Campus in Grand Rapids, Michigan. Likewise, this approach can be applied as one of the possible talent management strategies by companies. Much success in training talent and teaching a course in the past has applied a traditional instructional method of class lecture (and or computer lab time). Presently, the "flipped classroom" model allows more time for learners (employees) to problem solve in teams, review class lectures outside of class with pre-recorded slides, sound, and videos, and use valuable class time completing class exercises. Seeing more than 50% of the focus of the class requires weekly hands-on exercises applying the integrated business processes with enterprise resource planning (ERP/SAP) software, students are allowed more in-class time for problem-based learning (PBL) activities related to each weekly activity. Students have required reading assignments, quizzes, and instructor prepared recordings that are reviewed before class and applied to each weekly exercise.

This "flipped classroom" model allows students to work both independently to complete outside class assignments to allow the students to achieve mastery at their learning pace. Further, when students come to class, they spend more time working with the instructor (subject matter expert) applying their outside class activities with higher level learning activities. Therefore, the "flipped classroom" model can be effectively applied to the theoretical approach to "The Zone of Proximal Development" in this discourse.

The Zone of Proximal Development (ZPD) inside the classroom setting or cyberspace continuous learning environments has borrowed practices and techniques from Vygotsky (1978), Bandura (1977), Senge (1990), Lave and Wenger (1991), Brown and Duguid (1991), Jenkins (2009), Mupepi (2014) and SAP.Com(2015), among many others. Table 1 displays the responses of students enrolled in the Flipped Classroom Management 351 – Management Information Course which shows level of favorability and unfavorability of the Flipped Classroom strategy

Table 1 displays the responses by the students enrolled in the Management Information Course. Students indicated an 80 percent favorable response they were spending 2-4 hours per week watching course materials while 20 percent indicated unfavorable responses. The videos used in the course in addition to the recording for the power point presentations lectures were favorable at 61 percent while 39 percent indicated unfavorable. The student responses for the class format was favorable at 66.67 percent while

Table 1. N=32: Student responses to the flipped classroom survey

Description	Percentage favorable	Percentage unfavorable
Students who spent 2-4 hours per week watching course materials outside class	80.00	20.00
Students said videos were helpful in addition to the recordings for the power-point lectures	61.0	39.0
Students indicated the class format was helpful for their learning	66.67	33.33
Working in teams and problem solving exercises were helpful	77.8	22.22
Students indicated they were able to make contributions to others and provide assistance as needed with problem solving in the class	77.8	22.22

Source: Barrons (2017) Management 351 Class Survey

the unfavorable responses were 33.33 percent. A strong indication of working in teams and problem solving exercises was favorable at 77.78 percent while 22.22 percent was unfavorable. Students indicated a 77.78 percent favorable and 22.22 percent unfavorable response they were able to make contributions to others and provide assistance as needed with problem solving in class.

At the beginning of this survey, 20 percent of the participants in the class possessed the dexterity was lower compared to 80 percent whose proficiency was superior to the others in the class. Thirty nine percent lacked the necessary technology skills while 66 percent demonstrated acceptable skillfulness in applying the review of videos for instructional purposes. Twenty two percent did not participate in team activities immediately. There was a need to explain what they were expected to do as part of the course requirements. The summer population in this survey are those who also hold full time employment. Which are necessarily in education or work force development. Further, in the last group 77.78 percent demonstrated that they could work in teams and were knowledgeable about experiential learning and its usefulness in advancing organizational goals.

The Zone of Proximal Learning

Adapting the learning technologies progressed by Bandura (1977), Vygotsky (1978) and Senge (1990) I have contrasted their proposition to a zone of proximal learning. Vygotsky (1978) suggests that the Zone of Proximal Development (ZPD) can be adopted to develop the skillfulness of learners in different learning environments such as MIS. In the ZPD, Vygotsky propounds that competencies can be enhanced by the expert(s) demonstrating the "how to" in developing competencies. In the ZPD, Vygotsky demonstrates three stages of skills development by the novice. The lower limit of ZPD is the level of skill reached by the learner working independently. The upper limit is the level of potential skill that the learner can reach with the assistance of a subject matter expert. Bandura (1977) propounded that learning begins at home. If learning begins at home, we begin learning at an early stage. It a truism that charity begins at home. Senge appreciates learning in a different but similar way. He suggests in organizations, the need to create is a shared vision, personal mastery, systems thinking, team learning and mental models in this learning strategy.

The centricity of the ZPD is illustrated to be surrounded by three equal circles (see figure 1). If the circles are misaligned, the ZPD will not be real and the potential will of learning not be achieved. Vygotsky also makes reference to a community of practice. The ZPD develops concepts that can be applied to understand job specifications and the competencies required to do certain jobs. Mupepi (2014) suggests that the division of labor enables the managers to understand the skills dexterity in the job and the explicit knowledge to be successful. The division of labor is expanded and analyzed to understand the knowledge, skills, technology and disposition required by a worker to be become proficient.

Bandura (1977) posits that the socialization process must be understood for learning to take place. The socialization process constitutes the environment of the learner at work, at home and in social contexts. This environment is argued by Bandura to be critical for successful skills and language acquisition. According to Bandura, he discusses the importance social learning theory in skills acquisition where people learn through observing others. As MIS students imitate the teacher, this can be applied to the concept of socialization and learning. In the MIS area of study, the students develop the MIS confidence and increase self-efficacy in their ability to apply their skills to execute a set of courses of action.

Roehl, Reddy, and Shannon (2013), suggest various ways in which we can use technology to free class time from the lecture. Certainly, increasing learning activities during class time provides improved teacher-to-student mentoring, peer-to-peer collaboration and cross-disciplinary engagement. Most recently, the Flipped Classroom has been approached in various formats. This may include self-learning packages, problem-based learning, project-based learning, pre-recorded video lectures and or, demonstrations for personal review. It is important to focus on the level of knowledge transfer when one identifies the ZPD in this discourse. The Flipped Classroom is a step ahead of the ZPD model because of the emphasis on experiential learning, problem-based learning and the relationship to solving problems in social contexts.

An Overview of Pedagogical Practices

An overview of current pedagogical perspectives has been drawn from a careful selection of literature to answer the questions: 1) How did the SAP software development start?; and 2) How does the shared experience enable learning?

In 1972, the idea of creating a corporate software company was unheard of. SAP's five founders refused to let that stop them. They set out on a path that would transform the world of information technology and forever alter the way companies do business. Since then, SAP has moved on to what it is today to deliver, cloud solutions, enterprise resource planning, banking, customer relationship management, human resources, retail and mobile solutions. According to SAP (2015a), the company is the world leader in enterprise applications regarding software and software-related service revenue. Based on market capitalization, the company asserts that it is the world's third largest independent software manufacturer proceeded by Oracle and Microsoft at the helm. SAP has more than 291,000 customers in 190 countries, greater than 74,500 employees located globally, a 43-year history of improvement and evolution as a true industry leader and yearly income exceeding 18 billion Eurodollars (SAP, 2015b).

The concern of researchers, Bandura (1977) Vygotsky (1978) and Senge (1991) has been focused on organizational learning and competence development. The research on skills transfer and knowledge acquisition in socially constructed learning environments have been expanded very well in Bandura, Vygotsky and Senge. In the case of the MIS approach, the skills transfer occurs in defined places such as; using the workstations, exploring the software, the application usage, computer labs and real business problems. Vygotsky (1978) argues that the ZPD is the space where the learner acquires desirable skills after consultation with the subject matter experts. Long after the experts have left, the novice continues to practice to make perfect his/her skillfulness. Bandura (1977) suggests that the learner is influenced by the environmental factors to acquire knowledge and skills necessary to function in the ways the community desires. Bandura introduces a community of practice concepts positioned in the environment. This community can be the family, the school, and workplace. Thus, the socialization of the learner is critical to the acquisition of explicit practices.

Both Bandura and Vygotsky used children in their research. We are now applying the business model approach as the focal point of an older age group. Bandura and Vygotsky used their research with children and did not have a business organization in mind. The ZPD context can now be focused in the context of student's learning in a business simulation in a computer lab in this situation. It was Bandura who defined the socialization process as a continuum of learning from home to school and work. Thus, a student appreciates skills, knowledge, and attitudes from this experience. The same can be said where the child can develop attitudes at home which can be shared at school or many social contexts.

Senge, Kleiner, Roberts, Ross and Smith (1994), provide a point of view about learning techniques. They identify five learning modules that can be applied to progress organization. The first learning model is "personal mastery" which constitutes the skills sets an individual must possess in doing a given job. Personal mastery allows the learner to build the capacity to use his/her skills to produce the goods and services demanded by the customers. In the MIS area of study, students build their confidence to use software such as SAP by constantly conversing and consulting with experts and sharing knowledge with other students. The second is "the mental model" which is applied. This model includes reflection, clarification, and the ability to improve a shared window of the world. This model allows a community of practice in which to create, diffuse and distribute co-constructed practice. Senge suggests that a "shared vision is co-constructed as well. A shared problem is a problem solved.

The fourth model is the "team learning" approach. The shared learning concept leads us to Lave and Wenger (1991) about knowledge creation in distributed cognitive environments. They suggest that an organization can build a community of practice based on the notion of highly cohesive teams. They propound that a community of practice can be composed of a group of people preferably from the same organization that meets in defined places at agreed times or in cyberspace at any time. A community of practice becomes a tool which can be deployed to enhance learning in the value creation process. The Flipped Classroom embraces the social interaction in the community of practice. In the MIS course, students learning the SAP software use the interaction of business problems to increase knowledge and skillfulness at solving problems. This process continues to build as the course progresses until the job is complete. In all, this problem-solving experience amongst the team members builds confidence in the learning process.

Figure 2. Team learning (Barrons 2015)

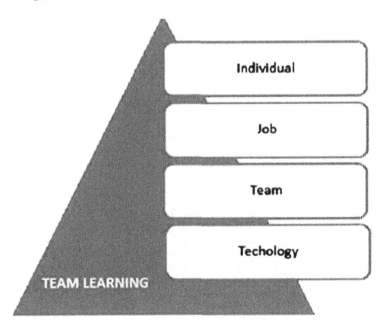

Senge, et al. (1994) alludes to the fact that the fifth learning discipline "systems thinking" which enables the entire organization to operate on the same page. Because a community of practice shares the same language, it implies they are aware of the organizational mission in which each individual deduces his job description which resonates with the mission statement.

According to Roehl, Reddy and Shannon (2013), it is suggested that the advantages of the Flipped Classroom are easy and use readily accessible technology. This allows for an expanded range of learning opportunities in a given time frame. The instructor gets to know each student "on a one-to-one basis" as they demonstrate how to use software or assists students as needed. These relationships continue by email, shared Google docs and with learning management systems online collaboration tools.

The Centricity of the Flipped Classroom

The Need to Know

Barrons (2015) suggested that there are five observations for the flipped classroom strategy. In the first part, the emphasis is placed on the "need to know" by the learner. The instructor will document this in the syllabus, which all those attending the class should have in hand. Prior knowledge is important for students as well as employees. They need to understand the syllabus. For example, the University of Michigan was engaged in a lawsuit for canceling classes because of snow and in the syllabus, this was not pointed out. The plaintiffs argued that the grades they received, in the end, could have been better if the class was not canceled. If they had prior knowledge of the canceled class, they could have received a higher grade. The court awarded damages to the plaintiffs leading to a refund of the tuition (Fraser, 2006). Further, we can continue the debate on the need to know about this issue; prior knowledge is an essential skill (see Figure 3).

Figure 3. The flipped classroom (Barrons, 2015)

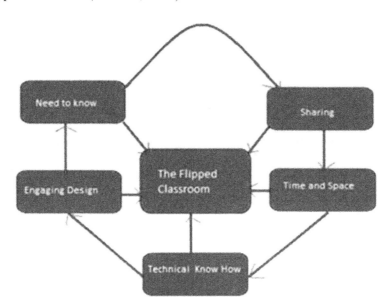

Appreciating Models

The classroom instructor must identify a pedagogical model that stresses the learning. This may include concepts such as project-based learning (PBL), problem-based learning (PBL), game-based learning (GML), understanding by design (UbD), and genuine literacy. Then the Flipped Classroom model can be assimilated to any of these concepts. Lave and Wenger (1991), allude to the fact that the above models could be implemented in the Flipped Classroom effectively by a community of practice. The ZPD, on the other hand, has been described distinctly by Vygotsky (1978) to be the area where the novice acquires competence (see Figure 3).

Simple Tools

The community of practice needs to know how to use the simple tools available in the classrooms, or within the learning community. Twenty-first-century students are highly engaged with the educational technology tools in the ZPD. The tools allow for higher motivation, stimulation, and comprehension. The technology enables students to interact among themselves, the virtual libraries, software, and instructors, which promotes higher level thinking skills.

Replication of Competencies

The use of technology and visual aids such as YouTube, pre-recorded videos, text, and PowerPoint presentations allow for reflection and enable students to benchmark competence in areas in which proficiency is sought. In the flipped model, students can review information materials before attending an in-classroom class which composes their prior knowledge before coming to class. Also, some activities can be assigned and completed as they pertain to the instructional objectives. Flavell (1979) suggests shared experiences are any conscious cognitive or affective familiarities that accompany and relate to intellectual exchange which happens in flipped classrooms.

Time, Stage and Location

In Argyris (1991) double-looped learning is introduced into the organization as imperative to successful business. We can apply this concept to the Flipped Classroom strategy. Both instructor and the learner receive constructive feedback (see Figure 4). Given the Flipped Classroom requires structure, the learning environment is important. The instructor will need to incorporate proficiencies to keep the students engaged. Most learners who are reviewing information before coming to class will need accountability. Allowing active learning to take place outside of class similar to hybrid or online learning techniques will require a means of formative assessment to evaluate student performance. These assessments will assist the educational leader in addressing the needs of the learners. Meyers and Jones (1993) discuss the active learning process and instructional tools which keep the learning environment "active" those include problem-solving exercises, cooperative student projects, informal group work, simulations, case studies, and role-playing as examples. Argyris (1991) propounds that feedback is critical in business environments which would apply to classrooms. He refers to this as double-looped learning.

Figure 4. Double loop learning (Argyris, 1991)

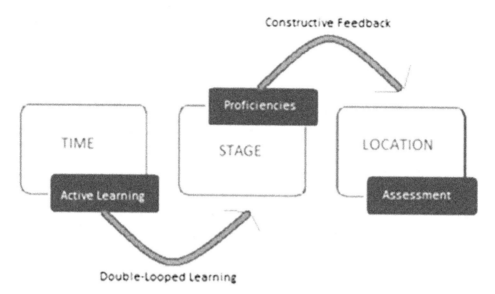

Epistemic Communities

The epistemic communities or knowledge communities have been described in Foucault (2002) as a group of people who meet regularly to create priorities in organizations. Foucault leads to the thought that an epistemic community co-constructs those priorities. Mupepi (2010) develops organizational strategy hinged on an epistemic community. For example, organizational efficiency and effectiveness can be advanced by a knowledge community. Mupepi gives the analogy of the Adam Smith pin production factory showing the division of labor. Adam Smith proposes that the division of labor into specialization units which can yield increased productivity. By determining the desired capacity and the set of skills that capture what the organization does best by utilizing appreciative inquiry (AI), the entire organization can advance to the next level. Adam Smith envisioned increased ratio of output as each man perfected his act. AI, a change management method can be deployed to determine the skillfulness required in avoiding wasted time and efforts. The AI methodology makes it possible for the entire organization to participate in the determination of what needs to be changed making it possible to distinguish between efficiency and effectiveness. It is essential to make this differentiation because successful corporations are both efficient and effective. By drawing from the Adam Smith pin-making enterprise, learning the best methods used to perfect the acts of different specialists, can be documented and communicated to all members of the epistemic community. Feedback on all the practices is imperative to developing specialist. The Flipped Classroom offers the opportunity to co-construct curricular by sharing experiences and drawing lessons from the instructors' syllabus.

The Impact of Communications

In Barrons (1993) organizational communications are viewed as critical to effective learning. In later research, Mupepi, Mupepi and Motwani (2015), posit that the centricity of organizational learning is clear and concise communications. In the Flipped Classroom, there should be an all-around communication among students and the instructor as they share information and experiences. Barrons suggests that the environment nowadays includes information from the media, social networks, and prevailing cultural trends. For example, if students attended a concert they would discuss the performance in class. This reflects that learning continued outside the classroom. Learning was influenced by the motivation from this experience. Mupepi et al., argue that the relationship between skills acquisition and motivation is highly correlated.

Instructors Role

Barrons (1993) considers the instructor is central to all the activities in the (flipped) classroom. The role of the instructor is still central in the reductions of dropouts and to increase the skillfulness of higher order learning. Barrons argues that the most critical problems of all times are to address the problem-solving skills of each student. Chall (1983) the scripts of Sesame Street which serves as an informal television classroom for pre-school children up to age 5 (Vygotsky and Bandura) were change to incorporate problem-solving skill development. In much later research Jacobs and Chall (2003) argue that the developmental stages of reading development, reading is conceptualized not as a process that is the same from beginning stages through mature, skilled reading, but as one that changes as the reader becomes more able and proficient. Therefore, problem solving is a developmental skill. In the flipped classroom, group exercises constitute problem solving and the conceptualization of explicit practices in relation to co-constructive epistemology.

One of the responsibilities of the instructor in the flipped classroom is dictate notes to students. This exercise enables the student to continue to develop their language arts skills. Lave (1988) suggests that there is a correlation between writing and memory. In the flipped classroom, it is important as students share information they write down what they want to remember. Lave argues that apprentices in the field of electrical engineering took notes as they saw the instructor provide demonstrations. In their final assessment, they were required to repeat those demonstrations. From the notes, they remembered the demonstration were learned in the classroom during the final exams.

MAIN FOCUS OF THE CHAPTER

This chapter focused on how the flipped classroom technology can be applied to develop a highly talented workforce. The Zone of Proximal Development is deployed to allow the instructor to demonstrate what needs to be done and how it will be done and setting performance standards. Instructional pedagogy techniques are applied to build the capability to enhance effectiveness and efficiency in the workforce.

Issues

It takes considerable resources to develop talent in an individual. Without making binding agreements, people soon find greener pastures elsewhere. When this happens turnover increases and so does operational costs. Employers situated in the same locality doing similar business can porch those who qualify by offering them competitive conditions of service. While making trainees sign a contract, some will offer to pay the agreement violation (usually with the help of their new employers) and leave.

SOLUTIONS AND RECOMMENDATIONS

Looking ahead, the concept of the Flipped Classroom strategy as applied to pedagogical models will continue to open alternatives to the learning community. Effective instructors (like employers) are looking for ways to provide the highest levels of achievement to their students (and employees). In business alike, the process of learning continues in a similar manner when it comes to new tasks.

Learning that has high-level relevance to the participants provides a high-level of engagement. Using the flipped strategy allows one to apply real-world problem-solving experiences by adding a high level of relevance to the process of developing explicit practices from tacit knowledge. In Figure 5 a practical model shows how flipped learning will move forward the pedagogical process which can be applied to talent management. However, this can only be done if one consider all the variables in this discourse and believing that the overall goal is to improve instruction and training.

The last but not least recommendation is to improve the conditions of service in the company as students' progress their skills development. This will reduce turnover and help to retain talented workers. Training of any kind is not cheap; it draws upon the resources of the company, and it is only fair to get the commitment of students by signing a binding agreement.

Lastly successful classrooms have teachers who have utilized a strategy that promotes successful learning. Most successful businesses today have a developed plan that encourages the cultivation of talent at every level of management. Figure 6 is a model representation of an approach to establish and retain talent. It starts with an introduction of personnel. Then a continuous loop of engagement, development, leadership and planning all occurs, all the while there are continuous measurements taken

Figure 5. The Making of Explicit Practices (Barrons, 2016)

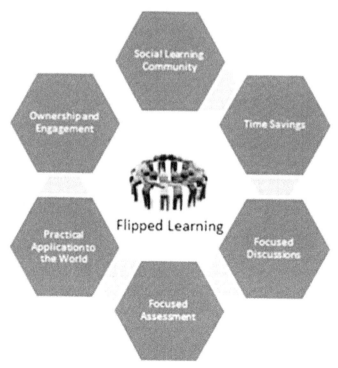

Figure 6. Talent management for superior business results (Barrons, 2016)

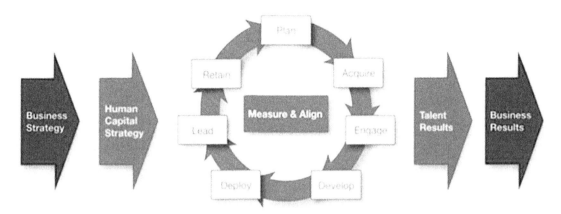

during this development and actions take to realign with the plan in necessary. This loop is never ending. However, the results of this process lead to better businesses. In education, the same rules apply for student achievement. The results are measurable by the objectives achieved and the level of information learned. Typically, you tend to see more productivity out of employees that have been trained and developed as well as a better atmosphere in the working environment. This is likely to come from the people feeling more positive about themselves and the work that they do when they see effort placed in their development and future.

A positive outcome for both employers and employees can manifest when proper leadership and training is provided (see Figure 6).

FUTURE RESEARCH DIRECTIONS

There is no substitute for on-job training for a number of reasons. OJT is easy to implement, and it is cost-effective. As technology is constantly evolving, the training of employees or stakeholders who are distributed in the world can be a challenge. Research on how to training employees virtually dispersed could be much needed.

CONCLUSION

One can continue to observe achievements as organizational learning such as the flipped classroom techniques, a process of creating, retaining, and transferring knowledge within an organization. Thus, an organization improves as it gains the capability to produce what the market demands. The flipped classroom offers learners the opportunity to continue to practice until desirable job proficiency are reached. A flipped classroom does not have a standard framework. However, there are many ways in which a classroom can be "flipped. This writing has offered only just one of the many approaches to talent management strategies.

REFERENCES

Argyris, C. (1991). Teaching Smart People How to Learn. *Harvard Business Review*, May- June, 99–109.

Axelrod, B., Handfield-Jones, H., & Michaels, E. (2001). Talent Management- A critical part of every leader's job. *Ivey Business Journal*.

Bandura, A. (1977). *Social learning theory*. Englewood Cliffs, NJ: Prentice-Hall.

Barrons, K. P. (1993) *Whittle Communications Channel One: The Effects of News and Advertising on Secondary Students* [Unpublished Ph.D. Dissertation]. Detroit: Wayne State University.

Bjorkman, I., & Farndale, E., et al. (2012). Six Principles of Effective Global Talent Management. *MIT Sloan Management Review, 53*(2).

Cappelli, P. (2008). Talent Management for the Twenty-First Century. *Harvard Business Review*, 86(3), 24–31. PMID:18411966

Chall, J. S. (1983). *Stages of Reading Development*. New York: McGraw-Hill.

Chall, J. S., & Jacobs, V. A. (2003). Poor children fourth-grade slump. *American Educator, 27*(1), 14–17.

Chen, C., & Hsieh, C. (2015). *Knowledge Sharing Motivation in the Public Sector: The Role of Public Service Motivation. International Review of Administrative Sciences, 81*(4), 812–832.

Chugh, R. (2015). Do Australian Universities Encourage Tacit Knowledge Transfer?*Proceedings of the 7th International Joint Conference on Knowledge Discovery, Knowledge Engineering and Knowledge Management* (pp. 128-135). doi:10.5220/0005585901280135

Dewey, J. (1940). *Education Today*. New York: Greenwood Press.

Dewey, J. (1966). *Democracy and Education*. New York: The Free Press.

Domjan, M. (2005). Pavlovian conditioning: A functional perspective. *Annual Review of Psychology, 56*(1), 179–206. doi:10.1146/annurev.psych.55.090902.141409 PMID:15709933

Donahue, B. K. (2001). Time to Get Serious About Talent Management. *Harvard Management Update*.

Flavell, J. H. (1979). Metacognition and Cognitive Monitoring: A New Area of Cognitive- Developmental Inquiry. *The American Psychologist, 34*(10), 906–911. doi:10.1037/0003-066X.34.10.906

Foucault, M. (2002). The Order of Things: An Archaeology of the Human Sciences. London, U.K.: Routledge classics.

Fraser, K. (2006, December 7). Why doesn't The University of Michigan have snow days? *The Michigan Daily News*.

Jenkins, C. (2009, February 2). The Australian Financial Review - ABIX via COMTEX -- SAP will supply software for a large revamp of Woolworths' merchandising systems.

Lave, J. (1988). *The culture of acquisition and the practice of understanding*. Palo Alto, CA: Institute for Research on Learning.

Lave, J., & Wenger, E. (1991). Situated Learning: Legitimate Peripheral Participation. Cambridge: Cambridge University Press. doi:10.1017/CBO9780511815355

Meyers, C., & Jones, T.B. (1993). *Promoting Active Learning, Strategies for the College Classroom*. San Francisco: Josey-Bass.

Mupepi, Mambo (2010). Appreciating social structures: a strategy for advancing the efficiency and effectiveness loci in organization. *International Journal of Education Economics and Development 1*(4), 306-319.

Mupepi, M. (Forthcoming). Using Communities of Practice to Identify Competencies.

Mupepi, M., Mupepi, S., & Motwani, J. (2015, March 25-27). Social Construct: Methods, Tools, and Applications in Re-Engineering Organizations. *Proceedings of the MBAA International Conference*, Chicago.

Mupepi, M.G. (2014). Can the Division of Labor Be Re-Engineered to Advance Organizational Dynamism? *SAGE Open*, 4(2).

Mupepi, M. G., & Mupepi, S. C. (2016). Applying Theory to Inform Competency Development: Bootstrapping Epistemic Communities in Growing Specialists. *International Journal of Productivity Management and Assessment Technologies*, 4(1), 28–38. doi:10.4018/IJPMAT.2016010103

Roehl, A., Reddy, S. L., & Shannon, G. J. (2013). The flipped classroom: An opportunity to engage millennial students through active learning strategies. *Journal of Family and Consumer Sciences*, 105(2), 44–49. doi:10.14307/JFCS105.2.12

SAP.COM. (2015a). SAP grows up but never grows old. Retrieved from https://www.sap.com/careers/about-us/history.html

SAP.COM. (2015b). SAP at a glance: Company Information. Retrieved from http://www.sap.com/corporate-en/about/our-company/index.html

Senge, P. M., Kleiner, A., Roberts, C., Ross, R., & Smith, B. (1994). The Fifth Edition Fieldbook. New York: Doubleday Books.

Young, T. P., Bailey, C. J., Guptill, M., Thorp, A. W., & Thomas, T. L. (2014). The Flipped Classroom: A Modality for Mixed Asynchronous and Synchronous Learning in a Residency Program. *Western Journal of Emergency Medicine*, 15(7), 938–944. doi:10.5811/westjem.2014.10.23515 PMID:25493157

KEY TERMS AND DEFINITIONS

Flipped Classroom Technology: The flipped classroom is an instructional strategy and a type of blended learning that reverses the traditional learning environment by delivering instructional content, often online, outside of the classroom.

Pedagogy: The theory and practice of education. it focuses on how actually to develop and implement curricula.

Socio-Technical Systems: Sociotechnical systems in organizational development is an approach to complex organizational work design that recognizes the interaction between people and technology in workplaces.

Zone of Proximal Development (Zpd): The zpd, is the difference between what a learner can do without help and what he or she can do with help.

Chapter 12
Single Factor Analysis in Grading Jobs:
The How-to Retain Talent

Mambo Mupepi
Seidman College, USA

ABSTRACT

Although human resources management is important in organization, its tenet of job evaluation is significant. Job evaluation is a management approach that enables employers to grade and reward jobs in comparison to what they are worth in the company in an equitable manner. The company will be able to craft a compensation plan aligned to performance. The Paterson derived job evaluation is a systemic way of determining the worth of a job in relation to other jobs in the organization using one single factor: decision making. This single factor is juxtaposed along the attributes of a selected multiple factors to progress the structuration of grades and compensation. Paterson defines six kinds of decisions or levels of work which are strategic intent, strategic execution, tactical management, advanced operational, operational and primary. These are found in any company and applied in the design and implementation of competitive conditions of employment to retain talent. There are more businesses floundering because of the failure to control costs. The single factor job evaluation system enables the firm to design and implement a sustainable performance strategy to retain talent in advancing the competitive advantage.

INTRODUCTION

Professor Thomas T. Paterson designed the job evaluation approach that carries his name at Strathclyde University in Scotland in 1972. The technique uses a single factor of decision making, to differentiate jobs from one another. It identifies six decision bands in organization. A rewards structure that accommodates the six levels of decision making bands can be developed to suit each organization and grade jobs according to the level of decision making each one of them may fall under. Paterson (1972) propounded that decision making factor was inherent in most jobs and fluid at all levels in a hierarchical structure in organization. Paterson postulated that jobs could be graded accurately and an equitable compensa-

DOI: 10.4018/978-1-5225-1961-4.ch012

tion plan put into place on a sliding scale where the top decision makers received the highest rewards compared to those at the bottom of the hierarchy.

Background

The ACAS (Advisory, Conciliation, and Arbitration Services) was created by the Labor Party administration in the mid-1970s in the UK to improve organizations and working life through the promotion and facilitation of effective industrial relations practices. Today ACAS is an independent and international organization that does not side with a particular party, but rather will help firms in designing and implementing of highly productive labor relationships. It offers organization development services such as workforce education and training and job evaluation, among many others. The ACAS (2016) handbook suggested that there are many job evaluation methods and techniques available in different industries and different countries. ACAS suggested that job evaluation takes time and a lot of patience to implement successfully. But a good job evaluation scheme can form the basis of a fair pay system. It's also a way for getting a hierarchy of jobs on which to base a grading system.

Reasons for Implementing Job Evaluation

Many employers carry out job evaluations when deciding on pay and grading, ensuring that there is a fair and equal pay system, determining on benefits such as bonuses or healthcare insurance coverage, comparing pay against other companies and reviewing all jobs after a major change within the company. At Ford Motor Corporation headquarters in Dearborn, the human resources organizational infrastructure includes recruiting procedures, job descriptions, job analysis, job evaluation of the classification type and other methodologies that change from plant to plant to accommodate different collective bargaining agreements or merely closed or open shops.

An international consulting company, Hay Group Inc., has developed a unique job evaluation system referred to as the Profile Method which is based on three factors, each of which has sub-factors (Hay Group, 2010). The methodology starts from the premise that all jobs exist to achieve a purpose---to create value in the business and evaluates this by analyzing what is the value that is created---(accountability), how it is created (problem solving) and what the job requirements are that the incumbent has to meet in order to deliver the value (know-how). These factors and sub-factors included under each are defined as follows:

Accountability

Every job exists to add organizational value by delivering some set of results or throughputs. Accountability measures the type and level of value a job can add. It has three dimensions:

1. **Freedom to Act:** The degree of empowerment to take action within the framework of guidance provided to focus on decision making
2. **Scope:** The business measure(s) the job is designed to positively impact.
3. **Impact:** The nature of the job's influence on business results (defined in scope) ranging from degrees of direct to indirect (Hays Group, 2010).

Problem Solving

The value of know-how is in its application to achieve results. Problem solving or throughputs refers to the use of know-how to identify, delineate, and solve problems. Problem solving measures the requirement to use know-how conceptually analytically and productively and has two dimensions:

1. **Thinking Environment:** The job's context regarding business matters to address and the degree to which the problems and solutions are clarified and focused by strategy, policy, precedents, procedures or rules.
2. **Thinking Challenge:** The inherent complexity of the problems faced and the difficulty in identifying solutions that add value (Hay Group, 2010).

Know-How

To achieve the accountabilities of a job requires know-how or inputs, which is the sum total of every capability or skill needed for fully competent job performance. Know-how has three dimensions:

1. **Practical/ Technical Knowledge:** Depth and breadth of technical or specialized knowledge needed to achieve desired results.
2. Planning, organizing and integrating (managerial functions, such as planning, organizing, staffing, directing and controlling financial, physical and human resources, to achieve business results over time.
3. **Communicating and Influencing Skills:** The interpersonal skills required for successful interaction with individuals and groups inside and outside the organization (Hay Guard, 2010).

In Eargle (2013), five popular approaches to job evaluation are listed as:

Non-quantitative methods consisting of

1. Ranking,
2. Comparison techniques approach to grading and evaluating jobs; Quantitative methods comprising,
3. Point ranking,
4. Factor comparison approach to grading and evaluating jobs, and
5. Emerging technology.

Technology is constantly evolving and for this reason Eargle propounded that a single factor analysis in evaluating emerging technology in hi-tech or knowledge-intensive organization was useful because the competences on such jobs were hinged on know-how.

An Overview of a Selected Literature Review

There are many other methods of evaluating jobs. The paper will attempt to describe some of them to enable comparisons to be made in the debate. Taber & Peters (2006) state that a Point-factor job evaluation system does not describe jobs equally the same. The Point-factor system uses defined attributes such as education, experience, decision making, and training, among others to establish job value. Taber & Peters argue that the perception of those who rate the jobs is bound to vary from one job to another. For example, educational qualifications vary from one institution to the other and may not be the same in terms of curricula. In the automobile engineering field, experience at designing engines for Ford Motors can be equated to be the same experience for doing the same work at General Motors.

The types of decision making and factors that influence decisions in this type of industry may also be the same. In this analogy the Peterson Derived Job Evaluation System (Decision Making) is valid when grading managerial jobs because there is defined Decision Making in management (See Table 1).

Decision making is reasoning underlying a managers' choices. Decision theory can be broken into two branches: normative decision theory, which gives advice on how to make the best decisions, given a set of uncertain beliefs and a set of values; and descriptive decision theory, which analyzes how existing, possibly irrational managers actually make decisions.

The Factor Comparison Job Evaluation System

The factor comparison job evaluation system is a quantitative approach in determining what jobs are worth and how they can be graded. The commonly used factors are Skill, Responsibility, Effort and Working conditions. These are weighted to give points towards a pay structure. The process establishes the rate of pay for each factor for each benchmark job. Slight adjustments may need to be made to the matrix to ensure equitable dollar weighting of the factors.

Retaining Talent

Leggit (2007) suggests that organizations must evaluate jobs and use intrinsic motivation to attract individuals into defined positions. Intrinsic motivation may arise from such perks as opportunities to train and grow from say grade B to C or D to E after a given period of training and experience. Leggit asserts that such a rewards package can help to recruit and retain people who seek challenges in their professions rather than those who are driven by money. Regardless of the motivation Valcour (2007)

Table 1. The Peterson Derived Job Evaluation Method (PSJEM)

Decision Band	Types of Decision	Decision Bands and Responsibilities	Benefits	Compensation
F	Strategic Intent		Package	Executive
E	Strategic Execution		Package	Executive
D	Tactical Management		Package	Structured Executive
C	Advanced Operation		Healthcare 401 K Tuition assistance PTO	Salaries
B	Operational		Limited	Hourly paid
A	Primary		Limited	Hourly paid

(Adapted from Paterson & Husband, 1970)

argued that work measurement, evaluation and work control were factors that led organizations to retain talented personnel. The competitive advantage is actually created by people who possess the skillfulness to produce goods demanded by customers.

Cognitive Ability in Effective Decision Making

In this model decision making is a factor inherent in all jobs. Drawing from the Perry Schema (1970), decision making can be placed into a dual realism: Good vs. Bad decisions, and Right vs. Wrong decisions. We as an organization vs. They, the competitors. Right answers exist somewhere for every problem, and authorities know them. Right answers are to be memorized by hard work. Knowledge is quantitative and agency is experienced in authority and responsibility, making the right decisions, and doing the right job. The Perry Schema compares cognitive abilities as necessary in effective decision making. Hofner & Pintrich (1997) state that the Perry scheme is a model for understanding how college students "come to know, the theories and beliefs they hold about knowing, and the manner in which such epistemological premises are a part of and an influence on the cognitive processes of thinking, reasoning and making decisions. Since Perry (1970) many scholars such as Knefelkemp & Slepitza (1978) have advanced the debate on cognition development and decision making. They assert that critical thinking can be understood as the ability to weigh evidence, examine arguments, and construct rational bases so as to make effective decisions. Knefelkemp & Slepitza have adapted Perry's developmental sequence to analyze the discourse on students at different levels in their courses and how they make decisions could be equated to grading managerial jobs.

A Case Study at Williamson Foods Group of Companies

Williamson Inc. was engaged in the food and wine processing industry and it introduced the Paterson Derived Job Evaluation Method (PDJEM) in the early 1990s as a way of rationalizing its operations to effectively compete with similar organizations. A collective bargaining agreement had existed in the industry for a long time and the Company decided to evaluate all the jobs using the PDJEM. The flexibility of the methodology implied that the Decision Bands were extended to accommodate the levels of decisions between the bands (e.g. E and F, or D and C bands. Further the F band accommodated the many executives who were in charge of companies within the group. Band F was created to accommodate the chief executive and chairman of the group. All this flexibility is part of the dynamic characteristics of the PDJEM. The workforce's perception focused on equal opportunities and fairness in the grades and the wages structure. The problem was exacerbated by management's failure to communicate with the workforce as to what they were hoping to achieve. The issue became a labor complaint and the hourly paid went to their union for arbitration. The labor division equivalent to ACAS ruled in favor of the organization citing that management had the prerogative to manage the business and to be fair to all stakeholders. However management was required to explain how the job evaluation worked in a series of workforce training programs and to produce a manual on how the system worked which could be referred to by stakeholders at all times. In addition the company was required by the labor laws to train first line supervisors how to write the required job descriptions and how the job evaluation was implemented.

At Williamson Company, there were 1500 people employed in all operations. The first company to be to receive the PDJEM was the head office employees and Table 2 lists a cross section of the key jobs that were graded.

Table 2. The decision band method

Band	Decision	Title	Grade	Decision	Title
E	Policy-Making	Top Management	10 9	Coordinating Policy	Managing Director Director
D	Programming	Senior Management	8 7	Coordinating Programming	General Mgt Works Mgr
C	Interpretive	Middle Management	6 5	Coordinating Interpreting	Dept. Mgr First line Mgr
B	Routine	Skilled Operator	4 3	Coordinating On Process	Lead Operator Craftsman
A	Automatic	Semi-skilled Operator	2	Coordinating On Process	Charge hand Machinist
A	Define	Unskilled Operator	1	On element	General Hand

Adapted from Paterson & Husband (1970)

Decision Bands E and F

In these bands the jobs entail designing policy. The incumbents must have absolute knowledge about the business. They must provide answers to all the difficulty questions regarding what to do in terms of policy. Perry (1970, p. 1) suggests that in these positions there is no conflict facts remain as facts, beliefs are not selected but given. In organization commandments only come from those who are at the helm of the hierarchical structure. Perry considers that in positions 1 and 2 the quality of thinking demands smart memories, attention, inferences and reasoning. The way jobs are organized in modern corporations allow the incumbents in the E band to employ people who can do the thinking, the actual drafting of policy, just to mention a few of the tasks that can be assigned to incumbents with job titles as "General Manager", "Personal Assistant to the CEO", or "Projects Manager"

Decision Band D

Multiplicity (Perry's positions 3 and 4 Multiplicity Correlative.) Most knowledge is still viewed as absolute, as in Dualism. But in some jobs all the answers can be obtained by asking those incumbents in position 1 and 2 or in Decision Bands E and F.

This decision band is responsible for interpreting and programming policy decisions made in Decision band E. who are viewed by Perry (1970, p. 3) as faultless and the keepers of the organization's values. Decisions in this band require knowledge, skills and experience that are directly related to the business of the company. In Perry's study this knowledge equate to that of sophomores in college, a knowledge that would grow with studying and experience. The incumbents may mature and be ready to move into the E and F decision bands.

Decision Band "C"

Relativism (Perry's 4 Relativism Subordinate, 5, and 6). Students recognize such strategies as analysis of evidence, comparison of interpretations, or designing experiments. Paterson (1972, p. 2) suggests that in the Decision Making Band "C" the incumbents are concerned with routine aspect of the job. They report to those in Decision Band "D" unless there are five sub-grades, 6, 5, 4, 3, 2 and 1 in which case the lower number may report to the next highest number within the same band. Decision Band constituted talent needed to produce the goods and services demanded by customers. The incumbents were artisans, toolmakers and electricians who served a post-high school apprenticeship lasting at least four years. The conditions of service for this group deviated from the norm in order to retain the talent (see Figure 1). Thus the toolmaker earns more than the supervisor and the manager because accountability, know-how, and problem solving decisions contribute to more to organizational profitability. At times the reporting structure can overlap sub-grades and jump straight to report to the next decision band. This may occur between say a production cost clerk who can be in grade C4 reporting to the Works manager who is in grade D4. The point here is about the types of decisions made in the job rather than the reporting structure. In this decision band qualifications are important as entry attributes. For example, the health and safety officer may be required to possess a registered nurse certificate, and not just a certificate of first aid.

Decision Band "B"

Perry (1970) suggests that the Commitment in Relativism (Positions 7, 8, and 9) is about students who are skilled in rational (formal operational) processes and drawing upon the accumulated learning and experience of the school years, the student can commit herself to the opinions, ideologies, values, and interests with which he will identify. A student may reaffirm or reject old beliefs; either way, the decision is based on a conscious consideration of alternatives as opposed to the blind acceptance of the Dualist. The Peterson (1972) systems can equate Positions 7, 8 and 9 to Decision Band *B* Paterson suggested that incumbents in Decision Band "B" are expected to make routine decisions and such decisions tend to improve with experience.

Figure 1. Salary scales and decision bands

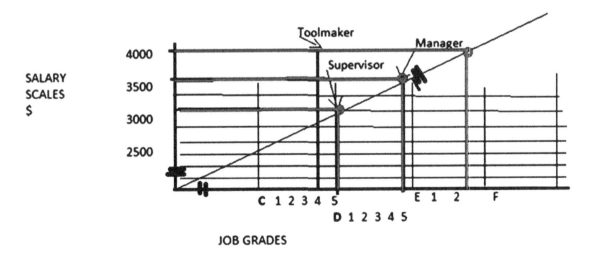

Decision Band "A"

Decision Band "A" is restricted to menial jobs such as general hands. Usually general hands can be hired to do day's job such as cleaning the yard after annual shutdown fore holidays or to offload goods from a truck.

MAIN FOCUS OF THE CHAPTER

The focus of this chapter is to illustrate the importance of job evaluation in organization and that the competitive advantage is created by the people doing the job. Compensation plans have to take cognizance of the fact that salary structure are merely reflect what a job is worth compared to similar jobs in the same organization. However if the organization must maintain competitiveness there is a need to retain the talent by providing a competitive contract for employment.

Issues, Controversies, Problems

The Paterson Derived Job Evaluation has been criticized by scholars such as Brannick Levine & Morgenson (2007) arguing that The Decision Band "A" was not applicable in most industries since recruits were often "skilled" in many other areas for which they were no vacancies. They took the "general hand" position as a job that was available when the incumbents were unemployed. The second argument raised was that the Decision Making Factor tended to benefit more managerial staff than the blue collar workers.

SOLUTIONS AND RECOMMENDATIONS

The change in business terrain is accelerated by globalization, which has opened many avenues of growth. To survive in this environment, the organization requires alignment of its strategic goals and available human resources. The need is to manage the performance of the employee who is the most important resource of the organization. The focus has now shifted to the highly skilled workforce in order to leverage technology. Job evaluation is a strategy to create the competitive advantage. The PDJEM is consistent, fair, and easy to implement. The workforce should be informed about how their jobs are graded and rewarded. A company can have all the technology but the know-how possessed by the people doing the job make the difference.

FUTURE RESEARCH DIRECTIONS

Emerging trends in organization indicate that there is a constant shift in method of working in nearly all industries. Performance evaluation should be a periodic activity which should start by looking at how work is divided and graded. Because newer technologies continue to evolve in organization it implies that newer methods to evaluate jobs should be created. Research about techniques to evaluate and grade jobs in emerging technologies could contribute to organizational effectiveness and efficiency.

CONCLUSION

There are many methods of job evaluation and some are easy to understand and implement and others are very complicated. Job evaluation using the Paterson method is a proposition to grade jobs fairly and to design and implement a compensation strategy appropriate to the means of a company. It is easy to understand and it can be implemented successfully.

REFERENCES

ACAS. (2016). *Job Evaluation Handbook*. Kingstone-Upon Thames, UK: HMGS.

Armstrong, M., & Cummins, A. (2005). *Job Evaluation*. London, UK: Kogan Page Business Books.

Brannick, M. T., Levine, E. L., & Morgenson, F. P. (2007). *Job analysis: Methods Research and Applications for Human Resources Management (2nd ed.)*. London: Sage.

Eargle, F. (2013). Job evaluation: Traditional Approaches and Emerging Technology. Lulu.com.

Hofer, B. K., & Pintrich, P. R. (1997, Spring). The development of epistemological theories: Beliefs about knowledge and knowing and their relation to learning. *Review of Educational Research, 67*(1), 88–140. doi:10.3102/00346543067001088

Johnstone, F. (1976). *Class, Race and Gold: A Study of Class Discrimination in South Africa* (p. 158). London: Routledge and Kegan Paul.

Knefelkamp, L. L., & Slepitza, R. (1978). A cognitive-development model of career development: An adaptation of the Perry scheme. In C. A. Parker (Ed.), *Encouraging Development in college students*. Minneapolis: University of Minnesota Press.

Kuhn, D. (1991). *The skills of argument*. Cambridge, UK: Cambridge University Press. doi:10.1017/CBO9780511571350

Leggit, R. (2007, November 22). Letting go too easily: human resources management. *Accountancy Age*.

Paterson, T. T. (1972). *Job Evaluation: A New Method* (Vol. 1). New York: Random House ISBN.

Perry, W. G. Jr. (1970). *Forms of Intellectual and Ethical Development in the College Years: A Scheme*. New York: Holt, Rinehart, and Winston.

Valcour, Monique (2007). Work-based resources as moderators of the relationship between work hours and satisfaction with work-family balance. *Journal of Applied Psychology, 92*(6), 1512-1524.

KEY TERMS AND DEFINITIONS

Accountability: Accountability is the acknowledgment and assumption of responsibility for actions, products, decisions, and policies including the administration and implementation within the scope of the role or job position and encompassing the obligation to report, explain and be answerable for resulting consequences.

Cues to Respond To: The cues in a job include how precise duties have to be carried out. In some jobs such as accounting and costing there is no margin of error precision is imperative in additions, subtractions and calculations.

Decision Band: The decision band divides decision making into six bands. The level decision band is A. In this band the decisions are routine and automated e.g. the room is dirty it should be cleaned. The top band is td is responsible for policy decisions such as the annual statements should be ready by November 1st each year.

Job Evaluation: A job evaluation is a systematic way of determining the value/worth of a job in relation to other jobs in an organization. It tries to make a systematic comparison between jobs to assess their relative worth for the purpose of establishing a rational pay structure.

Job Scope: The scope of the job is the range of duties and responsibilities and the cues the incumbent needs to pay attention to be successful in performance.

Know-How: Know-how is a term for practical knowledge on how to produce the goods demanded by the customers. Know-how is often tacit knowledge, which means that it is difficult to transfer to another person by means of writing it down or verbalizing it. Know-how is useful in crafting explicit practices to differentiate the business.

Chapter 13

Why the Zebra's Stripes are Important:
Protecting the Core Competences of the firm

Mambo Mupepi
Seidman College, USA

Aslam Modak
Seidman College, USA

Robert Frey
Kirkhof College, USA

ABSTRACT

This article progresses the argument that the core competences of the company must be created, diffused, and distributed and protected, to effectively exploit the market. Companies compete on what they know best and in management theory organizations draw a repertoire of multiple resources and skills to effectively differentiate the business in vying for market leadership. The core competence or capability of the firm can be described as talent and a special ability that allows the enterprise to produce the goods demanded by customers exceptionally well. The core competences can also be referred to as explicit practices constituting measurable or observable knowledge, skills, abilities, and behaviors critical in meeting the needs of clients. The capability should be crafted in a manner that makes imitation by similar entities impossible.

INTRODUCTION

This paper is spread out in four parts. The first provides an introduction and offers a definition of some of the key dimensions applied in the discussion. The second part reviews a selected literature to appreciate the management of knowledge in its various forms including core competences and how they can

DOI: 10.4018/978-1-5225-1961-4.ch013

be applied to make ends meet in successful organization. In the third part, a synthesis of the literature is provided to craft a conceptual model that characterizes organizational core competences critical in sustaining the organization. A conclusion is drawn in the fourth part mentioning the limitations of the arguments presented.

BACKGROUND

A Selected Literature Review: Some Dimensions in Knowledge Creation

Many scholars argue that a company needs to create its own practices that are unique to the environment in which it operates. For example, Menon, Bhardwaj, Adidam & Edison (1999), propounded that an internal assessment of the firm's strengths and opportunities was antecedent to the development of organizational strategy. The model they proposed was hinged on discovery-approach yielding a multifaceted conceptualization of strategy that can be implemented taking cognizance of the capability of the enterprise to succeed. Menon et al allude to the need in organization to create diffuse and distribute explicit knowledge to cognitive areas where the knowledge can be converted into practices to enhance sustainability.

Core Competences are a Construct

In an article that has become a Harvard Business Review classic entitled the *Core Competence of the Corporation*, Prahalad & Hamel (1990) suggested that what constituted the essential capacity of an enterprise were the ability to access markets successfully, produce and deliver the goods demanded by customers and Should make a significant contribution to the perceived customer benefits of the end product. Zook (2001) found that nine out of ten companies had succeeded because they had focused on their core competences. Those that did not had diversified operations into areas they did not have specific talent. In later research Zook & Allen (2016), proposed that there were at least three principles: Managing the business and responding to the necessary cues to enable efficiency and effectiveness to occur; solving problems; and focusing on productivity. Zook & Allen viewed this three-step approach as antecedent to growth of the firm. Solving problems enabled the firm to be effective and efficient. Zook & Allen argued that managers spent most of the time in efforts to understand why profitability was hard to achieve and sustain.

Core Capability is a Social Construct

In Burnes & Cooke (2013) the field force analysis technique developed by Kurt Lewin in 1943 has remained viable as a proposition in strategy management. Force-field analysis is an influential development in change management which provides a framework for looking at the factors (forces) that influence behavior in organization. It looks at forces that are either driving movement toward a goal achievement or blocking movement toward a goal. This proposition has been republished by the APA (1997) and remains in use today. Following this assumption managers spent a considerable time developing strategy using this technology commonly referred to as environmental analysis. Zook & Allen argued that executives managed their companies as if the solution to problems lay in the external environment such as finding an attractive market, or formulating the right strategy to win new customers. Zook & Allen claimed that when companies fail to achieve their growth targets, 90 percent of the time the root causes are internal, not external--increasing distance from the front lines, loss of accountability, proliferating processes and bureaucracy were some of the causes. The key insight from Zook & Allen's research is that managing these choke points required a "founder's mentality"--behaviors typically embodied by a bold, ambitious founder--to restore focus, and connection to customers. At the Apple Company, it was the opposite when the board of directors decided to fire Steve Job for failing to share the vision of the company. The founder's mentality enables management to appreciate the historical foundation of the company. The ideas of the founder of the business and what he wanted to do and achieve can be the beginning in the design of a better future. Re-visiting the founder's mission at De Beers Diamond Company after the Supreme Court upheld $295million settlement in antitrust suit demonstrated the importance of the historical foundation in organization. The capability of a company to recreate itself lay in what the founding fathers Alfred Beit and Ernest Oppenheimer set out to do nearly a century ago. Zook b& Allen propounded that there is a strong relationship between these three traits in companies and their ability to sustain performance and increase production capacity (see Figure 1).

Systems Thinking

In Danko (2015), Karl Ludwig von Bertalanffy was an Austrian biologist known as one of the founders of general systems theory (GST). The GST is an interdisciplinary practice that describes systems with interacting components, applicable to biology, cybernetics, and other fields. An analogy of an organism referred to as the amoeba an organism that thrives in marshy or wetlands, is made to understand the systems theory. The amoeba reproduces itself so many times by breaking into two parts which are identical and have the same genes. These parts continue to do the same until the entire pond or swampy area an open system, is populated by the amoeba. This theory illustrate how germs can spread using the medium of water. It can also be used to understand organizational behavior in varied environments such as competition Bertalanffy (1934)'s mathematical model alludes to the fact that those organisms that fail to adapt to their environment fail to exist (Bertalanffy, 1968).

Archetypes

In William Douglas's biography of Carl Gustav Jung who coined the word archetype observed that Jung was in a class of his own where most psychologists could not understand his arguments. For example, the principle of synchronicity, and perhaps even more in his central concept of the archetypes of the collective unconscious, Jung still not 'make sense' to most American psychologists. He is disturbing, therefore valuable, precisely because he does force scholars to reexamine their most cherished presuppositions. Douglas asserted that Jung's analytic practice and scholarly studies of symbolic productions, has brought forth data which do into the currently available categories of psychological theory and psychiatric practice. In archetypes Jung meant first of its kind. It is a technique that has been adapted not only in psychology or behavioral studies but in business accounting practices.

In Brown (2013), archetypes are highly developed elements of the collective unconscious. Being unconscious, the existence of archetypes can only be deduced indirectly by examining behavior, images, art, myths, religions, or dreams. Carl Jung understood archetypes as universal, archaic patterns and images that derive from the collective unconscious and are the psychic counterpart of instinct. Brown (2013) suggested that archetypes are inherited potentials which are actualized when they enter consciousness as images or manifest in behavior on interaction with the outside world. Holt & Cameron (2012) contended that archetypes were autonomous and hidden forms which can be transformed once they enter consciousness and are given particular expression by individuals and their cultures. They content themselves with understanding culture as mere ideology - as ideas that are shared resulting in system-wide motivation. Archetypes are part of culture and physical objects possessed by the organization. They influence organizational behavior. Holt & Cameron's model illustrates how archetypes can be rituals in organization. For example, in conducting financial audits reports have formats or archetypes and any deviation from the standard of presentation raises alarm and further investigation.

An archetype is a computable expression of a domain content model in the form of structured constraint statements, based on some reference model. Holt & Cameron allude to the fact that some business documents such as contracts, bills of laden, or invoices, contain universal knowledge such as the names parties in an agreement, date when the agreement could have been made, and the consideration leading to a binding contract. An invoice contains universal knowledge too about the supply of goods or services between two parties. In Golden (2016), the term archetype is deployed to represent fundamental human motifs of experiences. Archetypes represent fundamental human motifs of our experience as we evolved; consequentially, they evoke deep emotions and impact the way the job is done, and how customers are served, among many other outcomes associated with productivity. The archetype means original or old and typos, which imply pattern, model or type. The combined meaning is an original pattern, of which all other similar persons, objects, or concepts are derived, copied, modeled, or emulated (Golden, 2016). The psychologist, Carl Gustav Jung, used the concept of archetype in his theory of the human psyche. He believed that universal, mythic characters—archetypes—reside within the collective unconscious of many people around the world (Senge & Kleiner et al, 1994).

In Senge et al (1994), tools and methods referred to as stock-and-flow modeling are also archetypes valuable in limiting knowledge leakage in large-scale human systems. An archetype is a protocol model of a desirable construct. For example, a protocol for receiving dignitaries at one's function includes a greeting method such as "We welcome your excellency to our fundraising event" and this can be followed by escorting the visitors to their seats and so forth. An archetype can also include an acceptable way to behave. In organizations the acceptable way to behave is derived from a shared construct of the mission. Any behavior outside what has been envisioned as desirable is not acceptable. For example, leaking information to third parties can also be treated as both criminal and civil infraction of proprietary information. The loss of this information can lead to the demise of a business.

Explicit Knowledge

Brown Collins & Duguid (1989), proposed that situated cognition was a concept in which separating knowledge from skills was a difficult thing to do. The two are inseparable because knowledge is situated in an activity bound to social, cultural and physical contexts. In this notion Brown Collins & Duguid argued that a model of knowledge and learning required thinking on the spot to solve problems and use resources effectively rather than a model that waited for the retrieval of conceptual knowledge. In much later research Hung, Looi, & Koh (2004), suggested that the situated cognition learning approach could be applied situated learning in a dualistic orientation. Hung et al propounded that authenticity and problem-based learning were anchored in instruction or situated learning. These fundamental ideas are in practice in most organizations who focus assignments to projects or positions based on what needs to be done in those jobs and the capability of those selected for jobs.

Boland & Tenkasi (1995) suggested that a knowledge community (KC) could create and distribute the practices useful in effective business organization. Explicit knowledge is expressed and recorded as words, numbers, or codes in organizations. It is written in job specifications, product formulations and when applied can lead to the products and services demanded by customers. Explicit knowledge is easy to communicate, store, and distribute and is the knowledge found in work orders, on assertions made on web by businesses or corporations. Explicit knowledge can be presented visually in logos or orally in adverts on television or radio. Taking the concept of the KC further into effective workforce communications Fisher & Bennion (2005) propounded that the KC is an old idea on collaboration which has been given rebirth by many scholars including Mupepi Tenkasi Sorensen & Mupepi (2013) and Mupepi (2017), among many others. Working beneath the common umbrella of an overarching organizational structure and mission, technical communicators represent many distinct skill groups. To be successful practitioners in each skill area must demonstrate the unique value they add to the overall mission and at the same time find ways to further develop and hone their specialized skills. Fisher & Bennion argued that structures could place professionals with similar skills to diffuse innovation throughout the rest of the enterprise.

Explicit Practices

Carter (2013) propounded that a systems theory could be deployed to understand how groups could create explicit practices. Several key principles from systems thinking perspectives inform groups how they can position themselves as the interveners of a company. Groups make meaning of what they see and what actions they take. Carter suggested that the principle of embeddedness stated that every part was a whole and every whole was a part. Thus, in systems thinking any aspect to be analyzed is more fully understood when viewed within the context of its larger system and fully explained within its role in that larger system. Mupepi (2017) argued that the collective experience of a KC made it possible for them to understand the functioning of the different units or departments as parts of a whole system. This perception is enhanced by the experience and qualifications possessed by a KC. They are in a position craft practices difficult for similar businesses to mimic. Explicit practices define professions or the core business of a company. A practice can be described as an organization requiring mastery of a complex set of knowledge and skills through formal education and/or practical experience. Explicit practices can be understood as proprietary information which can be stored in software or work specifications. The practices can be protected legally by patents. Formalized and patented practices constitute proprietary information. Fisher & Bennion proposed that the simplest technique to implement the KC concept was to support skill-based works councils across the departments. In Boland & Tenkasi (1995), the KC is viewed as an opportunity to create different perspectives about the business in the development of explicit practices. Perspective making and perspectives taking were imperatives in the design of the ever-changing needs in organization. Boland & Tenkasi argue that know is incomplete and that there is no universal knowledge. It implies that the creation of explicit practices requires to draw perspectives of what is happening in the environment in which the company is doing business.

The Importance of the Zebra's Hoofs and Stripes

Sometimes a company may need to take additional steps to protect a brand or its raison d'être. For example, we see Adidas successfully protecting the exclusivity of its logo by suing Payless Shoes to prevent it from selling shoes with stripes that may seem similar to those of the Adidas shoes (Daly, 2010). Tomorrow, we may find a horse suing a zebra for having similar hoofs.

Patents Protect Intellectual Assets

Companies can protect intellectual property that may differentiate them from their competitors by patenting any significant innovations. Patenting prevents competitors from using similar technology. Amazon was granted a patent for 1-click technology (or one-click buying) that allows customers to make an online purchase in a single click, using a previously stored billing address and payment info. Barnes & Noble offered a checkout option called "Express Lane," which also enabled shoppers to make an online purchase with one click. Amazon sued Barnes & Noble successfully and forced them to stop using technology that seemed similar to one that Amazon had patented just a few weeks earlier (Reilly, 1997).

Patents can be Gold Mines: Google Purchase of Motorola

Google purchased Motorola for $12.5 billion and sold it to Lenovo at loss of $2.8 billion. Rarely does a company offload a $12.5 billion purchase for less than $3 billion and call the deal "a success," but that's exactly what Google's head of mergers and acquisitions Don Harrison called the Motorola deal. In an interview with Forbes, Harrison did the math on the deal and said that in the end, Google came out on top. Jain (2014) took a closer look and examined the deal to understand Google's claim of success. What Google received from Motorola was a treasure trove of Motorola's patents that it retained after selling the company to Lenovo. Jain lists 5 points why Google was thinking in terms of acquiring the elephant in order to get to the ivory. The first was that Google's mobile strategy was to get their Android operating system onto as many phones as possible, as almost all of the company's revenue came from advertising, including on mobile devices. This was very different from Apple, BlackBerry, and Microsoft, which are all now integrated hardware-software businesses. The second point was related to patents. Google wanted Motorola for the patents, not for the manufacturing. Apple's patent attack on Android licensees was slowing down and worrying Google's customers. Motorola had a massive patent library that can be used defensively. The third reason was that once Google bought Motorola, some of its major licensees started hedging their bets by developing or buying their own non-Google operating systems: Samsung with Tizen and LG with WebOS, for instance. They were worried Google would compete directly with them. Lastly, by reselling Motorola, Google could be seen by other phone companies as a reliable provider of operating systems, and make money doing so.

Outsourcing

The activities of purchasing goods and services from external sources, as opposed to internal sourcing either by internal production or by purchasing from subsidiaries of the business, is referred to as outsourcing (see Figure 1).

Figure 1. Outsourcing

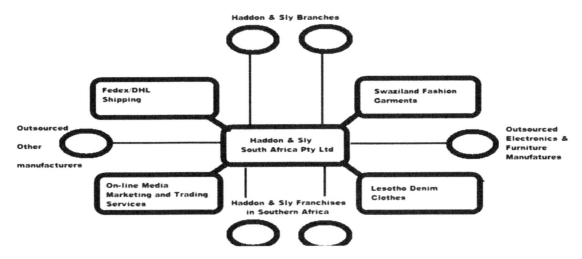

The idea of core competences is one of the most important business strategy currently shaping high performance in successful organizations. It is the key idea behind outsourcing, as businesses concentrate their efforts on things they do well and outsource as much as they can of everything else. In Chang (2007), outsourcing tends to be used in connection with a purchasing decision to change from an internal source to an external source.

Using Haddon & Sly of South Africa (see figure 1), and some other international trading corporations such as Aldi (Germany), Debenhams or Mark & Spencer (British), Carrefour (French) Walmart (USA) and Kiko Espana (Spain), as examples, we see that outsourcing part of manufacturing and distribution operations could be cost-effective to an organization. By purchasing certain activities as contracts for the provision of specific services such as producing goods according to provided specifications and delivery of finished goods or raw materials according to specifications on delivery notes, the companies can realize remarkable savings in operational costs. The advantages of outsourcing can include cost reduction, access to specialist expertise and greater concentration on an organization's core competence by avoiding peripheral operations. Chang (2007) suggests that the potential disadvantage of outsourcing can include reduced control over operations involved and so less flexibility in responding to unexpected developments.

Outsourcing could have had its beginnings in Europe during the rise of trade unionism. The unions raised wages which are part of prime costs and the action leads to a reduction in the marginal productivity and managers could not determine the short-run optimal level of employment of capital and labor in the production process. They were left with no other choice but to outsource to places such as India, Bangladesh, or Swaziland in South Africa, where there were/are viable operations due to workforce flexibility, low rent and wages and potential greater returns on investment (see figure 1). Essentially economies of scale exist when increasing all inputs in production causes output to rise by more than the percentage change in inputs. These advantages existed in India and Swaziland, among many other fast developing economies. The European and North American unions sustained a work-to-rule philosophy that brought governments to a halt in Britain and other states (Webb & Webb, 2005).

Raison D'être

The reason why a company exists can be referred to as the raison d'être in the French Language. In most organizations it is reflected, if not mentioned directly, in mission statements. The raison d'être as part of the organizational vision is used to communicate the purpose and goals of the organization in many written and visual formats such as mission statements or logos. Organizations are evolving entities and as such they must change and adapt to changing cultural conditions. When this happens the raison d'être and the mission statements will also need to be modified to reflect changing cultural conditions.

Limitations of the Arguments Presented

The concept of core competences is an honorable proposition that can be put into practice as a short term measure. Continuous learning and improvement should be an on-going exercise in organization, they say there is no rest for the weary.

There is truism in the argument that there is no substitute for experience. Yet it is difficult to impart experience to others. At best the technology can be transferred by showing the novice how the job is done and in most circumstances the learner can acquire the bad habits of the trainer too such as taking breaks to have a cigarette or a cup of tea.

Protecting the core competences is very difficult especially when employers compete for the same sources of expert labor such as conurbations or agglomerations. Human beings are gregarious animals protecting who they are at the same time learning to understand their enemies and differentiate themselves. The Zebra uses his stripes to create a mirage in flight to confuse the predators. In these environments learning and sharing experiences continues when the experts and novice meet in social clubs. What can be a secret at Ford Company can soon be known across the road at General Motors. Unified communications can limit access to proprietary information. In all outsourcing agreements there are caveats. With proper monitoring knowledge leakage aspects of outsourcing agreements can become less risky and more productive.

MAIN FOCUS OF THE CHAPTER

The focus of this discussion is on creating, diffusing, and distributing and protecting the core competences required in effective organization. Talent is also viewed as competency and the special ability to produce goods valued more by customers with ease. Core competence is also perceived as the talent necessary to sustain the enterprise and requires periodic updates and continuous learning and improvement to make differentiation possible. Talent and explicit practices are part of proprietary information which requires protection.

Issues and Controversies

The effectiveness of a knowledge community (KC) depends with how the business is structured and controlled. Pluralism in organization is acquiescent to democracy in organization and when a KC can be empowered to construct explicit practices. When there is no authority accorded to the forum, the owners of the business call all the shots. Building capacity to enable technology transfer can be problematic when proprietary information can be misappropriated causing a decline in the core competences of the enterprise. Knowledge leakage is a huge problem in knowledge-intensive organization. The expanded role of consultants in developing information systems pose risk in the leakage of explicit knowledge. The role of the consultant expands from merely programing information to that of editors of whole IT strategy. Technology transfer in outsourcing contracts is another source of knowledge leakage.

SOLUTIONS AND RECOMMENDATIONS

Suggestions and Recommendations

In the model in Figure 2, technology skills experience and *continuous* learning and improvement constitute the dynamic parts of the *core competences* enabling to the practices to become a habit. These parts will tend to gravitate towards the center as the marginal benefits equal costs resulting in an efficient and effective enterprise. Technology as part of the dynamic parts is constantly evolving and there is a need to collaborate constantly and make improvements. Technology also refers to the body of skills and knowledge involved in use of resources in value creation. Arnold (2014) argued that an advance in technology commonly increased the ability to produce more output with a fixed quantity of resources or the ability to produce same output with smaller quantity of resources. In Defeo & Juran (2016), continuous learning and improvement is argued to be the *modus operandi* in maintaining the edge. It is

Figure 2. Core Competencies (Mupepi, 2017)

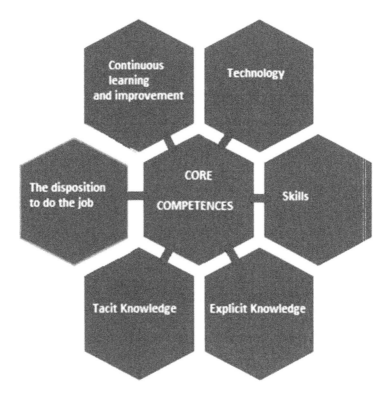

the route to creating organizational excellence. Mupepi Tenkasi Sorensen & Mupepi (2013) argued that sustainability in organization could be enhanced deploying a socially constructed competency model (SCCM). The model is based on the premise that collective intentionality expressed through one voice of the knowledge community (KC) enabled the co-construction of organizational reality. The SCCM makes it possible to collectively identify explicit knowledge, skills, and the technology necessary to sustain the core competence (see Figure 2).

Prahalad & Hamel (1990) suggested that there three requirements in the development of core competences and these were: to provide potential access to a wide variety of markets, make a significant contribution to the perceived customer benefits of the end product and that they should be difficult to mimic. Prahalad & Hamel argue that core competences are some of the most important sources of uniqueness: these are the things that a company can do uniquely well, and that no-one else can copy quickly enough to affect competition. They used examples of slow-growing and now-forgotten mega corporations that failed to recognize and capitalize on their strengths. They compared them with star performers of the 1980s (such as GEC or Honda), which had a very clear idea of what they were good at, and which grew very fast. Because these companies were focused on their core competences, and continually worked to build and reinforce them, their products were more advanced than those of their competitors, and customers were prepared to pay more for them. And as they switched effort away from areas where they were weak, and further focused on areas of strength, their products built up more and more of a market lead.

Continuous Learning

Core competencies are developed through the process of continuous improvements over the period of time rather than a single large change (see Figure 2). In Senge & Kleiner et al (1994) personal mastery is drawn from an individuals' ability to learn and improve continuously to perfect performance. The collective experience of people in the organization can make a difference. Experience is the knowledge or mastery of an event or subject gained through involvement in or exposure to it (Senge, 1990). Terms in philosophy, such as *empirical knowledge* or *a posteriori knowledge* are used to refer to knowledge based on experience (Audi, 2015). A person with considerable experience in a specific field can gain a reputation as an expert. The concept of experience generally refers to know-how or procedural knowledge, rather than propositional knowledge: on-the-job training rather than book-learning.

Confidential Information

Documents containing confidential information should be marked as such. Access to computer information system should be by way of a series of login and password controls. Authorization to access proprietary information must be done by top management.

FUTURE RESEARCH DIRECTIONS

On-job training (OJT) is very useful in improving performance in organizations. The system has been around for a while. There does seem to be scant OJT literature particularly in know-intensive and hi-tech industries. Research could focus on how the OJT intervention can be applied to improve performance in technology-led industries.

CONCLUSION

Systems perspectives should be linked to the explicit practices of the organization. The effective distribution of technology and practices required in successful enterprise is a continuous learning and improvement process aimed at sustaining the core competences. Failure to do this can result in obsolete competences.

REFERENCES

American Psychology Association. (1997). Defining the Field Force at a given time by Kurt Lewin. In *Resolving Social Conflicts & Field Theory in Social Science*. Washington, D.C.: American Psychological Association.

Audi, R. (2015). *The Cambridge Dictionary of Philosophy* (3rd ed.). Cambridge, UK: Cambridge University Press. doi:10.1017/CBO9781139057509

Boland, R. J. Jr, & Tenkasi, R. V. (1995). Perspective Making and Perspective Taking in Communities of Knowing. *Organization Science*, *6*(4), 350–372. doi:10.1287/orsc.6.4.350

Brown, J. S., Collins, A., & Duguid, S. (1989). Situated cognition and the culture of learning. *Educational Researcher*, *18*(1), 32–42. doi:10.3102/0013189X018001032

Brown, R. S. (2013). Beyond the evolutionary paradigm in conscious movement. *Journal of Transpersonal Psychology*, *45*(2), 159–172.

Burnes, B., & Cooke, B. (2013, October). Kurt Lewin's field theory: A review and re-evaluation. *International Journal of Management Reviews*, *15*(4), 408–425. doi:10.1111/j.1468-2370.2012.00348

Carter, I. (2013). *Human Behavior in the Social Environment: A Social Systems Approach* (6th ed.). London, UK: Aldine Transactions.

Chang, H. (2007). *Cultural Communities in a Global Labor Market: Immigration Restrictions as Residential Segregation*. Pittsburgh: University of Pennsylvania Law School.

Daly, E. M. (2010). Payless drops appeal of $305 million Adidas Trademark win. Retrieved from http://www.law360.com/articles/145508/payless-drops-appeal-of-305m-Adidas-trademark-win

Danko, N. (2015). Practopoiesis: Or how life fosters a mind. *Journal of Theoretical Biology, 373*, 40–61. doi:10.1016/j.jtbi.2015.03.003 PMID:25791287

Defeo, J. A., & Juran, J. M. (2016). *Juran's Quality Handbook: The Complete Guide to Performance Excellence* (7th ed.). New York: McGraw-Hill.

Douglas, W. (1961). Carl Gustav Jung: 1875-1961. *The American Journal of Psychology, 74*(4), 639–641. PMID:13887552

Golden, C. (2016). Introduction to Soul Craft. Retrieved from http://www.soulcraft.co/

Holt, D., & Cameron, D. (2012). *Cultural Strategy: Using Innovative Ideologies to Build Breakthrough Brands Reprint Edition*. Oxford, UK: Oxford University Press.

Hung, D., Looi, C.-K., & Koh, T.-S. (2004). Situated Cognition and Communities of Practice: First-Person "Lived Experiences" vs. Third-Person Perspectives. *Journal of Educational Technology & Society, 7*(4), 193–200.

Jain, A. (2014). Why did Google buy Motorola for $12.5 billion and sell it off for $2.91 billion? *Quora.* Retrieved from https://www.quora.com/Why-did-Google-buy-Motorola-for-12-5-billion-and-sell-it-off-for-2-91-billion

Lewin, K. (1943). 1997). Defining the Field at a Given Time. *Psychological Review, 50*(3), 292–310. doi:10.1037/h0062738

Menon, A., Bharadwaj, S. G., Adidam, P. T., & Edison, S. W. (1999). Antecedents and Consequences of Marketing Strategy Making: A Model and a Test. Retrieved from https://archive.ama.org/archive/ResourceLibrary/JournalofMarketing/Pages/1999/63/2/1830349.aspx

Menon, A., Bhardwaj, S. G., Adidam, P. T., & Edison, S. W. (1999, April). Antecedents and Consequences of Marketing Strategy Making: A Model and a Test. *Journal of Marketing, 63*(2), 18–40. doi:10.2307/1251943

Mupepi, M., Tenkasi, R. V., Sorensen, P. F., & Mupepi, S. (2013). Creating High Impact Organizations: Adapting OD Methods and Practices. In J. Vogelsang & M. Townsend et al. (Eds.), *Handbook For Strategic HR Best Practices in Organization Development from OD Network*. New York: Amacom.

Mupepi, M. G. (2017). Using Communities of Practice to Identify Competencies. In K. Rasmussen, P. Northrup, & R. Colson (Eds.), *Handbook of Research on Competency-Based Education in University Settings* (pp. 157–167). Hershey, PA, USA: IGI Global. doi:10.4018/978-1-5225-0932-5.ch008

Prahalad, C. K., & Hamel, G. (1990). The core competence of the corporation. Harvard Business Review, 68(3), 79–91.

Reilly, P. (1997, May 13). Barnes & Noble sues Amazon over rival's book selling claims. *Wall Street Journal.*

Reisinger, D. (2015). Apple, Samsung to remain bedfellows for next iPhone – report. *CNET.* Retrieved from http://www.cnet.com/news/apple-samsung-still-bedfellows-as-they-eye-next-iphone-report-says/

Senge, P., Kleiner, A., Roberts, C., Ross, R. B., & Smith, B. (1994). *The Fifth Discipline Field book: Strategies and Tools for Building a Learning Organization*. New York: Doubleday.

von Bertalanffy, L. (1968) General System Theory: Foundations, Development, Applications. New York: George Braziller.

Webb, S., & Webb, B. (2005). D. Martin (Ed.), The Webbs on Industrial Democracy. London, UK: Palgrave Macmillan.

Zook, C. (2001). *Profit from the Core: Growth Strategy in an Era of Turbulence*. Boston: Harvard Business School Press.

Zook, C., & Allen, J. (2016). *The Founder's Mentality: How to Overcome the Predictable Crises of Growth*. Boston: Harvard Business School Press.

KEY TERMS AND DEFINITIONS

Capability: The extent of the firms' ability and strength to produce goods and services distinguishing an enterprise from its competitors.

Competitive Advantage: The ability of one firm to outperform other organizations because it produces desired goods or services more efficiently and effectively than they do.

Core Competences: A defining capability or advantage that distinguishes an enterprise from its competitors.

Effectiveness: A measure of appropriateness of goals an organization is pursuing and the degree to which the organization achieves those goals.

Knowledge Creation Diffusion and Distribution: The process of designing and implementation of techniques and practices useful in the organization.

Patents: Protection for inventors allowing exclusive control of the invention.

Performance Repertoire: In organizations a performance repertoire is the application of skills, technology, explicit knowledge combined with the disposition to effectively do a job leading to increased productivity.

Sustainability: Sustainability is the property of organizations to remain viable and productive indefinitely. it is the endurance of organizations and their methods of producing goods and services to meet demand.

Tacit Knowledge: A unique knowledge that is difficult to transfer to another person by means of writing it down or verbalizing it.

Section 3
Managing Talent in Global Environments

Chapter 14
Engaging the Diversified Workforce Sustaining Productivity

Mambo Mupepi
Seidman College, USA

Yolanda M. Ross-Davis
Seidman College, USA

Jaideep Motwani
Seidman College, USA

Monica Allen
Seidman College, USA

ABSTRACT

The argument presented in this article is that highly productive workplaces can be inclusive, and purpose-fully built to produce the goods and services demanded by customers. A socio-technical system approach can be inclusive in terms of talent and technology and is subject to deconstruction. The characterization of diversity can be made in at least two ways: based on the attributes possessed by the employees; and racial composition of the workforce. A co-constructed competency model can be applied to understand the nature and description of prevailing cultural conditions to effectively engage people to be more productive. An inclusive circle of deeply involved people can design and support the necessary change and generate the synergy, techniques, and the heuristics, to increase productivity.

INTRODUCTION

This paper answers the following questions in four objectives: Is it possible to increase productivity in diversified workplaces? How can a sociotechnical system engage people to be more productive? The first objective offers an introduction to the discussion which will be followed by a definition of some of the key terms. The second objective reviews prudently selected literature about productivity in diverse work environments. This review enables the deduction of the notion that the collective performance espoused in focus groups generate the synergy to impact productivity. The third objective examines the application of positive psychology in advancing organizational efficiency and effectiveness. The last part proposes a sociotechnical systems (STS) model to increase productivity in diversified organizations.

DOI: 10.4018/978-1-5225-1961-4.ch014

Increasing Diversity

In Bell (2014), White men and women are the majority of the population followed by Latinos, Blacks, and Asians. The current population is more diverse than it was last century and the White workforce remain the dominant group. The workforce is aging and younger workers are more diverse in race and ethnicity than in the past (see Table 1). Recession-related economic changes have prevented many aging workers from retiring, resulting in even more age diversity in organization than in the past. The trend on higher education is rising among women compared to men. Bell argued that demographic changes impacted individuals, employers, and organizational diversity. Proposing the application of the sociotechnical system technology to progress diversified employers makes organizational sense.

Butner, Lowe, & Billings-Harris (2010) concur with Bell (2014) that the American workforce is increasingly becoming diverse. This implies many things including the fact that minorities and women will need to access the job market in terms of the equal employment opportunities regulations. It also implies that employers will be looking more for talented individuals to add value to their companies. Diversity and representation politically integrate a diverse nation with a measure of legitimacy. Butner et al assert that the impact of diversity on organizational outcomes such as organizational performance employee satisfaction and turnover has become essential. Numerous studies including Sungloo & Rainey (2010) and Butner et al (2010) suggest that employee perceptions and feelings impact productivity. Sungloo & Rainey indicated that employee job satisfaction was reflected on how customers were served and how the job was done. A satisfied employee performed above average and those who are dissatisfied in their jobs were inattentive to the details of the task at hand. Butner et al propounded that employee turnover was costly. The costs associated with lost business could be added to the costs of absence, turnover, and discrimination lawsuits that are commonly associated with mismanagement of diversity.

Table 1. Highlights from the US 2000 and 2008 Census Demographic Profiles

General Characteristics	2000 Percent 2008	Percentage
Total population	281 421 906 100 304 059 728	100
Male	138 053 563 49.1 149 863 485	49.3
Female	143 368 343 50.9 154 196 243	50.9
Median age	35.3 36.9	
One Race	274 595 678 97.6 297 045 856	97.7
White	211 460 626 75.1 228 182 410	75.0
Black	34 658 190 12.3 37 586 050	12.4
American Indian & Alaska Natives	2 475 956 0.9 2 443 422	0.8
Asian	10 242 998 3.6 13 413 976	4.4
Native Hawaiian & others Pacific	398 835 0.1 427 810	0.1
Economics characteristics		
Participating in labor force (16 years or over)	138 820 935 63.9 157 465 113	65.9
Median earnings male fulltime	n/a $45 556	
Median earnings female fulltime	n/a $35 471	

A Sociotechnical system (STS can be employed to configure people and technology in the value creation system (see Figure 1). In Bell (2014) people of color left jobs because of frustration. For example, studies in Bell (2014) assert that those who took part in the survey indicated that they were denied promotions, pay increase, and opportunity to make economic progress because of racism. Stereotypes and glass ceiling barriers prohibited individuals to self-actualize. Bell argued that talent was unevenly distributed in any given community. If employers were looking for a particular talent, there was a need to search all possible avenues including among people of color. In Mupepi & Taruvinga (2014), the ownership of the company or business is very important. It can determine the composition of ethnicity or race in employment. For example, a family owned business is likely to hire family members first followed by those they feel comfortable to work with. These could be members from the same Church or ethnic group. The STS model enables management to accurately chart organizational efficiency and effectiveness (see Figure 1). Giddens (1984) posited that the first step managers can take is to structure the enterprise to secure inputs which can be transformed into outputs and provide direct support in the value creation process (see Figure 2). The second proposition Giddens provides is to secure the right talent to supervise the workforce, allocate resources, and structure planning, and control systems. One of the challenges management have is conflict resolution and appreciate multicultural differences managing a diverse workforce. The hiring manager will be able to compare experiences, skills, explicit knowledge, technology and the disposition to effectively do the job as the attributes necessary in progressing organizational goals (see Figure 2). In Triana, Garcia & Colella (2010), it is suggested that when employees perceive their employer to be inclusive, they work extra hard in anticipation to be promoted on merit. On the other hand, Triana et al propound that when employees feel that their employer is insincere dissatisfaction lowered commitment and distrust can result.

Meaning Making

There are two contrasting definitions that are critical to appreciate what can be socially constructed in a socio-technical system. The first is the term: organizational structure. This implies structures of mutual

Figure1. A STS Model can be applied to recruit and retain talent (Mupepi, 2017)

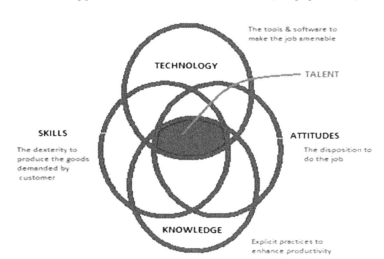

expectations, attached to roles that define each of its members shall expect from others and from the self. The structures are referred to as sociotechnical systems (STS) implying that technology is applied within the structures to make ends meet (see Figure 1). The second definition is that of social construction. In Mupepi (2017), social constructionism is viewed as instrumental in remodeling grounded theory. In attempting to make sense of the social world, social constructionists view knowledge as constructed as opposed to created. Thus effective socio-technical systems are a collaboration of people working together using similar tools to create goods and services demanded by customers. In this process the architects envisage a world and as such, it is unconcerned with ontological issues. Mupepi (2017 argued that the STS can be viewed as existing both as a subjective and an objective reality. Meaning is shared, thereby constituting a taken-for-granted reality.

Diversity in STS is viewed as multicultural as in any society. However, in organizations diversity is imminent because talent is unevenly distributed in society. Certain skills are common among a race. For example, during the early days of the settlers in 1800s the Irish were notable masons, bricklayers and so forth. Latin American cuisine competency is common among the Hispanic community and so is Indian or Japanese foods among the Asians. The African Americans tend to excel in sports such as basketball or football. Among the White community entrepreneurship is a historical competency developed by the settlers and has been passed on from one generation to another. However, there is a need to have the capacity to operate in global economy regardless of the structure and ownership of the business. In this sense diversity is viewed as a construct or strategy to recruit and hire the people who can progress the mission regardless of their color, religion, ethnicity or historical origins but who possess the talent useful in the enterprise (see Figure 2).

Self-Importance

In Campbell & Campbell (2010), leaders who are arrogant, dishonest or self-centered are not doing their organizations any favor. Productivity in such organization is on a low ebb. Narcissism is a personality trait that exists across the population of individuals. That is some individuals have high levels of narcissism and some have low levels, with the average individual somewhere in the middle of the continuum. Campbell & Campbell suggested that narcissism is often measured with the narcissistic personality inventory (NPI). The NPI included items like: "I think I'm a special person" "If I ruled the world it would a much better place" "I like to look at myself in the mirror" and "I'm a born leader"

Workplace Narcissism

Narcissism has an influence throughout organizational context. Narcissism benefits other individuals while hurting others. Risk-taking narcissistic leaders are up to take big risks which can put an entire organization in jeopardy. An example is that of Senator John Edwards who put his entire campaign into ruin when his "love child" and affair leaked to the press (Edwards & Auchard, 2003). Another example is that of Tiger Woods after his numerous affairs were revealed (BBC, 2010). Leaders who perceived themselves as important people failed to learn from their mistakes and they often liked to blame others for their mistakes.

Workplace Discrimination

Discrimination on the grounds of race, color, and national origin, sex and gender, age, physical and mental disability, religion, and military recruitment are all illegal in the US in terms of the Civil Rights Act, 1964 and as amended in 1991. Still unrelated to the requirements of the position, only 9% of Chief Financial Officers (CFOs) are women while they are over 60% among accountants and auditors. According to a 2013 report, those who reach a high responsibility position are paid on average 16% lower than their male colleagues (Carmichael & Woods, 2010).

In the US Bureau of Labor Statistics (2005), women's participation in the workforce has steadily grown from 43% in 1970 to 60% in 2004 (see Table 2). Restrictions on women's access to and participation in the workforce include the wage gap, the glass ceiling, inequities most identified with industrialized nations with nominal equal opportunity laws; legal and cultural restrictions on access to education and jobs, inequities most identified with developing nations and unequal access to capital, variable but identified as a difficulty in both industrialized and developing nations. In the United States, women's median earnings were 83 percent of male full-time workers in 2014 (Elsbach et al, 2016). Women are prevented from achieving complete gender equality in the workplace because of the "ideal-worker norm," which "defines the committed worker as someone who works full-time and full force for forty years straight," a situation designed for the male sex (Kinnear, 2011). Women, in contrast, are still expected to fulfill the caretaker role and take time off for domestic needs such as pregnancy and ill family members, preventing them from conforming to the "ideal-worker norm." With the current norm in place, women are forced to juggle full-time jobs and family care at home (Cabrera, 2007).

More detailed statistics show large differences even within these regions (see Table 2). For example, 11% of employed women in East Asia are employed in agriculture, a number that rises to 55% in South Asia; 70% of women in Southern Africa are employed in the service sector, while in Eastern, Middle, and Western Africa this number is 26% (UN, 2010).

Cultural Differences

During the early 1980s cultural differences were the subject of sizable research efforts in an attempt to understand how managers could sympathize with multiple ethnic groups with contrasting cultures compared to their own. It is important to recognize that people from different cultures perceive experiences differently as a result of socialization, education, and their subcultural influence. In the workplace, work

Table 2. The World's Women (2010)

Sectoral Distribution of Employed Persons by Sector & Sex (2004-2007)						
Region	Agriculture		Industry		Service	
	Women	Men	Women	Men	Women	Men
Africa	43%	42%	11%	20%	46%	39%
Asia (Exc. China)	32%	26%	12%	25%	56%	49%
Latin America	7%	22%	13%	27%	80%	51%
Europe & other	6%	8%	15%	36%	79%	55%

(Adapted from United Nations, 2010)

205

styles, disability, and education are attributable to the cultural differences. Culture is defined in various ways and attached to numerous adjectives in an attempt to describe a specific group's behaviors, beliefs, ideas, values, and shared knowledge transmitted and reinforced by those affiliated. Mupepi & Taruvinga (2014) asserted that culture was the collective programming of the human mind that distinguishes the members of one human group from those of another. This classification determines that culture is the accumulation of values by a group of like-minded individuals. As times passes, these liked minded individuals will transfer their behaviors, beliefs, ideas etc., on to the new members of their culture. This is essentially how culture is built within a community more or so in a business organization.

In this debate organizational culture is viewed as the values and norms encircling the STS. In Mupepi, Tenkasi, Sorensen & Mupepi (2007), organizational culture is defined as a pattern of basic assumptions that a given group has invented, discovered, or developed in learning to cope with its problems of external adaptation and internal integration. The patterns work well enough to be considered valid, and therefore, are taught to new members as the correct way to perceive, think, and feel in relation to those problems. Understanding why the members of the organization operate the way that they do, and what external and internal elements affect the business, provides a greater insight for needs to be changed within the organization.

Employee's performance or development is often influenced by environmental factors that are both external and internal. Some external factors include, but are not limited to, economy, politics, climate, geography, technology, education attainment, employment status, and criminal history. Internal elements may be considered as financial stability, personal relationships, subcultural affiliation, health, security, and job role. Lewin (1951) suggests that if an organization cannot respond positively to its environment, the chances of succeeding in its endeavors would be lowered.

A subculture is a sub-set group that has beliefs and behaviors that are different from the main groups within a culture or society. If the Christian community is the larger group, then the Catholics are a subculture of the Christians. Note that often times, those who are of ethnic minority descent are associated with the terminology of subculture. However, ethnicity or Catholics, are not the only factors in membership to a subculture. Disabilities, gender, religion affiliation, sexual orientation, and several other factors can be accounted for as markers for admittance into a subculture.

Diversity in an organization refers to differences among members. There is nearly an endless variety of ways in which members are unlike each other. Some of the differences are visible, but others are invisible. Bell (2014) defined diversity as real or perceived differences among people in race, ethnicity, sex, age, physical and mental ability, sexual orientation, religion, work and family status, weight and appearance, and other identity-based attributes that affect their interactions and relationships. The diversity, if utilized correctly, can fortify the company's presence in the industry of operations, recruit and retain talented individuals in addition to positioning the company to surpass their desired goals.

Multiculturalism is about different ethnicities and is used to describe the ethnic makeup of an organization. This term can be used to describe Africans who come from different parts of the African continent or Latinos who originate from South America. Even though 'multiculturalism' can be applied to describe the example above, commonly it is used to identify that the organization has employees who are ethnically different than those who are a part of the dominant ethnicity. If it is used for that purpose, generally the term 'diversity' is used to describe what multiculturalism is.

BACKGROUND

What is the Nature and Description of Diversity in the USA?

Diversity can arise by describing people's color, religion, language, ethnicity, or skills. The STS can also be viewed as a structure that is pursuing multiple objectives through the coordinated activities and relations among members and objects.

The Punctuated Cultural Equilibrium

In Givel (2006), the punctuated cultural equilibrium is a method of understanding change in multifaceted organizations such those found in the US. For example, there was a cultural equilibrium when the Native Americans, bison and deer, among other animals, roamed the prairies. This equilibria was punctuated with the arrival of the European colonists. It was further fractured when the colonists introduced slavery and indentured workers. Givel asserted that the punctuated equilibrium theory was useful in appreciating diversity to effectively exploit talent in the labor markets. Shrewd enterprises understand demographics to postulate and design exploitable databases.

Charting the Modus Operandi

Force-field analysis is an influential development in social science. It provides a framework for looking at political, economic, societal and technological factors that impact organization to successfully chart the *modus operandi* in organization. The field force analysis exams these factors which must be understood with a relative degree of precision in strategic planning. Example society or communities can be understood in demographic distribution such the population of Whites, Blacks, Asians or Latinos in the USA, in a given period. This population can also be understood in terms of income levels, employment or unemployment rates. The same demographics can be appreciated according to the health or education needs. Mupepi (2017) asserts that the complete analysis pinpoints at the driving forces as well as those causing a drag or resistance to change. The principle was developed by Kurt Lewin in 1943 and is still in use in strategic management in successful organizations.

Companies compete on what they know and it is critical to effectively manage what gives the business the competitive advantage. Managing intellectual capital include workforce diversity and talent management. Managers constantly face the questions of how to utilize diversity as a positive driving force within the organization, and how to resolve potential conflicts it may bring. As the nature of work shifted from being done by sociotechnical teams deploying appropriate technologies, Mupepi (2017) argues that organizations must meet stakeholder expectations. Shrewd HR professionals have increased the use of STS in the design and implementation of democratic workplaces that are extremely useful in producing the products and services valued by customers.

Performance Management and Diversity

In a case study presented by Johnson (2013), a soap manufacture based in Chicagoland the management committed to employing a diverse workforce drawn from the Latino Americans, African Americans and White immigrants from Poland. The company had contemplated relocating to Mexico in pursuit of lower operational costs. Johnson argues that the success of the workforce was based on a co-shared American Dream. The company put together a mentoring team who were instrumental in building a highly coercive team. It also organized a work-based adult education program to teach English as a second language to the Polish and Mexicans. The management organized events to promote the acculturation of American society to the immigrants. The work ethic of the three groups enabled the company to be profitable once and decided to remain in its present location. Johnson was able to conduct a comprehensive competency development program which has been very successful.

A Systems Approach to Culture

Mupepi & Motwani (2015) suggested that an extensive body of literature was growing devoted to productivity in diversity environments. It makes sense to employ a Latino driver to perform the duties of the door-to-door salesman in a Latino suburban. The sales driver will be able to coup the market successfully because he or she will comprehend easily the Latino customs, values and language. Mupepi & Motwani posited that it was imperative for companies to deconstruct local knowledge to develop different propositions. For example, alliances or focus groups can be enacted to get to understand consumer behavior. In Moran & Moran (2014), there are different anthropological approaches to cultural analysis and many prefer to use a coordinated systems approach as an alternative to appreciating other cultures. A system in this sense refers to an ordered assemblage or combination of correlated parts that form a unitary whole. Moran & Moran view a workforce in terms of economic system, religious system, or educational system. The economic system enables organizations to understand how organizations produce and distribute its goods and services in some ways as an extension of the family. The religious system means how a community that subscribes to a religion provides meaning and motivation beyond the material aspects of life i.e. the spiritual side of culture. Diverse national cultures can be somewhat unified under a shared religious belief in Islam or Christianity. The educational system examines how young or new members of a society are provided with information, knowledge, skills and values may be formal and informal within any culture. How people learn and acquire skills varies with culture.

Surface and Deep Level Diversity

In Trinh (2016) the effects of surface-level diversity i.e. age, sex, and ethnicity and deep-level diversity which includes personality characteristics such as conscientiousness, openness to experience, extraversion, emotional stability, and agreeableness, in teams need to be understood to be able to utilize the intellectual capital available to the organization. Trinh argues that a mismatch on diversity research designs and organizational needs can lead to the underutilization of talent in diversified companies. Trinh drew analysis from team data from 55 teams of volunteers from Shanghai, and recommended that HR training and selection should take specific team contexts into account and increase attention on functions that support important team processes such as communication and mutual support among team members. These results did not produce anything significant in terms of American culture where interpersonal communications tantamount to efficiency and effectiveness in organization. But in China, Trinh's study found that the sharing of information among team members to reach a common understanding was at times hampered by state censorship of the internet that made electronic communications erratic.

Performance in STS Value System

In Pieterse, van Knippenberg & Dierendonck (2012), the research found that teams with diverse talents positively contributed to team performance due to their different points of view, expertise, and experience. Brown & Duguid (1991) found that workplace practices indicated that the ways people actually worked usually differed fundamentally from the ways organizations described that work in manuals, training programs, organizational charts, and job descriptions. They then related its conclusions to compatible investigations of learning and of innovation to argue that conventional descriptions of jobs mask not only indicate the ways people work, but also significant learning and innovation generated in the informal communities-of-practice in which they work. Brown & Duguid argued that communities of practice generated synergy and the explicit practice and the technology the organization needed in defined situations. The composition of a community of practice can be made of people who share the same passion regardless of their religious beliefs, color or race. Pieterse et al (2012) posited that the way a community of practice progressed the job was an approach to accentuate the *modus operandi* from the *opus operatum.* The difference recognized that the job changes over a period of time, there will then be a need to re-design and implement practices to accommodate the current situation *modus operandi.* The *opus operatum* examined the efficacies in the way the job was done. It provided a way of analyzing the cost effectiveness of technology and labor in the value chain system. The same techniques can be applied to understand a diverse labor force, its skillfulness and disposition to effectively do the job continue to shift due to the dynamics of a labor market and changing rules and regulations. For example, the LGBT community has human rights too.

Diversity is everywhere in the value chain system. There are teams and individuals working to produce what has been ordered by customers. In a hypothetical situation in Figure 1, Plant A received produce from the Cabbages & Kings Farms who use a mechanized harvesting system manned by teams (see Figure 2). The price of lettuce is probably $0.50 per pound. The job of the teams is to ensure that only quality produce is dispatched to Plant A. In Plant A the produce is refreshed, sorted, weighed, packed and dispatched. The value of the lettuce is indicated on the barcodes say $1.00 per pound before it is dispatched to Plant B. In Plant B the lettuce is packed into different plastic bags and customized plastic containers. The packed produce is barcoded again and priced according to the customer specifications and dispatched to Plant C for onward transportation to customers. Value is added onto the produce in each plant (see Figure 2). The talent useful in the plants varies from horticulturalists, packaging specialists and toolmakers (who make molds to produce plastic bags, cartons, or containers) and many others. In White (2016), only a fraction of the 18000 migrant farm laborers from Mexico who go to Canada work in the north. These migrant workers were only engaged in the harvest season and very few were retained to work in the greenhouses. White alluded to the fact that the work ethic of the Mexican farm workers enhanced the ability of farms to compete effectively. According to the NAFTA local farmers also competed with producers from Mexico. Thus, any opportunity to lower prime costs in American produce is more than welcome.

Knowledge Diffusion and Flocking

In Emery a knowledge community (KC) is a group described the reverse of an autonomous work group. It is a temporary organization of similar thinking people, from different units or locations, who meet occasionally for consultation. Such a meeting is referred to as a flocking session (Davis & Cherms, 1975).

Figure 2. Value creation in the supply chain

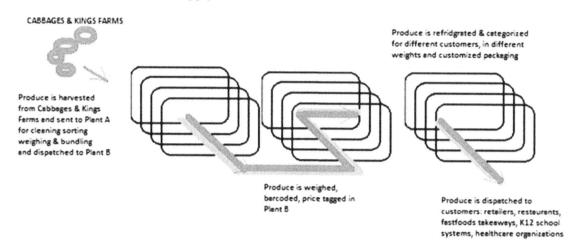

Flocking is a phenomenon that involves different people with common interests coming together for a few days to intensively confer with common interests.

Annual meetings can be viewed as flocking where the diffusion of new principles can start within the existing structure, and in a way flow from one level of a KC to the next. In annual meetings flocking or knowledge diffusion can be documented in the minutes or proceedings and is characterized by statements such as: It was resolved to…or a decision was arrived at to implement…The primary function of knowledge diffusion is learning. The process consists of stimulating one another in reaching a common defined objective (see Figure 3).

Figure 3. Knowledge community can emanate from the same unit

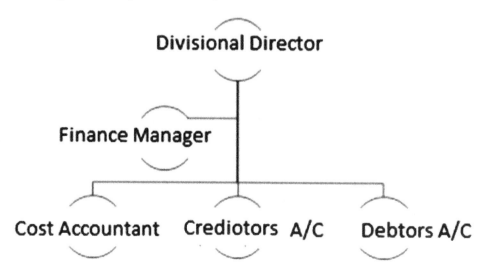

Sociotechnical Systems

In the field of organization development, a sociotechnical systems (STS) is an approach to complex organizational work design that recognizes the interaction between people and technology in workplaces. In Westlund (2006), Ludwig von Bertalanffy (1950) is credited with the concept of STS in technology studies. The STS perspective has made it possible to improve work processes and pinpoint the critical success points within the value making system. The STS adapts and redesigns the work contents and composition of technology and human task enabling the creation of new internal working relationships, determination of organizational needs and the implementation of effective on-job training programs. Bertalanffy proposed that organism such as the amoeba thrived in water and swampy environments where it recreated itself by breaking into two parts which were identical. These two parts also joined the recreation process until the pond or water was fully populated by the organism. The amoeba is invisible to the naked eye. However, its reproduction is very efficient and the organism has adapted successful in water or swampy environments. Mupepi & Mupepi (2014), human beings need to understand the environment in which they live to thrive. Organizations too, need to appreciative the competitive environment in which they operate. The competition must be understood in terms of prices, demand or supply. The company needs to know its competitors very closely. Lewin (1943) suggested a method of change referred to as the Unfreeze, Change, Freeze (or Refreeze). It is possible to take these stages to quite complicated levels and engage the entire organization. In Mupepi (2017), the Unfreeze theory has been extremely relevant in organization and is valid to this day. By identifying the system of behaviors and psychological processes occurring within a social group, Lewin developed group dynamics an assertion on how to develop and implement successful work groups.

Positive Scholarship

Positive psychology is a relatively new field of study that can be applied to advance organizational efficiency and effectiveness. In Seligman & Csikszentmihalyi (2000), positive psychology is concerned with three issues: positive emotions, positive individual traits, and positive institutions or organizations. Positive emotions are concerned with being content with one's past, being happy in the present and having hope for the future. Positive individual traits focus on one's strengths and virtues. Finally, positive organizations are based on strengths to better serve customers. Appreciative inquiry is a change management approach developed by David Cooperrider (1986) derived from positive scholarship. The six-dimension model can be applied to assess and evaluate the efficacies required in a successful organization (see Figure 4). The entire organization can participate to determine the change required to progress organizational goals. The Topic of choice is posed to the entire group to discover the talent that gives life to the business, and describe the nature and characteristics of diversity in the organization. The group will proceed to define the idle or dream stage. The group should produce the job specifications, product or services demanded by customers and continue to interpret their dreams or idle situation into practical designs. From the design the deliberations proceed to the implementation phase. Putting into practice the blue prints. These will be reviewed and evaluated to determine moving forward or back to the drawing board for modifications. If all is well the deliberations will proceed to the destination stage or goal achievement. The process can be repeated if the results are not satisfactory. Cooperrider (1986) argued that Appreciative Inquiry enabled to bring the best in people.

Figure 4. The Six-Dimension Assessment Technology. Adapted from Appreciative Inquiry (Mupepi & Mupepi, 2014)

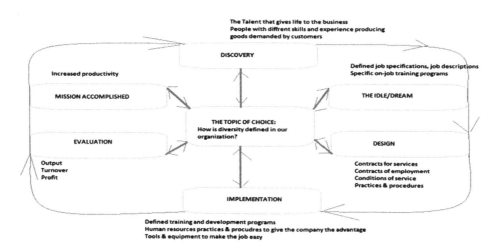

In Elsbach Kayes & Kayes (2016), diversity describes similarities and differences among people. In the context of organizations, diversity involves the processes of valuing difference, background, and perspective. Elsbach et al propound that there are different types of organizational diversity such as generational variety which focuses on differences among generations and the environmental forces that influence values beliefs and behaviors. There are others that focus on ethnicity or different races in a given community. A survey conducted by the Society for Human Resource Management and the on-line Wall Street Journal identified a list of organizational behavioral skills for success in contemporary enterprises (Salas, 2012). These skills included diversity learning and organizational culture, among many others.

People from Different Backgrounds

The term diversity is also used to recognize the fact that any other organization's workforce includes people from all walks of life and backgrounds. Diversity does not exist at individual level; differences among the people who comprise a team, department, or organization create diversity (Jackson, May & Whitney 1995). Different backgrounds can be similar to country of origin or members of the same religious denomination. It could imply differences in education and training and the disposition to do the job effectively. For example, in the hypothetical Cabbages & Kings Farms the Mexican workers tend to excel in the agro-industry because of their disposition to get the job done at competitive rates (White, 2016).

Talent in Different Types of Diversity

Gender diversity in increasingly apparent organizations throughout the world. There are more women participating in the workplace compared to ten or more years ago. Also gender-based occupational discrimination is declining compared to the last decade. Men and women are now seen working side by side in many occupations including the military or aviation. Many industrialized countries are experiencing population growth decline which push employers to hire both more youth and older employees.

Scholars such as Eijnatten (1998) and Wieck (1979) introduce the concept of democracy in the workplace. Eijnatten suggested that the participative democracy in the workplace was not about work to rule. But a strategy to leads to highly productive workplaces. Its basic mission is to increase the human conditions at the workplace while at the same time paying equal attention to the production goals. Wieck asserted that effective organizing encompassed taking into consideration of the talent available in the enterprise. Duties and responsibilities are allocated in proportionate to qualifications experience and the disposition to effectively do the job. In order to implement participative democracy Mupepi & Mupepi (2014) consider a set of workable human values serve as norms. The theoretical commodity of the STS is open-systems thinking with self-regulation as its characteristic feature. Mupepi & Mupepi assert that the use of the division of labor is substantially reduced in all sorts of work setting. There is a focus on the use of metaphor of the enterprise as an adaptive whole, giving rise to the concept of a sociotechnical system as a predominant frame of reference for description, analysis and design purposes. Participative democracy enables effective cohesion among a diverse workforce.

MAIN FOCUS OF THE CHAPTER

The aim of this chapter is to show that talent can be a product of diversity and that organizational effectiveness can be enhanced in multicultural firms. Organization development techniques and tools can be applied to advance a talented enterprise. The STS approach can be employed to bring out the best in people and for innovation to happen as antecedence to increase in productivity.

Issues

Discrimination and narcissism are illegal but companies can practice overt discrimination without being caught. Although the Whistleblowers are protected by a 2012 law, at times individuals can marked and are dismissed by and by. Women are still discriminated against especially in the corporate world. The majority of the top management in organizations are men. In almost all the states same sex marriages are now legal. However, the LGBT community is still experiencing issues regarding who they really want to be. The implementation of diversity in companies depend largely with its social responsibility plans. Some organizations are controlled and owned by families and that alone can be problematic to recruiting diverse people.

RECOMMENDATIONS

Creating a Vision for the Future

Widening the circle of involvement will make change happen very fast. The STS approach increases ownership of the organization and reducing the resistance to change. The STS offers a lens critical different perspectives in complex diverse societies. It is cost-effective and easy to understand and employ. Widening the network also increases innovation adaptation and learning.

Complex adaptive systems look at innovation from the perspective of variety. Axelrod & Cohen argue that unless diversity is introduced into a system innovation and adaption are unlikely. The division of labor is still in practice in many organizations. There is only one method to develop specialists and that is through the division of labor, or hiring talented individuals from elsewhere.

Diversity can be introduced into the system in a number of ways:

- Employees who come from different orientations produce innovation in the workshop design.
- The pulse-taking of the knowledge community (KC) provides the information necessary to make adjustment.
- The KC made up of both workshop leaders and participants continue the process of introducing diversity into the workshop design.
- Extensive usage of mixed groups and rotating memberships in the KC to introduce diversity.

CONCLUSION

Talent is unevenly distributed among men and women of all races and walks of life. Gender diversity is increasingly apparent with nearly all the states concurrence on sex marriages. The STS approach can be employed in the design of highly productive diverse organizations. Ethnic and cultural diversity are increasingly important to business. It is therefore important to include diversity in strategic planning.

REFERENCES

Aparna, J., & Roh, H. (2012). The role of context in work team diversity research: A meta-analytic review. Academy of Management Journal Vol. 52 No3 (599-6270.

Axelrod, R., & Cohen, D. (2001). *The Complexity of Cooperation: Agent-Based Models of Competition and Collaboration*. Princeton, NJ: Princeton University Press.

BBC. (2010). Tiger Woods makes emotional apology for infidelity. Retrieved from http://news.bbc.co.uk/sport2/hi/golf/8521060.stm

Bell, M. P. (2014). *Diversity in Organization (2nd ed.)*. Mason, Ohio: South-Western Learning.

Brown, J. S., & Duguid, P. (1991). Organizational learning and communities of practice: Toward a unified view of working learning and innovation. *Organization Science*, 2(1), 40–57. doi:10.1287/orsc.2.1.40

Buttner, H., Lowe, K. B., & Billings-Harris, L. (2010). The Impact of Diversity Promise Fulfillment on Professionals of Color Outcomes in the USA. *Journal of Business Ethics*, 91(4), 501–518. doi:10.1007/s10551-009-0096-y

Cabrera, E. F. (2007). Opting out and opting in: Understanding the complexities of womens career transitions. *Career Development International*, 12(3), 218–237. doi:10.1108/13620430710745872

Campbell, W.K., & Campbell, S.M. (2016). Narcissism and its role in organizations. In K.D.; Elsbach, D.A. Kayes, C. Kayes (Eds.), Contemporary Organizational Behavior: From Ideas to Action (pp. 53-59). New York: Pearson.

Carmichael, F., & Woods, R. (2010). Ethnic Penalties in Unemployment and Occupational Attainment: Evidence for Britain. *International Review of Applied Economics*, *14*(1), 91–98.

Carvalho, P. V. R. (2006). Ergonomic field studies in a nuclear power plant control room. *Progress in Nuclear Energy*, *48*(1), 51–69. doi:10.1016/j.pnucene.2005.04.001

Choi, S., & Rainey, H. G. (2010). Managing Diversity in U.S. Federal Agencies: Effects of Diversity and Diversity Management on Employee Perceptions of Organizational Performance. *Public Administration Review*, *70*(1), 109–121. doi:10.1111/j.1540-6210.2009.02115.x

Civil Rights Act. (1964). *The Civil Rights Act of 1964 (Public Law 88–352, 78 Statute 241, enacted July 2, 1964.* Washington DC: Congress of the United States

Cooperrider, D. L. (1986). *Appreciative Inquiry: Toward a methodology for understanding and enhancing organizational innovation* [Unpublished Ph.D.]. Cleveland: Case Western Reserve University.

Edwards, J., & Auchard, J. (2003). *Four Trials*. New York: Simon & Schuster.

Elsbach, K., Kayes, A.B.D., & Kayes, C. (2016). Contemporary Organizational Behavior: From Ideas to Action. New York: Pearson

Givel, M. (2006). Punctuated Equilibrium in Limbo: The Tobacco Lobby and U.S. State Policy Making From 1990 to 2003. *Policy Studies Journal: the Journal of the Policy Studies Organization*, *43*(3), 405–418. doi:10.1111/j.1541-0072.2006.00179.x

Jackson, S. E., May, K. E., & Whitney, K. (1995). Understanding the dynamics of diversity in decision-making teams. In R. A. Guzzo & E. Salas et al. (Eds.), *Team Effectiveness and Decision Making in Organizations* (pp. 204–261). San Francisco: Jossey-Bass.

Johnson, J. H. (2013). *Urban Geography: An introductory analysis* (2nd ed.). Ontario, Canada: Pergamon.

Kinnear, K. L. (2011). *Women in developing countries. A reference Book. Praeger*. NJ: Greenwood.

Lewin, K. (1943, May). Defining the Field at a Given Time. *Psychological Review*, *50*(3), 292–310. doi:10.1037/h0062738

Lewin, K. (1951). *Field theory in social science; selected theoretical papers. D. Cartwright*. New York: Harper & Row.

Lewin, M. (1992). The Impact of Kurt Lewins Life on the Place of Social Issues in his life. *The Journal of Social Issues*, *48*(2), 15–29. doi:10.1111/j.1540-4560.1992.tb00880.x

Mupepi, M. G. (2017). Using Communities of Practice to Identify Competencies. In K. Rasmussen, P. Northrup, & R. Colson (Eds.), *Handbook of Research on Competency-Based Education in University Settings* (pp. 157–167). Hershey, PA, USA: IGI Global. doi:10.4018/978-1-5225-0932-5.ch008

Mupepi, M. G., & Motwani, J. (2015). Deconstructing the Value Creation Process: Positioning Diversity to Increase Output. *International Journal of Sociotechnology and Knowledge Development, 7*(4), 15–30. doi:10.4018/IJSKD.2015100102

Mupepi, M. G., & Mupepi, S. C. (2014). Appreciating Rapid Technology Integration in Creating Value in Enterprises. *Journal of Electronic Commerce in Organizations, 12*(1), 53–75. doi:10.4018/jeco.2014010104

Mupepi, M. G., & Taruwinga, P. (2014). Cultural Differentials Modify Change: Comparativeness of the SADC and the US. *International Journal of Sustainable Economies Management, 3*(2), 50–79. doi:10.4018/ijsem.2014040105

Mupepi, S. C., Mupepi, M. G., Tenkasi, R. V., & Sorensen, P. F. Jr. (2007). Creating high impact organization in the SADC: Adapting OD Methods and Practices. *OD Practitioner, 32*(2), 34–39.

Pieterse, A. N., & van Knippenberg, D. (2012). Retrieved from http://leeds-faculty.colorado.edu/dahe7472/Pieterse%202012.pdf

Salas, E. (2012). So much Training, so little to show for it. Retrieved from http://www.wsj.com/articles/SB10001424052970204425904578072950518558328

Triana, M. C., Garcia, M. F., & Colella, A. (2010). Managing diversity: How organizational efforts to support diversity moderate the effects of perceived racial discrimination on affective commitment. *Personnel Psychology, 63*(4), 817–843. doi:10.1111/j.1744-6570.2010.01189.x

Trinh, M. P. (2016). Which Matters More?: Effects of Surface- and Deep-Level Diversity on Team Processes and Performance. In J. Prescott (Ed.), *Handbook of Research on Race, Gender, and the Fight for Equality* (pp. 213–239). Hershey, PA, USA: IGI Global. doi:10.4018/978-1-5225-0047-6.ch010

United Nations. (2010). The World's Women. Retrieved from unstats.un.org/unsd/demographic/products/Worldswomen/WW_full%20report_color.pdf

United States Bureau of Labor Statistics. (2005). Databases Tables and Calculators by Subject. Retrieved from http://data.bls.gov/timeseries/LNS14000000

von Bertalanffy, L. (1950). An outline of General Systems Theory. *The British Journal for the Philosophy of Science, 1*, 139–164.

von Eijnatten, F.M. (1993). *The Paradigm that changed the work place: Social science for social action: toward organizational renewal (Vol. 4)*. Stockholm: The Swedish Center for Working Life.

Westlund, H. (2006). *Social capital in the knowledge economy: Theory and Empirics*. New York: Springer.

White, E. (2016). Some northern Ontario farms bringing in migrant Mexican workers. Retrieved from http://www.cbc.ca/news/canada/sudbury/migrant-farm-workers-northern-ontario-1.3795537

Wieck, K. E. (1979). *The Social Psychology of Organizing*. New York: Random House.

KEY TERMS AND DEFINITIONS

Cultural Difference: Cultural diversity is the quality of diverse or different cultures, as opposed to monoculture, as in the global monoculture, or a homogenization of cultures, akin to cultural decay.

Deconstruction: Deconstruction is a management approach that exams text and meaning to develop different scenarios and perspectives.

Diversity: The term diversity is used to recognize the fact that any organization's workforce includes people from many different backgrounds.

Strategic-Fit: The strategic fit expresses the degree to which an organization is matching its resources and capabilities with the opportunities in the external environment.

Synergy: The interaction or cooperation of two or more organizations, substances, or other agents to produce a combined effect greater than the sum of their separate effects.

Talent Retention: A growing concern for businesses today is retaining skilled employees.

Chapter 15

Highly Productive 21st Century Workforce:
Tech-Savvy Women in-Charge

Sylvia Mupepi
Kirkhof College, USA

Mambo Mupepi
Seidman College, USA

Aslam Modak
Seidman College, USA

ABSTRACT

Some leadership behaviors are more frequently applied by women than men in the management of teams. These attributes have been proven successful in enhancing corporate performance and will be a key factor in meeting tomorrow's business challenges. Talent is unevenly distributed in diversified work environments and promoting women and gender leadership variety is of strategic importance in companies. Results from a recent study show an unprecedented amount of CEO turnover in 2015 and a growing tendency to look for new leadership outside the company. Nearly a quarter of the world companies replaced their CEOs during the same year and it is the highest turnover for the past two decades. Those new top executives were increasingly hired from elsewhere even during planned leadership changes. The data indicates that fewer women are the incoming list of top executives indicating that some of the old habits still linger in 21st century organizations. The organization development of effective capability deduces new viewpoints to advance the best talent for all time.

DOI: 10.4018/978-1-5225-1961-4.ch015

INTRODUCTION

This section examines the organization development intervention of diversity management and leadership and its role in effective talent management. Leadership and management are human resource techniques that attempt to transfer knowledge and skills to the entire organization. When diversity is taken into consideration it implies that the transference of knowledge practices, as well as, opportunities must be distributed equitably among employees. Leadership is critical in an organization for many reasons. For example, the leader is the captain who must provide a clear vision of where the organization is going and guidance must be inclusive of all employees. Management has a distinct role to play in the enterprise which is planning, organizing, leading and controlling, and coordinating activities in the value creation system. In Anderson & Hanson (2011) and Bell (2012), leadership can be defined as the process through which an individual guides and motivates a group towards the achievement of common goals. Research has examined whether or not there are sex differences in leadership. The differences can be seen from a relationship based or task based perspective. Anderson & Hanson (2011) have argued that until recently, leadership positions have predominantly been held by men who were often stereotyped to be more effective leaders. Women were rarely seen in senior leadership positions leading to a lack of data on how they behave in such positions. Current research has found a change in trend where women have become more prevalent in the workforce over the past two decades, especially in management and leadership positions, as more women enter leadership roles. Bell (2012) suggests that the gender gap is decreasing and these stereotypes are fading out as more organizations embrace equality. The objective of this chapter is to discuss diversity management in effective organizations. Secondary data is reviewed to illustrate that workplaces that embrace equal opportunities and the application of appropriate technology are highly productive.

BACKGROUND

Research conducted at Harvard Business School by Robert Sutton in 2007 indicates that women can effectively adapt in new environments with no additional costs to settling in. Men on the other hand needed to bring the team they worked with in the last job to be functional. Perhaps the reason for this is anthropological going back to the old-boy network and old shoes being more comfortable than new ones. In Giddens (1984), relationships in the structure are viewed as important in the execution of strategy. Cadres with a proven track record in related jobs tend to be hand-picked for newer assignments. In Mupepi (2014), the division of labor characterizes an enterprise manned by specialists and those with similar aspirations. The enterprise can make more wealth in this structure. However, handsome profits can be real when costs are contained. The former team could prove costly, all things being equal.

Women in High-Tech Enterprises

The mission of the General Motors Company indicates that the top position has been occupied by a lady engineer, Mary Barra since 2014. Mary Barra is Chairman and Chief Executive Officer of General Motors Company. Barra was elected Chairman of the GM Board of Directors on January 4, 2016, and has served as CEO of GM since January 15, 2014. This appointment was the first where a woman had been appointed to the top seat. It was deviation from the unexpected. Talent played a critical role in this selection. The Board unanimously elected Barra an electrical engineer by training and a daughter of one of the assembly line blue collar worker.

Under Barra's leadership, GM is focused on strengthening its core business of building great cars, trucks and crossovers, while also working to lead the transformation of personal mobility through advanced technologies such as connectivity, electrification, autonomous driving and car sharing. Barra has also established a strategic direction based on putting the customer at the center of everything the company does, all around the world (General Motor Company, 2016).

Women in the Race on Capitol Hill

The current GOP race is characterized by candidates who possess exceptional leadership talent. This competition has punctuated a cultural equilibrium in existence since the founding of the United States; no woman had reached the nomination of presidential candidate and Hilary Clinton has broken that record. Clinton is also the third woman to occupy the top government position of Secretary of State. In the corporate world, results from a recent study show an unprecedented amount of CEO turnover in 2015 and a growing tendency to look for new leadership outside the company. Seventeen percent of the world's 2500 companies replaced their CEOs during the same year and it is the highest turnover for the past two decades. Those new top executives were increasingly hired from elsewhere even during planned leadership changes. The data indicates that fewer than three percent incoming CEOs were women, indicating that some of the old habits still linger in 21st century organizations. The organization development of effective talent deduces new viewpoints from civil and corporate organizations to advance the best talent for all time.

Women Excel as Corporate Drivers

In McKinsey (2007), women leadership is viewed a corporate performance driver. McKinsey has been using a performance diagnostic tool that measures a company's organizational excellence against nine key criteria: leadership team, direction, work environment and values, accountability, coordination and control, capabilities, motivation, and external orientation. McKinsey suggested that using the tool his company established as a correlation between a company's level of excellence in these nine areas and its financial performance. On average the companies ranked most highly according to these organizational criteria tended to have operating margins twice as high as those of the lowest ranked (see Figure 1).

McKinsey (2007) argues that an additional correlation between the presence of a critical mass of at least three women in a corporation's management team and its organizational and financial performance. McKinsey then sought to establish whether women made a specific contribution to organizational performance that could explain such a positive correlation. Among the many levers of organizational performance (strategy, processes, systems, skills, and many others), McKinsey chose to focus on a lever which depended on individual practices: managers' leadership behaviors. The study identified nine key leadership behaviors that improve organizational performance (see Table 1):

Differences in the Frequency of Leadership Behavior

Women apply five of the nine leadership behaviors more frequently than men. They involved the team in decision making, people development expectations and rewards, role modeling and inspiration. On

Figure 1. A positive correlation exists between women team and effective organizational performance (McKinsey, 2007)

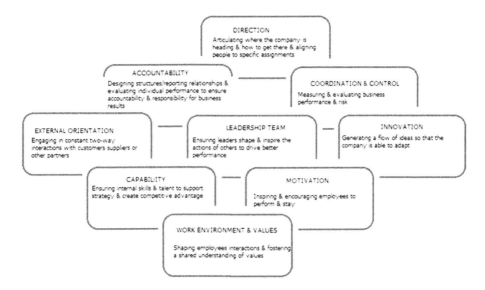

Table 1. Assessment tool (Adapted from Bass & Stogdill 1990)

LEADERSHIP BEHAVIORS	IMPROVE PERFORMANCE DIMENSION
1. Participative decision making…building a team atmosphere in which everyone is encouraging to participate in decision making 2. Role model…Being a role model, focusing on building respect and considering the ethical; consequences of decisions 3. Inspiration …Presenting a compelling vision of the future and inspiring optimism or hopefulness about its implementation 4. Expectations and rewards...Defining expectations & responsibilities clearly & rewarding achievement of target 5. People development…Spending time teaching, mentoring, and listening to individual needs and concerns 6. Intellectual stimulation…Challenging assumptions and encouraging risk taking & creativity 7. Efficient communication…communicating in a convincing way & with charisma 8. Individualistic decision making…Preferring to make decisions alone & engaging others in executing them 9. Control & corrective action…Monitoring individual performance including errors & gaps against objectives & taking corrective action when needed (Sanctions management)	1. Work environment & values 2. Building effective leadership team 3. Direction & motivation 4. Accountability 5. Leadership team capabilities work environment & values 6. Innovation 7. Direction 8. External orientation 9. Coordination

the other hand men adopted two behaviors; control and corrective action and individualistic decision making, more than women did. The latter behavior resonates with Hofstede (2001) cultural differences.

The Gender Scorecard

In Fagenson (1990), gender and leadership is a subject that is concerned with the following two main questions: What are the determinants of male/female differences in who assumes leadership positions and in leadership behavior? And, how is leadership a gendered concept?

Fagenson suggests that researchers distinguish between gender and sex as follows: sex refers to the basic, biologically given physiological differences between males and females whereas gender refers to a culture's social construction of differences between the sexes (see University of Michigan Student Life (2016) below). Fagenson argues that the variances include the different traits, roles, behaviors, attitudes, and aptitudes males and females are expected to display. Gender displays and reinforce claims of membership in a sex. Other scholars such as Fletcher (1994) propound that expressions such as gendered practices, gendered language and gendered jobs are used to emphasize the precept that gender involves a process of social construction, and to make gender a more central explanation of organizational behavior phenomena such as leadership.

Fletcher suggests that the term leaders refers to persons holding formal positions of leadership in complex organizations in industry, government, education, politics, the arts, sciences, and professions. Historically, gender precluded most females from becoming leaders in such organizations; as a result, the assumption that males were better suited than females for leadership roles was, until recently, rarely questioned. Since the early 1970s, the foundation of that assumption has been shaken by the large number of women who have (1) been elected prime minister, president, or highest office (in Britain, Canada, India, Germany, Malawi, Pakistan, the Philippines, Norway, Rwanda, Sri Lanka, and Zimbabwe, among many other countries) and to other high government offices; (2) been elevated to managerial positions in business organizations; and (3) earned professional qualifications in business management. In addition, the assumption those leaders are to be men have come under scrutiny by a growing body of scholarly writings on the subject of gender and leadership. In Llopis (2014), the argument progressed implies that it is impossible to respect, value, and admire great leadership if you can't identify what makes a leader great. Because of this, the identity crisis that exists in today's workplace is something that women leaders in particular have been facing for much too long. While the tide is changing and more women are being elevated into leadership roles, there is still much more work to do. Llopis (2014) asserts that as of July 2013, there were only 19 females elected presidents and prime ministers in power around the globe. In the business world, women currently hold only 4.6 percent of Fortune 500 CEO positions and the same percentage of Fortune 1000 CEO positions. As women continue their upward trajectory in the business world, they have yet to be fully appreciated for the unique qualities and abilities they bring to the workplace. Thus, gender does not impact the way a person does his or her job. It's the disposition to do the work, possessing the explicit knowledge and skills to produce the goods and services demanded by women.

The LGBT are Part of the Community

The members of the LGBT are part of any given organization or community. Some have come out to admit who they say they are. Talent is also unevenly distributed among the LGBT members of any workforce. The terms LGBT, LGBTQ, LGBTQA, or TBLG, are acronyms referring to Lesbian, Gay, Bisexual, Transgender, Queer or Questioning, and Asexual or Ally. Although all of the different identities within "LGBT" are often lumped together (and share sexism as a common root of oppression), there are specific needs and concerns related to each individual identity. Five elucidated examples are drawn from the University of Michigan Student Life Spectrum Center (2016):

1. **The Asexual:** Refers to a person who generally does not feel sexual attraction or desire to any group of people. Asexuality is not the same as celibacy or a person who voluntarily stays, unmarried.
2. **The Term Ally:** Typically, any non-LGBT person who supports and stands up for the rights of LGBT people, though LGBT people can be allies, such as a lesbian who is an ally to a transgender person.
3. **Gender Expression:** A term which refers to the ways in which we each manifest masculinity or femininity. It is usually an extension of our "gender identity," our innate sense of being male, female, etc. Each of us expresses a particular gender every day – by the way we style our hair, select our clothing, or even the way we stand. Our appearance, speech, behavior, movement, and other factors signal that we feel – and wish to be understood – as masculine or feminine, or as a man or a woman.
4. **Gender Identity:** The sense of "being" male, female, genderqueer, agender, etc. For some people, gender identity is in accord with physical anatomy. For transgender people, gender identity may differ from physical anatomy or expected social roles. It is important to note that gender identity, biological sex, and sexual orientation are separate and that you cannot assume how someone identifies in one category based on how they identify in another category.
5. **Genderqueer:** A term which refers to individuals or groups who "queer" or problematize the hegemonic notions of sex, gender and desire in a given society. Genderqueer people possess identities which fall outside of the widely accepted sexual binary (i.e. "men" and "women"). Genderqueer may also refer to people who identify as both transgendered and queer, i.e. individuals who challenge both gender and sexuality regimes and see gender identity and sexual orientation as overlapping and interconnected.

Times are Changing

The Secretary of State is a senior official of the Federal Government of the United States of America. For the sake of job evaluation the position is comparable to that of a minister of foreign affairs in other countries. However, in the United States the position is responsible for foreign affairs, inter alia, other duties as assigned by the President. Since the founding of the United States, only three women have been appointed to this position. Madeline Albright (1997-2001) broke the ice on the discrimination of women on Capitol Hill. Condoleeza Rice (2005-2009) followed and Hillary Clinton (2009-2013) is the third, in addition to be the first woman to clinch the Democratic Party nomination for the 2016 GOP Race. All candidates for the GOP race or any high office are talented in many business or civic affairs of the community. The trend shows incremental change in women occupying top government as well as corporate positions.

A Slow Train Coming: Incremental Change

Results from a recent study show an unprecedented amount of CEO turnover in 2015 and a growing tendency to look for new leadership outside the company. Seventeen percent of the world's 2500 companies replaced their CEOs during the same year and it is the highest turnover for the past two decades. Those new top executives were increasingly hired from elsewhere even during planned leadership changes. The data indicates that fewer than three percent incoming CEOs were women, indicating that changes in behavior can be slow. Comella—Dorda, Gnanasambandam, & Shah (2015) argue that chief financial officers are evolving around better ways to make more money as follows: (1) Moving to the Cloud- One in five companies has replaced its accounting systems and financial tracking applications with cloud-based alternatives. (2) They want to predict the future- About ninety six percent of senior executives believe that analytics will be more important in the next three years. (3) There is money at stake- Companies will spend more than $23.1 billion on financial management software during 2016.

Structure Built for Success

In Giddens (1984) structures can be designed to suit what the owners of the business want. There is flexibility in the theory of structuration particularly in creating an enterprise. Giddens has been in the forefront of developments in social theory for the past decade. In the book *The Constitution of Society* first published in 1984, he outlines the distinctive position he has evolved during that period and offers a full statement of a major new perspective in social thought, a synthesis and elaboration of ideas touched on in previous works but described in the book in an integrated and comprehensive form. CEOs and managers will find the book useful in designing and implementing the talent required in effective organizations. For example, if women managed teams have been successful in the past; they could be repeated in the new structures.

Comell-Dorda et al (2015) propound that at least ninety two percent of leaders believe that is critical to redesign their organization to meet global demand. More than forty five percent are either in the middle of restructuring or planning to do so. At least eighty nine percent cited strengthening re-engineering and improving organizational leadership as an important priority in the current year and fifty eight percent suggested that their companies were not structured to produce the leaders they needed hence the externally driven CEO recruitment. Re-engineering is an intervention that focuses on dramatically re-designing core business processes. Successful re-engineering is often closely related to changes in an organization's information systems. In Mupepi (2014), Adam Smith's division of labor increased the productivity of the pin makers by a factor of hundreds. It was re-engineering in 19th century and it is still valid to this day. Smith argued that productivity had increased for three reasons. The first was that the dexterity of the pin makers had increased. They had developed an understanding of what was required in the job. The second reason was attributed to savings of time which was commonly lost in passing from the cutters to pin sharpeners. Efficiency became a norm in the plant. The last was caused by the invention of great machines such as the foot-driven grinder, pin-head press machine or electroplating plant that facilitated and bridged labor, enabling one man to do the work of many. Effectiveness in pin production led to more orders of pins and both the pin maker and the owner of the pin production plant prospered.

Automation and the Professions

The education profession has been around since biblical times. The institution has gone through many changes from the feudal times when it was viewed as a noble profession. Those who entered it were mostly the daughters of the landlords who did the job out of interest and not rewards. As time has moved on the earnings of teachers are still lower than those of other professions that grew out of feudal times such as the City and Guilds blacksmith, ironmongers, steel fabrication among many others. Automating the teaching profession can be contested by many parents. For example, can homework and reading assignments be automated? Chui et al (2011) suggest that capabilities which could possibly be automated involve cognitive activities such as logical problem solving and creativity, among others. This automation in teaching students may not be successful. For example, Bloom (1958) suggests those successful learning take place when there are cognitive, skills, and affect changes. This change becomes even better when the student is given feedback to progress effective learning. Argyris (1993) suggest that there is more to learning than just defined objectives and introduces double loop learning characterized with feedback to the learner and the modification of what must be understood by the learner in light of his/her experience. The first loop uses the goals or decision-making rules, the second loop enables their modification, hence "double-loop". Argyris asserts that double-loop learning acknowledges the way a difficulty is defined and solved can be a source of the problem. For example, patients in the healthcare industry rely on narrative reports given to the nurse or doctor on the nature and description of pain or chief complaint. If this presentation is misunderstood by the care provider and patient, there will be possibilities of prescribing the wrong treatment interventions. Where automation could happen is probably in hospital billing and accounting. Other than that, automation can be limited as one move from one industry to the other.

The Impact of Technological Automation

Technology has forced finance corporations to review their operations and activities. For example, the automated teller (ATM) machine, has eliminated some of the activities of a bank teller or cashier. At Delloitte (2016), it is suggested that capital markets are experiencing serious existential threats. As the industry is being transformed, there is uncertainty around what the future of the banking industry will look like over the next decade.

Delloitte (2016) propound that in the future the capital markets will be over simplified in sync with changing societal and technological factors. For example, recruitment, will focus more at talent and experience rather than gender and qualifications. In the new organizational paradigms, maintaining an organizational identity and creating a cohesive culture and employee loyalty when most of the talent is not in-house will be an entirely new challenge (see Figure 2). In the view of Delloitte, a more globally-

Figure 2. Futuristic scenario

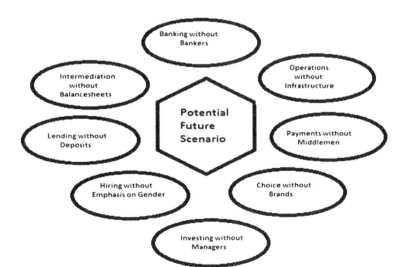

based talent will necessitate greater cultural sensitivity and the willingness to be more flexible with work protocols.

In Chui, Manyika, & Miremadi (2011) four fundamentals of workplace computerization are defined as the automation of activities, redefinition of jobs and business processes, impact of high-wage occupations, and future of creativity and meaning (see Figure 3)

The ATM has made money available to customers all the time and not only when the bank is open. Figure 4, provides a summary of automation activities developed by Chiu, Manyika, & Mirendi (2011).

The bottom line is that forty five percent of work activities could be automated using already demonstrated technology. If the technologies that process and "understand" natural language were to reach the median level of human performance, an additional thirteen percent of work activities in the US economy could be automated. The magnitude of automation potential reflects the speed with which advances in artificial intelligence and its variants, such as machine learning, are challenging our assumptions about automatable (Chui et al 2011:2).

Translating Innovation Growth

In Chui & Manyika et al (2011), leadership is both a research area and a practical skill encompassing the ability of the organization to innovate, guide others, and develop useful teams, alliances and communities of practice. They suggest executives need to be cognizant of the types of data they need to deal with. There are three types of data regardless of whether or not a company is using big data, unstructured data, structured data, and semi-structured data. The data needs to be analyzed to create exploitable structured databases. Decision making on matters of recruitment, training, compliance, and compensation can be made by using information drawn from the databases. A company's conditions of service are part of what gives the business the competitive advantage. A collaboration forum consisting of the company's

Figure 3. Technologies automation (Chui, Manyika, & Mirendi, 2015)

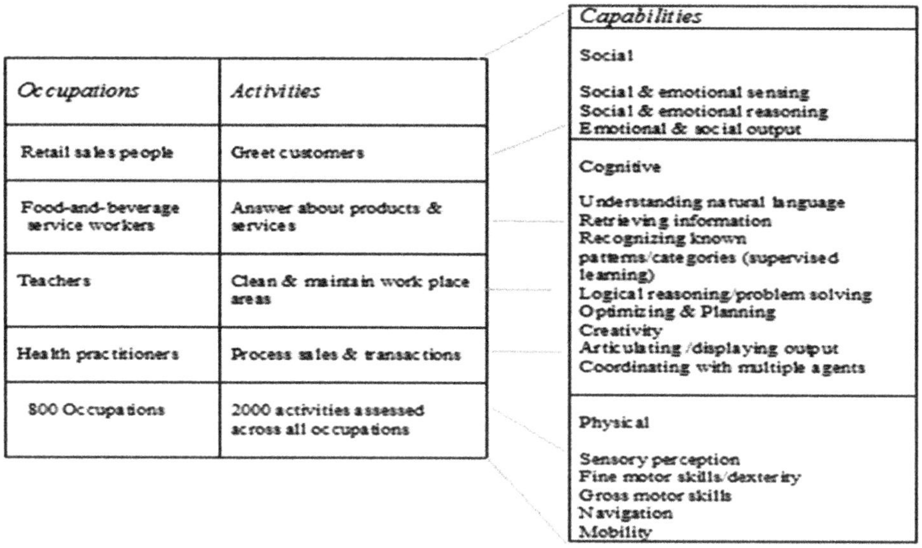

specialists can design and implement a diversity team to create and distribute the practices and procedures necessary to progress the business.

How does Exclusive Organization Impact Output?

Exclusive organization could be good or bad for the business. It could be good if a business was designed to cater for an exclusive audience or consumers. For example, customized food catering firms on Broadway or Hollywood exist to serve a few clients who pay the right price for what they want. On the other hand an exclusive business employing only one race such White, Black, Hispanic, or People of Color, is unlikely to succeed in a market segment with low income and a diverse community.

Employee Turnover and Litigation

The cost associated with doing a poor job of integrating workers from different backgrounds can be extremely high. Lower job satisfaction and the subsequent costs of turnover among women, minorities, and people of various religious faiths are often devalued in organizations. Bertrand & Mullainathan (2004) have reported lower satisfaction and higher turnover of women and minorities when compared to men and Whites. This finding is an important organizational concern, particularly as the number of women and minorities in the workforce increases.

Business Lost

Costs associated with lost business should be added to the costs of absence turnover and discrimination lawsuits that are commonly associated with mismanagement of diversity. When employees or customers learn of or personally experience unfair treatment toward their group by an organization they are less likely to patronize it. In addition, other groups who were not personally affected may find overt discrimination or other negative behavior offensive and choose to spend their money elsewhere (Benedick, Jackson & Reinoso 1994).

Access Discrimination

Minority job applicants frequently experience access discrimination based on stereotypes, prejudice, stated instructions to discriminate, skin tone with those with darker skins faring worse than those with lighter skins or even that their names *sound Black* (Harrison & Thomas, 2009). Women of all races are also discriminated in certain professions. For example up to 2010 women were not allowed to fly combat planes in the military. The Editorial Board of New York Times (2014) reported that three years after the demise of "don't ask, don't tell," an estimated 15,000 members of the military still must lie about themselves in order to go on risking their lives for their country. When Congress eliminated the law against gay men and lesbians serving openly in the military, the Pentagon left in place an equally unfounded prohibition on transgender people.

In the same report it was gratifying to hear the Defense Secretary, Chuck Hagel say in an interview on ABC's "This Week" on Sunday, "Every qualified American who wants to serve our country should have an opportunity if they fit the qualifications and can do it." After all, unlike the ban on openly gay soldiers, the rule on transgender people is just a rule. There is no law prohibiting them from serving openly (New York Times May 14, 2014).

Accessing Top Level Jobs

Ownership and control in the publicly quoted companies is dependent on who owns the majority of voting shares. The majority of the corporations have roots in family owned small businesses. They have expanded and spread the risk by enlisting on the stock exchange. The majority of such corporations are controlled by the dominant White group. The "Fortune 500" is a list of the 500 largest companies in the United States as compiled by Fortune magazine. Only 15 black executives have ever made it to the Chairman or CEO position of a "Fortune 500" listed company. Of these 15 executives, there are currently 5 active. In 1987, Dr. Clifton R. Wharton Jr. became Chairman and CEO of TIAA-CREF distinguishing him as the first black CEO of a Fortune 500 company. Franklin Raines became the second black person to lead a "Fortune 500" company, when he became CEO of Fannie Mae in 1999. On July 1, 2009, Ursula Burns became the first black woman to head a Fortune 500 company. There is currently no black majority owned company in the Fortune 500 rankings (Black Entrepreneurs, 2015).

The Glass Ceiling and Walls

The glass ceiling is an invisible barrier preventing women, disabled persons, and people of color from progressing beyond a certain level in organizations. Hurley, Fagenson-Eland, & Sonnenfeld (1997) propound that the glass ceiling and walls are invisible barriers created by the owners of the organization to target discrimination to women, people of color, and those with disabilities. The practices include assigning less challenging work leading to fewer developments of skills thus affecting qualifications. Failure to provide constructive performance feedback for fear of being perceived as racist leads to identify and achieve necessary improvement and assignment to certain minority neighborhoods and clients on the basis of presumed fit or connection or other employees' unwilling-ness to work there which can negatively impact employees' earnings and career progress.

Benefits of Inclusion

Cummings & Worley (2015) suggest that the advantages of inclusion include greater access to wider range of skillsets, abilities, ideas, and innovation at work, expansion of positive influence by an organization on a worldwide scale, reduction of discriminatory behaviors and racism in the workplace which impact

Table 2: Black CEO's from America's 500 Largest Corporations (Black Entrepreneurs, 2015)

Chairman / CEO	Company	Rank	Revenue (Billion)	Profits (million)
John W. Thompson	Microsoft Corporation	35	73.7	16,978
Kenneth C. Frazier	Merck & Co. Inc	58	47.3	6,168
Kenneth I. Chenault	American Express	90	33.8	4,482
Roger W. Ferguson Jr.	TIAA-CREF	97	32.2	2,060
Ursla M. Burns	Xerox Corporation	131	22.4	1,195

productivity, and the ability to increase profitability. The diffusion of innovation happens much faster in environments where everyone is appreciated. A diversified workforce shares similarities and appreciates differences among people. It appreciates the contribution of women and gender in an organization and recognizes that talent is unevenly distributed in an organization. This understanding can lead to highly productive organizations.

Workforce Diversity the Way Forward

In Cummings & Worley workforce diversity is more than a euphemism for cultural or racial differences. Diversity results from people who bring different resources and perspectives to the workplace and who have distinct needs, preferences, expectations, and lifestyles. Gender work design reward system and career development are among the more interventions for addressing issues arising out of gender trend. For example jobs can be designed to accommodate working moms. A job can be modified to be shared by three people. One person can be available during the early part of the day. Another takes over in the afternoon shift while the third covers the midnight shift. This arrangement is not new in health care or manufacturing industries. However, in knowledge-intensive organizations such SAS, Oracle, or Booz Allen knowledge sharing has been instituted to provide coverage to internet booming trade.

Sexual Orientation

Diversity in sexual and affectional orientation, including gay, lesbian, bisexual, and transgender (LGBT) individuals and couples, increasingly is affecting the way that organizations think about human resources. The primary organizational implication of sexual orientation diversity is discrimination. Members of the LGBT could be reluctant to discuss how human resources practices and procedures can be less prejudiced lest their openness will lead to unfair treatment.

The LGBT are a recent development in human resources management. The Title VII Civil Rights Act 1964 Chapter three prohibits discrimination on the basis of sex in employment-related matters. This law has been in existence over fifty years but intentional and unintentional discrimination still occurs.

Disparate treatment on the basis of sex occurs when an applicant or employee, typically a woman, is intentionally treated differently than males are treated. Such blatant or overt discrimination is less common than in the past, it is far from obsolete. (See Table 2 for the best practices).

MAIN FOCUS OF THE CHAPTER

The centrality of this chapter is on increasing opportunities to gender in executive situations. Research results indicate that some of the women in top management positions possess the talent needed to advance highly productive work environments. Modern workforce is characterized by highly talented multicultural individuals capable of taking the business to the next level. Discrimination hampers the ability of a diversified workforce to be creative and solve problems. A proposition to increase equal opportunities is made.

Issues

Diversity and equality in corporations has been sustained by the Title VII Civil Rights Act, 1964. The trend is that the majority of corporations comply with the diversity laws. There are issues in small to medium businesses whose ownership and control is in the hands of families. The majority of the small businesses employ family members. For example Indian retail small businesses in South Africa or Indiana have been consistent in employing what they considered as family. In other cases the small business has been moving towards employing talent from outside to warrant successful enterprise. Exception is made to huge corporations that were started as family owned grocery stores such as Frederick Meijer of Grand Rapids Michigan, DuPont Chemical Company, Rothschild Merchant Bankers, or Sam Walton of the international giant retailers, Wal-Mart, that have had to employ external professional corporate affairs leadership to progress operations.

SOLUTIONS AND RECOMMENDATIONS

It can be difficult for organizations to understand how women think, act, and innovate unless they have examples to go by. On July 1, 2009, Ursula Burns became the first black woman to head a Fortune 500 Company and she should not be the last. The Enron scandal involved the top three executives who were all male. In Healy & Palepu (2003) the Enron scandal led to the enactment of the Sarbanes-Oxley Act 2001 which has introduced more stringent measures in financial management. Soon after the Enron scandal the biggest financial fraud occurred at MCI WorldCom Inc. In Malik (2003) the following year saw the biggest fraud ever in the world. This was that of WorldCom MCI and the key executives were also men. McKinsey (2007) found that women made in-charge of teams or the entire organization made exemplary leaders. They were highly productive in an arena dominated by men. Probably their sixth sense of responsibility and motherhood discourages men from misbehaving or to follow established practices and procedures. In Table 3, Cummings & Worley propose a structure and format to articulate diversity.

Giving a Chance to the LGBT Community

The University of Vermont (2016) offers a unique course designed to fulfill the business leadership aspirations for students who are openly gay, lesbian or bisexual. The emphasis on this course is about good leadership and people management skills. The LGBT community should be given access opportunities in leadership positions. There is no known research that suggests that the LGBT professionals are not capable of leadership position. Instead there are highly talented members of the LGBT community who have openly expressed their sexual orientation such as Melissa Etheridge or Elton John (Goodall 1993) among many others (Landadio, 2008).

The Importance of Diversity

Studies have shown that diverse groups create better solutions than non-diverse groups. That's very good. But what is not very good is the fact that diverse work groups can sometimes produce work environments that create tensions among group members. These tensions can be between men and women, union

Table 3. Work diversity dimensions (Cummings & Worley 2015:500)

Workforce Differences	Trends	Implications and Needs	Interventions
Age	Median age up Distribution of ages changing	Health care Mobility Security	Wellness programs Job design Career planning and development Reward system
Gender	Percentage of women increasing Dual-income families	Child care Maternity / paternity leave Single parents	Job design Career planning and development
Disability	The number of people with disabilities entering the workforce is increasing	Job challenges Job skills Physical space Respect and dignity	Performance management Job design Career planning and development Employee involvement Reward system
Culture and value	Rising proportions of immigrant and minority group workers Shift in rewards	Flexible organized policies Autonomy Affirmation in mission statements Respect	Career planning and development Employee involvement Reward system
Sexual orientation	Number of single sex households up More liberal attitudes toward sexual orientation	Discrimination	Equal employment opportunities Fringe benefits Education and training

leaders and managers, older and younger people, people with differing spiritual beliefs, or countless other variations. However there are ways to move from discomfort to respect and higher productivity.

Williams, Dempsey & Slaughter (2014) suggest that women succeeded in their careers by recognizing the realities of today's workplaces and mastering the politics of offices which often benefit men. They argue that the maternal wall is the actual glass ceiling which they must be able to overcome given the support of Title VII Civil Rights Act 1964. Chambers et al (1998) asserts that companies succeed by engaging radically with society and explain why it is critical to look beyond corporate-social-responsibility initiative to truly engage with consumers and communities. Meeting the needs of stakeholders including women employees was critical in growing highly productive workplaces.

Executive director Phumzile Mlambo-Ngcuka, a Black woman has made a difference at the World YWCA in New York. There are numerous others such as Cynthia Bowman Chief Diversity and Inclusion Director at Bank of America. In Federal government, Nancy Pelosi is Minority Leader of the United States House of Representatives and has served as 52nd Speaker of the United States House of Representatives 2007-2011 and Loretta E. Lynch is the 83rd Attorney General of the United States. Around the world there are many other women who have contributed effectively to their communities in business or government.

In studies on talent management, Sutton (2007) suggests that if a company hired a woman for the top job, she was bound to succeed in that new position. If the same company hired a man as a CEO, Sutton argues that there would be a need to hire his previous team or he would fail.

The way forward is to create a workplace built upon common respect and values, providing equal opportunities to all employees, and to hire individuals who possess the talent useful in organization.

The Demise of Discrimination

Efforts to combat stereotypes must be purposeful. Employee involvement is strategy to increase productivity by providing: equal opportunity to all employees, people with enough authority to make work-related decisions covering various issues such as work methods task assignments, performance outcomes, customer service, and employee selection. Information that is relevant to employees should be easily accessed. For example, vacant notices should be posted on notice boards in cafeteria or meeting venues and should all be circulated by email where appropriate. The vacant notices should also include phrases such as "Women are encouraged to apply" Timely access to relevant information is vital to making decisions. Organizations can also adapt parallel structures which involve selected employees in resolving ill-defined complex problems and build adaptability into organizations. These parallel structures are also referred to as shadow structures or dualistic structures. These structures operate in tandem to the formal structure to address quality, equal opportunities, and, overall productivity matters.

CONCLUSION

The gender leaders seeking a chance to be significant see the world through a lens of opportunity; they are especially in search of those opportunities previously unseen. They should be given these chances not because of the law and social responsibility but as opportunity to advance productivity and humanity. Research results are conclusive that women are capable of the top job. Gender does not affect the outcome of the job. Therefor individuals should be hired according to their talent and skills.

REFERENCES

Andersen, J. A., & Hansson, P. H. (2011). At the end of the road? On differences between women and men in leadership behavior. *Leadership and Organization Development Journal*, 32(5), 428–441. doi:10.1108/01437731111146550

Argyris, C. (1993). *On Organizational Learning*. Cambridge, Mass.: Blackwell.

Bell, M. P. (2012). *Diversity in Organizations* (2nd ed.). Mason, Ohio: Cengage.

Bendick, M. Jr, Jackson, C., & Rainoso, V. (1994). Measuring employment discrimination through uncontrolled experiments. *The Review of Black Political Economy*, 23(1), 25–48. doi:10.1007/BF02895739

Berdahl, J. L., & Anderson, C. (2005). Men, women, and leadership centralization in groups over time. *Group Dynamics*, 9(1), 45–57. doi:10.1037/1089-2699.9.1.45

Bertrand, M., & Mullainathan, S. (2004). Are Emily and Greg more employable than LaKisha and Jamal? A Field Experiment on Labor Market Discrimination. *The American Economic Review*, 94(4), 991–1011. doi:10.1257/0002828042002561

Chambers, E.G., Foulon, M., Handfield-Jones, H., Hankin, S.M., & Michaels, E.G., III (1998). The War on Talent. *The McKinsey Quarterly Number, 3*.

Chui, M., Manyika, J., & Miremadi, M. (2015). Four fundamentals of workplace automation. Retrieved from http//:www.mckinsey.com/business-functions

Comella-Dorda, C.G., & Shah, B. (2015). From box to cloud. Retrieved from http://www.mckinsey.com/business-functions/from-box_to_cloud

Cummings, T., & Worley, C. G. (2015). *Organization Development & Change*. London, UK: Cengage.

Cummings, T. G., & Worley, C. G. (2009). *Organization Development and Change*. London, UK: Cengage.

Delloitte (2016). A new organizational paradigm: Agile, collaborative, and exposed. Retrieved from http://www2.deloitte.com/us/en/pages/financial-services/articles/banking-industry-outlook.html

Editorial Board New York Times. (2014, May 15). Discrimination in the military. Retrieved from http://www.nytimes.com/2014/05/15/opinion/discrimination-in-the-military.html?_r=0

Entrepreneurs, B. (2015). Black chairman and CEOs from America's 500 Largest Corporations. Retrieved from https://www.blackentrepreneurprofile.com/fortune-500-ceos/

Fagenson, E. A. (1990). Perceived Masculine and Feminine Attributes Examined as a Function of Individuals Sex and Level in the Organizational Power Hierarchy: A Test of Four Theoretical Perspectives. *The Journal of Applied Psychology*, *75*(2), 204–211. doi:10.1037/0021-9010.75.2.204

Fletcher, J. K. (1994). Castrating the Female Advantage: Feminist Standpoint Research and Management Science. *Journal of Management Inquiry*, *3*(I), 74–82. doi:10.1177/105649269431012

General Motors Corporation. (2016). Mary Barra is Chairman and Chief Executive Officer of General Motors Company. Retrieved from http://www.gm.com/company/leadership/corporate-officers/mary-barra.html

Giddens, A. (1984). *The Constitution of Society*. Berkeley: University of California Press.

Goodall, N. (1993). *Elton John*. London, UK: Omnibus press.

Hofstede, G. (2001). Culture's Consequences: comparing values, behaviors, institutions, and organizations across nations (2nd ed.). Thousand Oaks, CA: SAGE Publications.

Hurley, A. J., Fagenson-Eland, E. A., & Somerfield, J. A. (1997). Does cream always rise to the top? An investigation of career determinants. *Organizational Dynamics*, *26*(2), 65–71. doi:10.1016/S0090-2616(97)90006-1

Landadio, M. (2008). Melissa Etheridge ties the knot again. *People*. Retrieved from http://www.people.com/people/article/0,20230169,00.html

Llopis, G. (2014). The most undervalued leadership traits of women. *Forbes*. Retrieved from http://www.forbes.com/sites/glennllopis/2014/02/03/the-most-undervalued-leadership-traits-of-women/#36485b0c690c

McKinsey. (2007). Women matter: Female leadership, a competitive edge for the future. Retrieved from http//:www.mckinsey.com/women-matter

Schmidt, M. M. (2002). Female dominance hierarchies: Are they any different from males? *Personality and Social Psychology Bulletin, 28*(1), 29–39. doi:10.1177/0146167202281003

Sinclair, A. (1998). *Doing Leadership Differently: Gender, Power, and Sexuality in a Change.* Melbourne: Melbourne University Press.

Sutton, R. (2007). The War for Talent is Back. *Harvard Business Review*. Retrieved from https://hbr.org/2007/04/the-war-on-talent-is-back

University of Michigan. (2016). Terms and definitions of LGBT. Retrieved from https://international-spectrum.umich.edu/life/definitions

University of Vermont. (2016). Leadership development course for LGDP students. Retrieved from www.vermontbiz.com/news/may

Williams, J. C., Dempsey, R., & Slaughter, A.-M. (2014). *What works for women at work: Four patterns working women need to know*. New York: New York University Press.

KEY TERMS AND DEFINITIONS

Corporate Culture: This is the pattern of values, beliefs and expectations shared by organization members. It represents the taken-for-granted and shared assumptions that make about how work is done and evaluated and evaluated and how employees relate to one another and to significant others, such as suppliers, customers, and external stakeholders.

Corporate Performance Management: Corporate performance is the area of business intelligence involved with monitoring and managing an organization's performance according to key performance indicators such as revenue, return on investment, overhead and operational costs.

Leadership Behaviors: A set of measurable performance encompassing organizational, psychological, technological, and political and other factors used to assess the behavior expected of persons in a leadership role.

Structured Data: Structured data refers to any data that resides in a fixed field within a record or file. This includes data contained in relational databases and spreadsheets.

Tech-Savvy: Well-informed about or proficient in the use of modern technology especially computers or production systems.

Chapter 16
Managing Talent in Global Environments:
Effective Communication in Multinational Enterprise

Yiheng Deng
Southwestern University of Finance and Economics, China

ABSTRACT

In response to the call to elucidate the conditions necessary for successful multinational organization, this discussion is centered on effective communications between a subsidiary company located in China and an American parent organization (multinational company, MNC) based in the USA. Semi-structured interviews were conducted with 37 participants including the expatriate managers and the local employees. The findings show that the challenges facing the MNC mainly include confrontation in the contexts of conflict based on cultural differences and supervisor-subordinate interaction, and collectivity reflected in two themes including group dynamics and collective activities. The MNC incorporates local knowledge systems into its administration schema when conducting business worldwide. The study shows that perceptions of both management and employees vary. The challenge is to increase understanding of the job and what needs to be done in different environment as antecedent to increased outputs.

INTRODUCTION

Since 2000, a growing number of multinational corporations have relocating to the inland cities where rent is affordable compared to the seaside locations. One of the major decisions the MNC has to make is whether to maintain their foreign identity and incorporate local knowledge in the organization of their subsidiaries. Some multinational corporations choose to integrate both cultures into a unique culture as the *modus operandi* for the subsidiary company. For some other multinational corporations, it could be an on-going process with both sides constantly negotiating their roles and ways of doing things. This study is intended to explore management communication issues in a U.S.-based multinational corporation in Chengdu city, China, in terms of cultural adaptation on the side of the management and the local

DOI: 10.4018/978-1-5225-1961-4.ch016

employees' take on the issue. This study is unique in that (1) it is qualitative, thus, analyzes the MNC convergence-divergence in the process, and focuses on discovering the variables involved; (2) Both the managerial and the ordinary employees were interviewed to understand the perceptions of both sides on the managerial adaptation outcomes were obtained;(3) it looks into an MNC subsidiary in inland southwestern China, and thus, differs from most of previous studies that investigate the enterprises in the coastal cities of eastern China.

BACKGROUND

Global markets are characterized by economic agents in any given part of the world that are more affected by events elsewhere in the world than before; the growing integration of the national economies of the world to the degree that we may be witnessing the emergence and operations of a single worldwide economy. In such a setting the best companies are those that succeed at meeting desirable goals regardless of their nationalities. Boyacigiller & Adler (1991) reviewed a selected global business literature and concluded that the understanding of multinational organizations by then was inappropriate and parochial. The companies focused on markets in which they had interest. It is part of a strategy to design and implement a market structure in which it could influence prices.

International Human Resources Management

According to Jain, Lawler & Morishima (1998), after reviewing a series of articles dealing with international human resource management practices of MNCs in different countries, concluded that HRM policies and practices can impact developing countries more deeply than developed countries. Among this stream of literature, there exist arguments concerning the divergence vs. convergence approaches in MNC subsidiary HRM practices. To study the global practices of MNCs, one needs to look at the local subsidiary practices because the convergence vs. divergence dynamic is an on-going process at the local level (Geppert & Williams, 2006; Martin & Beaumont, 1998). Chen (2000) posited that for multinational corporations in China, problems exist regarding the local employees' understanding and acceptance of MNC management styles as well as management understanding of employees' cultural assumptions; thus, mutual cultural and organizational learning is imperative for both management and the local employees.

Culture has a significant influence on people's choice of communication patterns such as conflict management styles. For example, Ting-Toomey (1991) and her colleagues have found that Americans tend to use dominating style while Chinese tend to use avoiding and obliging styles. Since then, a number of scholars have conducted studies on the Chinese's conflict management styles in multinational organizations (e.g., Chen, Tjosvold, & Fang, 2005; Knutson, Hwang, & Deng, 2000; Liu &Chen, 2000; Peng, He & Zhu, 2000; Wang, Jing, & Klossek, 2007; Yuan, 2010), and found that the Chinese tend to be non-confrontational in conflict situations. They prefer using mediation or third party intervention in conflict management (Deng & Xu, 2014; Jia, 2002). Scholars have also identified harmony as a cardinal value in Chinese conflict resolution (Chen & Starosta, 1997; Kirkbride, Tang, & Westwood, 1991; Knutson et al., 2000).

Globalization and the Need for Efficacies

The globalization discourse can thus be summarized as follows: MNCs are becoming increasingly stateless enterprises. Corporate structures and strategies are following Anglo-Saxon business patterns, as they increasingly a higher role to corporate finance and shareholder value. Divergent interests and local power resources of key subsidiary managers are employee representative bodies are played down or are ignored altogether by this course. (Levy, 2005).

Productive efficiency occurs when there is maximum output produced with the given resources and technology. The firm is able to compete with what the people doing the job know. The core competency presented in Prahalad & Hamel (1990) assumes that similar companies will not be able to replicate its performance. The firms' products should be perceived by the consumers to possess the benefits they seek. While strategic planning is viewed in business management as a co-construct, there is a need for participants in the planning team to appreciate that successful strategy happens as a collective learning experience.

In Mupepi (2017), the community of practice approach is applied to inform the development of the core competences needed in effective organization. The core competency approach is a great strength in organization enabling a multinational firm to examine its capability and to build upon it to access markets easily (see Figure 1).

Managing the Local Context

In Gupta & Govindara (1991), international human resources management is concerned with managing the factors dealing with persons employed in various aspects of the business in global environments. These factors include planning for human resources needs such as staffing, training and development, developing compensation systems and evaluating the performance of the employees. Edstron & Lorange (1984) assert these factors are same as those for domestic operations except that international HRM

Figure 1. Productive efficiency (Mupepi, 2017)

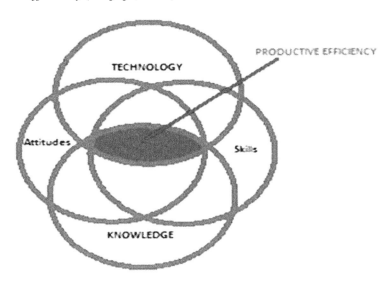

involves keeping a balance between employees' countries of origin, language differences, religious preferences, and a myriad of other factors which differ from country to country. Edstron & Lorange propound that international HRM involves keeping a balance between all employees, thereby allowing employee transfer from country to country as a strategy to diffuse knowledge and technology transfer.

Cultural Differences

In Mupepi & Taruvinga (2004), a mixed research methodology was instituted to understand cultural difference between American and South African owned family enterprises to show that cultural differences and perceived risk-taking must be considered in charting competences in advancing household enterprises in the Southern African Development Communities and the USA. The consequences were that triumphant households were those that took cognizance of multiculturalism in assessing and measuring performance. Multiple Linear Regression analysis demonstrated that capacity must be customized to suit organizational vision and that the vital predictor of perceived success in the USA was performance orientation while uncertainty avoidance topped the list in the SADC. Results indicate that diversity was understood in all successful enterprises. The results also show that difference management styles should be adapted as management make decisions that influence activities from one location to the other.

Sheer Strength

Taylor, Beechler, & Napier (1996) proposed a model that considered the situation of the employees in the subsidiary companies. The process of planning staffing, organizing, and controlling international business activities can be made easier by hiring local management consultant firms. Normally international strategic management is different from local strategy. In Anastasia & Vojtech (2015) defined the business strength and weaknesses that can arise in foreign countries drawing from experiences in Czech Republic. The object of their research was a family business as an economical phenomenon. The article was prepared on the basis of general theoretical scientific methods, particularly on those of analysis, synthesis, analogy, comparison, generalization and deduction, or the method of expert estimates. For the analysis of the actual situation in large Czech family business enterprises, it was decided to use the secondary data of a top research-journal for this area, namely the Forbes.cz. In accordance with one of the study, a SWOT analysis was applied to find out the basic strengths and weaknesses of family business. The results of this study have allowed the finding of a definition for the family business based on family ties and the laws of the Czech Republic. Another finding is that family business as a motor of the Czech economy has a real potential for its development and it is able to enhance the Czech economy competitiveness on the world market. The Czech Republic has numerous multinational firms such as Bata Shoe Company operating in many countries around the world including Canada, USA, South Africa, Australia, and India, among many others.

Global Mindset

In Levy (2005), a proposition indicating how global competition continues to intensify is made as more countries liberalize their economies. As global competition continues to intensify, global mindset has emerged as a key source of long-term competitive advantage in the global marketplace. A growing number of scholars view global mindset, or the cognitive capabilities of key decision-makers, as a critical success factors impacting a variety of organizational outcomes. For example Gupta & Govindarajan (2002) suggested that the idea of a global mindset is critical in performance management. It is a growing consensus that successful outcomes can arise from a people working collectively to forge ahead a shared vision of the future. Gupta & Govindarajan posit that the mental action of management and its understanding of the organizational situation encompassed problem solving and comprehension of prevailing cultural conditions. The notion that global mindset, or the cognitive capabilities of senior managers in multinational companies (MNCs), is important to firm performance dates back to the early works on foreign direct investment by Aharoni (1966) and Kindleberger (1969). However, it was Perlmutter (1969) who focused attention on managerial cognition by offering a formal typology of MNCs that explicitly incorporates the prevailing mindsets of senior management.

Multicultural Communication

In Rogers Hart & Yoshitaka (2002), effective cross-cultural communications were imperative in managing international business organizations successfully. They define cross-cultural communication is a field of study that looks at how people from differing cultural backgrounds communicate, in similar and different ways among themselves, and how they endeavor to communicate across cultures. Rogers et al propound that effective cross-cultural communications occur in a multidisciplinary environment where efforts to bring together such relatively unrelated areas as cultural anthropology and established areas of communication. Its core is to establish and understand how people from different cultures communicate with each other. Its charge is to produce some guidelines with which people from different cultures can better communicate with each other.

Cultural Differences

During the last three decades or so researchers have increasingly focused on cultural differences as a global phenomenon. In Hofstede (1984) developed a theory of cross-cultural communication he referred to as cultural dimensions. It is a framework for cross-cultural communication which describes the effects of a society's culture on the values of its members, and how these values relate to behavior, using a structure derived from factor analysis. Hofstede developed his original model as a result of using factor analysis to examine the results of a world-wide survey of employee values by IBM between 1967 and 1973. It has been refined since (Hofstede, 1991). The original theory proposed four dimensions along which cultural values could be analyzed: individualism-collectivism; uncertainty avoidance; power distance (strength of social hierarchy) and masculinity-femininity (task orientation versus person-orientation). Independent research in Hong Kong led Hofstede to add a fifth dimension, long-term orientation, to cover aspects of values not discussed in the original paradigm. In 2010, Hofstede & Hofstede (2010) added a sixth dimension, indulgence versus self-restraint.

Hofstede's work established a major research tradition in cross-cultural psychology and has also been drawn upon by researchers and consultants in many fields relating to international business and communication. The theory has been widely used in several fields as a paradigm for research, particularly in cross-cultural psychology, international management, and cross-cultural communication. It continues to be a major resource in cross-cultural fields. It has inspired a number of other major cross-cultural studies of values, as well as research on other aspects of culture, such as social beliefs.

Differences Between Cultures on the Values Dimensions

Although there are six cultural differences, here the focus is on those differences that impact business organization in the context of China. Putting together national scores (from 1 for the lowest to 120 for the highest), Hofstede's six-dimension model allows international comparison between cultures, also called comparative research (Hofstede & Hofstede 2010):

Power distance index shows very high scores for Latin and Asian countries, African areas and the Arab world. On the other hand, Anglo and Germanic countries have a lower power distance (only 11 for Austria and 18 for Denmark (2010, p. 2).

Uncertainty avoidance scores are the highest in Latin American countries, Southern and Eastern Europe countries including German speaking countries, and Japan. This could be the case because of socialistic as opposed to capitalistic tendencies in those countries. Management must make decisions that resonate with state policy most of the time. In capitalistic environments managers make decisions that give the best advantage to the business. Uncertainty avoidance is lower for Anglo, Nordic, and Chinese culture countries. For example, Germany has a high UAI (65) and Belgium even more (94) compared to Sweden (29) or Denmark (23) despite their geographic proximity. However, few countries have very low UAI (2010:3)

Cognitive Orientation

In Geppert & Williams (2006), the centricity of cognitive orientation of management is viewed as a practice deduced from cultural dimensions. Management cognitive processes can be analyzed from different perspectives within different contexts, notably in the fields of linguistics, culture or local knowledge systems. Geppert & Williams propound that different approaches to the analysis of cognition are synthesized in the developing effective decision making and problem solving techniques in international management.

Adaptation

Even though the global discourse has been predominant in the sphere of ideology, as well as in practice, local adaptation is still necessary (Geppert & Williams, 2006). Based on comparative research conducted at the UK and Chinese firms, Easterby-Smith, Malina, and Yuan (1995) concluded that there are strong cultural factors that limit the adoption of many features of Western HRM in China. MNCs' 'best practices' are inevitably influenced by the local practices and the culture of the host country. Despite the heated debate about the discourses between the global and the local, little was known about 'how local managers and employee representatives develop, negotiate and even resist the implementation of global best practices' (Geppert & Williams 2006: p. 52). Similar observation has been made by Temple and Walgenbach (2003). In the tug-of-war of globalization and localization of MNC subsidiaries, i.e. 'conflicting isomorphic pulls' in MNCs, the subsidiary managers need to make daily decisions on their own to adapt to the local environment in order to be effective (Geppert & Williams, 2006; Westney, 1993). Hence adaption process is not just one way that employees adopting the 'best practices' diffused from the parent company to the subsidiaries, and their mentality and behaviors conforming to the company policy and norms.

Hofstede in China

Since Hofstede (1980) proposed the dimensions of cultural variability, China has been identified at the higher end of the power distance dimension. The Chinese are more likely to accept that power is unequally distributed, and to be more willing to conform to the authority and be careful about it in the organization, than most western cultures such as the United States. Thus, many scholars argue that such cultural factors would preclude implementation of Western HRM methods in China and suggest that Western management must be adapted to fit better with Chinese culture (Easterby-Smith, Malina, &Yuan, 1995; Jackson & Bak, 1998; Lockett, 1988). However, recently, some scholars have found the cultures of the MNC subsidiaries in China can be very different from what Hofstede found about the Chinese culture. For example, King-Metters & Metters (2008) have found that Chinese hotel workers in western-brand hotels in Shanghai scored much lower on the dimension of power distance with an average score of 41, the same as the US, and much higher on the dimension of individualism with an average score of 71, than the results in Hofstede's study. Gamble (2003, 2006) found that a UK chain store in Shanghai has been successful in transferring a flat hierarchy and the Chinese employees view the UK management style as "modern," "egalitarian," and "civilized." Deng & Xu (2014) studied a Chinese subsidiary of an American MNC and found that the company norm and practices of conflict management were accepted and even internalized by some local employees as "appropriate" and "necessary," though the local employees have mixed views about this norm named "constructive confrontation" that violates the Chinese cultural practices.

While Western MNCs tended to adapt their HRM practices to the Chinese environment in the 1980s and early 1990s, Bjorkman & Fan (2002) argue that this is because MNCs at that time were mainly joint ventures and had less control than their Chinese counterparts, and recent MNCs tend to introduce more Western HRM practices because they have greater control over joint ventures than those set up in the earlier period or more MNCs are fully foreign owned. Nevertheless, these studies were conducted in the late 1990s and early 2000s when the Chinese state-owned enterprises (SOEs) were experiencing difficulties and many of them were privatized and many employees were laid off, while MNCs were more profitable than Chinese SOEs because MNCs received tax benefits and could make use of the cheap labor and sell their products in their home markets at relatively high prices. As the number of Chinese SOEs largely decreased and they have been very successful in the past decade, and MNCs are less profitable than before due to the increasingly expensive labor and fierce competition from the Chinese SOEs, we are not sure how Chinese employees view Chinese and Western management practices. Given the limited number of studies on the recent cultural change on the value dimensions, more studies are needed to investigate the communication patterns of the Chinese employees and expatriates in MNCs. Multinational corporations provide an ideal place for scholars to examine these intercultural communication issues.

Chinese Firms in International Markets

Gamble & Huang (2009) carried out a case study on the Chinese branches of a UK retailer, specifically, in Beijing and Shanghai. Taking on a diachronic perspective, he argues that there should not be a clear cut line between global and local when it comes to the transfer of the organizational practices. Besides, the local subsidiaries or branches take on different approaches according to different subcultural contexts, and also depending on who are the ones implementing the corporate practices. They borrowed Ferner (1997)'s statement that quantitative method might overlook important details in the process of convergence or divergence. Hence, they adopted the methods of survey, interview and participant observation to avoid missing the richness of the insights or the process and motives involved (Ferner, 1997; Hodson, 2005). What should be noted is that the studies (Gamble and Huang, 2009) were carried out in Shanghai and Beijing, the two biggest cities representing the highest level of economic power and living standards in China. In terms of the socio-economic indicators (Human Development Index, Marketization Index, foreign direct investment per capita, gross domestic product per capita, average income), the two cities enjoy all higher scores than most of the inland provinces, such as Human, Sichuan, and Anhui (Gamble, 2015).

With regard to China, researchers have suggested that with rapid economic development, Chinese society has become more diversified and some regions have a greater tendency to move towards a more individualistic side of the continuum (Stanat, 2005; Ralston, et al. 2008; Cao, 2009). For example, Koch and Koch (2007) indicate that a less developed region, Wuhan, was significantly more collectivistic than Beijing, a more developed region. The studies on MNC subsidiaries in China, especially those in inland China were still rare, considering the important economic status of China and its rapidly changing socio-cultural environment. Given the vast area and diverse local cultures in China, this study focuses on one case of an inland city in Southwestern China to illustrate how managers in multinational corporations have tried to adapt to the local culture. We also hope that the qualitative approach to the study would provide insights on how the managerial employees adapt to or converge with the local culture while transferring their organizational practices, and how the ordinary local employees perceive the outcomes of the adaptation.

Accordingly, this study proposes the following research questions: What are the major cultural differences or challenges in terms of communication in the multinational corporation (MNC), how did the MNC management reacts to these cultural differences (i.e. converge vs diverge, local vs global), and how did the local employees view the "adaptation or hybridization of practices", that is, the transfer outcomes (Ferner et al., 2012: p164) of the organization?

THE CASE STUDY

Company X is a world renowned U.S. –based IT company in Chengdu, which was moved from an economically more developed coastal city in Eastern China. The company started building its Chengdu subsidiary in 2004. Now, almost ten years have passed, the subsidiary has grown to have over 3000 employees. Among them, around 2000 are factory workers and about 1000 are administrative personnel including mid-level and upper level management.

Semi-structured interviews were employed for the study. The employees and expatriates were contacted through the manager of human resource, soliciting via email their voluntary participation in the interview study. 37 people volunteered to participate. In the first round, 27 interviews were carried out. Among the 27 interviewees, eight of them are expatriate managers, while the rest are Chinese managers, staff, engineers, and independent contractors. The interviews were conducted in a closed meeting room of the company during their work hours upon approval of the head of Human Resources. For each interview, only the interviewer and the interviewee were present in the room. All the interviewees were asked the same set of questions that are consistent with the research questions of this study: What are the major cultural differences in terms of communication in the multinational organization (MNC), and how did the MNC management reacts to these cultural differences? Depending on their answers, some probing questions were asked further for more in-depth information. The interviewees ranged from upper-level managers who report directly to the headquarters in the United States, to office staff with no subordinates. There are expatriates from the United States and other foreign countries, local Chinese employees with no overseas experiences, as well as Chinese employees and managers with overseas experiences. Their positions cover all the major departments of the company, from the human resources to manufacturing, from training and development to testing and quality control, from product engineers to accountants. Most of the expatriate managers have worked for the company for a long period of time, with the shortest being 14 years and longest over 20 years. Out of the seven expatriate managers who participated in this study, five are U.S. Americans, and two have been working for the headquarters in the United States for more than 10 years. Using the words of one of them, they are quite 'seasoned' and 'tenured.'

The 37 interviews, ranging from 45 minutes to 2 hours, were recorded and transcribed. English was used in the interviews with expatriates, and Chinese was used in the interviews with the Chinese employees. In data collection, we encouraged the interviewees to illustrate, elaborate, and give examples or anecdotes to support their views. We used constant comparative method (Strauss, 1998; Strauss & Corbin, 1998), to conduct thematic analysis of the interview data. The identification of repeated content is a major means of identifying key themes – recurrent themes embody in repeated content in the same interview data or across interview data of different interviewees. The second round of interview, focusing on the main themes identified in the first round of interview, were carried out with 10 workers and team leaders working on the manufacturing line. These workers and leaders have worked for the company for 5-9 years, and have had very little direct contact with expatriate managers or the mid to upper-level management, i.e., they represent the bottom level of the company pyramid. The excerpts in Chinese were translated into English to serve as examples to demonstrate the main findings in the following sections.

FINDINGS

The findings two salient themes were derived from the transcript in terms of the cultural differences requiring adaption-confrontation and collectivity. Two contexts were identified with each theme. In each context, the managerial transfer efforts and perceptions, as well as the employees' perception of the transfer outcomes were illustrated with excerpts from interview transcript.

Confrontation

The Chinese, I think, when you get this far west in China, I think it's a little different than you are in Shanghai, Beijing, or Dalian, where I think they have more of a mindset that's similar to the Malay and the US where they know they can confront, and they could be aggressive, and it's OK. I think it is in west central China, where they don't confront; they are all about a harmonious society, right? Confrontation is not harmonious, right? So it's not part of their culture, I would say, their DNA, right?

The human resource manager of Company X, a U.S.-based large-scale multinational corporation that moved from a coastal city in East China to Chengdu, an inland Chinese city, made the above comment when asked about his impression of the local culture. He admitted that he had heard and read a lot about these points of view but he also experienced scenarios pertaining to what he heard.

In Conflict

Research has shown that the Chinese tend to be non-confrontational when conflict arises. They would prefer maintaining a superficial harmony in conflict situations, and thus choose avoiding and obliging styles. Our study found that the cultural differences are even more real in the subculture of Chengdu compared with their coastal counterparts, such as Shanghai, in terms of conflict management. Although the MNC promotes constructive confrontation, the local employees find it hard to be confrontational and challenge each other although they can understand its benefits. What is worth noting is the process how the managerial employees come to realize the existence of and reasons underlying the obstacles for the local employees to overcome, and how the local employees perceive the transfer outcome?

In terms of the managerial perception, J, an expatriate manager in training and development explained to me about 'constructive confrontation,' the company's conflict handling value, and how different it is from Chinese values:

Constructive confrontation inside company X means anybody can challenge anybody about anything at any time in a very professional way... So in China, a lot of this is, it seems like the employees are very cautious about their supervisor and not willing to push back on their supervisor and challenge them that way...Well, my personal observation is that they are very hierarchical and authoritative on both sides, meaning the supervisor and the employees. The supervisor is very direct and, you see that the soft skill, emotional intelligence and the skills are not so refined as I have seen in other locations; at the same time, the employees are more willing to just accept directions than push back and question. They are more willing to just say, 'OK, my boss asked me to do this, I will go do it...' Constructive confrontation conflicts with the culture of China.

In the excerpt above, J explains how authoritative hierarchy is accepted among Chinese employees. The communication between the two observed by J is described as 'direct' and 'not so refined' on the supervisor side, while the subordinates 'are more willing to accept directions than push back and question.' Thus, we see a communication pattern of one way that entails giving orders and receiving orders. According to J, this communication pattern results from the Chinese culture and is in conflict with the company's norms in conflict management. Later, J added that confrontations being difficult in the Chengdu subsidiary might not only be due to the influence of the Chinese culture, but the result from its being a newer subsidiary and employees' lack of maturity compared with other subsidiaries of Company X.

F, a senior expatriate manager who has worked in the MNC for 20 years and has witnessed the growth of the Chengdu subsidiary, made the following remarks on the local employees when dealing with conflicts:

I can tell you that some of them cried...too emotional...It [confrontation] is very hard for them at the beginning...They are not used to it. They are only child, right? So, I told them they have to work a little bit more to turn a 'no' into 'yes', right? ... I told them, 'no use, crying is no use. (Being) emotional is no use. So you cried, but the problem won't go away. It is still there, right?'

Many years' working experience in the company has made F an authoritative figure whose own Pilipino culture has been integrated very well with the MNC culture. His job partly is to coach and train the newly hired local employees to be adapted in the company environment. He attributed such extreme cases as 'cried' and 'too emotional' to the employees/workers' being young and being the only child of the family. He thought that these young people growing up lacking the experience fighting with their siblings to cultivate conflict management skills and to be tough in pursuing their goals, and in handling stress. However, he also commented, "Today, fewer people are that emotional any more." He added that it is probably because that the company now puts much emphasis on training the newcomers to be prepared for the confrontational and high-stress situations.

In the interviews with the local employees, we find that the norm of 'constructive confrontation' has already been successfully established in the subsidiary. This shows that the training programs have achieved its goals in preparing new employees for the communication climate at work. Some of them viewed it as "better", "necessary", "not personal" and "beneficial", although it is not the most comfortable way for them to handle disagreement. For example, a local employee thinks that it provides a channel for the employees to express their views and emotions:

First of all, regardless of whether it can truly solve problems or not, if there is a channel for employee feedback, it could avoid suppressing complaints and the complaints can be expressed in time. Then, when problems are just arising, it can be discovered and then be solved in time so that [we] can avoid the worsening and escalation of problems.

W, a local engineer who has worked in the company for two and half years, when asked whether she was uncomfortable in a conflict confrontation situation, answered, 'It is uncomfortable, but you have to face it because anybody in conflict situation will be uncomfortable.' This seems to be a standard view towards conflict, as a result of the training she received from the company. Some other local employees also showed their concerns about its potential weaknesses. A local employee pointed out,

It is in conflict with the Chinese culture. Chinese prefer harmony. You are good, I am good, and every-body is good. When there is problem, and there is conflict, people will avoid confrontation as much as they can. Therefore, it takes a long time at the beginning to get used to it....So I feel that the weakness is that when it is not applied well in some situations, it will hurt relationships and emotions.

Between Superior and Subordinate

C, an expatriate manufacturing manager who has worked for the company for 14 years, including 11 years in the United States and three years in Chengdu, made the following comment:

Chinese culture is more hierarchical, and people don't feel comfortable challenging their boss, which is something I try to encourage them to do. In the US, I can have a conversation with my boss, and I feel comfortable challenging them in an objective manner, and I don't have to worry about someone or that person is going to revenge on me. Versus in China, the biggest thing I am not used to is that people are not willing to say what they feel until it costs them to do so, costs them to perform not well, or costs the relationship to be so broken before they speak up. That's one thing I really absolutely do not like.

C sees that the problem that the employees find it hard to confront their superiors lies in the Chinese culture being hierarchical. C compares himself while working in the United States as a subordinate with the local Chinese employees in Chengdu subsidiary and found a huge difference. C demonstrated strong negative feelings towards Chinese employees' being indirect and submissive in front of their superiors. Chinese employees' rather reserved and non-confrontational approach is in line with the culture being on the higher end of power distance in Hofstede's cultural dimensions. It seems that C's efforts to educate and train her subordinates – mostly line workers – did not pay off as much as he would like to see.

C, an expatriate manager who has worked in the Chengdu subsidiary for three years, made the following complaints when explaining about how he tried to accommodate the Chinese culture and the local employees:

They tell me how I have to adjust so that I don't holler people so badly or damage them permanently while helping them to grow…It makes my job tougher from the standpoint of I am not being natural, right? I have to control this control that thinking I have to do a lot more things… It just, it's changing me. Changes usually make people uncomfortable including myself… That's part of the challenge I come to China. I've never come to China before… That's another reason why, I struggled a lot in the beginning…

C is originally from Hong Kong, but was educated and worked in the US for many years, had a hard time understanding and adapting to the culture of mainland China. The frustration was shown in his feeling of being 'not natural' and the need to do many things and constantly monitor his own communication style.

Page 14 of 33

A, a female expatriate industrial engineering manager, having worked for the Chengdu subsidiary for five years, also expressed her frustration with the Chinese culture on supervisor-subordinate relationship:

With the Chinese culture, they are more quiet, and so it's kind of hard for both of us (she and her Chinese peer)…it is one thing that both of us have to help the local culture grow, you know, being open and direct, and us being not too direct…In the discussions with the group leaders and with the staff, Chinese employees don't know how to do that because they want to make their boss happy. They feel that they have to do everything. So there is a ton of self-pressure that they won't necessarily tell me that they don't have the time or resources to get something done. You know, so I get very frustrated because if they would tell me, I can reassign it, or I can do something differently or I can do it myself.

Due to the high power distance in the Chinese culture, the local employees felt reluctant to express their ideas and feelings in front of their superiors. The above comment partly explains her frustration. On one hand, A and her peer try to 'help the local culture grow'; on the other hand, they need to watch themselves not to be 'too direct'. The following conversation demonstrates that she is taking measures to help handle the communication problem that frustrates her:

A lot of times, they talk among themselves. I don't, I can't speak the language, so I don't necessarily hear all the conversations. I've got a couple of people in the department they seem to trust me, and those people will come to me and let me know what's going on. So you use kind of communication chain…

Using personnel who are bilingual and bi-cultural as 'communication chain' is an effective approach A has taken. This approach fills a gap in the communication between her and the workers due to language and cultural differences. The discrepancy in the value dimension of power distance between the Chinese and the US culture contributed partly to the outburst of the strike. If more local employees could speak up and treat supervisor-employee relationship in an egalitarian spirit, or the management could rely on the 'third-party/go-between' staff who are good at English and are adept at both cultures, more workers' voices would be heard, and problems such as the strike could be prevented.

The following excerpts from the transcript demonstrates how D, in the front-line manager development, realized the cultural difference, and then, helped the local managers to speak out their objections and to grow up to the company culture:

...At that point I realized there was a disconnect between my long experience in Company X compared to their experience level which was only three or four years, right? Here is how I am as a manager, right, and how I embrace X's values, right? So if you have a concern, you know, you can voice it to me. If it is confidential, it is between the two of us. If it is something that I am doing wrong, we can discuss and I can correct, and that was a new concept, eh, eh to them.

In terms of the local employee's perception and adaptation, when asked about how she would deal with her boss, W, a local employee, described a training session she had from the company:

I have attended a training session recently. It is very good...It's about communication. The training talked about the basic concepts on superior – subordinate interaction... I don't necessarily consult my boss on everything; sometimes I don't need to discuss with him. For example, I am an expert in my field and my boss does not know much about this field. Although he is my boss, I do not need to discuss with him. I will tell him directly, 'Mike, based on my experience and what I did previously, this is the best (way).' However, if I am talking to the little sister whom I am mentoring, or if I am to arrange training for her, I won't say, 'you come here at 4 this afternoon.' [Instead] I will ask her when it is convenient for her and when she feels comfortable, and when her time fits my schedule...

W thinks that this training session she attended is 'very good' and she learns that it is acceptable to be self-directed without asking and following her boss's order all the time when it is her who has the proper expertise. She also learns to treat her subordinates equally and be considerate with them. The purpose of the training is to foster a less hierarchical mentality in the employees and bring an egalitarian superior-subordinate relationship. According to J, from the training and development department, 'the soft skills', or people skills are what is lacking in the superior-subordinate relationship among Chinese employees. W's remarks told us that she would favor the values and ideals reflected in the training and would be willing to carry out what she has learned. In fact, there is a general receptive and supportive attitude among employees toward the company's promotion of egalitarian relationship.

Similarly, the second round of interviews conducted later shows that the perceptions generally held by the local workers were positive. In comparison, they are much more satisfied with the supervisor-subordinate communication than the expatriate managers. All the workers and team leaders interviewed found their company culture 'equal,' 'without hierarchy,' 'free and open,' the communication 'smooth and good,' and their supervisors 'easy to talk to,' 'accessible,' 'approachable,' 'open-minded,' 'considerate,' 'nice' and 'friendly'. Most of them looked at themselves as not being nervous or anxious when talking with their managers after getting familiar with each other, and saw themselves as someone who can openly and directly talk with their superiors when their opinions are not in line. The following are excerpts from the second round of the interviews:

I experienced four bosses within these nine years…All four bosses are quite good, all very good. I will speak out my different opinions directly. If I have difficulties, I will let my boss help me, which means I will point out [things] for him. Besides, sometimes we may have different opinions, then the boss will say what's on his mind, and if I find it right, I will accept it. If I think my boss failed to consider something, I will tell him, 'I feel I should insist on my idea' or things like that…My relationship with my boss is of no problem. I have always felt that it is easy to interact [with him].

The Chinese workers are sensitive to the term 'challenge the boss' or 'go against the boss.' They were more willing to say that they spoke out their opinions, or talked with their boss about their different views. Challenging one's boss has a negative connotation and seems an inappropriate way to go. They prefer using the term 'talking about my questions' or 'discuss my different opinions.' The following excerpts express the workers' carefulness in dealing with disagreement with their boss when asked if they have ever challenged their boss when they feel the boss's idea is not doable or not good:

Normally, we have not gone that far [challenge the boss]. In general, his ideas are not that bad. And we would have some constructive discussions. In the end, our ideas would combine. Nobody would insist on his own ideas. We would normally negotiate to have a common result. For example, if I have a question, I may tell my boss, by a variety of means, such as face-to-face, text message, or email. All are good as long as your words are not too oppositional. All are OK. We are fairly careful to maintain a friendly environment.

Several workers also provided examples that reflect the superior-subordinate relationship:

For example, when the biggest boss is here on site, we would call him Brother B. We would not call him boss or anything else. [We] greet him directly 'Brother B, how are you doing today?' when we see him playing badminton. He is just very equal. [He] won't be like thinking 'you are a very low level staff member.' He won't. He often greets us with a smile.

There are many such examples. Another worker mentioned:

When having meals together at the cafeteria, there is no hierarchy, say, where the managers sit and where the employees sit, things like that. Sometimes, when taking a walk, he may join us. The main thing is that when we go out to have TB (Team Building), he will be there too.

Another worker mentioned that he has even gone to his boss regarding his personal life:

If I have encountered some problem in my personal life, I may go and talk with my boss. For example, while I was dating before marriage, all of a sudden, we broke up, then I felt I could not control my emotions and my work would suffer. I went to find my boss and said: 'I have bad mood recently.' I communicated with boss, then he gave me some advice on how to balance life and work…It shows that our relationship is harmonious, so I am not afraid of telling him about it.

Collectivity

Also, evidences exist that the Chinese in coastal cities, which are economically more developed, are more individualistic than the inland provinces or cities (Gamble, 2015; Koch and Koch, 2007). Hence, we had expected to find expected to find that the Chengdu subsidiary of Company X still kept most of the collectivist tendencies and it was indeed supported. In this study, two subtopics concerning the collectivity arose from the interview data, they are, group dynamics and collective activities.

Group Dynamics

In terms of the managerial perception and measures, J, the director of the training and development department, had to integrate what he observed and heard into his training program with new employees. The following shows how he made the newcomers speak up through training:

Also, you exempt yourself from the conversation, but put them together in groups and give them a topic to talk on. Then, they'll give you all their ideas. You can sit back, and it works better if you are not even in the conversation. So it is facilitated working group. You're saying here is an activity, read this, talk about it, here is what I want you to come out with and then turn it over to them, and they will talk about it. So you remove the authoritative figure out of the work group.

J noticed that Chinese employees are often quiet in group discussions, especially when some supervisors or managers are present. Hence, he has made an adjustment and tried to 'remove the authoritative figure out of the work group' and thus created "facilitated working groups". However, when asked if he has tried to accommodate to or tried the Chinese communication style, he said firmly:

No, no, personally, I don't believe that's the right way to manage people, and I don't do that. I mean I am more of 'hey, this is…' If you have to set the direction, you explain the rationale for it and try and bring them along. If you don't have to set the direction and you are not sure what to do, you bring the group together to help them decide cos you want to get a better result…

Hence, the bottom line of his adaptation is not to violate the basic organizational values and his own cultural beliefs. His principle is to adapt to the local communication style to the extent to facilitate the discussion, and for the purpose of training the locals in order to bring them in line with the organizational values, without sacrificing these values in the long term.

F contributed similar views that there has not been much change with the company to adapt to the local culture. He tried to teach the company culture to the new hires and prepares them for the environment. He even invented a battle slogan, 'Chengdu can do!' (成都,都成!) 'teaching the culture, asking the culture what can be done, and how we can do it, to build a culture – Chengdu can do.' Jo has been trying to influence the local employees by creating a new spirit that conforms to the organizational values – the 'can do' spirit.

Sh, an expatriate factory manufacturing manager who has been on the Chengdu subsidiary for nine months, described what she found in terms of communication difference in the following account:

I think people understand what I am saying, and I understand what they are saying. Now the perspectives may be different sometimes, right? However, it's the thinking that you have to spend time trying to understand more, so I don't think the communication is much a challenge as the thinking, the beliefs, the values behind it...

Sh attributes the challenge to the core of the culture, i.e. 'the thinking, the beliefs, the values.' She realized that the deeper level of culture influences the way people communicate, and thus thought patterns, beliefs and values are the root of the problems in communication. Even though she thinks that she and her subordinates understand each other, they may understand each other at a superficial level, and it might not be so effective as she wants it to be. This is reflected by the following example she gave:

So an example, one of the things we struggle with sometimes is, I want to hear more of the local voice, and I want to hear it early on. I want to hear you know I put an idea on the table, and I want to hear the local people talking about the idea and talking about it loud, working it out in public together... However, what often happens is that when you're in a room, and there are expats in the room, then what I'm gonna hear is that the expats talking about it and somewhere about half way through; then, I may hear something from the local perspective...

Sh has identified the same problem as her colleagues have with Chinese employees being quiet during group discussions: the expatriates' or managers' presence in the groups makes the local employees unwilling to have open discussions. The solution she worked out in the example given above is to 'tone down a little bit the Westerners, and pull up the local folks, so that we get the right mix, because I think power comes from being diverse and being able to leverage the diversity instead of ignoring it ...' She made conscious efforts to create an environment where the local employees could feel free to express their opinions.

Sh arranged discussions to hear each team member's reflections on their own behavior and tried to tackle the mentality that goes against the open and direct company culture:

We have some individuals who, you know, said that it's really hard for them to go and talk to somebody if something is not going well or something has happened because they don't want to damage the relationship between them and the other person. And so by having that discussion and by providing their feedback, we know their mindset. If their mindset says if I go and talk to you about this problem, it's going to damage our relationship and we become further apart, so I don't want to do that; we have to replace that mindset with a different model, which is actually they come talk to me that makes us closer, and really people are getting to believe that...

The line workers, however, do not think that they cannot speak out their mind. Many of them said that everyone could express their opinions freely in group meetings where a decision needs to be made. For instance, a worker explained the process of making a decision:

Say, I am leading this project, and my boss, other colleagues and I are having a meeting. Everybody can speak in group discussion. The boss may speak more at the beginning and he will ask what's on your mind on this. Then, it was open time, and everybody can put forward some ideas. The views and choices of the majority will be considered. It is impossible to consider everybody's opinion. It must be only three choices A, B, C. [Decisions would be made] based on the majority's opinions. [We] would also consider if the idea is doable even though most people hold it.

There are often times when the workers do not want to speak against the boss in group meetings. However, it is not due to the power distance. The following excerpts manifest their concerns:

Because he (the leader) has many questions to answer in the meeting, and mine was just one of them, and [it] will take too much of everybody's time, and everybody is so busy, and you can't delay everybody just because of you, a single person.

Several interviewees mentioned that they would talk with colleagues first, and if all think the same way, then they would talk to the leader about it. One of them explained, 'If you put forward [the question] all by yourself and everybody opposes you, you would appear very embarrassed and stupid.'

Chinese workers, grown up learning to think for others and minimize one's own needs in a group setting, are reluctant to speak up in a big group for the fear of occupying too much time of others, or attracting too much attention to oneself. Furthermore, the face maintenance strategies include avoiding face loss for others and oneself in front of the public. Speaking up without others' agreement or support is one of the serious face losing situations. Therefore, although the company encourages open discussion and challenging the superior, many workers still prefer talking about their disagreement and concerns after the meeting, or when they are one on one with their boss. The company, in adaptation to this local culture, put forward several channels or platforms to hear the employees' voice. These include Brother B's (the CEO of Chengdu Site) Q/A, through which employees can write to him anonymously concerning almost anything; one-on-one time, when the boss and one of his subordinates meet regularly or by appointment to discuss things; having employee representatives, who are widely trusted among the workers and collect workers' ideas and advice to report to the supervisor or the manager; and MFP, through which employees can evaluate their direct boss anonymously and give comments. These measures taken by the company has won the ordinary employees trust and satisfaction as reflected in the interviews with them.

Collective Activities

In terms of the managerial perception and measures, Sh found it very beneficial to arrange group overnight excursion without a formal structure to foster solidarity of the team, which she has never done before in the United States. She described the after-effect of a recent overnight hiking trip to the E'mei Mountain which she organized for her team, and her own feelings as follows:

...While with this group, after this weekend passed, you know, the group just got very close, right? It was very good, cos it is a relationship based culture. People value that and they want to know, you know they want to know more about each other, and so forth. So I leave that open, and for me personally, very uncomfortable, because I grew in Company X and the US culture, right? So I am having to put in my mind, I am going to let this go, and the company's paying for it...Anecdotally, from both the locals as well as the expats, everybody thought the whole thing, that it was really good, and I can see it in the way they are working with each other. It's been really good...If I were to do this in the US, this wouldn't work.

Group-oriented activities highlight the nature of collectivism and the culture where Chinese employees are raised to enjoy them. Hence, Sh has tried the correct approach to cultivate the group bonding within her team. This female director has taken adjusting measures to the furthest degree in her effort to facilitate group dynamics within her team. However, she admits that such an adjustment brings uncomfortable feelings on her side as she 'grew in Company X and the US culture.' Intercultural adjustment and adaptation involves feelings of discomfort for the person in a new culture. The pain does lead to gain as her Chinese team members thought highly of the over-night excursion and the group has been unified to a great extent in this way.

L, an expatriate manager, who is a Chinese but had many years of education and work experience in the US and Canada, mentioned the following in our conversation:

Our group activity has been localized. You see, this is a young site with many young people. The locals like to sing karaoke ...they would often go together to the karaoke, and even do the foot massage thing together! ...And not only the group activities have been increased, but the content has been catering to the locals.

The workers showed even more enthusiasm toward the activities than the managers' observation. A variety of collective activities have been carried out, including team building every three months, annual sports meeting, bi-annual gourmet festival, monthly or even weekly team meals, activities by all kinds of social clubs, volunteer community service, and some other seasonal or festival activities. Team building was mostly mentioned and has the richest content, including 2-3 days' excursion, Karaoke, Mahjong, talent show, working on the farm, outward bound, to name a few. The workers summarized the advantages of having these activities as follows from the workers' perspective:

1. For leisure –to release stress from work, and to enrich the employees' pastime.
2. To exchange feelings and improve communication.
3. To improve interpersonal relationship and resolve conflict.
4. Fun to hang out with a large group of people whom you are familiar with.
5. To interact with the boss(s) more equally out of work, and to improve mutual understanding; (f) get to know more friends from other departments and sections.
6. Learn skills and knowledge.
7. A kind of company benefits.
8. Good advertisement for the company image.

A worker described the first collective activity that she experienced and impressed her: Our manager, our supervisor and colleagues of several work units were together. It was my first team building experience. We were on a Happy Farmhouse Tour. Every one of us needs to give a performance. In fact, I could not perform but I sang a song. In fact, I could not sing well, but they still applauded. For the first time, I found there were many talents in our team. Some play an instrument, some tell jokes, and all are talented. Our manager went to the stage to talk about which teams did well and gave us award. We all went up to the stage to take pictures together. Then some went fishing, some played mahjong, some played games...It was a lot of fun.

Another worker mentioned the volunteer work his team did on behalf of the company:

We went to the nursing home. It was touching. In fact, some colleagues seldom cook at home, and have been impatient with elderly people, but they are very willing to do some work, such as, cleaning, for people at the nursing home. At other times we went to some empty-nest elderly [people who don't have children or whose children were not nearby], and we helped them sort out their home. Sometimes it could be very dirty and messy, but we represent the company and were willing to do so. We felt good after we saw their home became clean.

Many workers enjoyed outdoor activities or company sponsored group travel. One of the interviewees was impressed with a trip to the famous scenic spot Jiu Zhaigou:

Once we went to Jiu Zhaigou. Because we all felt it was expensive going there, when the company will pay a large part of the expenses and we pay very little, all the colleagues in our department went. We were there for three days and everybody had fun. Because there were fairly a good number of people and people are familiar with each other, our department arranged two buses for that. It was a lot of fun...It was probably the farthest place we went as a group, and because many colleagues went and it was all company money and it was a lot of fun...

As we can see from the above narration, the Chinese workers enjoy being together and experiencing the journey as a group. For them, the more people that participate, the more fun. They also enjoy interacting with their managers on occasions out of work. Even for community services that may not be so fun, they see these activities as something very meaningful because what they do represents the image of the company.

DISCUSSION

As Gamble and Huang (2009) pointed out that there is no clear-cut line between global and local in terms of the company's approach to transfer their headquarter organizational practices. In some aspects, the subsidiary may adapt to the local culture. In some other aspects, the subsidiary may insist on implementing the organizational norms and practices, and thus increasingly resemble their headquarters. This study has confirmed their study. With the first identified theme, the company diverge with the local culture when transferring organizational practices of confrontation in conflict and egalitarian supervisor-subordinate relationship, and the local employees perceive these values and practices as positive changes. With the second theme of collectivity, the company adapt their approaches partly in order to help the group dynamic to diverge with the local practice, while organizing collective activities to converge with the local culture in to make the most of the local value of collectivism and solidarity.

Specifically, this study contributed to the literature of cross-cultural management and intercultural communication in several ways. First, our study indicated that both the local employees and the expatriate managers find it frustrating at the beginning stage when the MNC subsidiary was promoting the organizational norm of 'constructive confrontation' and the local employees were adapting to the norm. In spite of the cultural differences that lead to obstacles in conforming to the company norms, many

Chinese employees appreciate and endorse such company values as being open, equal and direct in the contexts of conflict and supervisor-subordinate relationship. This confirms Tjosvold and Sun's studies (2000, 2001) on Chinese conflict management, in which they concluded, "Chinese and Western partners in joint ventures and in other international arrangements may be able to agree that they should strive to disagree directly and respectfully and develop underlying cooperative goals so that they can work productively and synergistically" (p266). Furthermore, our study answered their call for researches on how this process could happen. We find that the company needs to provide mechanisms and channels such as off-line talk, the one-on-one session, and asking questions anonymously or through a representative to the managers, so that the Chinese can express their opinions without worrying about being viewed as attracting attentions to oneself and bragging in front of the group.

Second, the findings show that both the expatriate managers and the local employees understand the cultural differences regarding supervisor-subordinate relationship. The expatriates realize that the salient hierarchy embedded in Chinese culture and the superior-subordinate communication style resulted are hard to change but can only be adjusted over time. The local employees realize that their own cultural heritage could impede their adaptation process, and they have made efforts to adapt, although with slow and bumpy progress. At the same time, although most of the expatriate managers do not think the Chinese way would work, they have tried to understand the Chinese culture, to coach and train the local employees, and to make accommodations (e.g., paid team excursions on weekends, karaoke, and other collective activities) that are consistent with the local culture and would enhance team spirit.

Thirdly, the expatriate managers and the local Chinese employees have different views about group dynamics. The expatriate managers think the local employees are often quiet in group discussions, especially when some supervisors or managers are present. Hence, they tried different means, e.g., 'remove the authoritative figure out of the work group,' 'tone down a little bit the Westerners, and pull up the local folks, so that we get the right mix,' to facilitate group discussions for the local employees. On the local employees' side, many workers still think they can talk freely in many situations, but they are not willing to talk about their disagreement during the meeting. Speaking up without others' agreement or support is one of the serious face losing situations. The face maintenance strategies include avoiding face loss for others and oneself in front of the public. Therefore, although the company encourages open discussion and challenging the superior in group discussions, many workers still prefer talking about their disagreement and concerns after the meeting, or when they are one on one with their boss. This finding partly debates Tjosvold and Sun (2000, 2001) who conducted experiment and found that Chinese people can use open discussion effectively, especially if they confirm social face, and when persuasive rather than coercive tactics are adopted.

Fourth, not much research has so far touched upon the function of collective activities including team building in the Chinese subsidiaries of MNCs. We find that these activities provide many benefits psychologically and socially for both the employees and the company at this Chengdu subsidiary. In this case, the individual interest coincides with the collective interest, hence, the company chose to converge with the local culture in the content of the activities. Scholars have studied how group activities are related to the well-beings of individuals and the community in some cultures (Hylton, 2003; Schaaf, 2010). Our study found that these team building activities, mostly recreational, serve as the lubricant that mends and facilitates the interpersonal communication in the company, and increase the employee satisfaction. Future studies on group activity or team building could try to gain more insights on if and how these desirable activities could help the Chinese employees adapt to the organizational values and practices.

Finally, multinational corporations that moved from economically more developed cities to the inland cities of China such as Chengdu, have encountered with difficulties as well as advantages they had expected or unexpected. The local culture in inland areas remain more intact than the coastal cities. Hence, it embodies the unique characteristics of the local (As both S and A pointed out). Whether the local employees can adjust and adapt to the organizational culture of the multinational corporation depends, to a large extent, on the organization's training and management strategies and the managers' continual efforts to facilitate this process. The expatriate managers need to be willing to adjust their styles so that the locals can work in an environment where they do not feel oppressed while the core organizational values are not lost. For example, one implication from our study is that it is beneficial for both sides when the company conform to the Chinese employees' collective mentality to organize all sorts of team building activities to bond people together and maintain high work satisfaction.

The findings echo Chen's (2000) view that mutual cultural and organizational learning is imperative for both MNC management and the local employees. However, it will never be a meet-each-other-halfway deal because multinational organizations have always been keeping close bond with the home culture that makes up their identity, and the management will always represent the core MNC values. Nevertheless, they cannot bear to lose the diversity in the workplace, which brings them advantages in the process of expansion and growth. Multinational corporations can do well only by making use of the local culture, the local workforce and resources, and the local market. How to maintain a balance between the home management philosophy and the local cultural values is an endless exploration for every multinational corporation. MNCs need to acknowledge the limits to transfer their 'best practices' and make modifications to adapt to the local culture. Perhaps understanding the local culture is the first step, as Sh, an expatriate factory manager who managed her team successfully, when reflecting on the Chinese culture in the group discussion, put it:

A Chinese proverb (first bird out gets shot) which kind of tells me, ok, would I rather be first or rather be right? Probably, rather be right. And is it safe to be on my own, or is it better to kind of come from the middle, right? And so I think the values from the Chinese perspective or even from the Asian perspective is, you know, really thinking through things more deeply, understanding how things are connected, right, and it's not all about me, or I want to show myself and how great I am, so I am ok to sit back, and really think about what I am hearing and really play out different scenarios in my mind and then maybe come forward and say something... I can certainly understand that, you know, there are reasons why we are the way we are, right...but neither side is 100% good...

This study has a limitation that future studies need to overcome. Due to the company policy that does not allow outside researchers to observe or participate in meetings in the company, we did not have an opportunity to investigate live meetings or interactions of the employees and expatriates. The discussions in such meetings should be able to provide more details and insights about the cross-cultural differences and challenges both the expatriates and the local employees may encounter in the MNC. This should be a direction for future research.

ACKNOWLEDGMENT

This paper was written with funding from the Chinese government 2016/2017.

REFERENCES

Anastasia, P., & Vojtech, K. (2015). Family business in the Czech Republic: Actual situation. *Trendy Ekonomiky a Managementu*, *9*(23), 32–42.

Arnold, R. (2014). *Economics 11e*. Mason, Ohio: Cengage.

Bjorkman, I., & Fan, X. (2002). Human resource management and the performance of Western firms in China. *International Journal of Human Resource Management*, *13*(6), 853–864. doi:10.1080/09585190210134246

Boyacigiller, N. A., & Adler, N. J. (1991). The parochial dinosaur: Organizational science in a global context. *Academy of Management Review*, *1*(6), 262–290.

Chen, G. M. (2002). The impact of harmony on Chinese conflict management. In G. M. Chen, and R. Ma (Eds.), Chinese conflict management and management (pp. 3-17). Ablex Publishing.

Chen, G. M., & Starosta, W. J. (1997). Chinese conflict management and resolution: Overview and implications. *Intercultural Communication Studies*, *9*, 163–175.

Chen, L. (2000). Connecting to the world economy: Issues confronting organizations in Chinese societies. *Management Communication Quarterly*, *14*(1), 152–160. doi:10.1177/0893318900141008

Chen, Y., Tjosvold, D., & Fang, S. S. (2005). Working with foreign managers: Conflict management for effective leader relationships in China. *The International Journal of Conflict Management*, *16*(3), 265–286. doi:10.1108/eb022932

Coelho, D. A. (2011). A study on the relation between manufacturing strategy, company size, country culture and product and process innovation in Europe. *International Journal of Business and Globalization*, *7*(2), 152–165. doi:10.1504/IJBG.2011.041830

Deng, Y., & Xu, K. (2014). Strategy to motivate and facilitate compromise in Chinese mediation: A discourse analysis of contemporary Chinese mediation sessions. *The International Journal of Conflict Management*, *25*(1), 4–20. doi:10.1108/IJCMA-11-2011-0076

Easterby-Smith, M., Malina, D., & Yuan, L. (1995). How culture sensitive is HRM? A comparative analysis of practice in Chinese and UK companies. *International Journal of Human Resource Management*, *6*(1), 31–59. doi:10.1080/09585199500000002

Ferner, A., Edwards, T., & Tempel, A. (2012). Power, institutions and the cross-national transfer of employment practices in multinationals. *Human Relations*, *65*(2), 163–187. doi:10.1177/0018726711429494

Fischer, R. (2009). Where is Culture in Cross-Cultural Research?: An Outline of a Multilevel Research Process for Measuring Culture as a Shared Meaning System. *International Journal of Cross Cultural Management*, *9*(1), 25–48. doi:10.1177/1470595808101154

Gamble, J. (2003). Transferring human resource practices from the United Kingdom to China: The limits and potential for convergence. *International Journal of Human Resource Management, 14*(3), 369–387. doi:10.1080/0958519022000031807

Gamble, J. (2006). Introducing Western-style HRM practices to China: Shop-floor perceptions in a British multinational. *Journal of World Business, 41*(4), 328–343. doi:10.1016/j.jwb.2006.08.002

Gamble, J., & Huang, Q. (2009). The transfer of organizational practices: A diachronic perspective from China. *International Journal of Human Resource Management, 20*(8), 1683–1783. doi:10.1080/09585190903087032

Gamble, J., & Tian, A. W. (2015). Intra-national variation in organizational commitment: Evidence from the Chinese context. *International Journal of Human Resource Management, 26*(7), 948–970. doi:10.1080/09585192.2012.722122

Geppert, M., & Williams, K. (2006). Global, national and local practices in multinational corporations: Towards a sociopolitical framework. *International Journal of Human Resource Management, 17*(1), 49–69. doi:10.1080/09585190500366243

Gupta, A. K., & Govindara, V. (1991). Knowledge flows and the structure of control within multinational corporations. *Academy of Management Review, 16*, 768–792.

Hofstede, G. (1980). *Culture's consequences: International differences in work-related values*. Beverly Hills, CA: Sage.

Hofstede, G. (1984). *Culture's Consequences: International Differences in Work-Related Values* (2nd ed.). Beverly Hills, CA: SAGE Publications.

Hofstede, G. (1991). *Cultures and organizations: software of the mind*. New York: McGraw-Hill. Hofstede, G. (2001). *Culture's nations* (2nd ed.). Thousand Oaks, CA: Sage.

Hofstede, G., & Hofstede, G. (2010). *Cultures & organizations: software of the mind* (3rd ed.). New York: McGraw-Hill.

Hylton, C. L. A. (2003). African-Caribbean group activities, individual and collective consciousness, and enforced leisure. *Community Work & Family, 6*(1), 103–115. doi:10.1080/1366880032000063932

Jackson, T., & Bak, M. (1998). Foreign companies and Chinese workers: Employee motivation in the Peoples Republic of China. *Journal of Organizational Change Management, 11*(4), 282–300. doi:10.1108/09534819810225869

Jain, H. C., Lawler, J. J., & Morishima, M. (1998). Multinational corporations, human resource management and host country nationals. *International Journal of Human Resource Management, 9*(4), 553–566. doi:10.1080/095851998340892

Jia, W. S. (2002). Chinese mediation and its cultural foundation. In G. M. Chen and R. Ma (Eds.), Chinese conflict management and management (pp. 289-295). Ablex Publishing.

King-Metters, K., & Metters, R. (July 7, 2008). Misunderstanding the Chinese worker. *The Wall Street Journal,* from http://online.wsj.com/article/SB121441282707703883.html

Kirkbride, P. S., Tang, F. Y., & Westwood, R. Y. (1991). Chinese conflict preferences and negotiating behavior: Cultural and psychological influences. *Organization Studies*, *12*(3), 365–386. doi:10.1177/017084069101200302

Knutson, T. J., Hwang, J. C., & Deng, B. C. (2000). Perception and management of conflict: A comparison of Taiwanese and US business employees. *Intercultural Communication Studies*, *9*(2), 1–32.

Koch, B., & Koch, P. (2007). Collectivism, individualism, and outgroup cooperation in a segmented China. *Asia Pacific Journal of Management*, *24*(2), 207–225. doi:10.1007/s10490-006-9004-5

Levy, O. (2005). The Influence of Top Management Team Attention Patterns on Global Strategic Posture of Firms. *Journal of Organizational Behavior*, *26*(7), 797–819. doi:10.1002/job.340

Levy, O., Beechler, S., & Naylor, S. (2007). What we talk about when we talk about global mindset: Managerial cognition in multinational Corporations. *Journal of International Business Studies*, *38*(2), 231–258. doi:10.1057/palgrave.jibs.8400265

Liu, S., & Chen, G. M. (2000). Assessing Chinese conflict management styles in joint ventures. *Intercultural Communication Studies*, *9*(2), 71–90.

Martin, G., & Beaumont, P. (1998). Diffusing best practice in multinational firms: Prospects, practice and contestation. *International Journal of Human Resource Management*, *9*(4), 671–695. doi:10.1080/095851998340955

Mupepi, M. G. (2017). Using Communities of Practice to Identify Competencies. In K. Rasmussen, P. Northrup, & R. Colson (Eds.), *Handbook of Research on Competency-Based Education in University Settings* (pp. 157–167). Hershey, PA, USA: IGI Global. doi:10.4018/978-1-5225-0932-5.ch008

Mupepi, M. G., & Taruvinga, P. (2014). Cultural Differentials Modify Change: Comparativeness of the SADC and the US. *International Journal of Sustainable Economies Management*, *3*(2), 50–79. doi:10.4018/ijsem.2014040105

Nicotera, A. M., & Cushman, D. P. (1992). Organizational ethics: A within-organization view. *Journal of Applied Communication Research*, *20*(4), 437–462. doi:10.1080/00909889209365348

Peach, L. (1985). Managing corporate citizenship. *Personnel Management*, *17*(7), 32–35.

Peng, M. W., Lu, Y., Shenkar, O., & Wang, D. Y. L. (2001). Treasures in the China house: A review of management and organizational research on Greater China. *Journal of Business Research*, *52*(2), 95–110. doi:10.1016/S0148-2963(99)00063-6

Peng, S., He, Z., & Zhu, J. H. (2000). Conflict management styles among employees of Sino-American, Sino-French, and state-owned enterprises in China. *Intercultural Communication Studies*, *9*(2), 22–46.

Rogers, E. M., Hart, W. B., & Mike, Y. (2002). Edward T. Hall & the History of Intercultural Communication: The United States & Japan. *Keio Communication Review*, (24): 1–5.

Schaaf, R. (2010). Do groups matter? Using a wellbeing framework to understand collective activities in Northeast Thailand. *Oxford Development Studies*, *38*(2), 241–259. doi:10.1080/13600811003753370

Stage, C. W. (1999). Negotiating organizational communication cultures in American subsidiaries doing business in Thailand. *Management Communication Quarterly, 13*(2), 245–280. doi:10.1177/0893318999132003

Strauss, A. (1987). *Qualitative analysis for social scientists.* Cambridge, United Kingdom: Cambridge University Press. doi:10.1017/CBO9780511557842

Strauss, A., & Corbin, J. (1998). *Basics of Qualitative Research – Techniques and Procedures for Developing Grounded Theory* (2nd ed.). London, UK: Sage Publications.

Tempel, A., & Walgenbach, P. (2003). Global Standardization of Organizational Forms and Management Practices? Combining American and European Institutionalism. *Paper presented at the 3rd EURAM Annual Conference*, Milan.

Ting-Toomey, S., Gao, G., Trubisky, P., Yang, Z., Kim, H. S., Lin, S. L., & Nishida, T. (1991). Culture, face maintenance, and styles of handling interpersonal conflict: A study in five cultures. *The International Journal of Conflict Management, 2*(4), 275–296. doi:10.1108/eb022702

Tjosvold, D., & Sun, H. (2000). Social face in conflict: Effects of affronts to person and position in China. *Group Dynamics, 4*(3), 259–271. doi:10.1037/1089-2699.4.3.259

Tjosvold, D., & Sun, H. (2001). Effects of influence tactics and social contexts in conflict: An experiment on relationships in China. *The International Journal of Conflict Management, 12*(3), 239–258. doi:10.1108/eb022857

Wang, G., Jing, R., & Klossek, A. (2007). Antecedents and management of conflict: Resolutions styles of Chinese top managers in multiple rounds of cognitive and affective conflict. *The International Journal of Conflict Management, 18*(1), 74–97. doi:10.1108/10444060710759327

Westney, E. (1993). Institutionalization theory and the multinational corporation. In E. Westney (Ed.), *Organization theory and the multinational corporation* (pp. 53–76). Basingstoke: Macmillan. doi:10.1007/978-1-349-22557-6_3

Yuan, W. (2010). Conflict management among American and Chinese employees in multinational organizations in China. *Cross Cultural Management, 17*(3), 299–311. doi:10.1108/13527601011068388

KEY TERMS AND DEFINATIONS

Collective Activity: Activities which a group of people participate in for the purposes of enhancing group cohesion and relationship building among members.

Conflict Management: Managing differences or disagreement among people.

Confrontation: Face-to-face or direct interaction involving conflict or disagreement.

Cross-Cultural Management: Management involving more than one culture.

Group Dynamics: The state of a group including but not limited to leadership, power dimension, and communication style.

Intercultural Adaptation: Adjustment due to encounters with people of different cultural background(s) or due to relocation at a different culture.

Multinational Corporation: Corporations which operate or have branches in one or more countries other than their home countries.

Chapter 17

Fundamentals of Talent Management:
Capitalizing on Intellectual Assets

Kijpokin Kasemsap
Suan Sunandha Rajabhat University, Thailand

ABSTRACT

This chapter explains the overview of talent management (TM); the characteristics of global talent management (GTM); TM and human capital; TM and career development; the emerging trends of TM in the modern workforce; and the significance of TM in the digital age. TM is a continuous process that involves sourcing, hiring, developing, retaining, and promoting talented employees while simultaneously meeting organization's requirements. TM involves individual and organizational development in response to a rapidly changing business environment. The best TM plans should be effectively aligned with organization's strategic goals and business needs. Business leaders who implement the best TM processes are more prepared than their competitors to compete in the global economy and quickly capitalize on new opportunities. Executives and HR managers need to support the TM-related development of their talented employees to make necessary progress in the modern workforce.

INTRODUCTION

Talent management (TM) focuses on developing and retaining talented people that are important for an organization's future (Kim, Williams, Rothwell, & Penaloza, 2014). TM has become one of the most prevalent topics in the field of people development for practitioners and researchers (Collings, 2014). TM relates to the leadership studies that increasingly tries to measure the tangible contributions that individuals make to the improved organizational performance (Kirwan, 2009). As modern businesses have to be globally integrated, talent should serve as an influential source of competitive advantage (Tajuddin, Ali, & Kamaruddin, 2015). Most TM processes are driven by the need to define and identify characteristics which indicate greater ability when compared to others (Ross, 2013). Effective TM is a major contributor to the success of businesses (Joyce & Slocum, 2012).

DOI: 10.4018/978-1-5225-1961-4.ch017

Talent is associated with innate ability and creation, and can be effectively developed through training and development programs in the organization (Butter, Valenzuela, & Quintana, 2015). Talent includes human capital, social capital, reputational capital, and intellectual capital (Sparrow, Scullion, & Tarique, 2014). Talent is the collective knowledge, skills, abilities, experiences, values, habits, and behaviors of workforce brought to bear on achieving organizational mission (Schiemann, 2014). TM strategy tries to ensure that the existing talented, worthy, and committed people are contributing in achieving the existing and future needs of organization, and this procedure is called the talent pool. Talent pool describes an accumulation of talented employees who have been identified as talented (Tansley, 2011).

TM literature reflects a belief in systems and tools that can help executives and human resource (HR) professionals solve TM challenges in modern organizations (Thunnissen, Boselie, & Fruytier, 2013). TM raises institutional awareness and is a supportive tool for human resource management (HRM) (Karatop, Kubat, & Uygun, 2015). TM includes various processes (e.g., performance management, succession planning, career development, workforce planning, recruitment, and selection) in order to optimize talented people in the organization (Farley, 2005). The staffing of an organization's key positions is a major element of TM (Claussen, Grohsjean, Luger, & Probst, 2014). Organizations need talented employees to maximize their organizational performance (Vural, Vardarlier, & Aykir, 2012).

This chapter aims to bridge the gap in the literature on the thorough literature consolidation of TM. The extensive literature of TM provides a contribution to practitioners and researchers by describing the theory and applications of TM in order to maximize the business impact of TM in the modern workforce.

Background

Interest in TM in the business context came in the 1990s by a group of McKinsey consultants coined the phrase, "war for talent" in the late 1990s to emphasize the critical importance of employees to the success of top performing companies (Michaels, Hanfield-Jones, & Axelford, 2001). The HR planning movement of the 1980s and early 1990s provided the intellectual roots of TM (Sparrow, Cooper, & Hird, 2014). By the late 1990s and early 2000s, TM was being utilized as a label in its own right, with debate focusing on how organizations could develop, sustain, and manage the pools of talent, execute a talent mindset into organizational culture, align various HR programs to the needs of talent, pursue external recruitment, and develop internal talent development.

In early 2000s, TM emphasized the forecasting of staffing needs to meet business needs, succession planning, and short-term management accomplishments (Cascio & Boudreau, 2016). TM expands as a theory and practice across countries and emerging markets (Sidani & Ariss, 2014). TM is a relatively new research stream (Scholz, 2012). Businesses and consulting firms have been driving the practice and discourse on TM, while the academic field of TM is characterized by a lack of theoretical frameworks (Ariss, Cascio, & Paauwe, 2014). Many researchers consider the multi-stakeholder perspectives on the impact of TM and on the improvement of organizational effectiveness (Schuler & Jackson, 2014).

The academic interest in TM has partly arisen because, as in various areas of HRM (Jackson, Schuler, & Jiang, 2014), multinational corporations (MNCs), supported by consultancies, have adopted the terminology as they have begun to search for new options. A key to these options is people who can perform as the organizational boundary spanners between the local context and headquarters by having dual cultural schemas and bilingual skills (Furusawa & Brewster, 2015). Many academicians contextualize TM by investigating its utilization in various areas, such as small and medium-sized enterprises (SMEs)

(Valverde, Scullion, & Ryan, 2013), cross-organization partnerships, and emerging markets with national business systems (Cooke, Saini, & Wang, 2014).

PERSPECTIVES OF TALENT MANAGEMENT IN THE MODERN WORKFORCE

This section emphasizes the overview of TM; the characteristics of GTM; TM and human capital; TM and career development; the emerging trends of TM in the modern workforce; and the significance of TM in the digital age.

Overview of Talent Management

Talent management (TM) is a unique function that integrates the activities associated with the management of the talent lifecycle regardless of geography, from attracting and acquiring talent to developing and retaining it (Schiemann, 2014). The major aims of TM practice are to develop future leaders and to warrant the succession for management positions (Cohn, Khurana, & Reeves, 2005). The logic of TM meets individuals where they develop their skills through effective training, rather than simply selecting them based on the skill level they currently have (Cerdin & Brewster, 2014). Individuals' intercultural skills must be recognized by executives in order to effectively develop them in modern organizations (Mendenhall, 2006).

TM can be defined as the creative and competitive way by which organizations meet their human capital needs (Tatli, Vassilopoulou, & Ozbilgin, 2013). Collings and Mellahi (2009) viewed strategic TM processes as the important activities that involve the systematic identification of main positions that contribute to the sustainable competitive advantage of the organization and the development of HR structure to fill up these positions with competent employees. Collings (2014) considered TM as the development of high-performing and high-potential incumbents in organizational roles. TM refers to the process by which the organization identifies employees who are able to play leadership role in the future (Beheshtifar, Nasab, & Moghadam, 2012). Talented individuals produce the outstanding performance that helps firms achieve a competitive advantage (Collings & Mellahi, 2013).

Potential is the significant term in the context of TM because it has initiated the curiosity of organizations and consulting firms (Silzer & Church, 2009). Potential has a partly innate basis but has to be developed to become manifest in outstanding performance (Meyers, van Woerkom, & Dries, 2013). Only a small percentage of the workforce gets identified as having high-potential aspect (Ulrich & Smallwood, 2012). High-potential employees are frequently assigned to the international positions so that they may develop new skills, but it is also a way to test their abilities as tomorrow's top managers (Cerdin & Brewster, 2014). Organizations do not always communicate to their employees whether or not they belong to the high-potential category (Campbell & Smith, 2010).

Although TM is typically approached from the HRM perspective, different streams of the psychology literature offer the interesting theoretical perspectives on talent (Huselid & Becker, 2011). Organizations must organize their internal processes, policies, and procedures (i.e., the broader TM architecture) in order to exploit the organizational resource potential if they aim to sustain competitive advantage (Sparrow & Makram, 2015). In resource-based view (RBV) perspective, talent resources are the strategic assets that have the potential to create value and execute business strategies (Barney & Clark, 2007). The major concept of the RBV on TM is that talented people can be a source of sustainable competitive advantage

(Gallardo-Gallardo, Nijs, Dries, & Gallo, 2015). HRM researchers tend to be more accepting of subjective evaluations of talent, attempting to achieve reliability designs, thus reflecting the importance it attaches to the fit between individual talent and its interpersonal context (Silzer & Church, 2010).

TM is a significant component to business success in the current economy as it allows companies to retain top talent while increasing productivity (Kasemsap, 2016a). TM needs to advise business on empowering employees to better manage personal events as they affect job performance (Kumar & Raghavendran, 2013). Organizational leaders often find it difficult to distinguish talent as the person from the talent as the attributes of the person (Boudreau, 2013). TM is the bridge field, drawing various ideas from HRM, supply chain management, marketing, the RBV, and capability theory.

Critical success factors for effective TM include alignment with strategic goals, active chief executive officer (CEO) participation, and HRM (Kehinde, 2012). There are the positive relationships among TM, employee retention, and organizational trust (Chitsaz-Isfahani & Boustani, 2014). Organizational trust and perceived organizational support are positively related to organizational commitment in modern organizations (Kasemsap, 2013a). TM and performance management become the key strategic HRM issues for universities (van den Brink, Fruytier, & Thunnissen, 2013). TM in HR planning involves the process of identifying, selecting, developing, and retaining talented employees in organizations (Tajuddin et al., 2015).

It is an organizational practice to utilize performance appraisals for the purpose of talent identification (Dries & Pepermans, 2008). When companies invest in either the wrong people or the wrong programs, destined-to-fail teams are assembled and TM efforts are ultimately eroded (Russell & Bennett, 2015). Employee-oriented HRM practices tend to have a positive impact on TM and organizational performance (Preece, Iles, & Chuai, 2011). Incorporating a knowledge-sharing socialization mechanism with talent development programs has a supporting effect on learning and development (Wang-Cowham, 2011). Creating opportunities for research, innovation, and entrepreneurship can stimulate the flow of talent, as well as provide access to the international innovation networks (Cervantes & Guellec, 2002).

TM has a positive effect on organizational performance and individual's outcome (Bethke-Langenegger, Mahler, & Staffelbach, 2011). TM approaches need to be more equalized among organizational needs and they should be more closely linked with individuals' goals and expectations in order to retain high-potential talents (Farndale, Pai, Sparrow, & Scullion, 2014). Establishing the legitimacy of TM as an intellectual area of study remains a key challenge in the modern workforce (Collings, Scullion, & Vaiman, 2015). Organizational approaches to TM are often concerned with the ways that a small proportion of the relatively high-performing employees are identified and managed in relation to the majority (Swailes, 2013).

Björkman et al. (2013) indicated that informing talented individuals of their status has a motivational effect in line with the predictions of social exchange theory, and thus support the general logic of TM. Highly talented individuals can be characterized through a variety of characteristics, such as competencies, skills, abilities, experience, knowledge, intelligence, and character, or the ability to learn and grow within an organization (Ulrich, 2008). Highly talented people are valuable, rare, and difficult to imitate (Barney, 1995), and are recognized as the strategic resources (Schuler & Tarique, 2012) because they have the most important impact on organizational performance (Collings & Mellahi, 2009).

Characteristics of Global Talent Management

The core functions of global talent management (GTM) include talent planning, talent acquisition, talent development, and talent retention (Scullion, Collings, & Caligiuri, 2010). Talent is developed through international work experiences (Shaffer, Kraimer, Chen, & Bolino, 2012). The effective management of talent on a global scale represents a critical challenge for modern organizations (Vaiman, Haslberger, & Vance, 2015). Regarding the internationalization of businesses, GTM has emerged. The origins of GTM can be traced back to the 1800s and to the fields of entertainment management, sports management literatures, and early education (Tarique & Schuler, 2010). GTM has become a complex phenomenon in the marketplace with enhanced talent mobility and national-level competition for talent (Khilji, Tarique, & Schuler, 2015).

In order to be successful in the highly complex business environments, it is critical for firms to possess the well-developed global mindsets (Raman, Chadee, Roxas, & Michailova, 2013). MNCs are increasingly reliant on their ability to effectively manage their international operations, realizing the need to develop the key talent into the future leaders (Mendenhall, Reiche, Bird, & Osland, 2012). MNCs develop GTM strategies, concentrating on the movement of talent around the organization through expatriate assignments (McDonnell, Scullion, & Lavelle, 2013). This perspective not only enables the company to perform services in the global marketplace (Neal & Cavallaro, 2007), but also serves as a tool for developing managers with global competencies and global mindset to lead the MNCs of the future (Javidan, Teagarden, & Bowen, 2010).

Khilji and Keilson (2014) indicated that the global generational divide is likely to emerge as a workforce issue, where a majority of the young people come from developing countries, and aging from the developed countries. Managers need to fully recognize the broad scope of GTM and develop new organizational capabilities that enable them to globally acquire, grow, and retain talent with the purpose of improving their innovation performance in the modern workforce (Manning, Massini, & Lewin, 2008). Within GTM, MNCs often face the ongoing challenge of achieving the strategic balance among local adaptation, global coordination, business processes, and TM practices (Sidani & Ariss, 2014).

Despite the growing awareness of the importance of effective GTM to the success of global operations (Tarique & Schuler, 2010), MNCs face considerable challenges in implementing their GTM strategies (Scullion & Collings, 2011). The approach to GTM taken in MNCs is driven by a range of organizational goals, including business control and client demands, moderated by cost considerations (Li & Scullion, 2010). Managers need to develop organizational policies that promote environments conducive for organizational learning, as it is essential to develop the effective GTM outcomes (Khilji et al., 2015). National policymakers need to develop more integrated and collaborative GTM policies in order to effectively compete for talent (Manning et al., 2008).

The main question for organizations is where best to invest a limited pool of resources to maximize the contribution of talent in the organization (Becker & Huselid, 2006). In developed countries, they are forging global partnerships with other universities and exchange programs worldwide to train talent and get greater access to global talent pool (Wildavsky, 2010). In order to emphasize the significance of GTM, researchers have referred to many factors, including competitive global environment (McDonnell, Lamare, Gunnigle, & Lavelle, 2010), demographics (Khilji & Keilson, 2014), the rise of emerging economies and international mobility (Tyman, Stumpf, & Doh, 2010), talent shortages (McDonnell, 2011), and the need for the global integration of HR processes (Collings, 2014).

Talent Management and Human Capital

TM is an important process of expecting the need for human capital management in the modern workforce (Cappelli, 2014). The human capital perspective on talent assumes the RBV of the firm, with an employee's contribution to the organization as the main criterion of interest (Dries, 2013). Human capital and HR involve human beings who react emotionally, cognitively, and behaviorally when differently treated from other people (Paauwe, 2004). Organizations that embed the practices of human capital and competency across a range of HRM activities effectively create and develop a boundary spanning culture connecting with various organizational disciplines in the global knowledge economy (Kasemsap, 2016b).

Regarding current economic downturn and volatile market environments, TM has become an important tool to gain sustainable competitive advantage through human capital (Tarique & Schuler, 2010). Despite the efforts of HR professionals, TM remains a disjointed endeavor that rarely meets the human capital needs of today's organizations (Toterhi & Recardo, 2013).

TM aims at fulfilling the quantitative and qualitative needs for human capital, thus narrowing the supply-demand gap organizations are confronted with (Beechler & Woodward, 2009). The categorization of TM philosophy makes two assumptions about value generation from the human capital perspective: the characteristic of work has changed the potential value of talent and increased the level of power, business and social opportunity open to those with intellective skills; and an elite-group of talent generates value for an organization in a disproportionate manner, and therefore organizations should be expected to prioritize limited investment resources toward these people first (Sparrow & Makram, 2015).

Talent Management and Career Development

The labor market is characterized by outsourcing, increasing mobility, and declining job security and organizational commitment (Nilsson & Ellstrom, 2012). The fast-tracking knowledge workers seek the constant challenges and personal development in the virtually boundary-free careers (Brown & Hesketh, 2004). The demand for highly skilled labor focuses on the global level (Frank & Taylor, 2004). One example of integrative thinking in talent processes is the mass career customization (Benko & Weisberg, 2007) framework, which demonstrates integrative thinking by delivering an innovative solution to meet the needs of modern workforce, which desires flexibility in career growth and has the changing expectations for how and where work gets done.

Mass career customization goes well beyond flexible work arrangements to enable employees to create their own career paths by taking into account an individual's role and preferences for desired workload, workplace, and schedule (Kumar & Raghavendran, 2013). Career commitment, job involvement, and learning motivation are positively related to learning transfer in the modern learning environments (Kasemsap, 2013b). Career future, proactive personality, and affective commitment have a favorable impact on intention to remain (Kasemsap, 2013c). Career adaptability and participation in decision making beneficially lead to affective commitment in modern organizations (Kasemsap, 2013d).

GTM is centered on the development of employees, and it includes both high-potential development and global career development (Cerdin & Brewster, 2014). Recent work has examined company-assigned expatriates within GTM as involving high-potential talent development and global career management (Cerdin & Brewster, 2014). Vaiman et al. (2012) stated that GTM contributes to attracting, selecting, developing, and keeping the best employees in the most important roles worldwide. From the individual employee's perspective, there is an equal but different variety of goals, extending from personal and career development, to a desire to follow family members to another country or an ambition to experience the challenges of working abroad (Andresen, Biemann, & Pattie, 2013).

Executives and HR managers have to consider how to interact with talented employees, what strategies to use in order to benefit from their expertise, what reward mechanisms to use in order to retain them, and how to plan their careers if they are not willing to assign their careers into strategic corporate plans (Carr, Inkson, & Thorn, 2005). Individuals' careers are placed at the center of expatriation management as a crucial aspect of TM (Cerdin & Le Pargneux, 2009). While the advantages of GTM to the organization are apparent, expatriation assignments potentially provide a unique opportunity for the individual, setting him or her on a path of career development with global mobility opportunities (Baruch, Dickmann, Altman, & Bournois, 2013).

Emerging Trends of Talent Management in the Modern Workforce

TM has been one of the most debated themes in HRM theory and practice in recent years (Thunnissen et al., 2013). TM has gained prominence in the last few years with the advent of the global financial crisis when it is critical for firms to properly identify and retain talented employees while downsizing (Whelan, 2011). TM practices can be considered as communication mechanisms, that signal the expectations of the organization regarding the desired behaviors of employees, and also the organization's reciprocal promises to these employees (Sonnenberg, Koene, & Paauwe, 2011). Global talent is not only influenced by country reputation, but also produces reputations which manifest at the individual level through the inflow and outflow of talent (Harvey & Groutsis, 2015).

Becoming one of the most important topics of HRM, talents positively affect organizational success (Aksakal, Dağdeviren, Eraslan, & Yüksel, 2013). Workforce differentiation is the key principle between TM and strategic HRM (Boudreau & Ramstad, 2005). Studies on workforce differentiation have emphasized the positive influences on outcomes, such as employee retention, organizational productivity, and profitability (Huselid & Becker, 2011). Although workforce differentiation among employees can be reasonable from a strategic point of view, it promotes inequality among employees, making it a sensitive matter in organizations (Gelens, Dries, Hofmans, & Pepermans, 2013).

TM encompasses the instrumentation of unifying strategies in order to enhance workplace outcomes by deploying the processes matched with the business needs (Sahai & Srivastava, 2012). Organizations that are defined by a sense of purpose, and that prioritize employees as stakeholders, generally have higher levels of alignment between organizational and employee goals, more highly motivated employees, and ultimately more sustainable performance (Collings, 2014). Organizations must seek a balance between sourcing great individual talent and building such talent into a collective organizational capability (Lawler, 2008); or reflects a cultural discomfort with a differentiated approach to talent, thus calling for a more egalitarian, universal, and inclusive focus (Schuler, Jackson, & Tarique, 2011). While HR has made the significant strides in gaining the awareness of the need for a more strategic role, implementing information systems and establishing structures that combine centralized policies with decentralized business partnership, the actual practice of HR remains focused on practices not strategy, business leaders lack information about the quality of their own talent decisions, and the implementation of advanced analytics is very slow (Lawler & Boudreau, 2015).

The segmentation approach to TM addresses not only top positions, but also key positions in organizations (Cerdin & Brewster, 2014). Although access to the best talent has always been essential if organizations are to be successful, TM and talent-differentiation strategies have taken on heightened importance in the discipline of HRM as a result of a combination of demographic perspectives, labor market, and competitive pressures (Cheese, Thomas, & Graig, 2008). It is important to understand the influence of organizational choices associated with TM and talent differentiation for individual employee (Sonnenberg, van Zijderveld, & Brinks, 2014). Developing talented individuals means a single training initiative in one company, whereas it stands for a long-term development program including job rotation or expatriation in another company (Festing & Schäfer, 2014). Within a broader logic of HRM, the chance of expatriate management leading to the satisfactory results for organization and employee is higher (Cerdin & Brewster, 2014).

Organizations that aim to achieve competitive advantage have to make optimal use of their organizational resources, such as HR activities (Joyce & Slocum, 2012). The management of talented people has been proposed as the decisive factor for gaining competitive advantage through people (Heinen & O'Neill, 2004). Exclusive TM approaches face two central challenges that are unlikely to dissolve in the near future. The first perspective is the global scarcity of talent, meaning talent as defined according to exclusive philosophies (Farndale, Scullion, & Sparrow, 2010), and the second perspective relates to the highly dynamic organizations operate in, which restricts the prediction of future talent needs (Yost & Chang, 2009).

Repatriation management remains an organizational weakness in international mobility (Kraimer, Shaffer, & Bolino, 2009). Although the expatriation is a success for those individuals who went abroad, they often leave the company upon return (Suutari & Brewster, 2003). Given the investment that the organization has made in their development and the fact that they are likely to find work with competitors, this is hardly an example of good TM. Short-term approaches to repatriation, devoid of strategic management, result in repatriation not being effectively managed (Farndale et al., 2010). Repatriation is more likely to be a success for those individuals who were sent abroad with the explicit goal of developing their skills as the talented employees in the organization (Suutari, Riusala, Brewster, & Syrjakari, 2013).

Significance of Talent Management in the Digital Age

Organizations worldwide are facing the challenge of effectively managing talent (Meyers et al., 2013). Due to the economic crisis, demographic changes, and globalization, there is a growing need to develop HRM approaches that enhance the retention and development of talented employees (Lockwood, 2006). Competition and the lack of availability of highly talented and skilled employees make finding and retaining talented employees major priorities for organizations (Fegley, 2006). TM has become a popular topic among practitioners and a reoccurring phenomenon within organizations (Gelens et al., 2013). TM has gained a greater strategic role within organizations (Zagelmeyer, 2013). Organizations should recognize talent as both a strategic resource and a source of competitive advantage (Silzer & Dowell, 2010).

TM becomes a strategic area for the success of both multinational and local businesses across the globe that compete for attracting and retaining talented individuals (Selmer, Ebrahimi, & Mingtao, 2002). TM is critical to organizational success, being able to give a competitive edge through the identification, development, and redeployment of talented employees (Iles, Chuai, & Preece, 2010). Talented employees are both an organization strategic asset and a valuable resource, contributing to value creation (Sparrow & Makram, 2015). Information technology (IT) infrastructure capability can increase organizational performance through TM and sustainability programs (Benitez-Amado, Llorens-Montes, & Fernandez-Perez, 2015).

TM systems necessarily underline the importance of HR development and make use of a diverse set of HR practices that aim at expanding employees' knowledge, skills, and abilities (Meyers et al., 2013). HR practices include training, the provision of early leadership experiences, job assignment, job rotation, coaching, and mentoring (Dries & Pepermans, 2008). Yost and Chang (2009) indicated that TM initiatives often fall short of capitalizing on the value of all employees because they only focus on those workers who display leadership perspectives.

Top management, line management, and HR are the significant issues in TM (Burbach & Royle, 2010). Adopting the TM strategy to encourage talented employees has a positive impact on employee engagement and retention (Bhatnagar, 2007). Benko et al. (2014) indicated that uncertain global market conditions have heightened leadership awareness to developing effective TM that help organizations attract and retain the best talent. Without responsible leadership committed to a business strategy which addresses the development of talent and its retention, the long-term viability of an organization is weak (Doh, Stumpf, & Tymon, 2011).

Yi et al. (2015) indicated that talent is the competitive force of a hospital's development. Developing a broad variety of talents can be an essential advantage for organizations operating in the dynamic markets or business environments (Yost & Chang, 2009). Workforce demographics and skill shortages are likely to make the "war for talent" fiercer than ever before making effective TM a competitive necessity (McDonnell, 2011). Talented individuals with proven records of superior performance find difficulties performing at the same or higher level when they move to a new organization (Collings & Mellahi, 2013).

TM perspectives and knowledge management (KM) indicate organizational interventions that can facilitate knowledge-intensive organizations in exploiting their HR activities in order to maximize innovative capabilities (Gallardo-Gallardo et al., 2015). Both knowledge and TM lead to the improved organizational performance (Chadee & Raman, 2012). Economic development requires high rates of productive entrepreneurship, and this requires an efficient matching between entrepreneurial talent and production technologies (Bianchi, 2010). Economic development can be enhanced through the knowledge-based organizations to create new market and new industry platforms (Kasemsap, 2016c).

Meta-competencies (e.g., knowledge, intelligence, and learning agility) are positively related to TM (Dries, Vantilborgh, & Pepermans, 2012). Regarding human capital management, TM has a positive relationship with KM and organizational performance in the modern workforce. The integration of KM and organizational innovation is important for modern organizations to acquire better organizational performance (Kasemsap, 2016d). Lifelong learning and KM have become a fundamental goal of education policies, both at a national and international level (Kasemsap, 2016e). Effective KM is the key driver of new knowledge and new ideas to the innovation process, innovative products, services, and solutions (Kasemsap, 2016f). IT and KM applications effectively improve the strategic tools for providing the direct link between customers and tourism organizations, thus encouraging the communication channels in global tourism (Kasemsap, 2016g). Organizational culture, organizational climate, and KM are positively related to job performance (Kasemsap, 2016h).

TM is of a theoretical foundation and empirical research at the level of the individual (Gelens et al., 2013). The highly talented employees are only valuable to an organization if they occupy the specific positions that add to the organization's strategic objectives (Becker & Huselid, 2006). Concerning TM, the personnel appointment and selection are the typical decision-making concerns in the presence of various selection criteria and a set of possible alternatives (Karatop et al., 2015). Chabault et al. (2012) indicated that successful TM needs to be based on an understanding of three categories of factors (i.e., internal, external, and interconnecting perspectives). The perspective of talent development builds on the idea that everyone can become a top performer in any domain through adequate training (Colvin, 2010).

FUTURE RESEARCH DIRECTIONS

The classification of the extensive literature in the domains of TM will provide the potential opportunities for future research. Leadership is an important function of management which helps to maximize efficiency and achieve organizational goals. Leaders are responsible for training employees to perform their tasks effectively, as well as supervising the actual completion of those tasks on a regular basis. Social capital is a collective societal connection and understanding that enables individuals or groups to build trust and work together. A focus on social capital allows an organization to understand the dynamics of a situation and create effective frameworks for managing it. Learning organizations encourage organizational members to improve their personal skills and qualities, so that they can learn and develop (Kasemsap, 2016i). The relationships among leadership, social capital, and TM in the learning organizations will be the beneficial topic for future research directions.

CONCLUSION

This chapter highlighted the overview of TM; the characteristics of GTM; TM and human capital; TM and career development; the emerging trends of TM in the modern workforce; and the significance of TM in the digital age. TM is a continuous process that involves sourcing, hiring, developing, retaining, and promoting talented employees while simultaneously meeting organization's requirements. TM involves individual and organizational development in response to a rapidly changing business environment. Executives and HR managers should emphasize the basic TM perspectives (e.g., acquiring, hiring, developing, and retaining talented employees). Organizations need to have integrated TM processes in place to ensure they can attract, identify, develop, reward, and retain top performers, and address skill shortages before they become critical.

Effective TM leads to the improved human capital, career development, professional development, and organizational performance in modern organizations. The best TM plans should be effectively aligned with organization's strategic goals and business needs. As HR plays an important role in organizations, HR professionals should organize the integrated TM processes that deliver data in order to inform their strategic TM plans, enhance organizational goals, and provide the effective training programs for organizational employees toward enhancing TM strategies. TM and succession planning become the important components of organizational performance management and career development. Executives and HR managers need to support the TM-related development of their talented employees to make necessary progress in the modern workforce.

Regarding TM, goal alignment is an influential management tool that not only clarifies job roles for individual employees, but also demonstrates ongoing value of employees to the organization. Effective TM requires clarity on technical and behavioral requirements for the roles as well as specific experiences, such as international and specific market experiences. Business leaders who implement the best TM processes are more prepared than their competitors to compete in the global economy and quickly capitalize on new opportunities. Positioning HR functions and TM to contribute to overall effectiveness and financial performance of the organization is the best way the HR functions can add value to corporations and businesses. Facilitating TM has the potential to increase organizational performance and reach strategic goals in the digital age.

REFERENCES

Aksakal, E., Dağdeviren, M., Eraslan, E., & Yüksel, I. (2013). Personnel selection based on talent management. *Procedia: Social and Behavioral Sciences*, *73*, 68–72. doi:10.1016/j.sbspro.2013.02.021

Andresen, M., Biemann, T., & Pattie, M. W. (2013). What makes them move abroad? Reviewing and exploring differences between self-initiated and assigned expatriation. *International Journal of Human Resource Management*, *24*(3), 533–557. doi:10.1080/09585192.2012.697476

Ariss, A. A., Cascio, W. F., & Paauwe, J. (2014). Talent management: Current theories and future research directions. *Journal of World Business*, *49*(2), 173–179. doi:10.1016/j.jwb.2013.11.001

Barney, J. B. (1995). Looking inside for competitive advantage. *The Academy of Management Executive*, *9*(4), 49–61.

Barney, J. B., & Clark, D. N. (2007). *Resource-based theory: Creating and sustaining competitive advantage*. Oxford, UK: Oxford University Press.

Baruch, Y., Dickmann, M., Altman, Y., & Bournois, F. (2013). Exploring international work: Types and dimensions of global careers. *International Journal of Human Resource Management*, *24*(12), 2369–2393. doi:10.1080/09585192.2013.781435

Becker, B. E., & Huselid, M. A. (2006). Strategic human resources management: Where do we go from here? *Journal of Management*, *32*(6), 898–925. doi:10.1177/0149206306293668

Beechler, S., & Woodward, I. C. (2009). The global "war for talent". *Journal of International Management*, *15*(3), 273–285. doi:10.1016/j.intman.2009.01.002

Beheshtifar, M., Nasab, H. Y., & Moghadam, M. N. (2012). Effective talent management: A vital strategy to organizational success. *International Journal of Academic Research in Business and Social Sciences*, *2*(12), 227–234.

Benitez-Amado, J., Llorens-Montes, F. J., & Fernandez-Perez, V. (2015). IT impact on talent management and operational environmental sustainability. *Information Technology & Management*, *16*(3), 207–220. doi:10.1007/s10799-015-0226-4

Benko, C., Bohdal-Spiegelhoff, U., Geller, J., & Walkinshaw, H. (2014). *Global human capital trends 2014*. New York, NY: Deloitte University Press.

Benko, C., & Weisberg, A. C. (2007). *Mass career customization: Aligning the workplace with today's nontraditional workforce*. Boston, MA: Harvard Business School Press.

Bethke-Langenegger, P., Mahler, P., & Staffelbach, B. (2011). Effectiveness of talent management strategies. *European Journal of International Management*, *5*(5), 5524–5539. doi:10.1504/EJIM.2011.042177

Bhatnagar, J. (2007). Talent management strategy of employee engagement in Indian ITES employees: Key to retention. *Employee Relations*, *29*(6), 640–663. doi:10.1108/01425450710826122

Bianchi, M. (2010). Credit constraints, entrepreneurial talent, and economic development. *Small Business Economics*, *34*(1), 93–104. doi:10.1007/s11187-009-9197-3

Björkman, I., Ehrnrooth, M., Mäkelä, K., Smale, A., & Sumelius, J. (2013). Talent or not? Employee reactions to talent identification. *Human Resource Management, 52*(2), 195–214. doi:10.1002/hrm.21525

Boudreau, J. W. (2013). Appreciating and "retooling" diversity in talent management conceptual models: A commentary on "The psychology of talent management: A review and research agenda." *Human Resource Management Review, 23*(4), 286–289. doi:10.1016/j.hrmr.2013.08.001

Boudreau, J. W., & Ramstad, P. (2005). Talentship and the evolution of human resource management: From professional practices to strategic talent decision science. *Human Resource Planning Journal, 28*(2), 17–26.

Brown, P., & Hesketh, A. (2004). *The mismanagement of talent: Employability and jobs in the knowledge economy.* Oxford, UK: Oxford University Press. doi:10.1093/acprof:oso/9780199269532.001.0001

Burbach, R., & Royle, T. (2010). Talent on demand? Talent management in the German and Irish subsidiaries of a US multinational corporation. *Personnel Review, 39*(4), 414–431. doi:10.1108/00483481011045399

Butter, M. C., Valenzuela, E. S., & Quintana, M. G. B. (2015). Intercultural talent management model: Virtual communities to promote collaborative learning in indigenous contexts. Teachers' and students' perceptions. *Computers in Human Behavior, 51*, 1191–1197. doi:10.1016/j.chb.2015.01.030

Campbell, M., & Smith, R. (2010). *High-potential talent: A view from inside the leadership pipeline.* Greensboro, NC: Center for Creative Leadership.

Cappelli, P. (2014). *Strategic talent management: Contemporary issues in an international context.* Cambridge, UK: Cambridge University Press.

Carr, S. C., Inkson, K., & Thorn, K. (2005). From global careers to talent flow: Reinterpreting "brain drain." *Journal of World Business, 40*(4), 386–398. doi:10.1016/j.jwb.2005.08.006

Cascio, W. F., & Boudreau, J. W. (2016). The search for global competence: From international HR to talent management. *Journal of World Business, 51*(1), 103–114. doi:10.1016/j.jwb.2015.10.002

Cerdin, J. L., & Brewster, C. (2014). Talent management and expatriation: Bridging two streams of research and practice. *Journal of World Business, 49*(2), 245–252. doi:10.1016/j.jwb.2013.11.008

Cerdin, J. L., & Le Pargneux, M. (2009). Career and international assignment fit: Toward an integrative model of success. *Human Resource Management, 48*(1), 5–25. doi:10.1002/hrm.20264

Cervantes, M., & Guellec, D. (2002). The brain drain: Old myths, new realities. *The OECD Observer. Organisation for Economic Co-Operation and Development, 230*, 40–42.

Chabault, D., Hulin, A., & Soparnot, R. (2012). Talent management in clusters. *Organizational Dynamics, 41*(4), 327–335. doi:10.1016/j.orgdyn.2012.08.008

Chadee, D., & Raman, R. (2012). External knowledge and performance of offshore IT service providers in India: The mediating role of talent management. *Asia Pacific Journal of Human Resources, 50*(4), 459–482. doi:10.1111/j.1744-7941.2012.00039.x

Cheese, P., Thomas, R. J., & Craig, E. (2008). *The talent powered organization: Strategies for globalization, talent management and high performance.* London, UK: Kogan Page Limited.

Chitsaz-Isfahani, A., & Boustani, H. (2014). Effects of talent management on employees retention: The mediate effect of organizational trust. *International Journal of Academic Research in Economics and Management Sciences, 3*(5), 114–128.

Claussen, J., Grohsjean, T., Luger, J., & Probst, G. (2014). Talent management and career development: What it takes to get promoted. *Journal of World Business, 49*(2), 236–244. doi:10.1016/j.jwb.2013.11.007

Cohn, J. M., Khurana, R., & Reeves, L. (2005). Growing talent as if your business depended on it. *Harvard Business Review, 83*, 63–70. PMID:16250625

Collings, D. G. (2014). Towards mature talent management: Beyond shareholder value. *Human Resource Development Quarterly, 25*(3), 301–319. doi:10.1002/hrdq.21198

Collings, D. G., & Mellahi, K. (2009). Strategic talent management: A review and research agenda. *Human Resource Management Review, 19*(4), 304–313. doi:10.1016/j.hrmr.2009.04.001

Collings, D. G., & Mellahi, K. (2013). Commentary on: "Talent–innate or acquired? Theoretical considerations and their implications for talent management." *Human Resource Management Review, 23*(4), 322–325. doi:10.1016/j.hrmr.2013.08.003

Collings, D. G., Scullion, H., & Vaiman, V. (2015). Talent management: Progress and prospects. *Human Resource Management Review, 25*(3), 233–235. doi:10.1016/j.hrmr.2015.04.005

Colvin, G. (2010). *Talent is overrated: What really separates world-class performers from everybody else.* New York, NY: Penguin Group.

Cooke, F. L., Saini, D. S., & Wang, J. (2014). Talent management in China and India: A comparison of management perceptions and human resource practices. *Journal of World Business, 49*(2), 225–235. doi:10.1016/j.jwb.2013.11.006

Doh, J. P., Stumpf, S. A., & Tymon, W. G. Jr. (2011). Responsible leadership helps retain talent in India. *Journal of Business Ethics, 98*(1), 85–100. doi:10.1007/s10551-011-1018-3

Dries, N. (2013). The psychology of talent management: A review and research agenda. *Human Resource Management Review, 23*(4), 272–285. doi:10.1016/j.hrmr.2013.05.001

Dries, N., & Pepermans, R. (2008). "Real" high-potential careers: An empirical study into the perspectives of organizations and high potentials. *Personnel Review, 37*(1), 85–108. doi:10.1108/00483480810839987

Dries, N., Vantilborgh, T., & Pepermans, R. (2012). The role of learning agility and career variety in the identification and development of high potential employees. *Personnel Review, 41*(3), 340–358. doi:10.1108/00483481211212977

Farley, C. (2005). HR's role in talent management and driving business results. *Employment Relations Today, 32*(1), 55–61. doi:10.1002/ert.20053

Farndale, E., Pai, A., Sparrow, P. R., & Scullion, H. (2014). Balancing individual and organizational goals in global talent management: A mutual-benefits perspective. *Journal of World Business, 49*(2), 204–214. doi:10.1016/j.jwb.2013.11.004

Farndale, E., Scullion, H., & Sparrow, P. R. (2010). The role of the corporate HR function in global talent management. *Journal of World Business*, *45*(2), 161–168. doi:10.1016/j.jwb.2009.09.012

Fegley, S. (2006). *2006 Strategic HR management: Survey report*. Alexandria, VA: Society for Human Resource Management.

Festing, M., & Schäfer, L. (2014). Generational challenges to talent management: A framework for talent retention based on the psychological-contract perspective. *Journal of World Business*, *49*(2), 262–271. doi:10.1016/j.jwb.2013.11.010

Frank, F. D., & Taylor, C. R. (2004). Talent management: Trends that will shape the future. *Human Resource Planning*, *27*(1), 33–41.

Furusawa, M., & Brewster, C. (2015). The bi-cultural option for global talent management: The Japanese/Brazilian *Nikkeijin* example. *Journal of World Business*, *50*(1), 133–143. doi:10.1016/j.jwb.2014.02.005

Gallardo-Gallardo, E., Nijs, S., Dries, N., & Gallo, P. (2015). Towards an understanding of talent management as a phenomenon-driven field using bibliometric and content analysis. *Human Resource Management Review*, *25*(3), 264–279. doi:10.1016/j.hrmr.2015.04.003

Gelens, J., Dries, N., Hofmans, J., & Pepermans, R. (2013). The role of perceived organizational justice in shaping the outcomes of talent management: A research agenda. *Human Resource Management Review*, *23*(4), 341–353. doi:10.1016/j.hrmr.2013.05.005

Harvey, W. S., & Groutsis, D. (2015). Reputation and talent mobility in the Asia Pacific. *Asia Pacific Journal of Human Resources*, *53*(1), 22–40. doi:10.1111/1744-7941.12047

Heinen, J. S., & O'Neill, C. (2004). Managing talent to maximize performance. *Employment Relations Today*, *31*(2), 67–82. doi:10.1002/ert.20018

Huselid, M. A., & Becker, B. E. (2011). Bridging micro and macro domains: Workforce differentiation and strategic human resource management. *Journal of Management*, *37*(2), 421–428. doi:10.1177/0149206310373400

Iles, P., Chuai, X., & Preece, D. (2010). Talent management and HRM in multinational companies in Beijing: Definitions, differences and drivers. *Journal of World Business*, *45*(2), 179–189. doi:10.1016/j.jwb.2009.09.014

Jackson, S. E., Schuler, R. S., & Jiang, K. (2014). An aspirational framework for strategic human resource management. *The Academy of Management Annals*, *8*(1), 1–56. doi:10.1080/19416520.2014.872335

Javidan, M., Teagarden, M., & Bowen, D. (2010). Managing yourself: Making it overseas. *Harvard Business Review*, *88*(4), 109–113.

Joyce, W. F., & Slocum, J. W. (2012). Top management talent, strategic capabilities, and firm performance. *Organizational Dynamics*, *41*(3), 183–193. doi:10.1016/j.orgdyn.2012.03.001

Karatop, B., Kubat, C., & Uygun, O. (2015). Talent management in manufacturing system using fuzzy logic approach. *Computers & Industrial Engineering*, *86*, 127–136. doi:10.1016/j.cie.2014.09.015

Kasemsap, K. (2013a) Strategic knowledge management: An integrated framework and causal model of perceived organizational support, organizational trust, organizational commitment, and knowledge-sharing behavior. Paper presented at the 1st International Conference on Computing Engineering and Enterprise Management (ICCEEM 2013), Bangkok, Thailand.

Kasemsap, K. (2013b). Practical framework: Creation of causal model of job involvement, career commitment, learning motivation, and learning transfer. *International Journal of the Computer, the Internet and Management, 21*(1), 29–35.

Kasemsap, K. (2013c). Establishing a unified framework and a causal model of proactive personality, career future, affective commitment, and intention to remain. *International Research Journal of Humanities and Environmental Issues, 2*(2-1), 33–36.

Kasemsap, K. (2013d). Innovative business management: A practical framework and causal model of participation in decision making, career adaptability, affective commitment, and turnover intention. Paper presented at the 2nd International Conference on Economics, Business Innovation (ICEBI 2013), Copenhagen, Denmark.

Kasemsap, K. (2016a). Promoting leadership development and talent management in modern organizations. In U. Aung & P. Ordoñez de Pablos (Eds.), *Managerial strategies and practice in the Asian business sector* (pp. 238–266). Hershey, PA, USA: IGI Global. doi:10.4018/978-1-4666-9758-4.ch013

Kasemsap, K. (2016b). Analyzing the roles of human capital and competency in global business. In S. Sen, A. Bhattacharya, & R. Sen (Eds.), *International perspectives on socio-economic development in the era of globalization* (pp. 1–29). Hershey, PA, USA: IGI Global. doi:10.4018/978-1-4666-9908-3.ch001

Kasemsap, K. (2016c). Advocating entrepreneurship education and knowledge management in global business. In N. Baporikar (Ed.), *Handbook of research on entrepreneurship in the contemporary knowledge-based global economy* (pp. 313–339). Hershey, PA, USA: IGI Global. doi:10.4018/978-1-4666-8798-1.ch014

Kasemsap, K. (2016d). The roles of knowledge management and organizational innovation in global business. In G. Jamil, J. Poças-Rascão, F. Ribeiro, & A. Malheiro da Silva (Eds.), *Handbook of research on information architecture and management in modern organizations* (pp. 130–153). Hershey, PA, USA: IGI Global. doi:10.4018/978-1-4666-8637-3.ch006

Kasemsap, K. (2016e). The roles of lifelong learning and knowledge management in global higher education. In P. Ordóñez de Pablos & R. Tennyson (Eds.), *Impact of economic crisis on education and the next-generation workforce* (pp. 71–100). Hershey, PA, USA: IGI Global. doi:10.4018/978-1-4666-9455-2.ch004

Kasemsap, K. (2016f). Creating product innovation strategies through knowledge management in global business. In A. Goel & P. Singhal (Eds.), *Product innovation through knowledge management and social media strategies* (pp. 330–357). Hershey, PA, USA: IGI Global. doi:10.4018/978-1-4666-9607-5.ch015

Kasemsap, K. (2016g). The roles of information technology and knowledge management in global tourism. In A. Nedelea, M. Korstanje, & B. George (Eds.), *Strategic tools and methods for promoting hospitality and tourism services* (pp. 109–138). Hershey, PA, USA: IGI Global. doi:10.4018/978-1-4666-9761-4.ch006

Kasemsap, K. (2016h). A unified framework of organizational perspectives and knowledge management and their impact on job performance. In A. Normore, L. Long, & M. Javidi (Eds.), *Handbook of research on effective communication, leadership, and conflict resolution* (pp. 267–297). Hershey, PA, USA: IGI Global. doi:10.4018/978-1-4666-9970-0.ch015

Kasemsap, K. (2016i). The roles of e-learning, organizational learning, and knowledge management in the learning organizations. In E. Railean, G. Walker, A. Elçi, & L. Jackson (Eds.), *Handbook of research on applied learning theory and design in modern education* (pp. 786–816). Hershey, PA, USA: IGI Global. doi:10.4018/978-1-4666-9634-1.ch039

Kehinde, J. S. (2012). Talent management: Effect on organizational performance. *Journal of Management Research*, 4(2), 178–186. doi:10.5296/jmr.v4i2.937

Khilji, S. E., & Keilson, B. (2014). In search of global talent: Is South Asia ready? *South Asian Journal of Global Business Research*, 3(2), 114–134. doi:10.1108/SAJGBR-05-2014-0033

Khilji, S. E., Tarique, I., & Schuler, R. S. (2015). Incorporating a macro view in global talent management. *Human Resource Management Review*, 25(3), 236–248. doi:10.1016/j.hrmr.2015.04.001

Kim, Y., Williams, R., Rothwell, W. J., & Penaloza, P. (2014). A strategic model for technical talent management: A model based on a qualitative case study. *Performance Improvement Quarterly*, 26(4), 93–121. doi:10.1002/piq.21159

Kirwan, K. S. (2009). Practicing talent life cycle management. *The Journal of Leadership Studies*, 3(1), 65–66. doi:10.1002/jls.20101

Kraimer, M. L., Shaffer, M. A., & Bolino, M. C. (2009). The influence of expatriate and repatriate experiences on career advancement and repatriate retention. *Human Resource Management*, 48(1), 27–47. doi:10.1002/hrm.20265

Kumar, H., & Raghavendran, S. (2013). Not by money alone: The emotional wallet and talent management. *The Journal of Business Strategy*, 34(3), 16–23. doi:10.1108/JBS-11-2012-0073

Lawler, E. E. (2008). *Talent: Making people your competitive advantage.* San Francisco, CA: Jossey–Bass.

Lawler, E. E., & Boudreau, J. W. (2015). *Global trends in human resource management: A twenty-year analysis.* Stanford, CA: Stanford University Press.

Li, S., & Scullion, H. (2010). Developing the local competences of expatriate managers for emerging markets: A knowledge based approach. *Journal of World Business*, 45(2), 190–196. doi:10.1016/j.jwb.2009.09.017

Lockwood, N. R. (2006). Talent management: Driver for organizational success. *HRMagazine*, 51(6), 1–11.

Manning, S., Massini, S., & Lewin, A. Y. (2008). A dynamic perspective on next-generation offshoring: The global sourcing of science and engineering talent. *The Academy of Management Perspectives, 22*(3), 35–54. doi:10.5465/AMP.2008.34587994

McDonnell, A. (2011). Still fighting the "war for talent?" Bridging the science versus practice gap. *Journal of Business and Psychology, 26*(2), 169–173. doi:10.1007/s10869-011-9220-y

McDonnell, A., Lamare, R., Gunnigle, P., & Lavelle, J. (2010). Developing tomorrow's leaders: Evidence of global talent management in multinational enterprises. *Journal of World Business, 45*(2), 150–160. doi:10.1016/j.jwb.2009.09.015

McDonnell, A., Scullion, H., & Lavelle, J. (2013). Managing human resources in large international organizations. In G. Sarikades & C. Cooper (Eds.), *How can HR drive growth* (pp. 4–25). Cheltenham, UK: Edward Elgar Publishing. doi:10.4337/9781781002261.00008

Mendenhall, M. E. (2006). The elusive, yet critical challenge of developing global leaders. *European Management Journal, 24*(6), 422–429. doi:10.1016/j.emj.2006.10.002

Mendenhall, M. E., Reiche, B. S., Bird, A., & Osland, J. S. (2012). Defining the "global" in global leadership. *Journal of World Business, 47*(4), 493–503. doi:10.1016/j.jwb.2012.01.003

Meyers, M. C., & van Woerkom, M. (2014). The influence of underlying philosophies on talent management: Theory, implications for practice, and research agenda. *Journal of World Business, 49*(2), 192–203. doi:10.1016/j.jwb.2013.11.003

Meyers, M. C., van Woerkom, M., & Dries, N. (2013). Talent–Innate or acquired? Theoretical considerations and their implications for talent management. *Human Resource Management Review, 23*(4), 305–321. doi:10.1016/j.hrmr.2013.05.003

Michaels, E., Hanfield-Jones, H., & Axelford, B. (2001). *The war for talent*. Boston, MA: Harvard Business School Press.

Neal, A., & Cavallaro, L. (2007). Action learning accelerates innovation: Cisco's action learning forum. *Organization Development Journal, 25*(4), 107–123.

Nilsson, S., & Ellstrom, P. E. (2012). Employability and talent management: Challenges for HRD practices. *European Journal of Training and Development, 36*(1), 26–45. doi:10.1108/03090591211192610

Paauwe, J. (2004). *HRM and performance: Achieving long-term viability*. New York, NY: Oxford University Press. doi:10.1093/acprof:oso/9780199273904.001.0001

Preece, D., Iles, P., & Chuai, X. (2011). Talent management and management fashion in Chinese enterprises: Exploring case studies in Beijing. *International Journal of Human Resource Management, 22*(16), 3413–3428. doi:10.1080/09585192.2011.586870

Raman, R., Chadee, D., Roxas, B., & Michailova, S. (2013). Effects of partnership quality, talent management, and global mindset on performance of offshore IT service providers in India. *Journal of International Management, 19*(4), 333–346. doi:10.1016/j.intman.2013.03.010

Ross, S. (2013). How definitions of talent suppress talent management. *Industrial and Commercial Training, 45*(3), 166–170. doi:10.1108/00197851311320586

Russell, C., & Bennett, N. (2015). Big data and talent management: Using hard data to make the soft stuff easy. *Business Horizons, 58*(3), 237–242. doi:10.1016/j.bushor.2014.08.001

Sahai, S., & Srivastava, A. K. (2012). Goal / target setting and performance assessment as tool for talent management. *Procedia: Social and Behavioral Sciences, 37,* 241–246. doi:10.1016/j.sbspro.2012.03.290

Schiemann, W. A. (2014). From talent management to talent optimization. *Journal of World Business, 49*(2), 281–288. doi:10.1016/j.jwb.2013.11.012

Scholz, T. M. (2012). Talent management in the video game industry: The role of cultural diversity and cultural intelligence. *Thunderbird International Business Review, 54*(6), 845–858. doi:10.1002/tie.21507

Schuler, R. S., & Jackson, S. E. (2014). Human resource management and organizational effectiveness: Yesterday and today. *Journal of Organizational Effectiveness: People and Performance, 1*(1), 35–55. doi:10.1108/JOEPP-01-2014-0003

Schuler, R. S., Jackson, S. E., & Tarique, I. (2011). Global talent management and global talent challenges: Strategic opportunities for IHRM. *Journal of World Business, 46*(4), 506–516. doi:10.1016/j.jwb.2010.10.011

Schuler, R. S., & Tarique, I. (2012). Global talent management: Theoretical perspectives, systems, and challenges. In G. Stahl, I. Björkman, & S. Morris (Eds.), *Handbook of research in international human resource management* (pp. 205–219). Cheltenham, UK: Edward Elgar Publishing. doi:10.4337/9781849809191.00017

Scullion, H., & Collings, D. G. (2011). *Global talent management.* London, UK: Routledge.

Scullion, H., Collings, D. G., & Caligiuri, P. (2010). Global talent management: Introduction. *Journal of World Business, 45*(2), 105–108. doi:10.1016/j.jwb.2009.09.011

Selmer, J., Ebrahimi, B. P., & Mingtao, L. (2002). Career management of business expatriates from China. *International Business Review, 11*(1), 17–33. doi:10.1016/S0969-5931(01)00045-2

Shaffer, M. A., Kraimer, M. L., Chen, Y. P., & Bolino, M. C. (2012). Choices, challenges, and career consequences of global work experiences: A review and future agenda. *Journal of Management, 38*(4), 1282–1327. doi:10.1177/0149206312441834

Sidani, Y., & Ariss, A. A. (2014). Institutional and corporate drivers of global talent management: Evidence from the Arab Gulf region. *Journal of World Business, 49*(2), 215–224. doi:10.1016/j.jwb.2013.11.005

Silzer, R., & Church, A. H. (2009). The potential for potential. *Industrial and Organizational Psychology: Perspectives on Science and Practice, 2*(4), 446–452. doi:10.1111/j.1754-9434.2009.01172.x PMID:19580727

Silzer, R., & Church, A. H. (2010). Identifying and assessing high-potential talent: Current organizational practices. In R. Silzer & B. Dowell (Eds.), *Strategy-driven talent management: A leadership imperative* (pp. 213–279). San Francisco, CA: Jossey–Bass.

Silzer, R., & Dowell, B. E. (2010). Strategic talent management matters. In R. Silzer & B. Dowell (Eds.), *Strategy-driven talent management: A leadership imperative* (pp. 3–72). San Francisco, CA: Jossey–Bass.

Sonnenberg, M., Koene, B., & Paauwe, J. (2011). Balancing HRM: The psychological contract of employees: A multi-level study. *Personnel Review*, *40*(6), 664–683. doi:10.1108/00483481111169625

Sonnenberg, M., van Zijderveld, V., & Brinks, M. (2014). The role of talent-perception incongruence in effective talent management. *Journal of World Business*, *49*(2), 272–280. doi:10.1016/j.jwb.2013.11.011

Sparrow, P. R., Cooper, C., & Hird, M. (2014). *Do we need HR?: Repositioning people management for success*. London, UK: Palgrave MacMillan.

Sparrow, P. R., & Makram, H. (2015). What is the value of talent management? Building value-driven processes within a talent management architecture. *Human Resource Management Review*, *25*(3), 249–263. doi:10.1016/j.hrmr.2015.04.002

Sparrow, P. R., Scullion, H., & Tarique, I. (2014). Multiple lenses on talent management: Definitions and contours of the field. In P. Sparrow, H. Scullion, & I. Tarique (Eds.), *Strategic talent management: Contemporary issues in international context* (pp. 36–70). Cambridge, UK: Cambridge University Press. doi:10.1017/CBO9781139424585.004

Suutari, V., & Brewster, C. (2003). Repatriation: Evidence from a longitudinal study of careers and empirical expectations among Finnish repatriates. *International Journal of Human Resource Management*, *14*(7), 1132–1151. doi:10.1080/0958519032000114200

Suutari, V., Brewster, C., Riusala, K., & Syrjakari, S. (2013). Managing non-standard international experience: Evidence from a Finnish company. *Journal of Global Mobility: The Home of Expatriate Management Research*, *1*(2), 118–138. doi:10.1108/JGM-10-2012-0014

Swailes, S. (2013). The ethics of talent management. *Business Ethics (Oxford, England)*, *22*(1), 32–46. doi:10.1111/beer.12007

Tajuddin, D., Ali, R., & Kamaruddin, B. H. (2015). Developing talent management crisis model for quality life of bank employees in Malaysia. *Procedia: Social and Behavioral Sciences*, *201*, 80–84. doi:10.1016/j.sbspro.2015.08.133

Tansley, C. (2011). What do we mean by the term "talent" in talent management? *Industrial and Commercial Training*, *43*(5), 266–274. doi:10.1108/00197851111145853

Tarique, I., & Schuler, R. S. (2010). Global talent management: Literature review, integrative framework, and suggestions for future research. *Journal of World Business*, *45*(2), 122–133. doi:10.1016/j.jwb.2009.09.019

Tatli, A., Vassilopoulou, J., & Ozbilgin, M. (2013). An unrequited affinity between talent shortages and untapped female potential: The relevance of gender quotas for talent management in high growth potential economies of the Asia Pacific region. *International Business Review*, *22*(3), 539–553. doi:10.1016/j.ibusrev.2012.07.005

Thunnissen, M., Boselie, P., & Fruytier, B. (2013). Talent management and the relevance of context: Towards a pluralistic approach. *Human Resource Management Review*, *23*(4), 326–336. doi:10.1016/j.hrmr.2013.05.004

Toterhi, T., & Recardo, R. J. (2013). The talent funnel: How to surface key human resources. *Global Business and Organizational Excellence*, *32*(5), 22–44. doi:10.1002/joe.21501

Tyman, W. G., Stumpf, S. A., & Doh, J. P. (2010). Exploring talent management in India: The neglected role of intrinsic rewards. *Journal of World Business*, *45*(2), 109–120. doi:10.1016/j.jwb.2009.09.016

Ulrich, D. (2008). Call for talent: What is the best solutions? *Leadership Excellence*, *25*(5), 17.

Ulrich, D., & Smallwood, N. (2012). What is talent? *Leader to Leader*, *2012*(63), 55–61. doi:10.1002/ltl.20011

Vaiman, V., Haslberger, A., & Vance, C. M. (2015). Recognizing the important role of self-initiated expatriates in effective global talent management. *Human Resource Management Review*, *25*(3), 280–286. doi:10.1016/j.hrmr.2015.04.004

Vaiman, V., Scullion, H., & Collings, D. G. (2012). Talent management decision-making. *Management Decision*, *50*(5), 925–941. doi:10.1108/00251741211227663

Valverde, M., Scullion, H., & Ryan, G. (2013). Talent management in Spanish medium-sized organizations. *International Journal of Human Resource Management*, *24*(9), 1832–1852. doi:10.1080/09585192.2013.777545

van den Brink, M., Fruytier, B., & Thunnissen, M. (2013). Talent management in academia: Performance systems and HRM policies. *Human Resource Management Journal*, *23*(2), 180–195. doi:10.1111/j.1748-8583.2012.00196.x

Vural, Y., Vardarlier, P., & Aykir, A. (2012). The effects of using talent management with performance evaluation system over employee commitment. *Procedia: Social and Behavioral Sciences*, *58*, 340–349. doi:10.1016/j.sbspro.2012.09.1009

Wang-Cowham, C. (2011). Developing talent with an integrated knowledge sharing mechanism: An exploratory investigation from the Chinese human resource managers' perspective. *Human Resource Development International*, *14*(4), 391–407. doi:10.1080/13678868.2011.601573

Wanzel, K. R., Matsumoto, E. D., Hamstra, S. J., & Anastakis, D. J. (2002). Teaching technical skills: Training on a simple, inexpensive, and portable model. *Plastic and Reconstructive Surgery*, *109*(1), 258–264. doi:10.1097/00006534-200201000-00041 PMID:11786823

Whelan, E. (2011). It's who you know not what you know: A social network analysis approach to talent management. *European Journal of International Management*, *5*(5), 484–500. doi:10.1504/EJIM.2011.042175

Wildavsky, B. (2010). *The great brain race: How global universities are shaping the world*. Princeton, NJ: Princeton University Press.

Yi, L., Wei, L., Hao, A., Hu, M., & Xu, X. (2015). Exploration on construction of hospital "talent tree" project. *Cell Biochemistry and Biophysics, 72*(1), 67–71. doi:10.1007/s12013-014-0405-7 PMID:25413963

Yost, P. R., & Chang, G. (2009). Everyone is equal, but some are more equal than others. *Industrial and Organizational Psychology: Perspectives on Science and Practice, 2*(4), 442–445. doi:10.1111/j.1754-9434.2009.01171.x

Zagelmeyer, S. (2013). Tackling the crisis through concession bargaining: Evidence from five German companies. *International Journal of Manpower, 34*(3), 232–251. doi:10.1108/IJM-04-2013-0080

ADDITIONAL READING

Böhm, M. J., & Watzinger, M. (2015). The allocation of talent over the business cycle and its long-term effect on sectoral productivity. *Economica, 82*(328), 892–911. doi:10.1111/ecca.12143

Burkus, D., & Osula, B. (2011). Faulty Intel in the war for talent: Replacing the assumptions of talent management with evidence-based strategies. *Journal of Business Studies Quarterly, 3*(2), 1–9.

Cairns, T. D. (2015). Disruptive talent-acquisition strategies. *Employment Relations Today, 42*(3), 29–35. doi:10.1002/ert.21522

Cajigas, T. J., & McGrath, J. A. (2015). Formalizing a talent management strategy through a competency model framework. *Strategic Enrollment Management Quarterly, 3*(2), 132–144. doi:10.1002/sem3.20065

Calvo, N., Bastida, M., & Feás, J. (2013). A simulation tool for talent management in knowledge-intense firms. An opportunity for HR managers? *Global Business Perspectives, 1*(3), 261–273. doi:10.1007/s40196-012-0003-2

Cole, C. R., & McCullough, K. A. (2012). The insurance industry's talent gap and where we go from here. *Risk Management & Insurance Review, 15*(1), 107–116. doi:10.1111/j.1540-6296.2011.01212.x

Connell, J., & Stanton, P. (2014). Skills and the role of HRM: Towards a research agenda for the Asia Pacific region. *Asia Pacific Journal of Human Resources, 52*(1), 4–22. doi:10.1111/1744-7941.12021

Doherty, N. (2013). Understanding the self-initiated expatriate: A review and directions for future research. *International Journal of Management Reviews, 15*(4), 447–469. doi:10.1111/ijmr.12005

Dunnagan, K., Maragakis, M., Schneiderjohn, N., Turner, C., & Vance, C. M. (2013). Meeting the global imperative of local leadership talent development in Hong Kong, Singapore, and India. *Global Business and Organizational Excellence, 32*(2), 52–60. doi:10.1002/joe.21472

Festing, M., Schäfer, L., & Scullion, H. (2013). Talent management in medium-sized German companies: An explorative study and agenda for future research. *International Journal of Human Resource Management, 24*(9), 1872–1893. doi:10.1080/09585192.2013.777538

Gelens, J., Hofmans, J., Dries, N., & Pepermans, R. (2014). Talent management and organisational justice: Employee reactions to high potential identification. *Human Resource Management Journal, 24*(2), 159–175. doi:10.1111/1748-8583.12029

Glenn, T. (2012). The state of talent management in Canada's public sector. *Canadian Public Administration*, *55*(1), 25–51. doi:10.1111/j.1754-7121.2012.00204.x

Höglund, M. (2012). Quid pro quo? Examining talent management through the lens of psychological contracts. *Personnel Review*, *41*(2), 126–142. doi:10.1108/00483481211199991

Huang, J., & Tansley, C. (2012). Sneaking through the minefield of talent management: The notion of rhetorical obfuscation. *International Journal of Human Resource Management*, *23*(17), 3673–3691. doi:10.1080/09585192.2011.639029

Jones, J. T., Whitaker, M., Seet, P. S., & Parkin, J. (2012). Talent management in practice in Australia: Individualistic or strategic? An exploratory study. *Asia Pacific Journal of Human Resources*, *50*(4), 399–420. doi:10.1111/j.1744-7941.2012.00036.x

Kim, S., & McLean, G. N. (2012). Global talent management: Necessity, challenges, and the roles of HRD. *Advances in Developing Human Resources*, *14*(4), 566–585. doi:10.1177/1523422312455610

Kwan, L. Y. Y., & Chiu, C. Y. (2015). Country variations in different innovation outputs: The interactive effect of institutional support and human capital. *Journal of Organizational Behavior*, *36*(7), 1050–1070. doi:10.1002/job.2017

Loyeung, A., & Matolcsy, Z. (2015). CFOs accounting talent, compensation and turnover. *Accounting and Finance*, *55*(4), 1105–1134. doi:10.1111/acfi.12085

Maltais, D. (2012). Take a coordinated approach to talent-management strategies and solutions. *Employment Relations Today*, *39*(2), 47–54. doi:10.1002/ert.21364

McDonnell, A., Collings, D. G., & Burgess, J. (2012). Asia Pacific perspectives on talent management. *Asia Pacific Journal of Human Resources*, *50*(4), 391–398. doi:10.1111/j.1744-7941.2012.00035.x

McGee, R., Jr., Saran, S., & Krulwich, T. A. (2012). Diversity in the biomedical research workforce: Developing talent. *Mount Sinai Journal of Medicine: A Journal of Translational and Personalized Medicine, 79*(3), 397–411.

Nieto, J., Hernández-Maestro, R. M., & Muñoz-Gallego, P. A. (2011). The influence of entrepreneurial talent and website type on business performance by rural tourism establishments in Spain. *International Journal of Tourism Research*, *13*(1), 17–31. doi:10.1002/jtr.794

Nijs, S., Gallardo-Gallardo, E., Dries, N., & Sels, L. (2014). A multidisciplinary review into the definition, operationalization and measurement of talent. *Journal of World Business*, *49*(2), 180–191. doi:10.1016/j.jwb.2013.11.002

Olszewski-Kubilius, P., Subotnik, R. F., & Worrell, F. C. (2015). Conceptualizations of giftedness and the development of talent: Implications for counselors. *Journal of Counseling and Development*, *93*(2), 143–152. doi:10.1002/j.1556-6676.2015.00190.x

Rajgopal, S., Taylor, D., & Venkatachalam, M. (2012). Frictions in the CEO labor market: The role of talent agents in CEO compensation. *Contemporary Accounting Research*, *29*(1), 119–151. doi:10.1111/j.1911-3846.2011.01082.x

Sheehan, M., & Anderson, V. (2015). Talent management and organizational diversity: A call for research. *Human Resource Development Quarterly*, 26(4), 349–358. doi:10.1002/hrdq.21247

Tansley, C., Kirk, S., & Tietze, S. (2013). The currency of talent management–A reply to "talent management and the relevance of context: Towards a pluralistic approach." *Human Resource Management Review*, 23(4), 337–340. doi:10.1016/j.hrmr.2013.08.004

Vivas-Lopez, S., Perris-Ortiz, M., & Rueda-Armando, C. (2011). Managing talent for organizational learning. *European Journal of International Management*, 5(5), 540–557. doi:10.1504/EJIM.2011.042178

Wiblen, S., Dery, K., & Grant, D. (2012). Do you see what I see? The role of technology in talent identification. *Asia Pacific Journal of Human Resources*, 50(4), 421–438. doi:10.1111/j.1744-7941.2012.00037.x

KEY TERMS AND DEFINITIONS

Career: The progress and actions taken by a person throughout a lifetime, especially those related to that person's occupations.

Human Resource: The resource that resides in the knowledge, skills, and motivation of people.

Knowledge: The understanding of a circumstance, gained through experience.

Leadership: The activity of leading a group of people or an organization or the ability to do this.

Resource: The productive factor required to accomplish an activity, or as method to establish an enterprise and achieve desired outcome.

Resource-Based View: The management device utilized to assess the available amount of strategic assets.

Talent Management: The organization's attempts to recruit, develop, and retain the high-potential people that they can find, afford, and hire.

Workforce: The group of people who work in an organization and industry.

Chapter 18
Global Perspective on Talent Management:
The South African Experience

Neeta Baporikar
Namibia University of Science and Technology, Namibia

ABSTRACT

Today, no country can claim that its business can be local or national due to the effects of globalization. The world of business has become international. In this new millennium, few economies can afford to ignore global business opportunities. The globalizing wind has broadened the mind sets of executives, extended the geographical reach of firms, and nudged international business into some new trajectories. One such new trajectory is the concern with national culture. This has a tremendous impact on the subject matter of talent management for any country, economy or nation. Africa is no exception. Though there is a considerable body of research suggesting a link between language, communication and how gender – and leadership – gets 'done' in organisations, there is very little research on global perspective for managing talent especially in the African context. This chapter intends to fill that gap and in particular deals with global perspective of talent management in the African context.

INTRODUCTION

Africa has shown tremendous potential in recent years, with 27 of its 30 largest economies expanding rapidly since 2000. Once considered the "hopeless continent", the average purchasing power in the region has risen by a third in the past decade, nations are showing signs of political stability and foreign investment is accelerating. Looking to lay the groundwork for the next stage of growth, many of these countries are committed to investing in their people. Currently constrained by a lack of talent, today's leading African organizations are raising their sights, assuming responsibility, broadening their leadership development focus and learning forward. These corporations recognize the quality of leaders as a key strategic differentiator, and they are not waiting for public sector literacy programs and education initiatives to deliver results. However, in markets depressed by low skill sets, how do you best engage

DOI: 10.4018/978-1-5225-1961-4.ch018

the broad spectrum within an organization, from illiterate employees to experienced, highly educated professionals? How do you immerse employees in an experience that will build critical business, leadership and management capabilities? In today's competitive and fast-paced economy, how do you bridge talent gaps faster, accelerate skill development and increase application on the job?

With the liberation of trade policies, transnational companies moving production to low-cost areas and the corresponding growth of global supply chains, increased globalization has resulted in socio-economic and cultural challenges. Further, talent now takes many forms, from migrants, crossing borders (temporarily or seeking new homes), students gaining degrees and expatriates on assignment to tourists, refugees and business travelers (Baporikar, 2013a). Consequently, the demand for skills has countries working hard to develop policies that will attract talent with human and technological skills to support economic growth, retain talent and even reverse talent migration. In a "reverse brain drain" effect, China and India, for example, encourage their educated nationals to return and fill jobs at home (Kuptsch, & Pang, 2006). Along with the understanding the need to hire, develop, and retain talented people, organizations are aware that they must manage talent as a critical resource to achieve the best possible results. Few, if any, today have an adequate supply of talent. Talent is an increasingly scarce resource, so it must be managed to the fullest effect. Are today's leaders able to do more with less? The idea of managing talent is not new. Four or five decades ago, it was viewed as a peripheral responsibility best relegated to the personnel department, today talent management is an organizational function that is taken far more seriously (Baporikar, 2013a). Though there is a considerable body of research suggesting a link between language, communication and how gender – and leadership – gets 'done' in organisations, there is very little research on global perspective for managing talent especially in the African context. This chapter intends to fill that gap. After delving in detail on the existing literature on talent management the chapter will in particular deal global perspective of talent management in the African context and thereby hopes to contribute and add to the talent management knowledge base in African context.

Country Perspective: South Africa

With the Government struggling to act, businesses confront the talent shortage head on. Coined in 1997, the "war for talent" has echoed throughout the corporate world and remains a critical concern today. For South African organizations, this challenge is especially real. Despite significant advancements, for the past five consecutive years South African corporations have identified an inadequately skilled workforce as the greatest challenge inhibiting business growth (Pennington, 2013). The government has proven slow to respond. Relative to the international community, the nation's education system ranks near the bottom, considered 138 out of 144, in maths and science (Moolman & Breidenthal, 2013). Although secondary enrolment remains high, few students successfully graduate from a tertiary institution. Even after achieving an advanced degree, many South Africans do not necessarily have the skills demanded by businesses (Wits, 2013).

With rising rates of emigration, retaining the top talent capable of driving organizational competitiveness is increasingly difficult (Kerr-Phillips & Adèle Thomas, 2010). To outpace competitors in growth and profits, South African organizations are not relying on the public sector to address the talent gap. Instead, many companies are taking responsibility, elevating the organization's profile by investing in foundational business, leadership and management skill development. However, to drive competitive advantage on a global scale, companies are challenged to move beyond general capability building, align leadership and management skills to the organization's strategic objectives and close the "theory-to-application" gap (EIU, 2011).

DAWN OF TALENT MANAGEMENT

Despite a global recession on an unprecedented scale (CIPD, 2009) and consequential high unemployment rates, evidence suggests that organisations continue to face recruitment difficulties (CIPD, 2012). In fact, CIPD (2012) report that the recession is creating a perfect recruitment and retention storm, with 82% of organisations finding it difficult to recruit and retain suitable staff, particularly the UK public sector with its double-bind of pension's cuts and pay freezes. Against a backdrop of a confirmed UK double-dip recession, the Eurozone crisis, a 12-year high for unemployment and the highest recorded level of underemployment (individuals accepting part-time work because they cannot find full-time jobs) (CIPD, 2012): ".... competition for talent is rife in many industries" (CIPD, 2012, p. 2).

In addition to recessionary effects, a number of enduring environmental shifts are creating a climate in which competition for talent is increasingly intense. Demographic changes are predicted to be amongst the key factors likely to influence business over the next 30 years. All major research councils and future work commentators (such as Donkin, 2010 and Gratton, 2010) agree that an ageing population - combined with the recent abolition of the default retirement age – will create particular challenges for organisations attempting to fill key strategic roles. As the nature of work continues to shift away from manufacturing, through service and then to an increasing centrality of a pool of 'knowledge workers' (Handy, 2001; Williams, 2007; Goede, 2011) in a knowledge economy, this similarly creates a competitive pressure on organisations to recruit and retain these knowledge workers. There is also evidence to suggest that employee values are morphing over time, with arguably less organisational loyalty (Parry & Urwin, 2011), which again serves to render resourcing and talent management key strategic priorities (Carmichael et al., 2011; Iles et al., 2010), some two decades after the inception of the phrase 'talent management' following research at McKinsey in 2001.

Marchington and Wilkinson (2012) suggest that effective talent management is essential for 'competitive edge and future survival' (Marchington and Wilkinson, 2012, p. 200), specifically relating to leadership talent (the original focus in the work at McKinsey) in a global workplace. Of course, a depressed economic context tends to render talented leadership even more crucial to organisational success. CIPD (2012) similarly identify the crucial role of talent management in filling managerial, professional and technical vacancies, with a growing problem of limited specialist and technical skills in the labour market. The CIPD 2012 annual survey of resourcing and talent planning (CIPD, 2012) identified several strategies that organisations are now deploying in the fight for talent, including growing use of apprenticeships and professional networks (e.g. LinkedIn). Given the current apparent escalation of the 'war for talent', both male and female leadership talent might be deemed central to organisational success. However, previous research suggests that female leaders continue to be disadvantaged, with a continuing notion of 'leadership as male', despite evidence indicating that female leaders might actually be better suited to lead in the brave new global workplace (see, e.g. Powell, 2011). There is also a considerable body of research suggesting a link between language, communication and how gender – and leadership – gets 'done' in organisations.

Talent Management: Getting it Right

Notwithstanding its increasing prominence, there is still considerable ambiguity around the exact meaning of talent management. As Lewis and Heckman (2006) indicate:

A review of the literature focused on talent management reveals a disturbing lack of clarity regarding the definition, scope and overall goals of talent management." (Lewis and Heckman, 2006, p. 139) In this context, "...the field would benefit from a clear and comprehensive definition of the concept. (Collings & Mellahi, 2009, p. 304)

Some would contend that talent management is simply a case of old wine in new bottles (see, e.g., Mellahi and Collings, 2010), whilst others would suggest that talent management is clearly distinct from other HR practices and approaches (both practitioner and academic). Lewis and Heckman's (2006) analysis identifies three current perspectives on the possible definition of talent management: firstly, a suitable bundle of HR activities, practices or functions such as recruitment, selection and career planning; secondly, the development of a suitable talent pool, through (largely) internal processes; and finally a highly generic approach to talent and the management thereof, with talent perceived as something to be developed, almost irrespective of organisational strategy, direction or key success areas. The first two add little to traditional connotations of HRM while the latter is arguably one of the most fundamental problems with many approaches to talent management – it pays no heed to which talent should be developed, alignment with the organisation's strategy or effective resource deployment. Tarique and Schuler's (2010) re-working of Lewis and Heckman's third perspective improves the position slightly, through incorporation of a strategic imperative, but suffers from a highly generic conceptualisation of talent per se. Collings and Mellahi (2009) add an emergent fourth perspective whereby key positions (with the potential of having a significant impact on the organisation's performance) are identified prior to any attempt at filling such positions. Collings and Mellahi's approach is thus exclusive and seeks neither to embrace all employees in the talent pool nor to manage poor performers, which is seen as the remit of other imperatives and practices. Collings and Mellahi's model of 'strategic talent management' clearly identifies an HR architecture (an internal and external labour market feeding into a talent pool, combined with the identification of pivotal positions) and consequential outcomes (e.g. motivation, organisational commitment), though it is interesting to note that this does not, prima facie, differ significantly from current HRM practices and could be deemed to be simply a re-packaging of traditional concepts. However, a useful call here – focusing on the importance of identifying talent with a range of broad competencies (given uncertainty over future role requirements) – is for a contingency approach to the deployment of HR practices.

Thus, a critical perspective would suggest that talent management is essentially nothing new, but rather a repackaging of certain aspects of existing human resource management practice. Indeed, "... some argue that TM (talent management) is potentially the "new HRM"...." (Stewart and Harte, 2010, p. 506). Carmichael et al. (2011), for example, suggest that talent management may essentially be a 're-wrapping' of a range of related activities and Ford et al. (2010a) conclude that, within several Yorkshire and Humber SHA trusts, an incremental approach to implementation is resulting in the retrospective 're-labelling of existing practices' and little or no development of a strategic talent management approach in practice. CIPD's own definition appears to add little of value to the debate, essentially conceptualising the approach as a 'bundle' of HRM activities and as: "... the systematic attraction, identification, development, engagement, retention and deployment of those individuals with high potential who are of particular value to the organization." (CIPD, 2009)

Torrington et al. (2011) similarly focus on perceived core aspects of talent management, including: recruitment and retention (through the use of differential offerings for 'talent'); identification and placement of talent (with a focus on current staff); management and support of engagement (ensuring opportunities for risk taking (but with 'freedom to fail') and space to 'grow' (with appropriate resources and opportunity)); talent development (inclusive, but 'focused'); promotion and succession planning (which involves development of a 'talent pipeline'); and valuing employees' perspectives and meeting needs (of all staff, not just 'talent'). However, closer analysis of this approach suggests a continuing focus on traditional HRM, albeit with specific inclusion or mention of 'talent' and an inclusive (thus not differentiated) approach. Torrington et al. (2011) review a number of difficulties with the talent management concept – notwithstanding limitations with their own definition. Firstly, as suggested above, there is the notion that talent management is simply a case of old wine in new bottles. Essentially, there is nothing new to talent management - rather a more rapid and systematic approach to standard HRM practices such as workforce planning. Thus, there has been a tendency to include almost all of the activities inherent to the broader scope of human resource management (HRM) within talent management, hence weakening its differential base. Secondly, some cultural perspectives on talent management (likening this to a cultural 'mind-set') reveal the gap between reality and rhetoric in many cases (confirmed by Ford et al., 2010a, above); this is compounded by an extremely weak evidence base to support talent management. Moreover, identification and differential treatment of talented staff may have several undesirable, negative, consequences, such as rendering the organisation vulnerable to claims of discrimination, increasing competition and ignoring the multitude of 'the rest' of the workforce. Ford et al. (2010a) similarly posit that talent management – particularly in the current economic climate – may have detrimental consequences for those staff not identified as 'talent.' This is a significant point given Ford et al.'s research with practitioners in the field.

An emergent pattern within prior research and credible academic literature is one, therefore, of considerable ambiguity and confusion. In part, this may reflect one of the potential differentiators of talent management – a contingency approach. This is advocated by several commentators, including Ford et al. (2010a; 2010b) who suggest that:

… organizations are advised to develop their own talent management strategies and programmes that complement their culture, market and unique circumstances. (Ford et al., 2010b, p. 3)

Moreover, it is suggested here that a credible and differentiated definition of talent management should also include a strategic focus, as posited by Torrington et al. (2011). Essentially, this approach requires senior management sponsorship, integration across the organisation and with the organisation's strategic objectives, values and other HR practices. Similarly, Lewis and Heckman (2006) suggest that a strategic focus is central to the relevance of talent management. In an analogous manner, Zuboff (as cited in Lewis & Heckman, 2006) depicts a strategic approach to managing talent, akin to other strategLewis, R.E. & Heckman, R. (2006ic management models. According to Zuboff, organisations should pay heed to labour market conditions and product/service market relevance when determining talent pool strategy – thus also supporting a contingency perspective. This concept is further developed by Farndale et al. (2010), who call for a more strategic role for the HR function in organisations which are seen to require global (as opposed to national or regional) talent management strategies. Although Farndale et al.'s central focus is multinational corporations (MNCs), thus naturally gravitating towards a global concept of talent and talent management, this global dimension is absent from many of the approaches thus far considered. Interestingly, Mellahi and Collings' (2010) definition assumes a cultural perspective and also introduces the concept of '*global*' talent management as a distinctive approach:

Broadly defined, global talent management involves the systematic identification of key positions which differentially contribute to the organisation's sustainable competitive advantage on a global scale, the development of a talent pool of high potential and high performing incumbents to fill these roles which reflects the global scope of the MNE (multinational enterprise), and the development of a differentiated human resource architecture to facilitate filling these positions with the best available incumbent and to ensure their continued commitment to the organization. (Mellahi and Collings, 2010, pp. 143-144)

However, whilst attempting to introduce a global perspective, this definition ultimately reverts back to 'human resource architecture' or a traditional 'bundle' of HRM policies and practices, albeit within a multinational organisation, thus reinforcing the traditional definitional approach. This is similar to several other papers reviewing the relevance of talent management, for example Hartmann et al. (2010).

Fundamental to the entire talent management debate is the interpretation and lived experience of talent. For some, talent is to be sought out at all levels and the organisation staffed by 'A' players, with 'C' players being removed from the organisation. Talent here is a resource and an exclusive approach is warranted. Collings and Mellahi's (2009) approach suggests that the differentiator of talent management as opposed to strategic HRM is an exclusive focus on "high potential and high performing employees operating in key roles and not all employees in the organisation" (Collings and Mellahi, 2009, p. 306). Moreover, it is suggested that the focus should be on 'talent' in roles that are pivotal to organisational success. This becomes problematic, however, if one considers the limitations of exclusive approaches: overemphasis on the individual and risks of excessive competition and poor teamwork; a negative impact on motivation due to over-emphasis on external (not internal) talent in some cases; over-emphasis on talent at the expense of identifying process and cultural problems; and the development of an elitist culture (see, e.g., Mellahi and Collings, 2010).

In contrast, inclusive approaches suggest that all employees can be managed up to 'be' talent and that an organisation's culture should reflect this. Indeed, this distinction is central to the focal research topic, since it might be expected that less inclusive approaches might be more prone to bias, including gendered interpretation and implementation. However, many critics argue that an inclusive approach lacks strategic focus (at the extreme becoming little more than training), whilst others suggest that the *exclusive* connotation is equally non-strategic since, for some jobs, 'acceptable' performance is 'good enough'. Ford et al (2010b) consider that talent and its definition will surely vary with organisations' circumstances (suggesting that inclusive may be more relevant to the public sector, for example) and the key priorities at any point in time. Ulrich and Smallwood (2012) take this further and identify four categories of talent, although these appear to simply mirror organisational levels rather than embed strategic focus. Lewis and Heckman (2006) similarly identify a two-by-two classification matrix, suggesting that the treatment of employees should reflect their added value in addition to the ease or difficulty of replacing. The implication here is that talent management might become different things to different employees, thus again suggesting a contingency perspective. In conclusion, one might agree with Lewis and Heckman (2006) that:

It is apparent from the above that the term "talent management" has no clear meaning. It is used in too many ways and is often a means to highlight the "strategic" importance of a HR speciality .... without adding to the theory or practice of that speciality. (Lewis and Heckman, 2006, p.141)

That notwithstanding, the conclusion here (following, for example, Ford et al. 2010b) is that talent management builds upon some of the more traditional HRM concepts such as management development and resourcing, but that it also adds a unique focus and a fresh perspective – i.e. a talent 'culture' (see, e.g., Carmichael et al., 2011). As Beardwell et al. (2010) suggest:

There is nothing particularly new about the individual activities that comprise talent management but what is different is that these activities are 'bundled' together... (Beardwell et al., 2010, p. 162)

This analysis aligns well with practitioner understanding of the meaning and operationalisation of talent management (see, e.g., Davis et al., 2007) and continued use ensures that the 'talent tsunami' (Gordon, 2010) does not overwhelm HRM in the field. Moreover, a contingency perspective of the interpretation and implementation of talent management would appear to add most value and enable organisations to focus on the key strategic priorities at any one time. An acceptable definition and research framework for talent management, therefore, should include typical activities (the 'bundle') within a talent culture, but with a contingent frame of the possible meaning and treatment of 'talent'. Ultimately, categorisations such as those provided by Collings & Mellahi (2009), McDonnell et al. (2010), Iles et al. (2010) and Stewart and Rigg (2011) are helpful in summarising the potential variations on a theme. Thus, the position adopted here is that talent management can be either inclusive or exclusive, can focus on the individual and/or the pivotal nature of the role and can have a global, national and/or regional focus. Finally, one key notion deemed central to the focus and hitherto undeveloped in any empirical work or talent management literature is that suggested by Alvesson and Karreman (2007). Notably, that one common element of all talent management practice is that it at the very least influences the lived experience and social construction thereof. In other words, people are developed / created / produced through talent management and, indeed, HRM strategy. This position is fundamentally consistent with the ontological and epistemological position to be adopted in the focal research project and will be explored further in forthcoming empirical work.

Globalization Concerns

Globalization is a universal phenomenon which has benefited many countries all over the world. Four decades ago, it was not certain that countries like Korea, India, Brazil, South Africa, Russia and China would be recognized as strong economies with the capacity to make a global impact. Today, they have produced organizations that are competing successfully with multinational giants of the developed countries. As a result of globalization and the various economic and political reforms implemented by the developing world, particularly in Africa, there is emergence of an impressive array of manufacturing, telecommunications, banking, financial, and oil and gas companies. Many of them have performed so well within their national borders that they have now ventured into the international arena: they are becoming multinational corporations. However, the transformation is not generally accompanied by a change in the way these organizations manage talent. A major challenge which globalization therefore poses to these organizations is how to manage human resources effectively within the international setting. It is axiomatic to say that great organizations are the creation of great talent and great leadership. In his best-selling book, *Good to Great*, Jim Collins wrote: 'if you have the wrong people, it doesn't matter how great your strategy may be, you still won't have a great company' (2001, p. 42). Pfeffer (1998) noted that talent and the way in which it is managed is what gives companies competitive advantage. According to him, process and product technology, protected or regulated markets, access to financial resources, and economies of scale may provide competitive leverage but to a lesser extent than in the past and by far less than people will provide if properly managed. In other words, traditional sources of competitive advantage are no longer as effective, reliable and sustainable as talent management. Unfortunately, many managers are still fixated with the traditional sources of competitive advantage while ignoring this brutal truth. Although they probably appreciate the fact that people are the bastion of success for any organization, the challenge they face is how to fundamentally alter their paradigm about how to attract, hire, engage, develop and retain the talent which they so much need for their success.

Human resource management policies, systems and practices that were successful within national boundaries are still being deployed with the same vigour and frenzy to serve a completely different and diverse group of people working in different countries, cultures and socio-economic environments. It can safely be predicted that not only will the HR policies, systems and practices be inadequate to meet the value propositions of the diverse employees, but that they may also in fact be dysfunctional to talent management. In reality there is a disconnect between globalization and talent management even though we know that no multinational corporation can be effective or sustain its success for long without a strong, strategic and dynamic approach to the management of talent. Drucker (1993) wrote: "Making a living is no longer enough. Work also has to make a life." Maslow (1943), 30 years earlier, conceptualized a theory of human motivation called hierarchy of human needs. People have a basic desire to meet physiological needs, e.g., food, clothing, shelter. Next they seek safety, e.g., personal and financial security, and health and well-being. After physiological and safety requirements are fulfilled, they try to meet social needs, e.g., friendship, intimacy, and family. Next, all humans want to be respected and to have self-esteem and self-respect. Finally, at the top of the pyramid, is what Maslow called "self-actualization," the aspiration to fulfil one's self and become all that one is capable of becoming. After more than seven decades this still holds well when it comes to human motivation yet organizations across all countries struggle to motivate and retain employees. Moreover, knowledge economies call for people with global acumen, multicultural ease, technological skills, entrepreneurial mind sets, and the ability to manage organizations that are increasingly delayered and disaggregated. Rapidly changing lifestyles drive different expectations. Today, staffs are more interested in having meaningful and challenging work. They are therefore more loyal to their profession than to the organization. It follows that they are less accommodating of traditional structures and authority and more concerned about work–life balance. Therefore, they are better prepared to take ownership of their careers and development. Leadership supply, aka the "war for talent," is a perennial item on every executive's agenda. CEOs and other leaders devote considerable time and resources to finding, developing and deploying the people they need in critical jobs throughout the organization. But the conventional tools—recruitment and retention efforts, training programs and the like—often do no more than keep a company in the game. Essential as they are, they rarely help an organization pull away from the competition. And they're woefully inadequate for acute challenges such as expanding rapidly in a new market. A more fruitful approach, we have found, is to approach the talent issue from a different viewpoint entirely—that of decisions. Ultimately, any organization's performance depends on its decision effectiveness. Consistently high performers make good decisions, make them quickly and execute them well. They know which decisions are most important to creating value, and they make sure that those decisions get the attention they deserve. Research shows that decision effectiveness correlates tightly with financial results (Blenko, Rogers & Mankins, 2010).

Africa is larger than the United States, China, India, Japan and the whole of Europe put together, yet many in the West are ill-informed about it: If there's a riot in Liberia, companies want to pull out of Nairobi in Kenya more than 5,000 km away. A lot of attention is being paid to BRIC countries, but Africa hardly rates a mention, except in a negative context. Yet over the past decade, six of the world's ten fastest-growing countries were in Africa. With a population of over one billion – the fastest growing and youngest in the world – and an emerging middle class, Africa has consumers who are more prosperous today than ever. However, the sheer number of countries (54), currencies, languages and physical and cultural borders – not to mention poor infra-structure, corruption and political instability – are major obstacles for businesses interested in capitalizing on the Africa Opportunity. North Africa – which includes Algeria, Egypt, Libya, Morocco, Sudan, Tunisia and Western Sahara – provides a unique set of challenges and opportunities. IMD executive director Dr. Hischam El-Agamy pointed out that while this region is both part of Africa and part of the Arab world, it has never been able to exploit these dual identities. As a consequence, there has been little integration in North African markets and a failure to create an economic bloc. The trajectory of North Africa changed dramatically in just two months as a result of the Arab Spring, which started in late 2010. Disruptive changes are continuing and the ramifications are still being felt throughout the region as 100 million young Arabs remain in a system with low living standards, no freedom of expression, poor education and few job prospects. One of the direct consequences of the Arab Spring could be that the private sector will grow due to the new and important role it will play in the current political and socio-economic transformation.

While the region faces major challenges, including lack of fresh water, food insecurity, corruption and above all unemployment, it will also create great business opportunities especially in the field of developing infrastructure. For example, experts are estimating that the region will have to invest at least $300 billion over the next 10 years to repair the damage caused during the last two years and to meet the immediate needs of the population. These investments and more will be required to repair and develop oil fields, to construct social housing for a large portion of the population living in very rudimentary conditions, and of course to improve basic infrastructures for healthcare and education. There are also major investment opportunities in the telecommunications, tourism and renewable energy sectors. Real success will require open borders and free movement of goods and people. The journey to prosperity for North Africa, like the rest of the continent, will not be easy but may be shorter than commonly assumed.

Opportunities and Challenges

While most foreign investment targets the populous and more developed countries such as South Africa, Nigeria and Kenya, there are opportunities for doing business throughout the continent. Stéphane Paquier, president of Dow Africa, cited some positive megatrends:

- **Large and Growing Consumer Class:** A recent African Development Bank report found that Africa's middle-class consumers now constitute more than a third of its population, over 300 million people, which matches India (Ncube, Lufumpa & Vencatachellum, 2011).
- **Wealth:** Contrary to perceptions, several countries in Africa – including Libya, Algeria and Angola – have no debt and a considerable amount of money to invest in any vision for the future.
- **Nutrition and Agriculture:** Africa has most of the non-cultivated land in the world.

This is balanced with the recognition of common challenges that multinational corporations (MNCs) face:

- **Commitment:** MNCs have struggled with being consistent and having a long-term commitment to African markets. This is often down to ignorance and lack of direct experience.
- **Visibility from Headquarters:** It is hard to attract business partners and support within the executive team.
- **Cultural Differences:** Face to face relationships are valued above all others and patience is needed to cultivate them.
- **Supply Chain to the Continent is Long and Expensive:** Until infrastructure improves, there will be challenges in bringing products to Africa.
- **Corruption:** A zero tolerance approach to corruption is essential from the start of new alliances and joint ventures.
- **Threats to Intellectual Property Rights:** MNCs need to protect their IP and fight against counterfeit products.
- **Difficulty of Benchmarking:** How do you know what your competitors are doing?

Jonathan Ledgard, Africa Correspondent for *The Economist*, believes that there will be economic growth in many African countries, but the key issue is whether the growth is inclusive and if all of society benefits. The population of Africa will reach an estimated 2 billion in the next 30 years, and currently over 50% of the population in sub-Saharan Africa is under 19 years old. Africa is poised to benefit from a "demographic dividend" – a huge number of youth entering the workforce. This young talent must be harnessed to maximize opportunities and avoid political and social risk. The combination of economic growth and population growth means that the big future for Africa has not yet been written. However, factors such as frustrated youth due to unemployment; the effects of climate change, which could lead to food shortages; and non-inclusive cities could lead to a-disconnect, with some parts of Africa advancing while others are left behind. Technology and urbanization will be the big drivers, offering the chance to rethink what a city might be like – 800 million new people will be living in cities that do not even exist yet! Ramon Bastida, senior manager marketing, EMEA for Eaton Corporation, highlighted the megatrend of increasing power needs throughout Africa as the population explodes, and the imperatives of using resources, especially, energy more efficiently, sustainably and safely, the need to separate risks – political, ethical and economic. Asked about the biggest concerns over doing business in Africa, the message was loud and clear – it was quest for talent.

Africa isn't post-industrial, it's no industrial; growth will be based on agriculture and services. It is the right time to do business in Africa. After decades of slow growth and uncertainty, Africa's impressive growth looks likely to continue. Moreover, the private sector seems to be the future, whether SMEs or MNCs and not only the public sector or NGOs. Finally, from a strategic perspective, Africa may also enjoy the last-mover advantage and this could be very valuable. In the recent past, there are ongoing debates on how to retain talent within the boundaries and also how to maximise the talent usage from outside the boundaries. Ongoing debates, various workshops and seminars, have been going on in the region. Leading organizations like Standard Bank, Ecobank and Airways have undertaken studies on talent management, retaining knowledge workers, engaging employees, etc. Number of speakers at various forums has been reflecting on the challenges of attracting and retaining the right people in a difficult environment. Many believe an undersupply of leadership across all sectors is the root cause of many of Africa's problems.

Ecobank is a full-service bank with 10 million customers, 18,000 employees and a footprint that covers 32 African countries – more than any other bank in the world (Sjoblom & El-Agamy, 2012). According to Terrence Taylor, senior group manager, Learning & Development, at Ecobank, when it comes to retaining talent the bank has identified three success factors:

- **Keep Them Challenged:** Working on interesting assignments, projects and day-to-day work.
- **Pay Them Well:** Give them a total package with lots of value, including schooling, car allowances and status.
- **Keep Them Connected:** With the ethos.

Today, this has made, Ecobank a highly successful bank in a Pan-African context. Today it is a group of 1,200 visionary shareholders from 14 West African countries who in 1985 – with limited resources – decided to create a Pan-African bank to further the development of Africa. Thus, there is greater need now more than ever, to develop talent internally by offering training and internships to the many talented graduates unable to find work. Initiatives such as the African Leadership Academy launched to develop 6,000 leaders in Africa over 12 years, aim to develop strong leaders throughout society are good and needed. But what is equally if not more important is to realize that certification is not enough. Mentoring is an important part of the equation. Many people may not have technical competence, but they are willing to learn. Some companies send high potentials to factories in other countries on train-the-trainer programs. It requires advance planning and a medium-term outlook. To generate lasting growth and prosperity, additional leadership development initiatives are needed across the board. Moreover, the demographic dividend requires out of the box thinking. In Europe the goal is to employ the least possible labor because it is expensive; in Africa the opposite seems to be true. However, many disruptive innovations could come out of Africa; reverse innovation has been powerful in the mobile sector and could come to bear in a variety of industries. Therefore, there is a greater need to adopt a strategic approach to talent management, more so in the era of globalization. Thus, when building a strategic approach to talent management, one needs to demonstrate how organization will benefit overall in the changing business climate. Human capital, in all industries, is becoming an organization's most strategic asset and all trends indicate that human capital will become even more valuable in the future. To strengthen competitive position and drive business results, one need to invest in talent management processes; tools and technology that help to leverage human capital as the future depends on it. Though it takes time to adopt talent management best practices and build a world-class workforce that is aligned, inspired and delivers exceptional results by understanding the larger business value and impact of mature, strategic approach to integrated talent management, which address the executives' top concerns need to be adopted (Baporikar, 2013b).

The discussion herein has thus, considered the nature and lived experience of 'talent management', a concept which has ascended the ranks of human resource management (HRM) practice over the last decade, especially with the intent to relook at the talent management strategy in South African context. The phrase 'talent management', however, is neither simple nor uncontentious to define or explain. Moreover, whilst the concept is much cited by HRM practitioners, there is a relative paucity of credible academic literature in the field. Hereto the attempt is also to will evaluate the nature and meaning of 'talent management', specifically the two opposing claims that it is a revolutionary approach to ensuring a good supply of 'talent' (itself crucial to organisational success) as opposed to the stance that it is not a new HRM approach at all but merely a case of repackaging and re-labelling of existing approaches. The position adopted here is that talent management embraces many of the traditional aspects of HRM, but within a talent 'culture'. Moreover, it is suggested that a strategic and contingent perspective of the concept and its operationalisation is warranted and, most significantly, that talent management policy and practice at the very least influences the lived experience of managers and the construction of 'talent'.

SOLUTIONS AND RECOMMENDATIONS

However, to accelerate expansion into new markets, leading organizations increasingly recognize that basic general management skill development is not enough. Premier South African organizations recognize this reality and are leading the way forward. For Telkom, Africa's largest integrated communications company, the investment is delivering real returns. Build essential business and leadership skills. In the high-impact experience, participating employees engaged with a visually rich and hands-on board simulation reflective of the company's business. Through the risk-free competitive environment, leaders better understood the factors critical to driving profitability, recognized the importance of customer satisfaction and identified their role in the Telkom's success. This approach enabled application on the job, leading to tangible results. Following the experiential learning program, 99 percent of Telkom's front-line leaders had a more complete understanding of the business and its interrelationships as well as profitability drivers. Committing to action plans targeting revenue, expenses, capital and customer satisfaction, the total value of the initiatives implemented was assessed at over $50 million SAR. Adopting a strategic approach and connecting leadership skills to the overall company strategy through customized initiatives. Thus, there is a need to match individuals with jobs so as to reducing the demand for talent.

Once you know your critical positions and your top performers, you can assess the degree of overlap. One technology company, for example, identified its mission-critical positions and found that fewer than 30 percent were filled by top performers. When the company then asked how many of its top performers were in mission-critical positions, the answer was only 40 percent. Thinking about deployment from a decision perspective helped this company redeploy people to make the most of its talent pool and improve decision effectiveness. But some companies may find that they are facing a talent shortage even when they have carefully identified key jobs and top performers. That's when organizations typically step up long-term efforts aimed at boosting recruitment and retention. In the meantime, companies can redesign their organization and operations with decisions in mind; thereby making the best use of the talent they have right now (Buckingham & Clifton, 2001). To maximize the continent's full growth potential and drive further economic development, organizations are challenged to address the talent shortage and can no longer afford to wait for public programs and education systems to bridge capability gaps. "To be able to compete in Africa, you need skilled people on the ground who knows the business terrain," says Sim Tshabalala, Joint Chief Executive at Standard Bank (Dolan, 2011).

To effectively surmount the talent crunch, leading companies must place leadership development initiatives at the top of the business agenda. However, to overcome competitors and uplift employees, companies are advised to:

1. Move beyond generic skill-building programs that address a large number of non-specific competencies
2. Improve returns on learning and development investments by tying business and leadership capabilities to the company's strategic goals
3. Accelerate capacity building by leveraging innovative learning methodologies, including simulations, gamification and other experiential learning tools that deliver impact
4. Maximize results by incorporating the insights of senior leaders to transfer critical experience, increase relevancy and reduce the theory-to-application by closing the theory-to-application gap quicker, organizations can effectively accelerate competitive capability development and maximize their potential in the market—uplifting the people and economies on the Africa continent. The need is great, the business benefits are significant, and success demands courageous, bold action.

Aligning talent management to globalization must begin with a change in the paradigm of organizational leaders. So what need to be done are first things first.

1. First, they have to accept talent management and retention as their responsibility. For too long many organizations have abdicated this responsibility to the HR department. The role of the HR department is to develop policies and systems and guide managers, but the actual management of talent falls squarely on the shoulders of line managers.
2. Second, managers need to change their hedonistic philosophy about employees. Developing countries may be poor (in Africa about 300 million people live on less than a dollar a day), yet not every employee is necessarily an 'economic man'. People are motivated by factors other than pecuniary reward, and those factors should inform the way managers manage the abilities, potential, aspirations, needs, wants and concerns of their talented people.
3. Third, global executives have to perceive themselves differently – not just as managers but rather as entrepreneurial leaders who have a stake in the business. Yet, it is not enough to be leaders – they must be global leaders and have an entrepreneur's mind-set that enables them to see how critical talent is to the success of their firms, and also be able to manage talent with a passion and integrity amidst socio-cultural pressures to adopt a nationalistic or parochial approach which invariably vitiates diversity and creates a glass ceiling for certain categories of talent.
4. Fourth, the approach to attracting and hiring talent has changed from being a mere transaction to being a marketing enterprise. Managers must flow with the tide. Recruitment brand has become a preeminent feature, and information technology an incredibly useful instrument in the war or competition for talent. Hiring talent should be not only for the job, but also for a global career – not only for today, but also for tomorrow.
5. Fifth, recruiting talent is brutally hard but getting the best out of talent could even be harder. Managing the performance of talented people of different generations with conflicting value propositions in diverse cultures and countries is a huge challenge to organizations especially multinational corporations.
6. Sixth, merely setting objectives, providing resources and evaluating performance at the end of the year will not suffice. Rather, it is about how managers support and guide employees, proactively remove blockages to performance and reward performance equitably without any form of racial, ethnic or gender bias.

7. Seventh, there is a need to also identify, design and deploy appropriate employee engagement drivers taking cognizance of the fact that because of the diverse demographic, national and cultural differences and backgrounds of employees there can be no one size- fits-all engagement drivers.
8. Eighth, realizing that gone are the days of the 'organization man' with work–life balance becoming a cherished value, other things which are looming large due to social media and information explosion are issues like: empowerment, a socially amiable environment.
9. Ninth, with net worked society and structure taking shapes due to knowledge explosion, teams where interaction is devoid of excessive formality is also leading to non-acceptance of paraphernalia of status and hierarchy.
10. Tenth, growth, development and rapid advancement including career resilience are becoming crucial as these are the sine qua non for their engagement and retention.

FUTURE RESEARCH DIRECTIONS

Globalization has deepened the war on talent, in turn challenging many HR leaders, organizations and nations. Executives are looking to HR to source, recruit, develop and retain the best talent. This is a tall order but can be achieved with proper talent management strategies and systems support. However, for understanding the nation based uniqueness of talent management requirements, further research needs to be undertaken on how to develop intelligent recruiting process, optimization of social networking tools to explore and exploit social sourcing capabilities, designing and developing integrated models for internal social network to increase employee information sharing and engagement. Another interesting area of research would be to look into role-centric user experience designed to enhance accessibility, collaboration and productivity at all levels of the organization, methods to implement holistic yet flexible goal and performance management. How to do strategy mapping exercises for employee needs and organizational goals, IT enablement for ways to ensure integrated and embedded analytics to support informed data-driven decision making would be some of the multi-disciplinary areas for further research.

CONCLUSION

Global competition will change the world radically in the coming years, because for the first time it will not only be fought over goods or services but over 'people' that too smart people with creative abilities (Baporikar, 2009). Fact is that, fusing of the world markets has picked up speed and will continue to do in future with global talent and its issues becoming the key player. On the other hand, lifetime tenure has become history to such employees. Talented people are a high-risk and volatile asset. Hence previous national track record alone is not a sufficient determinant for succession. Potential is critical. The approach to preparing future leaders and successors deserves a review. Many years of executive training aimed at producing talented leaders have not yielded the desired results because development is not aligned to the context and strategy. Instead, it has tendency to focus primarily on today's needs with little or no regard for leadership of tomorrow. The change must begin with a paradigm shift in the thinking of government and policy makers about talent management. This change cannot take place unless they can see its urgency and criticality.

REFERENCES

Lewis, R.E. & Heckman, R. (2006) Talent management: A critical review. *Human Resource Management Review*, *16*(2), 139-154.

Alvesson, M., & Karreman, D. (2007). Unravelling HRM: Identity, Ceremony and Control in a Management Consulting Firm. *Organization Science*, *18*(4), 711–723. doi:10.1287/orsc.1070.0267

Baporikar, N. (2009). *Talent War - Myth or Reality? MBA Review*. India: ICFAI University Press.

Baporikar, N. (2013a). Understanding Talent Management in Borderless World. *MANAGEMENT TODAY – International Journal of Management Studies*, *3*(4), 10–16.

Baporikar, N. (2013b). Strategic Approach to Talent Management. *JIDNYASA Research Journal*, *7*, 20–26.

Baporikar, N. (2015). Effect of National Culture on Development of International Business in the Sultanate of Oman. In B. Christiansen (Ed.), *Handbook of Research on Global Business Opportunities* (pp. 268–288). Hershey, PA, USA: IGI Global. doi:10.4018/978-1-4666-6551-4.ch013

Beardwell, J., & Claydon, T. (2010). *Human Resource Management: A Contemporary Approach* (6th ed., pp. 161–195). Harlow: Pearson Education.

Blenko, M. W., Rogers, R., & Mankins, M. C. (2010). *Decide & Deliver: 5 Steps to Breakthrough Performance in Your Organization*. Harvard Business Review Press.

Carmichael, J., Collins, C., Emsell, P., & Haydon, J. (2011). *Leadership and Management*. Oxford: Oxford University Press.

CIPD. (2009). *The War on Talent: Talent management under threat in uncertain times, part 1*. London: CIPD.

CIPD. (2012). *Resourcing and Talent Planning: Annual Survey Report 2012*. London: CIPD.

Collings, D. G., & Mellahi, K. (2009). Strategic talent management: A review and research agenda. *Human Resource Management Review*, *19*(4), 304–313. doi:10.1016/j.hrmr.2009.04.001

Collins, J. (2001). *Good to great: Why some companies make the leap... and others don't*. HarperCollins Publishers.

Davis, T., Cutt, M., Flynn, N., Mowl, P., & Orme, S. (2007). *Talent Assessment: A New Strategy for Talent Management*. Aldershot: Gower.

Dolan, D. (2011). *Africa Banking Set for Growth*. Reuters.

Donkin, R. (2010). *The future of work*. Basingstoke: Palgrave MacMillan. doi:10.1057/9780230274198

Drucker, P. (1973). *Management: Tasks, Responsibilities, and Practices*. HarperCollins Publishers, Inc.

EIU. (2011). Banking in Sub-Saharan Africa to 2020: Promising Frontiers, *The Economist* Intelligence Unit, 2.

Elegbe, J. A. (2010). *Talent Management in the Developing World - Adopting a Global Perspective* (pp. xiii–xvi). UK: Gower.

Farndale, E., Scullion, H., & Sparrow, P. (2010). The role of the corporate HR function in global talent management. *Journal of World Business*, *45*(2), 161–168. doi:10.1016/j.jwb.2009.09.012

Ford, J., Harding, N., & Stoyanova, D. (2010a). *Talent Management in NHS Yorkshire and The Humber; The Current State of the Art*. Bradford: Bradford University School of Management.

Ford, J., Harding, N., & Stoyanova, D. (2010b). *Talent Management and Development: An Overview of Current Theory and Practice*. Bradford: Bradford University School of Management.

Goede, M. (2011). The wise society: Beyond the knowledge economy. *Foresight*, *13*(1), 6–45. Retrieved from http://search.proquest.com.libaccess.hud.ac.uk/852073314/ doi:10.1108/14636681111109688

Gordon, E. E. (2010). A new talent-investment metric is needed to advance technological leadership and increase jobs. *Employment Relations Today*, *37*(3), 9–14. doi:10.1002/ert.20304

Gratton, L. (2010). The future of work. *Business Strategy Review*, *21*(3), 16–23. doi:10.1111/j.1467-8616.2010.00678.x

Handy, C. (2001). *The Elephant and the Flea: looking backwards to the future*. London: Hutchinson.

Hartmann, E., Feisel, E., & Schober, H. (2010). Talent management of western MNCs in China: Balancing global integration and local responsiveness. *Journal of World Business*, *45*(2), 169–178. doi:10.1016/j.jwb.2009.09.013

Iles, P., Chuai, X., & Preece, D. (2010). Talent Management and HM in multinational companies in Beijing: Definitions, differences and drivers. *Journal of World Business*, *45*(2), 179–189. doi:10.1016/j.jwb.2009.09.014

Kaye Thorne and Andy Pellant. (2007). *The Essential Guide to Managing Talent: How Top Companies Recruit, Train, and Retain the Best Employees*. Kogan Page Limited.

Kerr-Phillips & Thomas, A. (2010). Macro and Micro Challenges for Talent Retention in South Africa. *South Africa Journal of Human Resource Management*, *7*(1).

Kuptsch, C., & Pang, E. F. (Eds.), (2006, January). *Competing for global talent*. Retrieved from www.ilo.org

Leif, S., Karugu, W., & Schuepbach, L.S. (2008). Kaskazi Network Ltd – Distributing to the Bottom of the Pyramid. *IMD*.

Lewis, R. E., & Heckman, R. (2006). Talent management: A critical review. *Human Resource Management Review*, *16*(2), 139–154. doi:10.1016/j.hrmr.2006.03.001

Marchington, M., & Wilkinson, A. (2012). *Human Resource Management at Work* (5th ed.). London: CIPD.

Maslow, A. M. (1943). A Theory of Human Motivation. *Psychological Review*, *50*(4), 370–396. doi:10.1037/h0054346

Mc Donnell, A., Lamare, R., Gunnigle, P., & Lavelle, J. (2010). Developing tomorrows leaders – Evidence of global talent management in multinational enterprises. *Journal of World Business*, *45*(2), 150–160. doi:10.1016/j.jwb.2009.09.015

Mellahi, K., & Collings, D. G. (2010). The barriers to effective global talent management: The example of corporate elites in MNEs. *Journal of World Business*, *45*(2), 143–149. doi:10.1016/j.jwb.2009.09.018

Moolman, T., & Breidenthal, J. (2013). How to Bridge South Africa's Talent Gap. Retrieved from www. Africa.com

Mupepi, M. G. (2017). Using Communities of Practice to Identify Competencies. In K. Rasmussen, P. Northrup, & R. Colson (Eds.), *Handbook of Research on Competency-Based Education in University Settings* (pp. 157–167). Hershey, PA, USA: IGI Global. doi:10.4018/978-1-5225-0932-5.ch008

Ncube, M., Lufumpa, C. L., & Vencatachellum, D. (2011). *The Middle of the Pyramid: Dynamics of the Middle Class in Africa*. Market Brief.

Parry, E., & Urwin, P. (2011). Generational Differences in Work Values: A Review of Theory and Evidence. *International Journal of Management Reviews*, *13*(1), 79–96. doi:10.1111/j.1468-2370.2010.00285.x

Pennington, S. (2013). *South Africa's Global Competitiveness 2013—Good News and Bad News*. South Africa: The Good News.

Pfeffer, J. (1998). *The Human Equation: Building Profits by Putting People First*. Boston, MA: Harvard Business School Press.

Powell, G. N. (2011). The gender and leadership wars. *Organizational Dynamics*, *40*(1), 1–9. doi:10.1016/j.orgdyn.2010.10.009

Sjoblom, L & El-Agamy, H. (2012). Ecobank: A Passion to build a World-Class Pan-African Bank. *IMD*.

Stewart, J., & Harte, V. (2010). The implications of talent management for diversity training: An exploratory study. *Journal of European Industrial Training*, *34*(6), 506–518. doi:10.1108/03090591011061194

Stewart, J., & Rigg, C. (2011). *Learning and Talent Development*. London: CIPD.

Tarique, I., & Schuler, R. S. (2010). Global talent management: Literature review, integrative framework, and suggestions for further research. *Journal of World Business*, *45*(2), 122–13. doi:10.1016/j.jwb.2009.09.019

Torrington, D., Hall, L., Taylor, S., & Atkinson, C. (2011). *Human Resource Management* (8th ed.). Edinburgh: Pearson Education.

Ulrich, D., & Smallwood, N. (2012). What is Talent? *Leader to Leader*, *63*(63), 55–61. Retrieved from http://onlinelibrary.wiley.com/doi/10.1002/ doi:10.1002/ltl.20011

Williams, C. C. (2007). *Rethinking the future of work: directions and visions*. Basingstoke: Palgrave MacMillan.

Pannell, M. (2013). Talent Management: A Global Context and a South African Perspective. *Wits Business School Journal*.

KEY TERMS AND DEFINATIONS

Competence: Refers to the capacity of individuals/ employees to act in a wide variety of situations. It's their education, skills, experience, energy and their attitudes that will make or break the relationships with the customers and the products or services that are provided.

Competitive Advantage: An advantage that firms has over its competitors, allowing it to generate greater sales or margins and/or retain more customers than its competition. There can be many types of competitive advantages including the knowledge, skills, structure, product offerings, distribution network and support.

Globalization: Globalization is the tendency of businesses, technologies, or philosophies to spread throughout the world, or the process of making this happen. Worldwide integration and development, the process enabling financial and investment markets to operate internationally, largely as a result of deregulation and improved communications.

Perspective: It is a way of regarding situations, facts or topics or a mental view or the state of one's ideas; prospective means concerned with or related to the future and judging their relative importance.

Strategy: The science and art of employing, a careful plan or method, the art of devising or employing plans or stratagems toward a goal, an adaptation or complex of adaptations (as of behavior, metabolism, or structure) that serves or appears to serve an important function in achieving evolutionary success.

Chapter 19
Amplifying the Significance of Systems Theory:
Charting the Course in High Velocity Environments

Mambo Mupepi
Seidman College, USA

ABSTRACT

In system theory organizations are viewed as closed or open systems. An open system interacts with the environment for its sustainability. The closed system does not interact with its setting consequently its behavior depends largely on internal dynamics of its parts. The centricity of an open organizational structure is one created and empowered to learn and change very fast to successfully achieve desired goals. However open systems need to embrace change as follows: transform inputs of energy and information to produce the products demanded by the customers, transact with key stakeholders to access resources, regulate system behavior to achieve stable performance, and adapt to continuously changing high velocity competition to increase productivity.

INTRODUCTION

The discourse progressed in this chapter is about the importance of systems theory and how it is applied to design and implement profound self-awakening change. The technology can be described a broad meta-theory for explaining the structure and behavior of complex wholes called systems. In Davidson (1989), Karl Ludwig von Bertalanffy an Austrian biologist is credited to have invented the general systems theory (GST). This is an interdisciplinary practice that describes systems with interacting components, applicable to biology or organizational studies. In his thesis Bertalanffy (1943) proposed that the classical laws of thermodynamics applied to closed systems, but not necessarily to open systems such as living things. His mathematical model of an organism's growth over time, published in 1934, is still in use today (see Figure 1).

DOI: 10.4018/978-1-5225-1961-4.ch019

Figure 1. The firm cushioned by key stakeholders tends to excel and grow (Mupepi, 2017)

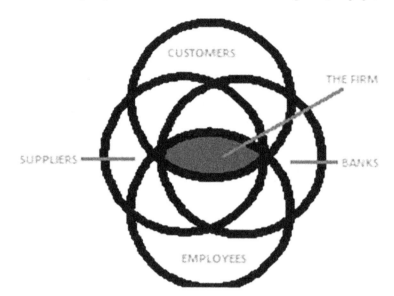

A decade later Kurt Lewin one of the founding fathers of the field of organizational behavior developed the field force analysis to provide a framework for looking at the factors that influence a situation such as increasing productivity. Lewin (1946) examines the forces that are either driving movement toward a goal, helping forces or blocking movement toward a goal i.e. the hindering forces (see Figure 1). The principle is a significant contribution to the field of organizational behavior. French & Bell (1999) have related the field force proposition to organizational and industrial settings. They place emphasis on the ever-changing paradigms in organizational systems and describe some of the important interventions such as the learning organization or quantitative and qualitative research methods. Organization discussions and thinking are critical in the rapidly-evolving contexts of globalization, intensified competition and collaboration.

BACKGROUND

One of the key feature of the systems theory is the notion of the system itself and how it forms an organized whole. Bertalanffy (1943) illustrated the importance of organism adapting to their ecology using the reproduction system of an amoeba. An amoeba is an organism that thrives in marshland or water. An amoeba is often referred to as amoeboid, and is a type of cell or organism which has the ability to alter its shape, primarily by extending and retracting pseudopods (see Figure 2). The amoeba reproduces itself by breaking into two parts one at a time and each part comes complete with identical DNA and continues to replicate itself too until the water is well populated by the organisms. The amoeba adapts to its ecology to thrive.

Bertalanffy argued that human beings were organisms too and for them to succeed they had to adapt to the environment in which they were operating. In organizational systems, this draws attention to identifying the constituent members or subunits of the system and examining relationships among them.

Figure 2. Amoeba organism thrives by understanding its ecology (Yamashita & Emerman, 2005)

There was a need to know the stakeholder groups and to appreciate how they contributed to effectiveness and efficiency in competition.

Mullins (2015) suggested that efficiency and effectiveness are enhanced by creating exploitable database. Collaborating with a computer programming company TechTarget Incorporated, Mullins (2015) asserted that a database management software (DBMS) provided users and programmers with a systemic way to create retrieve update and manage big data. Mullins propounded that the DBMS served as an interface between the end users and database. They argued that the DBMS managed three important aspects in creating the competitive advantage and these are the data, database engine that allows data to be locked and modified and the database schema which defined the database's logical schema. Christensen & Hall et al (2016) proposed that creating appropriate databases which enhanced management decision making capability enabled companies to grow. They viewed the environment in which companies operated and posited that those that thrived did so by producing the products they were sure customers would buy.

Innovation could be planned and implemented successfully drawing information for decision making from exploitable databases (see Figure 3). Exploitable databases about competitors should be made to understand their productivity basis for competition and how they manage their business. The various types of market segments should be described and the ways in which the rival companies function should be part of the information analyzed and developed to enable management to map and chart organizational effectiveness.

Table 1. Prep for creating database: stakeholder analysis

Stakeholder	Needs
Customer	Quality priced goods & services
Employee	Better return on invested competencies
Supplier	Timeous payments
Bank	Daily banking
Management	Increased shareholder value

Questionnaires are Part of the System

The questionnaire has been developed based upon the quality performance model of Garvin (1986) and improved by Fynes & Burca (2005) and Soliman (2014) where quality performance can be divided into: (1) product quality performance; and (2) process quality performance. The customers' questionnaire consists of nine questions where respondents are asked to assess degrees of importance and degrees of actual delivery of seven software product quality performance indicators. Questionnaires hosted on the portals of the company are part of data mining and the collection leading to big data acquisition. It is part of information analytics critical in producing cutting-edge practices necessary in differentiating the firm in highly competitive environments.

System Thinking (ST)

ST is a unified way of looking at organizational schemata that allows all members to be on the same pages when making decisions and producing products demanded by the consumers. ST was made popular by Peter Senge in his book: The Fifth Discipline: The Art and Practice of the Learning Organization, first published in 1990. In that book, *Systems Thinking* is the *Fifth Discipline* that integrates personal mastery, team learning, mental models, and building a shared vision. Senge described extensively the role of what he referred to as mental models which he argued was integral in focusing on the openness needed to unearth shortcomings in organizational perceptions.

Zooming In and Out

In Kanter (2011), organization systems can be observed from zoom buttons on digital devices. They also provide an apt metaphor for modes of strategic thinking. Some people prefer to see things up close, others from afar. Both perspectives have virtues. Kanter argued that the perspectives should not be fixed positions, there was a need to consider the systems dynamics. Kanter asserted that for management to get a complete picture they needed to zoom in and zoom out. A close-in perspective is often found in relationship-intensive settings. It brings details into sharp focus and makes opportunities look large and compelling. But it can have significant downsides. Leaders who prefer to zoom in tend to create policies and systems that depend too much on politics and favors. They can focus too closely on personal status and on turf protection. And they often miss the big picture. Kanter argued that when leaders zoomed out, they could observe events in context and as examples of general fashion.

Archetypes

The word archetype is derived from the Greeks and it implies first of its kind. Archetypes can be illustrated diagrammatically to represent the most commonly seen behaviors or translations of generic structures. Archetypes illustrate structures in a value-creation process (Mupepi & Mupepi, 2015). Archetypes can be applied in the design and building of effective capacity, databases, and organizational structures. The structure in system theory implies the inter-relationships among key components of the system such as those that can be found in a value creation process and characterized by defined inputs and outputs, cost centers, process maps and job specifications to mention just a few.

Figure 3. Archetypes can be applied in developing exploitable databases (Mupepi & Mupepi, 2015)

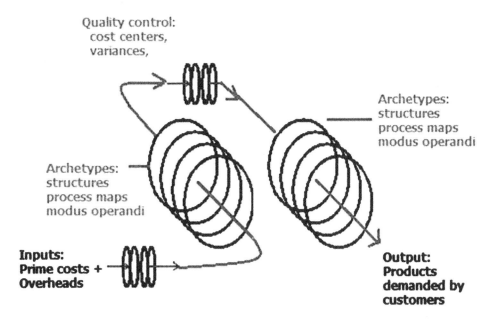

Figure 4. Exploitable databases (Mullins, 2015)

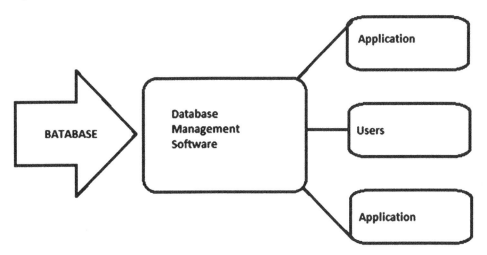

Systems marketing provide total solutions to customer problems. In Christensen & Hall et al (2016), vendors of management information systems such as TechTarget Incorporated, will design, develop, and implement, including the training of users, a database management system to meet the information requirements of customers and the value creation system.

THE FOCUS OF THIS CHAPTER

The focus of this chapter is on how the systems theory ontology can be applied to create and maintain the competitive advantage. The collective assumption in systems theory about performance is that the collective assumptions regarding systems thinking learning and strategic planning can be applied to craft strategy difficult for similar companies to mimic.

RECOMMENDATION

Building portals to recruit and hire talent, provide on-line learning opportunities for stakeholders, trade and mine data continuously provides opportunities to increase organizational efficiency and effectiveness. Customer questionnaires can be hosted on the portals and hard copies made available for those who visit the physical sales sites. The customer questionnaires could have variables on customer quality preference indicators, and the actual degrees of these quality performance. Telephone operators can also adapt some of the on-line questionnaires to call prospective customers and offer them the company's products. The databases for sales and marketing can be deployed to make promotions. The database for human resources development and training can also be employed to headhunt talent and provide the training needs in on-job training, simulations, and others.

ANALYSIS AND CONCLUSION

Organizations that continue to learn and improve performance will keep abreast of change. The ability to change is enhanced through effective decision making. In high velocity environments characterized by knowledge-intensive organization firms must develop the dynamic capabilities and open innovation strategies. Systems theory and informatics considerations can be applied in building high performance organization critical in creating the competitive advantage.

REFERENCES

Christensen, C., Hall, T., Dillion, K., & Duncan, D. S. (2016). *Competing against luck: The story of innovation & customer choice*. New York: Harper Business.

Davidson, M. (1983). *Uncommon Sense: The Life and Thought of Ludwig Von Bertalanffy*. Los Angeles: J. P. Tarcher.

French, W.L., & Bell, C.H. (1998). *Organization Development: Behavioral Science Interventions for Organization Improvement* (6th ed.). New York: Pearson.

Garvin, D. A., & Burca, S. D. (2005). The effects of design quality on quality performance. *International Journal of Production Economics, 96*. doi:10.1016/j.ijpe.2004.02.008

Gino, F., & Pisano, G. P. (2008). Toward a Theory of Behavioral Operations. *Manufacturing & Service Operations Management, 10*(4), 676–691. doi:10.1287/msom.1070.0205

Kanter, R. M. (2011). Zoom In, Zoom Out. *Harvard Business Review, 89*(3). PMID:21513265

Lewin, K. (1946). Action research and minority problems. *Journal of Social Issues, 2*(4), 34-46.

Mullins, C. (2015). An overview of today's leading DBMS Platforms. Retrieved from https://www.datavail.com/blog/an-overview-of-todays-leading-dbms-platforms/

Mupepi, M. G. (2017). Using Communities of Practice to Identify Competencies. In K. Rasmussen, P. Northrup, & R. Colson (Eds.), *Handbook of Research on Competency- Based Education in University Settings* (pp. 157–167). Hershey, PA, USA: IGI Global. doi:10.4018/978-1-5225-0932-5.ch008

Mupepi, M. G., & Mupepi, S. C. (2015). Charting Highly Productive Organization: Wrapping it all in Social Constructs. *International Journal of Productivity Management and Assessment Technologies, 3*(1), 13–30. doi:10.4018/IJPMAT.2015010102

Senge, P. (1990). *The Fifth Discipline: The art and practice of the learning organization.* New York: Doubleday.

Soliman, F. (2014). Role of Cloud Systems as Enabler of Global Competitive Advantages. In I. Portela & F. Almeida (Eds.), *Organizational, Legal, and Technological Dimensions of Information System Administration* (pp. 120–138). Hershey, PA, USA: IGI Global. doi:10.4018/978-1-4666-4526-4.ch008

von Bertalanffy, L. (1934). Untersuchungen über die Gesetzlichkeiten des Wachstums. I. Allgemeine Grundlagen der Theorie; mathematische und physiologische Gesetzlichkeiten des Wachstums bei Wassertieren. *Arch. Entwicklungsmech., 131*, 613–652.

Yamashita, M., & Emerman, M. (2005). The cell cycle independence of HIV Infections is not determined by known Karyophilic viral elements. *PLoS Pathogens, 1*(3), e18. doi:10.1371/journal.ppat.0010018 PMID:16292356

KEY TERMS AND DEFINITIONS

Ecology: The study of interactions among organisms and their environment

High Velocity Markets: High velocity markets are characterized by rapid-fire technological change, short product life-cycles, rapidly evolving customer expectations, frequent launches of new competitive moves and entry of important new rivals.

Productivity: Productivity is an average measure of the efficiency of production.

Schema: A mental image of what an authority figure will look and act like.

Systems Theory: System theory is an interdisciplinary study of systems in general with the goal of discovering patterns and elucidating principles that can be discerned from and applied to all types of systems at all nesting levels in all fields of research.

Chapter 20

A Centricity on Survey Design Techniques:
Advancing Talent Management in Emerging Enterprises

Mambo Mupepi
Seidman College, USA

ABSTRACT

The primary objective of this paper is to demonstrate how questionnaire techniques can be applied to assess and evaluate data to develop the metrics necessary to progress efficiency and effectiveness in successful organization. An opinion poll is a tool associated with survey research and can be designed and employed to collect information pertaining to attitudes, practices, and skills prevailing in a given or random population. The information can be examined and construed to progress the efficacies necessary in triumphant enterprises. Surveys are used to measure behavior, knowledge, attitudes and opinions useful in the design and implementation of high performance organization. Opinion polls can be interpreted in crafting practices necessary in differentiating the business and making of goods and services demanded by customers.

INTRODUCTION

The OD practitioner has many tools and techniques available to apply when working with different organizations around the world. I have chosen the job of the OD practitioner to illustrate how surveys, questionnaires or poll surveys can be designed and implement to collect data from sample or target populations which can be analyzed to appreciate prevailing cultural conditions. Other techniques require the use of computers to record and process data. The questionnaire is a tool that can be simplified or made complex depending on what a practitioner wants to do. The questionnaire tool has at least three explanations: the first is a list of a research or survey questions asked to respondents, and designed to extract specific information. It serves four basic purposes: to

DOI: 10.4018/978-1-5225-1961-4.ch020

1.   Collect the appropriate data.
2.   Make data comparable and amenable to analysis.
3.   Minimize bias in formulating and asking question.
4.   To make questions engaging and varied (Creswell & Plano Clark, 2011).

The second definition is that of a survey, a method of gathering information from individuals. Surveys have a variety of purposes, and can be conducted in many ways. Surveys may be conducted to gather information through a printed questionnaire, over the telephone, by mail, in person, by diskette, or on the web. This information is collected through use of standardized procedures so that every participant is asked the same questions in the same way. It involves asking people for information in some structured format. Depending on what is being analyzed, the participants being surveyed may be representing themselves, their employer, or some organization to which they belong (HR Survey, 2016). The third explanation is provided in Mupepi (2010a), as a formalized set of questions for obtaining information from respondents drawn at random or sample population. In enterprises questionnaires can be deployed to collect data which can be analyzed and understood in the design of customer-centric organization. Data collected by the use of survey instruments can also be interpreted to develop the metrics necessary in differentiating the business in search for the competitive advantage. The questionnaire instrument is employed mainly in quantitative research.

BACKGROUND

In Silverman (2001), a the survey is a technique for collecting data which can analyzed to accurately measure say, production output in defined quantities. The OD practitioner studies such information to record changes in the characteristics of the organization's performance over time. The difference then between a survey and questionnaire depends on what needs to be done. A survey allows the OD practitioner to ask multiple choice questions to any given population. The questionnaire can be distributed in a given population. Here four things can happen. The OD practitioner can employ research assistants who can help the subjects to respond to the questionnaire. Secondly, the questionnaire can be distributed by mail and the subjects are expected to make their responses and mail back the completed responses in a pre-paid mailing envelop. The third is to use the telephone to call preselected participants in a given geographic area. The fourth is to use email system to post questionnaires as attachments. The OD practitioner has these choices to make to collect data needed to be analyzed to develop the metrics to align performance to strategy.

In Malhotra (1993), the precarious concern of questionnaire design is the minimization of measurement error, i.e. minimizing the difference between the information sought by researcher and that produced by the questionnaire. Malhotra suggests that some of the factors that need to be included in survey design are: specification of required information, question content, question wording, response format, question order, physical characteristics and pilot testing. In Silverman (2001), the sense of questionnaire instruments is drawn from qualitative research methods. Qualitative research assume a fixed preference or predefined evaluation of what is good and bad research. However, the choice between the different research methods should depend on what needs to be investigated. Silverman suggests that software is available to assist in the design of questionnaires suitable in telephone and computer interviewing techniques. For example, Novi Survey (2017), offer software for use in face-to-face and on-line surveys.

Novi Survey boosts easy and immediate access online survey service which can be incorporated in creating a professional web survey without the hassle of installing any software. The same software can be downloaded and used as a face-to-face questionnaire. The probes are in some form of sequential order and provide the basis for collecting the responses. The total responses obtained are the raw data which can be analyzed and understood in framing the research results.

An Overview of Quantitative Techniques

Quantitative techniques are part of research methodology that applies survey or questionnaires and other large scale data collection techniques to predict results and identify factors viewed as universal in the organization. In Givens (2008), quantitative techniques are a systematic empirical investigation of observable phenomena via statistical, mathematical or computational techniques. The objective of quantitative research is to develop and employ mathematical models, theories and or hypotheses pertaining to phenomena. Givens asserts that the process of measurement is central to quantitative research because it provides the fundamental connection between empirical observation and mathematical expression of quantitative relationships. A questionnaire is a set of typed or written questions for obtaining statistical useful information from individuals. It allows the organizational development practitioner (OD practitioner) to ask multiple choice questions from a defined population which usually is members of the organization he or she has been contracted to help improve performance. A questionnaire or survey allows the OD practitioner to ask multiple choice questions. Participants can choose from among answers that the OD practitioner predefines.

Organization-Wide Climate

In Fitzgerald (2016) the University of Michigan will launch a survey of students, faculty and staff to gauge the climate regarding diversity equity and inclusion. The survey is part of the University's five-year strategic plan for making the campus community more diverse, equitable, and inclusive. Fitzgerald suggested that the survey will help the university to create a base level of statistics for measuring the countrywide campus climate relating to diversity equity and inclusion that can be repeated across time to measure progress toward established goals. The human resources development office is responsible for coordinating the survey. It will send more than 3500 students 1500 faculty members and 3500 staff members spread the university community.

Etic and Emic Information

The OD practitioner must enter the research sites with two objectives in mind. The first is to obtain an emic perspective of existing culture determined by local custom, meaning, and belief (Mupepi, 2010a) and best described by a native of the culture (see Table 1). A structured survey tool can be used to make observations about the practices or culture of an organization. The second objective is to understand behavior within the research site. In Mupepi (2010a) this perspective has been referred to as etic knowledge. It is the generalizations of human behavior that are considered universally true, and commonly linked to cultural practices which can be observed in situ by the OD practitioner and recorded as variables that can be measured to understand their distribution in a normal curve (see Table 1)

Table 1. Assessing prevailing cultural conditions

Competency	Strongly Agree	Agree	Neutral	Disagree	Strongly Disagree	
Do you know how to do your job?	5	4	3	2	1	N/A
Do you possess the skills to effectively do the job?						
Can you apply technology to make your job easy?						
Do you feel you have what it takes to do your job?						

A sample questionnaire (Mupepi, 2010)

Individual Questions

Specification of the required information is an essential part of the research process and a necessary prerequisite of good questionnaire design. It is also useful to consider who the respondents and what the interview technique will be… computer, telephone, or personal (see Table 1). The next consideration is to determine individual question context. Are the data to be produced by a particular question needed? Will a particular question produce the specified data? Are several questions needed instead of one? A common error is to ask two questions in one, resulting in the respondent having difficulties in answering unambiguously. Will the respondent answer all the questions? Is the subject private or embarrassing to answer?

Presenting the Data on Spreadsheets

Data obtained from surveys or questionnaires can be entered into a computer using software such as statistical processing software (SPSS) or enterprise resource palling software (SAP). These technologies are useful for data analysis and producing analytics useful in building exploitable databases in marketing or production management strategy. Numerous software technologies can be used to make data, numbers or text to be entered and presented in a rectangular matrix. Data can be manipulated in a variety of different ways defined by the OD practitioner. For example column or rows of numbers can be added interchanged or multiplied by constants of say 5 or 10. Spreadsheets provide the OD practitioner powerful and relevantly simple means of analyzing performance and productivity.

Questionnaire Housekeeping

As the OD practitioner anticipates data collection there is a need to respect participants and the sites for research which can all be local or distributed in global environments. Cultural practices are relative in global environments. Creswell & Plano Clark (2011) suggested that it made sense not to put vulnerable populations at risk and to respect the consent of all participants. Consent forms should be explained to all participants and to seek their permission to participate in the survey. Thus the design and implementation of a survey be secondary after securing the consent of the participants in sample populations. In random surveys, the purpose of the data collection should be explained to participants and simultaneously seeking their permission to participate.

Wording Can Lead to Understanding

In Saris & Gallhofer (2014), the wording of the questions is treated cautiously. The respondents must not spend their time trying to understand what the questions are all about. Simple, frequently used and well-understood words are preferred. Organizations are constantly learning and improving. The variables in a questionnaire must be understood by those who will work with the survey as participants or researchers. Surveys or questionnaires are useful in advancing organizational goals. They make it possible to understand what customers or other stakeholders might feel about what the organizations does. Certainly the data drawn from these instruments can be analyzed to craft cutting-edge practices.

Realizing Knowledge

Leading questions such as "Most people agree that the Japanese Language is not easy to learn" or "Do you think the Japanese language is difficulty to learn?" should be avoided. Questions should give alternatives equal prominence, for instance a residence of Cape Town might be asked: Do you prefer to travel by rail air or road when going to Johannesburg? Just asking whether they prefer to travel by road would give the question a bias (Mupepi Tenkasi & Sorensen, 2005). When employing battery of rating scales such as the Likert Scales, the statements should be a positive and negative mixture (see Figure 1).

The argument that knowledge can be created objectively is sustained by many scholars including Mupepi, Tenkasi & Sorensen (2008) and Mupepi (2017), among many others. Mupepi et al suggest that knowledge can be created by a network of individuals who share a passion about many things often related to their profession or fraternity. Knowledge creation efforts typically focus on organizational

Figure 1. The constitution of capability (Mupepi, 2017)

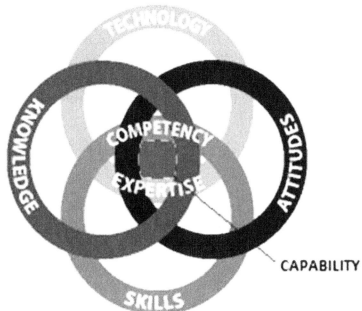

objectives such as improved performance, competitive advantage, innovation, the sharing of lessons learned, integration, and continuous improvement of the business.

In Mupepi (2017), different frameworks for distinguishing between different configurations of knowledge exist. It can be argued that the type of knowledge found in organizations constitute technology, explicit knowledge, skills, and the disposition to do the job. The questioning techniques encouraged in Mupepi (2017), focus on the capacity needed to expand operations. The assumption made in the construct of the competency development is that knowledge can be created by the people doing the job who have the expertise. The skunk works (SW) is a group of intrapreneurs who deliberate separately from the normal operation of the organization to focus their attention on improving existing products and developing new products. Their outfit can come up with new processes and technology to improve productivity. The SW can wield expert power conferred to it by top management to create, diffuse, and distribute explicit knowledge in the value creation system to effectively increase output (see Figure 1).

Can Knowledge be Applied Across Contexts?

Mupepi & Motwani (2015) contest that knowledge objectively obtained using the collaboration forums of skunkworks can be utilized across the organization to create new products and improve upon existing ones to meet customer demands. In Rodgers (1993), explicit knowledge can be disseminated from knowledge-intensive organizations to those who can put it into context to progress organizational goals. Rodgers pauses knowledge as something that can be shared through the diffusion process. Rogers proposes that four main factors stimulus the extent of a new idea: the innovation itself, communication channels, time, and a social system. This process relies heavily on the gregariousness of people in the organization. The invention must be widely adopted in order to self-sustain. The SW originated from Lockheed and Martin Aeronautics Engineering Company in 1943. Engineer Kelly Johnson and his team designed and implemented the first jet fighter plane using Skunk Works project as a title. The SW was composed of experienced and qualified and experienced engineers who developed the first jet fighter plane in the world. The techniques the SW developed have been adapted in peacetime as a *modus operandi* in new product design development and improvement. Engineer Kelly Johnson defined the attributes one had to meet to join his skunkworks project. The enriched skunkworks labs were equipped with all the necessary resources (Giddens, 1998) to make the project successful. Quantitative research techniques and applied sciences could have been used to advance many other subjects to progress the design and implementation of a stealth flying fighter plane. The collective experience of Johnson and his team led to successfully product design (see Figure 1).

The Survey

In Saris & Revilla (2015) a questionnaire is an instrument designed for data collection in human research surveys. A variable category that is often measured in survey research are demographic variables, which are used to depict the characteristics of the people surveyed in the sample. Demographic variables include such measures as ethnicity, socioeconomic status, race, and age. In organizations demographic variables can include stakeholders classified as management and non-management. Saris & Revilla suggest that surveys often assess the preferences and attitudes of individuals and a number apply self-report scales to measure stakeholder or sample population opinion.

THE FOCUS OF THE CHAPTER

The focus of this chapter is about how to design and implement useful surveys or questionnaires to collect data. The data can be analyzed and understood in advancing efficiency and effectiveness in varied organization operating in high velocity global markets. A survey is made for the purpose of understanding the experiences, beliefs, perceptions and feelings of a given group of people. Surveys may be used in a variety of fields including business, science and social studies. Opinion poll creates a more accurate picture regarding the way people view certain things in the community by collection of specific data.

In Mupepi (2010a) a questionnaire calibrated on self-rating scales to measure the knowledge, skills, attitudes, and technology of the Zambezi Valley Trading Company (Company from now onwards) that was growing fast. The Company needed to define its strength to make expansion a reality. The questionnaire was distributed among management and non-management stakeholders.

RECOMMENDATIONS

Creation of the Two Skunkworks (SW1 and SW2)

The sample used 40 participants, and within the sample, a further eight management and eight non-management staff were randomly selected to be the SW1 and SW2 respectively. The samples were drawn and assessments designed to answer these research questions:

- How does management rate itself in terms of competencies drawn by non-management?
- How does management rate itself in terms of the competencies it drew for itself?
- How does non-management rate itself in terms of competencies drawn by management?
- How does non-management rate itself in terms of the competencies it draws for itself?

(I refer to these competencies later in this text as Management and Non-Management Perceived Competencies)

Test of Significance and Interpretation of Results

This test investigated whether the competencies drawn by the two SW would represent statistically those of the population. The data was drawn from a random sample of 40 taken from a possible population of 90. The SW sample size of eight in each group was randomly selected from the 40 participants. Data was collected to test the hypothesis that competencies constructed by the communities of practice are more applicable than those developed elsewhere or by management alone.

The Chi square test of statistical significance result of 0.146 rejects the hypothesis that Management alone can draw effective competencies. We accept the null hypothesis that only SW can develop authenticated knowledge appropriate for what the organization does. To prove this hypothesis requires in-depth analysis of all data. In Table 1, 50% of the responses were below the expert threshold, necessitating analyses of each category to determine individual competency needs. The minimum expected count is 1.20 with a standard deviation of 3. The data can also mean that the Company simply was not as competent as it should be.

The scales for the measurement instrument. This research uses a competency range in the Likert Scale and is Described Below

1 = Little or No Skill, 2 = Basic Skill, 3 = Adequate Skill, 4 = Proficient Skill,
5 = Expert Skill, N/O = Not Observed

Analysis of Individual Categories

It is possible that management in its self-rating was not drawing a distinction between strategic planning and total quality control. The two types of competencies might be viewed by management as closely related. Management might view the outcome of total quality control as closely related. Is there any difference between how they rated themselves and how they were rated by non-management on the above competencies? Scholars argue that real work situations call for no more than minimal reading and writing skills related to the work requirements (see Table 2). Field experience indicates that the tillage operations required the calculations of the area of the field that must be ploughed. The tractor driver and his assistant would measure the tillage area and report their findings to the tillage supervisor with the names and location of the customer for approval. The supervisor would either re-check the area to allow for fuel and time budgets or can approve when the customer makes the 50% deposit required before the work can commence (FN1). There is very little writing at all and these findings concur with Mupepi Tenkasi & Sorensen (2007), who contend that language is much more important in such work environments. They suggest that the technical language developed in the field of the profession is much more important in advancing effective communications. In later research Mupepi (2017) posits that a language can impact the understanding of work practices as people coerce more with the spoken rather than the written word. Therefore, effective verbal and written communications are crucial in the transference of knowledge and technology in all cognitive areas. In much later research Mupepi (2017), propounds that

Table 2. The Pearson Chi-test

Techniques	Values	Differences (df)	Asymp. Significance (Two-sided)
Pearson Chi-Square	5.383[a]	3	0.146
Likelihood Ration	6.416	3	0.93
Linear-by-Linear	0.016	1	0.900
N of Valid Cases	40		

a. 4 Cell(50%) have expected count less than 5. The minimum expected count is 1.20 (Mupepi, 2010)

Table 3. N=8 (SW1) Management self-rating on perceived competencies

	Total Respondents	1	2	3	4	5	N/A	Average
Strategic planning	8		1			7		4
Total quality mgt.	8		1			7		4
Crop production	8					8		5

Table 4. N=8 (SW2) Non-management self-rating on management perceived competencies

Competencies	Total Respondents	1	2	3	4	5	N/A	Average
Strategic planning	8	2	4	2				
Total quality mgt.	8	3	5	0	0			
Crop production	8			2	3	3		

sharing the same language is critical in the development and implementation of organizational practices. People in the organization can make the difference if they all understand what needs to be done to create a successful enterprise (see Table 2).

Generally, the SW2 rated management lower on all competencies than management rated itself. But, like management, they made very little distinction between strategic planning and total quality control. They accorded crop production the highest rating. It appears that for both management and the other community of practice, crop production was a potentially independent competence. SWs have expertise in a defined area. Mupepi (2010) argues that knowledge requires contextual adaptation and that SWs should disseminate their knowledge of best practices and experience to the rest of the organizational members (see Table 3).

Based on the SW2's observations, the Company needs to develop a strategy to support its mission of sustaining the food security and poverty reduction initiatives in the Zambezi Valley. The Company must see to it that there is a coordinated plan for tillage, retail, haulage, and SMEs projects. Putting such strategy into place can also warrant that the Company must communicate effectively with all stakeholders to learn and chart the best courses of action available.

RECOMMENDATION

The design and implementation of survey instruments follows a proven pattern of sequences in questioning. The question sequence can impact the responses in many ways. Malhotra (1993) suggested the questions could start with a general topic and gradually moving on to more specific probes. In Mupepi (2010), a focus group is recommended to be used as a pilot to see if the same thing to the respondent as the researcher intended that lists of response categories are complete, that the questionnaire is not too long and that the routes through the opinion poll tool are appropriate and can be followed by the interviews or respondents.

ANALYSIS AND CONCLUSION

Questionnaires are useful in quantitative and qualitative research methodologies. In ethnography studies survey tools can be applied to obtain emic information as to the practices of an organization. They can be used to craft organizational practices difficult for firms doing similar things to mimic.

REFERENCES

Creswell, J. W., & Plano Clark, V. L. (2011). *Designing and conducting mixed methods research*. Los Angeles, CA: Sage.

Fitzgerald, R. (2016). Survey will gauge U-M campus climate on diversity equity and inclusion. The University of Michigan Record, 72(7), 1 & 9.

Giddens, A. (1998). *The Third Way: The Renewal of Social Democracy*. New York: Polity Press.

Given, L. M. (2008). *The Sage encyclopedia of qualitative research methods*. Los Angeles, Calif.: Sage Publications. doi:10.4135/9781412963909

Malhotra, N. K. (1993). *Marketing research: An applied orientation*. Englewood Cliffs, N.J.: Prentice-Hall.

Martin, L. (1943). The Skunk Works Origin Story. Retrieved from http://www.lockheedmartin.com/us/aeronautics/skunkworks/origin.html

Mupepi, M. (2010a). *Appreciating unlocking and building effective entrepreneurial capacity*. Saarbrucken, Germany: Lap Lambert Inc.

Mupepi, M. (2017). Using communities of Practice to identify workforce competencies. In R. Colson (Ed.), *Handbook of Research on Competency-Based Education in University Settings* (p. 35). Hershey, PA, USA: IGI Global. doi:10.4018/978-1-5225-0932-5.ch008

Mupepi, M., & Motwani, J. (2015). Deconstructing the Value Creation Process: Positioning Diversity to Increase Output. *International Journal of Sociotechnology and Knowledge Development*, 7(4), 15–30. doi:10.4018/IJSKD.2015100102

Mupepi, M., Tenkasi, R. V., & Sorensen, P. F. (2005). Building effective capability in the advancing economies in sub-Sahara Africa: *Proceedings of the Global Economy XI Conference Eastern Academy of Management June 26-30 University of Cape Town Graduate School of Business*.

Mupepi, M. G. (2009). The nature of a schematic description of a socially constructed organizational competency model (SCCM). *International Journal of Collaborative Enterprises*, 1(2), 224–240. doi:10.1504/IJCENT.2009.029291

Mupepi, M. G. (2010). Appreciating social structures: A strategy for advancing the efficiency and effectiveness loci in organization. *International Journal of Education Economics and Development*, 1(4), 306–319. doi:10.1504/IJEED.2010.034442

Mupepi, M. G., Mupepi, S. C., Tenkasi, R. V., & Jewell, G. D. (2008). Precision in managing organizational change: Identifying and analyzing needs using social constructs. *International Journal Management Practice*, 3(2), 150–163. doi:10.1504/IJMP.2008.018368

Mupepi, S. C., Mupepi, M. G., Tenkasi, R. V., & Sorensen, P. F. Jr. (2007). Creating high impact organization in the SADC: Adapting OD Methods and Practices. *OD Practitioner*, 32(2), 34–39.

Rogers, E. (2003). *Diffusion of Innovations* (5th ed.). New York: Simon and Schuster.

Saris, W. E., & Gallhofer, I. N. (2014). *Design, evaluation and analysis of questionnaires for survey research* (2nd ed.). Hoboken, NJ: John Wiley. doi:10.1002/9781118634646

Saris, W. E., & Revilla, M. (2015). Correction for measurement errors in survey research: Necessary and possible. *Social Indicators Research, 127*(3), 1005–1020. doi:10.1007/s11205-015-1002-x

Silverman, D. (2001). *Interpreting qualitative data: Methods for analyzing Talk, Text & Interaction* (2nd ed.). London, UK: Sage Publications.

Surveys, H. R. (2016). What is a survey? Retrieved from http://www.hr-survey.com/WhatIs.htm

Surveys, N. (2017). Survey Software. Retrieved from https://novisurvey.net/

KEY TERMS AND DEFINITIONS

Opinion Poll: An opinion poll, sometimes simply referred to as a poll, is a human research survey of public opinion from a particular sample.

Organization Development Practitioner (OD Practitioner): The OD practitioner role is varied and purposed with helping clients to improve the effectiveness of their organization developing both business processes and people processes within the context of the organization.

Organizational Design: Organizational architecture or organization design: the creation of roles, processes, and formal reporting relationships in an organization.

Questionnaire: A questionnaire is a research instrument consisting of a series of questions and other prompts for the purpose of gathering information from respondents

Respondent: A respondent is a person who is called upon to issue a response to a communication made by another. The term is used in survey procedure

Survey: A field of applied statistics, survey methodology studies the sampling of individual units from a population and the associated survey data collection techniques.

Compilation of References

ACAS. (2016). *Job Evaluation Handbook*. Kingstone-Upon Thames, UK: HMGS.

Achebe, C. (1958). *Things Fall Apart*. New York: William Heinemann.

Achtert, E., Böhm, C., Kriegel, H. P., Kröger, P., Müller-Gorman, I., & Zimek, A. (2006). Finding Hierarchies of Subspace Clusters. In *Knowledge Discovery in Databases. LNCS, 4213*, 446–453. doi:10.1007/11871637_42

AFNS. (2008). Bush family relation in diamond ring dispute. Retrieved from http://londonantwerpdiamonds.com/diamond-news-archive.php

Aggarwal, S., & Manuel, N. (2016). Big data analytics should be driven by business needs, not by technology. Retrieved from http://www.mckinsey.com/business-functions/mckinsey-analytics/our-insights/big-data-analytics-should-be-driven-by-business-needs-not-technology

Ahmad, A., Bosua, R., & Scheepers, R. (2015). Protecting organizational competitive advantage: A knowledge leakage perspective. *Computers & Security, 42*, 27–39. doi:10.1016/j.cose.2014.01.001

Akella, J., Marwaha, S., & Sikes, J. (2014). How CIOs can lead their company's information business. Retrieved from http://www.mckinsey.com/business-functions/business-technology/our-insights/how-cios-can-lead-their-companys-information-business

Akpolat, C. K., Soliman, F., & Schweitzer, J. (2014). Learning and Innovation in Uncertain Times: The Role of Organizational Systems and Managerial Perceptions of Uncertainty. In F. Soliman (Ed.), *Learning Models for Innovation in Organizations: Examining Roles of Knowledge Transfer and Human Resources Management* (pp. 209–221). Hershey, PA, USA: IGI Global. doi:10.4018/978-1-4666-4884-5.ch011

Aksakal, E., Dağdeviren, M., Eraslan, E., & Yüksel, I. (2013). Personnel selection based on talent management. *Procedia: Social and Behavioral Sciences, 73*, 68–72. doi:10.1016/j.sbspro.2013.02.021

Aldrich, R. (2005). Apprenticeship in England: Lessons from History of Education. In A. Heikkinen & R. Sultana (Eds.), *Vocational Education and Apprenticeships in Europe* (pp. 195–205). London, UK: Routledge.

Alford, C. J. (1906). Mining law of British Empire. Retrieved from https://archive.org/details/mininglawbritis01alfogoog

Alijafari, R., & Sarnikar, S. (2009). A framework for assessing knowledge sharing risks in inter- organizational networks. *Proceedings of the Americas Conference on Information Systems*. Retrieved from http://aisel.aisnet.org/amcis2009/572/

Altrichter, H., & Gstettner, P. (1993). Action research: A closed chapter in the history of German social science. *Educational Action Research, 1*(3), 329–360. doi:10.1080/0965079930010302

Alvesson, M., & Karreman, D. (2007). Unravelling HRM: Identity, Ceremony and Control in a Management Consulting Firm. *Organization Science, 18*(4), 711–723. doi:10.1287/orsc.1070.0267

Ambrose, D. (2003). Barriers to aspiration development and self-fulfilment: Interdisciplinary insights for talent discovery. *Gifted Child Quarterly*, *47*(4), 282–29. doi:10.1177/001698620304700405

American Psychology Association. (1997). Defining the Field Force at a given time by Kurt Lewin. In *Resolving Social Conflicts & Field Theory in Social Science*. Washington, D.C.: American Psychological Association.

Anastasia, P., & Vojtech, K. (2015). Family business in the Czech Republic: Actual situation. *Trendy Ekonomiky a Managementu*, *9*(23), 32–42.

Andersen, J. A., & Hansson, P. H. (2011). At the end of the road? On differences between women and men in leadership behavior. *Leadership and Organization Development Journal*, *32*(5), 428–441. doi:10.1108/01437731111146550

Andresen, M., Biemann, T., & Pattie, M. W. (2013). What makes them move abroad? Reviewing and exploring differences between self-initiated and assigned expatriation. *International Journal of Human Resource Management*, *24*(3), 533–557. doi:10.1080/09585192.2012.697476

Annansingh, F. (2015). Exploring the Risks of Knowledge Leakage: An Information Systems Case Study Approach. Retrieved from https://www.researchgate.net/publication/221924223_Exploring_the_Risks_of_Knowledge_Leakage_An_Information_Systems_Case_Study_Approach

Aparna, J., & Roh, H. (2012). The role of context in work team diversity research: A meta-analytic review. Academy of Management Journal Vol. 52 No3 (599-6270.

Argyris, C. (1991). Teaching Smart People How to Learn. *Harvard Business Review*, May- June, 99–109.

Argyris, C. (1993). *On Organizational Learning*. Cambridge, Mass.: Blackwell.

Ariss, A. A., Cascio, W. F., & Paauwe, J. (2014). Talent management: Current theories and future research directions. *Journal of World Business*, *49*(2), 173–179. doi:10.1016/j.jwb.2013.11.001

Armstrong, D. M. (1989). *Universals: An Opinionated Introduction*. Melbourne, Australia: Westview Press.

Armstrong, M., & Cummins, A. (2005). *Job Evaluation*. London, UK: Kogan Page Business Books.

Arnold, R. (2014). *Economics 11e*. Mason, Ohio: Cengage.

Arnold, R. A. (2016). *Economics* (11th ed.). Mason, Ohio: South Western Inc.

Aronson, D. (1998). An Overview of Systems Thinking. *Thinking.net.* Retrieved from http://www.thinking.net/Systems_Thinking/OverviewSTarticle.pdf

Ashkanasy, N.A. (2002). Cultivating communities of practice. *Personnel Psychology, 55*(3), 739-743.

Athanasopoulos, P., Damjanovic, L., Burnand, J., & Bylund, E. (2015). Learning to think in a second language: Effects of proficiency and length of exposure in English learners of German. *Modern Language Journal*, *99*(S1Suppl. 1), 138–153. doi:10.1111/j.1540-4781.2015.12183.x

Audi, R. (2015). *The Cambridge Dictionary of Philosophy* (3rd ed.). Cambridge, UK: Cambridge University Press. doi:10.1017/CBO9781139057509

Axelrod, B., Handfield-Jones, H., & Michaels, E. (2001). Talent Management- A critical part of every leader's job. *Ivey Business Journal*.

Axelrod, R., & Cohen, D. (2001). *The Complexity of Cooperation: Agent-Based Models of Competition and Collaboration*. Princeton, NJ: Princeton University Press.

Backstrom, L., Huttenlocher, D., Kleinberg, J., & Lan, X. (2006). Group formation in large social networks.*Proceedings of the 12th Annual International Conference on Knowledge Discovery and Data Mining*. doi:10.1145/1150402.1150412

Banathy, B. H. (1996). *Designing Social Systems in a Changing World*. New York: Plenum. doi:10.1007/978-1-4757-9981-1

Bandura, A. (1977). *Social learning theory*. Englewood Cliffs, NJ: Prentice Hall.

Bandura, A. (1977). *Social Learning Theory*. New York: General Learning Press.

Bandura, A. (1986). *Social Foundations of Thought and Action: A Social Cognitive Theory*. Englewood Cliffs, NJ: Prentice-Hall.

Bandura, A. (1997). *Self-Efficacy: The Exercise of Control*. NY: W. H. Freeman and Company.

Bandura, A., & Walters, R. (1959). *Social Learning and Personality Development*. New York: Holt, Rinehart & Winston.

Banton, M. (2007). Weber on Ethnic Communities: A critique. *Nations and Nationalism*, *13*(1), 19–35. doi:10.1111/j.1469-8129.2007.00271.x

Baporikar, N. (2009). *Talent War - Myth or Reality? MBA Review*. India: ICFAI University Press.

Baporikar, N. (2013a). Understanding Talent Management in Borderless World. *MANAGEMENT TODAY – International Journal of Management Studies*, *3*(4), 10–16.

Baporikar, N. (2013b). Strategic Approach to Talent Management. *JIDNYASA Research Journal*, *7*, 20–26.

Baporikar, N. (2015). Effect of National Culture on Development of International Business in the Sultanate of Oman. In B. Christiansen (Ed.), *Handbook of Research on Global Business Opportunities* (pp. 268–288). Hershey, PA, USA: IGI Global. doi:10.4018/978-1-4666-6551-4.ch013

Bareny, J. B. (1995). Looking inside for competitive advantage. *The Academy of Management Executive*, *9*(4), 9–61.

Barkema, H.G., & Vermeulen, F. (1997). What differences in the cultural backgrounds? *Journal of International Business Studies, 28*(4), 84-104.

Barlow, L. (2006). Talent development: The new imperative? *Development and Learning in Organizations*, *20*(3), 6–9.

Barney, J. B., & Clark, D. N. (2007). *Resource-based theory: Creating and sustaining competitive advantage*. Oxford, UK: Oxford University Press.

Barrett, F. (1995). Creating appreciative learning cultures. *Organizational Dynamics*, *24*(2), 36–4. doi:10.1016/0090-2616(95)90070-5

Barrons, K. P. (1993) *Whittle Communications Channel One: The Effects of News and Advertising on Secondary Students* [Unpublished Ph.D. Dissertation]. Detroit: Wayne State University.

Baruch, Y., Dickmann, M., Altman, Y., & Bournois, F. (2013). Exploring international work: Types and dimensions of global careers. *International Journal of Human Resource Management*, *24*(12), 2369–2393. doi:10.1080/09585192.2013.781435

BBC. (2010). Tiger Woods makes emotional apology for infidelity. Retrieved from http://news.bbc.co.uk/sport2/hi/golf/8521060.stm

Beardwell, J., & Claydon, T. (2010). *Human Resource Management: A Contemporary Approach* (6th ed., pp. 161–195). Harlow: Pearson Education.

Becker, B. E., & Huselid, M. A. (2006). Strategic human resources management: Where do we go from here? *Journal of Management, 32*(6), 898–925. doi:10.1177/0149206306293668

Beechler, S., & Woodward, I. C. (2009). The global "war for talent". *Journal of International Management, 15*(3), 273–285. doi:10.1016/j.intman.2009.01.002

Beheshtifar, M., Nasab, H. Y., & Moghadam, M. N. (2012). Effective talent management: A vital strategy to organizational success. *International Journal of Academic Research in Business and Social Sciences, 2*(12), 227–234.

Bell, M. P. (2012). *Diversity in Organizations* (2nd ed.). Mason, Ohio: Cengage.

Bell, M. P. (2012). *Diversity on Organizations* (2nd ed.). Mason, OH: South Western.

Bell, M. P. (2014). *Diversity in Organization (2ⁿᵈ ed.)*. Mason, Ohio: South-Western Learning.

Bendick, M. Jr, Jackson, C., & Rainoso, V. (1994). Measuring employment discrimination through uncontrolled experiments. *The Review of Black Political Economy, 23*(1), 25–48. doi:10.1007/BF02895739

Benitez-Amado, J., Llorens-Montes, F. J., & Fernandez-Perez, V. (2015). IT impact on talent management and operational environmental sustainability. *Information Technology & Management, 16*(3), 207–220. doi:10.1007/s10799-015-0226-4

Benko, C., Bohdal-Spiegelhoff, U., Geller, J., & Walkinshaw, H. (2014). *Global human capital trends 2014*. New York, NY: Deloitte University Press.

Benko, C., & Weisberg, A. C. (2007). *Mass career customization: Aligning the workplace with today's nontraditional workforce*. Boston, MA: Harvard Business School Press.

Benston, G. J. (2003). The Quality of Corporate Financial Statements and Their Auditors Before and After Enron. *Policy Analysis*, (497), 12.

Berdahl, J. L., & Anderson, C. (2005). Men, women, and leadership centralization in groups over time. *Group Dynamics, 9*(1), 45–57. doi:10.1037/1089-2699.9.1.45

Beregszaszi, J., & Hack-Polay, D. (2015). Off the overload: The growing HR outsourcing industry in emerging European economies - the case of Hungary. *European Journal of International Management, 9*(4), 409–424. doi:10.1504/EJIM.2015.070227

Berger, M. (2000, August 21). Harry Oppenheimer, 91, South African Industrialist, Dies. *New York Times*.

Berger, L. A., & Berger, D. R. (2011). *The Talent Management Handbook* (2nd ed.). New York: McGraw-Hill.

Berger, P. L., & Luckmann, T. (1966). *The Social Construction of Reality*. New York: Anchor Books.

Berger, P. L., & Luckmann, T. (1966). *The Social Construction of Reality: A Treatise in the Sociology of Knowledge*. Garden City, NY: Anchor Books.

Berger, R., & Gavish, Y. (2015). A gem in a hostile world: an evolutionary analysis of the diamonds industry: the case of the Israeli diamond industry. *International Journal of Strategic Change Management, 6*(3/4), 268–291. doi:10.1504/IJSCM.2015.075906

Bertrand, M., & Mullainathan, S. (2004). Are Emily and Greg more employable than LaKisha and Jamal? A Field Experiment on Labor Market Discrimination. *The American Economic Review, 94*(4), 991–1011. doi:10.1257/0002828042002561

Bethke-Langenegger, P., Mahler, P., & Staffelbach, B. (2011). Effectiveness of talent management strategies. *European Journal of International Management, 5*(5), 5524–5539. doi:10.1504/EJIM.2011.042177

Bevens, R.Q., & Raudenbaugh, R.A. (2004). A Model for Unified Science and Technology. *Journal of Technology Studies.*

Bhatnagar, J. (2007). Talent management strategy of employee engagement in Indian ITES employees: Key to retention. *Employee Relations, 29*(6), 640–663. doi:10.1108/01425450710826122

Bianchi, M. (2010). Credit constraints, entrepreneurial talent, and economic development. *Small Business Economics, 34*(1), 93–104. doi:10.1007/s11187-009-9197-3

Bian, J., Guo, X., Lai, K. K., & Hua, Z. (2014). The strategic peril of information sharing in Vertical-Nash Supply Chain: A note. *International. Journal of Production Management and Economics, 158,* 37–43. doi:10.1016/j.ijpe.2014.07.016

Bingham, T. & Galagan, P. (2007). Finding the right talents for critical jobs. *T&D, 30,* 30-36.

Bion, W. R. (1961). *Experiences in Groups.* London, UK: Tavistock Institute. doi:10.4324/9780203359075

Bizumic, B., & Duckitt, J. (2008). My group is not worthy of me: Narcissism and ethnocentrism. *Political Psychology, 29*(3), 437–453. doi:10.1111/j.1467-9221.2008.00638.x

Bjorkman, I., & Farndale, E., et al. (2012). Six Principles of Effective Global Talent Management. *MIT Sloan Management Review, 53*(2).

Björkman, I., Ehrnrooth, M., Mäkelä, K., Smale, A., & Sumelius, J. (2013). Talent or not? Employee reactions to talent identification. *Human Resource Management, 52*(2), 195–214. doi:10.1002/hrm.21525

Bjorkman, I., & Fan, X. (2002). Human resource management and the performance of Western firms in China. *International Journal of Human Resource Management, 13*(6), 853–864. doi:10.1080/09585190210134246

Blake, R. (1977). *A History of Rhodesia.* London, UK: Eyre Methuen.

Blasco, A., & Jorge, X. (2013). Bypassing information leakage protection with trusted applications. *Computers & Security, 31*(4), 557–568. doi:10.1016/j.cose.2012.01.008

Blass, E., & Maxwell, G. (2012). Inclusive talent management and diversity. In H. Francis, L. Holbeche, & M. Roddington (Eds.), *People and Organizational Development: A New Agenda for Organizational Effectiveness* (pp. 243–259). London: CIPD.

Blenko, M. W., Rogers, R., & Mankins, M. C. (2010). *Decide & Deliver: 5 Steps to Breakthrough Performance in Your Organization.* Harvard Business Review Press.

Bloom, N., Conway, N., Mole, K., Moslein, K., Neely, A., & Frost, C. (2004, March). Solving the skills gap. *Advanced Institute of Management Research.* Summary Report from the AIM/CIHE Management Research Forum.

Bloom, B. S. (Ed.). (1956). *Taxonomy of educational objectives: The classification of educational goals: Handbook I, cognitive domain.* New York: Longmans, Green.

Boas, F. (1963). *[1911]. The Mind of Primitive Man.* New York: Collier Books.

Boland, R. J. Jr, & Tenkasi, R. V. (1995). Perspective Making and Perspective Taking in Communities of Knowing. *Organization Science, 6*(4), 350–372. doi:10.1287/orsc.6.4.350

Boudreau, J. W. (2013). Appreciating and "retooling" diversity in talent management conceptual models: A commentary on "The psychology of talent management: A review and research agenda." *Human Resource Management Review, 23*(4), 286–289. doi:10.1016/j.hrmr.2013.08.001

Boudreau, J. W., & Ramstad, P. (2005). Talentship and the evolution of human resource management: From professional practices to strategic talent decision science. *Human Resource Planning Journal, 28*(2), 17–26.

Bourdieu, P. (1990). Structures, habitus, practices. In P. Bourdieu (Ed.), *The logic of practice* (pp. 52–79). Stanford, CA: Stanford University Press.

Boyacigiller, N. A., & Adler, N. J. (1991). The parochial dinosaur: Organizational science in a global context. *Academy of Management Review, 1*(6), 262–290.

Bradsher, K. (1996, March 9). G.M. Files a Lawsuit against VW and Some Executives. *New York Times.*

Brannick, M. T., Levine, E. L., & Morgenson, F. P. (2007). *Job analysis: Methods Research and Applications for Human Resources Management (2nd ed.)*. London: Sage.

Bratton, W. W. (2002, May). Does Corporate Law Protect the Interest of Shareholders and Other Stakeholders?: Enron and the Dark Side of Shareholder Value. *New Orleans. Tulane Law Review,* (1275), 61.

Breckman, W. (2010, July). Times of Theory: On Writing the History of French Theory. *Journal of the History of Ideas, 71*(3), 339–361. doi:10.1353/jhi.0.0082

Britannica (2016). Sir Ernest Oppenheimer: South African Industrialist. Retrieved from www.britannica.com/biography/Ernest-Oppenheimer

Brown, J. S., Collins, A., & Duguid, S. (1989). Situated cognition and the culture of learning. *Educational Researcher, 18*(1), 32–42. doi:10.3102/0013189X018001032

Brown, J. S., & Duguid, P. (1991). Organizational learning and communities of practice: Toward a unified view of working learning and innovation. *Organization Science, 2*(1), 40–57. doi:10.1287/orsc.2.1.40

Brown, L., Flavin, C., & French, H. (2000). *The State of the World 2000*. New York: Earthscan.

Brown, P., & Hesketh, A. (2004). *The mismanagement of talent: Employability and jobs in the knowledge economy*. Oxford, UK: Oxford University Press. doi:10.1093/acprof:oso/9780199269532.001.0001

Brown, R. S. (2013). Beyond the evolutionary paradigm in conscious movement. *Journal of Transpersonal Psychology, 45*(2), 159–172.

Brown, R. S. (2013). Beyond the Evolutionary Paradigm in consciousness Studies. *Journal of Transpersonal Psychology, 45*(2), 159–171.

Burbach, R., & Royle, T. (2010). Talent on demand? Talent management in the German and Irish subsidiaries of a US multinational corporation. *Personnel Review, 39*(4), 414–431. doi:10.1108/00483481011045399

Burby, J. (2009, June 2). What is Digital Analysis? (Click Z). Retrieved from http://clickz.com/print_article/clickz/column/1717832/what-is-digital-analysis#

Burnes, B., & Cooke, B. (2013, October). Kurt Lewin's field theory: A review and re-evaluation. *International Journal of Management Reviews, 15*(4), 408–425. doi:10.1111/j.1468-2370.2012.00348

Burns, J. R., & Balaji, J. (2007). Improved methods for task estimation and project tracking. *International Journal of Information Systems and Change Management, 2*(2), 167–189. doi:10.1504/IJISCM.2007.015118

Bushe, G. R. & Marshak, R. J. (2009). Re-visioning organization development: Diagnostic premises and patterns of practice. *Journal of Applied Behavioral Science On-line.* doi:10.1177/0021886309335070

Bushe, G. R. (2013). Generative process, generative outcome: The transformational potential of Appreciative Inquiry. In D. L. Cooperrider, D. P. Zandee, L. N. Godwin, M. Avital, & B. Boland (Eds.), Advances in Appreciative Inquiry. In *Organizational Generativity: The Appreciative Inquiry Summit and a Scholarship of Transformation* (Vol. 4, pp. 89–113). Bingley, UK: Emerald Group Publishing Limited. doi:10.1108/S1475-9152(2013)0000004003

Busine, M., & Watt, B. (2005). Succession management: Trends and current picture. *Asia Pacific Journal of Human Resources*, *43*(2), 225–237. doi:10.1177/1038411105055060

Butter, M. C., Valenzuela, E. S., & Quintana, M. G. B. (2015). Intercultural talent management model: Virtual communities to promote collaborative learning in indigenous contexts. Teachers' and students' perceptions. *Computers in Human Behavior*, *51*, 1191–1197. doi:10.1016/j.chb.2015.01.030

Buttner, H., Lowe, K. B., & Billings-Harris, L. (2010). The Impact of Diversity Promise Fulfillment on Professionals of Color Outcomes in the USA. *Journal of Business Ethics*, *91*(4), 501–518. doi:10.1007/s10551-009-0096-y

Cabraser, L. Heimann & Bernstein (December 21, 2011). Court Upholds $295 million settlement in De Beers Antitrust suit. Retrieved from http://www.diamonds.net/News/NewsItem.aspx?ArticleID=38343http://www.diamonds.net/News/NewsItem.aspx?Article ID=38343

Cabrera, E. F. (2007). Opting out and opting in: Understanding the complexities of womens career transitions. *Career Development International*, *12*(3), 218–237. doi:10.1108/13620430710745872

Callinicos, A. (2007). *Social theory: A historical introduction*. Cambridge: Polity.

Cameron, K. (1999). A framework for organizational quality culture. *Quality Management Journal*, *6*(4), 7–25.

Cameron, K. S., Dutton, J. E., & Quinn, R. E. (2003). *Positive Organizational Scholarship: Foundations of a New Discipline*. San Francisco, CA: Berrett-Koehler.

Campbell, R. H., & Skinner, A. S. (Eds.). (1976). The wealth of nations. The Glasgow Edition of the Works and Correspondence of Adam Smith, 2b, 47

Campbell, W.K., & Campbell, S.M. (2016). Narcissism and its role in organizations. In K.D.; Elsbach, D.A. Kayes, C. Kayes (Eds.), Contemporary Organizational Behavior: From Ideas to Action (pp. 53-59). New York: Pearson.

Campbell, M., & Smith, R. (2010). *High-potential talent: A view from inside the leadership pipeline*. Greensboro, NC: Center for Creative Leadership.

Cannon-Bowes, J., Tannenbaum, S. I., Salas, E., & Volpe, C. E. (1995). Defining team competencies. In R. Guzzo & E. Salas (Eds.), *Team effectiveness and decision making in organizations* (pp. 333–380). San Francisco, CA.

Capaldo, G., Iandoli, L., & Zollo, G. (2006). A situationalist perspective to competency management. *Human Resource Management*, *45*(3), 429–448. doi:10.1002/hrm.20121

Cappelli, P. (2008). Talent Management for the Twenty-First Century. *Harvard Business Review*, *86*(3), 24–31. PMID:18411966

Cappelli, P. (2008). Talent management for the twenty-first century. *Harvard Business Review*, *86*(3), 76–81. PMID:18411966

Cappelli, P. (2014). *Strategic talent management: Contemporary issues in an international context*. Cambridge, UK: Cambridge University Press.

Carifio, J., & Perla, R. J. (2007). Ten Common Misunderstandings, Misconceptions, Persistent Myths and Urban Legends about Likert Scales and Likert Response Formats and their Antidotes. *Journal of Social Sciences*, *3*(3), 106–116. doi:10.3844/jssp.2007.106.116

Carmichael, F., & Woods, R. (2010). Ethnic Penalties in Unemployment and Occupational Attainment: Evidence for Britain. *International Review of Applied Economics, 14*(1), 91–98.

Carmichael, J., Collins, C., Emsell, P., & Haydon, J. (2011). *Leadership and Management.* Oxford: Oxford University Press.

Carr, S. C., Inkson, K., & Thorn, K. (2005). From global careers to talent flow: Reinterpreting "brain drain." *Journal of World Business, 40*(4), 386–398. doi:10.1016/j.jwb.2005.08.006

Carruci, R. A., & Pasmore, W. (2002). *Relationships that enable enterprise change.* San Francisco, CA: Jossey-Bass/Pfeiffer.

Carter, I. (2013). *Human Behavior in the Social Environment: A Social Systems Approach* (6th ed.). London, UK: Aldine Transactions.

Carvajal, R. (1983). Systemic net-fields: The systems paradigm crises. Part I. *Human Relations, 36*(3), 227–246. doi:10.1177/001872678303600302

Carvalho, P. V. R. (2006). Ergonomic field studies in a nuclear power plant control room. *Progress in Nuclear Energy, 48*(1), 51–69. doi:10.1016/j.pnucene.2005.04.001

Cascio, W. F., & Boudreau, J. W. (2016). The search for global competence: From international HR to talent management. *Journal of World Business, 51*(1), 103–114. doi:10.1016/j.jwb.2015.10.002

Cerdin, J. L., & Brewster, C. (2014). Talent management and expatriation: Bridging two streams of research and practice. *Journal of World Business, 49*(2), 245–252. doi:10.1016/j.jwb.2013.11.008

Cerdin, J. L., & Le Pargneux, M. (2009). Career and international assignment fit: Toward an integrative model of success. *Human Resource Management, 48*(1), 5–25. doi:10.1002/hrm.20264

Cervantes, M., & Guellec, D. (2002). The brain drain: Old myths, new realities. *The OECD Observer. Organisation for Economic Co-Operation and Development, 230,* 40–42.

Chabault, D., Hulin, A., & Soparnot, R. (2012). Talent management in clusters. *Organizational Dynamics, 41*(4), 327–335. doi:10.1016/j.orgdyn.2012.08.008

Chadee, D., & Raman, R. (2012). External knowledge and performance of offshore IT service providers in India: The mediating role of talent management. *Asia Pacific Journal of Human Resources, 50*(4), 459–482. doi:10.1111/j.1744-7941.2012.00039.x

Chall, J. S. (1983). *Stages of Reading Development.* New York: McGraw-Hill.

Chall, J. S., & Jacobs, V. A. (2003). Poor children fourth-grade slump. *American Educator, 27*(1), 14–17.

Chambers, E.G., Foulon, M., Handfield-Jones, H., Hankin, S.M., & Michaels, E.G., III (1998). The War on Talent. *The McKinsey Quarterly Number, 3.*

Chang, H. (2007). *Cultural Communities in a Global Labor Market: Immigration Restrictions as Residential Segregation.* Pittsburgh: University of Pennsylvania Law School.

Chan, L., & Daim, T. (2012). High Technology Industrialization and Internationalization: Exploring International Technology Transfer. In A. Cakir & P. Ordóñez de Pablos (Eds.), *Social Development and High Technology Industries: Strategies and Applications* (pp. 70–98). Hershey, PA, USA: IGI Global. doi:10.4018/978-1-61350-192-4.ch006

Chan, P., & Cooper, R. (2006). Talent management in construction project organizations: Do you know where your experts are? *Construction Industry Quarterly, 194,* 12–18.

Charan, R. (2010). Banking on talent. *People Management*, October, 24-25.

Cheese, P., Thomas, R. J., & Craig, E. (2008). *The talent powered organization: Strategies for globalization, talent management and high performance*. London, UK: Kogan Page Limited.

Chen, G. M. (2002). The impact of harmony on Chinese conflict management. In G. M. Chen, and R. Ma (Eds.), Chinese conflict management and management (pp. 3-17). Ablex Publishing.

Chen, C., & Hsieh, C. (2015). *Knowledge Sharing Motivation in the Public Sector: The Role of Public Service Motivation. International Review of Administrative Sciences, 81*(4), 812–832.

Chen, G. M., & Starosta, W. J. (1997). Chinese conflict management and resolution: Overview and implications. *Intercultural Communication Studies, 9*, 163–175.

Chen, L. (2000). Connecting to the world economy: Issues confronting organizations in Chinese societies. *Management Communication Quarterly, 14*(1), 152–160. doi:10.1177/0893318900141008

Chen, Y., Tjosvold, D., & Fang, S. S. (2005). Working with foreign managers: Conflict management for effective leader relationships in China. *The International Journal of Conflict Management, 16*(3), 265–286. doi:10.1108/eb022932

Chitsaz-Isfahani, A., & Boustani, H. (2014). Effects of talent management on employees retention: The mediate effect of organizational trust. *International Journal of Academic Research in Economics and Management Sciences, 3*(5), 114–128.

Choi, S., & Rainey, H. G. (2010). Managing Diversity in U.S. Federal Agencies: Effects of Diversity and Diversity Management on Employee Perceptions of Organizational Performance. *Public Administration Review, 70*(1), 109–121. doi:10.1111/j.1540-6210.2009.02115.x

Christensen, C., Hall, T., Dillion, K., & Duncan, D. S. (2016). *Competing against luck: The story of innovation & customer choice*. New York: Harper Business.

Chugh, R. (2015). Do Australian Universities Encourage Tacit Knowledge Transfer?*Proceedings of the 7th International Joint Conference on Knowledge Discovery, Knowledge Engineering and Knowledge Management* (pp. 128-135). doi:10.5220/0005585901280135

Chui, M., Manyika, J., & Miremadi, M. (2015). Four fundamentals of workplace automation. Retrieved from http//:www.mckinsey.com/business-functions

Church, S. G. (2016). Beneath Thy feet: Secrets from the grave. *Beneaththyfeet*. Retrieved from http://beneaththyfeet.blogspot.com/2012/06/dunkelsbuhler-angels-and-diamonds.html

CIPD (2010a). The PM guide to reward and benefits: Engagement. *People Management*, December, 33-50.

CIPD. (2006). *Talent management: Understanding the dimensions. Change Agenda*. London: Chartered Institute of Personnel and Development.

CIPD. (2009). *The War on Talent: Talent management under threat in uncertain times, part 1*. London: CIPD.

CIPD. (2010b). *Opening up for business success: Integrating talent management and diversity*. London: Chartered Institute of Personnel and Development.

CIPD. (2012). *Resourcing and Talent Planning: Annual Survey Report 2012*. London: CIPD.

Civil Rights Act. (1964). *The Civil Rights Act of 1964 (Public Law 88–352, 78 Statute 241, enacted July 2, 1964*. Washington DC: Congress of the United States

Claussen, J., Grohsjean, T., Luger, J., & Probst, G. (2014). Talent management and career development: What it takes to get promoted. *Journal of World Business*, *49*(2), 236–244. doi:10.1016/j.jwb.2013.11.007

Coates, E. (2004). Knowledge management: A primer. *Communications of the Association for Information Systems*, *14*, 406–489.

Coelho, D. A. (2011). A study on the relation between manufacturing strategy, company size, country culture and product and process innovation in Europe. *International Journal of Business and Globalization*, *7*(2), 152–165. doi:10.1504/IJBG.2011.041830

Coelho, L., Goertzel, B., Pennachin, C., & Heward, C. (2010). Classifier Ensemble Based Analysis of a Genome-Wide SNP Dataset Concerning Late-Onset Alzheimer Disease. *International Journal of Software Science and Computational Intelligence*, *2*(4), 60–71. doi:10.4018/jssci.2010100105

Cohn, J. M., Khurana, R., & Reeves, L. (2005). Growing talent as if your business depended on it. *Harvard Business Review*, *83*, 63–70. PMID:16250625

Colletti, J. A., & Chonko, L. B. (1997). Change management initiatives: Moving sales organizations from obsolescence to high performance. *Journal of Personal Selling & Sales Management*, *17*(2), 1–30. Retrieved from http://search.proquest.com.ezproxy.gvsu.edu/docview/216748543?accountid=39473

Collings, D. G. (2014). Towards mature talent management: Beyond shareholder value. *Human Resource Development Quarterly*, *25*(3), 301–319. doi:10.1002/hrdq.21198

Collings, D. G., & Mellahi, K. (2009). Strategic talent management: A review and research agenda. *Human Resource Management Review*, *19*(4), 304–313. doi:10.1016/j.hrmr.2009.04.001

Collings, D. G., & Mellahi, K. (2013). Commentary on: "Talent–innate or acquired? Theoretical considerations and their implications for talent management." *Human Resource Management Review*, *23*(4), 322–325. doi:10.1016/j.hrmr.2013.08.003

Collings, D. G., Scullion, H., & Vaiman, V. (2015). Talent management: Progress and prospects. *Human Resource Management Review*, *25*(3), 233–235. doi:10.1016/j.hrmr.2015.04.005

Collins Dictionary (2016). Technical know-how. Retrieved from http://www.collinsdictionary.com/dictionary/english

Collins, J. (2001). *Good to great: Why some companies make the leap… and others don't*. HarperCollins Publishers.

Collins, J. C. (2001). *Good to Great: Why Some Companies Make the Leap--and Others Don't*. New York, NY: HarperBusiness.

Colvin, G. (2010). *Talent is overrated: What really separates world-class performers from everybody else*. New York, NY: Penguin Group.

Comella-Dorda, C.G., & Shah, B. (2015). From box to cloud. Retrieved from http://www.mckinsey.com/business-functions/from-box_to_cloud

Contu, A., & Willmott, H. (2005). You spin me round: The realist turn in organization and management studies. *Journal of Management Studies*, *42*(8), 1645–1662. doi:10.1111/j.1467-6486.2005.00560.x

Cooke, F. L., Saini, D. S., & Wang, J. (2014). Talent management in China and India: A comparison of management perceptions and human resource practices. *Journal of World Business*, *49*(2), 225–235. doi:10.1016/j.jwb.2013.11.006

Cooperrider, D. L. (1986). *Appreciative inquiry: Toward a methodology for understanding and enhancing organizational innovation* [Unpublished doctoral dissertation]. Case Western Reserve University, Cleveland, Ohio.

Cooperrider, D.L., & Dutton, J. (1999). *Organizational Dimensions of Global Change: No limits to Cooperation.* London, UK; Sage Publications

Cooperrider, D.L., & Whitney, D.K. (2005). *Appreciative Inquiry.* San Francisco, CA: Berrett-Koehler.

Cooperrider, D. L. (1986). *Appreciative Inquiry: Toward a methodology for understanding and enhancing organizational innovation* [Unpublished Ph.D.]. Cleveland: Case Western Reserve University.

Cooperrider, D. L. Jr, Sorensen, P. F., Whitney, D., & Yaeger, T. F. (2006). *Appreciative inquiry: Rethinking human organization: Toward a positive theory of change.* Champaign, Ill: Stipes LLC.

Cooperrider, D. L., & Sekerka, L. E. (2003). Toward a theory of positive organizational change. In K. S. Cameron, J. E. Dutton, & R. E. Quinn (Eds.), *Positive organizational scholarship: Foundations of a new discipline. San Francisco: Berrett-Kohler.*

Cooperrider, D. L., & Srivastva, S. (1987). Appreciative Inquiry In Organizational Life. *Research in Organizational Change and Development, 1*, 129–169.

Cooperrider, D., Whitney, D., & Stavros, J. M. (2003). *Appreciative Inquiry Handbook.* Bedford Heights, OH: Lakeshore Publishers.

Cowell, A. (2000). Controversy Over Diamonds Made Into Virtue by De Beers. *New York Times.* Retrieved from http://www.nytimes.com/2000/08/22/business/controversy-over-diamonds-made-into-virtue-by-de-beers.html?pagewanted=all

Cox, T., & Blake, S. (1991). Managing Cultural Diversity: Implications for Organizational Competitiveness. *The Journal of Academy of Management, 5*(3), 45–56.

Creswell, J. W., & Plano Clark, V. L. (2011). *Designing and conducting mixed methods research.* Los Angeles, CA: Sage.

Creswell, J., & Plano Clark, V.L. (2013). *Designing and Conducting Mixed Methods Research.* London, UK: *Sage.*

Cummings, T. G., & Worley, C. G. (2009). *Organization Development and Change.* London, UK: Cengage.

Cummings, T., & Worley, C. G. (2015). *Organization Development & Change.* London, UK: Cengage.

Cwiklik, J. S. (2006). *The story behind the numbers: How and why the appreciative inquiry summit process transforms organizational cultures.* Retrieved from http://search.proquest.com.ezproxy.gvsu.edu/docview/304910759?accountid=39473

Czarniawska, B. (2010). *Organizing in the face of risk and threat.* Cheltenham: Edward Elgar Ltd.

Daciulyte, Ruta & Katazina Stankevich (2015). A systemic approach to talent management: managers' perceptions versus employees. *International Journal of Business and Emerging Markets, 7*(3), 223 – 236.

Daly, E. M. (2010). Payless drops appeal of $305 million Adidas Trademark win. Retrieved from http://www.law360.com/articles/145508/payless-drops-appeal-of-305m-Adidas-Trademark-win

Danko, N. (2015). Practopoiesis: Or how life fosters a mind. *Journal of Theoretical Biology, 373*, 40–61. doi:10.1016/j.jtbi.2015.03.003 PMID:25791287

Davenport, T. R. H. (1991). *South Africa: A modern history* (4th ed.). London, UK: Macmillan. doi:10.1007/978-1-349-21422-8

Davidson, M. (1983). *Uncommon Sense: The Life and Thought of Ludwig Von Bertalanffy*. Los Angeles: J. P. Tarcher.

Davis, T. E. (2014). Newly Created Heterogeneous Groups: The Time to Adjust to Significant Race and/or Gender Differences. In V. Wang (Ed.), *Advanced Research in Adult Learning and Professional Development: Tools, Trends, and Methodologies* (pp. 224–235). Hershey, PA: Information Science Reference; doi:10.4018/978-1-4666-4615-5.ch009

Davis, T., Cutt, M., Flynn, N., Mowl, P., & Orme, S. (2007). *Talent Assessment: A New Strategy for Talent Management*. Aldershot: Gower.

Davis, W. P., Figgins, B., Hedengren, D., & Klein, D. B. (2011). Economics Professors' Favorite Economic Thinkers, Journals, and Blogs (along with Party and Policy Views). *Econ Journal Watch, 8*(2), 133.

De Beers Company Settlement. (2013). De Beers Company Settlement. Retrieved from https://www.diamongsclassaction.com

De Carvalho, P.V.R. (2006). Ergonomic field studies in a nuclear power plant control room. *Progress in Nuclear Energy, 48*(1), 51-69.

de Rothschild, D. (1979). Rothschilds at Waddesdon Manor. New York: Viking Penguin.

Defeo, J. A., & Juran, J. M. (2016). *Juran's Quality Handbook: The Complete Guide to Performance Excellence* (7th ed.). New York: McGraw-Hill.

Delbridge, R., Gratton, L., & Johnson, J. (2006). *The exceptional manager*. Oxford: Oxford University Press.

Delloitte (2016). A new organizational paradigm: Agile, collaborative, and exposed. Retrieved from http://www2.deloitte.com/us/en/pages/financial-services/articles/banking-industry-outlook.html

Deloitte (2005, February 15). Retiring workforce, widening skills gap, exodus of 'critical talent' threaten companies: Deloitte survey. *Canadian Corporate Newswire*.

Deng, Y., & Xu, K. (2014). Strategy to motivate and facilitate compromise in Chinese mediation: A discourse analysis of contemporary Chinese mediation sessions. *The International Journal of Conflict Management, 25*(1), 4–20. doi:10.1108/IJCMA-11-2011-0076

Derrida, J. (1967). *Of Grammatology*. Paris, France: Les Éditions de Minuit.

Derrida, J. (1998). *Of Grammatology (Corrected ed.)*. Baltimore: John Hopkins University Press.

Derrida, J. (2003). The world of the Enlightenment to come (Exception, Calculation, Sovereignty). *Research in Phenomelogy, 33*(1), 9–52. doi:10.1163/15691640360699591

Desanctis, G., & Poole, M. S. (1994). Capturing the complexity in advanced technology use: Adaptive structuration theory. *Organization Science, 5*(2), 121–147. doi:10.1287/orsc.5.2.121

Dewey, J. (1940). *Education Today*. New York: Greenwood Press.

Dewey, J. (1966). *Democracy and Education*. New York: The Free Press.

Diamond, L. L. (2016). The early days of the De Beers Company. Retrieved from http://www.gemgate.com/original-gemgate/Diamond/Advanced/Section1/early_De_Beers

Dias, J., Ionutiu, O., Lhuer, X., & van Ouwerkerk, J. (2016). The four pillars of distinctive customer journeys. *McKinsey*. Retrieved from http://www.mckinsey.com/business-functions/digital-mckinsey/our-insights/the-four-pillars-of-distinctive-customer-journeys

DiMaggio, P. (1997). Culture and cognition. *Annual Review of Sociology*, *23*(1), 207–267. doi:10.1146/annurev.soc.23.1.263

Doh, J. P., Stumpf, S. A., & Tymon, W. G. Jr. (2011). Responsible leadership helps retain talent in India. *Journal of Business Ethics*, *98*(1), 85–100. doi:10.1007/s10551-011-1018-3

Dolan, D. (2011). *Africa Banking Set for Growth*. Reuters.

Domjan, M. (2005). Pavlovian conditioning: A functional perspective. *Annual Review of Psychology*, *56*(1), 179–206. doi:10.1146/annurev.psych.55.090902.141409 PMID:15709933

Donahue, B. K. (2001). Time to Get Serious About Talent Management. *Harvard Management Update*.

Donkin, R. (2010). *The future of work*. Basingstoke: Palgrave MacMillan. doi:10.1057/9780230274198

Douglas, W. (1961). Carl Gustav Jung: 1875-1961. *The American Journal of Psychology*, *74*(4), 639–641. PMID:13887552

Drastal, M. (2010). The End of Apartheid: A racial revolution in South Africa. Retrieved from https://issuu.com/mason-drastal/docs/the_end_of_apartheid_-_a_racial_rev

Drew, S. W., & Wallis, J. L. (2014). The use of appreciative inquiry in the practices of large-scale organizational change. *Journal of General Management*, *39*(4), 3–26.

Dries, N. (2013). The psychology of talent management: A review and research agenda. *Human Resource Management Review*, *23*(4), 272–285. doi:10.1016/j.hrmr.2013.05.001

Dries, N., & Pepermans, R. (2008). "Real" high-potential careers: An empirical study into the perspectives of organizations and high potentials. *Personnel Review*, *37*(1), 85–108. doi:10.1108/00483480810839987

Dries, N., Vantilborgh, T., & Pepermans, R. (2012). The role of learning agility and career variety in the identification and development of high potential employees. *Personnel Review*, *41*(3), 340–358. doi:10.1108/00483481211212977

Driskell, T., & Salas, E. (2015). Investigative interviewing: Harnessing the power of the team. *Group Dynamics*, *19*(4), 273–289. doi:10.1037/gdn0000036

Drucker, P. (1973). *Management: Tasks, Responsibilities, and Practices*. HarperCollins Publishers, Inc.

Dube, S. (2016). Ex-Wenela employees demand pension dues. *Chronicle*. Retrieved from http://www.chronicle.co.zw/ex-wenela-workers-demand-dues/

Dubow, S. (2014). *Apartheid 1948-1994*. New York: Oxford University Press.

Eargle, F. (2013). Job evaluation: Traditional Approaches and Emerging Technology. Lulu.com.

Easterby-Smith, M., Malina, D., & Yuan, L. (1995). How culture sensitive is HRM? A comparative analysis of practice in Chinese and UK companies. *International Journal of Human Resource Management*, *6*(1), 31–59. doi:10.1080/09585199500000002

Easterby-Smith, M., & Prieto, I. M. (2007). Dynamic capabilities and knowledge management: An integrative role for learning? *British Journal of Management*, *19*(3), 235–249. doi:10.1111/j.1467-8551.2007.00543.x

Editorial Board New York Times. (2014, May 15). Discrimination in the military. Retrieved from http://www.nytimes.com/2014/05/15/opinion/discrimination-in-the-military.html?_r=0

Edwards, J., & Auchard, J. (2003). *Four Trials*. New York: Simon & Schuster.

Edwards, L., & Charlotte, W. (2005). *On-line Intermediaries and liability for copyright infringement*. Edinburgh, UK: University of Edinburgh.

Eggens, R. A., O'Brien, A. T., Reynolds, K. J., Haslam, S. A., & Crocker, A. (2007). Refocusing the Focus Group: Airing as a basis for effective workplace planning. *British Journal of Management*, 19(3), 235–249.

Eijnatten, F. M. (1993). *The paradigm that changed the work place: Social Science for social action: Toward organizational renewal* (Vol. 4). Stockholm, Sweden: Swedish Center for Working Life.

EIU. (2011). Banking in Sub-Saharan Africa to 2020: Promising Frontiers, *The Economist* Intelligence Unit, 2.

Elegbe, J. A. (2010). *Talent Management in the Developing World - Adopting a Global Perspective* (pp. xiii–xvi). UK: Gower.

Elsbach, K., Kayes, A.B.D., & Kayes, C. (2016). Contemporary Organizational Behavior: From Ideas to Action. New York: Pearson

Elsbach, K., Kaues, A., & Kayes, D. C. (2016). *Contemporary Organizational Behavior: From Ideas to Action*. Boston: Pearson.

Entrepreneurs, B. (2015). Black chairman and CEOs from America's 500 Largest Corporations. Retrieved from https://www.blackentrepreneurprofile.com/fortune-500-ceos/

Epstein, E. J. (1982). *The rise and fall of diamonds: The Shattering of a Brilliant Illusion*. New York: Simon & Schuster.

Erne, R. (2016). Change Management Revised. In A. Goksoy (Ed.), *Organizational Change Management Strategies in Modern Business* (pp. 1–23). Hershey, PA, USA: IGI Global. doi:10.4018/978-1-4666-9533-7.ch001

Etzioni, A. (1998). *The Essential Communitarian Reader*. New York: Rowman & Littlefield.

Fagenson, E. A. (1990). Perceived Masculine and Feminine Attributes Examined as a Function of Individuals Sex and Level in the Organizational Power Hierarchy: A Test of Four Theoretical Perspectives. *The Journal of Applied Psychology*, 75(2), 204–211. doi:10.1037/0021-9010.75.2.204

Farley, C. (2005). HR's role in talent management and driving business results. *Employment Relations Today*, 32(1), 55–61. doi:10.1002/ert.20053

Farndale, E., Pai, A., Sparrow, P. R., & Scullion, H. (2014). Balancing individual and organizational goals in global talent management: A mutual-benefits perspective. *Journal of World Business*, 49(2), 204–214. doi:10.1016/j.jwb.2013.11.004

Farndale, E., Scullion, H., & Sparrow, P. (2010). The role of the corporate HR function in global talent management. *Journal of World Business*, 45(2), 161–168. doi:10.1016/j.jwb.2009.09.012

Farnhill, K. (2002). Guilds and the Parish Community in Late Medieval East Anglia, 1470- 1550[book review]. *The Catholic Historical Review*, 88(4), 769–771. doi:10.1353/cat.2003.0054

Fastiff, E. B. (2016). A determined Advocate for Fair Competition. Retrieved from http://www.lieffcabraser.com/attorneys/eric-b-fastiff/

Fegley, S. (2006). *2006 Strategic HR management: Survey report*. Alexandria, VA: Society for Human Resource Management.

Ferner, A., Edwards, T., & Tempel, A. (2012). Power, institutions and the cross-national transfer of employment practices in multinationals. *Human Relations*, 65(2), 163–187. doi:10.1177/0018726711429494

Ferrer, D. (2016). A quiet role model for kids. *Acttwomagazine.com*. Retrieved from http://acttwomagazine.com/david-ferrer-quiet-role-model-kids/

Ferrer, J. N. (2011). Participatory spirituality and transpersonal theory: A ten year retrospective. *Journal of Transpersonal Psychology*, *43*(1), 1–34.

Festinger, L., & Carlsmith, J. M. (1959). Cognitive Consequences of Forced Compliance. *Journal of Abnormal and Social Psychology*, *58*(2), 203–210. doi:10.1037/h0041593 PMID:13640824

Festing, M., & Schäfer, L. (2014). Generational challenges to talent management: A framework for talent retention based on the psychological-contract perspective. *Journal of World Business*, *49*(2), 262–271. doi:10.1016/j.jwb.2013.11.010

Fischer, R. (2009). Where is Culture in Cross-Cultural Research?: An Outline of a Multilevel Research Process for Measuring Culture as a Shared Meaning System. *International Journal of Cross Cultural Management*, *9*(1), 25–48. doi:10.1177/1470595808101154

Fitzgerald, R. (2016). Survey will gauge U-M campus climate on diversity equity and inclusion. The University of Michigan Record, 72(7), 1 & 9.

Flavell, J. H. (1979). Metacognition and Cognitive Monitoring: A New Area of Cognitive- Developmental Inquiry. *The American Psychologist*, *34*(10), 906–911. doi:10.1037/0003-066X.34.10.906

Fleming, J.H. & Asplund, J. (2008, January 10). Understanding the nature of talent; managers must distinguish what's innate in their employees (talent) from what can be changed or acquired (knowledge and skills). *Gullup Management Journal*.

Fletcher, J. K. (1994). Castrating the Female Advantage: Feminist Standpoint Research and Management Science. *Journal of Management Inquiry*, *3*(I), 74–82. doi:10.1177/105649269431012

Forbes (2016). Africa's top 50 wealthy people. Retrieved from http://www.forbes.com/profile/nicky-oppenheimer/

Ford, J., Harding, N., & Stoyanova, D. (2010a). *Talent Management in NHS Yorkshire and The Humber; The Current State of the Art*. Bradford: Bradford University School of Management.

Ford, J., Harding, N., & Stoyanova, D. (2010b). *Talent Management and Development: An Overview of Current Theory and Practice*. Bradford: Bradford University School of Management.

Foschi, R., & Lombardo, G. P. (2006). Lewinian contribution to the study of personality as the alternative to the mainstream of personality psychology in the 20th century. In *J., Trempala, A. Pepitone, B. Raven (Eds.), Lewinian Psychology* (Vol. 1, pp. 86–98). Bydgoszcz: Kazimierz Wielki University Press.

Foucault, M. (2002). The Order of Things: An Archaeology of the Human Sciences. London, U.K.: Routledge classics.

Foucault, M. (1969). *The Archaeology of knowledge*. London, UK: Routledge.

Frank, F. D., & Taylor, C. R. (2004). Talent management: Trends that will shape the future. *Human Resource Planning*, *27*(1), 33–41.

Fraser, K. (2006, December 7). Why doesn't The University of Michigan have snow days? *The Michigan Daily News*.

French, W.L., & Bell, C.H. (1998). *Organization Development: Behavioral Science Interventions for Organization Improvement* (6th ed.). New York: Pearson.

French, W.L., Bell, C.H., Jr., & Zawacki, R.A. (2000). *Organization development and transformation: Managing effective change*. Boston, MA: Irwin McGraw-Hill.

Frishammar, J., Kristian E., & Pankaj C. (2015). The dark side of knowledge transfer: Exploring knowledge leakage in joint R&D projects. *Technovation, 41 & 42.*

Furusawa, M., & Brewster, C. (2015). The bi-cultural option for global talent management: The Japanese/Brazilian *Nikkeijin* example. *Journal of World Business, 50*(1), 133–143. doi:10.1016/j.jwb.2014.02.005

Gagné, F. (2007). Ten Commandments for academic talent development. *Gifted Child Quarterly, 51*(2), 93–118. doi:10.1177/0016986206296660

Gallardo-Gallardo, E., Nijs, S., Dries, N., & Gallo, P. (2015). Towards an understanding of talent management as a phenomenon-driven field using bibliometric and content analysis. *Human Resource Management Review, 25*(3), 264–279. doi:10.1016/j.hrmr.2015.04.003

Gamble, J. (2003). Transferring human resource practices from the United Kingdom to China: The limits and potential for convergence. *International Journal of Human Resource Management, 14*(3), 369–387. doi:10.1080/0958519022000031807

Gamble, J. (2006). Introducing Western-style HRM practices to China: Shop-floor perceptions in a British multinational. *Journal of World Business, 41*(4), 328–343. doi:10.1016/j.jwb.2006.08.002

Gamble, J., & Huang, Q. (2009). The transfer of organizational practices: A diachronic perspective from China. *International Journal of Human Resource Management, 20*(8), 1683–1783. doi:10.1080/09585190903087032

Gamble, J., & Tian, A. W. (2015). Intra-national variation in organizational commitment: Evidence from the Chinese context. *International Journal of Human Resource Management, 26*(7), 948–970. doi:10.1080/09585192.2012.722122

Garavan, T. N., Carbery, R., & Rock, A. (2012). Mapping talent development: Definition, scope and architecture. *European Journal of Training and Development, 36*(1), 5–24. doi:10.1108/03090591211192601

Garber, M. B. (2008). *Profiling Shakespeare.* New York: Routledge.

Gardner, H. R., Gino, F., & Staats, B. R. (2011). *Dynamically Integrating Knowledge in Teams: Transforming Resources into Performance* (Working paper). Harvard Business School.

Garvin, D. A., & Burca, S. D. (2005). The effects of design quality on quality performance. *International Journal of Production Economics, 96.* doi:10.1016/j.ijpe.2004.02.008

Gasson, Susan (2005). The dynamics of sensemaking, knowledge and expertise in collaborative, boundary spanning design. *Journal of computer-mediated Communications, 10*(4).

Gelens, J., Dries, N., Hofmans, J., & Pepermans, R. (2013). The role of perceived organizational justice in shaping the outcomes of talent management: A research agenda. *Human Resource Management Review, 23*(4), 341–353. doi:10.1016/j.hrmr.2013.05.005

General Motors Corporation. (2016). Mary Barra is Chairman and Chief Executive Officer of General Motors Company. Retrieved from http://www.gm.com/company/leadership/corporate-officers/mary-barra.html

Geppert, M., & Williams, K. (2006). Global, national and local practices in multinational corporations: Towards a sociopolitical framework. *International Journal of Human Resource Management, 17*(1), 49–69. doi:10.1080/09585190500366243

Gergen, K. (1999). *An invitation to social construction.* London: Sage Publications Ltd.

Gergen, K. J. (2001). An invitation to Social Construction. *Social Forces, 79*(3), 1190–1191.

Gergen, K. J. (2009). *Relational being: Beyond self and community.* New York: Oxford University Press.

Gibb, S. (2011). *Human Resource Development: Foundations, Process, Contexts* (3rd ed.). London: Palgrave McMillan.

Giddens, A. (1984). *Positivism and sociology*. London: Heinemann.

Giddens, A. (1984). *The Constituency of Society*. Cambridge, UK: Cambridge University Press.

Giddens, A. (1984). *The Constitution of Society*. Berkeley: University of California Press.

Giddens, A. (1984). *The constitution of society: Outline of the theory of structuration*. Cambridge, UK: Polity Press.

Giddens, A. (1989). A reply to my critics. In D. Held & J. B. Thompson (Eds.), *Social theory of modern societies: Anthony Giddens and his critics* (pp. 249–301). Cambridge: Cambridge University Press. doi:10.1017/CBO9780511557699.013

Giddens, A. (1998). *The Third Way: The Renewal of Social Democracy*. New York: Polity Press.

Giddens, A. (2009). *The Politics of Climate Change*. Cambridge, UK: Polity.

Giddens, A. (2014). *The role and nature of the European Union in Turbulent and Mighty Continent: What Future for Europe?* Cambridge, UK: Polity.

Giliomee, H., & Mbenga, B. (2007). *A New History of South Africa*. Cape Town: Tafelberg Pty Ltd.

Gino, F., & Pisano, G. P. (2008). Toward a Theory of Behavioral Operations. *Manufacturing & Service Operations Management*, *10*(4), 676–691. doi:10.1287/msom.1070.0205

Givel, M. (2006). Punctuated Equilibrium in Limbo: The Tobacco Lobby and U.S. State Policy Making From 1990 to 2003. *Policy Studies Journal: the Journal of the Policy Studies Organization*, *43*(3), 405–418. doi:10.1111/j.1541-0072.2006.00179.x

Given, L. M. (2008). *The Sage encyclopedia of qualitative research methods*. Los Angeles, Calif.: Sage Publications. doi:10.4135/9781412963909

Goede, M. (2011). The wise society: Beyond the knowledge economy. *Foresight*, *13*(1), 6–45. Retrieved from http://search.proquest.com.libaccess.hud.ac.uk/852073314/ doi:10.1108/14636681111109688

Goffman, E. (1959). *The presentation of Self in everyday life*. London: Anchor Books.

Golas, J. (2010). Effective teacher preparation programs: Bridging the gap between educational technology availability and its utilization. *International Forum of Teaching & Studies, 6*(1), 16-18.

Golden, C. (2016). Introduction to Soul Craft. Retrieved from http://www.soulcraft.co/

Goldschein, E. (2011). The Incredible Story Of How De Beers Created And Lost The Most Powerful Monopoly Ever. Retrieved from http://www.businessinsider.com/history-of-de-beers-2011-12

Goleman, D. (1996). *Emotional Intelligence: Why It Can Matter More Than IQ*. Bantam Books.

Goleman, D. (1998). *Working with emotional intelligence*. New York: Bantam Books.

Goleman, D. (2013). *Focus: The Hidden Driver of Excellence*. New York: Harper.

Goleman, D., Boyatzis, R., & McKee, A. (2004). *Primal leadership: Learning to lead with emotional intelligence*. Boston, MA: Harvard Business School Press.

Goodall, N. (1993). *Elton John*. London, UK: Omnibus press.

Gordon, E. E. (2010). A new talent-investment metric is needed to advance technological leadership and increase jobs. *Employment Relations Today*, *37*(3), 9–14. doi:10.1002/ert.20304

Gratton, L. (2010). The future of work. *Business Strategy Review*, *21*(3), 16–23. doi:10.1111/j.1467-8616.2010.00678.x

Green, R. E., Krause, J., Briggs, A. W., Maricic, T., Stenzel, U., Kircher, M., & Paabo, S. et al. (2010). A Draft Sequence of the Neanderthal Genome. *The Science Journal*, *328*(5979), 710–722. doi:10.1126/science.1188021 PMID:20448178

Gregory, E. T. (2013).Ernest Oppenheimer and the economic development of Southern Africa. Whitefish, MT: Literary Licensing, LLC.

Gupta, A. K., & Govindara, V. (1991). Knowledge flows and the structure of control within multinational corporations. *Academy of Management Review*, *16*, 768–792.

Habernas, J. (1972). *Knowledge and human interests*. Boston, MA: Beacon Press ISBN.

Handy, C. (2001). *The Elephant and the Flea: looking backwards to the future*. London: Hutchinson.

Harris, J. G., Craig, E., & Light, D. (2011). Talent and analytics: New approaches, higher ROI. *The Journal of Business Strategy*, *32*(6), 4–13. doi:10.1108/02756661111180087

Hartmann, E., Feisel, E., & Schober, H. (2010). Talent management of western MNCs in China: Balancing global integration and local responsiveness. *Journal of World Business*, *45*(2), 169–178. doi:10.1016/j.jwb.2009.09.013

Harvey, W. S., & Groutsis, D. (2015). Reputation and talent mobility in the Asia Pacific. *Asia Pacific Journal of Human Resources*, *53*(1), 22–40. doi:10.1111/1744-7941.12047

Hasse, C. (2004). Institutional Creativity: The Relational Zone of Proximal Development. *Culture and Psychology*, *7*(2), 199–221. doi:10.1177/1354067X0172005

Heider, Fritz (1959). On Lewin's Methods and Theory. *Journal of Social Issues Supplementary Series.*

Heinen, J. S., & O'Neill, C. (2004). Managing talent to maximize performance. *Employment Relations Today*, *31*(2), 67–82. doi:10.1002/ert.20018

Hills, A. (2009). Succession planning – or smart talent management? *Industrial and Commercial Training*, *41*(1), 3–8. doi:10.1108/00197850910927697

Hofer, B. K., & Pintrich, P. R. (1997, Spring). The development of epistemological theories: Beliefs about knowledge and knowing and their relation to learning. *Review of Educational Research*, *67*(1), 88–140. doi:10.3102/00346543067001088

Hofstede, G. (2001). Culture's Consequences: comparing values, behaviors, institutions, and organizations across nations (2nd ed.). Thousand Oaks, CA: SAGE Publications.

Hofstede, G. (1980). *Culture's consequences: International differences in work-related values*. Beverly Hills, CA: Sage.

Hofstede, G. (1980). *Culture's consequences: International differences in work-related values*. Beverly Hills, CA, USA: *Sage*.

Hofstede, G. (1984). *Culture's Consequences: International Differences in Work-Related Values* (2nd ed.). Beverly Hills, CA: SAGE Publications.

Hofstede, G. (1991). *Culture and Organization: Software of the mind: intercultural cooperation and its importance for survival*. New York: McGraw-Hill.

Hofstede, G. (1991). *Cultures and organizations: software of the mind. New York: McGraw-Hill. Hofstede, G. (2001). Culture's nations* (2nd ed.). Thousand Oaks, CA: Sage.

Hofstede, G. (2001). *Culture's consequences: comparing, values, behaviors, institutions and organizations across nations*. Thousand Oaks, CA: Sage.

Hofstede, G., & Hofstede, G. (2010). *Cultures & organizations: software of the mind* (3rd ed.). New York: McGraw-Hill.

Hofstede, G., Hofstede, G. J., & Minkov, M. (2010). *Cultures and organizations: Software of the mind* (3rd ed.). New York: McGraw-Hill.

Hogg, M. A., & Williams, K. D. (2000). From me to us: Social identity and the collective self. *Group Dynamics*, *4*(1), 81–97. doi:10.1037/1089-2699.4.1.81

Holt, D., & Cameron, D. (2012). *Cultural Strategy: Using Innovative Ideologies to Build Breakthrough Brands Reprint Edition*. Oxford, UK: Oxford University Press.

Hua, T. K., Wong, W. P., & Chung, L. (2015). Information and knowledge leakage in supply chain. *Information Systems Frontiers*. doi:10.1007/s10796-015-9553-6

Hughes, J. C., & Rog, E. (2008). Talent management: A strategy for improving employee recruitment, retention and engagement within hospitality organizations. *International Journal of Contemporary Hospitality Management*, *20*(7), 743–757. doi:10.1108/09596110810899086

Hughes, T. P. (1989). *American genesis: A century of invention and technological enthusiasm, 1870-1970*. New York: Viking.

Hung, D., Looi, C.-K., & Koh, T.-S. (2004). Situated Cognition and Communities of Practice: First-Person "Lived Experiences" vs. Third-Person Perspectives. *Journal of Educational Technology & Society*, *7*(4), 193–200.

Hurley, A. J., Fagenson-Eland, E. A., & Somerfield, J. A. (1997). Does cream always rise to the top? An investigation of career determinants. *Organizational Dynamics*, *26*(2), 65–71. doi:10.1016/S0090-2616(97)90006-1

Hurmelinna-Laukunnen, P., & Puumalainen, K. (2007). Formation of appropriate regime: Strategic and practical considerations. *Innovation Management Policy Practices*, *9*(1), 2–13. doi:10.5172/impp.2007.9.1.2

Huselid, M. A., & Becker, B. E. (2011). Bridging micro and macro domains: Workforce differentiation and strategic human resource management. *Journal of Management*, *37*(2), 421–428. doi:10.1177/0149206310373400

Hutt, A. E., Bosworth, S., & Hoyt, D. B. (1995). *Computer Security Handbook* (3rd ed.). Hoboken, NJ: Wiley.

Hylton, C. L. A. (2003). African-Caribbean group activities, individual and collective consciousness, and enforced leisure. *Community Work & Family*, *6*(1), 103–115. doi:10.1080/1366880032000063932

Iles, P., Chuai, X., & Preece, D. (2010). Talent management and HRM in multinational companies in Beijing: Definitions, differences and drivers. *Journal of World Business*, *45*(2), 179–189. doi:10.1016/j.jwb.2009.09.014

Iles, P., Preece, D., & Chuai, X. (2010). Talent management as a management fashion in HRD: Towards a research agenda. *Human Resource Development International*, *13*(2), 125–145. doi:10.1080/13678861003703666

IMF. (2011). IMF World Economics database. Retrieved from www.imf.org/external/na/ca.aspx?i.d.-28

Information Resources Management Association. (2016). Big Data: Concepts, Methodologies, Tools, and Applications. Hershey, PA, USA: IGI Global. doi:10.4018/978-1-4666-9840-6

Ingham, G. (2008). *Capitalism: reissued with a new postscript on the financial crisis*. Cambridge: Polity.

Jackson, S. E., May, K. E., & Whitney, K. (1995). Understanding the dynamics of diversity in decision-making teams. In R. A. Guzzo & E. Salas et al. (Eds.), *Team Effectiveness and Decision Making in Organizations* (pp. 204–261). San Francisco: Jossey-Bass.

Jackson, S. E., Schuler, R. S., & Jiang, K. (2014). An aspirational framework for strategic human resource management. *The Academy of Management Annals, 8*(1), 1–56. doi:10.1080/19416520.2014.872335

Jackson, T., & Bak, M. (1998). Foreign companies and Chinese workers: Employee motivation in the Peoples Republic of China. *Journal of Organizational Change Management, 11*(4), 282–300. doi:10.1108/09534819810225869

Jain, A. (2014). Why did Google buy Motorola for $12.5 billion and sell it off for $2.91 billion? *Quora*. Retrieved from https://www.quora.com/Why-did-Google-buy-Motorola-for-12-5-billion-and-sell-it-off-for-2-91-billion

Jain, A. (2014). Why did Google buy Motorola for $12.5 billion and sell it off for $2.91 billion? Retrieved from https://www.quora.com/Why-did-Google-buy-Motorola-for-12-5-billion-and-sell-it-off-for-2-91-billion

Jain, H. C., Lawler, J. J., & Morishima, M. (1998). Multinational corporations, human resource management and host country nationals. *International Journal of Human Resource Management, 9*(4), 553–566. doi:10.1080/095851998340892

James, P. (2015). Despite the Terrors of Typologies: The Importance of Understanding Categories of Difference and Identity. *International Journal of Postcolonial Studies., 17*(2), 174–195. doi:10.1080/1369801X.2014.993332

Javidan, M., Teagarden, M., & Bowen, D. (2010). Managing yourself: Making it overseas. *Harvard Business Review, 88*(4), 109–113.

Jenkins, C. (2009, February 2). The Australian Financial Review - ABIX via COMTEX -- SAP will supply software for a large revamp of Woolworths' merchandising systems.

Jia, W. S. (2002). Chinese mediation and its cultural foundation. In G. M. Chen and R. Ma (Eds.), Chinese conflict management and management (pp. 289-295). Ablex Publishing.

Jiang, X., Li, M., Gao, S. X., Baob, Y. C., & Jiang, F. F. (2013). Managing knowledge leakage in strategic alliances: The effects of trust and formal contracts. *Industrial Marketing Management, 42*(6), 983–991. doi:10.1016/j.indmarman.2013.03.013

Jindal, R., & Borah, M. D. (2016). A novel approach for mining frequent patterns from incremental data. *International Journal of Data Mining Modelling and Management, 8*(3), 244–264. doi:10.1504/IJDMMM.2016.079071

Johnson, J. H. (2013). *Urban Geography: An introductory analysis* (2nd ed.). Ontario, Canada: Pergamon.

Johnstone, F. (1976). *Class, Race and Gold: A Study of Class Discrimination in South Africa* (p. 158). London: Routledge and Kegan Paul.

Jolly, R. (2015). *Systems Thinking for Business: Capitalize on Structures Hidden in Plain Sight. Portland*. Oregon: Systems Solutions Press.

Joyce, W. F., & Slocum, J. W. (2012). Top management talent, strategic capabilities, and firm performance. *Organizational Dynamics, 41*(3), 183–193. doi:10.1016/j.orgdyn.2012.03.001

Kalonaityte, V. (2010). The case of vanishing borders: Theorizing diversity management in internal border control. *Organization, 17*(1), 31–52. doi:10.1177/1350508409350238

Kamoche, K. (2006). Managing people in turbulent economic times: A knowledge-creation & appropriation perspective. *Asia Pacific Journal of Human Resources*, *44*(1), 25–45. doi:10.1177/1038411106061506

Kanter, R. M. (2011). Zoom In, Zoom Out. *Harvard Business Review*, *89*(3). PMID:21513265

Kaplan, H. B. (1975). *Self-attitudes and deviant behavior*. Pacific Palisades, CA: Goodyear.

Kaplan, K. J. (1972). From attitude formation to attitude change: Acceptance and impact as cognitive mediators. *Sociometry*, *35*(3), 448–467. doi:10.2307/2786505

Karaganis, J. (2011). *Media piracy in emerging economies*. New York: Social Science Research Council.

Karatop, B., Kubat, C., & Uygun, O. (2015). Talent management in manufacturing system using fuzzy logic approach. *Computers & Industrial Engineering*, *86*, 127–136. doi:10.1016/j.cie.2014.09.015

Kasemsap, K. (2013a) Strategic knowledge management: An integrated framework and causal model of perceived organizational support, organizational trust, organizational commitment, and knowledge-sharing behavior. Paper presented at the 1st International Conference on Computing Engineering and Enterprise Management (ICCEEM 2013), Bangkok, Thailand.

Kasemsap, K. (2013b). Practical framework: Creation of causal model of job involvement, career commitment, learning motivation, and learning transfer. *International Journal of the Computer, the Internet and Management, 21*(1), 29–35.

Kasemsap, K. (2013c). Establishing a unified framework and a causal model of proactive personality, career future, affective commitment, and intention to remain. *International Research Journal of Humanities and Environmental Issues, 2*(2-1), 33–36.

Kasemsap, K. (2013d). Innovative business management: A practical framework and causal model of participation in decision making, career adaptability, affective commitment, and turnover intention. Paper presented at the 2nd International Conference on Economics, Business Innovation (ICEBI 2013), Copenhagen, Denmark.

Kasemsap, K. (2015). The Role of Total Quality Management Practices on Quality Performance. In A. Moumtzoglou, A. Kastania, & S. Archondakis (Eds.), *Laboratory Management Information Systems: Current Requirements and Future Perspectives* (pp. 1–31). Hershey, PA, USA: IGI Global. doi:10.4018/978-1-4666-6320-6.ch001

Kasemsap, K. (2016a). Promoting leadership development and talent management in modern organizations. In U. Aung & P. Ordoñez de Pablos (Eds.), *Managerial strategies and practice in the Asian business sector* (pp. 238–266). Hershey, PA, USA: IGI Global. doi:10.4018/978-1-4666-9758-4.ch013

Kasemsap, K. (2016b). Analyzing the roles of human capital and competency in global business. In S. Sen, A. Bhattacharya, & R. Sen (Eds.), *International perspectives on socio-economic development in the era of globalization* (pp. 1–29). Hershey, PA, USA: IGI Global. doi:10.4018/978-1-4666-9908-3.ch001

Kasemsap, K. (2016c). Advocating entrepreneurship education and knowledge management in global business. In N. Baporikar (Ed.), *Handbook of research on entrepreneurship in the contemporary knowledge-based global economy* (pp. 313–339). Hershey, PA, USA: IGI Global. doi:10.4018/978-1-4666-8798-1.ch014

Kasemsap, K. (2016d). The roles of knowledge management and organizational innovation in global business. In G. Jamil, J. Poças-Rascão, F. Ribeiro, & A. Malheiro da Silva (Eds.), *Handbook of research on information architecture and management in modern organizations* (pp. 130–153). Hershey, PA, USA: IGI Global. doi:10.4018/978-1-4666-8637-3.ch006

Kasemsap, K. (2016e). The roles of lifelong learning and knowledge management in global higher education. In P. Ordóñez de Pablos & R. Tennyson (Eds.), *Impact of economic crisis on education and the next-generation workforce* (pp. 71–100). Hershey, PA, USA: IGI Global. doi:10.4018/978-1-4666-9455-2.ch004

Kasemsap, K. (2016f). Creating product innovation strategies through knowledge management in global business. In A. Goel & P. Singhal (Eds.), *Product innovation through knowledge management and social media strategies* (pp. 330–357). Hershey, PA, USA: IGI Global. doi:10.4018/978-1-4666-9607-5.ch015

Kasemsap, K. (2016g). The roles of information technology and knowledge management in global tourism. In A. Nedelea, M. Korstanje, & B. George (Eds.), *Strategic tools and methods for promoting hospitality and tourism services* (pp. 109–138). Hershey, PA, USA: IGI Global. doi:10.4018/978-1-4666-9761-4.ch006

Kasemsap, K. (2016h). A unified framework of organizational perspectives and knowledge management and their impact on job performance. In A. Normore, L. Long, & M. Javidi (Eds.), *Handbook of research on effective communication, leadership, and conflict resolution* (pp. 267–297). Hershey, PA, USA: IGI Global. doi:10.4018/978-1-4666-9970-0.ch015

Kasemsap, K. (2016i). The roles of e-learning, organizational learning, and knowledge management in the learning organizations. In E. Railean, G. Walker, A. Elçi, & L. Jackson (Eds.), *Handbook of research on applied learning theory and design in modern education* (pp. 786–816). Hershey, PA, USA: IGI Global. doi:10.4018/978-1-4666-9634-1.ch039

Katz, D., & Kahn, R. (1978). *The Social Psychology of Organizations* (2nd ed.). New York: Wiley.

Kaye Thorne and Andy Pellant. (2007). *The Essential Guide to Managing Talent: How Top Companies Recruit, Train, and Retain the Best Employees*. Kogan Page Limited.

Keays, A. (2011). *The Crown Jewels* (Special Edition). London, UK: Thames & Hudson.

Kehinde, J. S. (2012). Talent management: Effect on organizational performance. *Journal of Management Research*, *4*(2), 178–186. doi:10.5296/jmr.v4i2.937

Kerr-Phillips & Thomas, A. (2010). Macro and Micro Challenges for Talent Retention in South Africa. *South Africa Journal of Human Resource Management*, *7*(1).

Khilji, S. E., & Keilson, B. (2014). In search of global talent: Is South Asia ready? *South Asian Journal of Global Business Research*, *3*(2), 114–134. doi:10.1108/SAJGBR-05-2014-0033

Khilji, S. E., Tarique, I., & Schuler, R. S. (2015). Incorporating a macro view in global talent management. *Human Resource Management Review*, *25*(3), 236–248. doi:10.1016/j.hrmr.2015.04.001

Kim, Y., Williams, R., Rothwell, W. J., & Penaloza, P. (2014). A strategic model for technical talent management: A model based on a qualitative case study. *Performance Improvement Quarterly*, *26*(4), 93–121. doi:10.1002/piq.21159

King-Metters, K., & Metters, R. (July 7, 2008). Misunderstanding the Chinese worker. *The Wall Street Journal,* from http://online.wsj.com/article/SB121441282707703883.html

Kinnear, K. L. (2011). *Women in developing countries. A reference Book. Praeger*. NJ: Greenwood.

Kirkbride, P. S., Tang, F. Y., & Westwood, R. Y. (1991). Chinese conflict preferences and negotiating behavior: Cultural and psychological influences. *Organization Studies*, *12*(3), 365–386. doi:10.1177/017084069101200302

Kirwan, K. S. (2009). Practicing talent life cycle management. *The Journal of Leadership Studies*, *3*(1), 65–66. doi:10.1002/jls.20101

Klein, A. (1016). South Africa's 10 Biggest Moments of the Rio 2016 Olympic Games. Retrieved from www.okayafrica.com/sports/rio-2016/south-africa-rio-2016- olympic-games/

Klie, Shannon (2008). Culture Guides Behaviors at Work. *Canadian HR Reporter.*

Knefelkamp, L. L., & Slepitza, R. (1978). A cognitive-development model of career development: An adaptation of the Perry scheme. In C. A. Parker (Ed.), *Encouraging Development in college students.* Minneapolis: University of Minnesota Press.

Knutson, T. J., Hwang, J. C., & Deng, B. C. (2000). Perception and management of conflict: A comparison of Taiwanese and US business employees. *Intercultural Communication Studies, 9*(2), 1–32.

Koch, B., & Koch, P. (2007). Collectivism, individualism, and outgroup cooperation in a segmented China. *Asia Pacific Journal of Management, 24*(2), 207–225. doi:10.1007/s10490-006-9004-5

Kraimer, M. L., Shaffer, M. A., & Bolino, M. C. (2009). The influence of expatriate and repatriate experiences on career advancement and repatriate retention. *Human Resource Management, 48*(1), 27–47. doi:10.1002/hrm.20265

Kreiner, K., & Lee, K. (2000). Competence and community. *International Journal of Technology Management, 20*(5-8), 657. doi:10.1504/IJTM.2000.002886

Kuhn, D. (1991). *The skills of argument.* Cambridge, UK: Cambridge University Press. doi:10.1017/CBO9780511571350

Kumar, H., & Raghavendran, S. (2013). Not by money alone: The emotional wallet and talent management. *The Journal of Business Strategy, 34*(3), 16–23. doi:10.1108/JBS-11-2012-0073

Kuptsch, C., & Pang, E. F. (Eds.), (2006, January). *Competing for global talent.* Retrieved from www.ilo.org

Kuratko, D. F., & Hodgetts, R. M. (2004). *Entrepreneurship: Theory, Process, Practice.* Mason, OH: South-Western Publishers.

Landadio, M. (2008). Melissa Etheridge ties the knot again. *People.* Retrieved from http://www.people.com/people/article/0,20230169,00.html

Landberg, S. (2004). Enabling profitable growth. *Best's Review, 104*(11), 99.

Lave, J. (1988). *The culture of acquisition and the practice of understanding.* Palo Alto, CA: Institute for Research on Learning.

Lave, J., & Wenger, E. (1991). *Situated Learning: Legitimate Peripheral Participation.* Cambridge, UK: Cambridge University Press. doi:10.1017/CBO9780511815355

Lawler, E. E. (2008). *Talent: Making people your competitive advantage.* San Francisco, CA: Jossey–Bass.

Lawler, E. E., & Boudreau, J. W. (2015). *Global trends in human resource management: A twenty-year analysis.* Stanford, CA: Stanford University Press.

Leggit, R. (2007, November 22). Letting go too easily: human resources management. *Accountancy Age.*

Lehrer, K. (2000). *Theory of knowledge.* Boulder, CO: Westview Press.

Leif, S., Karugu, W., & Schuepbach, L.S. (2008). Kaskazi Network Ltd – Distributing to the Bottom of the Pyramid. *IMD.*

Leisy, B., & Pyron, D. (2009). Talent management takes on new urgency. *Compensation and Benefits Review, 41*(4), 58–63. doi:10.1177/0886368709334323

Levy, O. (2005). The Influence of Top Management Team Attention Patterns on Global Strategic Posture of Firms. *Journal of Organizational Behavior, 26*(7), 797–819. doi:10.1002/job.340

Levy, O., Beechler, S., & Naylor, S. (2007). What we talk about when we talk about global mindset: Managerial cognition in multinational Corporations. *Journal of International Business Studies, 38*(2), 231–258. doi:10.1057/palgrave.jibs.8400265

Levy, P. (1979). *Moore: G.E. Moore and the Cambridge Apostles.* London, UK: Weidenfeld and Nicolson.

Lewin, K. (1946). Action research and minority problems. *Journal of Social Issues, 2*(4), 34-46.

Lewin, K. (1948). Resolving social conflicts; selected papers on group dynamics (G.W. Lewin ed.). New York: Harper & Row.

Lewin, K. (1943). Defining the Field at a Given Time. *Psychological Review, 50*(3), 292–310. doi:10.1037/h0062738

Lewin, K. (1947). Frontiers in Group Dynamics: Concept, Method and Reality in Social Science; Social Equilibria and Social Change. *Human Relations, 1*(1), 36. doi:10.1177/001872674700100103

Lewin, K. (1951). *Field theory in social science; selected theoretical papers* (D. Cartwright, Ed.). New York: Harper & Row.

Lewin, K. (1951). *Field theory in social science; selected theoretical papers. D. Cartwright.* New York: Harper & Row.

Lewin, M. (1992). The Impact of Kurt Lewins Life on the Place of Social Issues in his life. *The Journal of Social Issues, 48*(2), 15–29. doi:10.1111/j.1540-4560.1992.tb00880.x

Lewis, R.E. & Heckman, R. (2006) Talent management: A critical review. *Human Resource Management Review, 16*(2), 139-154.

Lewis, R. E., & Heckman, R. (2006). Talent management: A critical review. *Human Resource Management Review, 16*(2), 139–154. doi:10.1016/j.hrmr.2006.03.001

Liam, M., & Scerri, M. et al.. (2013). Reframing social sustainability reporting: Towards an engaged approach. *Environment, Development and Sustainability, 15*(1), 225–243. doi:10.1007/s10668-012-9384-2

Likert, R. (1932). A Technique for the Measurement of Attitudes. *Archives de Psychologie, 140*, 1–55.

Li, S., & Scullion, H. (2010). Developing the local competences of expatriate managers for emerging markets: A knowledge based approach. *Journal of World Business, 45*(2), 190–196. doi:10.1016/j.jwb.2009.09.017

Liu, S., & Chen, G. M. (2000). Assessing Chinese conflict management styles in joint ventures. *Intercultural Communication Studies, 9*(2), 71–90.

Llopis, G. (2014). The most undervalued leadership traits of women. *Forbes.* Retrieved from http://www.forbes.com/sites/glennllopis/2014/02/03/the-most-undervalued-leadership-traits-of-women/#36485b0c690c

Lockwood, N. R. (2006). Talent management: Driver for organizational success. *HRMagazine, 51*(6), 1–11.

Majchrzak, M., & Jarvenpaa, S. L. (2010). Safe context for inter-organizational collaboration among homeland security professionals. *The Journal of Strategic Information Systems, 27*(2), 55–86.

Malhotra, N. K. (1993). *Marketing research: An applied orientation.* Englewood Cliffs, N.J.: Prentice-Hall.

Mandela, N. (1995). *Long Walk to Freedom: The Autobiography of Nelson Mandela Kindle Edition.* Cape Town: Little, Brown and Company.

Manning, S., Massini, S., & Lewin, A. Y. (2008). A dynamic perspective on next-generation offshoring: The global sourcing of science and engineering talent. *The Academy of Management Perspectives*, 22(3), 35–54. doi:10.5465/AMP.2008.34587994

Mantel, M. J., & Ludema, J. D. (2000). From local conversations to global change: Experiencing the worldwide ripple effect of Appreciative Inquiry. *Organization Development Journal*, 18(2), 42–53.

Manyika, J., Chui, M., Bughin, J., Brown, B., Dobbs, R., Roxburgh, C., & Byers, A. H. (May, 2011). Big Data: The next frontier for innovation, competition, and productivity. Retrieved from http://www.mckinsey.com/business-functions/business-technology/our-insights/big-data-the-next-frontier-for-innovation

Marchington, M., & Wilkinson, A. (2012). *Human Resource Management at Work* (5th ed.). London: CIPD.

Martin, L. (1943). The Skunk Works Origin Story. Retrieved from http://www.lockheedmartin.com/us/aeronautics/skunkworks/origin.html

Martin, G., & Beaumont, P. (1998). Diffusing best practice in multinational firms: Prospects, practice and contestation. *International Journal of Human Resource Management*, 9(4), 671–695. doi:10.1080/095851998340955

Maslow, A. M. (1943). A Theory of Human Motivation. *Psychological Review*, 50(4), 370–396. doi:10.1037/h0054346

Mason, D. C., & Leslie, J. B. (2012). The Role of Multicultural Competence and Emotional Intelligence in Managing Diversity. *The American Psychological Association*, 15, 219–236.

McCreadie, K. (2009). *Adam Smith's The Wealth of Nations: A Modern-Day Interpretation of an Economic Classic*. Oxford: Oxford University Press.

McDonnell, A. (2011). Still fighting the "war for talent?" Bridging the science versus practice gap. *Journal of Business and Psychology*, 26(2), 169–173. doi:10.1007/s10869-011-9220-y

McDonnell, A., Lamare, R., Gunnigle, P., & Lavelle, J. (2010). Developing tomorrow's leaders: Evidence of global talent management in multinational enterprises. *Journal of World Business*, 45(2), 150–160. doi:10.1016/j.jwb.2009.09.015

McDonnell, A., Scullion, H., & Lavelle, J. (2013). Managing human resources in large international organizations. In G. Sarikades & C. Cooper (Eds.), *How can HR drive growth* (pp. 4–25). Cheltenham, UK: Edward Elgar Publishing. doi:10.4337/9781781002261.00008

McKinsey. (2007). Women matter: Female leadership, a competitive edge for the future. Retrieved from http//:www.mckinsey.com/women-matter

Mellahi, K., & Collings, D. G. (2010). The barriers to effective global talent management: The example of corporate elites in MNEs. *Journal of World Business*, 45(2), 143–149. doi:10.1016/j.jwb.2009.09.018

Meltzer, D. (1978). *The Kleinian development Part I: Freud's Clinical Development; Part II: Richard Week-by-Week; Part III: The Clinical Significance of the Work of Bion*. London, UK: Harris Meltzer Trust Publishers Ltd.

Mendenhall, M. E. (2006). The elusive, yet critical challenge of developing global leaders. *European Management Journal*, 24(6), 422–429. doi:10.1016/j.emj.2006.10.002

Mendenhall, M. E., Reiche, B. S., Bird, A., & Osland, J. S. (2012). Defining the "global" in global leadership. *Journal of World Business*, 47(4), 493–503. doi:10.1016/j.jwb.2012.01.003

Mendonca, J. (2016). US Court slapping nearly $1billion penalty TCS could impact entire Indian IT sector. Retrieved from http://economictimes.indiatimes.com/tech/ites/us-court-slapping-nearly-1-billion-penalty-on-tcs-could-impact-entire-indian-it-sector/article show/51870656.cms

Menon, A., Bharadwaj, S. G., Adidam, P. T., & Edison, S. W. (1999). Antecedents and Consequences of Marketing Strategy Making: A Model and a Test. Retrieved from https://archive.ama.org/archive/ResourceLibrary/JournalofMarketing/Pages/1999/63/2/1830349.aspx

Menon, A., Bhardwaj, S. G., Adidam, P. T., & Edison, S. W. (1999, April). Antecedents and Consequences of Marketing Strategy Making: A Model and a Test. *Journal of Marketing*, *63*(2), 18–40. doi:10.2307/1251943

Meredith, M. (2008). *Diamonds, Gold and War: The British, the Boers, and the making of South Africa*. New York: Public Affairs.

Merriam-Webster. (2015). Definition of Subculture. Accessed 05/18/15 http://dictionary.reference.com/browse/subculture

Meyers, C., & Jones, T.B. (1993). *Promoting Active Learning, Strategies for the College Classroom*. San Francisco: Josey-Bass.

Meyers, M. C., & van Woerkom, M. (2014). The influence of underlying philosophies on talent management: Theory, implications for practice, and research agenda. *Journal of World Business*, *49*(2), 192–203. doi:10.1016/j.jwb.2013.11.003

Meyers, M. C., van Woerkom, M., & Dries, N. (2013). Talent–Innate or acquired? Theoretical considerations and their implications for talent management. *Human Resource Management Review*, *23*(4), 305–321. doi:10.1016/j.hrmr.2013.05.003

Michaels, E., Handfield-Jones, H., & Axelrod, B. (2001). *The War for Talent*. Boston: Harvard Business School Press.

Michaels, E., Hanfield-Jones, H., & Axelford, B. (2001). *The war for talent*. Boston, MA: Harvard Business School Press.

Minchon, C. (2013). Diamonds may not be forever…but now, they look pretty good. Retrieved from http://jewishbusinessnews.com/2013/06/11/diamonds-may-not-be- for-ever-but-at-the-moment-they-look-pretty-good/

Mintz, H. (2015). Apple Vs Samsung: Samsung slapped with injunction. Retrieved from http://www.siliconvalley.com/apple-vs-samsung/ci_28829405/apple-v-samsung-samsung-slapped-injunction

Mlambo, A. S. (2014). A History of Zimbabwe. Cambridge, UK; Cambridge University Press.

Modak, F. (2016). *Policy: Protection of Confidential & Proprietary Information*. Denver, CO: Staples Inc.

Mole, K. F., & Mole, M. C. (2010). Entrepreneurship as the structuration of individual and opportunity: A response using a critical realist perspective. *Journal of Business Venturing*, *25*(2), 230–237. doi:10.1016/j.jbusvent.2008.06.002

Moolman, T., & Breidenthal, J. (2013). How to Bridge South Africa's Talent Gap. Retrieved from www.Africa.com

Moore, W. S. (1994). Student and faculty epistemology in the college classroom: The Perry schema of intellectual and ethical development. In K. Pritchard & R. McLaren Sawyer (Eds.), *Handbook of college teaching: Theory and applications* (pp. 45–67). CT: Greenwood Press.

Morgan, P. (2012). How to build a Blair Latrine. Retrieved from http://www.wikihow.com/Build-a-Blair-Latrine

Morton, L. (2005). Talent management value imperatives: Strategies for successful execution (Research Report).

Mullins, C. (2015). An overview of today's leading DBMS Platforms. Retrieved from https://www.datavail.com/blog/an-overview-of-todays-leading-dbms-platforms/

Mupepi, M. G. (2010). Appreciating social structures: a strategy for advancing the efficiency and effectiveness loci in organization. International Journal of Education Economics and Development, 1(4).

Mupepi, M. G., Yim, J. Y., Mupepi, S. C. & Mupepi, K. B. (2012). Can a knowledge community situated in an African village create and advance human rights practices beyond love thy neighbor principle? *International Journal of Knowledge and Learning, 7*(3/4), 233 – 252.

Mupepi, M., & Mupepi, S. (2014). Certain change: multi-democratic movements punctuate the tyrannical paradigm in Africa. *African Journal of Economic and Sustainable Development, 3*(1), 1–30.

Mupepi, M., & Mupepi, S. (2015). Charting Highly Productive Organization: Wrapping it all in Social Constructs. International Journal of Productivity Management and Assessment Technologies, 3(1).

Mupepi, M., Motiwan, J., & Mupepi, S. (2015, April 13-15). Inside social constructs: Re-engineering organizations successfully. *Proceedings of theMBAA International Conference*, Palmer House, Chicago, USA.

Mupepi, M., Mupepi, S., & Motiwan, J. (2015, March 10-14). Social constructs: Methods Tools and Applications: Re-engineering organizations successfully. *Proceedings of the Southwest Academy of Management 57th Annual Meeting*, Houston, Texas, USA.

Mupepi, M., Mupepi, S., & Motwani, J. (2015, March 25-27). Social Construct: Methods, Tools, and Applications in Re-Engineering Organizations. *Proceedings of the MBAA International Conference*, Chicago.

Mupepi, M., Tenkasi, R. V., & Sorensen, P. F. (2005). Building effective capability in the advancing economies in sub-Sahara Africa: *Proceedings of the Global Economy XI Conference Eastern Academy of Management June 26-30 University of Cape Town Graduate School of Business*.

Mupepi, M.G. (2014). Can the Division of Labor Be Re-Engineered to Advance Organizational Dynamism? *SAGE Open*, 4(2).

Mupepi, M.G., Mupepi, S.C., Tenkasi, R.V., & Jewell, G.D. (2008a). Precision in managing organizational change: identifying and analyzing needs using social constructs. *International Journal Management Practice, 3*(2), 150- 163.

Mupepi, M.G., Mupepi, S.C., Tenkasi, R.V., & Jewell, G.D. (2012). Unlocking entrepreneurial capabilities: Appreciating knowledge and technology transfer in advancing micro-enterprises in Zimbabwe. In D. Laouisset (Ed.), Knowledge-Technology Transfer. New York: Hauppauge.

Mupepi, Mambo (2010). Appreciating social structures: a strategy for advancing the efficiency and effectiveness loci in organization. *International Journal of Education Economics and Development 1*(4), 306-319.

Mupepi, Mambo (2010). Appreciating social structures: a strategy for advancing the efficiency and effectiveness loci in organization. *International Journal of Education Economics and Development, 1*(4), 306 – 319.

Mupepi, Mambo (2014). Appreciating Rapid Technology Integration in Creating Value in Enterprises. *Journal of Electronic Commerce in Organizations, 12*(1), 53-75.

Mupepi, Mambo (2016). The passage of the coal train: the inevitable mosaic in technical systems in global and local organization. African J. of Economic and Sustainable Development, 5(2), 149-171.

Mupepi, Mambo (2016). The passage of the coal train: the inevitable mosaic in technical systems in global and local organization. *African Journal of Economic and Sustainable Development, 5*(2), 149 – 171.

Mupepi, Mambo Ram V. Tenkasi Peter F. Sorensen & Sylvia Mupepi (2013). *Creating High Impact Organizations in the SADC: Adapting OD Methods and Practices.* In J. Vogelsang & M. Townsend et al. (Eds.), *Handbook for Strategic HR best practices in Organization Development from OD Network.* New York: AMACON.

Mupepi, S., & Mupepi, M. (2007, October 4-6). Creating a shared mindset: Advancing organizational effectiveness and efficiency. *Proceedings of the Midwest Academy of Management 50th Annual Conference,* Kansas City, Missouri, USA.

Mupepi, S.C. Mupepi, M.G., Tenkasi, R.V., & Sorensen, P.F., Jr. (2006). Changing the mindset: transforming organizations into high energized and performance organization. *Proceedings of the 49ᵗʰ Midwest Academy of Management,* Louisville, KT, USA.

Mupepi, M. (2010a). *Appreciating unlocking and building effective entrepreneurial capacity.* Saarbrucken, Germany: Lap Lambert Inc.

Mupepi, M. (2014). *Can the Division of Labor Be Re-Engineered to Advance Organizational Dynamism?* Wiley Open. Doi:10.1177/2158244014536404

Mupepi, M. (2015). *British Imperialism in Zimbabwe: Narrating the organization development of the First Chimurenga 1883-1904.* San Diego: Cognella.

Mupepi, M. (2015). *British Imperialism in Zimbabwe: The Organization Development of the First Chimurenga (1883-1904).* San Diego, CA: Cognella.

Mupepi, M. (2017). Using Communities of Practice to Identify Competencies. In K. Rasmussen, P. Northrup, & R. Colson (Eds.), *Handbook of Research on Competency-Based Education in University Settings* (pp. 157–167). doi:10.4018/978-1-5225-0932-5.ch008

Mupepi, M. (Forthcoming). *Using Communities of Practice to Identify Competencies.*

Mupepi, M. G. (2005). *Transforming village entrepreneurs into sustainable development using social constructs. A Case of Zimbabwe.* Ann Arbor, Michigan: ProQuest Publications Inc.

Mupepi, M. G. (2005). *Transforming village entrepreneurs into sustainable organization. A case of Zimbabwe.* Ann Arbor, MI: ProQuest Inc.

Mupepi, M. G. (2009). The nature of a schematic description of a socially constructed organizational competency model (CCM). *International Journal of Collaborative Enterprise, 1*(2), 224–240. doi:10.1504/IJCENT.2009.029291

Mupepi, M. G. (2010). Appreciating social structures: A strategy for advancing the efficiency and effectiveness loci in organization. *International Journal of Education Economics and Development, 1*(4), 306–319. doi:10.1504/IJEED.2010.034442

Mupepi, M. G. (2014). Can Human and Technical Resources be In Sync to Advance Resourceful Inclusive Enterprise? In F. Soliman (Ed.), *Learning Models for Innovation in Organizations: Examining Roles of Knowledge Transfer and Human Resources Management* (pp. 173–191). Hershey, PA, USA: IGI Global. doi:10.4018/978-1-4666-4884-5.ch009

Mupepi, M. G., & Motwani, J. (2015). Deconstructing the Value Creation Process: Positioning Diversity to Increase Output. *International Journal of Sociotechnology and Knowledge Development, 7*(4), 15–30. doi:10.4018/IJSKD.2015100102

Mupepi, M. G., & Mupepi, S. C. (2014). Appreciating Rapid Technology Integration in Creating Value in Enterprises. *Journal of Electronic Commerce in Organizations, 12*(1), 53–75. doi:10.4018/jeco.2014010104

Mupepi, M. G., & Mupepi, S. C. (2015). Charting Highly Productive Organization: Wrapping it all in Social Constructs. *International Journal of Productivity Management and Assessment Technologies, 3*(1), 13–30. doi:10.4018/IJPMAT.2015010102

Mupepi, M. G., & Mupepi, S. C. (2016). Applying Theory to Inform Competency Development: Bootstrapping Epistemic Communities in Growing Specialists. *International Journal of Productivity Management and Assessment Technologies, 4*(1), 28–38. doi:10.4018/IJPMAT.2016010103

Mupepi, M. G., Mupepi, S. C., Tenkasi, R. V., & Jewell, G. D. (2008). Precision in managing organizational change: Identifying and analyzing needs using social constructs. *International Journal Management Practice, 3*(2), 150–163. doi:10.1504/IJMP.2008.018368

Mupepi, M. G., & Taruwinga, P. (2014). Cultural Differentials Modify Change: Comparativeness of the SADC and the US. *International Journal of Sustainable Economies Management, 3*(2), 50–79. doi:10.4018/ijsem.2014040105

Mupepi, M. G., Tenkasi, R. V., Sorensen, P. F. Jr, & Mupepi, S. C. (2007). Creating high impact organization in the SADC: Adapting Organization Development Methods and Practices. *OD Practitioner, 32*(2), 34–39.

Mupepi, M., & Mupepi, S. (2013). Creating high impact organization in the SADC: Adapting OD Methods and Practices. In J. Vogel et al. (Eds.), *Handbook for Strategic HR: Best Practices in Organization Development from the OD Network.* New York: AMACON.

Mupepi, M., & Mupepi, S. (2015). (in press). Is it possible to increase productivity in diversified workplaces? *Organization Development Journal.*

Mupepi, M., & Mupepi, S. (2016). Applying Theory to Inform Competency Development: Bootstrapping Epistemic Communities in Growing Specialists. *International Journal of Productivity and Assessment Technologies, 4*(1), 27–37.

Mupepi, M., Tenkasi, R. V., Sorensen, P. F., & Mupepi, S. (2013). Creating High Impact Organizations: Adapting OD Methods and Practices. In J. Vogelsang & M. Townsend et al. (Eds.), *Handbook For Strategic HR Best Practices in Organization Development from OD Network.* New York: Amacom.

Mupepi, M., Tenkasi, R., Sorensen, P., & Mupepi, S. (2007). Creating high impact organization in the SADC: Adapting OD Methods and Practices. *The OD Practitioner, 32*(2), 34–39.

Mupepi, M., Yim, J., Mupepi, S., & Mupepi, K. (2011). Can a knowledge community situated in an African village create and advance human rights practices beyond love thy neighbor principles? *International Journal of Knowledge and Learning, 7*(3/4), 233–252. doi:10.1504/IJKL.2011.044557

Mupepi, S. C., Mupepi, M. G., Tenkasi, R. V., & Sorensen, P. F. Jr. (2007). Creating high impact organization in the SADC: Adapting OD Methods and Practices. *OD Practitioner, 32*(2), 34–39.

Muroe, T., Hatamiya, L., & Westwind, M. (2006). Deconstruction of structures: An overview of economic issues. *International Journal of Environmental Technology and Management, 6*(3-4). doi:10.1504/IJETM.2006.009002

Ncube, M., Lufumpa, C. L., & Vencatachellum, D. (2011). *The Middle of the Pyramid: Dynamics of the Middle Class in Africa.* Market Brief.

Neal, A., & Cavallaro, L. (2007). Action learning accelerates innovation: Cisco's action learning forum. *Organization Development Journal, 25*(4), 107–123.

Ng, E. S. W., & Burke, R. J. (2005). Person-organization fit and the war for talent: Does diversity management make a difference? *International Journal of Human Resource Management, 16*(7), 1195–1210. doi:10.1080/09585190500144038

Nicotera, A. M., & Cushman, D. P. (1992). Organizational ethics: A within-organization view. *Journal of Applied Communication Research, 20*(4), 437–462. doi:10.1080/00909889209365348

Nielsen, A. C. (2000). Nielson Net Ratings: Nielson Media Research. Retrieved from http://www.nielsen-netratings.com

Nilsson, S., & Ellstrom, P. E. (2012). Employability and talent management: Challenges for HRD practices. *European Journal of Training and Development, 36*(1), 26–45. doi:10.1108/03090591211192610

Nolan, S. (2012). Analytics. *Strategic HR Review, 12*(1), 3. doi:10.1108/shr.2013.37212aaa.001

Oppenheimer, H. (2008). Sir Ernst Oppenheimer 1880-1957. Retrieved from http://www.brenthurst.org.za/sirernest.cfm

Oppong, N. Y. (2015). Localization of management in multinational enterprises in developing countries: A case study of policy and practice. *International Journal of Training and Development, 19*(3), 223–231. doi:10.1111/ijtd.12058

Oppong, N. Y., & Gold, J. (2013). Talent management in the Ghanaian gold mining industry: A critical exploration. *Universal Journal of Management and Social Sciences, 3*(10), 1–19.

Otteson, J. R. (2002). *Adam Smith's Marketplace of Life*. Cambridge, UK: Cambridge University Press. doi:10.1017/CBO9780511610196

Oxman, J. (2007). *Preventing value leakage in outsourcing through an alternative model for invoicing reporting and data ownership*. New York: Technology Partners International.

Paauwe, J. (2004). *HRM and performance: Achieving long-term viability*. New York, NY: Oxford University Press. doi:10.1093/acprof:oso/9780199273904.001.0001

Pangarkar, N. (2011). *High performance companies: successful strategies from the world's top achievers*. San Francisco: Jossey-Bass.

Pannell, M. (2013). Talent Management: A Global Context and a South African Perspective. *Wits Business School Journal*.

Paprock, K. E. (2006). National human resource development in transitioning societies in the developing world: Introductory review. *Advances in Developing Human Resources, 8*(1), 12–27. doi:10.1177/1523422305283055

Parry, E., & Urwin, P. (2011). Generational Differences in Work Values: A Review of Theory and Evidence. *International Journal of Management Reviews, 13*(1), 79–96. doi:10.1111/j.1468-2370.2010.00285.x

Parsons, N. (1993). *A New History of Southern Africa*. London, UK: Palgrave Macmillan.

Parsons, T. (1996, Winter). The Theory of Human Behavior in its Individual and Social Aspects. *The American Sociologist, 27*(4), 13–23. doi:10.1007/BF02692048

Paterson, T. T. (1972). *Job Evaluation: A New Method* (Vol. 1). New York: Random House ISBN.

Peach, L. (1985). Managing corporate citizenship. *Personnel Management, 17*(7), 32–35.

Peng, M. W., Lu, Y., Shenkar, O., & Wang, D. Y. L. (2001). Treasures in the China house: A review of management and organizational research on Greater China. *Journal of Business Research, 52*(2), 95–110. doi:10.1016/S0148-2963(99)00063-6

Peng, S., He, Z., & Zhu, J. H. (2000). Conflict management styles among employees of Sino-American, Sino-French, and state-owned enterprises in China. *Intercultural Communication Studies, 9*(2), 22–46.

Pennington, S. (2013). *South Africa's Global Competitiveness 2013—Good News and Bad News*. South Africa: The Good News.

Perry, W. G. Jr. (1970). *Forms of Intellectual and Ethical Development in the College Years: A Scheme.* New York: Holt, Rinehart, and Winston.

Perry, W. G. Jr. (1981). Cognitive and Ethical Growth: The Making of Meaning. In *The Modern American College* (pp. 76–116). San Francisco: Jossey-Bass.

Peterson, R. A., & Anand, N. (2004). The production of culture perspectives. *Annual Review of Sociology, 30*(1), 311–334. doi:10.1146/annurev.soc.30.012703.110557

Pfeffer, J. (1998). *The Human Equation: Building Profits by Putting People First.* Boston, MA: Harvard Business School Press.

Phillips, J. (2013). *Building a Digital Analytics Organization: Create Value by Integrating Analytical Processes, Technology, and People into Business Operations.* London, UK: Pearson FT Press.

Pieterse, A. N., & van Knippenberg, D. (2012). Retrieved from http://leeds-faculty.colorado.edu/dahe7472/Pieterse%20 2012.pdf

Porter, M. E. (1985). *Competitive Advantage.* New York: Free Press.

Potts, D. T. (2012). *A Companion to the Archaeology of the Ancient Near East.* London, UK: John Wiley & Sons. doi:10.1002/9781444360790

Pouroulis, A. (2008). Chairman of Petra Diamonds Company Annual Report. Retrieved from http://londonantwerpdiamonds.com/diamond-news-archive.php

Powell, G. N. (2011). The gender and leadership wars. *Organizational Dynamics, 40*(1), 1–9. doi:10.1016/j.orgdyn.2010.10.009

Prahalad, C. K., & Hamel, G. (1990). The core competence of the corporation. Harvard Business Review, 68(3), 79–91.

Prahalad, C.K., & Hamel, G. (2001). The Core competence of the corporation. *Harvard Business Review.*

Preece, D., Iles, P., & Chuai, X. (2011). Talent management and management fashion in Chinese enterprises: Exploring case studies in Beijing. *International Journal of Human Resource Management, 22*(16), 3413–3428. doi:10.1080/095 85192.2011.586870

Quinn, R. (2000). *Change the world: How ordinary people can achieve extraordinary results.* San Francisco: Jossey Bass Publishers.

Raman, R., Chadee, D., Roxas, B., & Michailova, S. (2013). Effects of partnership quality, talent management, and global mindset on performance of offshore IT service providers in India. *Journal of International Management, 19*(4), 333–346. doi:10.1016/j.intman.2013.03.010

Reed, M. (2005). The realist turn in organization and management studies. *Journal of Management Studies, 42*(8), 1600–1644. doi:10.1111/j.1467-6486.2005.00559.x

Reid, J., & Crisp, D. (2007). The Talent Challenge: Creating a culture to recruit, engage and retain the best. *Ivey Business Journal Online.* Retrieved from http://search.proquest.com.ezproxy.gvsu.edu/docview/216185457?accountid=39473

Reilly, P. (1997, May 13). Barnes & Noble sues Amazon over rival's book selling claims. *Wall Street Journal.*

Reisinger, D. (2015). Apple, Samsung to remain bedfellows for next iPhone – report. *CNET.* Retrieved from http://www.cnet.com/news/apple-samsung-still-bedfellows-as-they-eye-next-iphone-report-says/

Reisinger, D. (2015). Apple, Samsung to remain bedfellows for next iPhone. Retrieved from http://www.cnet.com/news/apple-samsung-still-bedfellows-as-they-eye-next-iphone-report-says/

Reports, E. (2012). After De Beers, What's next for the Oppenheimers? Accessed 07/26/16http://rough-polished.com/en/expertise/58666.html?print=Y

Roberts, J. P. (2007). *Glitter & Greed: The secret world of the Diamond Cartel (Kindle ed.)*. Disinformation Books.

Robinson, J. (2001). Skills gap is big concern of employers today. *Alabama Cooperative Extension System*. Retrieved from www.aces.edu/dep/extcom

Rodger, L. & J. Bakewell, J. (2011). Sir Ernest Oppenheimer. *Chambers Biographical Dictionary*. London, United Kingdom: Chambers Harrap.

Roehl, A., Reddy, S. L., & Shannon, G. J. (2013). The flipped classroom: An opportunity to engage millennial students through active learning strategies. *Journal of Family and Consumer Sciences*, *105*(2), 44–49. doi:10.14307/JFCS105.2.12

Rogers, P.J., & Fraser, D. (2003). *Appreciating Appreciative Inquiry*. Wiley Periodicals, Inc.

Rogers, E. (2003). *Diffusion of Innovations* (5th ed.). New York: Simon and Schuster.

Rogers, E. M., Hart, W. B., & Mike, Y. (2002). Edward T. Hall & the History of Intercultural Communication: The United States & Japan. *Keio Communication Review*, (24): 1–5.

Ross, S. (2013). How definitions of talent suppress talent management. *Industrial and Commercial Training*, *45*(3), 166–170. doi:10.1108/00197851311320586

Roth, C. (2007). *The Magnificent Rothschild*. New York: Kissinger.

Rubiner, B. (1997). Brain study has wide implications. *Gannett News Service*.

Russell, C., & Bennett, N. (2015). Big data and talent management: Using hard data to make the soft stuff easy. *Business Horizons*, *58*(3), 237–242. doi:10.1016/j.bushor.2014.08.001

Ruttan, V. W. (2003). *Social Science Knowledge and Economic Development An Institutional Design Perspective*. Ann Arbor: University of Michigan Press. doi:10.3998/mpub.22975

Sahai, S., & Srivastava, A. K. (2012). Goal / target setting and performance assessment as tool for talent management. *Procedia: Social and Behavioral Sciences*, *37*, 241–246. doi:10.1016/j.sbspro.2012.03.290

Salas, E. (2012). So much Training, so little to show for it. Retrieved from http://www.wsj.com/articles/SB100014240 5297020442590457807295051 8558328

SAP.COM. (2015a). SAP grows up but never grows old. Retrieved from https://www.sap.com/careers/about-us/history.html

SAP.COM. (2015b). SAP at a glance: Company Information. Retrieved from http://www.sap.com/corporate-en/about/our-company/index.html

Saris, W. E., & Gallhofer, I. N. (2014). *Design, evaluation and analysis of questionnaires for survey research* (2nd ed.). Hoboken, NJ: John Wiley. doi:10.1002/9781118634646

Saris, W. E., & Revilla, M. (2015). Correction for measurement errors in survey research: Necessary and possible. *Social Indicators Research*, *127*(3), 1005–1020. doi:10.1007/s11205-015-1002-x

Scerri, M., Scerri, J., …. (2013). Reframing Social Sustainability Reporting: Towards an Engaged Approach. Retrieved from http://www.academia.edu/4362669/_Reframing_Social_Sustainability_Reporting_Towards_an_Engaged_Approach_

Schaaf, R. (2010). Do groups matter? Using a wellbeing framework to understand collective activities in Northeast Thailand. *Oxford Development Studies*, *38*(2), 241–259. doi:10.1080/13600811003753370

Schaeffer, F. A. (1994). *Pollution and the Death of Man: The Christian View of Ecology*. Wheaton, IL: Crossway.

Schein, E. H. (2004). *Organizational culture and leadership*. San Francisco: John Wiley & Sons, Inc.

Schiemann, W. A. (2014). From talent management to talent optimization. *Journal of World Business*, *49*(2), 281–288. doi:10.1016/j.jwb.2013.11.012

Schmidt, M. M. (2002). Female dominance hierarchies: Are they any different from males? *Personality and Social Psychology Bulletin*, *28*(1), 29–39. doi:10.1177/0146167202281003

Scholz, T. M. (2012). Talent management in the video game industry: The role of cultural diversity and cultural intelligence. *Thunderbird International Business Review*, *54*(6), 845–858. doi:10.1002/tie.21507

Schuler, R. S., & Jackson, S. E. (2014). Human resource management and organizational effectiveness: Yesterday and today. *Journal of Organizational Effectiveness: People and Performance*, *1*(1), 35–55. doi:10.1108/JOEPP-01-2014-0003

Schuler, R. S., Jackson, S. E., & Tarique, I. (2011). Global talent management and global talent challenges: Strategic opportunities for IHRM. *Journal of World Business*, *46*(4), 506–516. doi:10.1016/j.jwb.2010.10.011

Schuler, R. S., & Tarique, I. (2012). Global talent management: Theoretical perspectives, systems, and challenges. In G. Stahl, I. Björkman, & S. Morris (Eds.), *Handbook of research in international human resource management* (pp. 205–219). Cheltenham, UK: Edward Elgar Publishing. doi:10.4337/9781849809191.00017

Schutt, S., & Linegar, D. (2016). Eight Years of Utilizing Virtual Worlds for Education: A View from the Trenches. In K. Terry & A. Cheney (Eds.), Utilizing Virtual and Personal Learning Environments for Optimal Learning (pp. 1–21). Hershey, PA, USA: IGI Global. doi:10.4018/978-1-4666-8847-6.ch001

Scullion, H., & Collings, D. G. (2011). *Global talent management*. London, UK: Routledge.

Scullion, H., Collings, D. G., & Caligiuri, P. (2010). Global talent management: Introduction. *Journal of World Business*, *45*(2), 105–108. doi:10.1016/j.jwb.2009.09.011

Searle, J. (1997). The Mystery of Consciousness. New York, New York Review Press Secretary of Labor Report (1918). Sixth Annual Report of the Secretary of Labor Report. Washington, D.C.: Department of Labor, Office of The Secretary. Retrieved from http://digital.library.arizona.edu/bisbee/docs2/dlrep.php

Selmer, J., Ebrahimi, B. P., & Mingtao, L. (2002). Career management of business expatriates from China. *International Business Review*, *11*(1), 17–33. doi:10.1016/S0969-5931(01)00045-2

Senge, M.P., Kleiner, A., Roberts, C., Ross, R.B., & Smith, B.J. (1994). *The Fifth discipline fieldbook: Strategies and tools for building learning.*

Senge, P. M., Kleiner, A., Roberts, C., Ross, R., & Smith, B. (1994). The Fifth Edition Fieldbook. New York: Doubleday Books.

Senge, P. (2006). *The Fifth Discipline: The art and practice of the learning organization* (2nd ed.). New York: Random House Business.

Senge, P. M. (1990). *The art and practice of the learning organization.* New York: Random House.

Senge, P., Kleiner, A., Roberts, C., Ross, R. B., & Smith, B. (1994). *The Fifth Discipline Field book: Strategies and Tools for Building a Learning Organization.* New York: Doubleday.

Sewell, W. Jr. (1992). A Theory of Structure: Duality, Agency, and Transformation. *American Journal of Sociology, 98*(1), 1–29. Retrieved from http://www.jstor.org/stable/2781191 doi:10.1086/229967

Shaffer, M. A., Kraimer, M. L., Chen, Y. P., & Bolino, M. C. (2012). Choices, challenges, and career consequences of global work experiences: A review and future agenda. *Journal of Management, 38*(4), 1282–1327. doi:10.1177/0149206312441834

Sharfman, M.P., & Dean, J.W. (1991). Conceptualizing and measuring the organizational environment: a multidimensional approach. *Journal of Management, 17*(4), 681-701.

Sharif, K. (2012). A Value Centric Study of Intention to use Internet as a Shopping Channel in an Introductory Online Market. *International Journal of Online Marketing, 2*(3), 1–20. doi:10.4018/ijom.2012070101

Shepard, S. (2004). Teamwork and technology shift drilling performance paradigm. *World Oil 225*(4), 35-45.

Sibson, R. (1973). An optimally efficient algorithm for the single-link cluster method. *The Computer Journal. British Computer Society, 16*(1), 30–34.

Sidani, Y., & Ariss, A. A. (2014). Institutional and corporate drivers of global talent management: Evidence from the Arab Gulf region. *Journal of World Business, 49*(2), 215–224. doi:10.1016/j.jwb.2013.11.005

Siegel, E. (2013). *Predictive Analytics: The Power to Predict Who Will Click, Buy, Lie, or Die* (1st ed.). Hoboken, NJ: Wiley.

Silverman, D. (2001). *Interpreting qualitative data: Methods for analyzing Talk, Text & Interaction* (2nd ed.). London, UK: Sage Publications.

Silzer, R., & Church, A. H. (2009). The potential for potential. *Industrial and Organizational Psychology: Perspectives on Science and Practice, 2*(4), 446–452. doi:10.1111/j.1754-9434.2009.01172.x PMID:19580727

Silzer, R., & Church, A. H. (2010). Identifying and assessing high-potential talent: Current organizational practices. In R. Silzer & B. Dowell (Eds.), *Strategy-driven talent management: A leadership imperative* (pp. 213–279). San Francisco, CA: Jossey–Bass.

Silzer, R., & Dowell, B. E. (2010). Strategic talent management matters. In R. Silzer & B. Dowell (Eds.), *Strategy-driven talent management: A leadership imperative* (pp. 3–72). San Francisco, CA: Jossey–Bass.

Simpson, C. (2002). Obituary: Jonas Savimbi, UNITA's local boy. *BBC News.* Retrieved from http://news.bbc.co.uk/2/hi/africa/264094.stm

Sinatra, M. (2015). Employee turnover: Costs and causes. *Air Conditioning, Heating & Refrigeration News, 255*(17), 30. Retrieved from http://search.proquest.com.ezproxy.gvsu.edu/docview/1718314845?accountid=39473

Sinclair, A. (1998). *Doing Leadership Differently: Gender, Power, and Sexuality in a Change.* Melbourne: Melbourne University Press.

Sjoblom, L & El-Agamy, H. (2012). Ecobank: A Passion to build a World-Class Pan-African Bank. *IMD.*

Soliman, F. (2014). Role of Cloud Systems as Enabler of Global Competitive Advantages. In I. Portela & F. Almeida (Eds.), *Organizational, Legal, and Technological Dimensions of Information System Administration* (pp. 120–138). Hershey, PA, USA: IGI Global. doi:10.4018/978-1-4666-4526-4.ch008

Solnik, B. (2008). *Global Investments* (6th ed.). Upper Saddle, NJ: Prentice Hall.

Sonnenberg, M., Koene, B., & Paauwe, J. (2011). Balancing HRM: The psychological contract of employees: A multi-level study. *Personnel Review, 40*(6), 664–683. doi:10.1108/00483481111169625

Sonnenberg, M., van Zijderveld, V., & Brinks, M. (2014). The role of talent-perception incongruence in effective talent management. *Journal of World Business, 49*(2), 272–280. doi:10.1016/j.jwb.2013.11.011

Souad, M., Mynors, D., Grantham, A., Chan, P., Coles, R., & Walsh, K. (2007). Unearthing key drivers of knowledge leakage. *International Journal of Knowledge Management Studies, 1*(3/4), 456–470. doi:10.1504/IJKMS.2007.012535

Sparrow, P. R., Cooper, C., & Hird, M. (2014). *Do we need HR?: Repositioning people management for success*. London, UK: Palgrave MacMillan.

Sparrow, P. R., & Makram, H. (2015). What is the value of talent management? Building value-driven processes within a talent management architecture. *Human Resource Management Review, 25*(3), 249–263. doi:10.1016/j.hrmr.2015.04.002

Sparrow, P. R., Scullion, H., & Tarique, I. (2014). Multiple lenses on talent management: Definitions and contours of the field. In P. Sparrow, H. Scullion, & I. Tarique (Eds.), *Strategic talent management: Contemporary issues in international context* (pp. 36–70). Cambridge, UK: Cambridge University Press. doi:10.1017/CBO9781139424585.004

Stage, C. W. (1999). Negotiating organizational communication cultures in American subsidiaries doing business in Thailand. *Management Communication Quarterly, 13*(2), 245–280. doi:10.1177/0893318999132003

Stahl, G., Bjorkman, I., Farndale, E., Morris, S. S., Paauwe, J., Stiles, P., & Wright, P. et al. (2012). Six principles of effective global talent management. *Sloan Management Review, 53*(2), 25–42.

Stanford University. (2016). The History of Apartheid in South Africa. Retrieved from http://www-cs-students.stanford.edu/~cale/cs201/apartheid.hist.html

Stein, A. D., Smith, M. F., & Lancionic, R. A. (2013). The development and diffusion of customer relationship management (CRM) intelligence in business-to-business environments. *Industrial Marketing Management, 42*(6), 855–861. doi:10.1016/j.indmarman.2013.06.004

Stewart, J., & Harte, V. (2010). The implications of talent management for diversity training: An exploratory study. *Journal of European Industrial Training, 34*(6), 506–518. doi:10.1108/03090591011061194

Stewart, J., & Rigg, C. (2011). *Learning and Talent Development*. London: CIPD.

Strauss, A. (1987). *Qualitative analysis for social scientists*. Cambridge, United Kingdom: Cambridge University Press. doi:10.1017/CBO9780511557842

Strauss, A., & Corbin, J. (1998). *Basics of Qualitative Research – Techniques and Procedures for Developing Grounded Theory* (2nd ed.). London, UK: Sage Publications.

Surveys, H. R. (2016). What is a survey? Retrieved from http://www.hr-survey.com/WhatIs.htm

Surveys, N. (2017). Survey Software. Retrieved from https://novisurvey.net/

Sutton, R. (2007). The War for Talent is Back. *Harvard Business Review*. Retrieved from https://hbr.org/2007/04/the-war-on-talent-is-back

Suutari, V., & Brewster, C. (2003). Repatriation: Evidence from a longitudinal study of careers and empirical expectations among Finnish repatriates. *International Journal of Human Resource Management, 14*(7), 1132–1151. doi:10.1080/0958519032000114200

Suutari, V., Brewster, C., Riusala, K., & Syrjakari, S. (2013). Managing non-standard international experience: Evidence from a Finnish company. *Journal of Global Mobility: The Home of Expatriate Management Research, 1*(2), 118–138. doi:10.1108/JGM-10-2012-0014

Swailes, S. (2013). The ethics of talent management. *Business Ethics (Oxford, England), 22*(1), 32–46. doi:10.1111/beer.12007

Swailes, S., Downs, Y., & Orr, K. (2014). Conceptualising inclusive talent management potentials, possibilities and practicalities. *Human Resource Development International, 17*(5), 529–544. doi:10.1080/13678868.2014.954188

Swan, B. (2004, May-June). Solving Problems through Action Research: Engaging the Teacher and Student through Exploratory Learning. *The Agricultural Education Magazine, 76*(6), 26–27.

Swanson, D. J., & Creed, A. S. (2014, January). Sharpening the focus of force field analysis. *Journal of Change Management, 14*(1), 28–47. doi:10.1080/14697017.2013.788052

Tajuddin, D., Ali, R., & Kamaruddin, B. H. (2015). Developing talent management crisis model for quality life of bank employees in Malaysia. *Procedia: Social and Behavioral Sciences, 201*, 80–84. doi:10.1016/j.sbspro.2015.08.133

Tansley, C. (2011). What do we mean by the term "talent" in talent management? *Industrial and Commercial Training, 43*(5), 266–274. doi:10.1108/00197851111145853

Tarique, I., & Schuler, R. S. (2010). Global talent management: Literature review, integrative framework, and suggestions for future research. *Journal of World Business, 45*(2), 122–133. doi:10.1016/j.jwb.2009.09.019

Tatli, A., Vassilopoulou, J., & Ozbilgin, M. (2013). An unrequited affinity between talent shortages and untapped female potential: The relevance of gender quotas for talent management in high growth potential economies of the Asia Pacific region. *International Business Review, 22*(3), 539–553. doi:10.1016/j.ibusrev.2012.07.005

Tempel, A., & Walgenbach, P. (2003). Global Standardization of Organizational Forms and Management Practices? Combining American and European Institutionalism. *Paper presented at the3rd EURAM Annual Conference*, Milan.

Tenkasi, R. V. (2000). Some contextual antecedents of cognitive over-simplification processes in Research and Development environments: An exploration of the influence of social context on reasoning and knowledge creation practices in research and development teams. Retrieved from www2.warwick.ac.uk/fac/soc/wbs/conf/olkc/archive/oklc3/papers/id

Thompson, L. J. (2004). Moral leadership in a postmodern world. *Journal of Leadership & Organizational Studies, 11*(1), 27–37. doi:10.1177/107179190401100105

Thunnissen, M., Boselie, P., & Fruytier, B. (2013). Talent management and the relevance of context: Towards a pluralistic approach. *Human Resource Management Review, 23*(4), 326–336. doi:10.1016/j.hrmr.2013.05.004

Ting-Toomey, S., Gao, G., Trubisky, P., Yang, Z., Kim, H. S., Lin, S. L., & Nishida, T. (1991). Culture, face maintenance, and styles of handling interpersonal conflict: A study in five cultures. *The International Journal of Conflict Management, 2*(4), 275–296. doi:10.1108/eb022702

Tjosvold, D., & Sun, H. (2000). Social face in conflict: Effects of affronts to person and position in China. *Group Dynamics, 4*(3), 259–271. doi:10.1037/1089-2699.4.3.259

Tjosvold, D., & Sun, H. (2001). Effects of influence tactics and social contexts in conflict: An experiment on relationships in China. *The International Journal of Conflict Management*, *12*(3), 239–258. doi:10.1108/eb022857

Torrington, D., Hall, L., Taylor, S., & Atkinson, C. (2011). *Human Resource Management* (8th ed.). Edinburgh: Pearson Education.

Toterhi, T., & Recardo, R. J. (2013). The talent funnel: How to surface key human resources. *Global Business and Organizational Excellence*, *32*(5), 22–44. doi:10.1002/joe.21501

Toubia, O., Hauser, J. R., & Simester, D. I. (2004). Polyhedral methods for adaptive choice-based conjoint analysis. *JMR, Journal of Marketing Research*, *41*(1), 116–131. doi:10.1509/jmkr.41.1.116.25082

Triana, M. C., Garcia, M. F., & Colella, A. (2010). Managing diversity: How organizational efforts to support diversity moderate the effects of perceived racial discrimination on affective commitment. *Personnel Psychology*, *63*(4), 817–843. doi:10.1111/j.1744-6570.2010.01189.x

Trinh, M. P. (2016). Which Matters More?: Effects of Surface- and Deep-Level Diversity on Team Processes and Performance. In J. Prescott (Ed.), *Handbook of Research on Race, Gender, and the Fight for Equality* (pp. 213–239). Hershey, PA, USA: IGI Global. doi:10.4018/978-1-5225-0047-6.ch010

Trist, E., & Bamforth, K. (1951). Some social and psychological consequences of the longwall method of coal getting. *Human Relations*, *4*, 3–38. doi:10.1177/001872675100400101

Turner, L. C. F. (1970). *Origins of the First World War*. New York: W. W. Norton & Co.

Tyman, W. G., Stumpf, S. A., & Doh, J. P. (2010). Exploring talent management in India: The neglected role of intrinsic rewards. *Journal of World Business*, *45*(2), 109–120. doi:10.1016/j.jwb.2009.09.016

Ulrich, R., & Meier, R. (2001). Towards a framework for knowledge management strategies: process orientation as a strategic starting. Retrieved from http://citeseerx.ist.psu.edu/viewdoc/similar?doi=10.1.1.200.1086&type=ab

Ulrich, D. (1998). Intellectual Capital = Competence X Commitment. *Sloan Management Review*, *39*(2).

Ulrich, D. (2008). Call for talent: What is the best solutions? *Leadership Excellence*, *25*(5), 17.

Ulrich, D., & Brockbank, W. (2002). *Organization, people and HR: The General Manager agenda. Prepared for the Portable Executive Program*. Ann Arbor: University of Michigan Business School, Business School Press.

Ulrich, D., & Smallwood, N. (2011). *What is talent?* The RGL Group.

Ulrich, D., & Smallwood, N. (2012). What is talent? *Leader to Leader*, *2012*(63), 55–61. doi:10.1002/ltl.20011

Ulrich, D., & Ulrich, W. (2010). *Management by shared mindset* (1st ed.). New York: McGraw-Hill Education.

Ungureanu, H. (2016). Samsung Reportedly Making 100 Million OLED Displays for Apple's iPhone 7s Plus. *Techtimes.com*. Retrieved from http://www.techtimes.com/articles/150568/20160416/samsung-reportedly-making-100-million-oled-displays-for-apples-iphone-7s-plus.htm

United Nations. (2010). The World's Women. Retrieved from unstats.un.org/unsd/demographic/products/Worldswomen/WW_full%20report_color.pdf

United States Bureau of Labor Statistics. (2005). Databases Tables and Calculators by Subject. Retrieved from http://data.bls.gov/timeseries/LNS14000000

University of Michigan. (2016). Terms and definitions of LGBT. Retrieved from https://internationalspectrum.umich.edu/life/definitions

University of Vermont. (2016). Leadership development course for LGDP students. Retrieved from www.vermontbiz.com/news/may

Uren, L. (2007, March). Uren, L. (2007). From talent compliance to talent commitment: Moving beyond the hype of talent management to realizing the benefits. *Strategic HR Review*, *6*(3), 32–35. doi:10.1108/14754390780000970

Vaiman, V., Haslberger, A., & Vance, C. M. (2015). Recognizing the important role of self-initiated expatriates in effective global talent management. *Human Resource Management Review*, *25*(3), 280–286. doi:10.1016/j.hrmr.2015.04.004

Vaiman, V., Scullion, H., & Collings, D. G. (2012). Talent management decision-making. *Management Decision*, *50*(5), 925–941. doi:10.1108/00251741211227663

Valcour, Monique (2007). Work-based resources as moderators of the relationship between work hours and satisfaction with work-family balance. *Journal of Applied Psychology, 92*(6), 1512-1524.

Valverde, M., Scullion, H., & Ryan, G. (2013). Talent management in Spanish medium-sized organizations. *International Journal of Human Resource Management*, *24*(9), 1832–1852. doi:10.1080/09585192.2013.777545

van den Brink, M., Fruytier, B., & Thunnissen, M. (2013). Talent management in academia: Performance systems and HRM policies. *Human Resource Management Journal*, *23*(2), 180–195. doi:10.1111/j.1748-8583.2012.00196.x

van der Helm, P., Stams, G.J., & van der Laan, P. (2011). Measuring Group Climate in Prison. *The Prison Journal, 91*(2), 158-176. DOI: 10.1177/0032885511403595

Van der Veer, R., & Valsiner, J. (1994). Introduction. In R. Van der Veer & J. Valsiner (Eds.), *The Vygotsky reader*. Oxford, England: Blackwell. doi:10.1016/S0070-2161(08)60974-0

van Eijnatten, F. M., Hoevenaars, A. M., & Rutte, C. G. (1992). Holistic and participative (re)design: STSDD modeling in the Netherlands. In D. Hosking & N. Anderson (Eds.), *Organizing changes and innovations: European psychological perspectives* (pp. 183–207). London, UK: Routledge.

von Bertalanffy, L. (1968) General System Theory: Foundations, Development, Applications. New York: George Braziller.

von Bertalanffy, L. (1934). Untersuchungen über die Gesetzlichkeiten des Wachstums. I. Allgemeine Grundlagen der Theorie; mathematische und physiologische Gesetzlichkeiten des Wachstums bei Wassertieren. *Arch. Entwicklungsmech.*, *131*, 613–652.

von Bertalanffy, L. (1950). An outline of General Systems Theory. *The British Journal for the Philosophy of Science*, 1, 139–164.

von Bertalanffy, L. (1968). *General System Theory: Foundations, Development, Applications*. New York: George Braziller.

Von Bertalanffy, L. (1968). *General Systems Theory: Foundations, Developments, Applications*. New York: Braziller.

von Eijnatten, F.M. (1993). *The Paradigm that changed the work place: Social science for social action: toward organizational renewal (Vol. 4)*. Stockholm: The Swedish Center for Working Life.

Voyat, G. (1982). *Piaget systematized*. Hillsdale, N.J.: Earlbaum Associates.

Vural, Y., Vardarlier, P., & Aykir, A. (2012). The effects of using talent management with performance evaluation system over employee commitment. *Procedia: Social and Behavioral Sciences*, *58*, 340–349. doi:10.1016/j.sbspro.2012.09.1009

Vygotsky, L. S. (1978). *Mind and society: The development of higher mental processes*. Cambridge, MA: Harvard University Press.

Vygotsky, L. S. (1978). *Mind in Society. Cambridge*. MA: Harvard University Press.

Vygotsky, L.S. (1978). *Mind in Society*. Cambridge, MA: Harvard University Press.

Wang-Cowham, C. (2011). Developing talent with an integrated knowledge sharing mechanism: An exploratory investigation from the Chinese human resource managers' perspective. *Human Resource Development International, 14*(4), 391–407. doi:10.1080/13678868.2011.601573

Wang, G., Jing, R., & Klossek, A. (2007). Antecedents and management of conflict: Resolutions styles of Chinese top managers in multiple rounds of cognitive and affective conflict. *The International Journal of Conflict Management, 18*(1), 74–97. doi:10.1108/10444060710759327

Wanzel, K. R., Matsumoto, E. D., Hamstra, S. J., & Anastakis, D. J. (2002). Teaching technical skills: Training on a simple, inexpensive, and portable model. *Plastic and Reconstructive Surgery, 109*(1), 258–264. doi:10.1097/00006534-200201000-00041 PMID:11786823

Warren, C. (2006). Curtain call. *People Management, 12*(6), 24–29.

Watkins, J. M., Mohr, B. J., & Kelly, R. (2011). *Appreciative inquiry: Change at the speed of imagination*. San Francisco: Pfeiffer. doi:10.1002/9781118256060

Webb, S., & Webb, B. (2005). D. Martin (Ed.), The Webbs on Industrial Democracy. London, UK: Palgrave Macmillan.

Webb, S., & Webb, B. (2005). D. Martin (Ed.), The Webbs on Industrial Democracy. London, UK: Palgrave Macmillan.

Weisbord, M. R. (1987). *Productive Workplaces: Organizing and Managing for Dignity, Meaning and Community*. San Francisco: Jossey-Bass.

Weisbord, M. R. (2004). *Productive Workplaces revisited: Dignity and Community in 21st Century*. New York: Wiley.

Wenger, E. & Lave, Jean (2008). Communities of practice. Retrieved from http://www.infed.org/biblio/communities_of_practice.htm

Wenger, E. (2004). The community structure of large scale learning systems: Learning as a journey. Retrieved from http://www.efios.com/pdf/aerakeynote.pdf#search

Werner, J. M., & DeSimone, R. L. (2006). *Human Resource Development* (4th ed.). Ohio: Thomson South-Western.

Westlund, H. (2006). *Social capital in the knowledge economy: Theory and Empirics*. New York: Springer.

Westmeyer, P. (1997). *A History of American Higher Education* (2nd ed.). Springfield, Illinois: C.C. Thomas.

Westney, E. (1993). Institutionalization theory and the multinational corporation. In E. Westney (Ed.), *Organization theory and the multinational corporation* (pp. 53–76). Basingstoke: Macmillan. doi:10.1007/978-1-349-22557-6_3

Whelan, E. (2011). It's who you know not what you know: A social network analysis approach to talent management. *European Journal of International Management, 5*(5), 484–500. doi:10.1504/EJIM.2011.042175

White, E. (2016). Some northern Ontario farms bringing in migrant Mexican workers. Retrieved from http://www.cbc.ca/news/canada/sudbury/migrant-farm-workers-northern-ontario-1.3795537

Whitney, D., Trosten-Bloom, A., & Rader, K. (2010). *Appreciative leadership: Focus on what works to drive winning performance and build a thriving organization*. New York: McGraw Hill.

Whitworth, A. (1985). *A Centenary History, A History of the City and Guilds College, 1885 to 1985*. London, UK: University of London Press.

Wieck, K. E. (1979). *The Social Psychology of Organizing*. New York: Random House.

Wildavsky, B. (2010). *The great brain race: How global universities are shaping the world.* Princeton, NJ: Princeton University Press.

Williams, B. (2015). Sitting next to Nellie. *Fenman.* Retrieved from http://www.fenman.co.uk/traineractive/cat/login_dl.php?act_id=PED04

Williams, C. C. (2007). *Rethinking the future of work: directions and visions.* Basingstoke: Palgrave MacMillan.

Williams, J. C., Dempsey, R., & Slaughter, A.-M. (2014). *What works for women at work: Four patterns working women need to know.* New York: New York University Press.

Wrigley, C. (2002). *A companion to Twentieth-Century Britain.* London, UK: Blackwell Ltd. doi:10.1111/b.9780631217909.2002.x

Yaeger, T. F., & Sorensen, P. F. Jr. (2001). What Matters Most in Appreciative Inquiry. In D. Cooperider, P. Sorensen Jr, T. Yaeger, & D. Whitney (Eds.), *Appreciative Inquiry: An Emerging Direction For Organization Development* (pp. 129–142). Champaign, Illinois: Stipes Publishing L.L.C.

Yamashita, M., & Emerman, M. (2005). The cell cycle independence of HIV Infections is not determined by known Karyophilic viral elements. *PLoS Pathogens, 1*(3), e18. doi:10.1371/journal.ppat.0010018 PMID:16292356

Yang, D. (2011). How does knowledge sharing and governances mechanism effect innovation capabilities?--from the coevolution perspectives. *International Business Research, 4*(1), 154–157.

Yasnitsky, A., & Van Der Veer, R. (2015). *Revisionist Revolution in Vygotsky Studies: The State of the Art.* London, UK: Routledge.

Yi, L., Wei, L., Hao, A., Hu, M., & Xu, X. (2015). Exploration on construction of hospital "talent tree" project. *Cell Biochemistry and Biophysics, 72*(1), 67–71. doi:10.1007/s12013-014-0405-7 PMID:25413963

Yost, P. R., & Chang, G. (2009). Everyone is equal, but some are more equal than others. *Industrial and Organizational Psychology: Perspectives on Science and Practice, 2*(4), 442–445. doi:10.1111/j.1754-9434.2009.01171.x

Young, T. P., Bailey, C. J., Guptill, M., Thorp, A. W., & Thomas, T. L. (2014). The Flipped Classroom: A Modality for Mixed Asynchronous and Synchronous Learning in a Residency Program. *Western Journal of Emergency Medicine, 15*(7), 938–944. doi:10.5811/westjem.2014.10.23515 PMID:25493157

Yuan, W. (2010). Conflict management among American and Chinese employees in multinational organizations in China. *Cross Cultural Management, 17*(3), 299–311. doi:10.1108/13527601011068388

Yulong, M. A., & Runyon, L. R. (2004). Academic synergy in the age of technology-A New paradigm. *Journal of Education for Business, 79*(6), 367–371. doi:10.3200/JOEB.79.6.367-371

Zagelmeyer, S. (2013). Tackling the crisis through concession bargaining: Evidence from five German companies. *International Journal of Manpower, 34*(3), 232–251. doi:10.1108/IJM-04-2013-0080

Zingheim, P., & Schuster, J. R. (1999). Dealing with scarce talent: Lessons from the leading edge (part 2 of 2). *Compensation and Benefits Review, 31*(2), 40–44.

Zook, C. (2001). *Profit from the Core: Growth Strategy in an Era of Turbulence.* Boston: Harvard Business School Press.

Zook, C., & Allen, J. (2016). *The Founder's Mentality: How to Overcome the Predictable Crises of Growth.* Boston: Harvard Business School Press.

About the Contributors

Mambo Mupepi Affiliate Professor Brooks College and Seidman College of Business, Grand Valley State University Adjunct MBA Faculty Saint Joseph College of Business, Indiana. Research interests: Knowledge Management, Organizational Development & Change Work Experience: Visiting Scholar University of Michigan Global Scholars Program (2010-2013) Publications: British Imperialism in Zimbabwe: Narrating the Organizational Development of the First Chimurenga (Cognella 2015) The Legendary Nehanda: the Essence of the Second Chimurenga (1966-1980) (Mellen, 2015) Appreciating Unlocking and Building effective entrepreneurial capacity (Lambert 2010) Inside social constructs. IGI Global (2015) Can human and technical resources be in sync to advance resourceful inclusive enterprise? IGI Global (2014) Can human and technical resources be in sync to advance resourceful inclusive enterprise? IGI Global (2014) Creating High Impact Organizations. Handbook for Strategy HR: Best Practices... McGraw-Hill (2014) Appreciating rapid technology integration: impacting wealth creation in enterprises. IGI Global Inc. (2013)

***

Neeta Baporikar is currently Director/Professor (Business Management) at Harold Pupkewitz Graduate School of Business (HP-GSB), Namibia University of Science and Technology, Namibia. Prior to this she was Head-Scientific Research, with Ministry of Higher Education CAS-Salalah, Sultanate of Oman, Professor (Strategic Management and Entrepreneurship) at IIIT Pune and BITS India. With more than a decade of experience in industry, consultancy and training, she made a lateral switch to research and academics in 1995. Dr. Baporikar holds D.Sc. (Management Studies) USA, PhD in Management, University of Pune INDIA with MBA (Distinction) and Law (Hons.) degrees. Apart from this, she is also an External Reviewer, Oman Academic Accreditation Authority, Accredited Management Teacher, Qualified Trainer, Doctoral Guide and Board Member of Academics and Advisory Committee in accredited B-Schools. Reviewer for international journals, she has to her credit 5 conferred doctorates, several refereed research papers, and authored books in the area of Entrepreneurship, Strategy, Management and Higher Education.

Tarek Ben Noamene earned a Ph.D in Management from the University of Nice (France) in 2009 Dr. Tarek's research interests include Employee ownership, Corporate Governance and Human Capital, Corporate Social Responsibility. Dr. Tarek has written in these topics in the Journal of Business Research, International Business Research, in la Revue du financier etc. The courses Dr. Tarek teaches include Occupational Health and Safety, Introduction to human resource management, and performance management. Prior to joining ECT in 2014, Dr. Tarek was Assistant Professor at the University of Jendouba and the University of Nice.

Mark L. Davis is a freelance writer and business consultant who specializes in small/medium business development. He has earned her Masters' in the Science of Management from Cornerstone University in Grand Rapids, MI and his Bachelors' in Behavioral Science from Grand Valley State University in Allendale, MI. He has extensive work experience in sales, operations, and management and specializes strategic planning and developing interdepartmental identity.

Yiheng Deng is Associate Professor at Southwestern University of Finance and Economics, China, and Visiting Scholar at Grand Valley State University. She obtained PhD in Communication at University of Arizona, and has specialized in conflict management, business communication, and intercultural communication. She has published in Management Communication Quarterly, Chinese Journal of Communication, International Journal of Conflict Management, and some other communication journals.

Kijpokin Kasemsap received his BEng degree in Mechanical Engineering from King Mongkut's University of Technology, Thonburi, his MBA degree from Ramkhamhaeng University, and his DBA degree in Human Resource Management from Suan Sunandha Rajabhat University. He is a Special Lecturer in the Faculty of Management Sciences, Suan Sunandha Rajabhat University, based in Bangkok, Thailand. He is a Member of the International Association of Engineers (IAENG), the International Association of Engineers and Scientists (IAEST), the International Economics Development and Research Center (IEDRC), the International Association of Computer Science and Information Technology (IACSIT), the International Foundation for Research and Development (IFRD), and the International Innovative Scientific and Research Organization (IISRO). He also serves on the International Advisory Committee (IAC) for International Association of Academicians and Researchers (INAAR). He has had numerous original research articles in top international journals, conference proceedings, and books on the topics of business management, human resource management, and knowledge management, published internationally.

Aslam Modak is an IT professional, trainer, and consultant. He has consulted in various areas of training and development, and currently is a senior visiting faculty member at Grand Valley State University. His interests include organizations and technology, enterprise systems, and business process optimization using IT. He has previously worked at various places as a computer programmer, data manager, networking manager, grant proposal writer, enterprise systems manager, information technology project manager, and Division Chair for Computer Information Systems. He is also involved with technology management and critical thinking training and is an area chair for technology for the University of Phoenix.

Sylvia Mupepi PhD., RN., Associate Professor Maternal Child Health Grand Valley State University. Area of academic interest: Cervical cancer knowledge and screening practices; Organizational Development. Teach undergraduate and graduate nursing programs at GVSU and the University of Cape Coast Ghana West Africa. Graduated with a PhD Nursing from the Univ of Michigan, M Ed Univ of

Zimbabwe, Grad Cert Ed Univ of London, Dip in Nursing University of Kingston UK, HV Cert Unv of Wolverhampton. Kellogg Fellow, Fulbright Scholar, Founding Member and Fellow ECSACON.

Nana Yaw Oppong has worked in varied private sector organisations in administration and human resource roles, both in Ghana and the UK. He has also taught in higher and further education institutions in Ghana, UK and Germany. Nana holds PhD in talent management and development from the Leeds Business School, UK after his MBA from the East London Business School, UK and a BA and Diploma in Education from the University of Cape Coast, Ghana. He is currently a senior lecturer in Human Resource Management in the School of Business of the University of Cape Coast, Ghana. He also teaches Industrial Relations; Executive Secretarial Practice; and Organisational Behaviour. His research interests include cross-cultural HRM practices; talent management and development; and indigenous methods of developing employees, with publications covering these areas, and has also shared knowledge in these areas through conference presentations in Ghana, Greece, United Kingdom, Germany, Australia and Hong Kong. He is as well a consultant in human resource management and development.

Yalonda M. Ross Davis is a Visiting Instructor in the Management department with Seidman College of Business; teaching Introduction to Business and Diversified Workforce. She has earned her Masters' in the Science of Management from Cornerstone University in Grand Rapids, MI and her Bachelors' in Business Administration from Tennessee State University in Nashville, TN. She has extensive work experience in sales within the pharmaceutical industry and prior to becoming a Visiting Instructor, she was an Adjunct Instructor at the Grand Valley State University. Research interest includes employee and managerial diversity along with the results of inequality within organizations.

Index

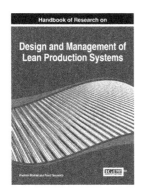

Stay Current on the Latest Emerging Research Developments

Become an IGI Global Reviewer for Authored Book Projects

The overall success of an authored book project is dependent on quality and timely reviews.

In this competitive age of scholarly publishing, constructive and timely feedback significantly decreases the turnaround time of manuscripts from submission to acceptance, allowing the publication and discovery of progressive research at a much more expeditious rate. Several IGI Global authored book projects are currently seeking highly qualified experts in the field to fill vacancies on their respective editorial review boards:

Applications may be sent to:
development@igi-global.com

Applicants must have a doctorate (or an equivalent degree) as well as publishing and reviewing experience. Reviewers are asked to write reviews in a timely, collegial, and constructive manner. All reviewers will begin their role on an ad-hoc basis for a period of one year, and upon successful completion of this term can be considered for full editorial review board status, with the potential for a subsequent promotion to Associate Editor.

If you have a colleague that may be interested in this opportunity, we encourage you to share this information with them.

CPSIA information can be obtained
at www.ICGtesting.com
Printed in the USA
BVOW04*1755250817
492936BV00011B/85/P

9 781522 519614